THE CONSOLIDATED B-24 LIBERATOR

THE CONSOLIDATED B-24 LIBERATOR

REUBEN FLEET, THE FACTORIES, AND THE PRODUCT

WILLIAM WOLF

This book is dedicated to all the men and boys who flew, crewed, and serviced the B-24, giving up their youth and often their lives to keep America free and the world safe again.

First published in Great Britain and the United States in 2025 by Fonthill
An imprint of
Pen & Sword Books Ltd
Yorkshire – Philadelphia
www.fonthill.media

Copyright © William Wolf 2025

ISBN 978-1-78155-840-9

The right of William Wolf to be identified as
Author of this work has been asserted by him in accordance
with the Copyright, Designs and Patents Act 1988.

A CIP catalogue record for this book
is available from the British Library.

All rights reserved. No part of this book may be reproduced or
transmitted in any form or by any means, electronic or mechanical
including photocopying, recording or by any information storage and
retrieval system, without permission from the Publisher in writing.

Typeset in Sabon LT 10/13
Typeset by Fonthill
Printed and bound in the UK by CPI Group (UK) Ltd, Croydon, CR0 4YY

The Publisher's authorised representative in the EU for product
safety is Authorised Rep Compliance Ltd., Ground Floor,
71 Lower Baggot Street, Dublin D02 P593, Ireland.
www.arccompliance.com

For a complete list of Pen & Sword titles please contact
PEN & SWORD BOOKS LIMITED
47 Church Street, Barnsley, South Yorkshire, S70 2AS, England
E-mail: enquiries@pen-and-sword.co.uk
Website: www.pen-and-sword.co.uk

Or
PEN AND SWORD BOOKS
1950 Lawrence Rd, Havertown, PA 19083, USA
E-mail: Uspen-and-sword@casematepublishers.com
Website: www.penandswordbooks.com

Foreword

Although many books have been published about the B-24, none has been a truly in-depth look at the aircraft itself, its development, manufacture/assembly, and post-war aftermath. Most have been superficial all-purpose, cursory descriptions of the bomber and its campaigns which tended to be similar from book to book and were intended for the general reader. This volume and two future companion volumes are directed at serious B-24 enthusiasts, historians, and modelers and are intended to be the definitive B-24 Liberator sources.

Among this volume's highlights are the relationship of Reuben Fleet and Consolidated Aircraft to the development of the B-24, which are chronicled in detail with special insight to Fleet, the man, and the aviation icon.

The development and construction of the plants of the original Consolidated San Diego Liberator manufacturer and the fabulous "modern Wonder of the World" Ford Willow Run Plant are extensively detailed in word and pictures. The manufacturing/assembly of Consolidated and Ford Liberators are examined and compared at length, also in words and photos. Of the 18,493 Liberators that were built, Ford Willow Run built 6,972 and 1,893 knock-down kits, while Consolidated San Diego built 6,506. The roles of the "other three" B-24 plants—Consolidated Fort Worth, Douglas Tulsa, and North American Dallas—are discussed. The disruptive effect of the numerous change orders on B-24 production is emphasized and the necessary development and use of Modification Centers is detailed. The important use of the Davis Wing, which defined the Liberator, and its inventor, Donald Davis, are examined in detail for first time anywhere. The manufacture and transport of the little-known Ford knock-down kits sent to NAA Dallas and Douglas Tulsa for assembly are also extensively described and pictured for the first time.

The major B-24 models D/E/G/H/J/L/M are generally described as they will be discussed and contrasted in much greater detail in a following volume: *The B-24 Liberator: In Detail and in Flight*. Meanwhile, minor models such as the B/C/F/K and special variants are discussed more thoroughly and will not appear in the following volume. B-24 transports and special duties aircraft are also discussed superficially as they will be documented extensively for the first time in a future third book: *Liberator*

Haulers: B-24 WWII Transports and Special Duties Aircraft. The PB4Y-2 Privateer is not covered as it would require a separate book, which Privateer guru Alan Carey has done in several excellent volumes.

The reader will find a number of repetitions and reiterations of certain specifics throughout the book, which I felt were necessary to include in order to keep track of the many different B-24 models produced by five factories and the numerous variants and British models—all of which endured numerous change orders. Even the five B-24 manufacturers had to initiate the production block designation system to keep track of the various changes. The post-war use and scrapping of B-24s is described in detail.

Note: During March 1943, Consolidated merged with Vultee, with the new company adopting the trade name Convair; however, the B-24 continued to be commonly referred to as a Consolidated product by the media, government, and even the company itself, and I will mostly refer to Liberators built at San Diego after the merger as Consolidated, rather than Convair or Consolidated Vultee.

Inflation Adjustor

$1 in 1940–45 = 2021 $

12/41 = $17.70
12/42 = $16.20
12/43 = $15.75
12/44 = $15.41
12/45 = $15.10
Based on Consumer Price Index (CPI) data

Caption Credit Abbreviations

AAF:	Army Air Force
AFSHRC:	Albert F. Simpson Historical Research Center
ATSC:	Air Technical Service Command (Logistics Planning Division)
CAC/AAF:	Consolidated Aircraft Corporation/Army Air Force
DAC/AAF:	Douglas Aircraft Company/Army Air Force
FMC:	Ford Motor Company/Army Air Force
LoC:	Library of Congress
NA:	National Archives
NAA/AAF:	North American Aviation/ Army Air Force
NMUSAF:	National Museum of the USAF
OWI:	Office of War Information
PASM:	Pima Air and Space Museum
SNASM:	Smithsonian National Air and Space Museum
USAF:	United States Air Force
USMC:	United States Marine Corps
USN:	United States Navy

Preface

By the time the last complete B-24M came off the Willow Run assembly line in July 1945, the five B-24 manufacturers built more B-24s—18,482 (or 18,188?)—than any other American aircraft. Although the B-24 edged out the B-17 on most performance criteria (speed, range, bombload), the B-17 was the media darling while the B-24 was considered the B-17's ugly sister. But of all the heavy bombers of World War II, Axis and Allied, the B-24 probably was the most adaptable and versatile of any. In the theaters it served, it had a profound influence assuming many roles, beginning its combat career as a heavy bomber in tandem with the B-17 in the MTO and ETO and then finding multiple roles as transports and special duty aircraft. With its great range, it performed anti-sub duties in the Atlantic and long-range, over-water heavy bomber support in the Pacific. By the end of the war, it and its rival the B-17 were superseded by the B-29, and the two become obsolete, discarded, and relics of the propeller age.

Acknowledgments

My lifelong hobby has been World War II aerial combat, and over the past forty years, I have collected over 25,000 books and magazines, along with hundreds of reels of microfilm on the subject. I probably have nearly every significant book written on World War II aviation and complete collections of every aviation magazine published since 1939. Also included in my collection are hundreds of aviation unit histories; intelligence reports; pilot, crew, flight, and training manuals; and technical, structural, and maintenance manuals for aircraft ordnance, armament, engines, and equipment. My microfilm collection includes vintage intelligence reports; hundreds of USAF, USN, and USMC Group, and Squadron histories and After Combat Reports; complete Japanese Monograph series; complete U.S. Strategic Bombing Surveys as well as complete USAF Historical Studies. Over the years, I have been fortunate to meet many fighter aces, other pilots, and fellow aviation buffs who have shared stories, material, and photographs with me (I have over 5,000 photos of fighter aces alone). I have made many multi-day expeditions to various military libraries, museums, and photo depositories with my copy machine and camera (later PC and scanner) accumulating literally reams of information and many thousands of photographs. I also had a photo darkroom where I developed thousands of rare photos from rare microfilm negatives. The author wishes that every person who contributed photos and materials during the past years could be specifically mentioned. Over the past forty years, the origin of many of the thousands of photos I have been lent to copy or have copied and collected myself have become obscured. Most are from military and government sources but many are from private individuals and I apologize in advance if some of the photos are miscredited. Also, some of the photos are not of the best quality because of their age and sources, especially those copied from microfilm and contemporary publications, but were used because of their importance to the book. Over the past two decades, I have scanned information and photos as I have found them and stored or printed them for future use (this B-24 volume is the result of ten years research; the final two years of concerted effort). Thanks go to the personnel at the Air Force Museum Archives at Wright-Patterson, Dayton, Ohio, the Library of Congress, National Archives, and the Ferndale Photographic facility, Washington, D.C., and Scott Marchand at the Pima Air and Space Museum, Tucson, Arizona. A belated thank you goes to Judy Endicott of the Albert F. Simpson Historical Research Center, Maxwell AFB, Alabama. Ms. Endicott was of great help during my ten-day expedition to that facility in the mid-1980s to collect materials and thousands of photos I have used in this and past books. Last, but not least many thanks go to my persevering wife, Nancy, who allows me to spend many hours researching and writing and patiently (mostly) waits while I browse bookstores and visit air museums, in search of new material and photos. I also need to thank her because her car sits out in the hot Arizona sun as my World War II library luxuriates in the remodeled, air-conditioned three-car garage.

Author Bill Wolf with the Museum of the U.S. Air Force's B-24D *Strawberry Bitch*. (*Author's collection*)

Contents

Foreword   5
Preface   7
Acknowledgments   8

Part I: Reuben Fleet, Consolidated Aircraft, and the B-24 Liberator

1	Introduction	17
2	Reuben Fleet: The Early Years	18
3	Fleet in the Service of His Country	21
4	Fleet Becomes an Aircraft Builder	29
5	The San Diego Plant Goes into Production	90
6	David Davis and the Davis Wing	96
7	Consolidated Model 31 Long-Range Patrol Boat and the Davis Wing	106
8	Consolidated Pre-XB-24 Four-Engined Bomber Proposals	108
9	Consolidated Model 32/XB-24: B-24 Precursor	112
10	Consolidated Heads toward B-24 Production	123
11	Consolidated Confronts the West Coast Labor Unions	134
12	Consolidated Merges with Vultee	140
13	Epilog: Reuben Fleet After the Merger	161

Part II: Liberator Production Pool, Committee, and Manufacturer Contracts

1	Liberator Production Pool	171
2	B-24 Committee	176
3	B-24 and Knock-Down Kit Contracts	179

Part III: Consolidated San Diego and Fort Worth B-24 Plants

Section 1: Consolidated San Diego		185
1	Developing the San Diego Facility	189
2	The San Diego Plant	198
3	The San Diego Consolidated Labor Force	215

4	Building the Liberator	232
5	Feeder Shop Plan and Subcontracting	265
6	Government-Furnished Equipment and Spare Parts	275
7	Consolidated Assembly Line	277
8	Consolidated San Diego: Summary and Conclusion	300

Section 2: Consolidated Fort Worth B-24 Plant	305
1 Fort Worth's Aviation Heritage	307
2 Enter Reuben Fleet	310
3 The Consolidated Fort Worth Plant	317
4 Fort Worth B-24 Knock-Down Assembly and Production	326
5 B-24 Manufacture is Terminated and B-32 Production Begun	338
6 Consolidated Fort Worth Plant Post-War to Present	340

Part IV: The Magnificent Ford Willow Run Plant

1	Henry Ford and Automobile Mass Production	349
2	The Trimotor *Tin Goose*: Ford's First Aircraft Manufacturing Endeavor	353
3	The Auto Industry Begins Aircraft Manufacture	355
4	Ford and Charles Sorensen Enter the U.S. Air Defense Program	365
5	The Willow Run Factory is Conceived	374
6	Plant Construction	381
7	The Plant	388
8	Mass Producing the B-24	407
9	The Willow Run Workforce	413
10	Production at Willow Run	439
11	Ford Implements the Plan	443
12	Engineering at Willow Run	458
13	Raw Materials and Purchased Parts	468
14	Subcontracting: Other Ford Plants and Outside Sub-Contractors	476
15	Spare Parts	484
16	Government-Furnished Equipment (GFE)	486
17	Inspection and Government Control	488
18	Rate of Production Acceleration	493
19	Willow Run Crises	500
20	Period of Rapid Production Acceleration	507
21	The Passing of Edsel Ford and Its Aftermath	511
22	The Fabled Willow Run Production Line	517
23	The Center Wing Section: The Essence of Liberator Manufacture	528
24	Knock-Down (KD) Kit Production and Transport	557
25	Was "Willit Run" a Success?	563
26	Willow Run Post-War	571

Part V: North American Dallas Plant

1	Planning and Building the Dallas Plant	579
2	NAA Builds Plant B for B-24 Production	585
3	Assembling KD and Scratch B-24s	587
4	NAA Dallas B-24 Production and Costs	592
5	NAA Dallas Plant Epilog	594

Part VI: Douglas Tulsa Plant

1	Planning and Building the Tulsa Plant	599
2	Assembling B-24s	605

Bibliography   613
Index   618

PART I

Reuben Fleet, Consolidated Aircraft, and the B-24 Liberator

1
Introduction

Along with other legendary American aviation icons, Glenn Martin and Donald Douglas, Reuben Fleet's hands-on approach was instrumental for his company's success as the development of the PBY Catalina and B-24 Liberator can be traced directly through him. In August 1933, Fleet's contemporary, Bill Boeing, retired at only fifty-one years old when his company was on the verge of finally emerging from financial limbo, and this within several years of developing the company's signature B-17, which would compete with Fleet's B-24 as America's premier early war heavy bomber. The development of the B-24 chronicles Reuben Fleet and his management of the Consolidated Aircraft Company.

2

Reuben Fleet: The Early Years

On 6 March 1887, David and Lillian Waite Fleet became the parents of Reuben Hollis Fleet in Montesano, Washington Territory. Young Reuben's father was elected as the county auditor and city clerk and became a successful, but heavily leveraged, property owner due to the railway boom in the area. During his first six years, Reuben lived in luxury, but unfortunately, the financial panic of 1893 that bankrupted one-third of all American railways also bankrupted the Fleets. While Reuben attended school in Montesano, his father worked to recoup the family's fortunes by taking jobs as a civil engineer in Alaska's gold fields and then returned to Montesano to form a successful abstract company. At age fifteen, Reuben was accepted to Virginia Military Institute where his father and his uncle, Alexander Frederick, had graduated; however, he was steered to the Culver Academy in Indiana—considered one of the most prestigious private military academies in the country—by his uncle, Col. Alexander Frederick, who founded the northern Indiana Academy after the Civil War and was the superintendent there. While there, Reuben became the editor-in-chief of the school paper and also its business manager. He also was the captain of the debating team and the 6-foot-tall Fleet played fullback on the football team as well as the center on the basketball team. In 1906, Fleet graduated second in his Culver class with the equivalent of an associate degree, but instead of continuing his college education, he returned to Montesano to become a high school teacher. Soon, Reuben's father persuaded him to resign his teaching position to join him in the abstract business. As a proviso to taking the job, the young Fleet requested that he would also be allowed to sell real estate on the side and soon he prospered in this undertaking. During this time, a romance developed between the twenty-one-year-old Fleet and his childhood sweetheart, Elizabeth Girton, whom he married in April 1908; over the next several years, they would have two children, Phyllis and David.

At age twenty-four, he was elected to the Washington State Legislature as its youngest member and was named to the Military Affairs Committee. Fleet joined the Washington National Guard in nearby Aberdeen where he was commissioned as a second lieutenant; after several years, he rose to the rank of captain. In March 1911, the National Guard was activated and dispatched to suppress a civil disturbance organized by the militant Industrial Workers of the World. Later, from April through May, Fleet and three other officers were assigned to San Diego to watch for agitators moving south to California and Mexico. During his stay in the area, Fleet became captivated with San Diego, and nearly a quarter of a century later, he would set up his aircraft business there. On his return to Washington, with a $1,500 loan from the Montesano State Bank, Fleet began investing in local real estate, buying large tracts of timberland that were subdivided and parceled out, often for railroad rights-of-way or logging, and all for a considerable profit.

Above left: During his first six years, an angelic Reuben Fleet lived in luxury, but unfortunately, the financial Panic of 1893 bankrupted the Fleet family. (*CAC/AAF*)

Above right: Uncle Col. Frederic Fleet, founder and superintendent of the prestigious Culver Academy, convinced nephew Reuben to attend, and Cadet Fleet excelled there. (*CAC/AAF*)

Left: Fleet family portrait: Reuben (R), childhood sweetheart and wife, Elisabeth Girton (L), whom he married in April 1908, and two children, Phyllis (lower) and David (upper). (*CAC/AAF*)

Below: Fleet hometown Montesano, Washington, where young, married Fleet would invest in local real estate and large tracts of timberland making a considerable profit. (*CAC/AAF*)

3

Fleet in the Service of His Country

Fleet is Introduced to Flying

In 1914, Fleet had read of the flying exploits of barnstormer Terah Maroney who was piloting flying boats off Lake Washington near Seattle, and soon Fleet flew with Maroney for his first time and became captivated by aviation. After this initial flight, Fleet flew at every opportunity with a nearby Tacoma seaplane operator. It is interesting to note that fellow Washington lumberman Bill Boeing also took his first flight with Maroney that same year and also became an aviation enthusiast, so much so he left the lumber business and would soon form the Boeing Airplane Company.

During 1915, Fleet became a Washington State Representative from the 29th District and was made chairman of the Military Affairs Committee of the House. Because of his interest in flying and some cajoling by Fleet, some of his house associates agreed that if he would fly around the Capitol building, they would support any bill that he would introduce in to help aviation. After he fulfilled the arrangement by, as reported by the *Daily Olympian*, "flying a hydro-aeroplane around the flagpole of the capitol and some of Olympia's other skyscrapers," Fleet introduced a bill to appropriate $250,000 for aviation with the Washington State National Guard, which was more than the Federal Government had allocated for national aviation.

Fleet Joins the Army as a Pilot

In 1916, Congress had appropriated $13 million for the Army Signal Corps Aviation Section, and in 1917, it set forth a provision to select one aviator from the National Guard of each state to qualify for a limited number of aircraft training positions. However, at the time, the War Department prohibited married men with children from learning to fly. Fleet and one other officer, a bachelor, were the last of eighty-three Washington Guardsmen to survive the three-day physical and mental examination for the pilot training position. The adjutant general chose the bachelor, but the persistent

Above: Fleet became captivated by aviation after he flew for the first time with barnstormer Terah Maroney who was piloting flying boats off of Lake Washington near Seattle. (*AFSHRC*)

Left: During the spring of 1917, at the relatively advanced age of thirty, Fleet closed his Montesano business and became a cadet in the Army's pilot training school in San Diego. (*CAC/AAF*)

Part I: Reuben Fleet, Consolidated Aircraft, and the B-24 Liberator 23

Fleet persuaded the AG to submit applications for two Washington representatives, and of only eleven National Guardsmen chosen from the entire country, Washington State had two. In the spring of 1917, at the relatively advanced age of age of thirty, Fleet closed his Montesano business and left for the Army's pilot training school in San Diego. Fleet reported on 5 April 1917 and the following day America declared war. Cadet Fleet received his wings as part of the sixth 1917 J.M.A. #74 (Junior Military Aviator) Class and was assigned to the 18th Aero Squadron as the Commanding Officer of the 260-man unit that trained in the Curtiss JN-4-A Jenny.

Fleet as Assistant XO of Training

In early 1918, now-Major Fleet was sent to Signal Corps HQ in Washington, D.C., to serve under Col. Henry "Hap" Arnold who had just been selected as the executive officer of the recently formed Air Division. Fleet was assigned to be the assistant executive officer to Lt. Col. Byron Jones, the chief of training who would be an influence on Fleet as a role model for his work ethic and administrative abilities.

Byron Jones was a pioneer aviator and an officer in the U.S. Army, beginning and ending his career as a cavalry officer; but in the Air Corps' formative years between 1914 and 1939, he served in various command and administrative positions and appeared to be on track in the 1930s to becoming one of the senior commanders of the Air Corps. Yet in early 1939 as a brigadier general (temporary), his views on the role of airpower diverged from those of his Air Corps contemporaries and he returned to the Army's ground forces at the beginning of World War II. Jones was an early and determined advocate of light aviation for air-armor coordination; retiring as a full colonel in 1944 due to health issues while serving in the Pacific.

Byron Jones: pioneer aviator and wartime chief of Air Corp's training. (*AAF*)

Between July 1917 and June 1918, Fleet and Jones established thirty-four primary and six advanced flight training schools for the more than 38,000 cadets who had volunteered for the rapidly expanding Signal Corps. After initial training in America, the combat training of American flying personnel was conducted in England and France.

Fleet, Officer-in-Charge of the New Aerial Mail Service

On 1 March 1918, Congress appropriated $100,000 for the War and Post Office Departments to organize air mail service jointly operated under War Department Secretary Newton Baker and Post Master General A. S. Burlsen. In earlier years, when the Post Office Department began to use new transportation systems such as railroads or steamboats, it contracted with the owners of the lines to carry the mail. Since there were no commercial airlines to contract, U.S. Army pilots and aircraft were selected to fly the mail.

From 15 May to 12 August 1918, in addition to his training duties, Fleet was appointed by Col. Hap Arnold as the officer-in-charge of the newly created Aerial Mail Service under the auspices of the Post Office Department. Fleet was tasked with setting up the first air mail service in the America, which was to be flown between New York and Washington, D.C., with a stop in Philadelphia for the exchange of mails or planes. The distance of the route was approximately 218 miles and the frequency of service was one daily round trip, except Sunday, with the service organized to begin on 15 May. On that day, Fleet left

Above left: From 15 May to 12 August 1918, in addition to his training duties, Fleet, as the officer-in-charge of the newly created Aerial Mail Service under the auspices of the Post Office Department, was tasked with setting up the first air mail service in the America. (*CAC/AAF*)

Above right: On 15 May, Fleet left Philadelphia's Bustleton Field with 300 pounds of mail and landed at Washington, D.C.'s Polo Grounds where he was greeted by President Woodrow Wilson. (*CAC/AAF*)

Philadelphia's Bustleton Field with 300 pounds of mail and landed at Washington's Polo Grounds where he was greeted by impressed dignitaries, including President Woodrow Wilson and his wife; Fleet informed the president that the Air Mail Service was operating on a wartime shoestring budget and of its problems. Six of seven flights were completed that day with one safely crash landing outside Washington.

Further World War I Assignments

After a commendable Air Mail stint, Fleet was assigned as temporary officer-in-charge of flying and commandant of cadets at the newly opened facility at Mather Field, Sacramento, California, where he spent two months. Fleet was then assigned on temporary duty to test foreign military aircraft at McCook Field, Dayton, Ohio, and after assisting in the testing of thirty-three aircraft there, Fleet was anxious to be transferred to England to observe the renowned Royal Flying Corps' Special Flying School at Gosport. Fleet arrived in England less than a month before the Armistice was signed but managed to attend and graduate from this advanced training school and was back in America just before Christmas 1918.

Fleet in the Post-war Air Service

In order to retain the talented Fleet in the post-war Air Service, Maj. Gen. Charles Menoher, chief of the Air Service, requested that Fleet be granted any position he desired. After observing the RAF Gosport facility and being involved in American air training, Fleet was convinced he could design a training aircraft superior and safer than the British Avro 504 or the U.S. Curtiss JN-4-A Jenny. To accomplish this undertaking, Fleet asked to be assigned to the engineering division at McCook Field, where Fleet's friend, Col. Thurman Bane, had been recently appointed as the commanding officer. McCook was in a war-to-peacetime transition with civilian contractors and top personnel leaving. The Air Service contracted with companies from throughout the country for new designs and Fleet's job at McCook was to act as a liaison with contractors, draw up contracts, and manage business negotiations.

McCook Field had a very influential effect on early U.S. aircraft design and designers, in 1917, six Dayton businessmen, including Edward Deeds, formed the Dayton-Wright Airplane Company, anticipating America's enormous need for military aircraft in her looming entry into World War I. During March 1917, Deeds purchased property along the Great Miami River approximately a mile north of downtown Dayton to build a public aviation field. Once America entered World War I, an urgent need developed for a research and development program for military aviation, and on 18 October 1917, McCook Field, Dayton, Ohio, was established on North Field leased by Deeds and was ready and opened on 5 December 1917. During World War I, McCook Field greatly contributed to aircraft and engine development, but its ultimate contributions came in the years after the war and for the next decade would serve as the center of American military aviation R&D.

Col. Bane has been given little credit for his contribution to American post-war advances at McCook. During the war, he headed the technical section of the Bureau

Left: After the war, Maj. Gen. Charles Menoher, chief of the Air Service, requested that the talented Reuben Fleet be granted any position he desired in the postwar Air Service and Fleet decided that he could design a training aircraft better and safer than the British Avro 504 or the U.S. Curtiss JN-4-A Jenny. (*AAF*)

Below: The Curtiss JN-4-A was initially produced as a training aircraft for the U.S. Air Service. Post-war, thousands of surplus Jennys were sold at bargain-basement prices to private owners and became the primary civil and barnstorming aircraft during the 1920s. (AAF)

of Military Aeronautics in Washington, where he formulated the requirements and specifications for all military aircraft and was responsible for the acceptance or rejection of finished aircraft. While operating with limited resources between 1918 and 1922, McCook engineers designed and built twenty-seven aircraft of various types and, in addition, the fledgling American aircraft industry also submitted many new designs while sharing their efforts and knowledge with the civilian aircraft industry. During these years, Col. Bane assembled perhaps an unequaled group of distinguished engineering and technical experts; this group pioneered research that led to the development of aircraft, engines, and instruments that contributed to American aviation's remarkable rise, resulting in world records for speed, altitude, endurance, and load. The first cantilever monoplane was designed and flown there, as well as the first all-metal aircraft. The inverted-in-line engine was developed and the exhaust-driven supercharger was first used successfully, its capabilities being demonstrated in altitude flights that broke world records. Revolutionary radial air-cooled engines were designed and developed and the first variable-pitch propeller was also developed during this time. In 1922, Col. Bane retired from the Army at his own request and returned to California and followed commercial and aeronautical pursuits. Afterward, urban growth impinged and larger aircraft were being developed, overtaxing McCook's landing areas; ultimately, the field became too small for its purpose, with no room for expansion. Dayton raised $400,673 for the purchase of 4,000 acres of land east of the city. Beginning in March 1927, 4,500 tons of McCook materiel and assets were relocated by truck to the new base, and on 12 October 1927, Wright Field was formally dedicated as the Air Corps' new test site and McCook Field passed into history.

In 1920, the struggling Boeing Airplane Company was the low bidder for an Army contract to build 200 Thomas-Morse designed MB-3 biplane pursuit aircraft. Ironically, Reuben Fleet was the contracting officer who signed the order that would keep his future competitor in business. While at McCook, Fleet was able to continue his active flying, and soon after his arrival, he and Capt. Earl White set an American long-distance and speed record, flying a de Havilland DH-9 to Hazlehurst Field, Long Island, over 664 miles in four hours and thirty-three minutes. The enthusiastic Fleet also could not resist testing several of the aircraft he would personally contract, rationalizing that he had to fly the aircraft himself in order to intelligently decide on its merits. Military life took its toll on the workaholic Fleet as the long hours, constant moving, and absences led to his divorce from Elizabeth and estrangement from his son, David.

By 1922, Fleet still had not accomplished his goal of developing his envisioned superior training aircraft, and the limitations and bureaucracy of a military career caused him to resign from the Air Service on 30 November, being awarded the Distinguished Service Medal for his service there. It was during this time at McCook that Fleet first made the acquaintance of Isaac Macklin Laddon, a civilian engineer contracted by the Army who had helped design an all-metal trainer that had been accepted by the Army as the TW-3 that had been contracted to the Gallaudet Company of East Greenwich, Rhode Island. Despite their later collaboration at Consolidated, their relationship at McCook was less than genial with Fleet considering Laddon as an "egotistical kid" while Laddon considered Fleet as a "gabby windbag."

Above: During World War I, McCook Field greatly contributed to aircraft and engine development, but its ultimate contributions to military aviation came in the years after the war. (*AAF*)

Left: Military life took its toll on the workaholic Fleet as the long hours, constant moving and absences led to his divorce from Elisabeth and estrangement from son, David. (*CAC/AAF*)

4

Fleet Becomes an Aircraft Builder

Fleet Enters Civilian Aviation Manufacture

With post-war budgets slashed and commissioned officers being reduced one rank, Fleet realized that his military aviation prospects were limited, and on 30 November 1922, Fleet resigned from military service to begin his distinguished career as an aviation industrialist. It was not long before the talented thirty-five-year-old Fleet was offered positions by three civilian companies. Boeing Airplane Company offered him a position as a vice president and general manager while Curtiss Aeroplane and Motor Company President Clement Keys offered him a position as his personal aviation advisor. However, Fleet accepted a position with the pioneering Gallaudet Aircraft Corporation that was highly respected in the industry due to its innovative founder, Edson Gallaudet, a former Yale physics professor and son of Thomas Gallaudet, founder of Gallaudet University for the Deaf. Edson Gallaudet is generally given the credit for organizing America's first aircraft factory, when in 1908, he formed the first aircraft engineering office and in 1910 established Gallaudet Engineering Company in Norwich, Connecticut, to build aircraft under contract. Over the years, Gallaudet created experimental aircraft with radical propulsion designs that while revolutionary were not viable at the time and the company was chronically in financial difficulties until America entered World War I. He reorganized as the Gallaudet Aircraft Corporation in 1917 and in May potential military orders prompted the company to open a large new factory in East Greenwich, Rhode Island; its first mass production aircraft was the 1918 production of Curtiss floatplanes. However, by 1922, it was having technical problems with its three Air Service contracts and the impractical Professor Gallaudet left the company in acute financial straits and disappeared from the aviation scene. Fleet knew of the company's problems through his Air Service contract dealings, so when new company investor and Wall Street multi-millionaire Harry Payne Whitney asked him to join Gallaudet as a company vice president and general manager, he took the position. Fleet had ulterior motives in his decision, as he knew that besides Whitney, there were many other leading Wall Street investors associated with the company whom he thought he could cultivate. Fleet's first

Above left: Professor Edson Gallaudet is generally given the credit for organizing America's first aircraft factory in 1908. (*NA*)

Above right: After joining the Gallaudet as a company vice president and general manager, Fleet untangled the company's financial problems by assuming a contract to modify fifty de Havilland DH-4 aircraft. (*AFSHRC*)

Gallaudet Factory, East Greenwich, Rhode Island. (*NA*)

step was to implement a financial analysis and found the company had lost $3 million and was worth less than $100,000. To forestall bankruptcy, Fleet terminated Gallaudet's problem contracts and assumed a contract to modify fifty de Havilland DH-4 aircraft.

TW-3

Fleet realized that Gallaudet had no promising designs and limited future prospects and looked to the General Motors subsidiary, Dayton-Wright Airplane Company, as an opportunity to build his envisioned trainer. Like Gallaudet, Dayton-Wright was having post-war problems as several of its commercial and private aircraft designs were failures and the company was under a corruption investigation for the issue of production contracts during the war. The situation was so serious that GM wished to disband the company and use its factories for automobile production. In mid-April 1923, Fleet made GM an offer to purchase its aircraft designs, good will, drawings, tools, design rights and patents. The company had built the TW-3 (Training, Water-cooled) advanced trainer powered by the 180-hp water-cooled Wright Model E engine (a license-built Hispano-Suiza V-8). The seats and dual controls of the trainer were placed side-by-side so that there was continual communication and joint observation between the student and instructor. This system was a version of the RAF Gosport system that Fleet had observed during the war. The TW-3 had mainly non-wood design features using commercial carbon steel tubing for fuselage structure, tail surface framework, struts, and landing gear components. Also the upper

The TW-3 water-cooled advanced trainer would be a future replacement for the Curtiss Jenny trainer that was to be withdrawn from service. (*AFSHRC*)

and lower wings of the biplane were interchangeable as were tail surface members. Fleet saw the TW-3 as a future replacement for the Curtiss JN-4-A Jenny trainer that was to be withdrawn from service. Wright's other contracts included the PS-1 Army pursuit version of the R.B. Racer monoplane and the Amphibian that was the Navy's W-A observation float biplane. As part of the Dayton-Wright deal, Fleet wanted the eccentric, unconventional, but brilliant TW-3 designer Col. Virginius E. Clark and his small engineering staff to be included for them to improve its design to keep it competitive and also to adapt it for the commercial market. In the negotiations GM wanted the Gallaudet Company to purchase the entire Dayton-Wright Company, not only the designs, drawings, tools, rights, and patents but also its contracts and buildings.

Fleet Creates the Consolidated Aircraft Company

Fleet did not want to take over the Dayton-Wright PS-1 and Amphibian contracts, which he thought were losing propositions; besides, Gallaudet could not afford to purchase Dayton-Wright's facilities. Fleet recognized that Gallaudet with its $3.5 million debt and past financial record was in no position to meet GM's demands and made a personal proposal to the Gallaudet Company hopefully receiving backing from Gallaudet's Wall Street investors that he had cultivated. Fleet wished only to acquire the TW-3, its drawings, tools, and patents along with the services of Col. Clark from GM with which he could profitably build twenty to twenty-five TW-3s. Fleet's proposal was to organize a new company, lease Gallaudet facilities, fulfill its contracts, and then terminate that company. Fleet offered Gallaudet a 40 percent stake in his new company, to pay rent from 10 percent of his profits, to divide his salary 50:50 between Gallaudet and the new company, to split overhead and to work out an agreement with the 400 Gallaudet's workers to finish existing contracts while building the TW-3s. Gallaudet's Wall Street investors balked at joining Fleet, and on 19 May 1923, Fleet formed the Consolidated Aircraft Corporation without them. Fleet had a good relationship with Gallaudet President Kelly Robinson who realized the financial benefits of associating with Fleet and an agreement was signed to lease the East Greenwich, Rhode Island, facility and for the employment of it labor force. The lease was to expire at the end of 1923 or until Consolidated completed its anticipated government contract for the TW-3 training aircraft (the lease was contingent on Consolidated receiving the order). In order for the proposed venture to be consummated, two major issues had to be resolved beginning with bankrolling the venture. The new company had an authorized capital of $60,000 (600 shares at $100 each). Fleet had $15,000 to invest and he received $10,000 from his sister, Lillian, and her lumberman husband, Edward "Ned" Bishop, back in Montesano. Thus, to meet the GM offer, Fleet was able to fund a $35,000 consideration. The final obstacle was hurdled when the Air Service signed a $200,000 contract with Fleet for twenty TW-3s and spare parts equal to three aircraft. This order came only two weeks before the Army's fiscal year production allotment would have reverted back to the Treasury

Department. On 10 June, Consolidated signed a contract with Dayton-Wright for which it received a sample TW-3, manufacturing equipment and tools, its design and production rights, and the services of Col. Clark. Fleet also received an unofficial agreement from GM that it would assign Dayton-Wright aviation patents to Consolidated.

As his first step, Fleet moved the TW-3 "Project A" and Col. Clark from Dayton-Wright's Ohio factory to the Gallaudet Rhode Island factory. As soon as the first TW-3 trainers rolled off the production line, Fleet stimulated sales by demonstrating them to the Army and Navy. Fleet flew the TWs back to Dayton and McCook Field for demonstration flights. Army inspectors at McCook decided to withhold approval charging that Fleet's design changes made at Gallaudet were solely to increase profits. Laddon, still at McCook, was sent to investigate the changes made to the aircraft he originally helped to design. Naturally, Fleet was pessimistic about the Laddon inspection but was surprised when Laddon admitted that that the changes actually improved the designed and reported so. By the end of the year, Consolidated had delivered the twenty TW-3s to the Army at Brooks Field, San Antonio, Texas. To get feedback on the trainer, Fleet, Gallaudet Factory Manager George Newman, and Col. Clark flew to Brooks Field. (Later, Newman would join Fleet and become instrumental in the company's hierarchy.) The Army instructors informed them that they did not find the side-by-side seating arrangement suitable, as they could not see the ground on the opposite side of the aircraft during the critical landing procedure. As a remedy, Fleet narrowed the fuselage and placed the instructor/student seating in tandem and this version of the TW-3 was dubbed the Camel because of the hump between the two cockpits. The large radiator and cowl of the in-line water-cooled Hispano-Suiza V-8 (Hisso Vee) engine made forward visibility difficult. The solution was to remove the top of the cowl and deduct $50 from the cost of future trainers that were manufactured without cowl tops. The large radiator core presented a more difficult resolution. The present costly radiator was an intricate twelve-sided core built from hexagonal brass tubing that had to be laborious fitted and dip-soldered. Fleet developed a successful cost-effective rectangular radiator core placed below the propeller so the pilot could see over it.

Virginius E. Clark

Clark was born at Uniontown, Pennsylvania, on 27 February 1886. After public schooling, he graduated from the Naval Academy in 1907 and crewed with the battleship fleet's round-the-world voyage of 1908–1909, and then joined the Coast Artillery and served at Boston, San Francisco, and Honolulu, 1910–1912. During the summer of 1913, he joined the Aviation Section, Signal Corps, and learned to fly at San Diego, earning FAI certificate #273 on 19 November. After a temporary return to the Coast Artillery, he was detailed in the Aviation Section on 5 October 1913, rated junior military aviator with rank of captain and would be rated military aviator after the required three years. During the fall of 1914, he participated in the new MIT aeronautical engineering course at his own expense as at the time the Signal Corps had no funds to grant for this purpose. He was MIT's first recipient of an aeronautical engineering degree and after graduation became the aeronautical engineer of the Signal Corps. During 1916, he was stationed in Washington, D.C., to test aircraft and inspect plants; was made a member of the National Advisory Committee for Aeronautics (NACA); and in 1917 was appointed as a member of the Joint Army and Navy Board on Rigid Airships. From 1917–1918, he was the first CO of McCook Field and had been the Army's chief aeronautical engineer at McCook while Fleet was there. The gifted and eccentric Clark left the Air Service in 1920, reportedly being drummed out of the service for "conduct unbecoming an officer and gentleman," which included a court martial and civil action for bigamy. He would become the Dayton-Wright Company's chief engineer (1920–1923) during the time the company won first place in the Navy shipboard amphibian competition and this success was followed by entering various models in Army competitions. In 1922, he became famous for his series of Clark flat bottom, deep mid-section "Y" airfoils widely used in general-purpose aircraft designs and has been much studied in aerodynamics over the years. The Lockheed Vega, Lindbergh's *Spirit of St. Louis*, the Waco F series, and the Stinson Reliant were a prominent examples of the Clark Y, giving these aircraft reasonable overall performance in respect to their lift-to-drag ratio and gentle and relatively benign predictable stall characteristics (which also makes the Clark Y useful today for RC model aircraft). The Clark YH foil was used by the Hawker Hurricane and several Russian World War II aircraft, including the ubiquitous Ilyushin Il-2 Sturmovik and the MiG-3. That same year, Clark also became vice president of the prestigious Society of Aeronautic Engineers (SAE).

In 1923, Fleet lured him into becoming vice president and chief engineer at Consolidated in order to develop the PT-1, which won first place in an Army competition. Over the years, the peculiar but extraordinary Clark had regularly submitted his resignation, often over petty squabbles with Fleet. In June 1927, Clark submitted his seventh resignation; unfortunately, it was during the development of the PT-3 and in the middle of the Patrick excess profit refund debate. The exasperated Fleet had put up with Clark's unconventional actions and accepted Clark's resignation. Clark later worked for the Duramold Division of Fairchild Aircraft in the mid-1930s. Similar to plywood, Duramold and other lightweight composite materials were considered critical during periods of material shortage in World War II, replacing scarce materials like aluminum alloys and steel. At Fairchild, he designed a series of single-engined monoplane utility transports with high-mounted wings: the Fairchild 100, Fairchild 150 (called the Clark GA-43), and the Fairchild F-46, in which was the first successful aircraft (first flight 12 May 1937) to use molded plywood. The fuselage was constructed of two halves bonded together and the wings used wooden spars with plywood covering. He later became a consultant at Hughes Aircraft Company, where his Duramold process would later be used to fabricate the infamous Howard Hughes' gigantic *Spruce Goose* flying boat.

Virginius Clark among notable companions. *Standing, left to right*: Capt. Edgar Gorell, Asst. Naval Consultant Jerome Hunsaker, Lt. John Towers, and Capt. Clark. *Sitting, left to right*: Lt. Cdr. Arthur Atkins and Maj. Benjamin Foulois (*AFSHRC*)

Hispano-Suiza V-8 (HS-8) Engines

In 1914, Hispano-Suiza 8A designer Marc Birgikt intended his 140-hp (the 8F reached 300 hp), water-cooled, eight-cylinder engine in 90-degree Vee configuration as a lightweight and powerful replacement for contemporary rotary engines that, due to their exaggerated torque, were physically and mentally demanding for a pilot to control. Popularly known as the "Hisso" or "Hisso Vee," it was the first mass-produced engine to have solid aluminum cylinder blocks into which steel sleeves were threaded to form the cylinder housing. The French government ordered production of the Model 8A to be started as soon as possible and issued a requirement for the new SPAD VII single-seat high-performance fighter aircraft to be equipped with the new engine, which would allow the Allies to regain air superiority the Germans. The Hisso also powered the Dayton-Wright SJ-1 trainer and the two Curtiss "Jenny" trainers (the JN-4H and JN-6H.) The 49,000 dependable and durable Hissos were the most commonly used and most successful engine powering the aircraft of the Entente Powers during World War I, often being referred to as the Rolls-Royce Merlin of World War I. HS-8 engines and variants produced by Hispano-Suiza and other companies under license were built in twenty-one factories in Spain, France, Britain, Italy, and the U.S. by Wright with derivatives of the engine also being used abroad to power numerous aircraft types.

Hispano-Suiza 8A: "Hisso" or "Hisso Vee." (*AFSHRC*)

Consolidated Produces the First Primary Trainers

Buffalo Plant Established

In May 1924, Fleet resigned as general manager of Gallaudet and began to look for a new factory to build the fifty PT-1s. Labor was a problem in the east as, to operate the 450-man Rhode Island Gallaudet plant, workers had to be imported from New York and Boston. After investigating a number of locations, Fleet settled on Buffalo, New York, as it had a large trained labor pool and had been the home to the Curtiss Aeroplane and Motor Company. The modern, government-built wartime Curtiss plant had been purchased by the American Radiator Company that leased it to Consolidated in September 1924 under a ten-year "accordion" lease that allowed Consolidated to expand or contract the leased square footage as dictated by the different demands of its various contracts. Fleet shipped Consolidated's equipment and records by rail from the Gallaudet plant and soon PT-1 production began.

PT-1 (Model 1) Trusty

In May 1924, the Army announced an official competition for its new PT (Primary Trainer) classification to replace the venerable discontinued Jenny. Fleet had a contender ready in the tandem Camel that Consolidated had redesignated as the PT-1 Trusty (Model 1), which had been heavily based on the TW-3. In a fly-off on 10 June 1924 against such companies as Fokker, Thomas-Morse, Vought, Cox-Klemin, and Huff-Daland, Consolidated was awarded an initial $500,000 contract for fifty of its

Above left: For his new Consolidated Buffalo Plant, Fleet purchased the former modern, government-built World War I Curtiss Aeroplane and Motor Company Plant during September 1924. (*AFSHRC*)

Above right: Buffalo Plant machine shop. (*CAC/AAF*)

Buffalo Plant main assembly hall with PT-1s being assembled in the background. (*CAC/AAF*)

Fleet's PT-1 (Model 1) Trusty design won the 1924 Army Air Service contract for a primary trainer, which would became the first trainer that was purchased in significant numbers following World War I because of its excellent ability to make a quick and effective recovery from the spins, which were dreaded by the cadets. (*AAF*)

Consolidated Buffalo meets the Army Air Service. *Left to right*: George Newman (works manager), Raymond Whitman (chief of inspection), Thomas Kenney (treasurer), Virginius Clark (chief engineer), Reuben Fleet (president), J. L. Kelley (AAS plant representative), 1Lt. Kenneth Wolfe (later major general), Carl Cover (AAS test pilot), Capt. Ralph Royce (later brigadier general), and PT-1 in background. (*CAC/AAF*)

trainers that were destined to continue as America's primary trainer for many years. The PT-1 trainer can be best described as a very unattractive but very functional and rugged aircraft that was the ideal for its intended job. The 27-foot 9.25-inch-long trainer had a wingspan of 34 feet 5.25 inches, and had a maximum take-off weight of 2,577 pounds. It was powered by a 180-hp Wright licensed Hispano E eight-cylinder, water-cooled Vee engine that gave it maximum speed of 92 mph and a cruising speed of 79 mph over a range of 350 miles. However, the trainer was prone to overheating and was ordinarily flown without its engine cowling.

Within a year, the Army had approved an additional 150 trainers to be contracted at fifty trainers initially and then fifty more in two months followed by fifty more in another two months. Subsequently, the PT-1 became the first trainer that the Army Air Service purchased in significant numbers following World War I. It was flown extensively by aviation cadets during the late 1920s and early 1930s. The easy to fly trainer earned its nickname "Trusty" due to its excellent ability to make a quick and effective recovery from the spins, which were dreaded by the cadets. It was so easy to fly that many cadets had problems when they graduated to faster, more advanced aircraft.

PT-3 (Model 2) Husky

With the success of the Navy's NY-1's switch to a Wright J-4 Whirlwind radial engine of the PT-1 airframe (see next), Fleet realized that the Army would soon require that the Hisso Vee would also be replaced with a Wright radial engine. The revised Consolidated Model 2 trainer was redesigned by the AAC as the PT-3. The Wright J-4 radial engine was reliable and offered an effective power-to-weight ratio. One PT-1 airframe was completed as XPT-2 with a 220-hp Wright J-5 Whirlwind radial engine. The XPT-3 was almost identical to the XPT-2 except for the tail, modified wing panels and a somewhat altered fuselage configuration. In September 1927, 130 production PT-3 aircraft were ordered (with one as the XO-17). Despite the engine change and Virginius Clark's resignation, Consolidated was nevertheless able to produce 310 of the new PT-3 Husky trainers in 1928, 177 to the Army, and 133 as NY-2s to the Navy, which was already using the Wright J-4 engine since they were introduced and adopted by the Navy as a stock power plant in 1925. The XPT-3 became the XPT-5 when equipped with the Curtiss Challenger R-600 two-row six-cylinder radial engine but was soon converted to PT-3 standard. In 1937, the PT-3 trainers were supplanted by another excellent, enduring trainer, the Boeing PT-13 Stearman.

NY-1/-2/-3 Huskys

After their experience in building the PT-1 and TW-3 trainers, Consolidated was again well-positioned for the Navy's 1925 competition for the procurement of a new training aircraft for which Consolidated offered its successful PT-1. The trainer was 31 feet 4.25 inches long, with a wingspan 40 feet, and a maximum take-off weight of 2,843 pounds. Fleet won the low bid competition against fourteen other companies. The first order was for sixteen model NY-1 (N=Navy, Y=Consolidated) trainers also nicknamed the Husky. Soon the Navy ordered forty more followed by ten more, all with spares. The Navy decided to use the air-cooled 200-hp Wright J-4 Whirlwind

Above: PT-3 (Model 2) Husky. (*AAF*)

Below left: Reuben Fleet (L) and Virginius Clark (L) pose with unnamed British Flying Corps representatives during the static test of the PT-3. (*CAC/AAF*)

Below right: Reuben Fleet poses proudly in later years with the PT-3, which gave Consolidated its start toward becoming one of America's great aircraft companies. (*CAC/AAF*)

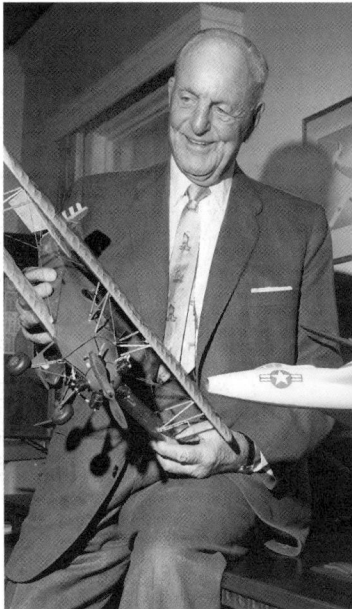

The success of the PTs-1/3 gave Consolidated a leg up for the Navy's 1925 new training aircraft contracts, which was won by its NY-1 Husky (N=Navy, Y=Consolidated) trainer. (*USN*)

Lt. James Doolittle flew the NY-2 in the first completely hooded 'blind' flight on 24 September 1929 for which he was awarded the 1930 Harmon Trophy. (*AAF*)

nine-cylinder engine in the NY-1 while the Army continued with the water-cooled Hisso Vee engine in the PT-1. This engine gave the NY's a maximum speed of 78 knots/90 mph, a cruising speed of 65 knots/75 mph over a range of 210 miles. The NY series could be operated from either wheels or floats but the most obvious feature was a fully rounded and much larger rudder that was necessary to compensate for the increased length of the seaplane versions. Lt. James Doolittle flew the NY-2 in the first completely hooded 'blind' flight on 24 September 1929 at Mitchell Field, Long Island, for which he was awarded the 1930 Harmon Trophy.

N2Y-1

During 1930, the Navy was preparing Curtiss F9C Sparrowhawk fighters for operational service for in-flight launching and recovery of aircraft by the Navy's massive rigid airships. To train pilots for this technique, the Navy purchased six specially-equipped Husky Junior two-seat trainers. All N2Y-1s were powered by the five-cylinder, 115-hp Kinner K-5 engine and were equipped with a "skyhook" mounted over the upper wings to be used with the airship's "trapeze" recovering gear. The specially-designed Sparrowhawk fighters were stored in the airship's large hangar and were to supply the airships with their own fighter protection. After training, airship flying operations became so routine that the Sparrowhawks had their fixed landing gear removed for better performance and longer range as reconnaissance aircraft. The pilots and their Sparrowhawks were first assigned to USS *Los Angeles* (ZR-3) and USS *Akron* (ZRS-4), then, with *Los Angeles'* retirement in 1932, and the loss of *Akron* in 1933, the remaining N2Ys were assigned to USS *Macon* (ZRS-5). In April 1933, *Akron* had crashed during a storm over the Atlantic, with one of the fatalities being the Navy's first chief of the Bureau of Aeronautics (BuAer) and airship advocate, R/Adml. William Moffett. After considering the airship's vulnerability in bad weather and during future wartime service, Moffett's loss, and the Navy's Depression era budget restrictions, the Navy wisely chose to concentrate on the more promising shipboard air operations.

O-17 Courier

In late 1926, the Army issued specifications for a new advanced trainer and Consolidated responded with the XO-17 Courier (CAC Model 8) that was a streamlined, modified PT-3/NY-2. The OX-17 was entered in a competition at McCook Field on April 4, 1927 and with its good performance and Fleet's powerful sales pitch, emphasizing his company's strong position in the training aircraft field, Consolidated was contracted to deliver twenty-eight O-17s in 1928. In 1929, Consolidated's primary trainer sales continued to be strong, as the Army purchased seventy-three PT-3s and the Navy purchased sixty NY-2s and twenty-five NY-1s. However, after the 1929 Depression, 1930 Navy sales slumped to twenty NY-2s and one NY-1, and sales to the Army also diminished substantially. After selling 865 trainers in seven years as the largest volume manufacturer of aircraft in the U.S., the Consolidated Aircraft Company era of manufacturing the best and safest training aircraft in the world was at an end.

During 1930, six specially-equipped N2Y-1 Husky Junior trainers were used to train future Curtiss F9C Sparrowhawk fighter pilots for in-flight launching and recovery by the Navy's huge rigid airships. (*USN*)

During late 1926, the Army issued specifications for a new advanced trainer and Consolidated responded with their XO-17 Courier (CAC Model 8). (*AAF*)

Consolidated's Excess Profits

The Consolidated Airplane Company had $213,975 in sales and a profit of $201.90 (yes, a correct number) during its first year, and by 1925, it passed $593,000 in sales and then did over $1 million over each of the next two years. The company was America's leading training aircraft producer selling 326 trainers, 260 to the Army, and sixty-six to the Navy. Consolidated had been awarded Army contracts only after open and competitive bidding, and through volume purchasing and an efficient production line, Consolidated had managed to reduce the cost per unit to both the Army and Navy and still boost its bottom line.

During 1927, the Buffalo Factory had seen orders increase to new levels and head for the $1 million Fleet envisioned. By mid-1927, cumulative profits on the trainers Consolidated had built since 1923 had reached $867,000 and profits so far in 1927 were $202,000. So impressive were these profits that the Army asked to inspect Consolidated's books, and although the laws of that time prevented the Army's inspection, Fleet agreed to the inspection. The Army declared that Fleet had made an excess $300,000 profit from the PT-1 contracts!

Maj. Gen. Mason Patrick, appointed chief of the Air Service during October 1921, seemed to have a particular axe to grind with the company and insisted it return $300,000 of the $800,000 in profits it had made in its first four years of business. Fleet confronted Patrick personally but soon saw he had no alternative but to pay the $300,000 as without the Army and Navy as customers, his company had no business. Fleet asked the Air Corps to negotiate; proposing that the Air Corps buy fifty trainers at $1 each at which the Army would lose nothing by agreeing and Fleet would save face and recover a margin of profit on each. Then, at the spiteful Patrick's urging, the Navy also received thirteen NY-1s at $1 each. The result of this excess profits penalty was that Consolidated was unable to pay a stockholder's dividends for nine and half years and Patrick's decision would be the first step in Fleet's disillusionment in doing business with the military and government over the next fifteen years.

Fleet received some solace when he found that the Navy had flatly refused to agree with the Army's charge of excessive profits. On 3 August 1927, Patrick received a memo from R/Adml. W. A. Moffett, chief of the Navy's Bureau of Aeronautics:

> The records of the Navy Department covering its transactions with Consolidated Aircraft Corporation show that all procurements from it have been subjected to competition in accordance with law.... It is evident that potential competitors put forth their best efforts to obtain this business. The Navy Department is not in a position to question the profits the company may have made.

Above left: Maj. Gen. Mason Patrick, chief of the Air Service. (*AAF*)

Above right: Medal of Honor recipient R/Adml. William Moffett is considered as the architect of U.S naval aviation. (*USN*)

Consolidated Enters the Large Aircraft Market

In late 1926, the Army issued a requirement for a twin-engined night bomber that came at a time when Fleet foresaw that the market for his PT-3 and NY-2 trainers would diminish (although not by a Depression) and decided to enter the competition. As an initial step, the savvy Fleet opened an office in Dayton to be close to the Army's new Wright Field engineering and testing facility and to his old base and contacts at McCook Field. Previously Fleet had optioned a parcel of land adjacent to the Army Wright Field facility for a new Consolidated design and research center but was forced to abandon the idea by Brig. Gen. William Gillmore, Wright Field commander, who believed that would give Consolidated an unfair advantage. During March 1927, Fleet engaged three design engineers from McCook Field when he hired Isaac Maclin "Mac" Laddon and then added Bernard Sheahan, from Design Branch 3, and Roy Miller, a structural engineer.

Issac Laddon

Issac Machlin "Mac" Laddon is considered Consolidated Aircraft's most important and influential persona after Reuben Fleet. Laddon was born in Garfield, New Jersey, on Christmas Day in 1894 but lived in Montreal as a child. He entered Montreal's prestigious McGill University studying mining engineering, but midway through his education there, he was compelled attend the University of Pennsylvania for a year, which offered no mining course; returning to McGill, he was awarded a civil engineering degree in 1915.

After graduation, Laddon was employed the Cadillac Motor Car Company Experimental Engineering Department. Two years later, the twenty-three-year-old Laddon left Cadillac because, as America readied for World War I, the Cadillac division of General Motors was asked to produce the new Liberty aircraft engine, but pacifist William Durant, the co-founder of General Motors with Frederic Smith, did not want General Motors or Cadillac facilities to be used for producing war material. With no work at GM, Laddon left for Washington, D.C., which was recruiting automotive engineers for experimental work on airplanes at the Smithsonian Institution's barn-like "Greenhouse" hangar, which was directed by future aviation icon, Donald Douglas. Laddon was considered a radiator expert and designed radiators for his first aircraft, a de Havilland and a Bristol fighter. From the Smithsonian, he was reassigned to McCook Field, but soon, in late 1918, because he spoke French (living in Montreal as a child), he transferred from McCook to the Packard Motor Car Company's Detroit aircraft division, where he worked with the French Mission. He was assigned as an aeronautical engineer under Capt. George LePere, developing the French-designed LePere C-11, O-11, and GH-1 two-seat fighters commissioned and built in America during World War I. The C-11 was later designated as the LePere USAC-11 or LUSAC-11 and was ordered in large numbers by the U.S. Army Air Corps, but were cancelled at the end of the war and only thirty were built and were used for experimental purposes. One LUSAC-11, equipped with one of the first turbochargers that Laddon helped to develop at McCook, was flown by Maj. Rudolf Schroeder who made an attempt for the world altitude record on 27 February 1920. Schroeder's oxygen supply failed after he reached 33,113 feet, a new world record, causing the pilot to black out, only regaining consciousness close to the ground. The same aircraft was flown to 34,508 feet on 28 September 1921 by Lt. John Macready, for which he won the Mackay Trophy.

After the Armistice, and remaining as a civilian employee of the War Department, Laddon returned to McCook and joined the U.S. Air Service Experimental and Engineering Test Center. Here he headed the Heavy Aircraft Design Branch 2, which was developing larger aircraft for the Army, with the emphasis on bombers and heavy armored aircraft. The twenty-five-year-old Laddon honed his engineering and design genius and conceived the large twin-engined triplane GAX Ground Attack Experimental bomber with an armor-plated fuselage and powered by twin Liberty pusher engines with a removable power plant installation encased in armor plate. Boeing produced ten GA-1s, which were assigned to the 3rd Attack Group at Kelly Field, Texas, but their 2,500 pounds of armor and armament made them too heavy to effectively fly combat missions. While designing the GAX, Laddon conducted the aviation's first fuselage stress analysis using his civil-engineering knowledge of structures. At this time, the whole field of aerodynamics was open for exploration, with no guidelines or set configurations to follow, and Laddon found the challenge immensely exhilarating.

Laddon is generally credited with designing America's first all-metal monoplane, the CO-1 observation aircraft. Two prototypes were built by the Army at McCook Field, one for static test and the other to be first flown on 26 July 1922. Two crewmen were carried along with 287 pounds of observation equipment and 300 pounds of defensive armament, two fixed Browning and two flexible Lewis guns. On 22 June 1922, the Gallaudet Aircraft Corporation received a contract to develop a production version. All three prototypes were Liberty-powered biplanes, except the first CO-1. Their version of the CO-1, improved with balanced ailerons and strengthened landing gear, first flew 20 June 1923 but only one example was built as the wing location detracted from the observer's vision.

During September 1924, the Naval Aircraft Factory in Philadelphia was assigned to design a long-range twin-engined flying boat, capable of flying 2,400 miles between San Francisco and Hawaii. In completing the initial design, Laddon assisted expert Navy aero-engineer Capt. Holden "Dick" Richardson who graduated from the Naval Academy in 1901 and received his master's degree in aeronautics from MIT. Laddon received much of his expertise in designing the future PBY Catalina flying boat during his tenure with Richardson. The aircraft was then sent to Boeing for detailed design and construction as the Boeing/Laddon Model 50 flying boat, a two-bay biplane with a beautifully streamlined lower metal hull design and with the upper hull half constructed of laminated wooden frames with a wood veneer covering. The cluttered wing superstructures were of metal construction, with wooden wingtips and leading edges supporting two 800-hp Packard 2A-2500 V12 engines, driving four-bladed propellers, mounted in tandem between the wings above the fuselage. From 1923–1927, Laddon was granted patents on aircraft wheels, brakes, and aerodynamic and structural developments.

Fleet's trainers had established Consolidated's reputation and given it a firm financial footing and the time was right for Fleet to branch out. He began by organizing the Products Corporation, which, because of its nearby location, was able to easily supply parts to Consolidated. Next, he supplemented Consolidated's Unit I (the designation for training aircraft) with newly established Unit II for heavy aircraft.

However, despite the popular influence of Lindbergh's epic transatlantic flight, the Air Service's interest in new designs had stagnated and was only concerned with small parts and accessory design. Laddon found that his creative genius was unchallenged as a civilian engineer at McCook and Reuben Fleet found that Laddon was ready for a change. Fleet approached Laddon to head the new section and as an incentive offered stock participation and virtual *carte blanche* as a designer.

Laddon accepted, and over a quarter of century, he became renowned as the man who was to design the PBY Catalina, the B-24 Liberator, and the B-36 Peacemaker, joining Douglas Aircraft's Ed Heinemann as the era's premiere designers. During his tenure at Consolidated, "Mac" possessed an inventiveness that was the result of his ability to apply his engineering knowledge to bring about practical solutions. Laddon would become the backbone of the Consolidated Design Department and would be

Above: Isaac "Mac" Laddon's design of the PBY *Catalina*, the B-24 Liberator, and the B-36 Peacemaker ranked him and Douglas' Ed Heinemann as the era's premiere aircraft designers. (*AFSHRC*)

Below: Isaac Laddon is generally credited with designing America's first all-metal monoplane, the CO-1 observation aircraft. (*AAF*)

the patent holder on a great variety of aircraft systems and aerodynamic and structural innovations. Laddon personally felt the ultimate designer's responsibility and he flew with his own designs on their every first flight. In 1939, Laddon became vice president of Consolidated engineering. Later, after Reuben Fleet had sold his majority stock to Vultee, Laddon became one of the directors of the Consolidated-Vultee Aircraft Corporation; as such, he was responsible for the design and development of great aircraft such as the B-36 intercontinental bomber and the Convair two-engined passenger aircraft that became very popular with airlines worldwide after World War II. Laddon was invested in the International Aerospace Hall of Fame in 1975. Isaac Machlin Laddon died in San Diego on 15 January 1976 at the age of eighty-one.

Sikorsky-Consolidated S-37B Model 11 Bomber

In April 1927, Fleet wished to associate with a designer and builder of large aircraft, and contacted Igor Sikorsky, head of the Sikorsky Manufacturing Company of Long Island, New York, who developed the all-metal, 100-foot wingspan, S-35 trimotor, bi-wing seaplane. The S-35 had impressed the Air Corps during flights at Bolling Field, Washington, D.C., in early 1926. Later that year, French World War I fighter ace Rene Fonck, whose seventy-five victories ranked him second after top world war ace von Richthofen's eighty, had selected the Sikorsky aircraft for his attempt to be the first to fly from New York to Paris non-stop. The S-35 was four-man twin-engined sesquiplane where one wing, usually the lower, had no more than half the surface area of the other (e.g. one-and-a-half wings). Fonck's 20 September 1926 flight met disaster on take-off as a landing gear failed and the overloaded S-35 crashed and burned off the end of the runway. Fonck and his co-pilot managed to escape, but two crewmen in the rear fuselage perished. The next year, Fonck returned to America with new funding to again attempt the first transatlantic flight and chose Sikorsky's new S-37 design that was similar to the S-35 but was powered by twin engines. When Charles Lindbergh flew solo across the Atlantic on 20–21 May 1927 in his Ryan monoplane, *Spirit of St. Louis*, Fonck canceled his plans and his S-37, *Ville de Paris*, reverted back to Sikorsky and would become the *Southern Star* that flew South American routes for American International Airways of Argentina.

During 1926–27, the Army had been funded to re-equip its bomber fleet and in 1927 announced its night bomber competition. Fleet discussed the conversion of the S-37 design with Sikorsky as an entrant, but Sikorsky's facilities limited his company to the production of only the prototype. The two men struck a deal that if the Consolidated-Sikorsky team won the competition, Consolidated would manufacture all the bombers but all design responsibilities were to be Sikorsky's with Consolidated's Mac Laddon and Roy Miller to direct armament installation and supervise structural stress analysis. However, due to Sikorsky's poor financial position, major investors refused to allow Sikorsky and his head engineer, Michael Gluhareff, to further develop the design and correct any faults. Consolidated would buy the prototype for $50,000, which also included a license to build aircraft on a

Above: After a disastrous attempt to fly the first transatlantic flight in the Sikorsky S-35, French World War I fighter ace Rene Fonck chose Sikorsky-Consolidated's new S-37 for his second attempt. (*AFSHRC*)

Left: Rene Fonck posing with Sikorsky S-37 *Ville de Paris* before his attempt to be the first to fly from New York to Paris non-stop, which was cancelled after Lindbergh was successful. (*NC*)

royalty basis when (if) the government awarded the contract. Consolidated was to be the primary contractor and would furnish engines and instruments but Consolidated would subcontract 30 percent of the airframe work back to Sikorsky. The bomber was named the Consolidated-Sikorsky Guardian (Sikorsky Model S-37B and CAC Model 111) and was adapted from Sikorsky's S-37 built for French Capt. Rene Fonck. It was powered by two Pratt and Whitney 525-hp Hornet engines, which sped the aircraft to a maximum speed of 128 mph. The fuel tanks were located in the nacelle behind the engine. The sesquiplane had a 100-foot wingspan and weighed 14,650 pounds including a 1,952-pound bombload. The five-man crew included a pilot, bombardier, relief pilot, and three gunners, one of whom acted as the radio operator. Once the prototype was completed on 27 December 1927, it was designated by the AAC as the XB-936. Fleet employed Lt. Leigh Wade, a friend from his McCook days, as the company's test pilot. Initial tests were conducted at Roosevelt Field, Long Island, and it soon was apparent that the bomber was grossly underpowered by 1,000 pounds and its performance was mediocre at best. At the Dayton competition that was won by the Curtiss B-2 Condor, the Consolidated-Sikorsky Guardian placed a poor third, an inauspicious entry for Fleet in the bomber market. (Note: Although the Curtiss B-2 had the best performance, the smaller and less expensive Keystone XLB-6 was awarded the contract for twelve XLB-6s in June 1928.) After its rejection, the aircraft was rebuilt in 1929 by Sikorsky as a twenty-one-seat transport with two 675-hp P&W Hornets, which were replaced by P&W Jupiters from the S-37-1. In 1934, it was rebuilt and reregistered as NR942M but crashed at sea that year. This joint venture, to be his last, was a major disappointment to Maj. Fleet and was to be Consolidated's last undertaking with the Army for the next decade.

Leigh Wade: During his lifetime, Wade was both a military and civilian pilot. He became a cadet in the Aviation Section of the Signal Corps in 1917 and received flight training from the Royal Canadian Air Force and in France, and then served as a flight instructor in 1918. In 1919, he was assigned as a test pilot to the Air Service Engineering Division at McCook Field where he met Reuben Fleet and set two altitude records. In 1924, Wade piloted the *Boston*, one of four Douglas World Cruisers attempting the first around-the-world flight and finished the flight in the *Boston II* after the original *Boston* crashed in the Atlantic. He then became chief of the Flight Test Branch at McCook in 1926. Fleet signed him as Consolidated chief test pilot from 1928 to 1929 and then he became a very successful Consolidated aircraft sales executive in the U.S. and South America until 1941. During World War II, Wade served in the AAF Air Intelligence Section, then with the First Bomber Group. He later commanded Batista Field, Cuba, and served with the 14th Air Force. After the war, Wade became air *attaché* to Greece in 1949 and to Brazil in 1952, and served as chief of the air section on the joint Brazil–United States military commission until he retired as a major general in 1955.

Above: The Sikorsky-Consolidated Guardian was Consolidated's especially unsuccessful entry in the 1927 Army night bomber competition. (*AAF*)

Left: Leigh Wade: Army Air Service and Consolidated chief test pilot and successful Consolidated aircraft sales executive in the U.S. and South America. (*AAF*)

Consolidated Designs and Builds Flying Boats

XPY-1 Admiral (Model 9)

Despite the Sikorsky-Consolidated S-37B Guardian semi-fiasco, Fleet was not dissuaded from entering the large aircraft market and was given another opportunity when the Navy issued specifications and requirements for a new long-range monoplane patrol aircraft, using twin 425-hp air-cooled P&W Wasp radials. The Navy's early patrol flying boats had been biplanes, but by the late 1920s, the Navy was interested in developing a large all-metal (except for fabric covered wings) monoplane with a 100-foot wingspan powered by radial engines with an operational range of 2,000 miles (not coincidentally, the approximate distance between California and Hawaii) and a cruising speed of 110 mph. Navy patrol planes had been exclusively designed by Navy designers or by the Naval Aircraft Factory with the hull design furnished by Capt. Holden Richardson of the Navy's Bureau of Aeronautics who was the world's leading expert on flying boat hulls. However, the Navy decided to open the new design to outside competition but using Richardson's hull design. Fleet moved Mac Laddon, Roy Miller, Bernard Sheahan, and the Consolidated design group back to the Buffalo home office to begin a new undertaking, the design and manufacture of flying boats, a domain in which Consolidated would become a world leader and purveyor through the end of World War II. While employed by the Air Service at McCook Field, Laddon, Miller, and Sheahan moonlighted in Laddon's basement, joined by Boeing engineer, Louis Marsh, who had designed the Boeing PB-1 biplane flying boat. At Buffalo, Laddon and Miller and Buffalo factory engineer, Joseph Gwinn, were given a thirty-man engineering and drafting team that, on 28 February 1928, won the Navy design competition. A $150,000 contract was let to build a prototype that was designated as the XPY-1, the first eXperimental Patrol aircraft built by Consolidated ("Y" was Consolidated's letter designator because Curtiss had previously used the "C" designator). The schmoozing Fleet decided to name the prototype the Admiral after R/Adml. William Moffett who was instrumental in administering the competition and drawing up the contracts. The XPY-1 was a five-man reconnaissance patrol plane powered by two 425-hp P&W Wasp engines mounted on struts between the hull and wing. Laddon also patented a design for a third engine that was to be mounted on the wing center section. Fleet, as the far-sighted and perpetual businessman, had the aircraft provisionally designed with a 60-foot cabin so it could be converted into a thirty-two passenger airliner. In March, the Consolidated Company began work on the XPY-1 prototype at its Buffalo factory. The company was inexperienced in producing what would be America's largest aircraft to that time, but the inevitable problems of a new design were met and solved, and in late December, the Admiral was ready for testing. The aircraft measured almost 62 feet long, over 17 feet high, had a wing span of 100 feet, and weighed 17,600 pounds. For testing, nearby Lake Erie and the Niagara River were frozen over and a new testing site was necessary. At the then-large cost of over $10,000 and requiring fourteen men, the XPY-1 was dismantled and the pieces were loaded on three railway flatcars that needed to be rerouted to avoid impassable bridges and tunnels. On Boxing Day (26 December), it arrived at the Naval Air Station on the Anacostia River near Washington, D.C. On 10 January, the Admiral made its first test flight with Navy test pilot Lt. A. W. Groton at the controls and Mac Laddon as an observer as he was on all the first flights of his aircraft designs. After several shake-down flights, the Admiral was ready for a public demonstration, and on 22 January, with Lt. W.G. Tomlinson piloting, hull designer Capt. Holden Richardson as a navigator, and assistant secretary of the Navy, Edward Warner as a passenger, the huge aircraft made a 655-foot take-off run on the Anacostia River. The successful flight signaled the end for the Navy's large biplane flying boats and Fleet's successful entry into the flying boat field.

In June 1929, to Fleet's extreme chagrin, the Navy announced that, despite the fact that Consolidated had invested an additional $500,000 more for its development than the original $150,000 Navy contract awarded, it would accept bids from "qualified companies" to manufacture nine Admiral flying boats to Consolidated's design. To recoup its costs, Consolidated was forced to bid for its own aircraft. The Glenn L. Martin Company, without any developmental costs, was able to under bid Consolidated by $500,000 and was awarded the contract. Fleet refused to supply Martin with any of Consolidated's engineering drawings and data, and Martin was forced to extrapolate the engineering details from the prototype itself. Fleet's vindictive gambit delayed Martin's production of the nine aircraft (three P3M-1s and six P3M-2s) by twenty-eight months, and the delay would tarnish Glenn Martin's standing as a major aircraft manufacturer.

The XPY-1 Admiral (Model 9) was Consolidated's answer to the 1928 Navy call for a new long-range monoplane patrol aircraft. (*USN*)

Fleet Organizes Tonawanda Products Corporation

It was not long after opening the Buffalo plant that Fleet realized the 200 local suppliers demanded high prices for the often-late delivery of poor-quality materials and decided to eliminate the middle man. During October 1927, Fleet organized Tonawanda Products Corporation to be a major parts supplier to Consolidated, also undertaking the parts engineering and inspection. The company was 80 percent owned by Consolidated and 20 percent allocated to Tonawanda employees. Tonawanda was to operate at the cost of labor, plus 60 percent for overhead and 10 percent of both for profit, which was 176 percent of labor cost for the finished product against the 240 percent cost of outside suppliers. Fleet invested $25,000 in machinery and rented space for Tonawanda Products near the Buffalo plant, which also greatly reduced transportation problems and costs. Fleet chose Charles Leigh to head Tonawanda as president and treasurer and also to oversee construction of a new building. Consolidated's machine shop foreman, Tonawanda native Henry Golem, had worked for the Curtiss plant in Buffalo, was named vice president. Secretary of the new corporation was Fleet's secretary, Lauretta Lederer Golem, Henry's wife, who soon would become an important part of Fleet's life. The Tonawanda endeavor was very successful, earning $225,299 the first year and Tonawanda paid twenty dividends of $25,000 each during its first five years.

At the time Fleet was organizing the first public offering of Consolidated shares, he also formed Frontier Enterprises Inc. as a holding company for various Consolidated Aircraft subsidiaries. Frontier held 225 of Tonawanda's 250 outstanding shares and also operated the company airport at Tonawanda and owned the Niagara-from-the-Air sightseeing business. Then, to promote pilot training and the sale of aircraft to the public, Fleet organized National Flying Schools Inc. with Leigh Wade, Consolidated's sales manager, as its operating head.

Consolidated Enters the Latin American Market

Commodore (Model 16)
Consolidated had spent $500,000 toward the engineering expenses for the XPY-1 Admiral and with the expectation of receiving the Navy contract Fleet had purchased the supplies and materials for its production. Fortunately, the Navy specification included a requirement for its convertibility to a thirty-two-passenger transport; again, the astute Fleet investigated the XPY-1's convertibility to carry passengers as the Commodore on potential Central and South American routes. The 61-foot 8-inch-long Commodore would have a 100-foot wingspan, weigh 17,600 pounds, and carry twenty-two passengers and a crew of three. It was powered by two 575-hp P&W R-1860 Hornet B engines that gave it a maximum speed of 128 mph over a range of 1,000 miles.

The aircraft was originally ordered by the Detroit and Cleveland Navigation Company to use on Lake Erie, but Capt. Ralph O'Neill, a World War I fighter ace with five shared victories with the 147th Aero Squadron, wanted to launch an airline with routes between North and South America and had represented Boeing in the area by selling its aircraft there. Juan Trippe's Pan American Airways with their Boeing-built flying boats had already gained a strong *entrée* to the South American airmail and soon passenger market. It was through Trippe's government and Wall Street connections that would ultimately give Pan American a virtual monopoly in Latin America for decades to come. O'Neill concentrated on the continent's east coast, particularly Brazil, Uruguay, and Argentina, with its many harbors, estuaries, and rivers that were suited to operating flying boats. The Argentine government advised O'Neill that if he could secure strong financial backing it would be interested establishing an airmail service on the Buenos Aires–New York route and it seemed that Uruguay and Brazil would also then commit. Meanwhile, Fleet had tried in vain to interest Trippe in purchasing the Commodores for Pan American, but Trippe had commitments to Boeing and its flying boats. In January 1929, O'Neill's airline, the Tri-Motor Safety Airways, came to fruition as James H. Rand, head of typewriter manufacturer Remington Rand Corporation of Buffalo, agreed to underwrite, through a consortium of investors, the design and manufacture of six Commodore flying boats for $150,000 each (plus spare parts). Soon Tri-Motor became the New York, Rio, and Buenos Aires Line Inc. (NYRBA). On March 1, Argentina officially signed the airmail contract and Fleet had recouped his XPY-1 developmental expenses with an initial order for six Commodores and went into profitability when an additional six Commodores were ordered followed by two more in October. NYRBA was able to deliver a reliable air service but there was a power struggle within the company in which several of Rand's large investors had tried to gain control of the company from O'Neill. Rand, devastated by the stock market crash of October 1929, was unable to help O'Neill. Meanwhile, Trippe made inroads on the Argentine market and with his influence on President Hoover's new postmaster general, Walter Brown, was able to promote the idea that there should be only one American overseas flag airline. The Argentine government exploited the rivalry between the two airlines and the stock market crash and convinced the two airline companies that PAA should remain the operating company and buy out the stock of NYRBA. In October 1930, NYRBA was officially merged into Pan American. The Commodore proved to be a dependable aircraft as nine years after they were built thirteen of fourteen were still flying (one burned in a hangar fire). Fleet had not only made a $208,000 profit on the fourteen Commodores that Consolidated had built in fifteen months, but the company gained valuable experience building large aircraft.

P2Y-1 and 2 Rangers (Model 22)

Even after recovering the costs of developing the XPY-1 by selling fourteen Commodores, Fleet and Laddon were still piqued by its contract being awarded to the Glenn Martin Company and decided to improve the design. After approval from the Navy, they enclosed the cockpit, added larger engines with streamlined cowlings, removed many of its wires and struts, redesigned the tail, and suspended the floats by a short sesquiplane wing extending from the fuselage. The result of the redesign was the XP2Y-1 Ranger whose prototype was equipped with three engines

Above left: With the expectation of receiving the Navy contract and using the engineering expertise and materials to be used for the XPY-1 Admiral, Consolidated developed and built the Commodore (Model 16). (*USN*)

Above right: Capt. Ralph O'Neill, World War I fighter ace, (shown) and founder of the New York, Rio, and Buenos Aires Line. Inc. (NYRBA) that flew Commodores. (*AAF*)

NYRBA and Consolidated officials pose by a Commodore flying boat. *Left to right*: Consolidated's George Newman, Mac Laddon, and Leigh Wade, Ralph O'Neill (NYRBA President), Lawrence Bell (new Consolidated GM), and William Grooch (NYRBA chief pilot). Reuben Fleet was not present as he was recovering from his near-fatal crash in the Fleetster. (*AFSHRC*)

(the third mounted on the top and center of the wing). Even before first prototype flew on 28 March 1930, the Navy ordered twenty-three Rangers. The three-engined design was abandoned and the twenty-three production P2Y-1 were manufactured with twin engines mounted below the upper wing and the first was delivered on 1 February 1933. The longer-range P2Y-2 succeeded the P2Y-1 and featured several factory modifications and improvements, the most important being the installation of larger twin 750-hp Wright Cyclone engines mounted into the upper wing. The Navy ordered twenty-three, and including thirty-four foreign orders, fifty-seven Rangers were sold. The Ranger became the Navy's stalwart scouting and patrol flying boat of the mid-1930s and its design was conspicuously similar to Consolidated's famed PB2Y Catalina, the Navy's stalwart scouting and patrol flying boat of the late 1930s and throughout the war.

P2Y-1 and 2 Ranger Reincarnations

The XP2Y-1 Ranger prototype was equipped with three engines. (*USN*)

Above: The twenty-three production P2Y-1s were manufactured with twin engines mounted below the upper wing. (*USN*)

Below: The longer-range P2Y-2 had the installation of larger twin 750-hp Wright Cyclone engines mounted into the upper wing. (*USN*)

Consolidated and the Private Aircraft and Mail Market

Husky Junior (Model 14)/Fleet

After Consolidated became a major player in the military training aircraft market, Reuben Fleet felt that there was potential for civilian trainers and private aircraft, an interest created by Lindbergh's May 1927 transatlantic flight. Also, previously, most private flyers utilized surplus World War I aircraft, which were becoming ever more difficult and costly to maintain because of the lack of spare parts. Consolidated had only its trainer designs to offer and Fleet considered the Husky as a possibility, but it was considered to be too large and expensive for the civilian market. Fleet ordered head engineer Joseph Gwinn to scale the Husky down to about 75 percent of its original size as the Husky Jr. (Consolidated Model 14) powered by the Kinner engine whose company stock Fleet had purchased in large blocks. However, the innovative design was too revolutionary for the time and Consolidated's skittish board of directors sold the aircraft and its rights directly to Reuben Fleet. The first Husky Jrs. were to be manufactured in Consolidated's Buffalo factory, but on 1 February 1928, Fleet formed the 100 percent Fleet-owned Fleet Aircraft Company in nearby Canada. Fleet renamed the Husky Jr. as the Fleet, contracting 110 to be manufactured on a cost-plus contract. To help him in his goal of entering the private aircraft market, Fleet astutely hired Lawrence Bell who had once been the general manager of the Glenn L. Martin Company in Los Angeles and then Cleveland, but now was a salesman in a Los Angeles second-hand store. Fleet had intended the Fleet airplane for the commercial market but shrewdly built it to military standards and the military air services purchased them as training aircraft with the Army designating them as the PT-6 and the Navy as the NY2Y-1. With the success of the aircraft Fleet profited as Kinner stock price climbed on the stock market due his use of over 1,000 engines in the Husky design. His profit soon equaled the cost of the engines and then each future engine installation would be at a no-cost basis! Consolidated board of directors reconsidered their mistake and issued 19,000 shares of company stock to purchase all Fleet's shares of his wholly owned Fleet Aircraft Company and Consolidated's shares were listed on the New York Stock Exchange. A twin-float seaplane version was ominously approved on 29 October 1929, the day of the Stock Market Crash. On that day, a Fleet airplane sold for $4,985, but during the Depression, the price was reduced by $1,000. A total 437 Fleets were sold, plus spares equivalent to 192 aircraft.

Fleet hires future aviation icon Lawrence Bell. (*AFSHRC*)

Above: Fleet renamed the Husky Jr. as the Fleet, to be manufactured on a cost-plus contract in his new Canadian plant. (*AFSHRC*)

Below: The Fleet airplane was intended for the commercial market, but Reuben Fleet shrewdly built it to military standards and the Army designated them as the PT-6 and the Navy as the NY2Y-1. (*AFSHRC*)

Fleet of Canada

As just described, in 1928, the Consolidated board decided to discontinue their light, training aircraft and Reuben Fleet founded Fleet Aircraft in Fort Erie, Ontario, Canada, to acquire the foreign rights to these aircraft and then Consolidated bought back Fleet Aircraft as a separate division in 1929 and formed Fleet Aircraft of Canada in 1930. The Canadian-based Fleet subsidiary manufactured aircraft for the American commercial market and for foreign military customers, but during the Depression of the early '30s, the volume of trainer sales decreased significantly; however, President Jack Sanderson was able to keep the company buoyant. Meanwhile, Consolidated had moved its headquarters from Buffalo to California, and the Canadian firm became somewhat isolated from the main company. In its seven years, a disappointing 112 aircraft had been sold for just under $1 million. During 1937, Canadian interests purchased the Fleet subsidiary and reorganized it under the new name Fleet Aircraft Ltd., with 50,000 shares of stock offered to Canadian public. Consolidated continued to hold 35,000 of the 90,000 shares of stock with Reuben Fleet and Joe Gwinn continuing to serve on the board of directors. The new company received exclusive rights to manufacture and sell Fleet trainers worldwide, except in America, China, and Romania, and it also acquired rights to the Model 21 advanced trainers, except for the U.S. The Fleet Model 1, originally the Consolidated Model 14 Husky Junior, and its derivatives were a series of orthodox two-seat trainer and sports biplanes that all shared the same basic design and varied mainly in their power plants. The Canadian manufacturing was a great success, with some 600 built for the Royal Canadian Air Force as the Fleet Fawn (Model 7) and Fleet Finch (Model 16). U.S. manufacturing rights were eventually sold to Brewster Aeronautical Corporation, which intended to produce the Brewster B-1 based on the Canadian Model 16F. Only one Brewster Fleet B-1 was built in 1939 by the Fleet Aircraft Company of Canada as a Fleet Model 16-F with a Warner 145 Super Scarab engine.

Gordon Mounce

Gordon Mounce served in Army Air Corps during war and post-war obtained his pilot's, transport, and engine mechanic's licenses. Mounce operated a small airfield from which he conducted an aerial mapping, advertising, and a student instruction business along with an auto dealership. In 1929, he joined the Fleet Aircraft Company, and over eight years, Mounce played a large part in Consolidated's biplane sales success, starting as a West Coast sales representative and as the division's principle pilot; he also became the company's European sales representative in 1932–1935. In 1935, he became Fleet Canada's assistant to Reuben Fleet but continued his European sales positon in which he became a well-known and popular aviation figure, performing aerial stunts for royalty and being decorated for demonstrating to national air force pilots how to escape from a spin—his specialty. In July 1938, thirty-eight-year-old Mounce was killed while demonstrating a Fleet biplane for Fleet Canada in Belgrade, Yugoslavia, when he crashed after completing twenty-four loops.

The Fleet, Fort Erie, Canada Plant shown with a number of Fleet Trainers purchased by the RAF. (*CAC/AAF*)

The Fleet Model 1, originally the Consolidated Model 14 Husky Junior, and its derivatives were a series of orthodox two-seat trainer and sports biplanes that all shared the same basic design and varied mainly in their power plants. (*AFSHRC*)

Gordon Mounce, Consolidated demonstration pilot and salesman (left), with (left to right) Charles Van Dusen (Consolidated's production manager), Reuben, and son, David Fleet. (CAC/AAF)

Fleet and Personal Secretary Lauretta Golem Crash in the Fleet

Fleet decided to publicize his Fleet aircraft during a 15,000-mile cross-country promotional and sales tour in August 1929. Forty-two-year-old Fleet raised eyebrows when he announced that his thirty-one-year-old secretary, Lauretta Golem, who was married to Henry Golem, the vice president of his Tonawanda Products Corporation, would accompany him. It seems as though Henry had no problem with this arrangement as he was also having an affair with his future wife, Lorraine. The two headed west to visit San Diego where Fleet proposed that the city sell him the newly established Lindbergh Field (for $1 million cash) in order for him to relocate his company, a proposal that would come to fruition. On 13 September 1929, on their homeward leg from Detroit to the Buffalo factory, they decided to fly the shorter route over Ontario, Canada, with Golem, who had recently gotten her pilot's license, at the controls in the rear cockpit and Fleet in the front cockpit. Over the north shore of Lake Ontario, the engine failed and Fleet took the controls and headed for a clearing and a crash landed. Lauretta suffered a broken neck and spinal injuries and died the next day. Her obituary dismissed the trip as "The trip from which they were returning, when the fatal crash occurred, was in the interests of business of the Consolidated Aircraft Company. They left Buffalo about two months ago and went all the way to the Pacific Coast."

Fleet spent seven weeks in the hospital in London, Ontario, and during his prolonged convalescence, his confidence in the capable Larry Bell paid dividends as he named him company general manager. Fleet then joined his parents on a New York to Panama to California cruise to recuperate and returned to work in November.

Before the accident, Fleet had met Dorothy Mitchell, Lauretta Golem's attractive niece, who was teaching a children's dancing class at a private school in New York City. It seems as though Dorothy had caught his attention as she relates in her vanity published biography, *Our Flight to Destiny*, that he invited her to Buffalo (ostensibly) to visit her grieving Uncle Harry Golem (Lauretta's husband) and "I felt that perhaps Reuben's suggestion was a good one. I accepted the invitation, recalling how we had taken a fancy to each other in our meeting a year earlier and again the past summer." Dorothy continues: "It was during the holidays that he persuaded me to move to Buffalo and take over Lauretta's job as his secretary. 'You have no idea how many things I have to do,' he told me. 'Now that Lauretta is gone I don't know how I'm going to manage.'" Dorothy had no previous secretarial experience and "no love for secretarial work," but Fleet told her that she was to be his "social secretary." Over the next several months, his social secretary learned to fly and to shoot trap. It seems Reuben had an attraction to secretaries as he would marry Dorothy in July 1930.

Above left: Reuben Fleet, the dashing, mustachioed forty-two-year-old president of Consolidated Aviation. (*CAC/AAF*)

Above right: Lauretta Golem, Fleet's beautiful married thirty-one-year-old personal secretary who would accompany him on a tragic cross-country sales trip. (*CAC/AAF*)

Fleetster (Model 17)

In the late 1920s, there was a need for a passenger and fast mail transport for the rapidly growing airline industry. Lockheed had introduced its streamlined wooden Vega in 1927, which had greatly influenced aircraft design at the time. At the time Consolidated's XPY-1 program was near completion and Commodore manufacture was underway. Because Fleet was involved with the organization of the NYRBA Line to Latin America, he authorized the design and production of the fast, high performance Model 17 Fleetster passenger plane for use by NYRBA. This cantilever high wooden wing monoplane was clearly inspired by the Vega except it would have America's first all-metal monocoque fuselage. The enclosed pilot's cockpit was located forward and above the six-passenger cabin and was streamlined into the wing's leading edge and could accommodate a co-pilot or another passenger. The 31-foot 9-inch-long Fleetster had a 45-foot wingspan and weighed 5,600 pounds. The aircraft could cruise at 150 mph (180 mph top speed) powered by a 575-hp Hornet engine that was covered by an advanced NACA-developed cowling that increased airspeed by 15 mph. The aircraft first flew on 27 October 1929, and a twin-float seaplane version was tested in Miami, Florida, soon afterward. The Model 20, a later version of the Fleetster, was designed mainly for airmail use. It was distinguished by its parasol wing configuration fastened to the fuselage by four struts about a foot above the fuselage. The pilot initially sat in an open (later closed) cockpit behind the passenger cabin.

Both the Model 17 and 20 were available as a landplane or twin-float seaplane. Tri-Motor Airways bought the first six Model 17s and then bought four more for mail and passenger service on NYRBA's South American routes. TWA leased then purchased seven Model 20s while the Army and Navy purchased one each as the XBY-1. Later, the Russian and Spanish governments were reported to have them in inventory. The Fleetster was somewhat of a failure as the company could not duplicate Vega's successful wooden design in metal. However, the Fleetster metal design and construction process was to be of later value to the company in fabricating their all-metal designs. About twenty-five Model 17 Fleetsters (about 20 percent of the number of Vegas sold) were built with the major customer being the NYRBA Line at $26,500 each.

Fast, high-performance Model 17 Fleetster six-person passenger plane would have America's first all-metal monocoque fuselage. (*AFSHRC*)

Model 17 Fleetster twin-float seaplane version. (*AFSHRC*)

Fleetster Model 20 was distinguished by its parasol wing configuration and the pilot in an open (later closed) cockpit behind the passenger cabin. (*AFSHRC*)

Consolidated Acquires and Retires the Thomas-Morse Company

During 1910, the Thomas Brothers Company was founded in Hammondsport, New York, by English expatriates William Thomas and his brother, Oliver. The company moved to Hornell, New York, and then moved again to Bath, New York, the same year. During 1912 and 1913, like Glenn Curtiss, the company operated the affiliated Thomas School of Aviation at Conesus Lake, New York. In 1913, the company became the Thomas Brothers Aeroplane Company based in Ithaca, New York, and in 1915, the brothers added the Thomas Aeromotor Company. That year, the Thomas Brothers built T-2 tractor biplanes designed by Englishman Benjamin Thomas (no relation) and formerly of Vickers, Sopwith, and Curtiss, and later the company's chief designer. The aircraft was sold to the Royal Naval Air Service and equipped with floats in place of wheels to the United States Navy as the SH-4. In 1916, the company was awarded an Army Signal Corps contract for two aircraft for evaluation, designated as the D-5. In January 1917, the company merged with Morse Chain Company headed by Frank Morse, and was recapitalized becoming Thomas-Morse Aircraft Corporation, continuing to be based in Ithaca. The company is best known for its S-4/TM-4 fighter-trainer, which first flew in June 1917 and was comparable in performance to 1916 World War I fighters. About 100 were built, and they were used as advanced trainers for Army fighter pilots and many saw post-war civilian use as sport and stunt aircraft. During this time, the company's workforce reached more than 1,200 employees, and it became one of the leading manufacturers in the country. The last company design was the O-19 observation biplane. In 1929, the company was acquired by Consolidated, becoming the Thomas-Morse Division. Under Consolidated Thomas-Morse continued to build seventy O-19Bs, seventy-one O-19Cs, and one O-19D converted as a staff transport for the secretary of war. Consolidated discontinued the company in 1934.

The P-30 (PB-2) Fighter Establishes Consolidated as an Innovator

The Detroit-Lockheed XP-900 prototype, first flew in September 1931 and was purchased by the Army as the Lockheed YP-24. As it was faster than any fighter then in AAC service, an order for five Y1P-24 pursuits and four Y1A-9 attack aircraft was placed, despite the loss of the prototype on 19 October 1931. The Detroit Aircraft Corporation went into bankruptcy eight days later, however, leading to the cancellation of the contract. After the Detroit Lockheed Company went into bankruptcy many of its designers and engineers were hired by Consolidated Buffalo, including YP-24 Chief Designer Robert Woods (future Bell Aircraft chief designer of the P-39 and supersonic Bell X-1-5 rocket-powered aircraft). Woods continued to develop the YP-24, the design becoming the Consolidated Y1P-2, Model 25, with all-metal wings replacing the wooden wings of the YP-24 and a larger tail. The Army Air Corps ordered two prototypes as the Y1P-25 in March 1932, to be powered by a Curtiss V-1570-27, equipped with a turbo-supercharger on the port side of the forward fuselage. The order for the second prototype was soon changed to an Y1A-11 attack aircraft, without a supercharger.

The Y1P-25 was delivered to the Air Corps on 9 December 1932, and was the first to fly, showing promising performance, reaching 247 mph but was destroyed in a crash on 13 January 1933, killing its pilot, Hugh Elmendorf (whose name was later given to Elmendorf Air Base in Alaska). The Y1A-11, armed with four forward-firing machine guns instead of the two of the Y1P-25 and racks for carrying 400 pounds of bombs was delivered to Wright Field on 5 January 1933. On 20 January 1933, the Y1A-11 disintegrated in midair, killing pilot Irvin Woodring. Despite the loss of both prototypes during two weeks in January, on 1 March 1933, the Air Corps placed an order for four P-30 fighters and four A-11 attack aircraft. The production aircraft differed from the prototypes in having stronger fuselages, simplified undercarriages, and more powerful engines.

The P-30 was an advanced all-metal two-place fighter whose development was impaired by crashes. However, the Army Air Corps considered that the accidents were no reflection on its design and ordered four more of these sophisticated models designated the P-30 for service evaluation. The result was the first American production all-metal pursuit aircraft to feature a fully retractable landing gear, fully cantilevered wing, enclosed heated cockpit, controllable pitch propeller, and exhaust-driven turbo supercharger. The high-altitude fighter had a rudimentary oxygen system, but the bulky flying suits made high-altitude flights too awkward and the rear gunner did not have a heated compartment. In 1936, Consolidated unsuccessfully entered a reconfigured P-30 in the AAC single-seat pursuit competition. The two-place pilot/rear gunner concept decreased performance and ultimately rear gunner proved to be impractical. However, the P-30 would later be the first aircraft to go into production at the new Consolidated San Diego plant because most of the parts had been previously manufactured in Buffalo and basically only required assembly.

P-30 (PB-2) was the first American production all-metal pursuit aircraft to feature a fully retractable landing gear, fully cantilevered wing, enclosed heated cockpit, controllable pitch propeller and exhaust-driven turbo supercharger. (*AAF*)

Fleet and Consolidated Face the Depression Years

The Depression years separated the success of the Husky/Fleet series of training aircraft and the development of the very successful PBY patrol bombers. Sales volume was acceptable but operational profitability was hard hit. Sales for the four years 1929–1932 totaled $10.2 million compared with $6.3 million for the company's first five and a half years. Total earnings during the period from the company's founding in 1923 through 1928 were $2.1 million, but during the next four years, the company about broke even because of net losses in 1931 and 1932. A new high sales volume was established in 1930 when the company produced, sold, and delivered more aircraft, 309, of a total value of $4,345,171, which was more than any other American aircraft manufacturer but the net profit was only 3 percent on the entire volume of business. The notable 1930 sales volume was due to deliveries of ten Commodore seaplanes and six Fleetster landplane transports for use on South American routes; to good customer acceptance of the Fleet biplanes, and to delivery of the Thomas-Morse O-19 observation aircraft to the Army.

The low profit margins on government contracts continued to irk Fleet since three years earlier when he had to sell fifty PT-3s at $1 each to compensate the Army for the claimed $300,000 of excess profits earned by Consolidated. In 1931 and 1932, the company had a net loss of $375,158 on sale of aircraft to the Army, but the government stepped forward to cover the company's loss. The chagrinned Fleet wrote: "Our losses to the Army put the shoe on the other foot, and it would seem fair that it should reimburse us at least for our outlay in its behalf, even if it were to pay us nothing for two years work." The year 1932 marked the low point for the company as only 100 aircraft were sold and sales volume dropped to $1.3 million. To compensate, all salaries and wages were cut 20 percent, and even Reuben's son, David, who had been a sales pilot and service manager for Fleet trainers, was laid off so as not to jeopardize the job of a married employee with a family to support. Then business gradually began to improve, though it was not until 1937 that sales volume surpassed the 1930 level.

Under an Army Air Corps design competition to develop an updated biplane trainer as successor to the PT-3, in 1931, Consolidated introduced the "convertible" Model 21 capable of conducting both primary and advanced instruction. The prototype aircraft was reported to have been designed, built, static tested, and ready for demonstration in only eight weeks. Smaller than the PT-3 but larger and more powerful than the Fleet, the 21 series trainers had a span of 31 feet 6 inches, compared with 28 feet for the 'Fleet' and 34 feet 6 inches for the PT-3, and were available with a wide range of power plants, depending on mission. For primary training, the 170-hp Kinner was used; for advanced training, either the 300-hp or 400-hp Wasp Junior was installed, but other engines could also be used. To provide longitudinal balance involving engine change from primary to advanced configuration, the wing was moved forward to additional fittings provided. In AAC service, the Model 21 carried the PT-11 and PT-12 designations for primary training and BT-7 for basic training. The Army purchased forty while the Navy and Coast Guard purchased the N4Y-1 model. Later, thirty of the Model 21 trainers were sold abroad, most to Colombia. The PT-11C version with 250-hp Wright engine and Townend cowling ring were sold to China.

Model 21/PT-11 was an updated biplane trainer as successor to the PT-3. (*AFSHRC*)

Model 18 XBY-1

During the Depression, Consolidated, like other aircraft manufacturers, initiated a number of development projects anticipating that one or more could be developed into a production model. The Model 18 XBY-1 (experimental bomber, "Y" for Consolidated, first model) was built in 1932 as an all-metal single-engined landplane designed for the Navy for use aboard aircraft carriers. It was based on the successful Fleetster commercial transport design and like the Douglas B-18, which was based on the commercial DC-2, was a unique example of a civilian aircraft in which bomb bay doors were installed in the fuselage in order to convert it into a military aircraft for bombing missions. The XBY-1 had the Fleetster's monocoque metal fuselage for which Larry Bell held the patents. It had a metal cantilever wing in place of the all-wood plywood-covered wing of the commercial Fleetster and was the Navy's first aircraft to employ stressed skin wing construction. Only the one XBY-1 bomber was built for the Navy, but the aircraft's metal wing leading edge contained the first integral fuel tank, a development on which Laddon later used.

Consolidated Meets the Depression

During the first four years of the Depression, 1929–1932, Consolidated's sales were $10.2 million as compared to the $6.3 million in sales during its first five years in business. However, its earnings for the first five years were $2.1 million, but the company only broke even during the 1929–32 Depression period even though in 1930 it produced more aircraft (309) for more dollars ($4.3 million) than any other American aircraft company. In 1932, the company sold only 100 aircraft on sales of only $1.3 million and it would not be until 1937 that sales would reach the 1930 level. Despite the lack of success of new

Model 18 was based on the successful Fleetster commercial transport, but the design was abandoned after the prototype was rejected for Navy use. (*AFSHRC*)

designs, the twenty-two P2Y-1 Ranger flying boats sold to the Navy and the sale of 130 Fleet and Model 21 trainers abroad led to a steady sales volume in 1933 and 1934 putting the bottom line at the breakeven point. To streamline Consolidated corporate structure, all subsidiaries were liquidated, except Fleet Aircraft of Canada, and their capital accounts reduced to almost nil and merged with the parent company.

Last Gasp of the Thomas-Morse Division

Other ventures undertaken by Consolidated during the Depression were the single Thomas-Morse Division's T-M Viper in response to the AAC's interest in a biplane fighter (designated as the XP-13) which was intended to use the 600-hp Curtiss Chieftain engine. The Model 23 was another Thomas-Morse project, the single Army Y10-41 two-place observation aircraft, the XO-932. During the fall of 1934, it was entered in the competition for Air Corps observation aircraft, but the competition was won by Douglas, and the aircraft was used as a Consolidated as a transport restricted to executives, engineers, and Consolidated company service workers. The Model 24 was the last Buffalo-based Thomas-Morse project which was intended to be a Navy carrier-based aircraft, which was found to be not sturdy enough for shipboard use and with this project Thomas-Morse ceased to be a Consolidated entity.

Consolidated Becomes a Major Industry Player with the Illustrious PBY Catalina

The success of the P2Y Ranger patrol boat series and the Navy's upcoming replacement of its existing patrol aircraft led Consolidated and Laddon to design a 3,000-mile/100-mph cruising speed successor, the Model 28. This aircraft would evolve into the PBY Catalina, which would become the foremost Allied patrol aircraft of World War II playing a major role in the both the war in the Pacific and the Battle of the Atlantic, serving in large numbers with the U.S. Navy and RAF Coastal Command.

On 28 October 1933, both Consolidated (XP3Y-1) and Douglas (XP3D-1) were awarded a contract by the Navy to build competing prototypes to replace the in-service Consolidated P2Y Ranger and the Martin P3M which was originally Consolidated's XPY-1 Admiral awarded to Martin. The XP3Y-1 prototype was ordered on 28 October 1933 for $268,476 and was built in Buffalo. The prototype was shipped by rail to Anacostia where it was first flown on 21 March 1935 by company test pilot William Wheatley where it tested very satisfactorily as did the Douglas XP3D-1, which had begun its earlier successful testing in its native California. The test performance results for the two were so similar that the final decision was made on price. Douglas estimated $110,000 per XP3D-1 but Consolidated was awarded the contract on 29 June 1935, for sixty P3Y-1s at $90,000 each, plus 20 percent spare parts, drawings, tests, etc., for a total of $6,506,000.

The XP3Y-1 was moved to San Diego by 20 October 1935, when Consolidated's new factory was dedicated. While the factory was being tooled up for production, the prototype was modified with a rotating nose turret, modified tail, and new 850-hp P&W R-1830-64 Wasps and flew again on 21 May 1936 with a new XPBY-1 designation. The aircraft's designation was changed to PBY-1 (PB for patrol bomber, Y for Consolidated) during August 1936 as the first flying boat was about to be accepted by the Navy.

The PBY-1 was an all-metal high wing monoplane, powered by two new fourteen-cylinder, twin-row, 800-hp P&W Twin R-1830-58 Wasp engines that were built into the leading edge of the wing center section that was supported by a pedestal to the hull. The elegant hull was streamlined with the simple main dorsal fuselage, containing the crew compartments, being the top half of a tube, with a circular roof. The flying boat's width remained constant from the pilot's compartment to the of the waist gunner's compartment and then tapered towards the tail. The cantilevered parasol wings, containing integral fuel tanks, were metal, except for fabric covering aft of the rear spar. Two out-board floats retracted upwards to become wing tips. The wing was connected to the fuselage by a single large pylon, which also contained the engineer's station, with only one pair of struts on each side, running from the side of the hull to a position just outside the engines. It was to be armed with four machine guns and could carry up to 2,000 pounds of bombs.

On 25 July 1936, the Navy placed a new contract for fifty P3Y-1's at $4,898,000, and in September 1936, the first production PBY-1 was accepted, with VP-11 the first Navy Patrol Squadron to be equipped on 5 October. The PBY-1 contract was completed in June 1937 and the first PBY-2 had been accepted in May. The remainder were accepted from September 1937 to February 1938. The PBY-1 through -5 was the most prolific and successful flying boat ever produced with its 1939 to 1945 production run producing more aircraft than all other flying boats combined: 3,272 Catalinas—1,854 flying boats and 1,418 amphibians were produced by Consolidated plants first few at Buffalo; then 2,160 at San Diego; 235 at New Orleans; along with licensed versions to the U.S. Naval Aircraft Factory (Philadelphia) 155; Boeing of Canada (Vancouver) 362; and Canadian Vickers (Montreal) 240; and twenty-seven in Russia. It would not be until 1 October 1941 that the U.S. Navy would adopt the name Catalina from the RAF, which gave the flying boat its name in 1939 from Catalina Island, a holiday island off the southern California coast.

The Catalina pre-war contracts gave Consolidated a viable production program and revenue source during a difficult time for the aircraft industry as the nation's economy labored to recover from the Depression. Thus, the Consolidated design department had the luxury of instigating many design studies for a wide assortment of both military and commercial aircraft, including the B-24.

The Air Corps' pre-war aircraft procurement policy would have a great effect on not only Consolidated but the entire American aircraft industry. The Air Corps Act of 1926 was to establish a statutory means to procure new aircraft. It provided for a design competition that would lead to the purchase of one or more prototypes, the issue of contracts for "experimental" aircraft by the secretary of war at "his discretion without competition," and competition where aircraft could be procured on grounds other than the first two provisions with the secretary able to "exercise discretion in determining the lowest responsible bidder." Another procurement possibility was for a negotiated purchase contract without competition of a design "of sufficient promise to justify immediate procurement." The act required the use of a design competition with the designs to be submitted to and evaluated at Wright Field, and a winner was to be selected and awarded a contract to build one prototype for service testing. If the service tests were successful, a production order was then to be issued. However, in effect, design competition was impractical as when bids went out Wright Field received a large number of design proposals that the designers claimed met or exceeded the specifications. Until a prototype was built, it could not be determined from the submitted design if specifications had been met, and if not, time passed and money was spent without result. Also, bidders were given inadequate time (several months) to design and submit their proposals and once the winner was chosen, its design had to be detailed and then it was often found that the original dollar bid was inadequate and the manufacturer would lose money on the building of the prototype and production models. This ineffective design competition gave way to the negotiated purchase contract, but the manufacturer with the winning bid also lost money as they intentionally low-balled the bid expecting to recoup this loss on the quantity production order. The act made no provision for a quantity order and a new bid for a quantity order needed to be issued and another manufacturer could be contracted to build the winning design of another manufacturer. In June 1929, the Navy announced that, despite the fact that Reuben Fleet's Consolidated Aircraft had invested an additional $500,000 more for the development of the Admiral Flying Boat than the original $150,000 Navy

Above: XP-3Y-1 was the prototype for the famed PBY Catalina. (*AFSHRC*)

Right: Company test pilot William Wheatley successfully first flew the XP-3Y-1 during March 1935. (*AFSHRC*)

One of the few PBY-1s manufactured at the Consolidated Buffalo factory before Catalina manufacture was moved to San Diego. (*CAC/AAF*)

The San Diego factory built 2,160 of the 3,272 Catalinas, which was the most prolific and successful flying boat ever produced. (*CAC/AAF*)

contract awarded, it would accept bids from "qualified companies" to manufacture nine flying boats to Consolidated's design. The Glenn Martin Company was then selected to build Consolidated's flying boat. Manufacturers were reluctant to submit designs and bids, and Army Regulation 5-240 was resurrected from the mass of regulations to accommodate procurement. This Regulation stipulated that "competition might be avoided in certain special circumstances in which competition was impractical." By interpreting AR 5-240 to classify the manufacturer of an experimental aircraft purchased under the Air Corps Act of 1926 as the only source that manufacturer could be awarded the production contract. Between 1926 and 1934, $16 million was awarded for contracts under the "experimental" provision of the Act and $22 million under the "impractical competition" provision; both of which were entirely legal under the terms of AR 5-240. Each year from 1926 to 1934, each procurement contract was on public record and annual aircraft procurement reports were made to Congress and all were completely legal. Nonetheless, in January 1934, the *Washington Post* reported that the House of Representatives was about to investigate seven years of wrongful aircraft procurement by the War Department in violation of the Air Corps Act of 1926.

In late 1933, the ambitious Democratic Alabama Senator Hugo L. Black was aggressively investigating the federal subsidies to private airmail contractors which were U.S. airlines. Black, who would become a Supreme Court Justice in 1937, was so strident and vocal that the newspapers soon led the public to believe that most of the nation's airlines were guilty of flagrant wrongdoing and excessive profits. Since many of America's aircraft manufacturers were associated with airlines (e.g. Boeing/United Airlines), they were also incriminated by the newspapers. When the Navy and Army came to Congress to present their appropriations bill, in January and February 1934 respectively, both were attacked with accusations of allowing profiteering and excess profits by the aircraft manufacturers at the expense of the taxpayers.

The chairman of the House Naval Affairs Committee, Georgia Representative Carl Vinson, appointed a subcommittee headed by New York Representative John Delaney to investigate the supposed widespread procurement corruption. In response to this subcommittee, Fleet sent the following letter to Delaney defending not only Consolidated but for the entire aircraft manufacturing industry:

> The profit on orders we have filled from our birth has not been great enough to justify the risks and hazards attending the creation, detailed design, building and guaranteeing of our aircraft.
>
> The risk involved in attempting to estimate in advance what military aircraft will cost in its experimental stages of development, especially where it must meet constantly changing military demands, is so great that it must yield higher profits to those who are successful, than they would have right to expect from production manufacturing of staple articles, if America is to have worthwhile brains and healthy companies engaged in this line of endeavor.
>
> Ten and three-quarters years sees us still without a factory of our own or a wind-tunnel or an experimental laboratory, and with no dividends to our stockholders for more than five years.

Lack of continuity of orders forces carrying costs that wipe out profits rapidly, for if we are to be a national asset we must not disband our organisation between contracts. Of course profits earned on specific orders must be drawn against for losses and for payment of at least the skeleton organisation of brains, trained engineers and lead men in 'lean' periods.

If the profit on any contract is to be restricted to 10%, who will carry the overhead in lean periods when there is little or no work on hand? Such a policy would destroy the aviation industry as a business and put each company in the category of a road or building contractor, a dangerously and woefully weak prop to our country in peace times and in times of emergency.

There is a gross misconception in the lay mind regarding negotiated aircraft contracts, namely that they are 'hand-outs' and perhaps involve collusion whereas they are awarded only after the severest competition. Government officers have then used every conceivable means of chiseling prices including threats to buy an admittedly inferior product, or to appropriate creator's design and invite formal competitive bids from other manufacturers therefor, or to have same manufactured by the Government, or to let the funds revert to the Treasury. Particularly unfair has been the government practice to try to force successful design creators to meet the prices of competitors with less satisfactory and 'cheap' aircraft.

Your basic aircraft procurement law should be amended to recognize design rights as proprietary if you expect to encourage the creation and development of better aircraft in this country. If samples are to be taken away from their originators by low-bidding competitors who have sat on the sidelines like vultures, it is discouraging beyond words.

You should also authorize procurement of aircraft, in cases where no one can intelligently estimate in advance their probable cost, on the basis of 'cost plus a fixed profit with a bogie saving.' Where the profit is fixed, no temptation exists to make the job run up in cost. By coupling the fixed profit with a bogie saving, the contractor gets part of all he can save as an incentive to make the cost as low as he can consistent with safe and satisfactory aircraft.

After two months and hearing 800 pages of testimony, the Delaney committee's final report found that that the charges against the Navy's procurement policies were unfounded and were "prudent and practicable" and fostered competition. The committee found that the major airframe manufacturers made only a very marginal 0.2 percent on cost profit on their sales to the military and commercial interests. The average profit earned by aircraft and engine manufacturers between 1926 and 1934 was also a not-too-excessive 9 percent on cost. Further figures showed that aircraft manufacturers lost an average of 50 percent on cost on "experimental" aircraft and when combining these losses with production profits (if the aircraft went into production) the return was 11.5 percent that was not considered excessive for the high risk involved. However, while *The New York Times* had headlined the committee's appointment of Delaney and the upcoming investigation and then printed titillating accusation feature articles during the committee's investigation, it only spent one day reporting the story exonerating the Navy and that was carried on page 15. To exacerbate the situation, one member of the committee charged publicly that the majority had "whitewashed" the Navy and then he wrote a minority report that reached the *Congressional Record* while the majority report languished in obscurity. Of course, the newspapers cited this minority report and referred to the "indication of new evidence of illegal procurement" alleged by the minority report author. Strangely, the majority members did not refute this minority report and the misleading indication of the "new evidence" that would never surface.

In the turmoil, the Air Corps also soon came under fire from South Carolina Representative (D) John McSwain, chairman of the Military Affairs Committee, who put New Hampshire Representative (D) William Rogers in charge of an eight-man committee that took his name. In closed hearings, the Rogers' Committee found the chief of the Air Corps guilty of "gross misconduct" and "deliberate and willful and intentional violation of the law" and the Air Corps both "inefficient" and "expensive" using "various subterfuges" for "pernicious" and "unlawful" procurement. It made the recommendation that there be a return to "aggressive design competition for experimental aircraft" and "competition on all contracts for procurement in quantity." Perhaps due to the closed nature of the hearings, Congress did nothing about the Air Corps Act of 1926 as there was no public outcry. Congress did pass a law limiting aircraft manufacturer's profits and provided for the recapture of all earnings in excess of 10 percent (but provided nothing to put a floor under losses). This excess profits law raised questions and a mandate for further revisions to it.

A new administrative procurement policy was devised by Assistant Secretary of War (1933–36) Henry Woodring who would later serve as secretary of war under Roosevelt (1936–40), resigning from office because he opposed Roosevelt's third term campaign. The policy essentially supported competitive bids and thus circumvented the Congress from amending the Air Corps Act by statute. During fiscal 1933, the Congress appropriated $10 million for the Army Air Corps, but the new Roosevelt Administration, under the economic pressure of the Depression, impounded $7 million as an economic emergency measure. The AAC urgently needed more than 700 new aircraft to equip active units and many more were needed to replace aircraft that were or were going to be obsolete soon. At the end of the year, the administration transferred $7.5 million to the AAC from the Public Works Administration (PWA). To expedite the purchase of the best aircraft available the AAC negotiated production contracts with the manufacturers of "top-quality aircraft" using Army Regulation 5-240 maintaining that the manufacturer was the "sole source" of the required aircraft. However, two companies complained about not getting the AR 5-240 negotiated contract awards. The Depression put the War Department under pressure to award contracts to a number of aircraft companies to keep them viable and Assistant Secretary of War Woodring was forced to reconsider the contract awards. In order to award contracts equably throughout the aircraft industry and also obtain aircraft of maximum performance at a minimum cost, Woodring was in a Catch-22 situation. Aircraft contracted on the basis of price competition would save the government money but not insure purchasing aircraft with the best performance.

On the other hand, aircraft contracted on the basis of having the best performance would cost more. Either way, the intention of spreading the wealth was not met as whether contracts were awarded on cost or performance, most of the contracts tended to be awarded to a few efficient companies who had the best designs and production capacity. Woodring asked the Air Corps to devise a policy before Congress reconvened in January 1934. The AAC responded with the 1934 War Department Aircraft Procurement Policy that had "competition" as its foundation. The AAC's solution was to allow each manufacturer to bid on its own design specifications, but the AAC required a minimum high speed thus allowing competition as to performance but disqualified all companies but those whose design proposals fell within a narrow margin of specified performance. The competition was also limited to companies that had previously submitted similar aircraft for approval to Wright Field for evaluation so that there was some assurance that the submitted aircraft proposal had some design and safety substance behind it. The 1934 Procurement Policy went on to state that if the aircraft with the highest performance was not the lowest bidder, the secretary would award the contract "at his discretion to the best advantage of the Government." Each submitting company was required to supply a prototype for flight testing eliminating "paper promises" and would provide a basis for an assessment of the aircraft for production contracts. The secretary's timely submission of the 1934 Procurement Policy undercut a Congressional Committee that was infuriated over the alleged profiteering by the aircraft industry and bent on amending the Air Corps Act.

Alabama Senator (D) Hugo L. Black. (NA)

Above left: New York Representative (D) John Delaney. *(NA)*

Above right: New Hampshire Representative (D) William Rogers. *(NA)*

Below left: Assistant Secretary of War Henry Woodring. *(NA)*

Below right: Handbook for Aircraft Designers. *(Author's Collection)*

 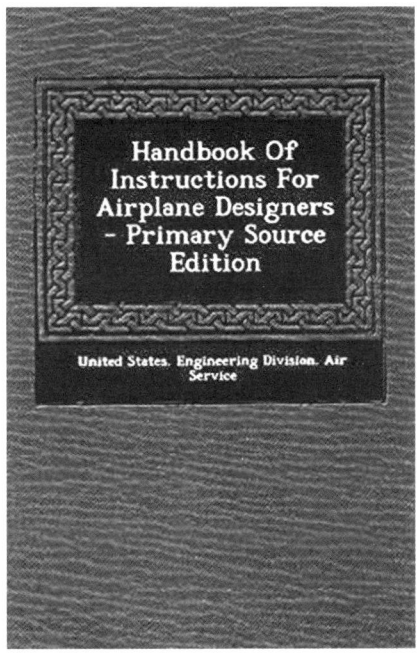

Now the competition procedure was to mail a circular containing "type specifications in terms of the minimum acceptable performance." The aircraft's maximum performance was then left to the talents of the manufacturer's design team whose design performance was to be verified by flight tests of the prototype aircraft. The AAC needed to require a necessary "degree of uniformity and standardization" on the aircraft industry to prevent the "collection of heterogeneous aircraft and equipment" and "insure a high degree of uniformity and interchangeability." The aircraft manufacturers were asked to submit designs based on the performance specifications issued by the AAC. With their invitations to the aircraft industry for designs and bids the AAC issued the *Handbook for Aircraft Designers* and an "index of all pertinent Army, Navy and Federal specifications for materials and subassemblies." In addition, the industry was required to use government-furnished equipment (GFE), which included instruments, armament, communications, oxygen equipment, etc., and use mandatory engine and propeller installations. The *Handbook* and use of GFE decreased the number of variables to be incorporated in the prototype design and thus limited the range of the competing designs and made the competition more evenhanded among the qualified competitors. In June 1936, the secretary of war reported to Congress that the new policy was a success as it had increased the number of bidders and the designs submitted were far advanced compared to contemporary aircraft. But the question remained as to equating price to performance. To which bidder should a contract be awarded when one manufacturer submitted a superior design at a higher cost while another submitted a much lower bid on an inferior design? If performance was the main prerequisite, then the manufacturer with the superior design could ask an unreasonable price for his design. During the design competition for an AAC transport, the larger, twin-engined Douglas DC-2, already in successful service as a commercial airliner, was clearly the far superior design over the single-engined transport designs submitted by Curtiss Wright (Condor) and Fairchild (C-8). But the Douglas bid was $49,500 per aircraft compared to the $29,500 for Curtiss Wright and $29,150 for Fairchild. The transport design proposal stipulated that the primary consideration would be performance, not price, and the Douglas DC-2 was given the production contract. But Fairchild protested and the comptroller general (CG) deferred payment to Douglas pointing out that the performance of the Fairchild transport "was far in excess of the minimum performance required." The comptroller general did not realize that, in combat, having the minimum acceptable performance would not be sufficient against the superior aircraft being designed in Europe. The CG believed that the AAC's competition was illegal as it did not provide any method of establishing a precise relationship between cost and performance and left the choice only on performance. The secretary of war held that no formula could evaluate price *v.* performance and that the Air Corps Act of 1926 gave him legal discretion to make decisions regarding the weight of price versus performance when evaluating bids "in order to serve the best interests of the air arm." Meanwhile, Douglas delivered aircraft on the contract but was not paid as the disagreement between the CG and secretary of war continued. The attorney general was asked to intervene and, after four months, ruled significantly in favor of the secretary of war, and Douglas was finally paid. Even though the attorney general had ruled in favor of the secretary of war, AAC procurement officers realized that price would remain a problem with the comptroller general and general accounting office. In order to expedite their procurement programs and for their aircraft contractors to receive timely payments, the AAC agreed to include price as a factor for evaluation in all future competition. The AAC's evaluation proposal was to determine a "figure of merit" on the basis of performance that was to be divided by the dollar cost bid by the manufacturer. This "price factor" would favor the bidder with the lowest price and the highest performance. However, the War Department continued to be adamant that final selection would be the decision of the secretary of war and the figure of merit and price factor would serve as a guide lines for the final selection.

With this procedure in place, the manufacturers found that drawbacks lingered. The circulars (design proposals) had to be composed so that the manufacturer's had enough design autonomy to incorporate innovations, but it also had to be specific as to the design requirements so that the manufacturer knew what the circular required. To make the competition as fair as possible, the manufacturers could not consult Wright Field engineers, which, in turn, prevented Wright from offering suggestions that could enhance the design. The manufacturers were also not allowed to submit mock-up aircraft to Wright for evaluation that could discover design defects that could be more easily corrected in this mock-up stage than in the prototype phase. Changes in the prototype phase once it reached Wright Field could only be made by change orders to amend the contract that was time and money intensive. The overriding factor in issuing a circular was getting a design into quantity production as soon as possible and the AAC assumed that the manufacturers would submit a wholly developed prototype that would be ready to go into production. But to win the competition, the manufacturers had to design aircraft with innovations that were not yet combat proven and thus the prototypes tended to be more experimental in nature and would later require numerous contract change orders (e.g. the B-24). Prototypes were very expensive to build, especially four-engined bombers, whose airframe costs could rise 300–400 percent and the time for their fabrication increased from months to as much as two years during the 1930s. Also the manufacturers always faced the possibility of not having their design and prototype accepted and having to absorb the entire cost of the project as there was a very slight chance that the rejected design could be sold to foreign air forces or used commercially. The manufacturers were caught in a "Catch-22" situation as they were forced into bidding simply because they needed the business in the poor economic environment of the Depression and failure to enter the competition would result in leaving the manufacturer behind its contemporaries in developing combat technology. But then not entering competition would save them the costs of developing a design and building a prototype without assurance of a contract. In the late 1930s, the result was a declining number of bidders for government contracts as the economic conditions improved and the large manufacturers were receiving contracts from commercial airlines and air transport. In 1938, manufacturers led by Consolidated Aircraft Corporation's Reuben Fleet suggested remedies to increase bidding. Fleet had once been a procurement officer for the Army in the early 1920s and had been committed to solving the problems of aircraft procurement and legislation. Over the years, Fleet had made several proposals that culminated in his suggesting that legislation be passed to authorize the War Department to procure aircraft in production quantities by negotiated contracts rather than bids involving prototypes. Of course, the War Department could not endorse this idea without rankling Congress and their desire for competition. When in a dilemma, the government's usual solution was to convene another board to study yet again another revised procurement recommendation. The AAC and various aircraft manufacturers testified and the new board recommended a solution that was a compromise between competition with prototypes and a simple design competition. Before issuing circular proposals for production aircraft, the AAC would invite aircraft manufacturers to submit designs for evaluation. One or more designs would be selected and be granted experimental contracts for the construction of one or more prototypes. There was also the proviso that a quality data from losing designs could be purchased. Detailed type specifications would not be prepared until the winning design(s) passed the final mock-up phase allowing the AAC and manufacturers to discuss changes. Once the design was finalized, the AAC was to issue its circular proposal for a prototype aircraft to be built by manufacturers interested in procuring a contract for the production aircraft. The War Department would subsidize the building of the prototype of the winning manufacturer(s). Usually the winner could expect to be awarded a production contract with his prototype but other manufacturers who could afford to build a prototype to specifications could also enter the competition and preclude any accusations that free competition was being thwarted. An impartial evaluation of the design was now based on the performance of the prototype and was to reduce the number of design changes and get the aircraft into production sooner. Finally a workable procurement proposal seemed to have been realized. The chief of staff approved the board's proposal in October 1938, but the threat of an impending European war soon made the proposal moot.

In February 1939, the chairman of the House Military Affairs Committee introduced a bill authorizing 6,000 aircraft for the fiscal year 1940 that was passed in April authorizing $57 million for new equipment. The next day, the AAC issued contracts worth $19 million to build 571 aircraft. In July, in response to an appeal by President Roosevelt, a request for a supplementary $89 million was authorized for immediate disbursement and authorized an additional $44 million. On 10 August 1939, the AAC issued $86 million in aircraft contracts. By 1941, the same Congress that was so adamant about financial prudence and competitive bidding in 1934 were now voting billions of dollars for defense and endorsing negotiated contracts to expedite the placement of contracts to meet the president's call for 50,000 aircraft. All the legislation from the Air Corps Act of 1926 onward and all the boards and committees and their investigations and recommendations were to be invalidated by the Japanese attack on Pearl Harbor and the procurement flood gates were to be opened.

While patrolling the Tijuana Mexican border during his Washington National Guard days in 1911, Fleet had become captivated with San Diego. As part of his ill-fated cross-country Fleet aircraft promotional and sales junket with Lauretta Golem in August 1929, Fleet had stopped at San Diego. While there, Fleet was contacted by Thomas Bomar, head of San Diego's Chamber of Commerce Aviation Division who enlightened him about his city's aviation virtues. Two years earlier, San Diego voters had approved a $650,000 bond issue to develop an airport and facilities on the tidal flats adjacent to San Diego Bay. Fleet was so impressed with the new Lindbergh Field facility that he offered to purchase it for an extraordinary $1 million and also acquired land in Mission Bay for a flying school. Encouraged by Fleet's interest, Bomar continued to send promotional information to Fleet who virtually ignored Bomar's efforts over the next two years. Meanwhile, E. P. Querl, representing the Los Angeles Chamber of Commerce, visited Buffalo to present his city's proposal to Fleet. In April 1933, Fleet and Larry Bell visited the Los Angeles and Long Beach areas that had previously made overtures to him to move to their localities. Fleet, playing one city against another, contacted Bomar, saying that Long Beach had made him an offer of 22 acres of free land on their municipal airport, which was on the "water." On the negative side, Fleet also mentioned the stench and sight of oil wells, which were proliferating during the Long Beach oil boom. In selling San Diego, Bomar told Fleet that the Long Beach land would be under water during the winter months and was 5 miles from the ocean, a disadvantage in the flying boat business. After investigating Bomar's (correct) assertions, Fleet and Bell then flew down to San Diego to meet with the Mayor, Bomar, the city manager, and the harbor commissioner. After the meeting, Fleet and Bell returned to Buffalo to consider moving to the West Coast and to present the possible move to the customarily conservative Consolidated Board of Directors. Meanwhile, not giving up, Los Angeles and Long Beach sent representatives to Buffalo to lure Fleet to their cities. When the city of Buffalo learned of Fleet's possible defection, it also made several ineffective offers to keep the company there. Fortunately for San Diego, Emil Klicka, the city's harbor commissioner and an influential banker, who been in the meeting with Fleet during his California visit, stopped at Buffalo on 29 May 1934 during his spring vacation. Klicka spent an hour with the Consolidated Board of Directors and was so persuasive that on that same day the board passed a resolution authorizing a conditional fifty-year lease with the West Coast city. Fleet then dispatched his son, David, and Vice President Charles Leigh to San Diego to contract the building of a new factory at Lindbergh Field and plan for the California end of the move from Buffalo. They retained architect L. B. Norman to design a modern aircraft factory using the basic elements Fleet had observed during his visits to other new purpose-built aircraft and automobile factories—particularly, continuous, uninterrupted production from raw materials to a finished aircraft. The plant was to be 1,000 feet long and 275 feet wide and total 275,000 square feet. In December, Consolidated took construction bids and applied for a $500,000 loan from the Reconstruction Finance Corporation (RFC) to build the $300,000 plant and spend the remainder of the loan on new equipment and to move the company from Buffalo. The limit for a RFC loan was $100,000, but Fleet and the San Diego faction influenced the area Congressman to persuade the RFC to grant all the $500,000.

Left: Thomas Bomar, head of San Diego's Chamber of Commerce Aviation Division, enlightened Fleet about his city's aviation virtues. (*CAC/AAF*)

Below: Buffalo Consolidated executives move to San Diego. *Left to right*: Raymond Madison, "Doc" Carpenter, Issac Laddon, Roy Miller, Harry Sutton, Ralph Oversmith, James Kelley, George Newman, Charles Leigh, Charles Van Dusen, Capt. Leland Hurd, Roy Nelt, Bernard Sheahan, and David Fleet. (*CAC/AAF*)

Fleet authorized $40,000 for the move, but it was imperative for Consolidated to make the it as quickly as possible as the company had been awarded two large contracts, one in December 1934 from the Army for fifty Model P-30 pursuit aircraft and one on 29 June 1935 for sixty PBY-1 Catalina flying boats from the Navy. Fleet assigned Howard Golem, the nephew of Henry Golem, Fleet's deceased wife's ex-husband, as the traffic manager of the move. Initially, the move by a single shipment by sea via the St. Lawrence Seaway and the Panama Canal was considered but was dismissed as too time consuming. However, Fleet used the sea route move as leverage in his negotiations with the railways to secure the best rates. The Buffalo factory continued production until mid-August when its contents were sequentially loaded into 157 freight cars for shipment to San Diego where they would be unloaded sequentially so that production could be resumed as soon as possible. Fleet selected about 311 key employees and paid their moving expenses and promised jobs to another 100 if they paid their own expenses (during the Depression, the promise of a good, steady job was persuasive). The employees drove from Buffalo to San Diego during the last two weeks of August (another 400 would be hired in California). Fleet stated: "We left all the bad radicals back there in Buffalo."

When the Buffalo city fathers learned that Fleet was actually going to leave, they offered to finance a new aircraft company if Larry Bell would remain behind to head it. Meanwhile, Bell was to take over the plant that Consolidated was renting from the American Radiator Co. When Bell broached Buffalo's offer to Fleet, the Consolidated president was taken aback as after Lauretta Golem's death in 1929, Fleet and George Newman had stepped down to policy and planning positions, respectively, and assigned the capable Bell as the company's general manager and operating head with Ray Whitman as the assistant general manager. Fleet biographer and former Consolidated PR man William Wagner glosses over Fleet's reaction as wishing Bell luck on this new opportunity that would force Fleet back into managing the company after Bell's five successful years. Wagner reports that Fleet promised he would send Bell "a couple million dollars of subcontract work to help him get started." But it seems as though such magnanimity was not in Fleet's nature as he was so upset with Bell that he demanded that Bell not offer a position to anyone he (Fleet) wanted to take with him to San Diego.

Bell resigned from Consolidated and remained in Buffalo, as did talented Robert Woods to serve as Bell's new chief designer and, most galling, so did Ray Whitman, Fleet's long-time assistant. Bell planned to lease the Consolidated factory that would became Bell Aircraft Company and would produce the P-39 Cobra fighter, designed by Woods. With the loss of Bell, Woods, and Whitman, Fleet named three new vice presidents with Mac Laddon serving as chief engineer, Charles Leigh as materials supervisor, and then, as a major coup, he hired Charles Van Dusen from the Glenn L. Martin Company where he had served as their works manager for twenty years

The triumvirate Laddon, Leigh, and Van Dusen would develop into a formidable team. After graduating from Worcester Poly Technical Institute in 1911, Nebraskan Leigh continued onto a varied career in mechanical and civil engineering, first in Washington state as the chief engineer at the Raymond, Washington, unit of the

Fleet hired Charles Van Dusen from the Glenn L. Martin Company where he had served as their works manager for twenty years. (CAC/AAF)

Airplane Spruce Division in 1917; then as service engineer for the Portland Cement Association for several years; and as general superintendent for the Grays Harbor Construction Company at Hoquiam, Washington, for four years until he joined Consolidated in 1926. Beginning as an assistant to Consolidated's factory manager, he would become a company vice president and assistant general manager.

By mid-September 1935, the San Diego factory began limited operations with 874 employees and was officially dedicated on 20 October. As the centerpiece of the ceremony Lt. Cdr. Knefler McGinnis flew the XP3Y-1 south from San Francisco after it had just set the seaplane non-stop distance record of 3,281.383 miles flying from the Canal Zone to Alameda, California in thirty-four hours and forty-five minutes.

In his dedication, Fleet proclaimed:

> Twice each year I flew around the country trying to find a suitable location with a publicly-owned waterfront on a good but not congested harbor. I needed to be in a city large enough to furnish a reasonable supply of labor and materials, and, of course, with all-year flying weather. So today is a culmination of a dream for a factory of our own in a city of our choice.

So on 20 October 1935, San Diego no longer was another "Navy town" that had retirees as its civilian base but, instead, would see its population grow by 41 percent between 1941 and 1944. The continual production backlog of Army, Navy, and foreign orders caused Consolidated to increase employment, engaging 797 workers in 1939 and 16,500 in 1942, and by the end of 1943, the number of workers almost tripled to 45,000. (Note: The new San Diego Plant will be extensively discussed later.)

Reuben Fleet, flanked by a Catalina, dedicated the new San Diego Factory on 20 October 1935 and afterward the city would no longer be a "Navy town." (*CAC/AAF*)

To showcase the San Diego factory dedication, Lt. Cdr. Knefler McGinnis arrived in the record-setting XP3Y-1. (*USN*)

5

The San Diego Plant Goes into Production

The fifty PB-2A (P-30) two-seat, high-altitude pursuit biplanes (PB) were the first aircraft to go into production at San Diego because most of its parts had been previously manufactured by the Buffalo plant and the fighter basically only needed to be assembled. The PB-2A was the first turbo-supercharged production aircraft to enter squadron service in any large numbers and heralded the thousands of high-altitude military aircraft that would follow.

However, the real challenge facing Consolidated was fulfilling the important $6.5 million contract for sixty PBY-1s, awarded only three months before the new factory was opened. The PB-2A contract was completed in July 1936, but then the Navy placed a second order for fifty of the improved PBY-2 valued at $4.9 million, which would keep the Consolidated fifty production lines busy but stressed.

PB2Y-1 Coronado (Model 29)

The Navy initiated a new design competition for a long-range, four-engined flying boat with an ordnance payload of 12,000 pounds. Competition was again between Consolidated and Sikorsky, and after a fly-off between the two, Consolidated was awarded the $600,000 contract for the prototype XPB2Y-1 (Model 29) in May 1936 (to which Consolidated added another $400,000). The Coronado's first flight would not take place until 17 December 1937 at which time serious directional stability problems were noted, which were not corrected after several attempted fixes involving its tail configuration. Coronado production was not begun until March 1939 due to these problems and to PBY Catalina production priority. The Coronado was only a moderate success, with 217 being produced; they were to be considered a drag on B-24 development and production.

Prosperity at Consolidated brought problems as space in the new factory was at a premium. For security reasons and so as not to interfere with normal production, the experimental XPB2Y-1 Coronado prototype would have to be built in its own facility. Factory additions of 450,000 square feet of inside space and 170,000 square feet of paved area for outside assembly were financed by the issue of 22,976 shares of convertible stock at $50 each that raised $1.15 million (1,024 shares were reserved for sale to "selected" employees). The PBY-2 proved to be such a success that on 3 October 1936, the Navy ordered another sixty-six of the improved PBY-3s with 1,000-hp Twin Wasp engines only two days before the first of the fifty PBY-1s were delivered and only two weeks less than a year after the dedication of the San Diego plant. Consolidated showed small profits in 1935 and 1936, but by the end of 1936, the Navy had ordered 176 PBYs and the company had an $18 million order backlog and its work force had grown from 900 in 1936 to 3,200 the next year. Finances were definitely on the upswing. In 1937, the Navy awarded a contract for thirty-three PBY-4s at $4.5 million. In 1937 and 1938, the company had sales of $12 million but in 1939 the sales fell to $3.6 million as after manufacturing 200 PBYs there were no new orders and the work force decreased from 3,700 to 1,200 by the end of 1938 in anticipation of the decrease in orders. As noted previously, the Coronado prototype was having continual control problems with its tail configuration and the first production order would not come until the end of March 1939 when the Navy ordered six of the deep-hulled PB2Y-2 patrol bombers, but the first would not be delivered until the end of December 1940.

PB2Y-1 Coronado (Model 29). (USN)

Boeing Gets an Early Start in the Four-Engined Bomber Competition

By the mid-1930s, the global situation had begun to change with the rise of Hitler and Mussolini in Europe and the Japanese militarism in the Far East. In 1933, the disciples of Billy Mitchell's strategic air power theories had been promoted to levels of some importance in the Army Air Corps, particularly in its research and development branch, the Air Materiel Command at Wright Field, Dayton, Ohio. Out of this branch came "Project A," a thorough feasibility study for a four-engined bomber that could fly 5,000 miles carrying a ton of bombs. However, also at the time, the top echelon of the Army general staff still was dominated by former cavalry officers, and on 14 April 1934, they grudgingly approved Project A but not as an "offensive" weapon but one for "hemispheric defense." Project A in relation to the long-range bomber program will be discussed in depth later.

In a memorandum of 14 July 1934, the Air Materiel Command had changed its philosophy and decided that a second bomber that was not as grand as the Project A bomber could be more easily realized and put into production. The new AAC bomber was to have the same 2,000-pound bombload, but its speed was to be 200 mph and its range was to be at least 1,020 miles—2,200 miles was much preferred. The AAC proposal was for "multi-engines," which to the AAC meant two, but to Boeing it meant four. On 26 September 1934, the Boeing Board of Directors of the newly independent Boeing Airplane Company met for the first time after parent United Aircraft and Transport was finally dissolved. The new board bravely voted $275,000 to design and build a bomber to meet the new AAC specification. Boeing President Claire Egtvedt assigned his project engineer, E. G. "Giff" Emery, with Ed Wells as his assistant, and Frederick Laudan as the construction supervisor to work on the Model 299. The bomber was to be a low-wing monoplane that would have four engines to power it and was essentially an up-scaled version of Boeing's streamlined Model 247 twin-engined airliner that had been first flown in February 1934. Concurrently, Egtvedt ordered Emery to develop a four-engined airliner based on Model 299 design that was to become the Model 307 Stratoliner. With Emery running the Model 307 project, Egtvedt placed twenty-four-year-old Edward Wells as the project manager for the development of the Model 299 that had been unofficially designated as the XB-17 by Boeing before it had been approved by the AAC. The Model 299 made its first flight on 28 July 1935 and the media was impressed by its large size and armament, dubbing it the "Flying Fortress." On 20 August, project test pilot Leslie "Les" Tower flew it cross-country 2,100 miles to Wright Field for evaluation at an impressive average speed of 232 mph.

During testing at Wright Field, the four-engined Boeing Model 299 was to challenge Douglas Aircraft's twin-engined DB-1 bomber, the XB-18, which had been developed from the company's successful DC-3 airliner design. From August and into October, the AAC examined both bombers and the Boeing's better range and reliability earned it the lead in gaining a contract. On 30 October 1935, Boeing test pilot Les Tower and AAC pilot Maj. P.P. "Pete" Hill and the test crew took off in the Model 299. But once it was airborne, the bomber became uncontrollable and, as it passed over the end of the runway, it crashed into a nearby pasture. Investigation revealed that the newly developed gust locks on the controls had not been removed. Hill was killed on impact and Tower survived with horrible burns but died twenty days later. Lt. Donald Putt of the test crew was pulled from the burning wreckage and given little chance of survival but Putt did survive and four years later was to become the project manager of the B-29 program. Investigation showed no problems with the bomber were involved but that the ground crew had not unlocked the tail control surfaces causing the crash that would put the Boeing program in jeopardy. The Douglas XB-18 had also done well in tests and two of these twin-engined Douglas bombers could be manufactured for the cost of one Model 299. On 17 January 1936, the Army general staff decided to order 133 production B-18s and only thirteen of the Model 299s now designated the YB-17 (the "Y" meant that the aircraft was not experimental but a "service test" model that could, or not, precede production aircraft). Once on the production line, the YB-17 was redesignated by Boeing as the Y1B-17 (the 1 because they were purchased out of F-1 fiscal year supplementary funds). The first Y1B-17 rolled off the Seattle line on 2 December 1936 and the last of the thirteen was finished on 5 August 1937. One Y1B-17 was sent to Wright for testing and the other twelve were assigned to the Second Bombardment Group at Langley Field, VA, under Lt. Col. Robert Olds. Meanwhile, the B-17 was slated to become America's four-engined bomber while Consolidated continued its flying boat endeavors.

After having the most bombers in American inventory at the time of Pearl Harbor, the B-18 faded into oblivion mainly flying unproductive U-boat patrols over the Caribbean.

Boeing Model 299 (future B-17) after its fatal 30 October 1935 crash that would place the Boeing heavy bomber program in jeopardy, even though it was the far superior bomber at the time. (*AFSHRC*)

At the time when rapid advances in airframe, aero engine, and propeller design were taking place, Fleet saw the potential market for long-range bombers and higher-performance and longer-range flying boats, not only for the Navy but also for the intercontinental commercial market. Consolidated engineers realized that to achieve these range and performance goals a study of wing form, structure, and aerodynamics would be necessary. At the time, the National Advisory Committee for Aeronautics (NACA) had compiled a catalog of wing profiles and their associated wind tunnel calculations from which airfoils could be selected. These wings sections had been tested in the 10-foot wind tunnel of the Guggenheim Aeronautics Laboratory of the California Institute of Technology (GALCIT).

During the summer of 1937, Walter Brookins, the first pilot trained by the Wright Brothers, called Fleet asking him to meet with David Davis, a freelance aeronautical engineer, who was trying to obtain development funds for his revolutionary low-drag, high-aspect-ratio wing design for use on Consolidated flying boats. When Davis was a teenager, his mother moved to California, only a few miles from where Glenn L. Martin was developing a biplane that Davis often helped to move from its hangar. In 1911, he made his first flight and four years later bought a used Curtiss pusher biplane with Grover Bell, Larry Bell's brother. After serving in the infantry during World War I, he purchased a second-hand Curtiss Jenny and, using family money, quickly became a millionaire sportsman and aviation enthusiast. In the spring of 1920, he wanted to build the first aircraft able to fly non-stop coast-to-coast and contacted Donald Douglas, head of a fledgling Santa Monica aircraft company. Douglas, though disappointed with the small, one-up order, realized that designing and building an aircraft that could fly non-stop cross-country would lead to other more lucrative projects. With $40,000 from Davis and borrowing family money, Douglas built the Cloudster, which was the first aircraft in history able to airlift a useful load exceeding its own weight. The aircraft showed promise when it broke the Pacific Coast altitude record of 19,160 feet on 29 March 1921. The first American cross-country flight was attempted by Davis and former Martin chief test pilot Eric Springer on 27 June 1921 but was cut short when its Liberty engine quit over El Paso. Before a second attempt could be made, two Army pilots, Lieutenants Oakley Kelly and John Macready, flew a Fokker T-2 monoplane from Roosevelt Field, Long Island, to Rockwell Field, San Diego—2,500 miles in twenty-eight hours and fifty minutes. With the record broken, Davis sold the Cloudster, which was then modified for sightseeing flights and was ultimately sold to T. Claude Ryan in 1925 who had established his aircraft company and airline in San Diego. Later Davis developed a variable pitch propeller for Bendix, but the 1929 Stock Market Crash ended the Bendix propeller project and ruined Davis financially. Broke and supporting his wife and daughter on a $5 a day job, Davis began working on a new revolutionary theoretical type of wing at his kitchen table.

Above left: Donald Davis (L) and Donald Douglas in 1921 when Douglas built Davis' Cloudster aircraft which was intended to be the first to cross the U.S. non-stop. (*CAC/AAF*)

Above right: Walter Brookins, the first pilot trained by the Wright Brothers, was the partner in the Davis-Brookins Aircraft Company. (*AFSHRC*)

6

David Davis and the Davis Wing

Consolidated Adopts the Davis Wing

The down, but not out, David Davis wanted to mathematically determine the optimum airfoil by varying the values assigned to the constants in his equations. Since Davis could not afford a wind tunnel test, he improvised by borrowing a large Packard automobile from a friend to act as an ersatz wind tunnel. To isolate his model from the aerodynamic turbulences of the car body, he mounted a large flat board horizontally on top and tested his airfoils cantilevered vertically above the board. The distribution of pressure at the surface of the airfoil were measured by photographing an array of manometers in the car as it was driven at high speed on Southern California rural roads. During 1935 to 1937, Davis arduously tested a number of airfoils and reluctantly decided that this procedure would require too much time and effort and decided to approach aircraft manufacturers.

Consolidated had recently flown its four-engined Navy XPB2Y-1 Coronado for the first time and already had some rudimentary plans for the twin-engined Model 31 flying boat that would be a significant advancement over it and the PBY Catalina design. The Model 31 wing design offered an opportunity for Davis to apply his wing airfoil design. The cautious Davis, who already had been rejected by one major U.S. aircraft company, had asked to meet with Fleet alone and was reluctant to share his now-named "Fluid Foil" with anyone else. But Fleet was a self-described "practical engineer," not an aerodynamicist, and demanded that Davis meet with Consolidated Chief Engineer Laddon and aerodynamicist George Schairer. Upon meeting the slight, mustachioed, bespectacled, and rather unassuming Davis, Fleet asked why he had not presented his idea to former partner Donald Douglas. Davis' answer made it quite obvious that he had differences with Douglas dating back to his 1920s Cloudster aircraft days. Davis disclosed that Brookins, his partner in the Davis-Brookins Aircraft Company, suggested Fleet on his wife's recommendation as she had been Col. Thurman Bane's secretary at McCook Field when Fleet was there in the 1920s. Though not a graduate engineer, Davis proceeded to outline his ideas on his Fluid Foil to Fleet and Laddon and described the work he had done to prove his theories, and concluded there must be some mathematically perfect airfoil section. Most airfoils had been developed by trying different sections in a wind tunnel, then calculating which were the most efficient. Davis thought that was doing things backward as, instead of testing an infinite number of sections, why not begin with a perfect sphere, followed by the teardrop-shape formed from it which Davis compared to a falling drop of water and feasibly drag could be virtually eliminated. Davis asserted that his airfoil designs were superior to other contemporary foils in performance, which made them particularly suitable for long-range aircraft. Fleet and Laddon were initially unconvinced as Laddon and his engineers were unable to discern a physical basis for Davis's equations and doubted that the untrained Davis could improve on the extensive NACA research. The main point of contention was that the equations in Davis' patent contained two unspecified, assignable constants for which Consolidated engineers would need values to be able to represent and examine his airfoils. Davis was unwilling to disclose this essential secret data without a commitment from Fleet and Laddon. Alternatively, Davis proposed that he build a wind tunnel model with the same planform and span-wise thickness as one of the Consolidated aircraft models but would integrate his own wing airfoil. Without specifying the shape of its sections, Davis would provide this model to GALCIT, at Consolidated's expense, for testing together with the Consolidated models without the Davis wing. Davis specified that if his wing proved superior and Consolidated signed a license to use it, he would then supply the shape of the profile. Although the airfoil design was still essentially empirical and had no physical basis or basis in fluid mechanics, Fleet and Laddon considered that the Fluid Foil had merit and decided to give it a chance.

Aircraft wing design of the 1930s generally positioned the thickest portion of the wing within the first 10–15 percent of the wing chord and the National Advisory Committee on Aeronautics and Davis were both looking for wing designs that provided the maximum lift and minimum drag. NACA studies had found that there was a direct relationship between turbulent air flow and friction drag, determining that rivets, lap joints, and even paint diminished aircraft horsepower simply due to the drag these created. NACA's conclusions were to have substantial consequences on future aircraft design. Davis' Fluid Foil was a wing design in reverse, starting with a basic low-drag teardrop shape and then modified as required to provide maximum lift. In comparison to contemporary designs, Davis' design was relatively thick but had a short chord and a high aspect ratio. Aspect ratio is the ratio based on the span and chord of an aircraft's wings; the span is the length of the wings measured wingtip to wingtip; and the chord is an imaginary straight line joining the extremities of the leading and trailing wing edges. Aspect ratio is equal to the square of the wingspan divided by the wing area; consequently, a long, narrow wing has a high aspect ratio, whereas a short, wide wing has a low aspect ratio. Davis maintained that his new wing would offer much lower drag than designs then in use and would offer considerable lift even at a small angle of attack (the angle between the wing chord line and the flight path). The wing's ability to generate lift at low angles of attack made it particularly appealing for use in flying boats as it would reduce the need to pull up the nose for take-off and landing, which was often limited in flying boats due to the way they floated on the water. Additionally, the thickness of the wing would allow for excellent fuel storage, or even embedded engines which were then a fashionable aircraft design trend.

Davis held U.S. Patent No. 1942688 (filed 25 May 1931 and issued 9 January 1934) that concerned mathematical formulae relating to the development of a group of wing sections, which he claimed gave substantially better performance and were much more efficient than any other existing airfoil. Thus, the so-called Davis Wing/Fluid Foil was not a patented specific physical wing but a mathematical formula for creating high-aspect, low-drag airfoils—one of the first laminar flow wings. Generally, a laminar flow wing delays the turbulence created by the wing passing through the air by placing the thickest part of the wing as far as possible from the leading edge consistent with maintaining lift.

Davis incorporated this airfoil on the Consolidated model to be delivered to GALCIT for testing in late August and early September 1937. At the time NACA had recently completed a comprehensive wind tunnel study on airfoil shapes, but the NACA airfoil study did not include a wing similar to the Davis Wing as existing wind tunnels were too turbulent to test laminar theories. Davis began by constructing an 8-foot model wing section for the new flying boat incorporating his formula-derived airfoil. Caltech put it into its Guggenheim wind tunnel and began a series of tests. Davis awaited the results for several weeks and then was informed that the wind tunnel was not performing properly and some equipment would have to be reworked. GALCIT Drs. Clark Millikan and Theodore von Karman were perplexed as the results could not be correct as the airfoil's efficiency was 102 percent, exceeding the theoretical maximum, and thought something must be wrong with the wind tunnel as 90 percent efficiency had always been considered about the maximum theoretical efficiency. Milliken and von Karman considered that, perhaps, the results were some unexplained phenomenon, leaving Fleet and Laddon without a basis for making a decision on the Davis Fluid Foil.

Meanwhile, as 1937 ended, Consolidated believed that the Davis foil formulae to be superior but did not know its shape and Davis would not divulge it until the company signed agreement with Davis-Brookins. Fleet assigned engineer George Schairer to determine (guess) the foil's profile by using drawings to represent hundreds of airfoils from the equations of Davis's patent and inserting a wide-ranging series of the assignable constants. It was not long before Schairer was forced to conclude that it was hopeless to guess these values.

Consolidated received the airfoil's ordinates on a sheet of paper on 9 February 1938 when it entered into a license agreement from which Davis would receive $2,500 for each prototype and a royalty on each subsequent aircraft using his airfoil, based on a sliding scale beginning at half of 1 percent of the selling price of the aircraft (less engines, propellers, other items of GFE and spares) and decreasing to one-eighth of 1 percent when and if orders reached $10 million. In addition, when total royalty payments reached $50,000, the rate was to be reduced to one-sixteenth of 1 percent. With the signing of a contract on 10 February 1938, Davis became a consultant to

Patented Jan. 9, 1934

1,942,688

UNITED STATES PATENT OFFICE

1,942,688

FLUID FOIL

David R. Davis, Los Angeles, Calif.

Application May 25, 1931, Serial No. 539,729
Renewed May 29, 1933

13 Claims. (Cl. 244—12)

This invention relates to a construction of foils to be driven through a fluid, and particularly concerns the profile of the foil in its front to rear section. While the invention may be applied to a foil used in any medium, it has its greatest usefulness when applied in the construction of airfoils for air vehicles.

The upper surface of a fluid foil should have a profile, which, when the foil is driven through the fluid, will develop a region of reduced pressure on the upper side of the foil, and the under side of a foil should have a profile which will de- regularly from each other can be readily tested to determine the most advantageous form of foil for certain purposes.

Further objects of the invention will appear hereinafter.

The invention consists of novel parts and combinations of parts to be described hereinafter, all of which contribute to produce an efficient fluid foil.

A preferred embodiment of the invention is described in the following specification, while the broad scope of the invention is pointed out in the

Above: The 9 January 1934 patent approval for Davis' mathematical formulae relating to the development of a group of wing sections. (*U.S. Patent Office*)

Right: The 1931 patent application drawing of wing foil submitted and signed by David Davis. (*U.S. Patent Office*)

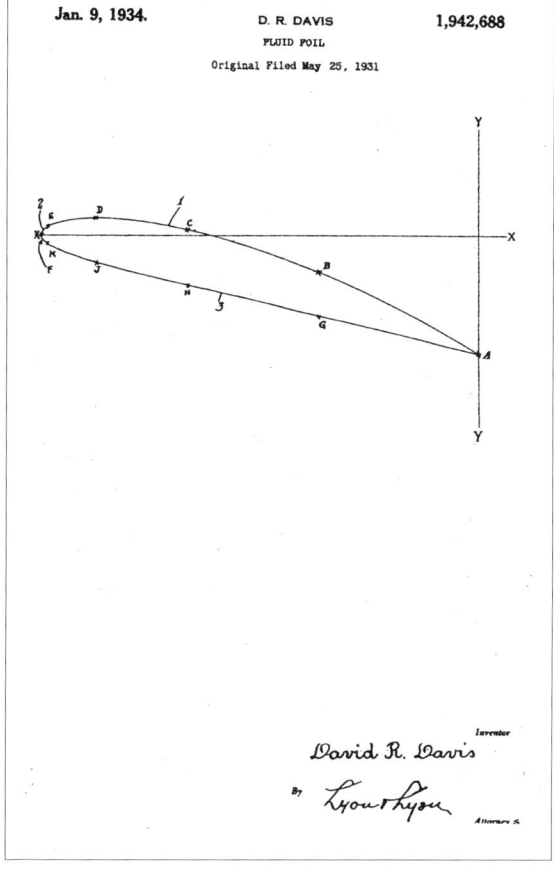

Consolidated at $200 per month for a minimum of eight days effort monthly for six months. Wind tunnel models of Davis-generated airfoil sections would be tested at Consolidated's expense at the California Institute of Technology. Particularly important to Consolidated's competitive position in the industry was the provision that for a year Davis would not disclose his method of generating airfoil sections to other aircraft companies or government agencies. Davis was also to move forward in obtaining full patent protection on his pending application and should his patent position be judged invalid, royalty payments would cease. Nonetheless, even at this time, Laddon and his engineers continued to have some doubt about the Foil as a provision was included that canceled Consolidated's commitment if tests of the same airfoils on larger scale models in the NACA full-scale wind tunnel indicated that the improvement demonstrated in the smaller scale models did not exist.

At this time, Laddon and his engineers had to make a realistic decision on adopting the Foil, despite Fleet's enthusiasm. During 1938, a new wind tunnel was built at the California Institute of Technology's (Cal Tech/CIT) Guggenheim Aeronautical Laboratory that enabled air flow smooth enough to finally test concepts like the Davis Fluid Foil. With the new Cal Tech wind tunnel available in late August, Laddon reconsidered that Davis could be right and a willing Reuben Fleet agreed to pay for a model and wind tunnel tests costing $40,000, a huge amount at the time. If the GALCIT full-scale comparison was valid then the Davis Airfoil offered a definite advantage for long-range performance, which was central for future Consolidated aircraft under consideration. If not, then the Davis Foil would likely be no worse than a conventional design. So aerodynamically, there could perhaps be something to gain and nothing to lose, but there could be some structural disadvantages. The salesman in Reuben Fleet saw an additional consideration to have something new to add sales appeal for the Navy and Air Corps. Continuing to explore these technical trade-offs, Consolidated engineers arranged for tests at GALCIT, from March to May 1938, of three Davis wings of greater thickness and one Consolidated wing.

The initial Guggenheim Wind Tunnel results were unsatisfactory as the test instruments did not "return significant readings" to support Davis' estimates. Although, allegedly among the most advanced wind tunnels of the time, Davis determined that the wind tunnel instruments were not sufficiently sensitive to record accurate performance measurements. Once the wind tunnel instruments were recalibrated, the results of the test showed significantly improved readings but were considered so good that they were again considered to be implausible. Cal Tech again checked the calibrations of their new wind tunnel and ran the tests twice more. When the GALCIT/Millikan Wind Tunnel Report was sent to Consolidated, it indicated that the wing appeared to deliver everything Davis claimed that the three wings with Davis profiles proved consistently superior to the one without and that the "remarkably high value for the Davis Wing is probably associated with a peculiar variation of boundary layer thickness with angle of attack but no real explanation for it has yet appeared." The report indicated that the wing actually could be a ground-breaking concept but also hedged that the good results could be an "idiosyncrasy" that could only occur in the wind tunnel.

In late September, three weeks after the GALCIT tests, an enthusiastic Fleet approached Adml. Arthur Cook, chief of the Navy's Bureau of Aeronautics (BuAer) relaying the wind tunnel test results and Millikan's Report, which when applied to flying-boat studies would increase performance and save significant fuel. Laddon forwarded a similar report to Cdr. Walter Diehl, senior engineering officer at the BuAer. Diehl soon forwarded Laddon's letter and data to the NACA's research laboratory at Langley Field, which replied that the data was much too tentative to be reliable. In late September, Walter Brookins continued to advocate for the Airfoil and contacted his old friend Gen. Henry Arnold, then-assistant chief of the Air Corps, sending him a copy of Millikan's Report, which Arnold immediately forwarded to Maj. A. W. Brock of the Materiel Division at Wright Field for evaluation. Brock also was unimpressed and, like NACA, had doubts about the report's uncertainties and the unreliability of wind tunnel testing.

Davis and the Consolidated engineers only knew that their airfoil had very low drag in the wind tunnel but did not realize that it was what would become known as a laminar flow airfoil. It was only later that the explanation for the Davis Wing's exceptional performance became apparent. Laminar Flow is the smooth, uninterrupted flow of air over the contour of the wings and is most often found at the front of a streamlined body and is an important factor in flight. If the smooth flow of air is interrupted over a wing section, turbulence is created, which results in a loss of lift and a high degree of drag. An airfoil designed for minimum drag and uninterrupted flow of the boundary layer is called a laminar airfoil.

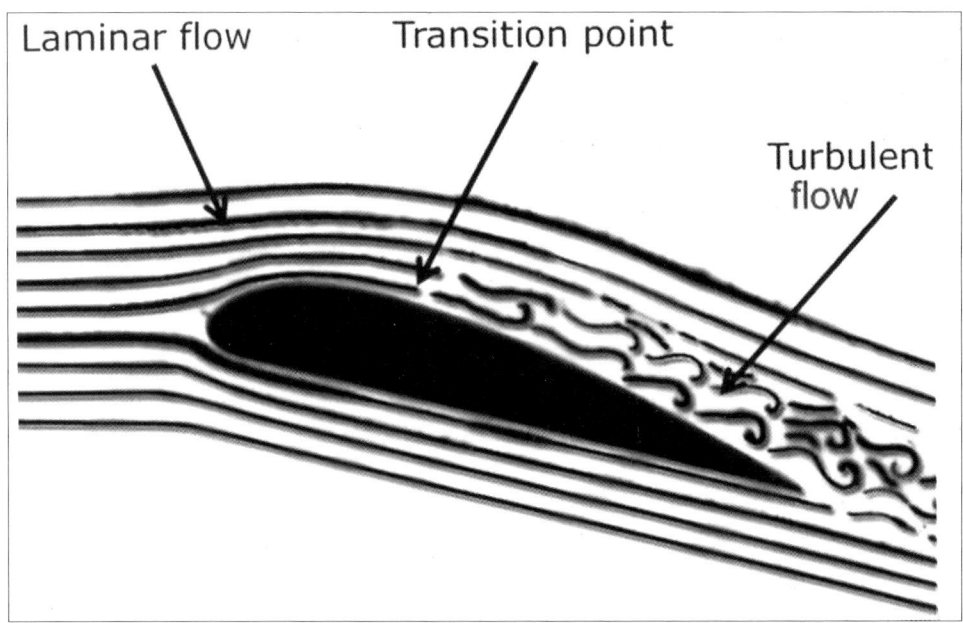

Laminar *v.* turbulent flow. (*Author's collection*)

The Davis wing shape was able to maintain laminar flow over a wider area of its leading edge, to about 20 percent or 30 percent of chord; while in comparison, most contemporary airfoils were more typically 5 percent to 20 percent. Although later designs were able to greatly improve on this, maintaining laminar flow to upwards of 60 percent of chord, the Davis Wing represented a great improvement at the time; its cross-section showing a distinct likeness to the famous NACA 6-Series Laminar Flow Airfoils used on the P-51 Mustang which had a purposely-designed laminar wing. Later, the wing when used on the Liberator revealed that its high aspect ratio Davis Wing, although meeting its promise of lift and speed, caused instability in flight when it was required to carry heavier loads in combat. The Liberator became difficult to fly, particularly at high altitude and in poor weather, and was also very sensitive to ice formation that distorted the airfoil section, causing lift.

Despite the continued uncertainty, only after considerable deliberation did Laddon and Schairer join Fleet in deciding that they would use the Davis Wing on Consolidated's new twin-engined Model 31 commercial flying boat, which was to be a private venture planned to be both a commercial transport and a possible successor to the PBY Catalina. Then, if the Davis Wing was successful it was to be considered for use on a projected land-based bomber for which Consolidated had several design studies underway. The Model 31 and its role in the decision to use the Davis Wing on the B-24 is described next.

Before Fleet left Consolidated he defended the highly efficient Davis Wing which had been credited as the main factor in the B-24's and Consolidated's success and Fleet did not begrudge the several hundred thousand dollars in royalties, which had been paid to David Davis and Walter Brookins for use of their patent. However, when the Navy initiated contracts for the single-tail PB4Y-2 Privateer version of the B-24, they examined the Davis Wing patent and found that the ordinates were not correct and, therefore, considered the patent invalid. Although nearly all the B-24 contracts had been with the Army, which had paid the royalties, the Navy notified Consolidated to stop paying further royalty and also to have Davis return any previous royalty payments. Fleet defended Davis to the Navy arguing that the wing carried more weight than any comparable wing and Davis had deserved the royalties. Davis explained that the ordinates were purposely wrong on the patent application as patents were open to the public and he falsified them so no one could poach the information in case his death. Despite Fleet's strong intervention, the Navy allowed its rather insubstantial royalty payments to stand but did not approve further payments.

For the year ended 30 November 1942, royalties paid to the Davis-Brookins Aircraft Co. totaled $92,665. Subsequently, some modification of the original royalty schedule was negotiated and a new license agreement signed on 29 June 1943. Payments totaling $44,005 were made between October 1943 and February 1946 and involved a royalty of $5 per aircraft on 8,801 aircraft, which included AAF B-24s, USN PB4Y-2 Privateers, and AAF B-32 Dominators.

The sleek, tapering Davis wing proves itself on the B-24. (*AAF*)

The Davis Wing at Consolidated After the B-24

The one year David Davis airfoil use prohibition in the Consolidated agreement expired before the first flight of the Model 31, and Davis used that publicity and the much-acclaimed use of his wing on the B-24 to launch an airfoil engineering service to interested manufacturers on a royalty basis but there were no offers. Douglas and Hughes conducted studies of the Davis Foil for their designs but never employed it. NACA received an inquiry from Vought-Sikorski about the Foil but informed them that was inferior to new "laminar-flow" sections recently developed at Langley Field. After George Schairer moved to Boeing from Consolidated in 1939 and was bound not to disclose the Davis data to Boeing, he was influenced by his San Diego experience during 1942 regarding the B-29's aerodynamic design (and its later derivatives, the B-50 and KC-97). These aircraft all had a high-aspect-ratio airfoil, which was somewhat similar to Davis concepts. During the war, the only other aircraft to employ the Davis Wing was Consolidated's B-32, a strategic bomber designed to the same Air Corps' specification as the B-29. This bomber was begun in mid-1940 and the prototype first flew in September 1942. Its wing configuration imitated the B-24's but with considerably increased size and a design maximum speed of 385 mph, which was significantly higher than the test values of about 300 mph for various modifications of the earlier aircraft. Tests in mid-1941 using NACA's 8-foot high-speed wind tunnel at Langley Field showed that the Davis Wing to be unsatisfactory for this higher speed. These tests showed a relatively high drag for the wing at high speeds and other adverse effects of the compressibility of air that occurs as flight speed increases. These results were partially attributed to the shape of the Davis Wing and partly to the relatively large section thicknesses used by Consolidated, but whatever the cause, the realization of the results were that the bomber could not reach its projected speed. Because the design had already been released for production, Consolidated decided it could not be changed. The B-32 had numerous teething problems, many due to the empennage configuration, and to what extent the wing contributed to them is unknown. The B-32 became irrelevant after the success of the B-29 and only 115 were manufactured, and it saw only limited use in the Philippines and Okinawa at the end of the war. (After its use on the B-32, the Davis Wing quietly disappeared and NACA's new laminar-flow sections and the increased obsession with high speeds came on the scene and culminated in the P-51 Mustang's laminar flow wing.)

David Davis and his Wing after Consolidated

Between 1939 and 1944, after Consolidated accepted the Fluid Foil and independently of Consolidated, Davis also conducted studies of his airfoil in the low-speed wind tunnel at the University of Washington at Davis-Brookins' expense. The results for Davis airfoils of various thicknesses combined in a variety of planforms (wing silhouette when viewed from above or below), some extreme and unconventional, were very similar to those completed by GALCIT. As part of this study, a thick-wing version with a very thick chord ratio and an aspect ratio of 6:1 $v.$ 11:1 was developed over two years in anticipation of producing a very long-range aircraft combining the performance of a bomber and interceptor able to cross the Atlantic non-stop at 40,000 feet.

Davis developed an engineless wind tunnel model was named the "Manta" due its wing (and horizontal tail) planform (looking at the wing from the top) resemblance to the oceanic Manta Ray. During 1942, a full-scale 40-foot-long, 50-foot wingspan/42-inch-thick leading edge, tri-cycle gear mock-up/prototype was built by the obscure Los Angeles-based Manta Aircraft Company, of which Davis was the vice president. In additional to its wing/tail configuration innovation, the Manta was to be powered by a mid-fuselage 1,150-hp Allison engine that drove twin contra-rotation props via a flexible shaft coupling (like the Bell P-39). The molded plastic skin covered a welded tubing framework. Wind tunnel tests indicated that the aircraft could cruise at 250 mph with a maximum speed of 430 mph, flying for over ten hours to cover 3,500 miles as a fighter escort for bomber formations. By removing underwing panels covering bomb shackles, the Manta could be converted to its bomber configuration. Its armament arrangement was to be four wing-mounted 20-mm cannon and four .50-caliber machine guns. I am unable to find any further information on this interesting, but scarcely documented aircraft.

During 1943, Davis signed an agreement with the government limiting the royalty paid to him on Davis wing aircraft bought by the United States. In the early 1950s, he sued the government, claiming that additional payments were owed him for B-24s sold as surplus to private buyers at the end of the war. Davis felt his $5 per plane royalty agreement with the government should not apply to Davis Wing B-24s sold as surplus. He tried, unsuccessfully, to collect an additional $795 for each Liberator

Donald Davis formed the Manta Aircraft Corporation to develop the Manta, a very long-range aircraft combining the performance of a bomber and interceptor able to cross the Atlantic non-stop at 40,000 feet. (*AFSHRC*)

disposed of in this way. The government contested the suit, arguing that the claims of Davis' patents were, in fact, not valid. The Court of Claims ruled twelve out of the thirteen claims of the original two Davis Patents were invalid; the first because it required experimentation with values of the constraints to be used in the formulas and the second on the ground of double patenting.

The Davis Wing Considered

The question arises as to whether the B-24 would have been as good an aircraft without using the Davis airfoil. The technical press, on reporting the Liberator's largely excellent performance, gave Davis and his airfoil their professional acclaim while the popular press portrayed Davis as the everyman who, against all odds, developed his "wing" when the engineering departments of America's aircraft industry could not. Aircraft performance is determined on many factors besides the wing and dependable performance data was difficult to quantify accurately with the available instruments at that time. The B-24's outstanding range can be attributed to the Davis Wing's high aspect ratio and its other features. Wind tunnel model Davis Wings or aircraft models using the wing had no directly comparable contemporary aircraft employing a conventional section. There was no data on how different aircraft would have performed using different airfoils. Another "real life" $v.$ wind tunnel factor was that manufactured aircraft wings had inherent surface roughness and inaccuracies that precluded the wind tunnel data gathered from highly polished models. (Note: A more extensive look at the dynamics and structure of the Davis Wing on the B-24 is included in Volume 2.)

7

Consolidated Model 31 Long-Range Patrol Boat and the Davis Wing

Detail design and construction of the Model 31 was authorized on 11 July 1938 as Consolidated undertook a $1 million private venture to create the Model 31, XP4Y prototype. Shortly after authorization, GALCIT conducted a month of model testing of the complete configuration in numerous detailed modifications while associated tests of the wing alone showed the same outstanding results. As a private project, Consolidated was able to build it more quickly (ten months) and have it be ready for flight testing than if the company was required to submit all pertinent design data for government approval before construction could begin, which was crucial in the months before and after Pearl Harbor. Consolidated streamlined its procedure of sending drawings from the engineering department to the prototype shop by reducing or eliminating unnecessary drawings for all parts, but also to have these fewer drawings maintain the ability to reproduce all parts. Although Consolidated's expedited procedures would allow the company to get a prototype bomber ready more quickly, later, when Ford was contracted to produce B-24s, problems arose and both Ford and the Air Corps rebuked Consolidated for its lack of engineering drawings. This rebuke would lead to the question: Was Consolidated just being obstinate for not wanting to divulge and share its proprietary data and methods or rather were Consolidated's engineering drawings not of the complexity and degree that was expected by an automobile manufacturer who had multiple drawings of every auto part that included in the mass-produced Model T?

The Consolidated Model 31 was designed as an all-metal, long-range maritime amphibian patrol flying boat using the untried Davis Wing, having the potential for both commercial and military applications. It featured twin engines, a deep fuselage (with upswept aft fuselage), and twin endplate fin and rudders. Consolidated engineers had designed the aircraft around the innovative, high-mounted, cantilever Davis Wing with the unusually high aspect ratio of 11.55 (for the time), which gave it a long and narrow appearance for such a large aircraft. It was a large aircraft with a wingspan of 110 feet, a length of 73 feet, height of 23 feet, an empty weight of 25,000 pounds, and a gross weight of 50,000 pounds. It had retractable floats installed under the wings and for the first time beaching gear that was carried within the aircraft. It was powered by two of the new Wright R-3350 Twin Cyclone radial engines. The civil version was to have fifty-two passenger seats or sleeper accommodation for twenty-eight.

On 5 May 1939, ten months after its start, the Model 31 made its first flight, with test pilot William Wheatley reporting that the aircraft had the performance of a "pursuit plane," vindicating the Davis Wing and Fleet's $1 million gamble. The Davis Wing gave the Model 31 about 20 percent better performance than any other comparable aircraft and by comparison, the Consolidated PBY only had a top speed of approximately 170 mph and a normal range of only 2,500 miles while the Model 31's maximum test speed was reported at 250 mph with an anticipated range of 3,500 miles.

The aircraft met expectations and considering its size and complexity, it was considered a major engineering and manufacturing achievement for the time. Due to a number of non-engineering reasons, the prototype Model 31 was extensively modified by Consolidated and the design approved by the Navy for wartime antisubmarine use in 1942, with 200 scheduled for procurement under the designation P4Y-1. The order was canceled after only the prototype was built and when the German U-boat threat diminished. The onset of war blocked its commercial application.

The importance of the Model 31 first lay in the design experience it provided to Consolidated engineers in preparation for their future land-based bomber, for which preliminary studies were in progress when go-ahead for this flying boat was given. The processes and procedures used to construct this aircraft would have a profound effect on the future B-24 and was instrumental in Consolidated's ability to progress from contract to prototype to finished B-24 in a very short time but, as will be described, would also cause a few problems.

Consolidated Model 31 long-range patrol boat was the first aircraft to use the Davis wing. (*USN*)

8

Consolidated Pre-XB-24 Four-Engined Bomber Proposals

During late 1937 and early 1938, Consolidated had a brief dalliance with the then-trendy flying wing concept. Consolidated's flying wing differed from the conventional wing-only version as it also included an orthodox Consolidated-style twin-tail empennage sustained by a very small fuselage. However, the crew, passengers, payload/cargo, equipment, engines, and fuel were all housed in the wing structure. The study encompassed a number of proposals including bombers, transports, commercial passenger versions, and some seaplane applications, which was Consolidated's niche. The initial configuration was a 50,000-pound twin-engined bomber (LB-37and LB-38) with buried experimental pusher Allison XV-3420-1 liquid-cooled engines, which were coupled Allison V-1710s (1710×2=3420) that drove the aircraft at 321 mph over a range of 4,520 miles while carrying 2,000 pounds of bombs externally under the wing center section. A crew of five to seven was positioned in the wing leading edge in the center section. The defensive armament included single 37-mm cannons mounted in two retractable fuselage turrets and two forward flexible guns in the wing leading edge between the flight deck and the engines. In addition to being a bomber, this aircraft was also configured for a ground attack mission with its armament then including eight .50-caliber and two .30-caliber forward-firing guns mounted in the leading edge of the wing.

Consolidated's advanced flying wing designs underwent continual development as two- and four-engined flying wing configuration proposals, both for military bombers and civilian applications, tending toward more and more conventional versions until the concept was abandoned by early 1938. The designers then returned to more conventional aircraft designs using a full fuselage to increase crew accommodation and payload of either military equipment and supplies or passengers. One of their ensuing designs was a twin-tail bomber featuring an aerodynamic blending between the wing and the fuselage, which was also an aeronautical engineering trend *de jour*. The blended fuselage design was a four-engined bomber with a buried pusher Allison XV-3420 liquid-cooled engine installation. This short nose design had a heavily glazed flight deck that included flexible forward-firing guns with the crew located at the blended area of the wing root. There

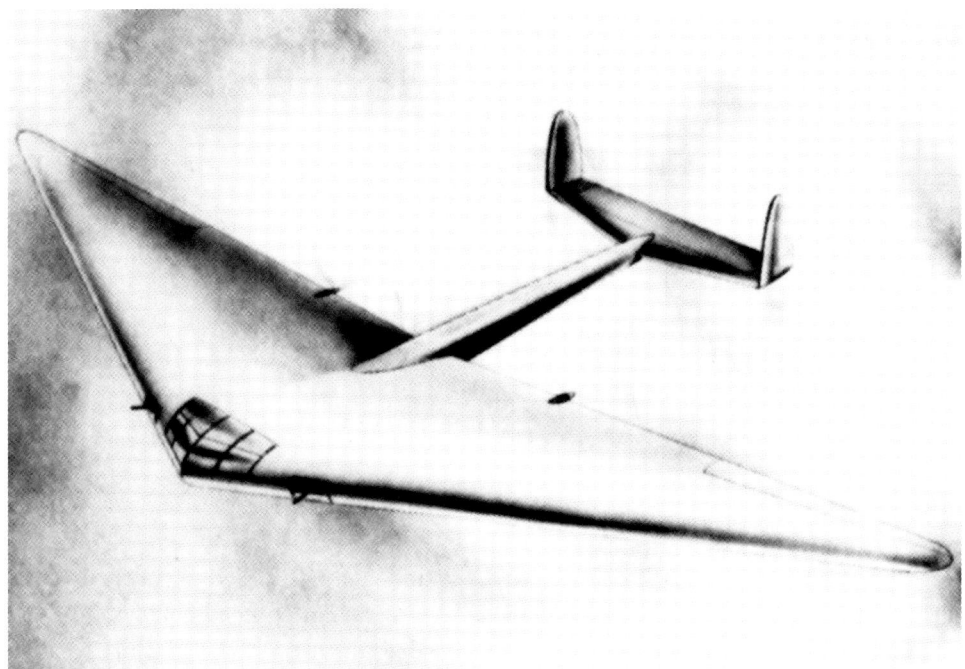

Consolidated's flying wing differed from the conventional wing-only version as it also included an orthodox Consolidated-style twin-tail empennage. (*AFSHRC*)

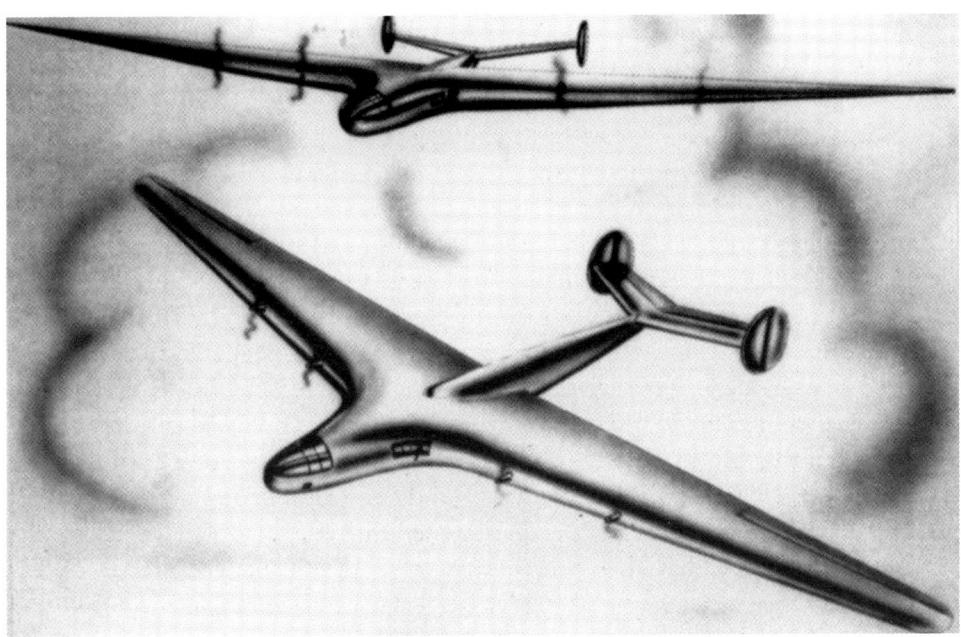

Consolidated blended wing design. (*AFSHRC*)

were two retractable turret installations similar to those of their flying wing design, one dorsal and one ventral, and two flexible guns in the fuselage waist section, one on each side. A tractor version was also considered, which was identical except for the engine installation but these designs were also abandoned in favor of full-fuselage, four-engined bombers of a much more conventional design in anticipation of a looming European war. There is little data available about these first bombers except they were of pusher or tractor engine versions of the same design.

The next design was the January 1939 nine-man LB-16, which was of conventional shoulder-wing configuration with Consolidated's hallmark twin-tail. This design retained the rounded-glazed B-29-type nose that had been incorporated on many other designs of the time. It included a large dorsal turret on the aft circular fuselage and a nose, tail, and a ventral gun position (three .50-caliber and two flexible .30-caliber). Four 600-pound bombs could be carried. (The LB-17 would have been the twin-engined version.)

During June 1939, a paper-only proposal appeared as the LB-29 in both a twin- and four-engined configuration, which showed the final familiar design of the B-24 with the deep fuselage and the stepped cockpit arrangement.

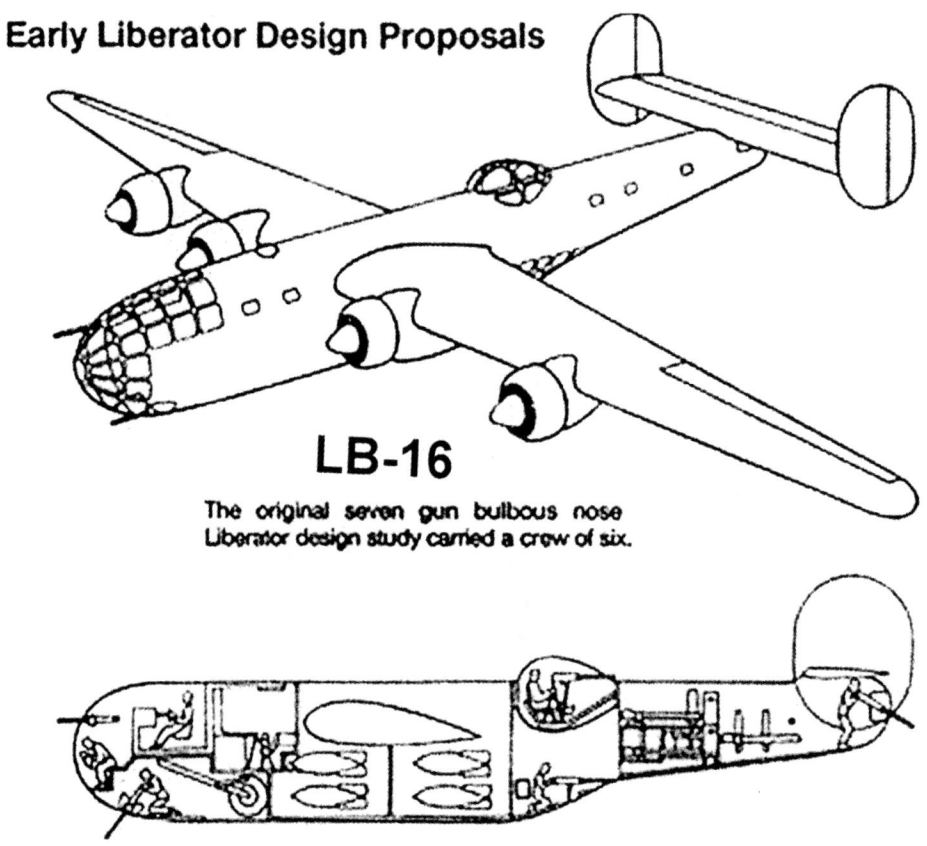

LB-16. (AFSHRC)

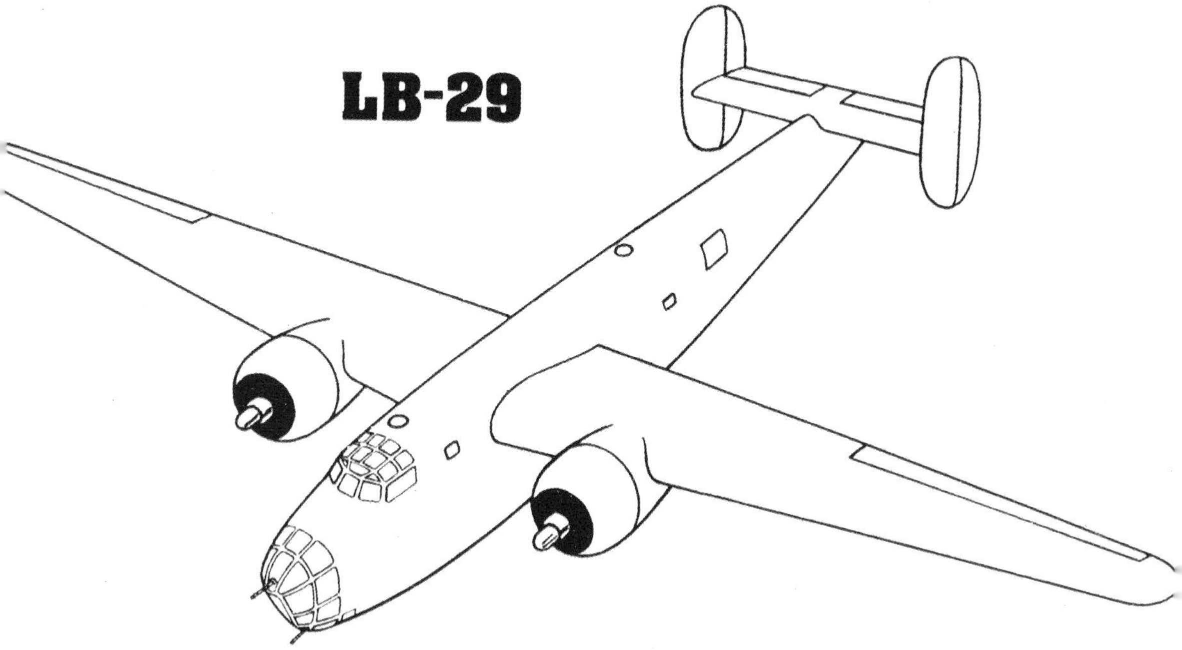

LB-29 twin-engine. (*AFSHRC*)

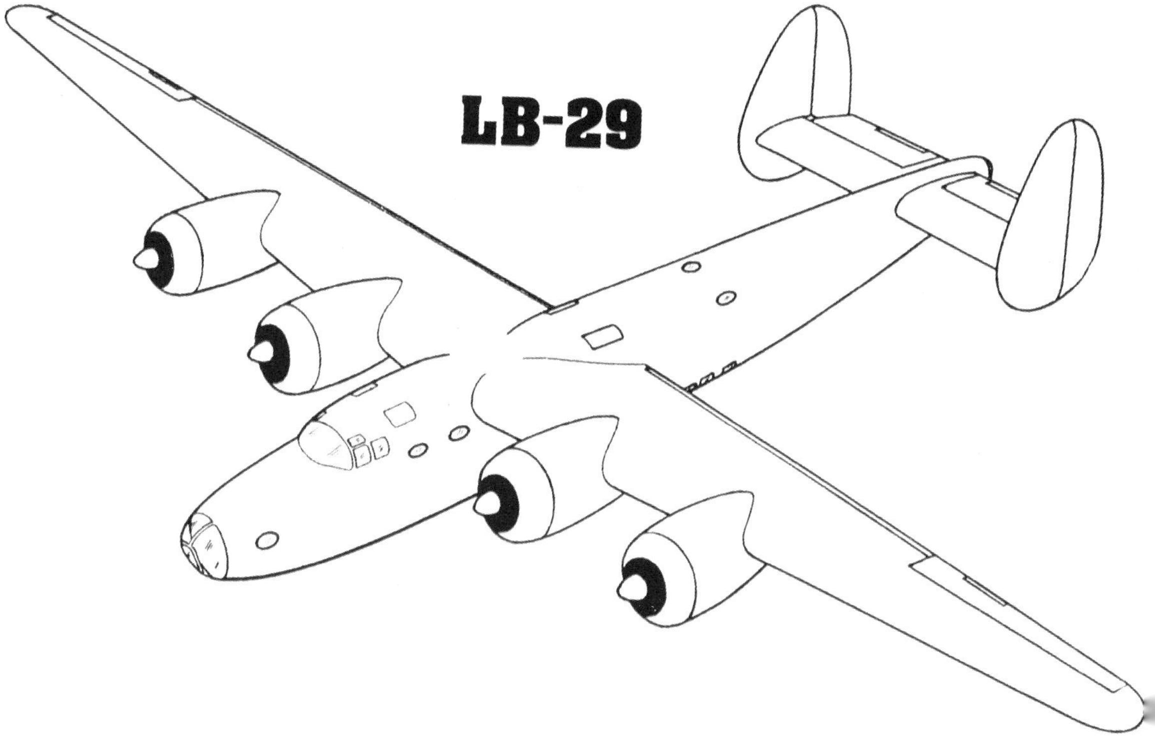

LB-29 four-engine. (*AFSHRC*)

9

Consolidated Model 32/XB-24: B-24 Precursor

Consolidated Model 32

By the autumn of 1938, Gen. H. H. Arnold, the recently appointed chief of the Air Corps, while confident that B-17 was a qualified success, was concerned that if war came Boeing would be unable to build sufficient numbers of their bomber. Arnold considered the possibility that Consolidated should manufacture the B-17 under license, and in December, Mac Laddon and Charles Van Dusen went to Seattle to discuss licensing with Boeing. They found that Boeing, itself, did not have enough work at that time to share orders and moreover the B-17 design was already four years old in an evolution of rapidly changing aircraft designs. During January 1939, the Air Corps had issued Type Specification C-212 for a bomber with a 3,000-mile range, 35,000-foot ceiling, a maximum speed of 300 mph, and a bomb load of 8,000 pounds. After the pair returned to San Diego, they prepared a report to the AAC that stated that the B-17 design was "incomplete" and would be difficult to adapt to Consolidated's manufacturing methods. The report stated that Laddon and his engineering staff were confident that they could design a new bomber that would be able to carry the same or greater bomb load than the B-17 but at higher speeds and most importantly at a longer range. Consolidated's confidence was based on its Model 31 Davis Wing experiments that improved performance by 20 percent.

Once Congress reconvened in January 1939, Roosevelt stated: "Our existing forces are so utterly inadequate that they must be immediately strengthened." Gen. Arnold concurred and issued a policy statement underscoring the need for the country to develop additional sources of supply of heavy bombardment aircraft. By the end of January 1939, Fleet sent Laddon and twenty-eight-year-old son David to Wright Field with specifications and primary data for the proposed Model 32 bomber (future B-24), which the company had been developing. Of the significant design features of Consolidated's Model 32 was use of the extremely narrow, highly efficient Davis Wing, mounted shoulder high on the fuselage, which assured meeting the long cruising range required by Air Corps specifications. The 110-foot wing and hydraulic flaps were virtually identical to that of the Model 31 flying boat. Four 1,200-hp P&W Twin Wasp engines powered the Model 32 (and later the B-24) in its initial 41,000-pound gross-weight configuration. Unpredictably, Consolidated's first large land-based bomber was designed with a tricycle undercarriage, an innovation that was to be adopted by all future heavy (B-29 and B-32) and medium (B-25, B-26, and A-26) American bombers. Unlike the tail-dragging B-17, the B-24 had a tricycle gear with the main wheels folding outward to be retracted into the long, thin wing between the inboard and outboard engines. Laddon also borrowed the proven twin fin and rudder features from the Model 31 seaplane and the earlier XPB2Y-1 four-engined flying boat. Laddon increased the flap area by utilizing the Fowler design, which slid back and down from the trailing edge of the wing, assuring good low-speed and landing characteristics.

In early January 1939, Consolidated engineer Frank Fink met with Fleet and Laddon and was informed he was to be the project engineer on the new Consolidated land bomber as the company could build a better bomber than the B-17 in the same time it would take to tool up to build B-17s under license. However, when Fink queried Fleet about the new bomber, he was only told that there were no drawings. He was also told that it was to use the Davis Wing and twin-tail from the Model 31, four engine nacelles from the PBY, and have a new fuselage that would have two bomb bays, with each being the same size as the B-17's one bomb bay. Fink was told to have the drawings completed from Fleet's verbal design description and a mock-up built by the experimental shop in fourteen days. Meanwhile, Fleet sent Laddon and David

Wind tunnel scale model used to test the classic B-24 Davis wing/twin tail configuration. (*CAC/AAF*)

Above: Four 1,200-hp Pratt and Whitney Twin Wasp engines powered the Model 32 and later the B-24. (*AAF*)

Left: The B-24 had a tricycle gear with the main wheels folding outward to be retracted into the long thin wing between the inboard and outboard engines. (*AFSHRC*)

to Wright Field to persuade the AAC to build their new bomber and to immediately appoint a mock-up board to travel west to inspect the mock-up.

Fink relied on the company's experience gained in the accelerated design and construction of the Model 31, using the same processes and procedures and appropriated entire design features from it and other earlier Consolidated models. The mock-up used the Model 31's 110 foot Davis Wing, a landing gear conversion for a land-based aircraft, and its twin box tail, and it added the four engine arrangement of the PBY and the waist gun from the old PB2Y design.

The Mock-up Inspection Team arrived from Wright Field, led by 1Lt. Donald Putt who was the co-pilot and fortunate survivor of the crash of the original Boeing Model 299 at Wright Field in 1935. The cause of that crash was ultimately linked to the failure to remove the control locks, so perhaps was not unexpected that the B-24's control locks were protected by an obvious red strap connecting the lock handle to the throttle pedestal.

After inspecting the initial mock-up layout, the AAC insisted on many expected changes, principally in gun placements, windshield arrangements, and the bombardier's position. As a result, Consolidated built a second complete fuselage mock-up that would become the design used for the new bomber, which was designated as the XB-24 by the AAC but for the meantime would be known by Consolidated as the consecutive Model 32. It was also allocated the export designation LB-30 for which the French and then the British would place orders.

As a formality to satisfy procurement regulations, the Air Corps had also made inquiries of the Glenn L. Martin Company and Sikorsky Aviation Corporation inquiring if they had any designs that could meet the C-212 Specifications; however, as expected, neither had anything on the drawing board as they had only three weeks to respond to C-212. On 21 February, the Air Corps declared that Consolidated was the only company that had a C-212 contender and the company's proposal was recommended for approval. A contract was tendered and signed on 30 March 1939, sanctioning the preliminary work already completed, authorizing one wooden mock-up, one wind tunnel test model, a set of engineering reports, and for a single XB-24 prototype (USAAC s/n 39-556), officially designated as the Consolidated Model 32, to be completed by 30 December 1939. Since the world situation was deteriorating in early 1939, seven YB-24 service test aircraft with spare parts for $2.88 million were contracted in April and thirty-eightB-24As were added in August.

Talented Consolidated engineers Isaac Laddon, Virginius Clark, George Hallett, Roy Miller, William Ring, Bernard Sheahan, and Harry Sutton had all worked with the AAC's engineering division at McCook Field, and had been recruited by Fleet to work for him. To expedite the development of the aircraft, these engineers now had to work with McCook successor Wright Field and continue to use the *Handbook for Airplane Designers* (which Fleet had helped write). The *Handbook* was intended as a guide for aeronautical engineers for "safe, good practice." Yet, over time, this guide was no longer a guide but an inflexible manual that had not been kept current with aircraft development and manufacture. The frustrated Fleet met with Wright Field and complained that "this restrictive thinking … was doing more to hold back aviation than the rest of the world put together." Fleet told the Air Corps that he "couldn't tolerate a lot of bureaucratic supervision and get the job done on time." As a result, the AAC sent Maj. E. R. McReynolds to San Diego as their resident representative and he was able to expedite many decisions that generally would have been referred to Wright. Later, McReynolds was transferred to head the Air Service Command and was replaced by Maj. Carl Brandt from the Wright Field Engineering School.

GALCIT wind tunnel tests during late February and March led to changes in the Model 32 that would determine the familiar slab-sided shape of the B-24, which would lead to one of its disparaging nicknames, "Flying Boxcar." The Model 32 prototype design concept was simple, but nonetheless sophisticated for its time as Consolidated designers integrated innovations into the design making it the first American bomber to employ the tricycle landing gear and the efficient, long, thin, high-aspect-ratio Davis Wing.

In early May 1939, with the initial Model 31 tests successfully completed, Laddon wrote to Gen. Arnold detailing the test pilot's favorable impressions, adding that "the above information is pertinent to the B-24 since the same wing, flap and tail are used thereon." As a final check, Consolidated engineers also conducted the usual tests of the aircraft configuration in the GALCIT tunnel in June, with the wing again showing the performance that had become accepted as typical of the Davis Airfoil. In further tests, Consolidated engineers constructed two comparative wings, one the Davis foil and the other the conventional NACA 230-series profiles, both with the same planform and spanwise thickness distribution employed on the two airplanes. Again, the Davis Wing proved superior.

Compared to the B-17, the proposed Model 32 was shorter and had a distinctive Consolidated twin tail. However, the significant difference was its Davis Wing that had 25 percent less wing area and a wingspan that was 6 feet longer, giving it a significantly larger load-carrying capacity. Since the wing was constructed of Duralumin sheet, instead of putting the unnecessary extra weight of a Dural fuel tank inside an already enclosed metal wing section, Fleet used newly-developed Dupree to seal all joints where the wing might leak, forming integral wing fuel tanks.

The long tricycle main undercarriage units retracted outwards to lie flat into open wing stowage bays behind small underwing blisters, which was necessary as the Davis Wing was attached to the top of the fuselage. The tricycle undercarriage design provided better visibility for the pilots on the ground and also allowed for the faster landing and take-off speeds required by the high wing loadings of the Davis design. This gear put the bomber in flying attitude, giving it a shorter take-off run as it did not have to lumber several hundred yards more on take-off to get the tail off the ground as did the B-17.

The B-17 was powered by four 850-hp, nine-cylinder Wright R-1820 Cyclone radial engines, while the Model 32 used four twin-row, 1,000-hp, fourteen-cylinder P&W R-1830-31 Twin Wasp radials. Laddon chose to use the Twin Wasp engines for the Model 32 rather than the B-17's Cyclones because of their smaller frontal area. The Model 32's 70,547-pound maximum take-off weight was one of the heaviest of the time.

The Model 32 fuselage had a central bomb bay, divided into front and rear compartments, which could accommodate up to 8,000 pounds of bombs. The two sections of the bomb

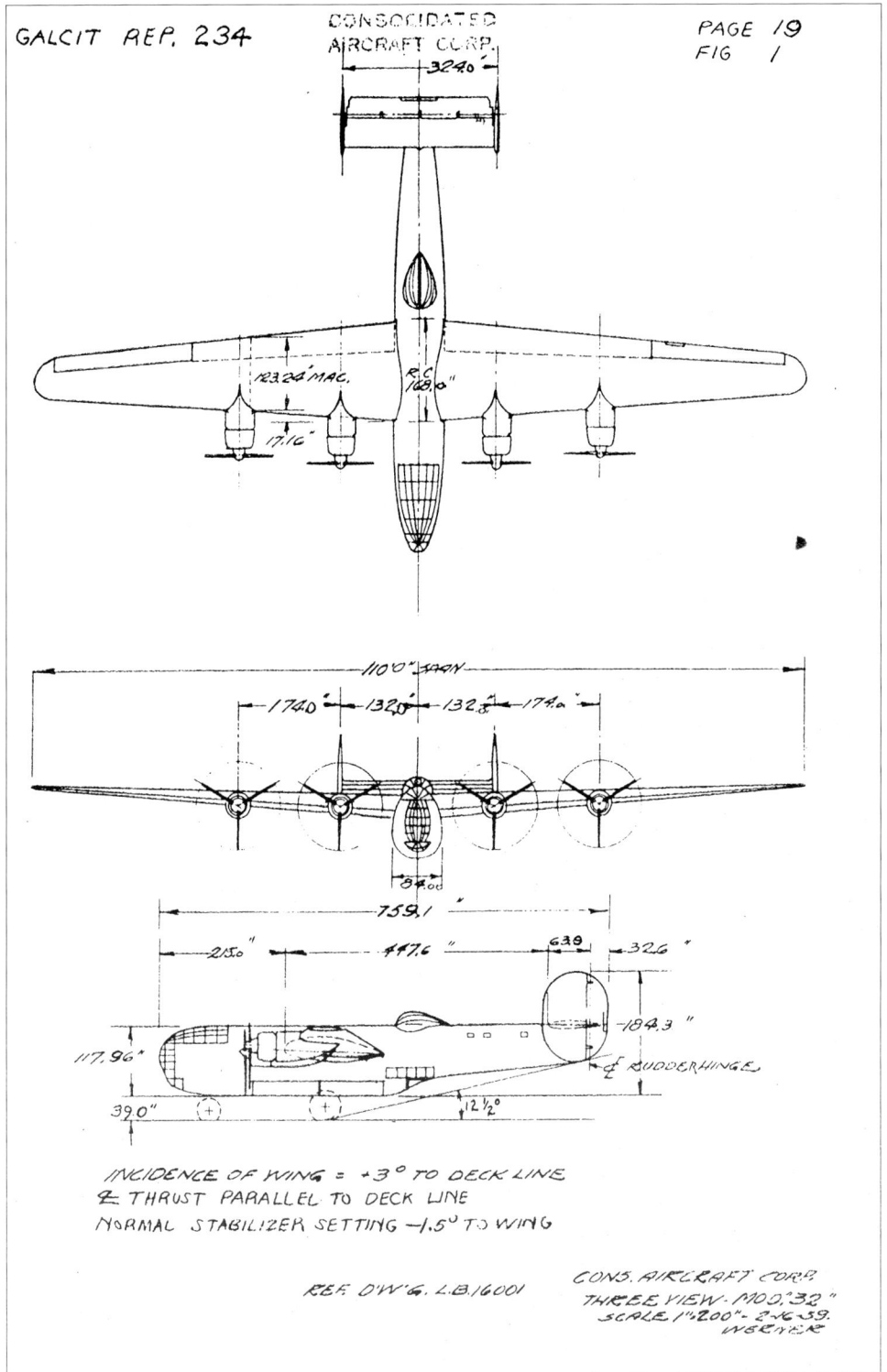

GALCIT Model 32 three-view drawings.

bay were further divided by a central, extremely narrow catwalk, which also served as the fuselage keel beam. Because the only entry and exit from the bomber was in the rear, it was almost impossible for the flight crew and nose gunner to move from the flight deck to the rear when wearing parachutes. The bomb bay doors were unusual, consisting of two roller-type segments that retracted upward into the fuselage from the keel beam. Being similar to the segments of a roll-top desk this arrangement had the advantage of contributing less aerodynamic drag when the bomb bay doors were open, as opposed to B-17 bomb bay doors hanging down into the slipstream.

The rapid pace of Consolidated Model 32 development was demonstrated by the short two-month timespan from when the Davis Wing was mated to the fuselage on 29 October 1939 to when the aircraft was first flown on 29 December 1939. However, this was still only one day less than the relatively short deadline specified in the AAC contract. On that date, Consolidated test pilot William Wheatley, with George Newman, John Kline, and Robert Keith aboard, flew the aircraft from Lindbergh Field adjacent to the San Diego Plant on its inaugural flight lasting seventeen minutes. Upon approval of the 30 March 1939 XB-24 contract by the assistant secretary of war for air, Robert Lovett stated:

> Consolidated is the designer and sole manufacturer of this particular Prototype Heavy Bombardment Airplane which is required for experimental purposes as a means of bringing in additional sources of supply.

Thus, America had another heavy bomber to compliment the B-17, which was at the time America's only proven heavy bomber.

Consolidated XB-24: The Redesignated Model 32

After the 29 December 1939 Company flight, the first Air Corps flight of the Model 32 was flown by Maj. Stanley Umstead and Capt. Jake Harmon on 17 February 1940, and on 18 March 1940, the Model 32 made its first official AAC flight as the AAC redesignated XB-24 with the Serial 39-556.

Control problems were revealed during the early tests, which led to substitution of its twin fins with those of the Model 31. Beginning with the twenty-third XB-24 test on 12 April 1940, the horizontal tail was increased from 22 to 26 feet, solving most of the control problems. The slots in the outer wings were found to be unnecessary and caused drag and were deleted.

While production plans progressed, development continued on the XB-24, which had failed to meet the AAC's maximum speed specifications under the original contract. Additional wind tunnel testing examined the possible benefits of wing and tail fillets, re-design of the engine nacelles, and a fully retractable main gear instead of the existing partially exposed and faired configuration. The pitot tubes were relocated from the wing to the forward fuselage. Ultimately, time was the controlling factor and only those changes that could be made quickly were completed.

Above: Consolidated Model 32. (*CAC/AAF*)

Right: On 29 December 1939, Consolidated test pilot William Wheatley flew the Consolidated Model 32 from Lindbergh Field on its inaugural seventeen-minute company flight. (*AFSHRC*)

Designer Laddon had originally chosen to use the P&W R-1830 engine over the contemporary Wright R-1820 because of its smaller frontal area that reduced the drag of the twin-row P&W design. The mechanically supercharged (R-1830-33) version installed in the XB-24, however, did not have the high-altitude performance of the forthcoming turbo-supercharged R-1830-41, which would soon be available in quantity and which the AAC preferred.

Early tests confirmed that XB-24 performance and stability was mostly as predicted and was generally better than the B-17. With a full bombload, the range of the 38,300-pound gross weight XB-24 was 200 miles more than the B-17 and with additional fuel tanks installed in the forward bomb bay, the range was 600 miles greater than that of a similarly equipped B-17, which in that configuration was unable to carry any bombload. Nonetheless, during the first thirty test flights, the XB-24 prototype's speed was computed at between 291 to 298 mph, instead of the 311 mph required by the specification, which was somewhat less than the 323 mph of the current 1,200-hp turbo-supercharged B-17C.

Like most American military aircraft of the late 1930s, the XB-24 had been designed without consideration for self-sealing fuel cells, armor protection for crew, provision for current defensive armament, and other vital equipment that was considered fundamental by Allied and Axis European air forces.

The integral fuel cells, which were installed inside the wings of the original XB-24, reduced the fuel capacity by approximately 300 gallons in each wing. While the Air Corps wanted new self-sealing tanks, they wanted the newer engines even more. As a result, six YB-24s and twenty B-24As would be "borrowed" from Army contracts and delivered against the British order so that the AAC could wait for these later, improved, up-engined aircraft. On 26 July 1940, the Air Corps ordered leak-proof fuel tanks and B-2 turbo-superchargers (to replace mechanically supercharged P&W R-1830-33s) for the XB-24. Each new B-2 turbo-supercharger would add 135 pounds but increased the critical altitude to 25,000 feet where the maximum speed could reach 320 mph.

The planned XB-24 armament consisted of several hand-held .30-caliber machine guns. One was to be mounted in the large transparent nose, another to be fired from removable hatches above, below, and on each side of the fuselage. An additional gun was positioned in a cupola in the extreme tail, which was a relatively new concept for American bombers at the time, being introduced on the Douglas B-23.

Meanwhile, additional AAF orders had been placed, so that production planning was already well under way for future B-24s and for an LB-30 export version that the French, and later the British, had added to the backlog. However, tool up for series production would take time and it would not be until December 1940 before the first production aircraft was accepted from the San Diego Plant.

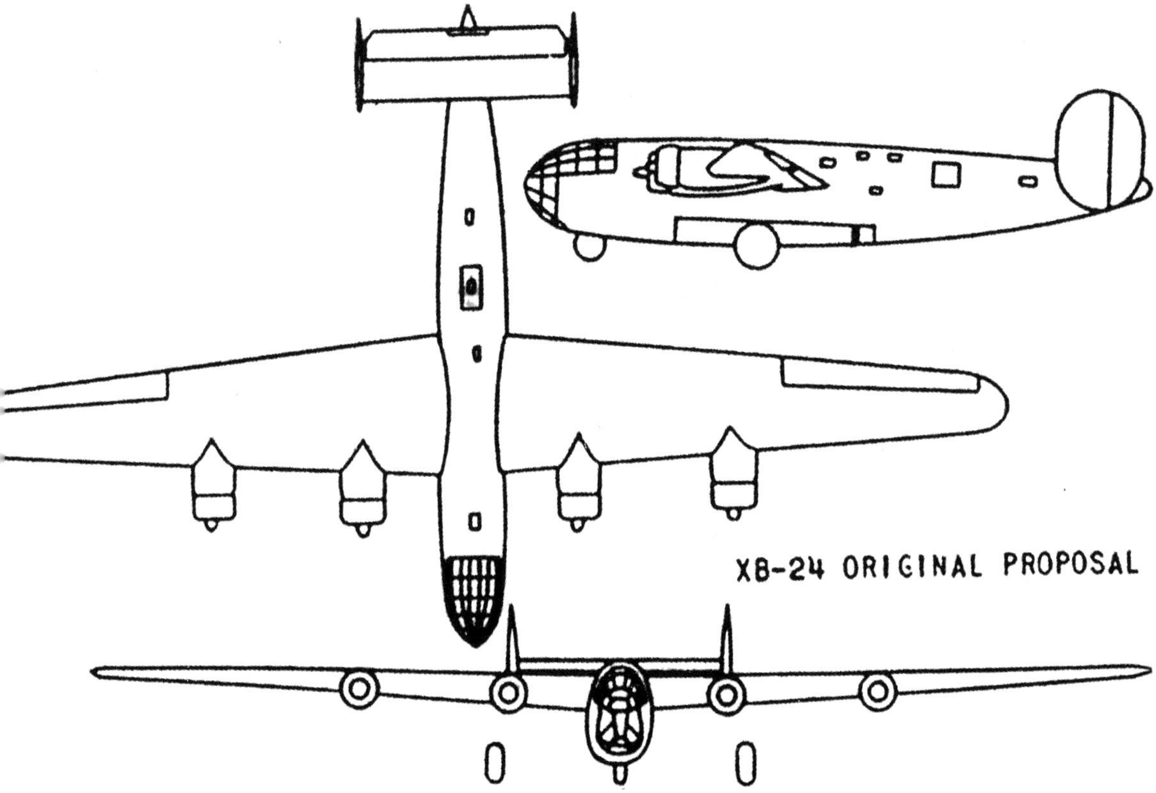

XB-24 ORIGINAL PROPOSAL

Above: Consolidated's original proposal drawing of the XB-24. (*ATSC*)

Right: The first Air Corps flight of the Model 32 was flown by Maj. Stanley Umstead and Capt. Jake Harmon on 17 February 1940. (*AAF*)

The Model 32 painted in AAC markings. (*AAF*)

On 18 March 1940, the Model 32 made its first official AAC flight as the redesignated XB-24 with the serial 39-556. (*AAF*)

10
Consolidated Heads toward B-24 Production

Fleet Acquires the Hall Aluminum Aircraft Company

The Hall Aluminum Aircraft Company of Buffalo was founded 1927 by Charles Ward Hall, the son of Charles Martin Hall, a vice president of the Aluminum Company of America (ALCOA) and developer of the inexpensive mass production process that made aluminum the first metal since iron to attain widespread use. Hall's new entity was an engineering company formed to develop the Hall PH-1 prototype naval flying boat based on the hull design of Britain's Felixstowe F.5 for the U.S. Naval Aircraft Factory. In this undertaking, Hall would develop methods of aluminum fabrication that would transform the aircraft industry. The twin-engined PH-1 was superseded by PH-2 and PH-3 variants, which served in small numbers with the U.S. Coast Guard during World War II. In 1936, Hall flew the XP2H-1 four-engined patrol bomber, the largest American-built flying-boat at that time. The Hall XPTBH was a prototype twin-engined seaplane, submitted to the Navy by the Hall Aluminum Aircraft Corporation in response to a 1934 specification for new bomber and scout aircraft. Constructed in an innovative approach that made extensive use of aluminum, the XPTBH proved successful in flight testing but failed to win favor with the U.S. Navy and no production contracts were let. During this time, the Hall Aluminum Aircraft Company produced twenty-nine all-metal flying boats. After Fleet moved to San Diego, Hall moved to Bristol, PA, but Hall and his company had always been an annoyance to covetous Fleet who had made several unsuccessful offers to buy it. In 1936, Hall was killed in a flying accident and his son, Archibald, became company president, but it was not until 1940 that Fleet bought the company and absorbed it. Hall would become an officer with Consolidated and his company's engineers and technical staff would be transferred.

The Effect of the British and French Purchasing Commissions

French Purchasing Commission
In May 1938, the French Air Ministry announced its intention to strengthen and modernize its *Armée de l'Air* fighter arm as an increasingly desperate French government was secretly attempting to gain authorization from the U.S. government to inspect and possibly purchase new American military aircraft. The French Purchasing Commission was formed with the responsibility for purchasing and organizing all other components from American manufacturers, including engines, propellers, and accessories such as instruments, radios, starters, pumps, and other components, which were to be shipped separately to France for the final assembly.

British Purchasing Commission (BPC)
In 1938, the British Air Ministry sent a mission headed by Sir Henry Self to America to make aircraft purchases and also to investigate Canadian aircraft production and the manufacture of British types under license. In August 1939, the British Lord Riverdale visited Washington and Ottawa and recommended establishing a purchasing commission in Washington. In November 1939, the Ministry of Supply, a British supply board in Canada, established a subsidiary in New York as the British Purchasing Commission (BPC), which was to be responsible for purchases from U.S. sources. The formation of this new organization, headed by Arthur Purvis, was announced on 7 November 1939, just three days after the repeal of the U.S. arms embargo under the revised Neutrality Act. The BPC was able to arrange purchases paying for the materiel with Britain's gold reserves.

British Air Commission (BAC)
The increased demand for the production of aircraft and air engines in America led to the formation of the British Air Commission (BAC) under the director generalship of Sir Henry Self, which initially operated as part of the British Purchasing Commission. In June 1939, the BAC returned to the U.S. and purchased 200 North American Harvards (AAC T-6 Texan) and 200 Lockheed Hudsons as training aircraft. The BAC became established as a separate entity in November 1940 in Washington, responsible to the newly formed Ministry of Aircraft Production. The BAC was to be a link between the Ministry of Aircraft Production and American and Canadian aircraft and equipment manufacturers.

Anglo-French Purchasing Board
In January 1940, the Anglo-French Purchasing Board was set up in New York with Purvis as chairman and Bloche-Laine as vice chairman. When it became apparent that the fall of France was imminent, the Purvis/Bloche-Laine association, backed by the authority of the Anglo-French London Committee, assigned existing French contracts over to the British Government on 17 June 1940, shortly before the U.S. froze French assets within America.

Copy of a newspaper photo of the British Air Commission led by Director-General Henry Self (in hat on left) with Consolidated VP Isaac Laddon (pointing) inspecting Liberator construction at San Diego. (*Author's collection*)

Effect of the British and French Purchasing Commissions

The effect the British and French Purchasing Commissions on American aircraft design and pre-war production has been underestimated, as has their financing of the expansion of the American aircraft industry of which the U.S. Government was later able to take advantage.

Increased Demand for Aircraft Changes the American Pre-War Aircraft Industry

From 1938 to Pearl Harbor, the demand for aircraft increased greatly causing major changes in the configuration of the American aircraft industry, especially the significant transfer of aircraft factory locations away from the East and West Coasts where there was a shortage of labor and housing and where a future enemy could possibly attack them.

During 1938, Air Corps mobilization plans projected a maximum size of 12,000 tactical and 2,000 training aircraft. However, at the time, there were no specific programs for the expansion of aircraft production, but it was generally supposed that if a rapid expansion was required, the automobile industry could be converted "overnight" to the mass manufacture of aircraft and aircraft engines. The automobile industry arrogantly concurred that this assumption to be viable.

While the U.S. Government expenditure on military aircraft grew steadily during the 1930s—from $13 million in 1934 to $68 million in 1939—the actual incentive for expansion came from foreign sources as the British, French, and Dutch, which were in an arms race in the face of the new military menace from Fascist Germany and Italy. In 1938, British and French Purchasing Missions arrived in the U.S. to acquire airframes and engines and as a result the American aviation industry accumulated a backlog of $680 million of orders in the immediate pre-war years, of which approximately two-thirds ($400 million) were foreign orders. It was estimated that tooling and plant expansion financed by the British and French advanced the volume of American aircraft production by a year.

When the Nazis invaded Poland in September 1939, the U.S. aircraft industry had been expanding slowly as its output in 1939 was 5,856 aircraft, of which 2,195 were military. However, military airframe weight produced was 10.1 million pounds while civil airframe weight was only 2.4 million pounds. The USAAC and USN each had about 800 "frontline" aircraft but most were inferior to contemporary British, German, and even Japanese designs. The aircraft industry ranked forty-first among American industries, with $280 million in production and with a workforce of 64,000. Yearly foreign and domestic aircraft requirements and capacity was estimated at 15,000 airframes and 14,000 engines of over 1,000 hp, and it was clear that expansion to meet these requirements would necessitate new factories and the conversion of other industries, particularly automotive.

In December 1939, President Roosevelt and upper echelon U.S. Government officials met with the British and French Purchasing Commissions where it was decided that the French and British be allowed to purchase an additional 8,400 aircraft consisting of 2,800 fighters and 5,600 bombers, plus 13,650 engines and 14,000 propellers for those aircraft. The effect of British aircraft orders, in particular, on American aircraft design was considerable. Although some of the aircraft the British ordered were "as is," most needed modifications to meet evolving combat requirements which completed by the eager-to-please U.S. aircraft industry. Additionally, because the RAF selected certain aircraft (better) types and rejected (inferior) others, American aircraft development was thus motivated toward the production of these certain types. By December 1940, British cash orders for aircraft had exceeded $1.2 billion with deliveries of 300–350 per month and were expected to reach 500 per month by early 1941.

On 29 December 1940, Roosevelt made his famous "Arsenal of Democracy" radio broadcast, during which he promised to help England fight Nazi Germany by supplying them with military materials while America remained neutral. Roosevelt's "Arsenal" was ready to supply its latest American warplanes to "friendly countries" with the proviso that they, in turn, furnish information on their operational use and service improvements and pay cash for them (before Lend-Lease). The beleaguered French government placed a rush order for sixty B-24s with options for 120 more while the British contracted for 164, but when France fell in June their order was transferred to the British. B-24s under these foreign orders were designated Model LB-30s. As Western Europe began to fall to the Nazi Blitzkrieg, Roosevelt urgently requested 50,000 aircraft and for the production capacity to build that number yearly. Therefore, though it would be eighteen months before Pearl Harbor, B-24 production was assured and Consolidated would take its place as a leading manufacturer of large in land-based bombers as it had in producing flying boats.

Roosevelt during his famous "Arsenal of Democracy" radio broadcast on 29 December 1940, during which he promised to help England fight Nazi Germany by supplying them with military materials while America remained neutral. (*NA*)

Consolidated Wins New Contracts and Expands for B-24 Production

In September 1939, Adml. John Towers, chief of the Bureau of Aeronautics, contacted Fleet, asking Consolidated to build 500 PBY-5s. Fleet advised Towers that Consolidated could fill the order in two years if the size of its factory was doubled. At the time, the factory was only running at half capacity and Fleet did not wish to invest any more company money and counter-offered to build 200 PBYs for $20 million if the Navy would build the new PBY factory. On 20 December, the contract, the largest single military aircraft contract ever awarded to that time, was signed for the 200 PBYs with the $20 million to be paid when the work was completed. The Navy let contracts to build a 441,000-square-foot factory that would double the Consolidated's plant capacity. With the machinery and associated equipment, the cost was $2.2 million. In May 1940, with the war in Europe going badly for Britain and France, President Roosevelt authorized 50,000 new aircraft. Consolidated spent $3 million to add 650,000 square feet to production that then totaled 1.5 million square feet in factory capacity and another 1.2 million square feet of paved outside area that could be used for assembly and final outfitting in the yearly good California weather. With the European and Pacific political situations threatening to escalate into a world war and the B-24 coming online, there would have to be new factories built for its large-scale production. In November 1940, construction was begun on the government-financed

1.6 million-square-foot facility just north of Consolidated's San Diego main factory. Another massive $45 million, 3 million-square-foot government-financed facility to be operated by Consolidated to build four-engined bombers and transports was to be built in Fort Worth adjoining Lake Worth. In May 1941, the government decided to construct an 800,000-square-foot B-24 factory near Tulsa, Oklahoma, that was to be operated by Douglas Aircraft. A third massive B-24 facility was to be constructed near Ypsilanti, Michigan. This $85 million Willow Run plant was to be operated by Ford Motor Co. and was originally to manufacture and supply parts for the Tulsa and Fort Worth B-24 factories but later would fabricate complete B-24s. The Consolidated facility quickly expanded from 14,000 employees to 35,000 in 1941, and it was adding 500 more per week. In April 1941, the government awarded Consolidated a contract for 700 B-24s worth $226 million. Sales had grown from the $3.6 million of 1939 to $95.5 million for eleven months of 1941 with a backlog of $755.5 million ($9.44 billion 2017) in unfilled orders. In 1942, a $28 million government-owned plant at Grand Prairie (Dallas), Texas, was constructed to build B-24s under the supervision of North American Aviation. By the end of the war, 18,482 B-24s and variants had been built, the largest production run for any American bomber. Consolidated-Vultee San Diego built 6,724 and Consolidated-Vultee Fort Worth built 3,034 to total 9,759 Consolidated-Vultee B-24s. Ford Willow Run built 6,792, Douglas Tulsa built 964, and North American Texas built 966. During 1944, its greatest year of production, Consolidated-Vultee produced more aircraft than any other manufacturer in the world. From Pearl Harbor to the victory in Europe, the company manufactured 33,000 aircraft that amounted to 13 percent of the U.S. output. In addition to the 18,482 B-24s, Consolidated-Vultee manufactured nearly 900 PB4Y-1s, 739 PB4Y-2s (the single-tail Navy Privateers), 2,393 PBY Catalinas, and 216 PB2Y Coronado flying boats.

Adml. John Towers, chief of the Bureau of Aeronautics (BuAer). (*NA*)

By mid-1940, Consolidated began to have problems with early B-24 and PBY-5 deliveries with the delays in B-24 shipments the direct result of the numerous design changes and inspections while the PBY-5's problems were due to Sub-Contractor Brewster's chronic wartime poor performance. Brewster's three eastern plants produced the inferior Buffalo fighter and subcontracted parts; it also had severe quality-control problems mainly due to its newly hired work force that was inferior in skills and often motivation and who engaged in illicit strikes—even outright suspected sabotage. Brewster was seized by the Navy in April 1942 to build licensed F4U Corsairs but the Navy contract was canceled in July 1944 after the company sustained huge losses that forced its dissolution in April 1946.

Fleet recommended in correspondence with "Dollar-a-Year Man" George Mead—the former United Airlines president/P&W founder and newly appointed chairman of the National Production Board—that a San Diego parts plant, controlled by Consolidated would solve this delivery problem. Fleet continued: "What we have here, George, is not a one-man show, it is a three-ring circus and when the Washington troupers stop clowning we will begin delivering real quantities of airplanes from the plant. Anything you can do toward elimination of dual inspection and the interminable petty arguments incident thereto will speed up deliveries."

George Mead

By 1939, Mead's policy disagreements with P&W co-founder and United Aircraft President Frederick Rentschler had become so vehement that he declined reelection to United Aircraft's board of directors. In October 1939, he became president of the National Advisory Committee for Aeronautics (NACA). In May 1940, he was named head of the Aeronautical Section of the National Defense Advisory Commission (NDAC) by President Roosevelt, acting on William Knudsen's recommendation. In this position, Mead would play a major role in America's pre-war/pre-Lend-Lease aviation buildup. The Lend-Lease program was still eighteen months from being created, and the U.S. did not yet have any certainty of being a combatant in the new war that had erupted; however, the program to build up materiel to send to Britain and France, and to augment the United States' own armed forces, had begun. Roosevelt had appointed Mead to help coordinate aircraft production.

The day before Christmas 1940, George Mead contacted Fleet regarding the deteriorating situation in Europe and the need to quickly establish the best secondary sources for bomber parts supply. Mead stated that the aircraft industry was currently unable to expand without significantly interfering with present aircraft delivery requirements. Mead advised Fleet that the Big Three (Ford, General Motors, and Chrysler) automobile companies had tentatively been assigned to bomber production and had agreed to accept educational contracts. Ford would be teamed with Consolidated on the B-24; General Motors with North American on the B-25; and Chrysler with Martin on the B-26. Mead informed Fleet that he and Charles Sorensen, Ford's production chief, would be in San Diego in two weeks to assess the situation. The government's concept was to have the auto companies build parts and subassemblies, which would then be assembled in new government-owned factories supervised by prime contractors.

Reuben Fleet with George Mead (L), the former United Airlines president/Pratt & Whitney founder and newly appointed chairman of the National Production Board. (*CAC/AAF*)

Consolidated Expands to Meet Demand

To expedite Navy flying boat production, Consolidated had doubled its plant facilities early in 1940 and followed that with another 650,000 square feet of factory space in anticipation of further defense orders. However, on 2 September, when the facility was dedicated, Fleet warned of the danger of the government's new role to free enterprise (e.g. nationalization):

> We had planned announcement today of further extensive plant expansion but the Bill recently passed by the Senate authorizing peacetime commandeering of industrial plants which may fail in any respect to please a high official of our Government, makes us hesitate, much as we have been striving with all our might as a private enterprise to do our bit. Nationalization of her aircraft industry by France was so disastrous that that country's production fell down terribly; even though she frantically resorted to foreign help at exorbitant expense, she collapsed as a nation. We hope our Government will not make this mistake, which would be the beginning of labor regimentation, the emasculation of labor unions, which our President has stated cannot strike against the Government, and the end in this country of free enterprise.

Nonetheless, Fleet proceeded with planning factory expansion despite the government's insistence that any new facilities be in the zone of the interior (continental U.S.) away from possible enemy attack on coastal cities. The Navy, too, wanted an inland plant for flying boat production. While this discussion was continuing, plans for participation of the Big Three automobile companies in aircraft production were being negotiated. Political considerations played a role in plans for new B-24 plants as Roosevelt promised Governors William "Alfalfa Bill" Murray of Oklahoma and Lee O'Daniel of Texas that their states would be granted B-24 plants. Roosevelt asked Fleet to choose the sites for both plants, to assist in the design of the production facilities, and then manage them. Fleet informed FDR that he did not have the personnel to operate the two new plants, and that he should be allowed to expand in San Diego. In doing so, Fleet convinced FDR that he could then develop additional personnel that could later be sent to Fort Worth and Tulsa. FDR approved yet another expansion of our San Diego facilities.

Above: Original San Diego Plant. (*ATSC*)

Below: The 1940–41 San Diego Plant expansion. (*ATSC*)

In November 1940, construction began on a huge government-financed parts plant located a mile north of the main San Diego factory and connected to it by a private road and overpass above busy Pacific Highway, the main route from the north into San Diego. The 1.6 million square feet of the new facility again doubled in size the original plant and all subsequent additions.

The government's plan for expanded B-24 production in Texas required a factory site survey. As an advisor, Fleet asked Tom Bomar, who had been instrumental in the Buffalo to San Diego move, to accompany him. During a whirlwind two-day trip, Amon Carter, wealthy and influential Fort Worth newspaper publisher, showed them Lake Worth and next the Dallas Chamber of Commerce showed them their site. That afternoon, they boarded the train to Houston. They were accompanied by Secretary of Commerce Jesse Jones, who showed them where an artificial lake and plant site could be built. At a luncheon the next day, Fleet said he appreciated everything but told a flabbergasted Texas audience that he "hadn't seen a damn thing that looked as good as Chula Vista on San Diego Bay." In the meantime, Fleet sent Van Dusen to Oklahoma to look over plant sites there.

The government's plan came to fruition with Consolidated operating the new Fort Worth government-built plant for the assembly and production of four-engined bombers and transports. The $45 million plant adjoining Lake Worth would have over 3 million square feet of production area. Another government decision in May 1941 was to build an 800,000-square-foot B-24 facility at Tulsa to be operated by Douglas Aircraft Company. The third component of the government's plan was the $85 million Ford Motor Company Willow Run bomber plant of the near Ypsilanti, Michigan. Initially the Willow Run plant was conceived as a parts factory to supply assemblies for the Douglas Tulsa and Consolidated Fort Worth plants; later, it would build complete B-24s as well.

During the war, Reuben Fleet desired to sub-contract transport aircraft manufacture with an eye on post-war manufacture of commercial aircraft. However, Hap Arnold informed Fleet that Donald Douglas would not "stand for (Fleet) to manufacture any commercial aircraft as that would be cutting into Douglas' domain upon which he was principally dependent for transports." Perhaps influencing Arnold's decision was that his son, Bruce Arnold, had married Donald Douglas' daughter, Barbara. However, Arnold also had a daughter, Lois, whom he had sent to San Diego where Fleet gave her a clerical job at Consolidated and Hap knew that his old friend, Reuben, would keep a fatherly eye on his daughter.

Exactly six years to the day since dedication of the first unit of the Consolidated San Diego facility, Plant 2, the new parts factory that was as large as the main plant, was completed in the fall of 1941 and dedicated on 20 October by Artemus Gates, assistant secretary of the Navy for Air and Admiral John Towers.

Plant 2 was dedicated on 20 October 1941 by (L-R) Adml. Arthur Lyster, Royal Navy; Adml. John Towers, USN; Artemus Gates, assistant secretary of the Navy for Air; and Reuben Fleet. (CAC/AAF)

11

Consolidated Confronts the West Coast Labor Unions

At the time when Fleet's company was located in Buffalo, Eastern industrial cities had more resolute unions that had greater leverage in contract negotiations than did those on the West Coast. Beginning March 1934 Consolidated was subjected to a fifty-seven-day strike by the Aeronautical Workers Federal Union at its Buffalo factory that was settled by arbitration under the same terms that were stated in the pre-strike labor contract.

However, when Fleet moved to San Diego, it was at a time when industrial unions there were becoming more aggressive. After about a year, Fleet and his 3,600 employees experienced their first confrontation with the unions in what Fleet described as distributing "propaganda tending to give them a biased point of view." The emerging International Association of Machinists (IAM) of the American Federation of Labor (AFL) condemned the company's only employee group, the loosely organized Consolidators Association, as a "company union, dominated by management." In April 1937, the National Labor Relations Board (NLRB) ordered an election to determine which labor organization the Consolidated employees wanted to represent them in collective bargaining: IAM Local 1125 or the Consolidators Association. In an unsophisticated and irrational attempt to embarrass the company, IAM Local 1125 sent a letter to R/Adml. Ernest King of the Bureau of Aeronautics accusing Consolidated of "shoddy" workmanship on PBYs that was tolerated by company inspectors and that the "Navy inspectors need to be disciplined very urgently." The Union's recording secretary noted in closing: "That I am not much of a writer but I am sure you will allow for mistakes."

The overwhelming vote, 1823 to 531, gave AFL Machinists Union the immediate mandate to present their demands; among them was a 10 percent wage increase, which Fleet signed off on after relatively painless collective bargaining agreements. This was the first aircraft agreement since the Supreme Court ruled that the National Labor Relations Act of 1935 (also known as the Wagner Act after NY Senator Robert Wagner) was constitutional. The Act is a basic statute of U.S. labor law that "guarantees basic rights of private sector employees to organize into trade unions, engage in collective bargaining for better terms and conditions at work, and take collective action including strike if necessary." The act also created the National Labor Relations Board, which conducts elections that can require employers to engage in collective bargaining with labor unions.

Because strikes in the east affected the delivery of materials necessary for production, Consolidated was forced to lay off 200 employees less than three months after the IAM contract had been signed. Soon IAM members were voting on whether to affiliate with the AFL's rival, the United Automobile Workers (UAW), as part of the Congress of Industrial Organisations (CIO), which was then gaining strength in San Diego and seeking to topple the AFL. The two rival union factions and Reuben Fleet were called to testify before an NLRB hearing in San Diego. Fleet testified that when Consolidated signed with the IAM, it promised to consider a second 10 percent wage increase effective in June 1938. At that time, the company assumed its bid sixty-four PBY-4 flying boats would be accepted and further wage raises would have been possible. Even though Consolidated was the lowest bidder, the Navy could not afford the contract. Fleet denied the Union's 10 percent wage increase request citing the Vinson-Trammel Act that placed a ceiling of 10 percent company profits on military profits. Six months later, the company submitted a substantially lower figure for the flying boats and received a contract but for only thirty-three PBY-4s, which did not allow a wage increase. The NLRB ordered new elections in July. Again, the IAM won another crushing victory, with a vote of 1,098 to 487 for the UAW-CIO.

The huge growth of wartime employment in the aircraft industry created huge demands for increasing wages and the repeated reopening of labor contracts. A new agreement between Consolidated and the IAM was negotiated in December 1940 providing for automatic increases from the beginning wage rates until a base of 60 cents an hour was quickly reached; thereafter, additional raises would depend upon merit. Fleet was proud to have closed the deal within three weeks without a single missed day of work or financial loss to any employee. In advising Admiral John Towers of the contract provisions, Fleet wrote:

> I find labor is not satisfied with "absent treatment," dislikes being shunted to subordinates, likes to talk itself out with the "boss," is pleased with concessions although not ever completely satisfied, and never willingly surrenders a concession once granted....
>
> The Union here is not dominated by radicals, is extremely patriotic, and is aiding us in detecting disloyal acts....
>
> I believe the offer is fair and will be well received; that we are doing our country a service in taking on greenhorns with at best only five weeks vocational training, permitting them to earn while they learn to do useful work with precision under our standard that nothing short of right is right....
>
> Our 50 hour work week, with two shifts, gives the lowest paid daytime beginner a weekly pay of $27.50 (with automatic raises to $33.00.) It is enough to enable him to live in decency and comfort, permits him to have off Saturday and Sunday, and recognizes the 40 hour week with a penalty of 50% for the overtime necessitated by the national emergency.

Meanwhile, management was troubled that the government planned to appoint a Federal Aircraft Wage Board to establish national wage guidelines and that its policies could override provisions of the contract just signed with the Union. Payment on government contracts for the increased direct labor cost was slow to take effect, although FDR stated that if the defense industries granted raises in their factories he would go to Congress and get permission to pay it.

A new two-year contract with the AFL Machinists Union was signed in June 1941 agreeing to match pay rates of Lockheed-Vega, a 10 cent hourly increase. It gave immediate increases to 14,500 hourly-paid workers and provided that there would be no strike or work stoppage, for any cause, on defense production. For the contract signing, Fleet, who had personally conducted all negotiations with labor since moving the plant to San Diego five years earlier, went to the union hall accompanied by Mrs. Fleet, by factory manager James Kelley and his wife, and by J. H. Waterbury, personnel director, and his assistant, Herman Wiseman.

Even while signing the new two-year contract, further problems were facing Consolidated. Labor leader Sidney Hillman—recently designated as co-director of the Office of Production Management (OPM) and a favorite of President Roosevelt—convened the first aircraft stabilization meeting of management and labor representatives in Washington, D.C. Hillman's basic plan to achieve labor-management harmony and uninterrupted defense production was to select the strongest board and give it the exclusive right to represent the workers in return for instituting wage and work standards and waiving the union's right to strike.

The Great Depression had strengthened pioneer labor leader Sidney Hillman's belief in the importance of a strong affiliation between labor and government, and so, he became an original supporter of Roosevelt and the New Deal. In turn, FDR appointed him to the Labor Advisory Board of the National Recovery Administration in 1933 and to the National Industrial Recovery Board in 1934. Hillman collaborated substantially with Senator Robert Wagner in the drafting of the 1935 National Labor Relations Act and with Secretary of Labor Frances Perkins in securing enactment of the 1938 Fair Labor Standards Act. In 1937, Hillman removed his pioneering (1914) Amalgamated Clothing Workers of America from the American Federation of Labor (AFL), joining John L. Lewis and others to found the to-be-influential Congress of Industrial Organisations (CIO) and was elected its first vice president in 1937. Hillman strongly opposed Nazi Germany and supported of U.S. aid to England and France. Roosevelt appointed Hillman to the National Defense Advisory Committee in 1940 and named him associate director of the Office of Production Management (OPM) in 1941; when FDR created the War Production Board (WPB) in 1942, he appointed Hillman to serve as the head of its Labor Division. He supported Roosevelt's use of Army troops to break up a strike at North American aviation in June 1941. Hillman and Philip Murray of the Steelworkers led Labor's agreement to a "no-strike pledge" in 1941. After Pearl Harbor, they supported Roosevelt's demand that workers comply with a freeze on and voluntarily relinquish (without any consultation with the rank and file) workers' right to receive time-and-a-half for Saturday work and double time for Sundays, all while the cost of living between January 1941 and January 1944 increased by 43.5 percent. The post-war would see the festering discontent of the war years fulminate into the largest number of strikes in U.S. labor history.

Wages and the union shop *v.* the open shop were the issues that continued to disrupt the labor-management relations. North American Aviation/Los Angeles had experienced brief but grueling strike before it was broken by an Army factory take-over forcing the employees to return to the production line. In late September, Lockheed Aircraft at Burbank had approved a comprehensive 10 cent per hour wage increase and the AFL Machinists Union asserted that Consolidated should follow Lockheed under the terms of its latest contract, signed in June, and reinforced its demand when its membership voted authorizing a strike. Fleet publicly and determinedly refused to negotiate and forced the subject before the National Defense Mediation Board, chaired by William Davis, a New York patent lawyer who had been at odds with Fleet years earlier concerning Consolidated's patent problems with General Motors' Dayton-Wright Company. Davis desired to have the matter concluded as soon as possible and instructed Fleet to grant the raise. Fleet adamantly refused stating that granting the raise would cost him $82 million and that there was no provision for pay raises in the contracts he had negotiated with the union and with the government. Fleet refused to sign any agreement unless the government held him completely harmless and agreed to absorb the increased costs not only of direct labor but also of overhead expenses.

After the hearings, the Mediation Board recommended that Consolidated accept the same agreement that had settled the North American strike: wage increases of 13 cents per hour across the board but not retroactive to 5 July as the Machinists had requested. Workers in the upper wage brackets influenced the union that now represented 24,000 Consolidated employees, not to accept the Mediation Board's suggestion. The board compromised by recommending retroactivity to 5 August and the union approved. However, Fleet felt the recommendation to be unacceptable without government guarantees to assume the increases and asked that the Mediation Board send William Knudsen or Sidney Hillman, co-directors of Office of Production Management (OPM), to San Diego to discuss the situation with community business and civic leaders.

Hillman flew west only to find himself berated by Fleet before the pro-Consolidated audience. The larger Fleet was reported to have shouted down and almost physically bullied the smaller Hillman:

> I'll have you know that I'm not going to have the business I've spent my whole life building up ruined by one branch of the Government not knowing what the other branch is doing....It's high time we were getting some encouragement for the hard work we are doing in preparing for the battle against Hitler. Aviation as an industry is being kicked around. We are being forced to expand more than any other industry, yet we are constantly being subjected to investigations and limitations by congressional committees and the like.
>
> The military should be getting down to brass tacks. The only way to lick Hitler is by aircraft, but we won't have the planes to do the job in short of five years. We mustn't get into a thing of this kind with the valor of ignorance. We must realize first of all that we are already in it. The question is how far we should go.

Above left: Labor leader Sidney Hillman, co-director of OPM and FDR favorite, with John L. Lewis (R), leader of the powerful CIO. (*NA*)

Above right: Robert Lovett, assistant secretary of war for air. (*NA*)

The Government should call in the heads of all the big plane companies and ask our advice instead of brow-beating us with Vinson Committees trying to figure out how every dollar we ever earned was gotten, and with constant labor trouble.

This new labor agreement the board proposes is going to cost $82 million. That would break Consolidated. I will never sign the document unless I am assured by the Government they will stand by their end of the bargain. Whenever the Government says they will take care of it we will be able to give our men a labor life of decency and comfort.

After Fleet finished his lengthy diatribe, Hillman briefly replied: "We must have the work done as quickly as possible. You will get the proper cooperation from the Government." Fleet told Hillman that he would not sign until he had received telegrams from the War Department, Navy, and Office of Production Management that they would hold Consolidated wholly risk-free. The next day he received telegrams from the War and Navy Departments but none from the OPM.

However, Fleet insisted on OPM approval and Assistant Secretary of War for Air Robert Lovett contacted him by telephone in the presence of James Forrestal for the Navy, Robert Patterson, War Department undersecretary, Hap Arnold, Air Force chief, and John Towers of the Navy Bureau of Aeronautics. In their presence, Lovett admonished Fleet as being the "only" aircraft manufacturer causing the government problems. All the other aircraft manufacturers, realizing that they would soon be in the same predicament, were waiting to see how the government would react toward Fleet. Lovett threatened a government takeover of Consolidated. Fleet countered Lovett's threat by telling him that he should do that if he thought it could do a better job and that the government would have to provide $82 million to keep the Consolidated viable in a takeover. Several hours later, Fleet received the OPM wire and only then did Consolidated sign a new one-year contract with the union.

After the Union contract settlement, W. J. Chudleigh, president of Aircraft Local 1125 of the AFL Machinists Union, announced that any future contracts between his union and Consolidated would be negotiated only if there was new management. While constant poor labor union relations contributed to Fleet's increasing sense that he should consider selling his Consolidated holdings, it was the government's intrusion into his business affairs, its delayed reimbursement for plant expansion, and the possible future infringement of the auto industry into aviation that probably led him to his decision to sell.

By the early 1940s, Fleet became increasingly frustrated with the government and military bureaucracy and interference that had occurred throughout his long years in the aviation industry. This frustration began with his forced selling of fifty PT-1s for $1 each for alleged "profiteering" and was followed by the government's award of his Admiral flying boat design to Glenn Martin and culminated with the favoritism shown to Pan American and Juan Trippe in the South American route awards. Fleet became increasingly concerned by the specter of the automobile industry's incursion into the aircraft industry, especially with Ford building his B-24 design at the Willow Run plant; North American allied with General Motors for B-25 production; and Martin with Chrysler for B-26 manufacture.

The Navy's order for 200 PBYs in 1939 had increased Consolidated sales from $3.6 million to $95.5 million and the company had a backlog of $775.5 million in orders which made Consolidated Aircraft and Fleet industrial icons. However, the powerful and autocratic Fleet had been a constant thorn in government's and the War Department's sides and they wished that he be removed as Consolidated's chairman and president. They believed that the company with 35,000 workers had become too large for Fleet, the everyday hands-on capitalist, to manage every detail. Fleet arrogantly replied that he did not feel that he was being adequately compensated for his management skills, which was true.

Fleet related that in 1910 at twenty-three years old in Montesano, Washington, he had earned $27,400 with no taxes withheld, and that in 1941, at fifty-four, he was only clearing $9,340 on his $60,000 Consolidated salary and at the time he had almost all his wealth invested in his company. Although his investment income totaled about $1.7 million, the Federal Government collected 93 percent and the State of California took another 6 percent, leaving him with a paltry $17,000. The 93 percent taxation was due to the government's new wartime Excess Profits Tax Act, intended to take the profit out of war and make the building of a quality aircraft economically as possible a priority. This was enacted to become effective in 1942, convincing Fleet that selling his controlling 34 percent interest in the company as the only economical and judicious decision he could make.

12

Consolidated Merges with Vultee

Premature publicity could have had a devastating effect on Consolidated's stock and Fleet was obliged to continue slowly and cautiously. When a daily aviation newsletter published a report that the War Department was seeking to change the Consolidated management, the story was zealously denied by Consolidated Vice President Edgar Gott. Fleet's son, David, also a Consolidated executive, stated that the reported sale "must be a mistake," adding that his father "does not own the controlling interest" and that reports he would be receiving $10 million for his holding were "ridiculous."

In mid-November 1941, Fleet was the subject of the cover story of a *TIME* magazine article, which led to rumors of the impending sale of Consolidated to begin to become widely circulated. Speculation in aviation circles was that the huge Consolidated aircraft complex was to be consumed by Vultee Aircraft, a comparatively small Los Angeles company building trainers of which the prolific (11,000) and profitable BT-13/BT-15 trainers would be produced.

Tom Girdler: The Force Behind the Merger

At the time, Vultee Aircraft was under the control of the AViation COmpany holding company (AVCO), and more rumors that would be substantiated later also had it that Republic Steel Chairman of the Board Tom Girdler was also behind the merger.

Rumors were rife and proved of special interest to Tom Girdler who writes in his autobiography, *Boot Straps*:

> Because of our ultimate goal, the development of a great aircraft manufacturing enterprise, there was temptation for us in a bit of gossip first heard some time in the spring of 1941. It was being whispered in Washington and in Wall Street that Major Reuben Fleet was disposed to sell control of Consolidated Aircraft Corporation. This was exciting. Consolidated was producing the best big airplanes in the world.... Behind each one of those current products even greater products

were in development. We were proud of the Vultee engineering department, but I dare say we were envious of the engineering department of Consolidated, headed by I. M. Laddon. If "Mac" Laddon ever designed a bad airplane I never heard of it. Consolidated's record was excellent. In fact, it had not been equaled in the industry. However, all we had to go on was, as I say, a bit of gossip to the effect that Rube Fleet wanted to cash in and retire.

Girdler did not trust Fleet:

Temperamentally Fleet was a benevolent czar. Although generous to the point of being a sucker for his friends, where Consolidated was concerned he would trade anybody, Uncle Sam included, right out of his boots.

Girdler also observed:

Moreover, when the war began and both army and navy were eager to see this great Consolidated property expanding fast, Rube wanted to take time and see where he was going. The whole thing was bound up with him. It was scarcely possible to buy a typewriter without Rube's O.K. He had been careful and smart in hiring people but in his own opinion he could play any position on the team. In the weeks before Pearl Harbor generals and admirals, especially admirals, desperately counting on the company's products were inclined to mention Rube in their prayers; they were praying he would be tempted by a favorable tax situation and sell out; they were hoping, too, that our company, Vultee Aircraft, Inc., would buy him out.

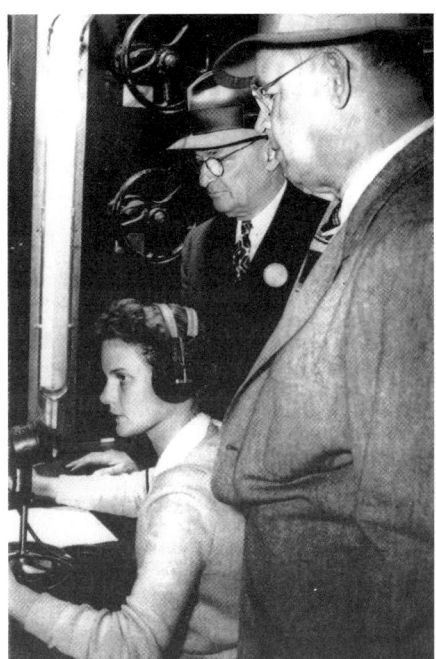

The new powers at Consolidated-Vultee: Powerful Republic Steel Chairman of the Board Tom Girdler (R) engineered the Consolidated Vultee merger with Reuben Fleet (L) and would install Harry Woodhead as its new president. (CAC/AAF)

Victor Emanuel

The real power behind any deal for Consolidated would be financier Victor Emanuel, a World War I Navy pilot and graduate of Cornell University and Dayton University Law School. He was the chairman and a member of the executive committee of AVCO and also served on the boards of Republic Steel and Vultee. He was described by *TIME* magazine as "a short, stocky and razor-brained young man who at the age of 42 had demonstrated his genius for making money." In 1941, he was president of the Aviation Corporation, which had had its origin in the mid-1930s when Emanuel had acquired control of the Cord properties. Errett Lobban ("E. L.") Cord had made his fortune by taking over the plant, assets, and liabilities of a failing automobile company and soon his the Auburn automobile and later the sensational Cord model were immensely successful in the pre-Depression upper-end automobile market. This success led Cord to grow rapidly to control various industrial concerns, including the 1929 purchase of the Stinson Aircraft Company and, in 1932, the formation of the Airplane Development Corporation (ADC) with Gerard "Jerry" Vultee.

Stinson Airplane Company

A new monoplane, the SM-1 Detroiter, made its first flight on 25 January 1926 and became an immediate success, enabling Eddie Stinson to quickly raise $150,000

Victor Emanuel (L) seen in the late 1950s as AVCO CEO. (*NA*)

in public capital to incorporate the Stinson Aircraft Corporation on 4 May 1926. In September 1929, Cord acquired 60 percent of Stinson's stock and his Cord Corporation provided additional investment capital to permit Stinson to sell its aircraft at a competitive price while still pursuing new designs. At the height of the Depression in 1930, Stinson offered six aircraft models, ranging from the four-seat Junior to the Stinson 6000 trimotor airliner. Eddie Stinson died in an air crash in Chicago, on 26 January 1932, while on a sales trip. The Stinson Company was reorganized in 1938 as a division of AVCO's Aviation Manufacturing Corporation and built a new plant in Nashville, Tennessee, with the prospect of a probable increase in military demand.

The Jerry Vultee and the Vultee Aircraft Company

In 1912, Gerard "Jerry" Vultee and his family moved to Ocean Park, California, and he attended prestigious Cal Tech from 1921–23, studying aviation science. In 1923, Vultee was hired as a structural aeronautic engineer at Douglas Aircraft where he met Jack Northrop who was also working there. In 1928, Northrop invited Vultee to join him at Lockheed to help build the Vega, one of the most popular planes of its day. That same year, Northrop left the company, and Vultee became Lockheed's new chief engineer and designed the successful Sirius floatplane for Lindbergh, who with his wife, Ann Morrow, flew it on promotional tours in the early 1930s. Vultee continued to add to his aviation reputations with the innovations he helped introduce: the engine nacelle or cowling, the fully retractable landing gear, replaceable fuselage panels, the V-type windshield, and Vultee large wing flaps that made it possible to reduce landing speeds. During the Depression, Lockheed went into receivership and Vultee was forced to accept a teaching position at the Curtiss-Wright Technical Institute and then became chief engineer for the E. M. Smith Corporation (EMSCO) but left there as there was little need for new designs. During 1932, entrepreneur E. L. Cord (Cord Auto Company) was seeking new ventures, had founded an airline, and needed a new commercial aircraft. With Cord's financial support, Vultee and Vance Breese established the Airplane Development Corporation (ADC), as a division of the Cord Corporation. Fortunately, Vultee had been working with Breese on the V-1 (V for Vultee), which met Cord's needs. Completed as an eight-passenger, ten-place low-wing monoplane in 1933, it was the fastest aircraft of its kind with a top speed of 235 mph, powered by the largest engine available: the 710-hp Wright Cyclone radial. During 1934, avid surfer Vultee met Sylvia Parker, a Hollywood debutant, while surfing in Southern California and they were married on 19 January 1935. Vultee's happiness was interrupted when the Federal Aviation Administration (FAA) decreed that all commercial passenger aircraft were to be multi-engine. The single-engined V-1 was grounded for passenger use and Cord reorganized his holdings, and Vultee Aircraft abandoned its commercial aircraft enterprises. Vultee redesigned the aircraft into the successful V-11 two-place military attack bomber, which with its three-place version was purchased by the AAC and several foreign air forces. In 1936, with increasing orders for the V-11, Vultee built a new plant in Downey, California, and changed the

Gerard "Jerry" Vultee. (*AFSHRC*)

name to Vultee Aircraft, Inc. The innovative new plant featured the first legitimate, though rudimentary, production line, producing bombers at an increasing rate using an overhead conveyor in the factory—an innovation copied from the automobile industry, which marked the beginning of mass-production technique for the aviation industry. In 1937, now employing 500, the Downey plant was renamed the Vultee Aircraft Division of the Aviation Manufacturing Corporation. Unfortunately, Vultee did not live to see his company's success as, in January 1938, Vultee and his wife, Sylvia, were killed in a snowstorm near Sedona, Arizona, while flying back home from Washington, D.C. After Vultee's death, Richard Millar succeeded Vultee as president and Richard "Dick" Palmer as general manager/chief engineer of the company, and both remained in those positions at the time of the Consolidated merger.

Richard Millar

In 1930, Millar was named president of BankAmerica Corp., the investment branch of what became Bank of America. Adept at financial restructuring, Millar helped reorganize the Richfield Oil Co. from 1932 to 1934 and Universal Pictures Co. Inc. in 1937 and 1938. With a lifelong attraction to flying and a holder of a pilot's license, in 1928, Millar became a director of Douglas Aircraft Co., a position he held for ten years. In 1932, he had formed a syndicate and raised $125,000 intending to buy Lockheed at the receiver's sale but Donald Douglas discouraged the deal. In 1938, Millar became vice president, and when Jerry Vultee died one year later, he became president of Vultee Aircraft Inc. Millar found that Vultee was a creative genius rather than a production person and factory production was far below AVCO's expected scale of operations and the company had no new business on the drawing boards. Spurred by the defense demands of World War II, Millar presided over the expansion of Vultee's manufacturing floor space from 273,800 square feet to 1,795,000 square feet in a mere fifteen months. In 1942, shortly before he left Vultee, he was elected president of the Aircraft War Production Council Inc., an organization of California's eight warplane plants that shared production information. Millar later organized a new company, Avion Inc., and after the war joined Northrop. He served as a member of Northrop's board of directors from 1946 until 1984, during which time he served as its chairman from 1947 to 1949. He was recalled to the position in 1975 to re-establish the company's credibility after Northrop was accused of making illegal political contributions and overseas payoffs.

Dick Palmer's Trainers Put Vultee on the Aviation Map

During 1938, about the same time as the AAC issued a solicitation for an advanced trainer, AVCO hired Dick Palmer away from Howard Hughes to become general manager/chief engineer of the Vultee Aircraft Division. Palmer began designing a single-engined fighter aircraft. However, with the promise of a substantial order, Palmer adapted his design concept from a fighter to an advanced trainer, resulting in the V-51 prototype (BT-13 Valiant) that first flew on 24 March 1939 as a cantilever low-wing monoplane of all-metal construction, with fabric-covered control surfaces, and powered by a 600-hp P&W R-1340-S3H1-G Wasp radial engine. It had an enclosed cockpit for the instructor and student, integral wing fuel tanks, and a hydraulic system to operate the flaps and retractable main landing gear. Palmer created the renowned BT-13, BT-15, and SNV Valiant trainers and oversaw other major production program such as the V-72 Vengeance, which served in the AAC as the A-31 and A-35. In August 1939, the U.S. government ordered the Vultee trainers in a contract worth $2,986,000, representing the largest order ever placed by the Air Corps and causing the plant to be redesigned and retrofitted to meet the new production orders. The company accepted an estimated loss $3.5 million on this contract in order to get the business, and the gamble paid off when subsequent orders for the BT-13 would total over 11,000. By 1940, Vultee had doubled the size of their plant and as World War II approached, both production and personnel continued to increase to build the Vultee Valiant Basic Trainer for the AAC. The next Vultee project was the Vengeance (A-31 and A-35) dive bomber, which was initially designed for Britain, and resulted in $90 million in orders in 1940 and 1941. By July 1941, Vultee was producing 15 percent of all America's military aircraft.

In 1939, Stinson Aircraft, which had plants in Tennessee and Michigan, became a division of Vultee, and on 14 November 1939, Vultee Aircraft, Inc. was established to acquire the assets of the Aviation Manufacturing Company, making Vultee a subsidiary of the AVCO parent company. When many of Vultee's male workers went to war, Vultee added hundreds of women to their work force to become the first military aircraft manufacturer to employ women directly in production and pay them the same as men for equivalent work.

AVCO Becomes a Force in the Aviation Industry

Eventually the Depression caused Cord serious trouble with the government and particularly with the IRS. The aging Cord chose not to contest the charges and left America; a large portion of his holdings were ultimately placed on the market, to be acquired by a well-heeled syndicate controlled by financier Victor Emanuel and Tom Girdler, president of Republic Steel, who had combined to buy Cord's AVCO stock in 1937 for $2,632,000. Late in 1939 Vultee Division, Aviation Manufacturing Corporation, became the Vultee Aircraft Corporation, largely to assist in financing with a quarter of the new company's stock issued to the public and the remainder retained by AVCO. Two of the aviation properties of Cord's holdings were Stinson Aircraft of Wayne, Michigan, which was selling its aircraft at a loss, and Lycoming Motors, Williamsport, Pennsylvania, which was manufacturing excellent aero engines but also at a cost that raised the selling price exorbitantly. The Emanuel syndicate solved both Stinson's and Lycoming's problems, and ultimately joined Vultee with them to form the Aviation Corporation, which added to the Emanuel's AVCO Syndicate's vast additional holdings. A year later, Vultee absorbed Stinson through transfer of stock within the AVCO structure.

The expanded Vultee organization began a remarkable production performance with its Downey plant improving Jerry Vultee's production line, using the first powered assembly line in the industry: an overhead track that carried fuselage frames in cradles through twenty-five assembly stations. Assembly time was decreased 75 percent and costs 40 percent. The Nashville plant was enlarged with British financial assistance to produce the Vengeance.

AVCO Pursues Reuben Fleet

In March 1941, the AVCO board of directors sent representative Francis Callery to San Diego to negotiate a deal with Fleet to purchase his company. Callery had served in the Marine Corps in World War I and graduated from Princeton in 1920 and became an investment banker. From 1932 to 1941, Callery was a partner in Emanuel and Co. Callery was able to negotiate with Fleet alone as Fleet's 34-percent share represented control as 25 percent of the shares would represent a quorum at a stockholder's meeting. In August, AVCO held their board meeting in Los Angeles and spent a day in San Diego, inspecting the Consolidated facilities, but the option was not exercised.

On the surface, the absorption of Consolidated by Vultee appeared similar to a minnow-swallowing whale; in 1941, Vultee had 9,000 employees compared to Consolidated's 30,000, and a $178,000,000 order backlog $v.$ Consolidated's $725,000,000, but the giant AVCO owned 71 percent of Vultee stock.

Negotiations were revived again in the fall after the AVCO board deliberated and drafted an agreement during the Saturday following Thanksgiving, only this time with Vultee Aircraft. Their proposal was for negotiations to be conducted between

Consolidated and Vultee Aircraft, which had been set up by Cord and subsequently acquired by AVCO. Callery arrived in Palm Springs, California, with the assurances of the AVCO board that if Fleet priced his company agreeably a sale could be arranged. The second conference with Callery took place in Palm Springs, where Fleet, Dorothy, and children were staying at the posh El Mirador Hotel.

The AVCO proposal included terms and conditions, which would net Reuben, and the rest of the stockholding members of the family, a then enormous $10 million before taxes ($186 million 2021). After the agreement was signed, Vultee was to pay $250,000 as evidence of good faith, and the whole deal was to be voided if Vultee could not complete the transaction before 31 December. The amount of $8.4 million was to be paid in cash, with the balance carried by a six-month note. The agreement provided, however, that the note could be paid either in cash or in $8 per share of Vultee stock. Technically, since Fleet was the seller, the choice of how the note was to be paid should have been his alone, but Vultee asked for this particular arrangement because it did not have enough available cash to make a firm bid. It was obvious that Vultee was wary that Fleet might use the proceeds from the Consolidated sale to go back in business, so also included in the agreement was a non-compete contingency on his staying out of the aircraft business for five years. This agreement was to be submitted to Vultee directors on 28 November 1941, but Fleet had warned Callery "that if someone else should show up with a concrete cash offer, without all these strings," he would accept that offer.

However, during the buyout process, Fleet had implied that other buyers, one, in particular, who was willing to buy the controlling interest in Consolidated but who also wanted Fleet to stay on and run the business. There had been rumors of Howard Hughes interest in Consolidated and possibly Ford. The Hughes' possibility was lent some credence when Hugh Fenwick, a Vultee vice president, arrived in Palm Springs recognized a private aircraft owned by Howard Hughes on the tarmac. Unknown to Fenwick and Callery, Hughes had been in Palm Springs to have Consolidated build aircraft for him and Fleet was not about to divulge the reason. Fleet was never inclined to positively identify the two unsuccessful prospective buyers. That Howard Hughes was even in Palm Springs caused Fenwick to call Callery who quickly authorized Fenwick to personally offer Fleet $50,000 option not to accept another offer until the end of the year. That night, Callery had dinner with Fleet and his wife, Dorothy, and presented the new offer. After Callery finished his pitch, Reuben looked to Dorothy for her opinion and she reports in her autobiography that she facetiously advised:

> I think you should take it that is, if you give me the fifty thousand. I was under the impression that I had made a feeble joke but Reuben looked thoughtful. We had finished dinner and were leaving the dining room when Reuben made up his mind. "You've got yourself a deal," he said to Callery. "Write the check out to Mrs. Fleet.

Dorothy Fleet was said to be very pleased with the $50,000 check.

Francis Callery would become Consolidated Vultee financial vice president until 1946 when he joined Lehman Brothers in 1946 and was a partner from 1949 to 1959.

The Final Finances of the Merger

On 25 November 1941, it was finally confirmed that Fleet had reached a merger agreement with Victor Emanuel. In this agreement, Vultee purchased 348,882 shares of Fleet's personal Consolidated stock and 440,000 shares owned by various family members, including Dorothy Mitchell Fleet, his wife; William Mitchell, her father; Edward Bishop, his brother-in-law; Barbara and Edward Bishop, his niece and nephew; and Elizabeth Fleet, his first wife. A share was valued at twenty-two and seven-eighths plus a $2 cash dividend per share to bring the sales total to the then-enormous sum of $10,945,000. These 788,882 shares gave Vultee control Consolidated's common stock that totaled 1,291,574 shares after a recent two for one stock split.

Under the specter of Pearl Harbor, on 19 December, Fleet received a cashier's check for $8,980,000, which was collected by Emanuel by netting $5.4 million through the sale of preferred stock; by the purchase of additional holdings amounting to $1.5 million by the AVCO parent company; and by $1.5 million borrowed from banks. The total, added to the funds already available to Vultee, closed the deal, with the balance covered through a company note promising to pay $1.6 million either in cash or in stock. Another plus for Emanuel was at the time Consolidated had a colossal $750 million ($14 billion today) in orders from the American and British Governments for multi-engined bombers while Vultee had $162 million in orders from the United States, Peru, and China for training aircraft.

On the same day, the payment of 440,000 common shares of Consolidated stock was issued as follows: In the name of Reuben Fleet, 347,622 shares, with the balance divided among father-in-law, William Mitchell; Edward Bishop, Reuben's brother-in-law; Elizabeth Girton Fleet, Reuben's first wife who he divorced in 1920; the trustees for Barbara and Edward Bishop, Reuben's niece and nephew; and Dorothy Mitchell Fleet, Reuben's second wife.

Before the merger, a disgruntled Fleet flew to Washington to privately discuss the sale of his company with FDR, whom he had known personally since 1931. The president was against the sale and have the company fall into "adverse hands." Fleet assured the president any prospective buyers would be "good Americans," and offered FDR the approval of the buyer. When the president saw that he could not persuade Fleet not to sell, he offered him a job as a consultant to the government for the same $60,000 he was receiving from Consolidated. The president offered to expedite the Consolidated sale and allow the Army and Navy to select the buyer.

Ever the astute businessman, Fleet saved a 10-percent capital gains tax by completing the sale before 1 January 1942 when the capital gains tax rate was to be raised from 15 percent to 25 percent, saving him $1.33 million. For serving as an advisor on the new Consolidated-Vultee board, Fleet had agreed to accept a salary of $60,000 a year. *TIME* quotes him as remarking that "if I can't earn this measly salary, I'll turn in my suit and take a shower."

The deal was closed.

The Merger: Aftermath and Clarification

It was common knowledge that the outspoken Major Reuben Fleet had become *persona non grata* in Washington as, too often and too vocally, he had accused the Administration of botching the nation's defense program, virtually biting the hand that fed him. Nevertheless, Fleet was able to succeed since he was a major aircraft producer and his aircraft were claimed as vital and unexcelled by the Army and Navy.

The 8 December 1941, *TIME* devoted several columns to reporting the sale of Consolidated, under the heading "Vultee Swallows Fleet."

> After formal contract signing in Consolidated's huge San Diego plant, Vultee's President Richard Millar, Rube Fleet, and an army of lawyers toasted the deal with Coca-Cola in paper cups. Thus Vultee took control of Consolidated through a 34 per cent stock interest and Rube Fleet will be US big-bomber-builder No. 1 no more.

Even today, there is the speculation the government forced Fleet to sell. Senators Gerald Nye of North Dakota and Burton Wheeler of Montana were particularly vocal in this assertion. Various aviation trade journals reported that the government had been seeking to effect a change in management at Consolidated.

Vultee's Vice President Hugh Fenwick issued a press statement denying that the government had played anything but a passive part in the transaction:

> With the government being the sole customer of the two aircraft concerns the proposed transaction has more or less had the Government's tacit approval.
>
> Never once have Vultee executives been approached by the Government concerning the plans. The deal was started by Vultee of its own volition. If the transaction is completed, Major Fleet, at our request and at that of the government, will remain as an executive in the concern. He has expressed his willingness to do so.

After the merger, Fleet held a press conference to explain his part in the merger and his future at the new company:

> The charges being made, that government dictation has forced me to withdraw as the controlling interest in Consolidated Aircraft and Vultee Aircraft Incorporated, are without any basis in fact.
>
> By no means am I withdrawing. The job before me is even bigger than before. Turning over management details to a younger man and becoming an adviser ... will enable me better to serve my country in this period of need than has been possible previously. I consider this my patriotic duty.
>
> The experience which has taught me the intricacies of the aircraft business has been accumulated over a quarter of a century. I helped nurse the business into being, helped it cling to life during the trying periods, and to expand into the most important industry in the nation today.

This is certainly no time for a man of that experience and training to turn his back on his countrymen and retire with a few dollars profit. No such thing is the case and never will be. I love my country and believe that aviation is the one means of bringing about world peace.

To further the ends of the American way of life and of world peace I would and will give my all.

There have been reports that severe criticism of the Administration, attributed to me, has brought about the present negotiations ... nothing could be further from the truth. I have sometimes disagreed with things that have been done, just as have thousands of other democratic Americans. But I subscribe entirely and wholeheartedly to the all-important foreign policy of our President and am with him one hundred per cent. Several members of the Roosevelt family are among my closest friends and we shall always be friends.

The idea of merging Consolidated and Vultee is a natural and the plan has come about in a perfectly normal way. The two companies' products, proximity of location (we are just 98 miles apart) and management are ideal complements. For a number of months we have discussed the possibility of a future association of the two organisations. We are approaching an agreement which should prove mutually beneficial. All of our discussions and plans have been wholly voluntary and the government had injected no dictation of any kind. On the contrary, the Army and Navy, with whom both companies do a large percentage of their business, have aided us in our planning.

One suggestion the government has made is that the President of Consolidated ... not retire and that there be no drastic changes in management. All through the proceedings these has been a fine spirit of obedience to our common interest in national-defense production.

My personal fortune is tied up in Consolidated. Members of my family have their interests in this company. It is obviously outlandish to consider that I would abruptly drop out of the picture at this particular time, when such a move might jeopardize the production of the most important aircraft items in our defense program, long-range Army and Navy bombers. It would be erroneous for my fellow Americans to get the idea that I am even thinking so unpatriotically.

In these times loyal Americans must make all sorts of sacrifices. We must devote our entire efforts to the purposes which each may best serve. For the common good we must be ready to brook the criticism which may come from any who disagree. It has developed that my duty in aviation is away from the myriad details which cluster about the building of big planes. My particular experience and background naturally place me best in the role of an advisor ... one who can thick in terms of aircraft which production men can only dream of in the little spare time they have.

We haven't even scratched the surface of aviation yet. We haven't had time ... to think far enough ahead. I will now have the time to think and plan for the future....

Before we are through, planes like the B-19 and the B-24 will be small fry. Despite my innate attachment for the duties of an aircraft factory boss, I belong in this new field. Thus I will be able to contribute my utmost to the leadership in aviation which America must take....

> And I urge all patriotic citizens immediately to get 100% behind our President and help him and his Administration in the leadership which they are all so ably giving our country.

A few weeks after the merger, Fleet and a group of new Convair officials were honored by San Diego during a luncheon at the El Cortez Hotel. Speakers were Tom Girdler, new chairman of the board, and Convair President Harry Woodhead, a long-time associate of Girdler who had been chosen to replace Millar.

Girdler: On Fleet: "The most outstanding thing about him is that he has gone and done the things that couldn't be done." On himself, he remarked: "If I can turn out one long-distance bombing plane that otherwise would not have been produced, I shall be happy." On his opinion of Consolidated: "[the] best aircraft concern not only in the United States, but in the entire world." "Give us credit," he remarked, "for knowing when to step into a good thing. That's what we did when we bought into Consolidated."

Fleet offered a rather altered version in his speech of why he had chosen to sell out his interest:

> It became apparent that the time might come when my heirs would have difficulty in raising sufficient money with which to pay the inheritance tax on my estate.
>
> I went to the Army and Navy people and explained the situation. At first they were reluctant, but finally gave their consent to the deal. Any stories you may have heard to the contrary are unfounded.
>
> We are very fortunate in the particular buyers who came into control of Consolidated. Our firm is the greatest builder of aircraft in the world. Now that I have left the office of President, I am on call for any service I can give Consolidated, even if it is on janitor work, if I am needed.

Although Reuben had offered this new explanation of why he had parted with Consolidated, it was only a veneer of the basic reasons of his belief that the constantly increasing power of the unions, linked with an equally increasing interference from the government going back to the $1 forced sale had really dictated this final course of action.

Fleet at the New Company

Soon after the Consolidated-Vultee merger, it became evident the Fleet's position on the board of directors was more honorary than advisory as it had been created by AVCO executives more or less as a precautionary measure. They were less concerned with his advice than they were in his whereabouts, as they intended to surveil and curtail all future business activities of Major Reuben Fleet, ex-president of Consolidated Aircraft. By committing him to a five-year board term, AVCO was able to monitor Fleet who had spent most of his fifty-four years in constant motion and was unable to slow down. He flew to Washington to sit in on government conferences; to Tulsa, where Douglas had begun to manufacture the B-24; to Kansas City, where the bomber was being turned out by North American Aviation—all trips were approved by AVCO.

After Pearl Harbor, ex-Company President Reuben Fleet gave a last inspirational talk to his employees proclaiming:

> We have a most profound duty to our country and for its national defense. We must buckle down to it with fervor and our best patriotic effort.... We have no place for foreigners or fifth columnists.... Most of our employees are of draft age; if a workman can serve his country better with us than as a soldier, we want him, otherwise he should go wherever his country calls.
>
> We in America must catch up. We cannot do it by working on small piecemeal orders totaling a few hundred bombers or flying boats, each order with changes in the craft, and all done under the strictest profit-limitation, where pennies must be watched lest we go broke.
>
> But these days are past, and we must not stand, like Lot's wife, paralyzed in the act of looking backward. The future is our Bible. So we must visualize the task ahead, for the Good Book says, 'Where there is no vision, the people perish.'

The New Consolidated Hierarchy

Tom M. Girdler: Chairman

The transfer of Consolidated stock from Fleet to Emanuel took place on 19 December 1941. After Fleet left Consolidated, Emanuel persuaded Tom Girdler, Republic Steel Board chairman, to immediately take control as the man he considered most able to keep production rolling to meet government requirements. Girdler succeeded President Fleet as Consolidated's chairman.

Girdler was the personification of the self-made, ruthless entrepreneur; in fact, his 1944 autobiography was entitled *Boot straps: The Autobiography of Tom M. Girdler*. Girdler grew up on a farm as the son of a father who managed a small cement mill and always had trouble making ends meet but Tom managed to earn a degree in mechanical engineering at Lehigh University. In an only-in-America story, he was hired as a steel salesman by Jones and Laughlin Steel Company and rose to company president and then became the first president and board chairman of newly-formed Republic Steel Company in 1930 by conspiring to get proxies and control of the company. Once in control, he single-handily built that company by acquisition, modernizing existing plants, and exploiting labor while deftly guiding it through the Depression to become a major producer of light alloys. To do so was expensive, and from 1930 to 1935, it cost Republic about $30 million while he drew a then-huge $130,000 yearly salary (over twice that of Reuben Fleet, whose company made a profit). At first Girdler supported Roosevelt's National Industrial Recovery Act, establishing a representation plan for Republic's employees, but when the Wagner Act outlawed such plans and promoted negotiations with regular unions, Girdler lost all attraction for the New Deal. He refused to bargain with the CIO, though conceding the need for collective bargaining, Girdler declined to do so by government decree. Girdler was so resolute that he stated: "I'll go back to the farm and dig potatoes before I sign with the CIO." In 1937, Girdler's

Republic Steel and the three other the so-called "Little Steel" companies (Bethlehem, Youngstown, and Inland) refused to sign a contract with the Steel Workers Organizing Committee (SWOC) of the CIO that had been previously accepted by "Big Steel," the U.S. Steel Company, the leading American steel producer. The SWOC called a strike on the Little Steel companies, but Girdler, who was vehemently anti-union, refused to close his Republic Steel plants and trouble began at the Chicago plant with the initial union picketing being dispersed by the police, who were clearly supportive of Republic Steel. On Memorial Day, 26 May 1937, about 1,500 SWOC sympathizers and their families gathered to show their support and about 1,000 members marched toward the Republic Plant. They were stopped by police who fired into the fleeing crowd, killing ten and wounding thirty with thirty-eight more being hospitalized by injuries suffered from beatings. The incident became known as the "Memorial Day Massacre," although Chicago's foremost newspapers portrayed the marchers as Communist conspirators and downplayed accusations of police brutality, which were verified during a later Senate investigation. Howard Fast (self-avowed Communist and author of 1951 best-seller and 1960 movie *Spartacus*) saw Girdler as "the front, the testing ground, the trial balloon of the most reactionary forces in American capitalism. He is a latter-day Morgan (the Pirate), a Jim Fisk (1870s 'Robber Baron'), and John D. Rockefeller but operating at a time when the tactics of these financial pirates were supposed to be outdated and hopeless." Fast criticized the major newspapers of the time for not branding "Tom Girdler, or his private police, as murderers" in the Memorial Day Massacre. After the Massacre, Girdler stated: "I will not sign a contract with that racketeering Communistic (union) unless the government passes a law to make me do it." During August 1943, just months before the Consolidated/Vultee merger, the Little Steel companies were legally forced to "cease committing acts of unfair labor practices" and a year later signed their first labor contract with the U.S. Steel Workers of America.

When Girdler took over as Consolidated-Vultee chairman, there was the distinct possibility of labor union problems from Aircraft Local 1125 of the AFL Machinists Union, which held the bargaining rights for most of Consolidated's 30,000 workers, and also at the Vultee Downey plant that had a contract with the CIO Auto Workers Union. However, President Roosevelt's unlimited national emergency declaration forestalled the threat as the Consolidated contract ended on 27 May 1943 or the end of the emergency declaration or whatever was shorter.

During the summer of 1944, Girdler and Consolidated faced charges of discrimination when Donald Ellinger, head of the Fair Employment Practice Committee (FEPC) in Dallas, and a small staff of investigators spent two years working to achieve entry for African-Americans into the all-white training facilities at Consolidated Fort Worth. Despite conferences, surveys, and appeals to management, the company virtually ignored Ellinger, and its discriminatory practices intensified, expanding into such areas as hiring, upgrades, and discharge for all employees. Ellinger unconvincingly threatened public hearings that would be too costly for his inherently weak Federal agency to carry out against the South's (e.g. everywhere except the Northeast and Midwest) racial system and its steadfast employer opposition. Upon resigning from Consolidated-Vultee in 1945, Girdler stated that he served as its chairman "Only in the service of the nation and in support of the Government's war effort." This from the man who several years earlier stated: "I don't think of the hope of reward as selfishness. Work is the prime mover of our economy and the fuel that makes people work is profit."

Girdler gives a rather tough self-assessment in *Boot Straps*:

> In the exercise of my special craftsmanship I have to be fair and I have to be tough. When I say "tough" I mean positive; in such a post as mine a man must have courage to act on his convictions, else he cannot be fair. There can be fairness only if there is "toughness." You dare not be soft simply because you are personally fond of someone who just been found wanting; for the sake of the organisation he must go. To be soft with a human misfit in your organisation you would have to be unjust to many other people. However, the consistent exercise of fairness and toughness in the running of an organisation gets magnificent results in industry and in my opinion it would get as great results in the administration of government.

Harry Woodhead: President

Harry Woodhead, president of AVCO and board chairman of Vultee, became Consolidated's president, rather than successful Vultee President Richard Millar. While Millar had been the Vultee president, Woodhead had frequently been called upon to resolve production problems. Millar and Girdler came to what Girdler termed an "amicable" parting at the time of the Consolidated-Vultee merger with Girdler explaining the situation:

> Sometimes good men get to working at cross purposes possibly through a failure to see each other's responsibilities in sharp focus. It had seemed to me that Dick Millar did not see where his job ended and the jobs of others began. It's as simple as that; a flaw had developed in the organisation.

Harry Woodhead was born on 29 January 1889 in Bradford, Yorkshire, England, and moved with his family to Canada. After graduating from Bradford Technology College, he became a supervisor at the Cleveland Metal Products Company, Sarnia, Canada (1913–1916). This was followed by works manager at Parish and Bingham Corporation, Cleveland (1916–1920); vice president of the Federal Pressed Steel Company, Milwaukee (1920–1921); general works manager A. O. Smith Corporation, Milwaukee (1921–1921); vice president of the Midland Steel Products Company, Cleveland, Detroit (1924–1928); vice president Truscon Steel Company (Pressed Steel Division), Cleveland (1928–1940); president of Aviation Manufacturing Corporation, Williamsport, Pennsylvania (1940–1942); chairman of the Board American Central Manufacturing Corporation, Connersville, Indiana (1941–1942); president of the Consolidated Aircraft Corporation (1942–1948); and finally the general manager of Western Pressed Metals Division, Douglas Aircraft Company. Woodhead died in 1961 at the age of seventy-two.

I. M. Laddon: General Manager

Laddon remained as general manager (he would become the vice president by 1945). When taking over Consolidated, Girdler wrote:

Harry Woodhead, new Consolidated-Vultee president. (*CAC/AAF*)

Yet at Consolidated I found an organisation far better than I had expected, one that was extraordinarily rich in talented men. Rich though it is in talent, and especially in engineering talent, I. M. Laddon is the genius. Laddon is the fundamental creative force which the Consolidated organisation is expressing. Every big ship he has designed has been a success and I do not know of another man in the aircraft field of whom that can be said unequivocally.

Vice Presidents: Charles Leigh and Charles Perelle

Charles Leigh remained as vice president while Woodhead brought in the forty-one-year-old Charles Perelle as a second Consolidated vice president. After being hired away from Boeing Seattle, Perelle had made Vultee the producer of more pounds of aircraft per man-hour than any other plant in the world.

David Fleet: Executive Vice President

After graduating from Culver Military Academy and Cornell University, Reuben Fleet's son David became executive vice president of his father's company. When it was sold, he remained with that company, as assistant to the president. In 1949, he retired at the age of thirty-nine to become a prominent San Diego real estate developer of the prestigious Fleetridge neighborhood and was involved in various philanthropic, cultural, and business organizations.

Consolidated-Vultee's Wartime Contributions

In 1943, Consolidated-Vultee manufactured more aircraft by weight than any other manufacturer and was the world's largest aircraft manufacturer. The company had produced 126 million pounds of aircraft $v.$115 million pounds by Douglas, which was second and North American in third place at 73 million pounds. The peak production year for Consolidated Vultee was 1944 when the combined Fort Worth and San Diego Plants out-produced every other aircraft manufacturer in the world. During World War II, all thirteen divisions of Consolidated Vultee combined ranked second in production among all American aircraft manufacturers. From the day the first B-24 rolled off the assembly line at San Diego until the war ended, the company produced 30,696 aircraft of all types. North American Aviation ranked first in producing 41,188 aircraft, Douglas, Curtis, and Lockheed ranked, third, fourth, and fifth with 30,696, 26,154, and 18,926 aircraft respectively. The Fort Worth division produced more than 3,000 warplanes: 2,750 were B-24 bombers, almost 300 were C-87 transport versions of the B-24, and about 125 were B-32 heavy bombers. In addition, the entire company built enough spare parts to equal 5,000 more aircraft delivered as spares, which represented nearly 13 percent of the total output of the nation's aircraft industry.

Epilog: Consolidated Post-War

Consolidated-Vultee

After the war, it soon became evident that Convair was having problems in its endeavor to enter the post-war commercial market and B-36 production was not proceeding smoothly. Convair had a development contract for the B-36, the first intercontinental bomber that could carry up to 72,000 pounds of bombs and sixteen crewmembers had two pressurized compartments and could fly 12,000-mile missions. The ten-engined Peacemaker strategic bomber was "burning four turbojets and turning six pusher propellers" driven by P&W R-4360 Wasp Major radial piston engines. The first flight of the B-36A was on 28 August 1947; it was not ordered into production until 1948 at Fort Worth and 285 were built through 1954. Meanwhile, its XB-46 four-engined bomber program was cancelled in August 1947, even before flight-testing had been completed as the North American B-45 Tornado had been ordered for production.

Victor Emanuel and AVCO

After the war, AVCO ranked thirty-second among American corporations in the value of World War II production contracts. Victor Emanuel, who bought out Fleet's stock in November 1941, was ready to leave the aircraft industry to concentrate on the conversion of AVCO from a producer of aircraft and heavy goods to a manufacturer of consumer goods into a $165 million business by a series of complicated financial deals. Emanuel acquired a number of companies including the Crosley Corporation for $20 million in 1945 and Bendix Home Appliances in 1950. These purchases helped to transform AVCO into one of the early conglomerates by the early 1950s.

Floyd Odlum

Floyd Odlum, a multimillionaire aviation investor, began buying AVCO Manufacturing Corporation (the renamed Aviation Corporation) stock in 1946, through his Atlas Corporation. In 1923, Floyd Odlum, a friend, and their wives pooled $40,000 to organize the United States Company to speculate in purchases of utilities and general securities. Within two years, the company's net assets had increased to nearly $700,000. In 1928, Odlum incorporated Atlas Utilities Company to take over the common stock of his other company. During the summer of 1929, Odlum was one of the few on Wall Street to believe that the boom could not continue much longer and he sold half of Atlas's holdings, as well as $9 million in new securities to investors. He had $14 million in cash and short-term notes when the stock market crashed, and during the next few years, Atlas Utilities bought stock in depressed investment companies at Depression-reduced prices. By 1933, Odlum was one of the ten wealthiest men in America. His second wife, whom he married in 1936, was famous aviatrix Jackie Cochran, and the two were close friends of Amelia Earhart and her husband, George P. Putnam.

On 4 September 1947, Odlum exchanged all of his AVCO stock for all of Convair's aviation operations in San Diego, Fort Worth, and Detroit. Odlum's Atlas Corporation took control of Convair in November 1947. In 1948, Odlum replaced President Harry Woodhead with La Motte Cohu, previously president of Trans-World Airlines. Odlum returned Convair to profitability in 1949, benefiting from an increase in military orders. Under Odlum, Convair established leadership in delta-wing design, and during 1950, Convair received a contract for the advanced supersonic F-102 Delta Dagger. Meanwhile, Convair enjoyed some success

Floyd Odlum and his second wife, famous aviatrix Jackie Cochran, whom he married in 1936. (*AFSHRC*)

in the military trainer (T-29) and civilian markets (CV-340) but, nonetheless, Odlum wanted to merge Convair or sell it completely. After many discussions with numerous interested parties, John Jay Hopkins of Electric Boat began negotiations with Atlas Group and Odlum in 1951, which led to their March 1953 agreement to purchase Convair from the Atlas. After the sale, Odlum and Atlas Corporation's business concerns had significant interests in mining operations. Odlum retired from Atlas in 1960, and from 1961–1969, he was the chairman of the board of Federal Resources Corporation, which concentrated on mining activities, particularly uranium. Odlum died on 17 June 1976.

The Atlas/Convair sale was approved by government oversight with the proviso that operations would continue from Air Force Plant 4 in Fort Worth. Over time, the Fort Worth plant became Convair's major production center. The merger became official on 29 April 1954, with Electric Boat renamed General Dynamics (GD), which had transformed itself into a major conglomerate of military and high technology companies. Its Convair Division would be a significant contributor to the American space program. In May 1965, GD reorganized into twelve operating divisions based on product lines. The board decided to build all future aircraft in Fort Worth, terminating aircraft production at Convair's original San Diego plant but continuing with space and missile development there. During the early 1960s until 1965, Convair manufactured its own line of jet airliners, the Convair 880 and Convair 990, which were not profitable and discontinued. Convair then commenced airframe subcontracting projects for other larger airliner manufacturing companies: McDonnell Douglas, Boeing, and Lockheed.

Convair's Atlas Rocket was originally developed in 1957 as an ICBM for the USAF and was replaced in 1962 by the liquid-fueled Titan II missile and the solid-fueled Minuteman missile. The Atlas then transitioned from military missiles into civilian launch vehicles and were used for the first orbital manned U.S. space flights during Project Mercury in 1962 and 1963. The Atlas Rocket became a very reliable booster for satellite launching and continued to evolve, remaining in use into the twenty-first century, when combined with the Centaur upper stage to form the Atlas-Centaur Rocket for launching geo-synchronous communication satellites and space probes.

By 1984, General Dynamics had four divisions: Convair in San Diego, General Dynamics-Fort Worth, General Dynamics-Pomona, and General Dynamics-Electronics. In 1985, a further reorganization created the Space Systems Division from the Convair Space division. The San Diego and Pomona Convair Missile Systems Division production units were sold to General Motors-Hughes Aerospace in May 1992 and Fort Worth aircraft production to Lockheed in March 1993. In 1994, General Dynamics split further and sold the original Convair Division, along with other General Dynamics aerospace units that had been absorbed by Convair over the years. The airframe manufacturing company and the space boosters company were sold to McDonnell Douglas. The Fort Worth factory and its associated engineering facilities and laboratories, which had been previously used for the manufacture of hundreds of General Dynamics F-111s and F-16s for the USAF, were sold, along with all intellectual property and the legal rights to the products that were being designed and built within, to the Lockheed Corporation. In 1996, General Dynamics deactivated all of the remaining Convair Division and concentrated on its land and sea products.

Convair 880. (*PASM*)

Convair 990. (*PASM*)

Atlas-Centaur rocket. (*PASM*)

13

Epilog: Reuben Fleet After the Merger

Reuben Fleet: Private Citizen and Air Power Advocate

After the merger, Reuben Fleet signed a five-year agreement with new Consolidated President Harry Woodhead to serve in an advisory and consulting capacity for $60,000 per year. The retaining of Fleet by Consolidated was widely seen as an effort to refute intimations that the merger had been prompted by the War Department to force the change in Consolidated management but actually was AVCO's ploy to keep tabs on Fleet.

President Roosevelt had valued Fleet's opinions during his time at Consolidated and he continued as a FDR consultant and air power advocate; even to the extent that the president requested that a direct private phone line be installed from the White House and into the Fleet home and office. Fleet also gave unsolicited advice to many congressman and senators, and appeared before congressional committees and public forums on the need to preserve free enterprise, on the iniquities of excessive taxation, and on the increasing importance of air power, which he placed first, sea strength second, land forces third. "Out of this war will come to humanity a particularly great blessing; namely, an instrumentality (air power) capable of enforcing world peace while peacefully spreading good will among men."

Once the outlook on the Pacific and European war improved because of American air power, Fleet began to focus his attention on the aircraft industry's post-war problems. In a 10 December 1943 letter to Undersecretary of the Navy James Forrestal, he wrote:

> Aircraft manufacturers are driving full blast to a precipitous abyss-the war's end. They fear the post-war holiday for their wares that will force them to discharge employees, and maybe break them (financially) before they can design and get into production of commercial products.
>
> They have been, and will continue to be, indispensable to our Nation; therefore, they should have fair treatment from a grateful country, whose post-war policy toward them should be decided upon and announced soon.

Reuben Fleet and Family

Soon after Reuben Fleet had moved the company to San Diego, his second wife, Dorothy Mitchell, whom he married in 1930, and two years later their son, Preston, nicknamed Sandy, was born. David, his oldest son by his first wife, Elizabeth, was already living in San Diego with his new wife. Soon, Reuben's mother, Elizabeth, and his sister, Phyllis, also moved to San Diego from Buffalo. Initially, Reuben, Dorothy, and her parents, and son, Sandy, leased a large, old home in Mission Hills where their daughter, Lillian, would be born. The house had a reputation as being haunted, causing the Fleets to move and purchase a huge Spanish baronial mansion atop posh Point Loma called Dias Felices (Happy Days). As a footnote, Fleet's son, Sandy, founded the Fotomat Corporation in 1967.

Managing the household, raising three small children (their daughter, Nancy, was born during August 1940), and serving as her husband's social host left Dorothy little time for travel with Reuben. As the pace of production at the factory increased, business matters in San Diego, and extensive travel east required more and more of Reuben's time away from home. In 1940, Reuben Fleet purchased a home in Los Angeles' exclusive Beverly Hills, and Dorothy Fleet, tired of Reuben's absences and attracted by the lure of a social life among Hollywood celebrities, moved there with their three children. Meanwhile, Fleet moved from the Point Loma home to San Diego's La Jolla Beach and Tennis Club where Consolidated maintained an apartment for the use of important customers and friends. After a while, there was reconciliation as Dorothy returned to San Diego and to the Point Loma castle, but the arrangement

Dias Felices, the Fleet baronial mansion atop posh Point Loma. (*CAC/AAF*)

did not last and the separation resumed due to an interesting provision of Fleet's merger package. The provision was the $6,000 per year stipend for two secretaries of his selection. Of course, one of the secretaries was Eva May Wiseman who would continue in her long-time position as Fleet's personal secretary, after which Fleet and Dorothy again separated.

Reuben Fleet: According to Ex-Wife Dorothy

In her 1964 biography *Our Flight to Destiny*, Dorothy, the second Fleet wife, writes her insights into Reuben Fleet, the man, husband, and father:

> Although I received flowers and candy, periodically convincing me that I was ever uppermost in Reuben's thoughts, I spent more than one solitary evening glaring at the clock. Reuben was too well mannered to disappoint me deliberately, but I wasn't long in learning that anything connected with Consolidated acted as an erasure on his social calendar. Hell or high water, either one or both, came after Consolidated. This I accepted; it was a facet of Reuben which I could not change even if I had wanted to. Consolidated Aircraft was a part of the man I married....
>
> (While) Reuben advocated turning the other cheek in the trivia department, he fought unceasingly for things which he considered important. When he was aroused he had a tremendous temper. He wanted always to have his own way; he wanted always to win. When he was crossed he was likely to explode in all directions even if, to a disinterested observer, the situation didn't warrant it....
>
> I remember a trap shoot at Travis Island, New York, when my husband demonstrated a typically Reuben reaction to a situation which did not please him. It should be remembered that trapshooting was important to him. He loved it, and what's more he was good at it. On this particular occasion he was trying out a beautiful, and expensive, new Parker gun. Unhappily he was thwarted by the wind. It blew in his face, it churned up the dust, it spoiled the normal direction of the clay pigeons. Shot after shot was ruined. Reuben was helpless, and when he was helpless he was furious. When the shoot was over and he learned that I, who was nothing but a female, had beaten him by two shots, he blew up. Since he couldn't take his wrath out on the wind, he seized the Parker gun and tried to break it over his knee. When that didn't work, raging more than ever, he finally managed to smash it over the barrel which stood nearby to receive empty shells....
>
> His competitive spirit, driving him always, extended to the bridge table, where I, as his generally unlucky partner, tried to respond to his constant demand bids. When we lost, as we did often enough, Reuben was wild. One evening when we had done badly, after our guests had left he began to smolder because I had not held good cards. As he talked, becoming angrier with every word, he began to fold the card table, which foolishly defied his efforts. After a few minutes of struggling, of cursing the whole contraption as a "Goddamned newfangled thing," he simply tore off the legs and hurled them, one by one, across the room....

On the domestic front, he has been known to shatter a stack of expensive China plates because he wasn't pleased with the progress the cook was making with an important dinner....

And yet Reuben had his quiet, patient, and even gentle times. Hopelessly addicted to the crossword puzzle, he always won the Sunday-morning skirmish for the proper newspaper section. Then he would sit quietly, pencil in hand, until the puzzle was finished....

He played a masterful game of chess, and one year when the world champion, Dr. Alexander Alekhine, stopped in Buffalo to match his skill against the top local players, Reuben was his only opponent to obtain a draw....

Reuben had several sayings he was fond of repeating to anyone in need of guidance. To be more accurate, he was always glad to repeat them to anyone at all. One was, "Pretend to virtue if you have it not"; another, "Better to keep your mouth shut and be considered a fool than to open it and remove all doubt." And still another, "Moderation is the silken string that runneth through the pearl chain of all virtue...."

Reuben seldom tried to cover up his mistakes and he was outspoken on every subject he considered important, which was another disarming quality that went to make up the complex personality of the unique Major Reuben Fleet....

Reuben attributed to a Divine intervention which had its beginnings in an idea, in a creative thought, which had been conceived, not by Reuben Fleet, but by an Infinite Power. His conviction of this was responsible for his own freedom from doubt, for his continuing certainty that the course he had chosen, the decisions he had made, were inalterably correct.

After the sale of Consolidated to AVCO and at the end of his five-year term on the Consolidated-Vultee board of directors, "the pressures upon Reuben decreased. In a business sense, he had begun the process of deceleration. His enthusiasms, his energies became directed more to local affairs, to politics, and closer to home, to his family."

In spite of his reputation for shrewdness, and even ruthlessness, Reuben at heart has a strong streak of sentimentality. When he had time to think about it, I know it caused him concern to realize how little his children actually knew their father. While they were growing up he must have seemed to them as a sort of combination Santa Claus and Ruling Monarch who appeared, sporadically, to distribute largess and edicts with equal generosity.

Too often Reuben had not had time for his children, and what he withheld of himself he tried to compensate for in material things. Certainly he was an indulgent parent. Though he went to school wearing overalls, Sandy and Dotty and Nancy wanted for nothing.

Of course, the reader must remember that the above was written by the disgruntled second wife of fourteen years. It seems that Dorothy should have known from her own personal experience as Reuben's "personal secretary" and that of her aunt, Lauretta Golem, what an important and personal role his secretary always played in his life. It was said that Fleet always seemed to have two wives: a homemaker to care for the children and be his in-home host and the "office wife/secretary" who could fill a social as well as business role outside the home. Fleet's longtime, efficient, and devoted secretary was Eva May Wiseman, who was employed after Fleet decided that his male secretary was no longer efficient. Eva had been married to Herman Wiseman, who earlier had been the assistant to Consolidated's personnel director (shades of the cuckolded Harry Golem). There were also insider rumors that Eva had previously thwarted "attempts of affection" from some Consolidated executives.

It would not be until May 1944 that Dorothy filed a divorce petition accusing Fleet of "inflicting great mental suffering and bodily injury." She later dropped these charges and moved on with an uncontested divorce that a year later netted her a very generous $1.55 million ($29 million today) settlement and custody of the three children. Dorothy would eventually remarry twice but both her husbands would pass away.

The Fleets. *Left to right*: Father William, Reuben, and son, David. (*CAC/AAF*)

Dorothy Fleet, the second Fleet wife. (*CAC/AAF*)

Tom Girdler on Reuben Fleet

Tom Girdler, in his autobiography *Boot Straps*, suggests that Reuben drove himself day and night to achieve a goal:

> Rube started to school at six in a little Lord Fauntleroy velvet suit but when he was seven had only overalls, which were ragged overalls when he was eight. Ever since he has been going at a gallop to get away from that situation....
>
> I can scarcely imagine a more impressive coincidence that the fact that just as Rube Fleet gained his ambition through creating something that was worth ten million dollars the Japs struck at Pearl Harbor. If you like, turn Rube Fleet's motive around and upside down; examine and smell it; the fact remains, it was Rube Fleet's interest in profit that had provided America with this source of vital weapons. This great aircraft plant existed when the United States needed it only because all those years Rube Fleet had been free to exercise his right to work.
>
> I know perfectly well that Rube Fleet hadn't made this thing by himself; better than anyone else I know what marvelous talents were built into the organisation. But the best men in it have said to me that it survived and grew and flourished because of Fleet's determination and drive. He was at once the boss of it and the slave of it.
>
> Reuben set his own price for giving the best that was in Rube Fleet.

Fleet Marries Secretary Eva Wiseman and Retires

In March 1947, Fleet crashed his car into a tree severely crushing his chest against the steering wheel, nearly losing his life. Two months later, the resilient Fleet, at sixty years old and true to his "marries his secretary" proclivity, wed Eva (whom he always called Eve). While married to Herman Wiseman, Eva gave birth to Sally and twins, Sandra and Susan. Fleet would adopt the two-year-old Wiseman twins and four-year-old Sally and was said to have considered them as his daughters. The two children, who were the product of Fleet's 1908 marriage to Elizabeth Girton, were Phyllis Fleet and David Fleet who became a Consolidated executive and later a real estate developer and the creator of the upscale Fleetridge neighborhood in San Diego.

Reuben Fleet: Philanthropist

On 12 April 1946, Fleet resigned from Convair, ending his involvement with the company he built. During his retirement, Fleet was known for his philanthropy. In August 1946, Fleet and his sister, Lillian, bought a parcel of land in Montesano and donated it to the city for use as a park named in honor of their parents. The city subsequently renamed Second Street to Fleet Street in their honor. During the war years, after the merger, Fleet found the time to devote his efforts toward the Institute of Aeronautical Sciences (IAS) (now the Institute of Aerospace Sciences), a valued

Reuben Fleet and third wife, Eva.
(*CAC/AAF*)

project in which he served as president in 1944. He was instrumental in raising funds to purchase a Fifth Avenue mansion to serve as the New York IAS Headquarters, and made generous personal contributions, which included endowment of the Reuben Fleet Foundation Library at the IAS building in San Diego. For his long service to the institute and to the aviation industry, he was presented with a Certificate of Honor during the Fifth Aeronautical Conference held in Los Angeles in June 1955. He also was instrumental in founding the San Diego Aerospace Museum in 1965 and then became a benefactor. In 1965, Fleet was inducted in the International Aerospace Hall of Fame. In the early 1970s, Fleet largely funded construction of the Bishop Center for Performing Arts at Grays Harbor College in Aberdeen, Washington, in honor of logging tycoon and early investor in Consolidated Aircraft E. K. "Ned" Bishop, and Fleet's sister, Lillian Fleet Bishop. In 1985, the Reuben H. Fleet Foundation donated $8 million in assets to the San Diego Foundation. Fleet died on 29 October 1975 at eighty-eight years old from injuries related to a fall, still married to Eva, for a Reuben Fleet personal marriage record of twenty-eight reportedly happy years.

Fleet Science Center, San Diego. (*CAC/AAF*)

PART II

Liberator Production Pool, Committee, and Manufacturer Contracts

1
Liberator Production Pool

In September 1939, when the Nazis attacked Poland, the American aircraft industry was manufacturing 5,856 aircraft, of which only 2,195 were military; more significantly, military airframe production weight totaled 10.1 million pounds $v.$ 2.4 million pounds for civilian airframes. The aircraft industry ranked forty-first among American industries, employing 64,000 workers with an output of $280 million, producing 15,000 airframes per year and 14,000 engines of over 1,000 hp.

With a probable war looming, American facilities would have to be expanded, and the principal airframe manufacturers immediately began to increase their manufacturing capacity, floor space, and warehousing. Because it was such a large undertaking, the U.S. government provided 89 percent of the $3.84 billion ($56 billion today) that would be invested in aircraft plants between 1940 and 1945.

Concerned about the possibility of enemy air attacks from aircraft carriers on factories built directly on the East and West Coasts, the War Department decided that new defense plants were to be built at least 200 miles from the Atlantic and Pacific Oceans. Another main reason for building factories throughout the country was that it distributed work among different congressional districts and also opened competition among contractors. In the late 1930s, Congress decided not to recognize design rights, which then allowed the government to take a design from one contractor, even if the contractor had financed its own research and development, and grant it to another contractor to manufacture. Although the government purportedly did this so that other contractors could support mass production in time of war, it also was a political tool that the government could take advantage.

In early 1941, the government established the Liberator Production Pool Program to facilitate the projected demand for the B-24. The program directed Consolidated to establish a new plant in Fort Worth to supplement its main San Diego Plant Liberator production and Douglas was to open a similar plant for Liberator production in Tulsa, Oklahoma. The initial plan was for the Douglas/Tulsa plant to assemble complete Liberators from sub-assemblies and components provided to it by Consolidated until it gained sufficient experience to build complete aircraft on its own. Soon, the Ford Motor

Company joined the Liberator Production Pool Program but intended to build complete Liberators at a new factory at Willow Run near Detroit. However, Ford was initially consigned to providing complete components, called knock-down kits (KD kits or KD assemblies) or less often, built-up units (BUs) from the Ford Line for final assembly by the government-financed Consolidated/Fort Worth and Douglas/Tulsa Plants. During October 1941, Ford was authorized to also assemble complete Liberators.

Each KD, which Ford initially contracted to supply at the rate of 100 per month, included all major components of the Liberator—fuselage, wings, tail, and landing gear. First production at the new plants was scheduled for early 1942. Somewhat later (January 1942), a fourth company was added to the pool when North American Aviation was issued a Letter of Intent, preceding a contract issued on 1 May, to operate a complete and independent B-24 fabrication and assembly complex at Dallas, Texas. The pool placed Douglas in a difficult situation as the company was responsible for a Consolidated product whose parts had been fabricated by Ford. Douglas had no authority or control over design, material procurement, detailed inspection, tooling, or assembly methods, but Douglas was ultimately responsible for on schedule delivery of the finished B-24D-DT.

By early 1942, the AAC's initial Liberator manufacturers were Consolidated/San Diego, which would manufacture the B-24D; Ford/Willow Run, the B-24E; and North American/Dallas, the B-24G. Consolidated/Fort Worth and Douglas/Tulsa were to complete the final construction of aircraft by completing sub-assemblies supplied by the other three plants. Eventually, Consolidated/Fort Worth was also to become a primary manufacturing center. The Ford Willow Run Plant was also selected to be the prime contractor for B-24 spare parts. The first AAC B-24Ds were manufactured by Consolidated/San Diego in January 1942. As part of its participation in the Liberator Production Pool, Consolidated/San Diego also began to supply subassemblies for B-24Ds to Consolidated/Fort Worth in May 1942 and to Douglas/Tulsa in August 1942.

However, since each plant in the pool would often use sub-assemblies and components provided by the other members, this D (Consolidated), E (Ford), or G (NAA) system could not completely identify which factory was actually the primary manufacturer responsible for the final assembly of any particular aircraft. The letters designating the five members of the pool, which was responsible for the construction of the aircraft, were the following manufacturers:

CO: Consolidated/San Diego
CF: Consolidated/Fort Worth
DT: Douglas/Tulsa
FO: Ford/Willow Run
NT: North American/Dallas

For example, the B-24D-CO was the primary version of the Liberator that was manufactured at Consolidated/San Diego. However, Consolidated/San Diego also shipped parts and components of B-24Ds to Consolidated/Fort Worth and to Douglas/Tulsa for final assembly, which was designated B-24D-CF and B-24D-DT, respectively. The B-24E was the B-24D version that was primarily manufactured by Ford/Willow Run. There were noteworthy differences between the B-24E and the other two versions. Ford not only built complete aircraft, but it also supplied components of B-24Es for final assembly at Douglas/Tulsa and at Consolidated/Fort Worth. B-24Es built and fully assembled at Ford were designated B-24E-FO, but those assembled by Douglas/Tulsa and Consolidated/Fort Worth from parts supplied by Ford were designated B-24E-DT and B-24E-CF.

The version of the Liberator that underwent primary manufacture at Consolidated/San Diego was designated B-24D. When the B-24D was completely assembled at San Diego, it was designated B-24D-CO. However, Consolidated/San Diego also shipped parts and components of B-24Ds to Consolidated/Fort Worth and to Douglas/Tulsa for final assembly. B-24Ds assembled by these plants were designated B-24D-CF and B-24D-DT respectively.

The B-24E was the version of the B-24D that underwent primary manufacture by Ford at Willow Run. There were significant differences between the B-24E and the other two versions. Not only did Ford build complete aircraft, but it also supplied components of B-24Es for final assembly at Douglas/Tulsa and at Consolidated/Fort Worth. B-24Es built and fully assembled at Ford were designated B-24E-FO, but those assembled by Douglas/Tulsa and Consolidated/Fort Worth out of parts supplied by Ford were designated B-24E-DT and B-24E-CF respectively.

The version of the Liberator built by North American/Dallas was designated B-24G, which differed little from the Consolidated/San Diego-built version. Since North American/Dallas was only a primary manufacturer and did not supply components to the other members of the Pool, all B-24Gs bore the NT manufacturer's letters.

Maintenance and Parts Interchangeability

The Production Pool system caused many problems with the standardization of components and equipment. Often there were significant differences between the various production blocks of the same model Liberator and even differences even within a production block. Variants originating from the various members of the pool would often have significant detail differences from each other that would cause significant spare parts and interchangeability difficulties. Parts for Liberators built at different factories often were not interchangeable with each other and all four factories involved in primary manufacturing produced Liberators of similar variants but of vastly different detail specification. Even the two Consolidated plants using Consolidated-manufactured parts experienced this problem.

The small differences between the four different Liberator Models produced by the various pool members caused maintenance problems in the field, causing each to require its own manuals, parts lists, and technical orders. Ford models, including the Douglas and Fort Worth KDs, had interchangeable parts, as did the North American models, although these two types were not interchangeable with each other. The other two types were those manufactured at San Diego and Fort Worth, and while all Consolidated engineering was controlled by San Diego, the lack of scrupulous dimensional control prevented these hypothetically identical versions from being completely interchangeable. A tooling sub-committee of the B-24 Liaison Committee was established in February 1944, to establish actual interchangeability among all manufacturers but had not achieved its purpose before production cutbacks made its work unnecessary.

From the beginning, however, Ford had demonstrated great interest in becoming a full-fledged producer of complete Liberators, as was substantiated by its huge Willow Run facility, which, although supposedly built as a knock-down and parts plant, was indeed a full-fledged production facility. During October 1941, the government contracted Ford to manufacture completed Liberators in addition to the KD assemblies at increased rate of 150 per month for Tulsa and Fort Worth. In less than three years, Ford built 6,792 B-24s, furnished 1,893 others in KD form to Tulsa and Fort Worth, produced a multitude of spare parts, and yet never operated Willow Run at full capacity.

All this production was not achieved as quickly as original plans had stipulated, and as a result, the Tulsa and Fort Worth plants were ready to receive KD kits before Willow Run could supply them. To expedite production, both Douglas and Consolidated Fort Worth began operations with sub-assemblies supplied by San Diego. The aircraft resulting from this temporary arrangement were, for all practical purposes, identical with the B-24D-COs then being built at San Diego, and carried the serial numbers originally allocated to the California plant.

The AAF accepted the first Willow Run Liberator on 1 September 1942, designated as the B-24E to differentiate it from the Consolidated B-24D from which it was virtually copied; followed by two dozen more before the end of the year. The first KD from Willow Run arrived at Tulsa during September 1942, and by February 1943, Douglas was in series production of the B-24E. Fort Worth received its initial Ford KD in January 1943 and, starting in July, began delivering assembled Willow Run E's as well as its B-24D production.

Initially, Ford had problems adapting automobile mass production techniques to the production of aircraft. They had to redo the 30,000 drawings they had copied from Consolidated so that their relatively unskilled workers could interpret them. They found that working with aircraft aluminum was different from working with automotive steel. The most important fact of aircraft production life Ford had to learn was to accept the inexorable design changes that characterized wartime aircraft production as contrasted to the yearly self-imposed automobile design freeze of the pre-war auto industry. Ford resolved these problems and many others, but by the time it had almost completed the entire B-24E production run, the E-model was considered obsolescent.

North American B-24G production progressed slowly. The first B-24G, which was basically a D model, was flight tested in January 1943 and accepted in March. By the end of July, only four more B-24Gs had been accepted by the AAF, and it was not until January 1944 that Dallas production exceeded one-a-day.

By 30 June 1943, the AAF had accepted 2,988 Liberators of all models, while on that same date, 1,867 of these were still in AAF inventory and hundreds of others flew for the U.S. Navy and RAF. However, D and E production was ending as, on 30

June 1943, the first B-24H was delivered from the Ford assembly line at Willow Run, and on 18 September 1943, the last of the early Liberators left the factory. With the introduction of the B-24J, all five members of the pool (both primary manufacturers and sub-assemblers) converted only to the production of this version.

With the advent of the front-turreted Liberator, the operational B-24 was near its design limit. There was little, if any, reserve power for take-off and the flight characteristics at high attitude (20,000 feet) were less stable. Before the end of 1944, the Liberator production by Willow Run was such that Ford was able to assume the production quotas of both Douglas and North American. Consequently, during July and November, respectively, Liberator assembly at Tulsa and Dallas was terminated. Fort Worth manufactured its final B-24 in December 1944.

During August 1944, San Diego Consolidated and Ford began B-24L production, which was an attempt to improve handling characteristics by reducing weight with the installations of a light rear turret. The new turret was about 200 pounds lighter and had an increased arc of fire. After nearly 1,700 model Ls were produced, they were followed the M model, which was almost identical to the L model except that it had improved aileron control. North American had pioneered a change involving the substitution of bell-cranks in place of the gearbox in the aileron control system, providing a single point system of aileron control that considerably reduced the 'stick' force required to fly the B-24. Nearly 2,600 M models were built.

By Germany's May 1945 surrender, Willow Run and San Diego had begun to decrease production. Although the last B-24s from Ford and Consolidated were recorded as being accepted during June 1945, this was actually an arbitrary contract termination point and many of the final Liberators were actually delivered after that point. However, by this time, Liberators were no longer needed, and hundreds of the last Liberators were flown directly to storage and were eventually scrapped.

2
B-24 Committee

Coordination of B-24 Program

At the beginning of the B-24 program, when a specific problem developed and demanded the combined efforts of Ford, Douglas, and Consolidated, coordination was carried out by direct discussions between representatives of the concerned companies. As the program progressed, difficulties arose because Consolidated procedures and plans were different from those used by Ford. These difficulties could not be satisfactorily settled by discussions between company representatives only, because a solution could be realized only if one of the companies altered their methods to satisfy the other. Because some of the changes would have involved significant time and expense, each company was unwilling to effect such changes, especially when it was not obvious that such a change would in fact benefit the entire program, or only delay one company as much as it helped the other. Subsequently, the B-24 Liaison or Production Committee (popularly known as the "B-24 Committee") was created to simplify coordination between the company's producing Liberators.

The B-24 Committee was established at a meeting held at Wright Field on 21 March 1942 and was patterned after the BDV (Boeing-Douglas-Vega) Committee established in May 1941 for the purpose of assisting Douglas and Vega Aircraft Companies in manufacturing the B-17. The committee was comprised of a member from each company involved who represented management and was authorized to make agreements for their company concerning schedules for delivery, data, parts, materials, coordination of subcontracting, tooling, facilities, and materials. The committee then appointed various sub-committees to handle specific items and procedures and advise the committee if changes were considered advantageous. The sub-committees were spares sub-committee, tooling sub-committee, and engineering sub-committee.

The committee functioned throughout the balance of 1942 and during the early part of 1943, then, as the sub-committees became more effective and difficulties decreased, it gradually cut its meetings from approximately once a month until early in 1944 when it met only when called. Because the majority of difficulties mostly concerned engineering, the engineering sub-committee operated during most of the manufacturing period while other sub-committees met less often as problems decreased. Sub-committees were composed of the contractor's personnel who were directly responsible for the departments concerned. These sub-committees were responsible for the reliable fulfilment of the directives of the executive committee.

The tooling sub-committee was an example of the function of the B-24 Committee's sub-committees. Because no previous resolute effort had been made to establish close tooling coordination between contractors, a tooling sub-committee was created on 18 February 1944 to oversee the interchangeability between B-24s being manufactured and assembled by the various contractors. In early 1944, a physical parts interchangeability assessment uncovered that there was an immediate need for contractor interchangeability coordination. The tooling sub-committee was comprised of one tooling representative from each contractor to act in an advisory role to the B-24 executive committee on "all detail duties and assignments directed by the execution committee." The tooling sub-committee made repeated calls to the various contractor's plants to assist in tooling problems, prepare tooling documents, interchangeability lists, lists of master tools, location of the control master, tool number of the tooling master, number of inspection gages, etc. The B-24 liaison committee and its tooling sub-committee continued to function until the summer of 1945, or at the termination of member contracts.

The B-24 Committee's authority depended mainly on the active cooperation and assistance of the AAF and its insistence that agreements of the executive committee were to be followed by the companies involved and the AAF. While Wright Field representatives on the executive committee always supported the decisions made, difficulties sometimes occurred because the various departments at the Materiel Command inaugurated independent actions, which unintentionally undermined or disregarded the AAF personnel concerned about the procedure to be followed. Generally, a much-improved coordination was finally realized, greatly decreasing the hostility between companies.

The B-24 Committee Program probably somewhat increased the direct cost in management time than would have occurred without a committee. Usually it was possible for sub-committee participants to also conduct the functions of company representatives, and at the height of the program, a number of committee men were required to act as company representatives. As examples, Consolidated furnished a substantial number of engineers to work at Willow Run and the AAC requested that Ford and North American be allowed to carry out independent design.

Early in the program, the B-24 companies agreed to have Consolidated's Field Division fabricate the common tools for power plant installations, but this agreement became unworkable because the number of changes was so excessive that the tools were never current. Additionally, this program, along with the later Interchangeability Program, was hindered by the fact that each company had tools in production and could not just institute new tools at random. The Interchangeability Program involved a sizable cost in special tooling but would not have been excessive had the Interchangeability Program been introduced earlier, but since it was started too late in the program, it was never completed.

The liaison committee decided that engineering data and information on all changes were to be interchanged between Ford, North American, and Consolidated, San Diego, so that each contractor could obtain all engineering data directly from the contractor completing the design. During May 1944, the liaison committee decided that because the effective point of interchangeability at Consolidated was only two or three months before termination, it was agreed that Ford would produce one set of masters for use, which would be delivered to San Diego for future spares production at the time Ford terminated B-24 production.

During May 1944, the executive committee decided that final termination of San Diego's B-24 production would end in April 1945 and Fort Worth in December 1944. With the termination of Consolidated's B-24 production prior to that at Ford and North American, Consolidated was to have the continued responsibility for accuracy of engineering data and information used by all B-24 producers. The executive committee decided that contractors producing Liberators when San Diego production was scheduled to terminate, would provide data to Consolidated to permit this prime contractor to continue its engineering responsibilities.

During its existence, the B-24 Committee encountered many problems, criticisms, and recommendations for improvement. Having only one committee was considered unsatisfactory because this committee was mainly interested in only one phase of the program and had no direct control over the methods used in other departments of the contractor plants. With committees composed of members from each department of a plant, the necessary adaptations to the program could be made by direct consultation between sub-committees without resorting to the executive committee, which was necessary when a single sub-committee attempted to carry out work not directly related to its own. The biggest problem with the B-24 program was that possible difficulties were not anticipated and rectified in advance and action was taken only after problems had occurred and rectified at considerable cost in time and money. In any future program, it was considered to be beneficial to inaugurate the committee system at the beginning of the program and that any future committees should also include specific sub-committees for tooling, inspection, purchasing, spares, contracts, etc. as required, as well as engineering. The members of these committees would all collaborate, preferably in the same offices.

3

B-24 and Knock-Down Kit Contracts

Consolidated Contracts

During the latter part of 1933, the Army Air Corps asked Consolidated to consider the building of Boeing's B-17 to provide two four-engined bomber sources. Consolidated San Diego sent representatives to Boeing's Seattle Plant in to explore the feasibility of this proposal. After their return, Consolidated determined that the B-17 design was obsolete and that the construction method would be difficult to use in their shop. Using its experience gained in building flying boats for the Navy, early in 1939, Consolidated submitted a proposal for building the XB-24.

Based on Consolidated's decision, the Army requested that the company supply preliminary designs and quotations for their new bomber. Work was immediately underway, and when completed in January 1939, the proposal was sent to Wright Field. Negotiated contract (W-535-ac-12436) was agreed upon in February 1939 and March 1939 for one prototype, one wind tunnel model, and one mock-up at a total cost of $2 million. The prototype was to be delivered in December 1939. This fixed-price contract was immediately followed on 26 April 1939 by contract No. W-535-ac-12464, calling for seven additional B-24s at a total cost of $2,330,000, including approximately 13 percent spares. Delivery was to begin with one bomber in May 1940 and one per month thereafter until completion.

During the early stages of production on the above contracts, the French government negotiated with Consolidated for the procurement of 139 "B-24-type airplanes" and signed a contract for this amount on 4 June 1940. This is considered the first real production contract as all preceding contracts were too small in quantity to enable the contractor to use production breakdowns to any extent. After the French capitulation, the British assumed the French contract aircraft as the LB-30. Then to aid the beleaguered British, the initial output was diverted to them by the AAC.

Contingent on satisfactory performance of the aforementioned contracts, and as additional appropriations became available, a large-scale production program for B-24-type airplanes was planned as evidenced by additional fixed-price orders outlined below.

Contract W-535-ac-13281 approved on 20 September 1939 called for the delivery of 138 B-24-type airplanes at a total cost of $8,613,674 including $123,274 for structural parts and test data at a unit cost of $223,300, with the following delivery schedule: one aircraft during October 1940; one during November 1940; two during December 1940; two during January 1941; three during February 1941; four during March 1941; four during April 1941; five during May 1941; five during June 1941; five during July 1941; and balance of six in August 1941.

Considering the combat experience gained by the British up to that time, certain improvements—such as leak-proof tanks, turbo-superchargers, and power turrets—were required by the Army; therefore, Change Order No. 5 to this contract, dated 24 June 1941, was issued to incorporate approximately 7 percent spare parts and redesignate the aircraft as the B-24D. This subsequently became the first production article for combat use after U.S. entry into the war. This change order increased the number of aircraft by fifty-six for a total of ninety-four, with an increase in total cost, including spares, of $13,704,343, or a unit cost of $228,405. This change order further revised the entire delivery schedule to be as follows: four aircraft during November 1940: five during December 1940; seven during January 1941; eight during February 1941; eight during March 1941; eight during April 1941; four during May 1941; seven during June 1941; ten during July 1941; 13 during August 1941; sixteen during September 1941; and balance of four in October 1941.

Contract W-535-ac-16005 approved on 20 September 1940 called for the delivery of 352 B-24s at a total cost of $85,006,000, including approximately 5 percent spares, at a unit cost of $230,000 with a delivery schedule as follows: fourteen aircraft during August 1941; twenty-nine during September 1941; thirty-two during October 1941; twenty-seven during November 1941; thirty during December 1941; twenty-six during January 1942; thirty-three during February 1942; thirty-three during March 1941; thirty-two during April 1942; thirty-two during May 1942; thirty-two during June 1942; and balance of thirty-two in July 1942.

Contract DA-W-535-ac-4; approved on 31 May 1941 called for the delivery of 700 B-24Ds at a total cost of $226,636,200, including approximately 17 percent spares at a unit cost of $269,605, with a delivery schedule as follows: fifteen aircraft during December 1942; thirty-five during January 1942; and thirty-five per month thereafter until completion of the contract.

Contract W-535-ac-24620 approved on 26 February 1942 called for the delivery of 1,200 B-24Ds at a total cost of $329,444,515.80 including approximately 13 percent spares at a unit cost of $238,727.91, with a delivery schedule as follows: forty-five aircraft during March 1943; 100 during April 1943; and 100 per month thereafter until completion of the contract.

Contract W-535-ac-30l46l approved on 6 July 1942 called for the delivery of 750 B-24Ds at a total cost of $150,937, 500 including approximately 13 percent spares at a unit cost of $175,000 with a delivery schedule as follows: ninety aircraft during September 1943; 136 during October 1943; and 136 per month thereafter until completion.

Contract W535ac-35312 approved on 30 November 1942 called for the delivery of 900 B-24Ds at a total cost of $181,125,000, including approximately 13 percent spares at a unit cost of $175,000, with a delivery schedule as follows: sixty-one aircraft during November 1943; 200 during December 1943; 210 during January 1944; 220 during February 1944; 209 during March 1944. Later, contractor voluntarily reduced the unit cost per plane to $139,000.

Joint Contracts: Consolidated San Diego and Fort Worth, Douglas and North American

Contract W-535-ac-40033 (approved on 4 February 1944) superseded letter contract dated 14 April 1944 and supplement dated 21 May 1943 and called for the delivery of 4,500 B-24Js (to be produced jointly by the San Diego and Fort Worth Divisions of Consolidated). This was at a total cost of $712,465,500, including approximately 13 percent spares, and also including the provision that the contractor was to furnish all special tools and ground handling equipment necessary to properly service B-24Js then being produced by Douglas Tulsa; North American Dallas; and Ford Motors at Willow Run, which amounted to $3,493,500 of the above stated amount. The unit cost of these airplanes was $137,000 with a delivery schedule as follows: 111 aircraft during February 1944; 275 during March 1944; 255 during April 1944; 268 during May 1944; 257 during June 1944; 251 during July 1944; 256 during August 1944; and 240 per month thereafter until completion of the contract.

It is to be noted that although the above contracts were awarded in sufficient numbers (except in the very beginning) to preclude gaps in the slowly growing production line, company policy dictated that the planning must always be ahead of contract issuance in order to meet anticipated schedules subsequently imposed upon production lines as the war progressed.

Generally speaking, contractual matters were very satisfactory to Consolidated, except for the question of spare parts, where company records indicate that at no time in the war was the contractor fully covered by approved spare parts lists to the extent necessary to insure payment for services rendered while at the same time being required to furnish parts that were crucially needed in combat without contract approval. At one time, approximately $6 million worth of spare parts had been shipped and payment could not be made because of the lack of contractual coverage.

The change in the bomber from the B-24D model to the B-24J came in time for delivery of 551 of the latter to be made against contrast AC-3041. Likewise, 500 B-24Js were delivered to the Army against contract AC-35312; 400 PB-Y2s were delivered to the Navy in this same contract.

On a previous contract, AC-16005, forty-seven airplanes were delivered by San Diego as knock-down sets. On contract DA#4, forty-four sets of knock-downs were delivered and twenty-seven sets were cancelled.

On the final contract, AC-40033, the AAF accepted 2,674 B-24s, in the J, L, and M models, but 585 of these were transferred to the Navy as PB-4Ys. Fabrication of 500 aircraft on this contract were transferred to the Fort Worth plant, of which 453 were actually built The balance of 1,373 aircraft was cancelled by termination of this contract.

Ford Willow Run Contracts

The Ford Motor Company operated under three cost-plus-fixed-fee contracts in building B-24s at Willow Run. Two were War Department contracts with Consolidated and Douglas, respectively, in which Ford was designated the major sub-contractor to furnish knock-down Liberators. The third was Ford's prime contract for the production of complete bombers.

Consolidated-Ford as a Subcontractor Contracts

The War Department contract with Consolidated Aircraft Corporation of San Diego W-535-AC-18723, naming the Ford Motor Company as a major sub-contractor was entered into on 21 May 1941 and called for 600 B-24D bombers, with Ford to furnish knock-down components to Consolidated for final assembly at its Fort Worth plant.

The first delivery schedule was in Supplement Number 1, issued 23 April 1942, which increased the total quantity to 1,400 aircraft. This schedule called for delivery of knock-down kits as follows:

1942: May: one aircraft; June: one; July: six; August: twelve; September: eighteen; October: twenty-four; November: thirty; December: forty-five.
1943: January: sixty-five; February: eighty; March: 100; and 100 each month thereafter.

This contract was an innovation in that an automobile company was to act as a 100 percent sub-contractor for an aircraft company, building its aircraft in knock-down condition for final assembly at another plant. Consolidated had designed the B-24 and was responsible for it from an engineering perspective. Consolidated, as stated by the contract, was to furnish Ford with engineering services and data, three complete sets of Van Dykes of all items, three complete sets of specifications, bills of materials, and parts lists. (A Van Dyke is a hand-coated, contact printing process that is greatly influenced by the paper and toner used for the print. It is a comparatively simple and inexpensive photographic alternative that does not require a darkroom.)

The original supply contract cost for 600 aircraft was estimated at $163,614,000 including a fixed-fee of $5,390,000 or $272,730 per aircraft. The first supplement added 800 aircraft at a unit price of $263,730. The total fixed-fee was set on a 2.6 percent basis. Spares at a cost of $55,337,500 were provided far in the April 1942 supplement. This supplement also recognized that this contract would represent 29 percent of the total output of the Willow Run plant.

The original plan to have Fort Worth receive all of its knock-downs from Willow Run did not prove feasible, and in May 1942, Supplement Number 3 issued to CVAC-Fort Worth called for their San Diego plant to furnish the Fort Worth plant with 150 sets.

Douglas-Ford as a Sub-Contractor Contracts

The War Department Contract with Douglas Aircraft Company of Santa Monica, W-535-AC-l8722, which similarly named the Ford Motor Company as the major sub-contractor, was entered into on 21 May 1941, and called for 600 B-24D bombers in knock-down form. Ford was to furnish these for assembly by Douglas at a government-owned plant in Tulsa, OK, completion date of which was set as 1 January 1942. The contract stated that it confirmed a Letter of Intent dated 8 February 1941.

The first delivery schedule was specified in the original contract and called for delivery of knock-down kits by Ford as follows:

1941: July: one aircraft; August: one; September: six; October: twelve; November: eighteen; December: twenty-four.
1942: January: thirty; February: forty: March: fifty; and fifty each month thereafter

The special stipulations of this contract were the same as those in the Consolidated Contract No. AC-13723, except that only Consolidated was to furnish special engineering data. Consequently, for a like number of aircraft the supply contract costs were cut to $158,850,000 and the fixed-fee reduced to $3,600,000.

The first supplement of 22 April 1942 increased the total to 1,600 aircraft, recognized Ford's prime contract, and set up 33.17 percent as the pro-rated costs of total Willow Run production to be assessed against the Douglas contract. It also advanced the delivery schedule some three months starting with two aircraft in May 1942 and reaching a peak of 155 per month in August 1943.

Among the other early supplements was one providing for the receipt of ten sets of components from Consolidated, San Diego, because of production delays at Willow Run.

Ford Prime Contract

The first Ford Contract, W-535-AC-18061, which was approved 9 April 1941, was essentially an educational order for one B-24; the estimated cost was $3,418,500.

Ford's working contract for complete B-24s to be assembled and delivered at the Willow Run plant was W-535-AG-21216. This contract was not formally approved until 14 October 1941, although a Letter of Intent had been sent to Ford in June of that year. The contract specified 795 complete B-24E bombers plus an estimated 10 percent spare parts.

The delivery was scheduled as follows:

1942: September: one; October: one; November: two; December: four.
1943: January: six; February: seven; March: nineteen; April: twelve; May: fifteen; June: twenty-five; July: thirty-six; August: fifty; September: sixty-five; October: seventy-five; and seventy-five each month there after

The contract provided that the plants to be furnished by Ford were to Consolidated's specifications as reported 18 March 1941 ED-32-009. The aircraft were to be manufactured concurrently with and by means of the same facilities used for the Consolidated and Douglas sub-contracts on which Ford was to furnish knock-downs. No changes were to be made on the Ford aircraft unless the change was also made on knock-downs being furnished to Consolidated and Douglas.

The aircraft were estimated to cost $250,000 each with the total cost estimated at $231,742,500 with 10 percent spares and a fixed-fee of 6 percent or about $13 million. Tooling and pre-production costs already expended were recognized as reimbursable under the contract.

The contract provided in detail the engineering and technical data that Consolidated was to furnish Ford and also provided for the training and work of 150 employees at the San Diego plant.

One of the most important changes in the Ford prime contract was supplement No. 9, which provided $50 million for otherwise unallocated changes. This supplement, which created an open-end contract, enabled Ford to do anything approved by the contracting officer not originally specified, such as converting GFE affected by engineering changes, etc. It was originally drawn up to cover the redistribution of large quantities of critical raw materials and parts which Ford had accumulated by mid-1942 as production acceleration fell below expectations.

The supplement was executed on 23 June 1943, although by that time it had the informal approval from Wright Field, Ford had already shipped $13 million worth of raw materials and parts to other aircraft manufacturers and in effect had become a central warehouse for the B-24 program. By 30 April 1945, $20 million of the supplement's authorized $50 million had been expended. At one time, Ford had 155 employees engaged in clerical work under this supplement alone.

Many other supplements and contract changes were issued from time to time and as more aircraft were purchased, both the price and fixed-fee were reduced

PART III

Consolidated San Diego and Fort Worth B-24 Plants

Section 1: Consolidated San Diego

Over the years, the Consolidated San Diego Plant, the original Liberator manufacturer, has been greatly over-shadowed by the immense and well-publicized Ford Willow Run B-24 Plant. When Ford Production Chief Charles Sorensen first visited the Consolidated San Diego production line in preparation to build the Willow Run Plant for producing Ford Liberators, he compared Consolidated's production methods to that of Ford producing the Model A some thirty-five years previously.

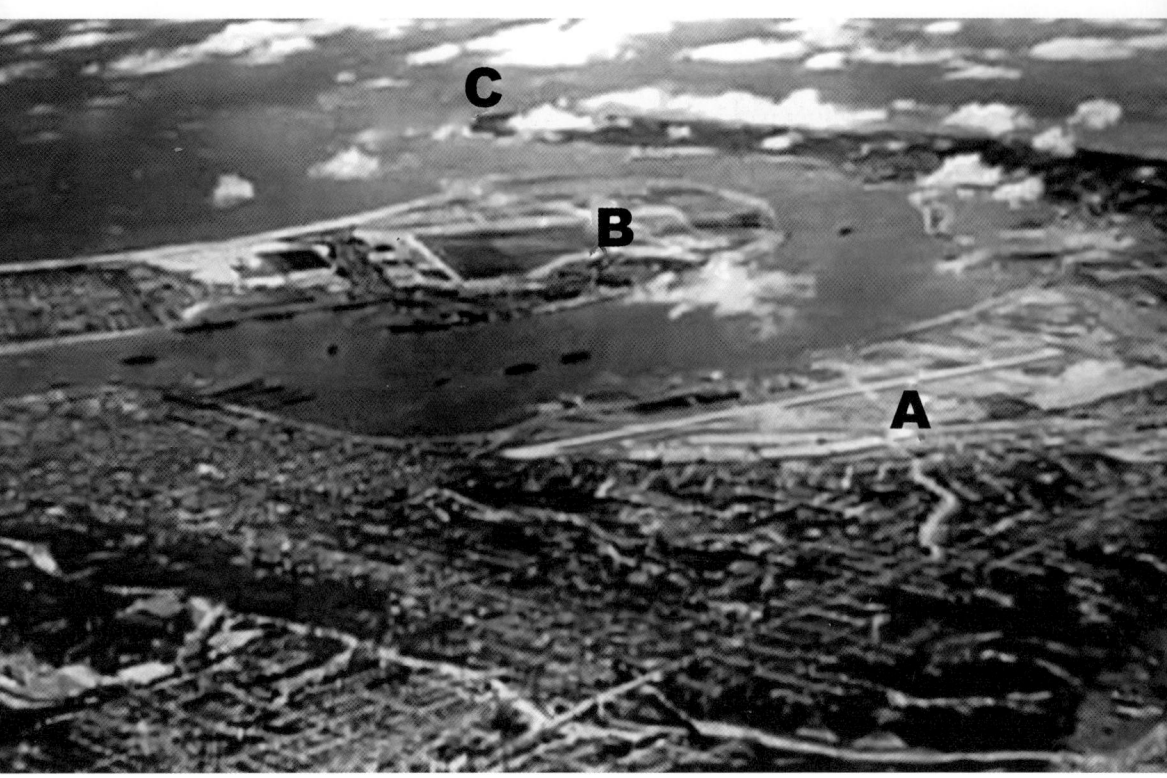

San Diego Bay Area late 1930s: (A) Lindbergh Field/Consolidated factory area, (B) North Island Naval Air Station, (C) Point Loma. (*ATSC*)

Opposite above: The original plant, called Building One, covered 247,000 square feet of continuous flow along the Pacific Coast Highway and Lindbergh Field. (*ATSC*)

Opposite below: Bayside/Lindbergh Field view of Building One showing apron with two parked PBYs (foreground), the Model 31 (top left), PB2Y-1 Ranger (middle center), and a PG2Y-2 Coronado (top right). (*ATSC*)

Part III: Consolidated San Diego and Fort Worth B-24 Plants

1

Developing the San Diego Facility

The Original Plant

The initial plant, originally called Building One, covered 247,000 square feet of continuous flow along the Pacific Coast Highway and included an unfinished parking lot and a landing field that at the time were grassy tracks. By the time of the open house in October 1936, attended by 30,000, Building One was ready for the production of the PBY.

Plant Expansion

Beginning with a completely integrated but small aircraft plant in the fall of 1939, Consolidated grew in three major expansion programs and several minor ones. The first two major programs expanded the then existing facilities to Plant #1 and the third program resulted in Plant #2.

Program	Date	Area Added	Cumulative Plant Area
1st Major Expansion	1939–40	410,000	1,000,000
2nd Major Expansion	1940–41	663,000	1,663,000
3rd Major Expansion	1941–42	1,700,000	3,363,000
Administration Bldg.	1942	157,000	3,520, 000
Plant #1 Addition	1943	10,000	3,530,000
Plant #2 Addition	1944	176,000	3,706,000
Miscellaneous	----	473,000	4,179,000

Early Planning

By 1939, it was obvious that the entire American aircraft industry was gearing up for wartime expansion. European countries, wary of Nazi military expansion, particularly the *Luftwaffe*, were contracting for American warplanes. Meanwhile, the Air Corps and Navy air services were becoming increasing aware of their current second-rate status in aircraft quantity and quality and the associated threat to national security and were planning for expansion and negotiating for increased procurement of modern and superior warplanes.

At the time, Consolidated had been involved in the production of flying boats, and when the Navy decided to acquire additional flying boats in the fall of 1939, Consolidated was contracted for 200 PBY Catalinas which was considered a substantial order. Consequently, it became evident that the existing Consolidated Plant would have to be expanded. Later expansions were planned and implemented as the necessity arose.

First Expansion

The architectural firm of Taylor and Taylor of Los Angeles was selected to prepare plans and specifications for the new buildings because of Consolidated's previous good experience and that these architects were thoroughly familiar with Consolidated's requirements. Taylor and Taylor was headed by brothers Edward Cray Taylor and Ellis Wing Taylor, but it was Ellis Wing, married to silent film actress Anne Cornwall, who became renowned as the designer of the Douglas aircraft plant in Long Beach. The architect was retained on 1 October 1939 to prepare plans and specifications for the general structure only and to furnish architectural supervision of the constructions. By 31 January 1940, all plans and specifications for general structures were completed and released for bids.

Meanwhile, plans and specifications for the mechanical trades, electrical, plumbing, heating, monorail, etc. were prepared by Consolidated's Plant engineering department. Detailed inspection of the construction work was also supervised by the corporation's engineers and inspectors.

Competitive bids were accepted on most of the project with the initial proposals covering the complete project. However, individual fixed-price contracts were let for the various phases of the work and Consolidated acted as general contractor in letting these contracts and in supervising and coordinating the construction operations.

Negotiations associated with the financing of this expansion were conducted over an extended period. The expansion was begun under a "closing agreement," which was approved in the fall of 1939 but after Consolidated had committed itself. This was subsequently changed to a Certificate of Necessity covering all work performed subsequently to 10 June 1940 and this was later modified by an additional Certificate of Necessity that covered all work performed after 1 January 1940 but previous to 10 June 1940. A final Certificate of Necessity was not issued until sometime after 1 January 1943.

This expansion consisted of a new assembly building, a new paint building for the final finishing of completely assembled bombers, additions to existing buildings, the erection of mezzanines in existing buildings and miscellaneous smaller service buildings, such as boiler house, storage sheds, etc.

At the time of the construction program, there was no government priority control, building materials were still available, and the design was suitable for quick construction so that there were no delays other than those commonly faced in any program of this large scale.

Because this type and method of construction required the use of floor space exclusively for construction purposes, it was necessary to wait for the completion of the facilities before they could be occupied and production could begin. Canvas covered shelters were used temporarily for manufacturing operations in the meantime.

The first major expansion, costing approximately $2,150,000, amounted to an additional area of 140,000 square feet, which increased the total plant area to nearly 1 million square feet. The approximate completion of construction and occupation of facilities and start of manufacturing operations was to be 1 August 1940.

Chronology of the Highlights of the First Expansion

Date	Event
10/1/1939	Taylor and Taylor selected as architects
10/31	Bids obtained on structural steel plans
12/6	Foundation drawings released for bids
1/15/1940	Excavation for footing on first building begun
1/31	All plans and specifications for general structure released for bids
2/13	General structure bids received
2/15	Electrical plans and specifications released for bids
2/16	Steel sash proposals received
2/29	Electrical bids received
3/6	Erection of steel in first building begun
3/14	Heating and ventilating plans and specifications released for bids
3/20	Plumbing and heating bids received
4/8	Erection of steel in assembly buildings begun
8/1	Approximate completion of construction
8/1	Approximate occupation of facility and start of manufacturing

First Expansion: This first major expansion, costing approximately $2,150,000, added 140,000 square feet, increasing the total plant area to nearly 1 million square feet. (*ATSC*)

Second Expansion

This expansion was divided into two parts, the first being a large assembly building, 200 feet by 1,500 feet (Building #4), and the second being another large assembly building, 360 feet by 720 feet (Building #3), an office building, additions to the boiler house and paint shop, and various other small structures.

Two firms, one for each part, were retained to design and supervise this expansion program. National Iron Works, San Diego, was selected to manage the first part on 2 April 1940 and Taylor and Taylor, Los Angeles, was selected as the architect on the second on 1 August 1940; final drawings were completed on 23 September. The purpose of this division was to compare construction under an engineer contractor agreement, with construction completed by sending out complete plans and specifications prepared by an architect and obtaining competitive bids from contractors. The major portion of the work was performed under cost-plus-a fixed-fee contracts.

The original plan was to utilize Building #1 for parts manufacturing, but after the preliminary design was completed, it was decided that the building would be used for assembly operations, which necessitated an increase of 10 feet in clear truss height. No other major design changes were made in this program.

The project was begun under a Navy-sponsored Emergency Plant Facilities Contract, which was later changed to a Certificate of Necessity. This program was begun six months before final government approval and at least three months before any financing agreement with the government.

As in the first major expansion, there were no building material priorities or no delays in construction other than those normally encountered except that a shipload of structural steel was sunk near New Orleans, and it was necessary to make some substitutions of steel section in order to prevent a delay in the fabrication of structural steel. Because of the type and method of construction, occupancy of the buildings was not practical until they were virtually completed, necessitating the use of some temporary structures for manufacturing operations.

This expansion increased the area of the plant by 663,000 square feet and the cost of the project was approximately $2,370,000 with the approximate completion of construction and occupation of facilities and start of manufacturing operations on 1 February 1941.

Chronology of the Highlights of the Second Expansion

Date	Event
4/2/1940	Engineer contractor selected for Assembly Bldg. #4
5/8	Design drawings for Building #4 completed
7/5	Decision made to increase ceiling height from 20 to 30 feet
8/1	Taylor and Taylor selected for Assembly Bldg. #4 and small bldgs.
8/15	CPFF proposals on Buildings #3 and #4 received
8/19	Construction drawings for Building #4 complete
9/10	Proposals on Paint Shop received
9/23	Architect's final drawings completed
October	Final Government approval on entire project received
10/2	Building #3 pile driving begun
10/5	Proposals for Plant Engineering Building received
10/20	Proposals for Tool and Die Fixture Building received
10/23	First structural steel erected (Bldg. #4)
11/3	Structural steel erected (Bldg. #3)
12/12	Proposals on service tunnel received
12/13	Proposals on Boiler addition received
2/1/1941	Approximate completion of construction
2/1	Approximate occupation of facility and start of manufacturing

Third Expansion

In this expansion, Plant #2 was an entirely new facility and consisted of the following buildings: three major manufacturing buildings, 400 by 750 feet; paint shop, 100 by 400 feet; boiler and compressor house, 80 by 125 feet; two-story shipping building 100 by 400 feet; two-story office building, 50 by 750 feet; three-story drop-hammer building, 80 by 250 feet. These facilities were designed and used for the production of major assembly parts.

Second Expansion: This expansion increased the area of the plant by 663,000 square feet and the cost of the project was approximately $2,370,000. (*ATSC*)

Erection of assembly building during the second expansion. (*ATSC*)

The firm of Taylor and Taylor was again selected as the architects for this program. Proposals, covering the complete project except for the fill and grading of the site and based on preliminary drawings and specifications, were received from several contractors with a separate contract let for this work.

After the delivery of the general proposals and the award of the contract, it was decided to remove the fabricating and erecting of the structural steel from the general contract and process this work under a separate agreement. The general contract was cost-plus-a-fixed-fee, and the structural steel contract was on the basis of a price-per-ton.

Negotiations concerning the financing of this expansion extended over approximately two months. The entire plant was constructed and equipped under a Navy-sponsored Defense Plant Corporation (DPC) Lease Agreement. During the summer of 1940, the entire Consolidated San Diego facilities were allocated to the Navy for administration and control by mutual agreement.

During the entire construction program, building materials of all kinds became more and more difficult to obtain, and in an attempt to control the use of these materials, priorities were first assigned in the early part of 1941. These priorities probably did not accelerate the delivery of construction materials although the system undoubtedly did help in procuring certain materials, which otherwise would have been unavailable.

There were two main causes of construction delay: bad weather and the late deliveries of fabricated structural steel. The first delay of seventeen days in completing foundations was caused by the extremely heavy rainfall in February 1941, which transformed the plant site and surrounding area into a 2-foot-deep pond. The second delay was caused by the local structural steel contractor who placed an order for steel with a Pittsburgh mill whose schedules were full. The mill apparently favored eastern over western companies, as steel delivery was held up three months and the AAF lost fifty bombers before February 1942 as a result. It was eventually necessary to send an expeditor to the mill and keep him there until all the steel had been shipped.

Buildings were occupied as soon as construction permitted with a minimum use made of temporary facilities. However, a large hydro-press was placed in operation before completion of its building by the erection of a local temporary housing. Throughout the war, an important though never very large part of all San Diego operations had to be completed under temporary canvas shelters,

This expansion increased the area of the San Diego facilities by 1,700,000 square feet at a cost of approximately $11 million. The first building was completed and occupied on 15 October 1941; complete plant operation occurred on 15 January 1942; and the completion of the entire project occurred in June.

Chronology of the Highlights of the Third Expansion

Date	Event
8/1/1940	Site selected
9/10	Taylor and Taylor Architects selected
10/31	DPC financial approval received
11/9	Preliminary Drawings completed
11/16	DPC Lease Agreement approved
11/20	CPFF proposals on buildings received
11/27	Site fill and grading contract approved
12/2	Filling of site begun
2/1941	Priorities on building materials assigned
4/11	First structural steel erected
10/15	First building completed and occupied
1/15/1942	Complete Plant operation begun
6/1942	Completion of the San Diego Plant Project

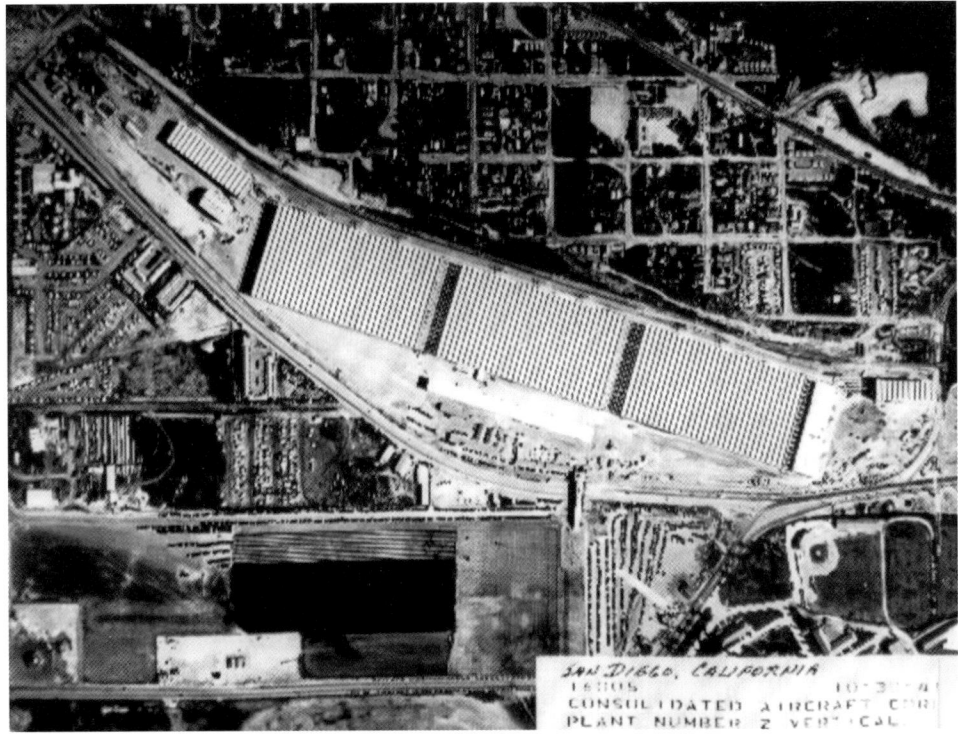

Third Expansion: This expansion greatly increased the area of the San Diego facilities by 1.7 million square feet at a cost of approximately $11 million. (*ATSC*)

Additional Expansions

In addition to the major expansion programs, there were smaller expansions that were continually in development. A company financed administrative office building was started in April 1942, but due to a four-month delay in steel deliveries and additional delays of other critical materials, it was not completed until March 1943. This building was a seven-story reinforced concrete structure, 140 by 140 feet, with a basement, an executive dining room, and rooftop penthouse. This building was designed and built without windows and used fluorescent lighting throughout and for an air cooling system utilized the largest steam-jet air conditioning unit in the U.S. This building had a floor space of approximately 157,000 square feet and cost $1.3 million.

In the spring of 1943, a Navy-sponsored emergency plant facilities expansion was embarked on, which was costly at $3 million and added only a small area. The expansion was mainly machinery and sprinkler equipment with only a few thousand square feet added as sheds, mezzanines, and small additions to existing working spaces.

Beginning in spring 1944 and finishing a year later, Consolidated, along with the City of San Diego and the USMC base, improved the existing facilities at Lindbergh Field and increased the length of the main runway to 8,500 feet at a combined total cost of approximately $3 million largely company financed.

Meanwhile, additional Plant #2 expansions were being completed as miscellaneous buildings, manufacturing, and service and storage areas, amounting to 176,000 square feet. This increased the Plant #2 area to 1,876,215 square feet, which added to the Plant #1 area of 2,303,469 square feet, resulting in a total area at San Diego of 4,179,711 square feet.

2

The San Diego Plant

The San Diego Division of Consolidated-Vultee Aircraft Corporation consisted of two plants that were designed and built by the company in part for general use with company funds and in part for the B-24 Project with Defense Plant Corporation funds. These two plants were located along Route 101, Pacific Highway, north of the San Diego business district. Plant #1 was approximately 1.5 miles north of the business district and was located along the east side of Lindbergh Field on San Diego Bay, 20 miles from the Mexican border. Plant #2 was approximately one mile north of Plant #1 and was located between Pacific Highway and the AT and SF Railroad right-of-way. All of the buildings of both plants were located on filled ground. The total area of Plants #1 and #2, Feeder Plants, and warehouses was 4,493,716 square feet.

Description of the San Diego Property

Location and Access
Plant #1 was located on both sides of Pacific Highway; the section west of the highway was occupied by manufacturing, experimental, and miscellaneous buildings; the section lying east of the highway was occupied by the seven-story administration building and parking lots. Two pedestrian overpasses spanned the highway, providing traffic-free connections between the two areas. This plant, valued at $19 million, was owned by Consolidated-Vultee.

The area comprising Plant #2 was also located on both sides of Pacific Highway; the section lying east of the highway was occupied by manufacturing, administration, and warehouse buildings; the section lying west of the highway was occupied by the salvage yard, storage yard, and parking lots. One pedestrian overpass spanned the highway, providing a traffic-free connection between the two areas. This plant was owned by Defense Plant Corporation and was valued at $22.84 million, roughly one-half of which was machinery and equipment.

The manufacturing areas of the two plants were connected by a private hard surface road that crossed Pacific Highway at the south end of Plant #2 by a concrete vehicular

Early 1944 view looking southwest of Plants One and Two. (*ATSC*)

Early 1944 view looking northeast of Plants One and Two with Lindbergh Field and seaplane base evident. (*ATSC*)

overpass and ran parallel to and on the west side of Pacific Highway between the highway and the Marine Corps base.

Overhead monorail type cranes served the main manufacturing areas in the buildings at both plants. In addition, the monorail systems within the buildings were connected by outside monorail trackage to the monorail systems in the adjoining manufacturing buildings.

The major manufacturing buildings at both plants were of steel frame construction, with corrugated sheet metal siding and roofing that was of saw tooth-type construction. The columns of all the buildings at Plant #1, except Building #1, were supported on driven steel piling while the floor slabs laid on the filled grounds. The columns as well as the floor slabs of the buildings at Plant #2 rested on driven steel piling.

Plant #1 Complex

There were fourteen main manufacturing buildings at Plant #1. The first of these buildings was 1,000 feet long (north to south) and 300 feet wide (east to west) with an addition built on the west side starting from the south end of the building. This west addition measured 550 feet long (north to south) by 150 feet wide (east to west). The south 275-foot section of the west addition had a second floor 16.7 feet above the main floor level while the north section of this addition was 200 feet long and was divided east and west into three 50-foot-long, 30-foot-high bays. The remaining 75 feet of the west addition was a clear span with a height of 30 feet. Columns were spaced throughout the building at 25-foot centers except in the two-story section at the southwest corner where columns are spaced 16.7 feet on centers. Starting from the east side of the building, there were two 100-foot-long and 114-foot-high bays and one 100-foot-long and 30-foot-high bay.

The second and third Plant #1 buildings were 360 feet (east to west) by 720 feet (north to south) with a 36-foot ceiling height. The buildings were divided east to west into three 120-foot bays. The columns along the east walls of these buildings were spaced on 30-foot centers. The two intermediate rows of columns were spaced on 60-foot centers and along the west walls they were spaced at 120-foot centers. In the west walls of each of these buildings there were four door openings each 118.8 feet wide by 36 feet high and two door openings 88.8 feet wide by 36 feet high. The south walls of each of the buildings had two door openings 118.8 feet wide by 36 feet high. One of these buildings had a door opening in the north wall 115 feet by 36 feet high.

The fourth building was 200 feet (east to west) by 1,500 feet (north to south) with 30 feet height and 26-foot crane clearance. The building was divided into two 100-foot bays (east to west) with columns spaced on 25-foot centers. There were two door openings on each end of the building of 92.8 feet wide by 30 feet high. There are four door openings in the east wall 48.8 feet wide by 30 feet high and 23.8 feet wide by 30 feet high. These door openings were closed by 12.5-foot-wide hangar-type doors that rolled on 12-inch-diameter wheels on standard tracks. The doors extended the full height of the openings and were guided by standard rolling door guides.

These four buildings, supplemented by office, engineering, experimental, storage, and miscellaneous buildings, as well as three cafeterias, comprised a total building area of 2,303,486 square feet. In addition, there was a yard and parking area of 1,072,211 square feet.

Plant #1 Buildings

1	Main Factory Building	17	Fire Station
2	Assembly Building #1	18	High Altitude Test Lab
3	Assembly Building #2	19	Administration Building
4	Major Parts Assembly	20	Garage
5	Experimental Building	21	Air Tech
6	Wood Mill	22	North Ryan Building
7	Storage Shed	23	South Ryan Building
8	Final Finish	24	Ryan Administration Building
9	Boiler House	25	Employment Office
10	Wood Shop	26	Cafeteria #1
11	Acetylene Generator	27	Cafeteria #2
12	Bump Hammer	28	Cafeteria #3
13	Tool and Die Storage	29	Educational Building
14	Plant Engineering Bldg.		
15	Hospital		
16	Personnel Office		

Wind Tunnel   (Not part of Plant #1 but built at same time)

Plant 1 Complex. (*ATSC*)

Plant #2 Complex

There were three main manufacturing buildings at Plant #2; measuring 400 feet (east to west) and 750 feet (north to south) with a 36-foot ceiling height and 32-foot spans clearance. The buildings were divided east and west into four 100-foot bays with columns spaced on 25-foot centers. The buildings were arranged end to end, with 100-foot spaces between served by continuous tramways, in a north and south direction. An addition, 75 feet north to south by 300 feet east to west, was added to the north end of the northernmost of the three buildings. The east walls of each of these buildings had three door openings 48.8 feet wide by 36 feet high. In the north and south walls of the south and center building and in the south wall of the north building, there were two door openings 98.8 feet wide by 36 feet high, two door openings 85 feet wide by 36 feet high, and one door opening 72 feet wide by 36 feet high. In the north wall of the north building there was one door opening 93.8 feet wide by 36 feet high.

In addition to these three buildings, there was a 100-foot by 400-fot paint shop; a three- story drop hammer building, 80 by 240 feet; a two-story warehouse and shipping building, 100 by 400 feet; a two-story office building, 90 by 750 feet; a boiler and compressor building; warehouses; three cafeterias; and other miscellaneous buildings comprising a total building area of 1,876,215 square feet. For service, there was yard, salvage, storage, and, a parking lot area of 1,374,943 square feet. There was adequate administrative and shop office space, cafeteria and dining room facilities, toilets, and rest rooms, training areas, special testing facilities, and automobile parking space.

The plants were originally designed and built for the production of large two- and four-engined naval aircraft and were readily adapted for production of the B-24. However, for the later very heavy bombers such as the B-32 and B-36, these present clearances were not sufficient for economical operations.

Plant #2 Buildings

1	Assembly	10	Maintenance Building
2	Assembly	11–21	Warehouses
3	Assembly and Machine Shop	22	Unnamed Building
4	Office Building	23	Wood Storage Shed
5	Boiler House	24	Education Building (Larson Bldg.)
6	Warehouse	25	Identification Office
7	Paint Shop	26	Cafeteria #1
8	Hammer House	27	Cafeteria #2
9	Garage	28	Cafeteria #3

Plant 2 Complex. (*ATSC*)

Factory Camouflage

Lt. Gen. John De Witt, in command of the Western Defense Command, was assigned to implement "passive defense measures" for all vital installations along the Pacific Coast. De Witt was also to be responsible for the relocation and internment of American-born Japanese citizens from the West Coast. Col. John Ohmer, who commanded a camouflage training center at March Field east of Los Angeles, was a pioneer in camouflage, deception, and misdirection methods. In late 1940, during the Battle of Britain, Ohmer had been in England and observed how carefully crafted and situated camouflage caused the *Luftwaffe* to drop thousands of tons of bombs on empty fields.

Due to his proximity to Hollywood, Ohmer was able to enlist aid from the movie studios and their set designers, painters, carpenters, landscape artists, and their lighting and prop departments. Ohmer's first mission was to employ Hollywood techniques to camouflage thirty-four air bases with replica foliage and structural cover and also to conceal important factories and assembly plants that would be likely targets for a possible Japanese carrier-borne air attack on the Pacific Coast. Camouflaged aircraft manufacturing facilities included the Los Angeles area Douglas Aircraft plant in Long Beach and the Lockheed-Vega aircraft plant in Burbank and the San Diego Consolidated and Boeing Seattle Aircraft plants.

The San Diego plant had 1.5 million square feet of netting covering the factory area while 1.2 million square feet covered outdoor parking and assembly space. The Consolidated Plant never was camouflaged to the detail or extent of the Douglas, Lockheed-Vega, or Boeing plants, which were mostly covered by netting and completely concealed beneath a complete suburban motif including rubber automobiles and peaceful rural neighborhood scenes painted on canvas. Hundreds of fake trees and shrubs were situated to give a three-dimensional presence. To give the "suburb" an active appearance to any possible enemy aerial reconnaissance observation fake automobiles were occasionally relocated and people appeared on top of the camouflage netting through hidden trap doors and appeared to take walks on hidden catwalks and pretended to do maintenance work. Test observation flights over these camouflaged areas showed that the camouflage was quite effective as pilots were unable to identify the bases, and factories. As the war continued and the threat of Japanese invasion subsided, especially after the Battle of Midway in June 1942 when the Navy neutralized the Japanese carrier force, the camouflage would be eventually removed.

Erecting camouflage netting. (*ATSC*)

Opposite above: Netting over factory area: The San Diego plant had 1.5 million square feet of netting covering the factory area. (*ATSC*)

Opposite below: Netting over open area: The San Diego plant had 1.2 million square feet covering outdoor parking and assembly space. (*ATSC*)

Part III: Consolidated San Diego and Fort Worth B-24 Plants 205

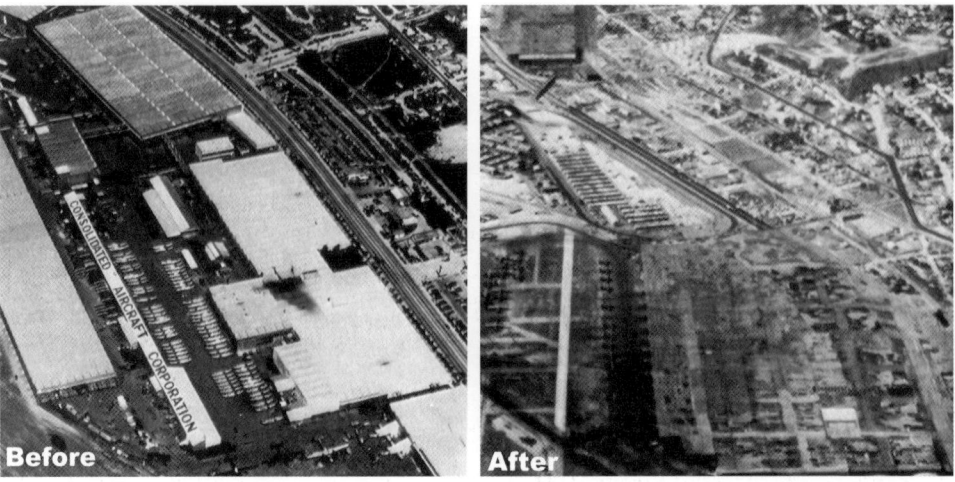

Factory Camouflage: before and after. (*ATSC*)

Airfields

The plant was situated on and used the facilities of the municipally-owned Lindbergh Field, which was the commercial airline airfield for San Diego. This field had two concrete landing strips of sufficient length and design strength to allow their use by modern, very heavy bombers. In addition and adjacent to the field there was a large marine ramp on San Diego Bay for the launching of amphibious aircraft and flying boats.

Lindbergh Field 1929–1944

Lindbergh Field, 1929. (*ATSC*)

Lindbergh Field, 1936. (*ATSC*)

Lindbergh Field, 1943, with seaplane base. (*ATSC*)

Lindbergh Field, late 1944. (*ATSC*)

Factory apron. (*ATSC*)

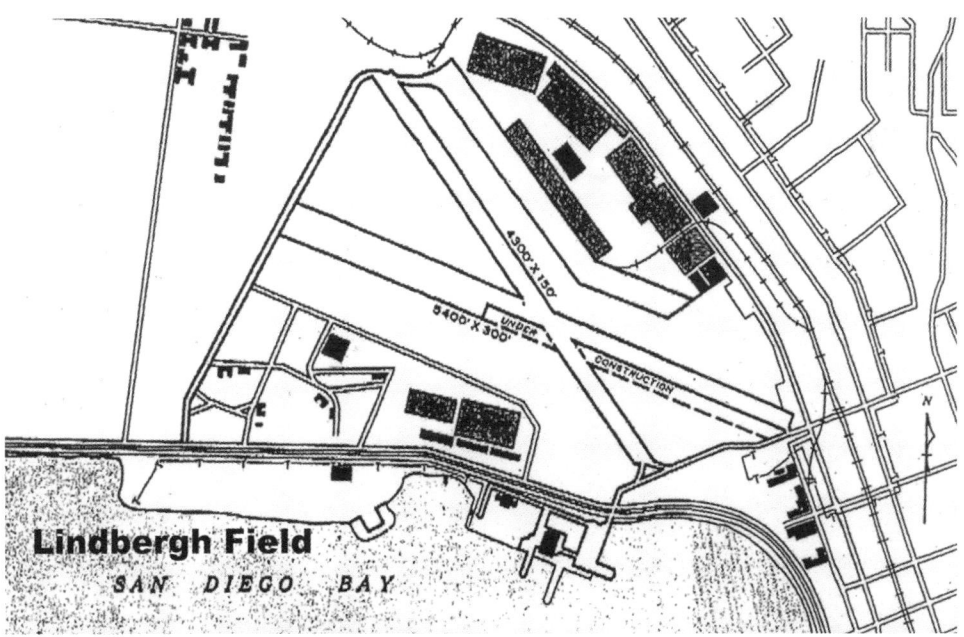

Lindbergh Field 1945, post-war.

Roads and Railways

The facility was adjacent to the Atchison, Topeka, and Santa Fe RR main line had 2,000 feet of spur tracks running into both Plants #1 and #2. The San Diego and Arizona Eastern RR also used the tracks. The public Pacific Coast Highway (Route 101) ran between Plant #1 and #2 was a modern divided six-lane highway artery connecting San Diego and Los Angeles. Adequate bus service to and from the plant was available.

FACTORY ROADS AND RAILWAYS

Above: Pacific Coast Highway passing in front of Building One. (*ATSC*)

Below: Public Transport: Overpass to buses and private car parking lot. (*ATSC*)

Above: Plant Two: Pacific Coast Highway with a modern overpass and a rail spur behind the facility. (*ATSC*)

Below: Rail Access: Atchison, Topeka, and Santa RR spur into Building Seven (note overhead camo netting). (*ATSC*)

Utilities and Services

Public utility companies furnished the gas and electricity, the latter being generated at Boulder Dam with a local steam plant used as emergency and peak activity standby. The buildings were lighted by both incandescent and fluorescent lights. Water and sewage services were furnished by the municipality and all service connections were single although they were backed up by standby capacity. The water supply proved to be barely adequate during peak operations and additional sources (Boulder Dam) were required to safeguard future peak operations.

Management

Consolidated published this rather saccharine overview of its management in its company magazine:

> First the company, then the Corporation, and the Division, but always the man who started the job with additions, changes, and subtractions worked continually at the job of getting B-24s to the flight line generally in accord with the original 1938 forecast and the overhanging schedules. With the ever loyal help of their associate workers at all levels they won all their objectives of delivery date and quantity. Based on this experience, they have voluntarily pointed out all of the many things which were wrong during the last war. They have clearly and forcefully set forth how the job can be done quicker and by how much. They have shown how much cheaper the airplane could be built, that is in a very general way. Most important of all they have pointed up all of the things both within and without the company which must be changed to make possible the accomplishment of the objective of the next war program, namely the utmost speed of acceleration and maximum economy of man-hours and material.
>
> The before, during, and after phase of organisation and merger represent not reorganisation but the orderly evolution of a very small to a very large organisation. This business was exploded rather than expanded. It grew more per month than the average "Blue Chip" company grew per year. As a result, a whole generation of personnel changes were compressed into the war period during which time manpower of every classification was critical.
>
> The first line protection for national security lies in this management and supervision "know how" which was so painfully acquired during the war emergency. This stockpile of knowledge and experience must be protected and increased through the years by means now unknown. This problem is as much of a challenge to the industry and to the Army as the technological development of the flying weapon itself.
>
> With the experience acquired during the past emergency, and the personnel who were finally knit together to form the organisation which did produce 270 airplanes a month, it is believed that Consolidated could undoubtedly accelerate to that figure in twelve months under proper conditions as stated in the foregoing pages and could no doubt greatly exceed this peak production figure even on new models of aircraft, in existing facilities and under proper conditions should they be required.

In considering the performance of the management of the San Diego Division, attention is invited to three particularly important facts:
1) For the first three active years of the project it was an independent company
2) It was one of fourteen major operating divisions of the Consolidated-Vultee Aircraft Corporation for more than a year before peak production was reached
3) It was the design prime contractor carrying heavy technical responsibilities for B-24 production at Willow Run, Douglas, North American, and its own affiliate at Fort Worth

While there may have been some, advantages accruing to the San Diego program from these factors, it is obvious that benefits were completely lost in the magnitude of the load imposed on the Division management by the complex situation.

The actual merger of Consolidated and Vultee taking place during 1942 and early 1943 appears from this date to have resulted not in the conventional reorganisation of B-24 management but rather in its being gradually strengthened and improved as the requirements steadily increased with the expansion of the war program generally.

Consolidated-Vultee Management 1944

Name	Position
Harry Woodhead	Corporation President
I.M. Laddon	Executive Vice-President
David Fleet	Assistant to the President
G.P. Tidmarsh	Assistant to the President
A.E. Lombard	Engineering Consultant
C.R. Dockstader	Assistant Industrial Engineering Director
D.L. Pratt	Assistant to the Executive Vice-President
R.R. Brewton	Executive Accountant
V.C. Schorlemmer	Controller
G.T. Bovee	Assistant to the Controller
B.W. Sheahan	Engineering Manager
W.A. Maloney	Plant Engineering Director
J.A. Kelley	San Diego Division Manager
H. Ezard	San Diego Division Works Manager
H. Golem	Plant 2 Works Manager
A.W. Abels	Chief of Contracts
E.H. Jones	Chief of Materials
G.F. Gerhauser	Chief Tool Engineer
W.G. Tuttle	Chief of Industrial Relations
W.W. Lampkin	Chief Industrial Engineer
F.W. Fink	Chief Division Engineer
D.R. DeMarce	Chief of Inspections
H.G. Golem	Purchasing Agent
E.T. Stewart	Production Control Superintendent
K.R. Aiken	Production (Ordering Scheduling) Supervisor
W.J. Wiley	Production (Ordering Scheduling) Supervisor

H.E. Pasek	Employment General Supervisor
T.W. Wills	Employment Records Supervisor
J.K Field	Employee Service General Supervisor
R.M. Andrews	Wage and Salary General Supervisor
L.C. Tomkins	Educational General Supervisor
J.M. Kite	Plant Engineering General Supervisor
W.P. Tabor	Industrial Engineering
R.S. Fleet	Plant Facilities Director
Maj. L.C. Hall	Assistant AAF Plant Representative
Capt. C. Albertson	Plant Clearance Officer
Capt. H.S. King	Contract Officer

3
The San Diego Consolidated Labor Force

San Diego and the Labor Supply

San Diego, California, lies directly on the Pacific Coast, 130 miles south of Los Angeles and 17 miles north of the Mexican border. In 1940, together with adjacent communities consisting mostly of farmers and tropical fruit growers, comprised San Diego County, which had a total population of 289,348. This population, exclusive of 150,000 military personnel, gradually rose to 415,875 in 1944 the year of peak production at Consolidated.

During this time, the major commerce of the area was fishing, boat building, and tourism with the U.S. Navy having a large presence in the area that contributed substantial revenue. Consequently, the industrial skill level was low and metal-working personnel were practically non-existent. However, the general education and intelligence of the population was assessed as well above the average of other American cities of comparable size. Since the city was not an industrial center when Reuben Fleet moved Consolidated to San Diego in 1935, the company was mostly reliant on outside workers from its beginning. As the war approached and finally came, many new Army, Navy, Marine Corps training stations and staging areas were established in and around this area. The arrival of these military personnel with their dependents significantly added to the ever growing problem of housing the defense workers and their dependents and certainly thwarted the recruiting of new workers from outside the area.

Due to lack of appropriations, the AAF was unable to let large production contracts in 1940 and because of the previous continual schedule changes, Consolidated was obligated to plan all phases of its operations "as a process of evolution." Using previous employment figures, Consolidated estimated that it would require 25,000 employees by November 1941, which would be an increase of approximately 12,000 during a twelve-month period over the number currently employed on Navy and British contracts. Consolidated's hiring was to be based on shop requisitions but their hiring qualifications were relatively high considering the available labor pool. Emphasis was to be placed on the hiring of skilled and semi-skilled male workers with no pre-schooling or no qualifying trade tests planned.

The Labor Build-up

Consolidated began hiring in November 1940, planning for an ultimate production of thirty-five Liberators per month by 25,000 workers a year later. At this time, the company employed approximately 13,000 workers mainly involved on the manufacture of flying boats for the Navy. Over the next twenty months, employment increased by 32,000 employees that, combined with a considerable turnover rate, caused the level of hiring at Consolidated to reach as much as 1,600 per week with the average during 1942 and 1943 being approximately 500 per week. The labor force reached a peak of 45,244 in July 1942 employees of whom over 60 percent were direct workers. Total employment of more than 44,000 was maintained throughout the remainder of 1942 and the first four months of 1943. Subsequently, employment declined somewhat steadily through 1943 and 1944, and when peak production was achieved in March 1944, the company had 36,246 employees on all production contracts, of whom approximately 43 percent were direct workers. The reason that peak employment was recorded twenty months before the peak production of 270 bombers per month was attributed by Consolidated to a "lack of prior knowledge and detailed planning" and to the time required to train workers.

During 1940, the labor supply was considered adequate but because of the previous lack of major industries in the area a large proportion of the employees needed to be recruited from outside the area. The area outside San Diego was agricultural without an available labor pool and Consolidated concentrated on local skilled and semi-skilled men who were mainly employed in pre-war automotive services and related fields. While this labor source was initially very useful, by early 1941 very few of these men remained available and Consolidated then relied on Aircraft Trade Schools throughout the U.S. to supplement this dwindling source of labor. These schools also proved to be a very effective labor source and would provide many valuable men who later were promoted to supervisory positions not only in San Diego but also in the company's other plants that later produced the B-24s.

By late 1941, the company was directed to increase production from thirty-five to 100 bombers per month and in order to meet this schedule, employment estimates were set at 35,000 by November 1942 (actual employment in November 1942, however, would be 44,334). When the company realized that the Aircraft Trade Schools could no longer fulfill their demands for labor, Consolidated, with cooperation of government and local schools, established a vigorous program to train the new outside recruits using the increasing source of experienced factory supervisors as instructors in these schools. Once this program was underway, the Japanese attacked Pearl Harbor and production schedules suddenly increased. However, this mandatory increase in production, along with the employee losses caused by the increasing number of men volunteering or being inducted into the military, caused the company to abandon all its estimates of the number new hires and implement hiring "any and all" personnel as quickly as possible. This strategy allowed Consolidated to meet or surpass all previously estimated employment schedules until the end of 1942 when the "hires" could no longer replace the "quits." At this point, the company was forced to turn to outside Feeder Plants and increased the amount of sub-contracting in order to meet production schedules.

Worker Training

As discussed, during the early stages of the B-24 production program, Consolidated had recruited most of its personnel from Aircraft Trade Schools and their skilled and semi-skilled help from automotive services, etc. As the production program was accelerated, these sources were unable to provide sufficient personnel and Consolidated began participating in government-sponsored programs that had been established with the collaboration of the local school system. The company sent a number of its best supervisors to these schools as instructors as did other local companies and over 100,000 persons were trained for aircraft work. This training program's main drawback was that the worker or those wanting work were obligated to train on their own time. In the summer of 1942, to overcome this shortcoming, Consolidated began sending newly hired employees to these schools where they were trained at no cost to them on company time. This scheme was so efficient that it was continued throughout the program.

An employee training school was finally established at the Consolidated Plant so that a more thorough four-week program was introduced to develop specific skills in fabrication, assembly, inspection, and to teach general subjects. Large-scale voluntary employee training was subsidized by Consolidated but only one out seven of employees, of whom only 20 percent were female, liked the scheme.

Stanford, California, Modesto, Denver, and other western universities and colleges assisted in the recruiting of engineering personnel. Before graduation the engineering undergrads visited the San Diego Plant and were trained mostly by Consolidated

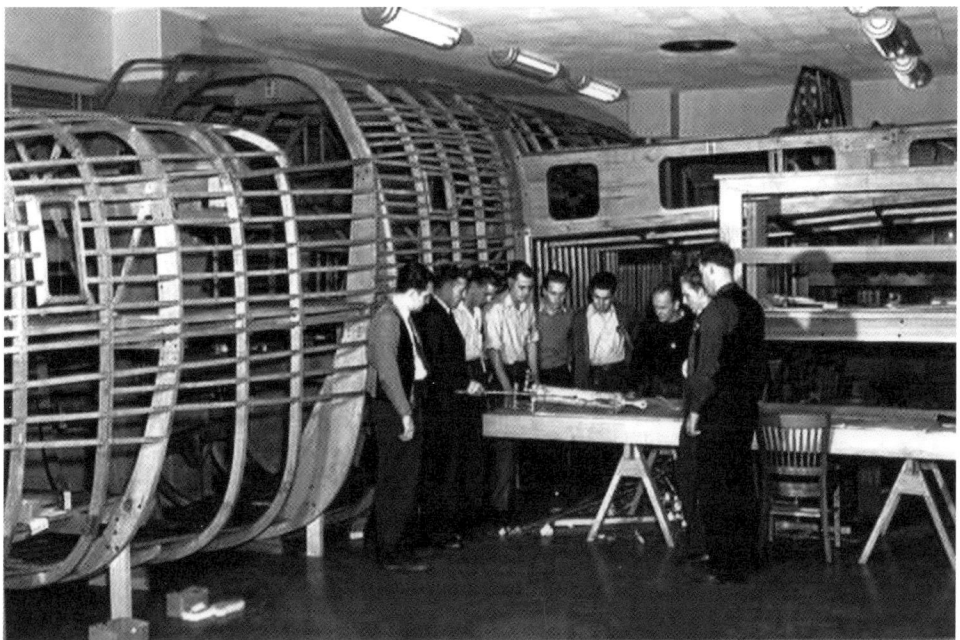

Students being instructed using a full-scale training mock-up. (*CAC/AAF*)

personnel. During this program, 200 engineers spent eight weeks and 800 draftsmen six weeks in training and were paid a nominal salary during the training period.

New employees were immediately given a half-hour orientation talk and then were personally escorted to their jobs and introduced to their new supervisors. During the next day, they were given an hour-and-a-half indoctrination lecture, and the following day, they heard another two-hour indoctrination lecture followed by a discussion. This three-day orientation/indoctrination program proved to be much more effective than the original practice of giving the new employees a half day of "concentrated advice and assistances" before, in most cases, they even reached the inside of the plant.

Generally, Consolidated considered that their training program was "entirely adequate"—as many as 5,400 employees were in training simultaneously with 107,000 total trained by the education section. Top management, individual departments, and other sectors made continual training requests and successful training programs were devised by the training section as required.

Work Force Growth and Production

The promise of good-paying war jobs lured people to the West Coast from everywhere in America, and San Diego's population grew by 41 percent between 1941 and 1944. Meanwhile, Consolidated increased employment from 797 in 1939 to 16,500 in 1942, and by the end of 1943, the number of Consolidated employees almost tripled to 45,000 employees. Before July 1940, Consolidated operated one forty-hour shift per week, but after Pearl Harbor, the work schedule was increased to a two-shift, fifty-three-hour week, and only two months later, this was increased to a three-shift, forty-eight-hour week. By thorough planning and training, and by increasing the work force and number of shifts, Consolidated achieved a steady increase in productivity. During January 1942, the direct man-hours expended per pound produced was a very poor 5.31, but from then on, the ratio was steadily reduced until June 1944 when the direct man-hours per pound was 0.47, an impressive 90 percent improvement in a short ten-month period. However, during the March 1944 peak production period, direct man-hours per pound increased to 0.52, and after June 1944, this efficient rate was not maintained, increasing to 0.66 two months later in August.

Utilization of the Available Work Force

Women

In September 1941, the Office of Production Management (OPM) requested that Fleet hire forty women on a trial basis to begin work at the covering and upholstering department ("women's work"). By 1942, these women had been transferred to clerking positions and then onto factory jobs with two women even earning positions in the engineering department as draftswomen. Women would become an essential part of the assembly line although initially they were mostly limited to "acceptable" roles and to particular

In September 1941, the OPM requested that Fleet hire forty women on a trial basis, and by May 1944, 42 percent of the San Diego Consolidated workforce were women. (*OWI*)

departments such as inspection. Soon, as the male workforce diminished to go to war and factory capacity increased, women became Rosie the Riveters and worked men's jobs on the assembly lines. However, hard work and long hours necessitated company-funded support for women employees who also had to manage their responsibilities at home. Special female counselors guided the women on such company-serving subjects as "try not to do a full day's work at home before coming to work." Special exercises were developed by the company doctors to relieve cramps and the company would allow them to work while pregnant if they had the permission of their own doctors. By May 1944, 42 percent of the San Diego Consolidated workforce were women.

Black Workers

Roosevelt's Executive Order 8802 of June 1941 had banned hiring discrimination, and his 1942 Columbus Day Speech reiterated that proclamation, stating that employers who discriminated against women and minorities hindered the war effort. The War Manpower Commission (WMC) reported that black employees at Consolidated numbered about 800 in early 1943 when the total employment reached over 40,000. It was estimated that there were 70,000 skilled black craftsmen available for hire in California's shipbuilding and aircraft industries. Elmer Davis, director of the Office of War Information, presented Senator Harry Truman and his Committee with quotes from W. Gerard Tuttle, the

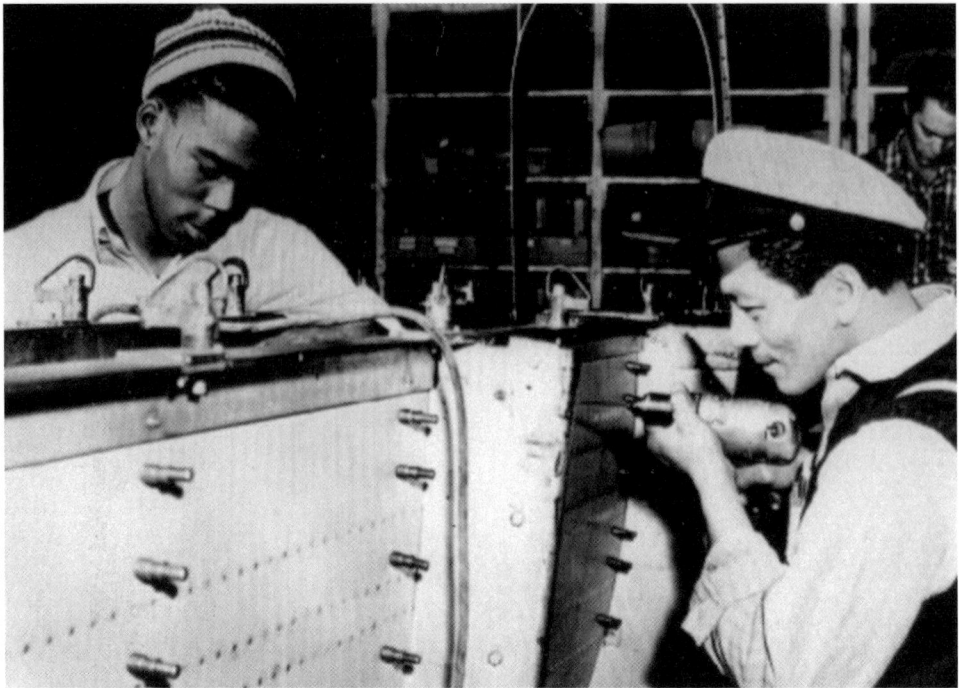

Consolidated never hired many black employees as the War Manpower Commission (WMC) reported that black employment at Consolidated was about 800 in early 1943 when the total employment reached over 40,000. Depicted is an Office of War Information propaganda photo touting the "industrial melting pot." (*OWI*)

manager of Industrial Relations at Consolidated, who acknowledged the company supported policy of "Caucasians only" while Vultee Aircraft had also candidly admitted to not hiring black workers.

Military Personnel

Consolidated employed approximately 700 military personnel from nearby Army camps along with over 1,500 Navy personnel on pass, which profited both the men and the company. They worked on a single shift, cash payment basis, performing all types of heavy work throughout the plant. This labor source was removed suddenly without notice by a Naval District Order placing Consolidated Plants "out of bounds" for all naval personnel which was upheld despite Consolidated's efforts and influence.

Marginal Workers

The company made extensive use of marginal workers but at a cost that did not justify the rather meager benefits it was to receive. In collaboration with the City of San Diego and County schools, the company used hundreds of minors both on a part-time and full-time basis. Through its Physical Placement Program, the company was able to utilize the service of thousands of handicapped, physically-limited, and elderly employees. There were a number of government employees, particularly teachers, who gave vacation time to work in the plant.

Once B-24 orders increased, Consolidated found that it did not have enough workers to meet the demand. This ad thanks San Diego teachers for giving up their vacations to assist in building bombers. (CAC/AAF)

Work Week and Shift Distribution

The work week in November 1940 consisted of fifty hours on two shifts; in October 1941, however, a two-shift, forty-five-hour week was instituted because of the arrival of a large number of new workers. After Pearl Harbor, the production schedules began to increase abruptly, and the company changed to a two-shift, fifty-three-hour week. This schedule was not entirely satisfactory to meet the demands and utilize the floor area and accordingly, in March 1942, a three-shift, forty-eight-hour week was established.

This work schedule corresponded to the hours worked by other industries in the area and was considered to be the most suitable work schedule. Any increase in hours worked per week would not have been advantageous considering the rapid increase in female employment and their special "home responsibilities." The female workforce increased from approximately 7 percent of the total employment in March 1942 to 40 percent of the total employment, and 50 percent of the direct employment in February 1943. The ratio of female employment remained close to the February 1943 figure throughout the remainder of production.

The shift distribution remained fairly constant throughout the production acceleration period. Approximately 60 percent of the employees were on the first shift, 38 percent on second shift, and 2 percent on the third cleaning and maintenance shift (with the exception of 1942 when the third shift, increased to approximately 7 percent). The continuous and critical shortage of personnel prevented any closer balancing of the first and second shifts.

Comparison of wage rates paid by Consolidated with those paid by other local factories and other military industries were considered by Consolidated to be "very favorable," although they actually were slightly lower. However, slightly lower wages were not considered by the company to be a serious detriment as only a small percentage of the total company employee large turnover was thought to be attributable to the slightly higher rates paid by local ship-building and construction industries. It is notable that there was no employee "pirating" of any consequence among San Diego companies despite the scarcity of available labor.

Employee Morale

In general, worker morale was considered only satisfactory in view of the many undesirable conditions prevalent in a city that had more than doubled its working population in a relatively short time. In an attempt to solve employee living problems, the company provided services to assist its employees in securing housing and transportation and maintained a special in-house board to assist them with the problems associated with rationing. Counseling service was established to help female employees in solving their special in factory and at home problems. Free child care centers were provided by the company to assist working mothers. Among other in factory morale-raising amenities were a comprehensive recreational and sports program and seven cafeterias to provide tasty hot nutritious meals. Again, following Glenn L. Martin's lead, Fleet organized leisure activities for its employees. Sports teams, baseball and basketball, were formed and individual sports, such as golf, bowling, tennis, and swimming, were encouraged. Consolidated employee teams were matched against other Southern California aviation factory teams. Events such as family days, beach days, treasure, and Easter egg hunts for the children were held. However, after the production peak was attained, the many unpleasant factors that occurred would have an inevitable cumulative effect and morale deteriorated. Quits outnumbered hires, and the decrease in direct workers interfered with production. Although Consolidated energetically pursued every possible avenue to remedy these many problems, it never achieved any very satisfactory outcome.

"NOTHING SHORT OF RIGHT IS RIGHT"

Celebrated wartime reporter Ernie Pyle chose Consolidated Aircraft as the topic for his 28 May 1942 nationally syndicated "Roving Reporter" column:

> Across the front of the immense plant of the Consolidated Aircraft Company (on the final assembly building) there is, to me, the most remarkable sign in America. It says: "NOTHING SHORT OF RIGHT IS RIGHT." The sign is 720 feet long and each letter is as big as a nine by twelve rug. It is painted, not with common paint, but with portrait artist's oil. It took twenty quarts to do the job.
>
> I passed the sign on the way into town, and as soon as I got here started asking people what it meant. Everybody laughed and shook his head and said, "Nobody knows."
>
> And then at Consolidated I asked what it meant, but nobody out there knows either. No, that isn't exactly correct. One man knows. And that's Major Reuben Fleet, the President of the company, who had the sign painted on his factory.

"NOTHING SHORT OF RIGHT IS RIGHT." (*AFSHRC*)

Major Fleet is a sloganeer. Like many other great production tycoons, he likes to scatter mottoes over the place to keep employees on their toes. (Fleet's fondness for slogans, dated back to the his real estate venture days in Montesano-Author)

Today you can see it for miles away: "NOTHING SHORT OF RIGHT IS RIGHT."

To me that tops all the others you see around great business institutions, such as "Think," "Pull Together," "Do It Now," and so on. Every one of them would decrease my efficiency about 50 per cent if I worked there.

But I don't work at Consolidated and after all, it is Major Fleet's plant, and I guess if he wanted to paint the Star Spangled Banner up there in Greek letters, it's none of my business ... and might well be selected as a fundamental American principle—not only as a measuring stick for those engaged in the construction of arms of defense, but also in the daily thought of all men to whom America looks for her destiny.

While I wouldn't venture an opinion on the daily thought content of "all men," I know without question that "Nothing Short of Right Is Right" has always served as Reuben's personal measuring stick.

Lodging and Housing

Of all the wartime shortages, housing shortages were the most critical and persistent as between 1942 and 1945, due to San Diego's voluminous population increase due to the influx of workers looking to find military and aircraft employment, the housing market was overwhelmed. So much so that people slept in shifts in hotel rooms or three families lived one small house. Even though fines discouraged discrimination, specific groups, such as families with children, single women, and blacks, found it particularly difficult to find housing.

By the fall of 1941, San Diego Consolidated employment was up to 25,000 and would rise by another 20,000 in the next nine months and accommodations plainly were not available. A trailer city near the USN Destroyer Base had a $7 weekly rental and permanent dormitories for 750 single men in a seventeen-building complex only briefly relieved the problem. But the greater need was for family housing. It was reported that 75–80 percent of the rental houses and apartment did not accept children despite the threat of fines.

Rents

Rents in San Diego quickly escalated to sums that defense workers found difficult to pay. Finally, in January 1942, after two years of landlord rental bonanza, Congress authorized a number of rent control measures. However, rents had increased so steeply that even a legislative directive was able to return them to prewar levels. Instead of increasing the supply of affordable housing, by limiting landlord monetary return, rent controls not only reduced the number of units for rent but also stimulated the sale of houses at inflated prices in a real estate bull market. In purchasing a house, the buyer was permitted to evict any occupying tenants, beginning a sequence of buying, evictions, and escalating rents. Lowered rents could have been achieved by an increased supply of new rental housing, but too little was built, too late to meet existing needs. Testimony before the Tolan Committee revealed that between 75 and 85 percent of those offering houses for rent would not accept children, despite heavy fines.

The House Committee, commonly known as the "Tolan Committee," named after the chairman, Representative John Tolan (Democrat/CA), began in 1940 as the Select Committee to Investigate the Interstate Migration of Destitute Citizens with its initial hearings centered on the problems that refugees from the Dust Bowl encountered as they moved west. By 1941, with the nation preparing for war, workers flocked to military production jobs, causing the committee to change its focus and its name to the House Select Committee Investigating National Defense Migration. In addition to investing migrant rents and housing, this committee became infamous during hearings in February and March 1942 about the possible removal of Japanese Americans from the West Coast.

Dormitories

The attempt to provide dormitories for single men was also a failure as San Diego had an abundance of private rooms of all types for rent for single men and single men without dependents were being drafted. However, the vast majority of arriving defense workers were married men with families, mothers with children, and single women of all ages. Even had it been desirable for men to leave their families behind, it would have been financially impossible to pay rents and provide for their distant families.

Women's Housing

Women encountered a prevailing resistance, not only in the job market, but also in the lodging and housing market. As increasing numbers of young, single men were drafted, the defense plants needed to make increased efforts to attract women. Preliminary recruitment efforts were mostly unsuccessful because of the rigid nature of most women's daily life: childcare, housework, laundry, and shopping, which made work outside the home difficult. There were no factory or community daycare or affordable private facilities to care for young children or older children after school hours. An awareness of women's needs and the impact on the war effort were overlooked and developed very slowly the normal high rate of employee turnover at the aircraft plants was even higher among women. Single women encountered similar levels of housing discrimination; many were forced to sleep in shifts in a single shared room.

Linda Vista

In 1940, to alleviate the national housing shortage, Congress had authorized the National Housing Agency (NHA) and the Lanham Defense Housing Act that made possible the construction of the Linda Vista Housing Project, America's largest planned community, which was located on the plateau northwest of San Diego's Mission Valley.

Fleet used his influence to have Treasury Secretary Henry Morgenthau provide streets and homes for 3,000 families, in a new self-sufficient city called Linda Vista, which was built in just six months using production-line techniques on a brush-covered mesa north of San Diego. Like Glenn L. Martin's planned 5,000 unit Aero Acres, Middle River, and Stansbury projects in Baltimore, Linda Vista, California's first planned community, was a city within a city, having its own schools, stores, and churches. Linda Vista was dedicated in 1941 by Eleanor Roosevelt, and by 1942, this community was to expand by 6,000 more new homes into Chesterton.

At the time it was built, Linda Vista was the largest single defense housing project and the largest low-income housing development in the world with a projected occupancy of 13,000 people. Because of the project's size, Federal site selection agents found a limited choice of suitable properties near the Consolidated factory or even in San Diego. Eventually they had to select a barren 1,240-acre plateau in the southwestern part of Kearny Mesa, north of Mission Valley. The site was relatively flat but was surrounded by steep, rugged canyons on three sides that posed problems for site planners. The main axis of the project was a 2-mile-long ridge running north to south and the major access route, Linda Vista Road, traversed the ridge and side roads radiating from it to form housing pods. The single-family and duplex units were sited on periphery to take advantage of the views and were served by secondary loops and cul-de-sacs. To separate cars and pedestrians in the central city area, the six-family dwellings situated along the highest ridge and the four-family dwellings one level below could only be reached by paved footpaths. When Linda Vista opened in 1941, the only route in and out of Linda Vista was a narrow, winding, very dangerous two-lane road usually clogged with traffic, with its grades too steep for buses to navigate.

Although Linda Vista was described by its architects as "a wonder of construction technology and efficiency," it was, in fact, rows of unimaginative homes built by using assembly line techniques adapted from automobile manufacturing. An entire street of houses could be built in days by using a carefully conceived sequence of construction trades. However, local officials were not consulted during the site selection or planning phases and because Linda Vista was two miles from the nearest built-up area of San Diego, it was difficult and costly to arrange basic public services such as police and fire protection, trash collection, street cleaning, ambulance service, and public transportation and so entirely new systems and services had to be provided for the initial 5,400 unit project. Six months after it had opened in May 1941, the population was 2,290 families, 9,200 people,

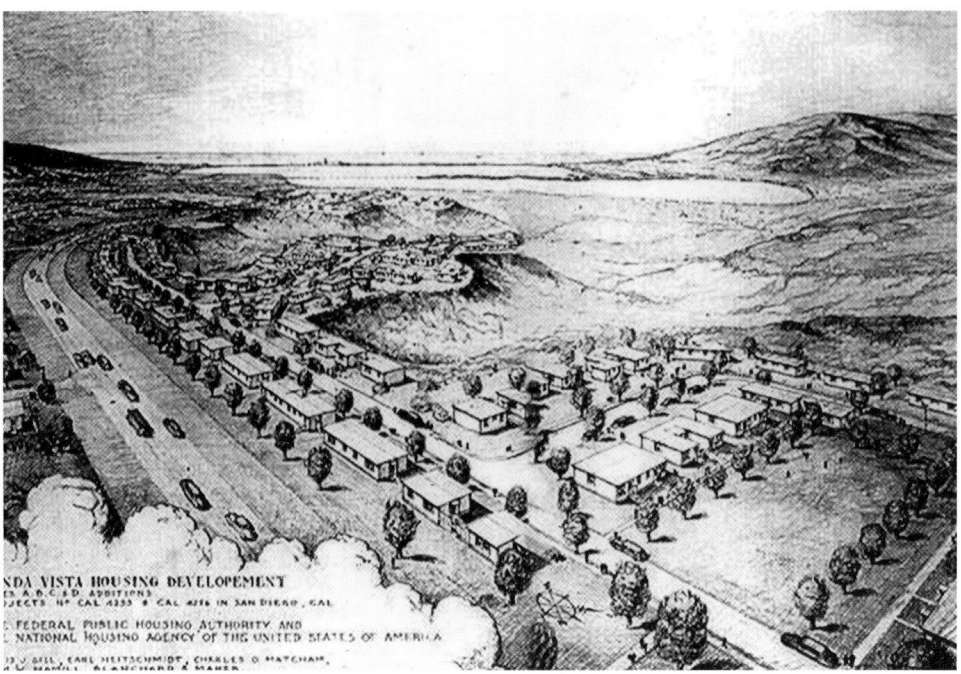

Architect's concept of Linda Vista Housing Project, America's largest planned community with an initial planned 5,400 units that was described by its architects as "a wonder of construction technology and efficiency." (*CAC/AAF*)

An aerial view of Linda Vistas' 3,001 permanent units and the additional 1,845 less-desirable temporary, movable units that were added between 1941 and 1943. (*CAC/AAF*)

Rows of unimaginative homes were built by using assembly line techniques adapted from automobile manufacturing. An entire street of houses could be built in days by using a carefully conceived sequence of construction trades. (CAC/AAF)

and by April 1943, it had a population of over 4,000 families, 16,000 people. Besides public services, there were no existing schools or recreational facilities anywhere in the vicinity. There were no shops, drugstores, service stations, or commercial facilities of any kind until a Safeway store opened in February 1943. This one store was insufficient to meet local needs and shoppers often waited an hour in checkout lines. The original Linda Vista development consisted of 3,001 permanent units, but an additional 1,845 less-desirable temporary, movable units were added between 1941 and 1943 for a total of 4,846 units.

Housing Problems Continue

By early 1942, the lack of housing became a serious threat to Consolidated production despite the addition of 6,000 new homes built in the adjacent city of Chesterton mainly due to the need of the many large Army and Navy bases in the San Diego area that also needed to house their personnel. New hires could not be recruited and many of those already employed were leaving the area because adequate housing for their families was non-existent. Even the effective effort of the Army and Navy to obtain private housing and their use of early Federal housing programs to accommodate their personnel did not relieve the housing situation for Consolidated. To relieve this situation, Reuben Fleet, through influence in Washington, was able to secure approximately 7,500 additional Federally-sponsored homes and 900 trailers for exclusive use of the aircraft companies in the San Diego area. Construction of the new homes over the next two years helped substantially but actually never relieved the overcrowding, as personnel continued to terminate as late as June 1944 because of this condition.

Rationing

After Pearl Harbor, there was a shortage of rubber for tires as the Japanese had quickly overran Southeast Asia's natural rubber yielding areas and America's synthetic rubber industry had yet not been developed. On 11 December 1941, tires became the first item to be rationed by the Office of Price Administration (OPA), and throughout the war, gasoline rationing was as much the result of wanting to conserve rubber as to conserve gasoline. A national speed limit of 35 mph was enforced to save fuel and rubber for tires. Automobile factories stopped manufacturing civilian models by early February 1942 and converted to military articles with the government as the only customer.

In 1942, *Consolidated News* explained to workers why automobiles had to be sacrificed for the war effort: "A four engine bomber, fully loaded, burns as much gas in one hour's top-speed cruising as the average family auto burns in six months" and the "rubber used to make garden hoses in the last three months of 1941 would provide bullet-proofed gas tanks on 400 Consolidated bombers."

Civilians first received ration books, *War Ration Book Number One*, the "Sugar Book," on 4 May 1942 followed by coffee in November 1942, and by the end of 1942, ration coupons were used for nine other items. During 1943, the rationed list expanded to numerous food stuffs and many other items such as nylons, typewriters, bicycles, etc. that were often unavailable anyhow. Although many workers were earning a steady income for the first time, they had few products to buy with rationing in effect.

Civilians first received ration books, the "Sugar Book," during May 1942 but during 1943, the rationed list expanded to numerous foodstuffs and many other items that were often unavailable anyhow. (AFSHRC)

Company Services

The company was concerned about the leisure time of its employees, especially to take their minds off their long and grueling work schedules, not having the comforts of a permanent home, and their lack of off-hours diversions. A radio station and daily newspaper, the *Consolidated News*, was launched to provide its employees with Company, local, state, and national news. Consolidated instituted a number of sports teams and leagues including baseball, golf, bowling, tennis, basketball, and swimming, which were organized with team names like "Parts Plant," Paint Shop," and "Maintenance." The *News* and company radio broadcasts reported news about and the standings of these teams and as the Southern California aircraft industry expanded, inter-company rivalries grew. The San Diego Consolidated employee sports teams would play the Los Angeles' North American Aircraft or Douglas Aircraft teams. The company also organized, with great hoopla, free family events such as "beach days" at Mission Beach that included treasure hunts, beauty contests, and dancing accompanied by an orchestra. Due to the central location of the company plants, the existence of adequate parking facilities, the full cooperation of the local bus system, together with the staggering of shopping hours by the businesses and other local war plants, transportation was never considered a serious factor at San Diego.

Consolidated News: The daily company newspaper. (CAC/AAF)

Community Factors
As a naval base city of long-standing and with its rapid wartime growth, the city of San Diego took no positive measures to make Consolidated Management and its workers part of the community even though of the city's peak increase of 50 percent in county population, nearly 80 percent was attributed to Consolidated. Consolidated and its employees were received by the community as definitely negative and verging on the hostile, which made recruitment and retention of personnel very difficult for Consolidated throughout the war.

Labor Relations
After a Union contract was signed in June 1941, the company continued a consistent and progressive labor relations policy through the establishment of an effective Industrial Relations Department that maintained active cooperation with Union leaders that enabled the company to maintain a record of no shut-downs or even minor work stoppages during the entire B-24 program.

Absenteeism and Turnover
Consolidated's absentee rate was consistently lower than the average rates of the Aircraft Industry. For the period March 1942 through December 1944, the rate was approximately 5.5, while the rate for the other Southern California aircraft plants averaged 6.5.

In late June 1942, to address the illness and injury situation, the company initiated a health care program at Plant #1, where a two-story hospital provided first aid, emergency care, exam rooms, and laboratories. There were fifty registered nurses who screened the patients to determine who was actually sick and administered or referred those who were. Consolidated joined with Aetna Life Insurance Company to provide an affordable hospitalization insurance plan and 85 percent of all employees took advantage of this benefit.

Nonetheless, in early 1944, the industrial relations department reported that in one month there were 72,554 employee workdays lost to absenteeism. Women had more absenteeism than men for reasons besides illness, injury, and dental problems. Women had family/child and personal issues, the need to visit their military spouses, and there were some women who could not cope with the demands of the industrial environment.

Consolidated's turnover rates were slightly higher than the industry average rate. In the one-year interval, 1 January 1943 through December 1943, the company's turnover rate was 7.8 percent as compared to 7.4 percent for the industry. The labor situation first became critical during August and September 1942 when departures exceeded hires by a very large margin of 1,200 men and, although occasionally relieved, this remained a serious problem affecting production. Then from 1 September 1942 through January 1943, the company lost an average of more than 1,000 production workers per month and an approximate monthly average of 8.8 percent of all employees. For example, from September 1942 through May 1944, the major period of major production, departures exceeded hires on an average of 470 per month. The major percentage of departures were male workers and to replace this loss, female employment was increased from 27 percent of total in September 1942 to 43.5 percent by September 1943. With manpower shortages continuing into 1944 with an 88 percent annual turnover rate, Consolidated considered virtually no one as unemployable. The manpower situation became so serious that James Kelley, division manager, announced; "We will fail to meet schedules for production of Liberator bombers, for the first time in 18 months if absenteeism does not stop and if workers continue to quit their jobs." He attributed the problem on war weariness, men being drafted or joining the military, and workers leaving with their accumulated earnings. The departures to the military mentioned by Kelley took as many as 1,300 employees in one month and a totaled of more than 13,000 during the war. Later in the hiring program, a personal interview was instituted in an effort to salvage employees who were quitting, and consequently many employees were retained through discussion and the solution of their personal problems.

Work Force Conclusions

The Consolidated Personnel Department excelled in its mission of hiring more people at peak production than the total increase in the number of those gainfully employed in all San Diego. It had employed nearly 20 percent of the county's pre-war population and its final manpower capacity would be far beyond supply by the local market. Consolidated succeeded in supplying personnel into the plant through its cooperation with all possible outside sources such as local schools, colleges, universities, trade schools, and government agencies, and also through their own efforts in the fields of training, selection, upgrading, promotion, and recruiting campaigns both local and national, and in the face of a continuous and growing shortage of living facilities. While the supply of workers was often too hurried for economical utilization, it was always within the capacity to sustain accelerating production. During this long period of work force evolution, "major elements of strength" were developed that plainly made possible the delivery of many more bombers per day from the San Diego Plant than had been required and planned.

4

Building the Liberator

Engineering

The XB-24 bomber was first conceived in late 1938 and designed, built, and first flown in 1939, which was considered extraordinary for an aircraft of this size. However, the result of this rapid development was that when high-volume production was begun, the necessary engineering data was deficient and a large amount of shop engineering became necessary. Later this became a serious problem and one of the major contributing factors, which, along with the large number of engineering changes, resulted in delaying all operations, especially of the associate prime and the design prime contractors.

The B-24 was considered well-engineered for the small-scale production requirements of the time and for the "high-type of mechanics" then available in the shops. However, the shops required a wholly different type of engineering design and information be available to them for the final high-level requirements and the multi-plant operation utilizing personnel who were not aircraft mechanics but who were also largely without any industrial experience. Although this type of engineering was generally practiced in the metal trades and other high-volume manufacturing industries, the Aviation Industry had not adopted it because of its small volume requirements prior to Pearl Harbor and afterward it was not necessary because the AAF had not yet issued any of its peak wartime requirements.

The basic problem was that Consolidated's shop organization built aircraft by the so-called "handicraft method" that were generally in use in the aircraft industry prior to the war. This method solved production problems in the shop making complete engineering drawings unnecessary. Any drawings, therefore, were rather superficial and did not attempt to indicate production breakdown, nor were they sufficiently comprehensive to assure that the detail parts could be individually produced and would be interchangeable.

It had been estimated that the peak production date for the B-24 at San Diego and associated plants and possibly the entire Liberator program could have been moved ahead by as much as a year providing that the AAF had immediately proposed its peak production requirements; second that the bomber had been originally been suitably production engineered for this peak volume requirement; and third, that if the AAF held up all engineering changes except those of the utmost tactical urgency.

The Plan

At the time engineering was begun on the XB-24, the Consolidated engineering department consisted of approximately seventy-five men operating all phases of this department and was mainly concerned with the Navy flying boat contract (then starting production) and since the XB-24 was to include many of the characteristics of this flying boat, no large increase in the engineering staff was contemplated. However, during the fall of 1939, a contract was let for the production of B-24s and management decided that the engineering department was much too small to deal with the requirements of this contract. During the spring and summer of 1940, the company initiated a recruitment program to procure the required engineers, which would prove to be an astute move because the LB-30 (British version of the B-24) was being manufactured and flown in combat in the Europe and numerous changes were revealed, both from the production and combat perspectives. This, together with the joint participation in the B-24 production program beginning in 1941 by Ford, Douglas, and North American, made it imperative for Consolidated to maintain a competent engineering staff that would peak at approximately 600 in the middle of 1944. The company encountered many difficulties in maintaining the required engineering personnel as the engineering turnover was approximately 75 percent annually, due to the same problems facing other workers: inadequate housing, uncertainty relative to Selective Service draft status, transportation problems, etc.

Initial Difficulties

Once the first Liberator production contract was underway in early 1940, it was found that the available engineering information was imprecise and the B-24 was not at all engineered from a mass-production stand point and simplifying the production process was embarked upon. Although this program was operated by the shop organization, it placed an additional burden on the small engineering department because of the inordinate number of engineering changes which were currently required and because of the department's lack of experience in production designing. At about the same time, the AAF added to the engineering obligation by their decision that B-24 would also be manufactured by Consolidated Fort Worth; by Ford at Willow Run; by North American at Dallas; and by Douglas Tulsa.

In its existing form, the status of engineering on the B-24 was not suitable for use by these new participating prime contractors. When Ford entered the bomber program in February 1941 and sent its engineers to the Consolidated Plant, they not only found that there was no production breakdown for mass-production purposes but

In anticipation of increased engineering requirements, Consolidated included a large engineering building in its second 1940–41 expansion. (*ATSC*)

The engineering department would peak at approximately 600 in the middle of 1944 despite an approximately 75 percent annual turnover. (*CAC/AAF*)

Once Ford entered the B-24 program, Consolidated became aware of value of lofting and included a lofting department in its expansion plans. (*CAC/AAF*)

the bomber had never been lofted. (Lofting is a drafting technique in which curved lines are generated from drawings, to be used in plans for streamlined objects such as aircraft and ships and is discussed in detail in the Willow Run section.) The changes and short cuts made by Consolidated's shop engineering during a brief time period caused discrepancies that its engineering department was unable to keep up with. The amount and accuracy of engineering information available was very inadequate and had to be carefully redeveloped by Ford Engineers working with Consolidated over many months. During this time, Consolidated became aware of the value of lofting and established a lofting department in its subsequent plant expansion.

Engineering Changes

The original engineering data difficulties in the entire B-24 program were further intensified by the large number of engineering design changes required beginning as early as the beginning of the first production contract. The initial effect of these engineering changes on both engineering and production was moderated by the diversion of twenty-six bombers, built substantially to the original specifications without engineering changes, to the British. This diverted order was in advance of the 139 (British) LB-30s, which had been originally ordered by the French. This order compromised all except the most urgent requirements and Consolidated's workforce and engineering staff was able to maintain operations and was thus available for the AAF Master Change Record (MCR) program in January 1942. This delay, which was agreed to by the AAF by a contract change, led to the delivery of the improved bomber, designated B-24D, and did not begin until September 1941 or ten months after delivery schedule designated in the original production contract. Several design improvements in the early AAF models had been the result of the combat-testing of the bomber by the British after they assumed the French LB-30 contract. The changes included turbo-superchargers, power turrets, .50-caliber machine guns, self-sealing fuel tanks, and other major changes were added.

The Master Change Record and the Treatment of Changes

During the approximately five years during which 6,725 B-24s were produced by San Diego, there were 1,820 master changes incorporated—or one for every 3.6 Liberators delivered. These changes were made early in the program by the engineering department, but as the program developed, it became evident that a new procedure was necessary. During 1942, the AAF instituted the master change record (MCR) system under the direction of the master scheduling supervisor for use in all airframe plants. Consolidated adopted the system but difficulties immediately became apparent when through the insistence of this supervisor the schedule on MCR changes must be met even though the engineering, tooling, and panning departments had not executed as scheduled. The confusion resulting in all departments from this practice was the leading reason why the company failed to meet its delivery schedule early in 1943.

To solve these problems, a master change board was formed to coordinate all engineering changes with the engineering, planning, and production departments before their release into the system, thereby giving everyone concerned an input in scheduling. This procedure functioned reasonably well but the changes began arriving so quickly that this board could not keep up with them, and it was again necessary to alter the system and establish an engineering control board to screen all such changes at time of arrival with the objective of deleting all unnecessary changes. This board performed satisfactorily and a large number of unimportant changes were eliminated or postponed by coordination with the Project Office at Wright Field and the local AAF Plant Representative.

Engineering Changes and the B-24 Committee

The B-24 Committee was established to coordinate the many production and engineering problems that appeared in the four B-24 plants. When this committee was activated, engineering changes were becoming more and more serious and were delaying production and the complicating factor was that all engineering changes originated from Consolidated. Many times the change data sent to the participating companies arrived too late for incorporation in the desired production block, or the design change was such so as to make it unworkable without redesign for production in that particular plant.

Ford, in particular, was affected primarily because Ford as an automobile manufacturer failed to understand the procedures and methods being used by the aircraft industry. These problems led to the establishment of an engineering sub-committee during May 1942 and was active in bringing Consolidated and Willow Run closer together by the coordinating and streamlining both company's engineering programs.

Production Methods and Tooling

Once the war began, Consolidated's production effort changed from a small job shop building bombers by hand to a very large integrated factory using modern industrial procedures. Fortunately, this change was very well suited to B-24 production in that the bomber had the flexibility necessary for the incorporation of the many design changes. Nonetheless, this production system was inadequate because little advanced detailed planning could be done to handle rapid changes and because it required great quantities of manpower.

Consolidated's Tooling Plan

Consolidated did not have a comprehensive overall plan for B-24 production as the facility had been sponsored by and set up as a Navy source for heavy flying boats. During a pause in continued Navy flying boat contracting and manufacture, the AAC placed a contract for the XB-24 and other contracts followed. When the first production contract was signed, $3 million was spent on expanding production facilities. The next production contract necessitated the expenditure of approximately $22 million to build and equip Plant #2. With each change in the delivery schedule, Consolidated created a production plan to fit that schedule.

Consolidated anticipated fabricating and assembling all the required parts in its own plant except standard parts, such as nuts, bolts, fittings, terminals, etc. and parts requiring special skills and equipment such as landing struts, pumps, electric motors, etc. The existing production and supporting departments were to be separated as soon as possible. Plant #2 was designed to fabricate and assemble sub-assemblies to supply the production line at Plant #1. The company's tooling plan consisted of duplicating the existing tooling to increase production.

To expand a plant that was building a small number of bombers by hand into high-capacity manufacture the following requirements had to be met:

1) Engineering had to be completed far enough in advance to allow for production planning. The lofting and templates had to be complete and accurate.
2) Engineering had to be complete so that production breakdown of the aircraft was available for shop planning in detail.
3) Engineering changes had to be kept to a minimum and the necessary changes had to be completely planned in advance.

4) The tool planning and design departments had to be adequately staffed and organized.
5) Tooling, dies, jigs, fixtures, and master controls had to be accurate and available for rapid acceleration,
6) Large tool making resources with many skilled workers had to be available at the beginning of each program and also available to handle necessary changes.
7) Raw materials and purchased parts had to be available and their control in the plant had to be accurately timed.

The company expected that all the above requirements would not be fulfilled and so Consolidated planned for a slightly increased production. However, under this plan, floor space and machine tools were mostly available on time to meet current schedules.

Throughout the war, in addition to the B-24, Consolidated had several Navy flying boats in production, which necessitated a large tooling department that was needed so that tooling for changes could be fabricated rapidly. The effective use of Plant #2 for fabrication and sub-assembly was possible as the bomber was broken down into smaller sections, thus allowing the use of more workers with greater efficiency. Compared to Ford, Consolidated's tooling was not as complex nor as inflexible, and as new techniques were instituted, they could be readily used. Since the company's tooling plan was more flexible, actual production could be achieved sooner and changes could be incorporated more quickly.

Due to the continuous shortage of skilled personnel in the engineering department, engineering data on the B-24 was never entirely accurate, up-to-date, nor complete, and neither was it ever basically revised to permit an appropriate breakdown for mass- production. This inadequacy seriously affected every other function in the production cycle and necessitated much shop engineering, thus resulting in turmoil in the tooling department. This lack of complete and accurate engineering data also adversely affected the development of tooling by Ford, North American, and Consolidated Fort Worth.

The AAF requested and Consolidated's engineers attempted to incorporate too many changes without sufficient time for suitable planning, which resulted in unnecessary disorder and delay on the production line. Consolidated's expansion from low-production using skilled "hand workers" and its lack of high-production "know-how" necessitated the use of excess labor compared to automotive mass production criteria. (Note: In factory documents, Consolidated called their production "high capacity" as opposed to Ford's "mass production.") Because skilled workers were not available, first local workers and later large numbers of outside, "immigrant," workers were hired and trained which delayed production. The shortage of manpower continued, limiting production at San Diego, so Feeder Plants and outside contracting had to be instituted "to take the work to the worker." The breakdown of the bomber into smaller sections was not completed until the shortage of skilled workers made it necessary. The tooling department was well-equipped and had a relatively large staff, which allowed rapid tooling. However, due to the large number of engineering changes, on occasion it was necessary to send some tool work to outside contractors.

The tooling used in the production of the experimental models and the LB-30 were on hand and were used to start the production of B-24s. Job-shop "know-how" of the original staff was available for starting the production line. The original production tooling plan for ninety B-24s per month had been substantially released to the tool fabrication department in the early fall 1941 and was substantially completed by the end of that year.

San Diego's initial B-24 production was completed without any changes in the nature of the original tooling or handicraft production methods. With major components built in assembly jigs, the installation of wiring, plumbing, etc. became a time consuming job, requiring workmen to actually crawl inside the separate assemblies. Next, the fuselage had to be constructed in sections in the same jig so that these sections could be removed and mounted on fixtures and have the necessary installation work done of their individual pick-up assembly lines.

A jig's (template) primary purpose is to provide accurate repeatability to increase productivity and interchangeability in the manufacturing of products. Jigs may be custom and durably made for frequent use or may be economically improvised for a single task. An example of a jig is when a house key is duplicated; the original is used as a jig so the new key can have the same path as the old one. A jig is often confused with a fixture; a fixture holds the work in a fixed location while a jig is a device that performs both functions (holding the work and guiding a tool). A fixture is an apparatus used to securely hold and support a workpiece (a piece of work in process of manufacture) in a specific position or orientation, ensuring that all parts produced using the fixture would accurate and maintain conformity and reliable interchangeability of the finished parts. The use of a fixture improves production economy by expediting smooth and accurate operation and quick transition from part to part, reducing the requirement for skilled labor by simplifying how workpieces are mounted and increasing conformity throughout a production run. A fixture differs from a jig in that when a fixture is used, the tool must move relative to the workpiece; a jig moves the piece while the tool remains stationary. Both jigs and fixtures serve to reduce working time by having quick set-up, and by easy transition from part to part. Both frequently reduce the complexity of a process, permitting unskilled workers to accomplish it and to effectively transfer have and unskilled worker perform the skills of a tool maker.

The original tooling expansion consisted of duplicating the scaffold-like fixtures designed for the early low-volume contracts in sufficient quantity to meet the increased production levels required. These scaffold-like fixtures lacked rigidity and became misaligned which became a serious problem in mating sections on the assembly line and it became necessary to employ a dozen full-time men to restore them. When restoration was found to be ineffective some of the fixtures were redesigned and rebuilt using 16-inch steel tubing in the place of four inch and the problem was solved and mating difficulties were eliminated.

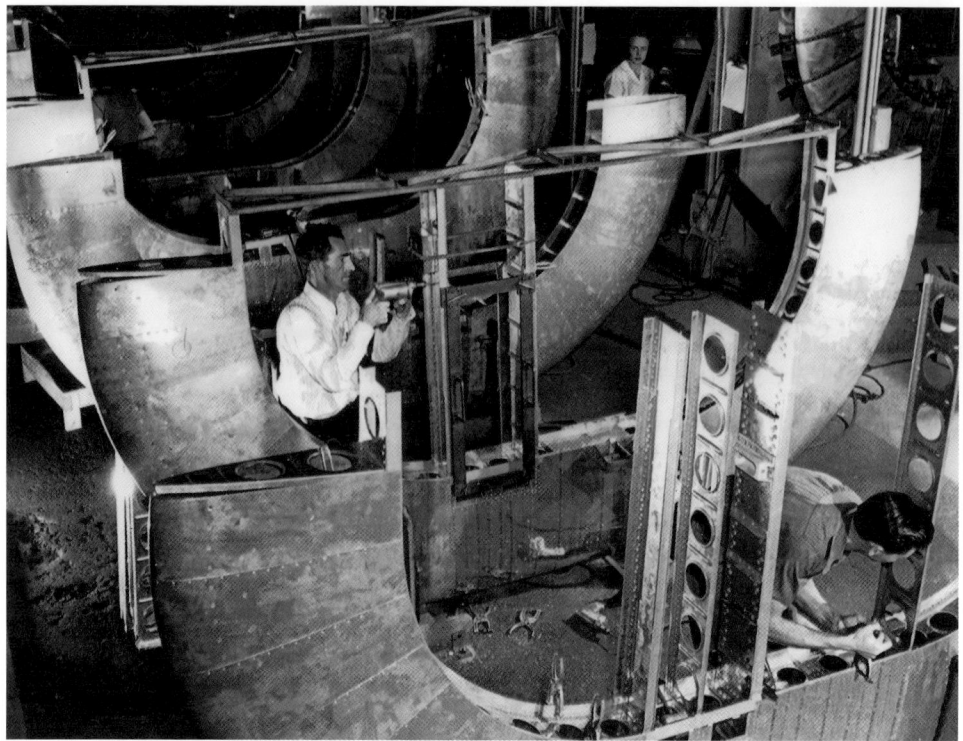

Jig. (*CAC/AAF*)

Fixture. (*CAC/AAF*)

Assembly Tooling

The assembly method at the start of the B-24 program was to build complete major assemblies in the final jigs. Consolidated's veteran workmen were skilled in building and installing operations, but as the production rate was increased and additional, skilled all-around mechanics became unavailable, these major assemblies were continually broken down into smaller and smaller sections. This breakdown allowed more workers to work on each section and also required only the development of one special skill by the worker for one simple operation. As production demands increased, a further division of labor became necessary and was achieved. The time in the main assembly jig was further reduced by using the main jigs only to align the parts and install the aligning rivets. Detail riveting and accessory parts were installed in adjacent moving assembly lines. Once this plan was operational, sub-assemblies fabrication at Plant #2 was complete and therefore only mating and assembly was required on the final assembly line Plant #1.

The B-24 moved down the final assembly line supported by an assembly fixture with several working levels and an angle to the line due to the space limitations of the building. The movement of the line was via by conveyor chains at floor level. Final assembly was completed in approximately fifty-four stations on the line with definite planned operations at each station.

An example of the flow for the wing department follows:

1) Cutting and forming of parts for wing.
2) Assembly and key riveting of wing members in the wing jigs.
3) Transfer of partially complete wing to moving wing line where detail riveting, installation of components, plumbing, and wiring was made.
4) Delivery of complete wing to final assembly Plant #1 where installation to the fuselage was made.

The thirteen wing jigs were made of heavy steel tubing construction served by overhead cranes, and having two working levels for convenience. The 700-foot-long moving conveyor line for detail work held the wing in flat position.

The fuselage and other sub-assemblies were built in a similar jig. After structural assembly, the fuselage was taken apart in four segments (roof panel, two side panels, and floor) for installation of components, plumbing and wiring, and then mated on the final assembly line.

Changes Made

Early in the B-24 program, use was made of pre-punched pilot rivet holes. These pilot rivet holes were punched to rivet size at assembly in the jigs. Later, when personnel became more experienced and the jigs in use more accurate, full-sized rivet holes were pre-punched in the aluminum skin, but this type of pre-punching was found not to be very successful.

The initial set-up for formed parts had been drop hammer Kirksite dies with the use of rubber for back-up. As production experience increased and the bomber design became more stable, zinc and Kirksite dies were used, which required much less hand work to finish parts. Kirksite is a moderate strength (less than steel) zinc (94 percent) and aluminum (6 percent) base alloy that was originally developed as a forming tool alloy for making sheet metal dies for low-volume manufacturing. Its primary advantage is its low melting temperature (725 degrees Fahrenheit), which is low enough that it can be poured into rubber molds. Dies cast from Kirksite provided low-cost tooling because the alloy can be accurately cast with low porosity, requiring a minimum of finishing. Throughout production, steel-faced blanking dies were used with rubber strippers. The forming of parts was done with stretch presses and drop hammers using zinc and Kirksite dies. Experimental and small run parts were made by hand-forming or by wood from blocks in drop hammers.

A drop hammer or press consists of a large steel chassis containing changeable dies, lifted by hydraulic rams above a similarly-sized steel chassis containing a reverse image of the upper die. When the press or hammer is in the open position, the operators place a sheet of metal into the hammer, and when all operators are clear of the dies, each operator presses a start switch and holds it down. The machine then will trip, causing the top dies to drop into the bottom dies, stamping a molded piece out of the blank metal.

One important change in manufacturing methods was the return of final assembly operations to sub-assembly departments so that when sub-assemblies arrived at the main assembly line, mating and rigging were the only operations required. This change required more complete and accurate tooling in sub-assembly departments. As manpower shortages in the San Diego Plant became more critical, more work was sent to the Feeder Plants and sub-contractors. Much of this outside work, such as the wiring harness and form tubing, required fixtures that had not been required in the original final assembly operations.

Kirksite die. (*CAC/AAF*)

Drop hammer building. (*ATSC*)

Drop hammer. (*CAC/AAF*)

Tooling Difficulties

1) The many engineering changes which required immediate incorporation onto the bomber made both tools and parts obsolete during manufacture.
2) Due to new engineering changes many tools were sub-contracted; then due to manufacturing and transportation time at the sub-contractor were obsolete upon receipt and required considerable rework, if not scrapping.
3) Engineering changes caused difficulty with sub-assembly and Feeder Plant production. Changes in tooling and material, again due to transportation and manufacturing time, fell behind the change schedule and, often, necessitated the setup of jigs at San Diego to correct assemblies received.
4) The shortage of manpower at San Diego necessitated an increase in the amount of work sent to Feeder and outside sub-contracting plants, which in turn, required more tooling to accompany the job.
5) The necessary use of unskilled assembly workers at San Diego required the reworking of many existing tools to improve accuracy of finished parts so they would "fall into place."
6) The ultimate use of a high percentage of female labor required special attention in tool design and considerable revision and rebuilding.

Cost of Tooling

The investment in the Consolidated San Diego Plants was approximately $60 million, of which about one-half was machine tools and fixtures. This represented a large investment in terms of "product produced" as compared to high-production industries. However, the aircraft industry was not a high-production industry, and very little automatic or semi-automatic machinery could be used and machine and man-hour costs per operation were high.

A large portion of the tooling expenditures were made to incorporate the large number of engineering design changes. The breakdown of "going costs" of the tooling department were approximately as follows:

1) Maintenance 20 percent (this expenditure of only 20 cents for maintenance out of every dollar of "going costs" of tooling clearly demonstrates the large additional expense of design changes).
2) AAF sponsored design changes 45 percent.
3) Consolidated sponsored design changes 14 percent.
4) Improvements in production methods 21 percent.

Tooling Developments

About 45,000 tools, jigs, and fixtures were actually used to produce the B-24, and with the replacement of tools required by design changes, the total quantity produced was much larger. Consolidated was too occupied and lacked the skilled manpower to develop very many new manufacturing processes and generally remained within the general practices of the aircraft industry.

Due to both the bomber's engineering status and subsequent design changes, the tooling program was slow in developing, requiring a considerable time to do so after initial acceptances. When the first seven B-24Ds were accepted in January 1942, tooling man-hours per month had increased to over 250,000, and a total of 3,359,330 hours had been expended through 1941. Factory tooling hours continued at a high volume through 1942 and reached its monthly peak of 264,013 in July 1943 when production of over 200 bombers per month was achieved. Even then, tooling expenses did not begin to decrease significantly until the latter part of 1944. Total tooling expenditures through June 1944 amounted to 9,541,309 man-hours. Consolidated, as the design prime contractor, was required to produce or make available to other contractors tool designs and many master gauges in addition to tooling for many of the sub-contractors and all Feeder Plants.

This large and ongoing expenditure on tooling was not only due to realigning and maintenance work but also to a considerable degree to rework and new tooling requirements again resulting from design changes. The cause of a significant portion of the rework was that the original type tooling was insubstantial and frequently required strengthening or rebuilding but in general was of the same type and character of tooling that was used until late in the B-24 program.

Some production shortcuts were developed, among the more important were the sheet deburring machine and master tooling dock. The sheet deburring machine passed the drilled sheet through rubber covered rollers and scraped the burrs against fixed steel knife.

Master Tooling Dock

Charles Perelle, Consolidated vice president of manufacturing, purchased the patents of inventor Leland Bryant of Beverly Hills, California, for the master tooling dock by which "many months can be saved in tooling for production a new type Aeroplane." In the foreword to a manual describing the principles, construction and use of the dock, prepared by the inventor for Consolidated Perelle, states that "Consolidated has been extremely fortunate to be the first manufacturer to utilize fully the principles of this remarkable new positioning device, which has opened up an important field in manufacturing."

The master tooling dock was a three-dimensional locating and positioning device, approximately equivalent to a three-dimensional pantograph. The key elements were three sets of coordinated straight-edges, fixed longitudinal straight-edges to establish length, movable vertical straight-edges to establish height, find movable transverse straight-edges to establish width. The longitudinal members were from 20 to 80 feet in length while the other members are usually 12 to 15 feet long.

This instrument was used to locate points precisely in space and to transfer these points to assembly or tooling gauges to obtain exacting dimensional control, thus insuring interchangeability. The dock transferred dimensions from drawings or lofts

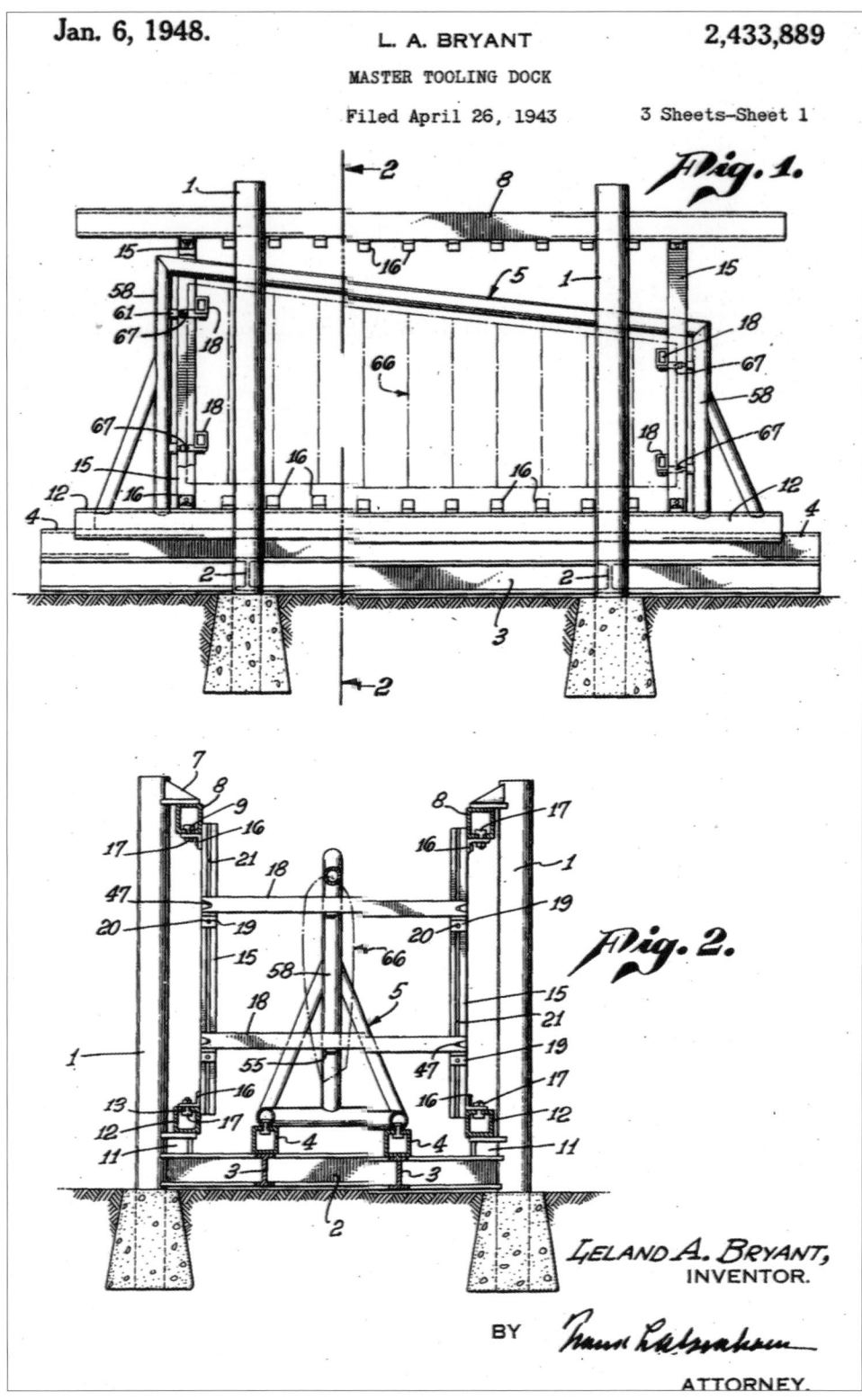

Master tool dock patent. (*U.S. Patent Office*)

Master tooling dock. (CAC/AAF)

to the tool through the use of strip templates which were steel strips three-eighths by 2 inches cut in convenient lengths, and index templates, which are flat steel sheets. The tooling dock later saved a considerable layout and construction time, particularly in Consolidated's manufacture of the PB4Y for the Navy.

Reproduction of Tooling Gauges by Tooling Docks

When a design contractor and the secondary contractors were to produce the same aircraft, and where absolute interchangeability was to be required, exact control of dimensions was possible by placing master tooling docks at each of the secondary contractor's plants.

Assuming that the design contractor had fabricated one set of high-production tooling it would be immediately possible to provide the necessary strip templates and index templates to the other secondary contractors. Thus, these secondary contractors could immediately begin to build their own tool gauges while the design contractor could devote its own manpower to building additional tooling and to aircraft production.

If the design contractor possessed only one set of high-production tooling, he would be required to build 100 aircraft of 25,000 pounds airframe weight per month, necessitating more than 1.1 million man-hours of additional tooling labor to meet requirements. If the tool gauges was were fabricated by the co-contractors, this would result in the saving of more than 250,000 hours at the prime plant. The time required to fabricate these gauges at the outside plants would be about 310,000 hours, or 60,000 hours more than (the 250,000) would be used at the design contractor's plant. However, it may be assumed that in the following months, manpower would be a most vital factor at the design contractor's plant where bombers were already in production, even at a low rate, and where a rapid acceleration would be possible.

Additional advantages of producing duplicate tool gauges at the secondary contractor's plants through use of the master tooling dock:

1) Avoid the serious difficulties which could arise through damage to these gauges if made at the prime plant and shipped to the associated contractors.
2) Changes in tooling could be made accurately to contend with design changes if all the plants involved had master tooling docks, merely by sending new templates to the outside plants. Otherwise, in order to insure interchangeability, it would often be necessary for the design contractor to manufacture new tool gauges and ship them to the other plants.
3) If master tooling docks were located at all involved plants, one or more sets of the strip templates and index templates could be made and stored at a one secure point. Thus, there would be protection against the loss of all tooling for the particular model "through the bombing of Consolidated's Plant." (At this time there remained the concern that the Japanese could bomb Pacific Coast plants.)

If engineering and tooling programs were coordinated and the employees properly instructed, considerable time and money could be saved by the design contractor in the construction of tool gauges. This saving was due to tool gauges being made in the tooling dock directly from the blueprints, thus avoiding the necessity of first making control masters. It was estimated that the use of the tooling dock in making tool gauges for aircraft of 25,000 pounds airframe weight would result in saving of approximately 170,000 man-hours.

If the secondary contractors did not have tooling docks, or if for other reasons it was thought prudent for the design contractor to create the tool gauges for the other plants, a large saving would be realized through the use of its tooling dock to reproduce additional sets of tool gauges. If the aircraft had an airframe weight of more than 25,000 and three additional sets of tool gauges were made, use of the dock would save approximately 42,500 man-hours, which at the then rate of $3 per hour would be a savings of $127,000 and at least twenty-five work days.

Manufacture of Tooling

Original tooling could be fabricated in the tool dock without first making control masters or tool gauges. However, then it would later be desirable to make tool gauges in the dock, in order that tooling could be tested during production without the delays and expense involved in disconnecting air hoses and electrical lines and physically moving the tooling back into the dock for testing purposes. Consequently, this program would make the tooling available for use earlier but would not affect an overall saving as compared with making the tool gauges in the dock and then using these tool gauges outside the dock for the manufacture of the tooling. These tool gauges primarily involved the assembly tooling which seldom exceeded 40 percent of a tooling program

Machine Tools

A machine tool is a machine that uses some type of tool for shaping or machining metal or other rigid materials, typically by cutting, boring, grinding, shearing, or other forms of deformation to produce machine parts as their principal function. All machine tools have some method of holding the workpiece and providing a guided movement of the parts of the machine. Consequently the relative movement between the workpiece and the cutting tool (the toolpath) is controlled or constrained by the machine, rather than being entirely "offhand" or "freehand." With their inherent precision, machine tools enable the economical production of interchangeable parts.

Consolidated's major purchasing of machine tools for the B-24 program occurred at several different times with some minor tool buying to fill production gaps and improve methods between the major buying periods. Machine tool purchase at the San Diego Plant was, to a large extent, coordinated with the plant expansion to accommodate production plans for the PBY-5 and PB2Y-3 as well as the B-24. While no actual production delays were caused by the lack of machine tools; some extra manpower was required at times to fabricate parts by hand which could have been better accomplished if machine tool delivery had been on schedule.

Consolidated planned the procurement of machine tools to meet the requirement of all major schedule changes with fill-in purchases to supplement production or to improve production methods. From August 1940 to April 1942, there were three major tool procurements programs; two were for production expansion and the other to complete the facility. After April 1942, a small volume of purchases were mainly for replacement or improved methods.

Machine Tool Procurement

Ordering under the first plan took place between August and November 1940 with about 200 machine tool items, the first machinery ordered for the B-24 program, were purchased to equip the expansion of Plant #1. Almost all of the equipment was delivered from dealer stocks or from factory floors within thirty to sixty days. The important large hydraulic press built by Birdsboro was delivered to San Diego behind schedule but within ninety days from placement of the order.

In the middle of the first ordering period in the fall of 1940, the B-24 machine tools for Plant #2 were ordered. This procurement began in October 1940 and item delivery was mostly completed in the early fall of 1941. This program was the largest of three major programs and included from ten to thirty each of most of the production equipment items ordered. Deliveries of tools purchased in this order took much longer than those on the first program, particularly on orders placed in the middle of 1941. Machine tool orders for Plant #2, which was under construction, were placed far enough in advance that delivery was made when equipment was needed at the completed plant, By December 1941, the equipment and tools procurement program for imminent schedules was complete.

During March and April 1942, the "filling in and rounding out" orders were placed for about 300 items requiring delivery by 1 July 1942. Actual deliveries were made by 1 July on much of the smaller equipment, but there were delays of four to five months on the larger items. During this time, the machine tool program was most chaotic and "urgency standings" were being adjusted to accommodate various war production programs. Rearrangement of the machine tools schedule of by the aircraft scheduling unit worked to the advantage of the B-24 program on many items. After the March and April 1942 ordering program, ordering of machine tools was not large and was restricted to improve methods or to make production capacity adjustments.

However, the worst delays in machine tool ordering occurred after spring 1943 when Wright Field control of War Production Board priorities was discontinued and the determination of machine tool needs was decentralized, with coordination undertaken between AAF Procurement District Offices and local War Production Boards (WPB). Local AAF plant representatives and procurement district officers questioned the need for additional equipment without having a proper appreciation of the required increase in labor efficiency possible. Under this system of priority approval, some orders required as much as a month to process the priority papers and then to place the purchase order.

Production Plan

As war seemed more and more inevitable, and with the tangible and invaluable French contract in hand, Consolidated continually planned to achieve more and more heavy bomber productive capacity. These general plans included:

1) The complete aircraft was to be built on site and with an insignificant amount of sub-contractor assistance. Facility expansion was coordinated directly to this policy.
2) Labor, material, equipment, etc., were all to be available in slightly larger quantities than the anticipated needs.
3) B-24 Production methods were to be those successfully used in building flying boats for the Navy and improved as schedules permitted.
4) Equipment was to be that used previously and already installed, supplemented by more of the same type.
5) Manpower in the plant was to be local, "native to the community." However, no studies were made or could be made to indicate that the ultimate manpower

requirement would deplete not only the local market but also overburden the practical possibilities of importation of outside labor.
6) No changes in management, procurement, or other functions or controls were made, contemplated, or appeared necessary.
7) The formation of the Production Control Organization, which was not set up until March 1941. This group, which numbered 2,500 at its peak employment, was of great assistance with master planning, detailed scheduling, order writing, dispatching, stock control, and the issue of all finished parts and assemblies to the line, and parts or assemblies to spare parts. It would require over a year before the actions of the new Production Control Organization would have any real impact.

The Ford-Willow Run Project, approved 25 February 1941, became a heavy burden on the already stressed Consolidated organization and definitely hindered operations at San Diego. While the company learned much from Ford that would be helpful in later months, Ford certainly gave no assistance in production planning at this critical stage. While deliveries of B-24s by Consolidated were specified during 1940, 1941, and 1942, and the company was more or less met AAF specified requirements, the problem was that these bombers were built, not manufactured. They were built, not as the product of any comprehensive manufacturing planning, but because Consolidated men knew how to build aircraft the "hard way" and because they had the determination to continue building more and more bombers this way.

During the summer of 1941, it became necessary to break down the bomber so that an increasing number of people per hour could be put on assembly operations and at the same time sub-contracting and Feeder Plant operations would gradually take more and more of burden off San Diego. Originally, seven designers and seventy-one toolmakers were engaged in producing the assembly jigs and the hand tools routinely used in pre-war aircraft plants. As production requirements grew, necessitating an increasingly total breakdown of the bomber to smaller sub-assembly units, the demands increased for more tooling, more tools, more rigid and more precise procedures; the demand for personnel increased to a peak of 564 on methods and tool design, plus 146 on lofting, and 1,420 toolmakers.

In addition to manpower problem, the tooling program was confronted by two other serious hurdles: engineering and know-how. Aircraft engineering, partly due to its peacetime conception and design and partly due to the continuous necessary changes, was never current. This condition resulted in a continuing urgent demand for tools which were made before the drawings were finished. Mass-production know-how did not exist at Consolidated, and as volume increased, the company had to gain experience along the way. The first set of tools was satisfactory when used as intended to build a few bombers at a time, basically by hand. But these tools failed completely to produce assemblies, which would "drop into place." Also, it was found to be impossible to get and/or keep the light tools lined up so exact duplicates could be made and much heavier fixtures had to be completely rebuilt

A program had to be developed to assist quality control, including masters and control masters. This and the constant demand for more and duplicate tools led

Consolidated to develop the excellent tooling dock. By the summer of 1942, the moving assembly lines, complete breakdown in sub-assemblies, sub-contracting operations, and the company-owned Feeder Plants all began to combine into the first defined framework of the final preparations to actually manufacture, not build, bombers.

As time passed, the following serious obstacles were encountered, making earlier success of the production objective impossible:

1) Consolidated was totally deficient in mass-production experience.
2) The pre-war B-24 was not engineered for volume production and under Consolidated's engineering procedures and practices at that time, could not have been designed for volume production. To make matters worse, no one at Consolidated knew the means to attain volume production.
3) Consolidated's engineering policy which had been satisfactory in building aircraft by hand during the peacetime was not helpful in preparing for volume production but frequently actually interfered as every element designed in the shop instead of on the engineering drawing board failed to seat in the jigs.
4) The multiple engineering changes dictated by combat experience in this peacetime design more than doubled the responsibility on tool design, tooling, production planning, and the procurement of materials. The importance of many of these early changes was known, although the handling and control of these changes was less than effective.
5) The building of the tooling was constantly delayed by the non-availability of mechanics and tool designers in the San Diego area and the continuing lack of housing and accommodations deterred attracting potential outside personnel.

Generally, while the bomber was designed, the plant built, and the shop equipment procured in peacetime, Consolidated found itself lacking in the experience and the means to more effectively manage the rapidly changing complications that war presented.

Production Acceleration

Consolidated's production department had had experience in building aircraft by "handicraft methods," which dated back to 1925. As has already been discussed, Consolidated's main work prior to and during the negotiation of their B-24 contracts was on flying boats for the Navy. Consolidated's overall record in producing PBYs, PB2Ys, and PB4Ys for the Navy, and B-24s for the AAF was actually excellent—especially Consolidated's production department's record on B-24s considering the problems that had to be overcome and that are more completely detailed next.

After the XB-24 prototype was flown in 1939 and accepted in August 1939, Consolidated gained substantial experience in building this bomber on the LB-30 order originally placed by the French, later taken over by the British. The contracts for the LB-30s were completed in January 1942 at which time Consolidated held an

AAF contract for 352 Liberators and a defense aid contract for 700 more aircraft. A month later, they were to receive another AAF contract for 1,200 more B-24s. These orders on their books, three months after Pearl Harbor, totaling 2,252 bombers and involving an estimated cost of $641,088,715 with the likelihood of more in the future, should have justified at least some planning for using mass-production methods. However, Consolidated failed to do this for various reasons.

As the B-24 was essentially identical to the LB-30, although with introduction of some major engineering changes, Consolidated gained considerable production experience building the LB-30 prior to the acceptance of the first B-24 in June 1941. Although six LB-30As had been accepted in December 1940, Consolidated's overall period of production acceleration should be considered from at least March 1941 when the first two LB-30Bs were accepted. From that time until the peak of acceleration in March 1941, when 270 B-24s were accepted, was a period of thirty-seven months of production that was equivalent to an acceleration rate from first acceptance to peak production rate of 7.3 bombers per month. Ford Willow Run reached a peak of 421 B-24s in March 1944, twenty-one months after first acceptance in July 1942, for an acceleration rate of twenty bombers per month.

Period of Production Acceleration

Company records indicate that production acceleration actually began in the summer of 1941, and except for the decline in January 1942 when the LB-30 contract had been completed and production of the B-24D model was begun, the production curve moved relatively smoothly upwards from that point to peak production. Prior to 1942, plant facilities were being developed, the growing company was in a "shaking down" phase and was not being "motivated" by the AAF, which, at the time, understood of the magnitude of the job. Nevertheless, warplanes in wartime quantities were not and could not be delivered until months later.

By the end of 1942, the ongoing manpower problem had become a serious issue and the unplanned policy of "taking the work to the worker" involving sub-contracting and Feeder Plant operations were becoming unavoidable. Recruiting, training, and engaging new employees on the assembly line had all been necessarily overhauled and improved. Solutions to relieve housing problems were being continually offered but never became effective until production reductions and employee terminations decreased housing requirements.

During 1942, the Consolidated merger with Vultee was developing, and by March 1943, it was completed with the assimilation of AVCO personnel and modifications in operating procedures, which generally were thought to have strengthened the company. Most importantly, Emanuel, Girdler, and Woodhead wisely allowed most of the established, responsible, and qualified personnel the San Diego Division that had advanced the B-24 venture to this point, to be delegated to complete the project. While functions, sections, and departments were moved, strengthened, or enhanced, none of these changes appeared to be caused by major failures or to have resulted from the "reorganizations" that typified many other programs during the war. Instead, they appear to have been the result of the company's rapid growth and the associated growing pains that were ordinarily spread over years instead of months.

As early as October 1942, and as a result of the Consolidated-Vultee merger, improved production methods were implemented. The Vultee faction implemented a trend toward more extensive and appropriate manufacturing breakdown of the work into sequences of simple operations suitable for the utilization of ordinary, mostly unskilled factory workers. These improvements were generally of three separate types as follows:

1) The long and complicated assembly operations which formerly had to be completed by craftsmen who had several years of experience were broken down into small sub-assemblies.
2) Improved skill and methods in tooling design.
3) Improved assembly fixtures.

Consolidated streamlined its production methods by requiring each of the plant's fabricating and sub-assembly departments to produce parts and components at the same rate that the bombers were coming off the final assembly line. Concurrently with this innovation, they installed stock bins along all sub-assembly lines, saving many man-hours previously spent in moving stock out of the previous stockrooms. The stock bins carried only an eight- to ten-day supply, which avoided the delay of raw and fabricated materials.

After considering several methods to reorganize their assembly lines, Consolidated decided to mechanize all assembly lines. However, the buildings in which the bomber was assembled had bays that were too narrow to accommodate the 110-foot wingspan at 90 degrees to the direction of production flow so the bombers were turned at 45-degree angles. This adjustment increased the production line by half, allowing one-third more stations to be placed on the line.

As of 1 May 1943, cost improvement plans put into effect during August 1942 resulted in a savings in more than 4.5 million man-hours per year. Employee suggestions, as of 1 May 1943, saved approximately 70,000 man-hours. Under the employees incentive plan workers had received awards in war bonds, stamps, and cash totaling approximately $30,000.

From September 1941, when the Liberator "conveyor" (assembly) line was first established, to May 1943, the over-all efficiency increase in the two San Diego Plants was estimated to be in excess of 20 percent, and in May 1943, the plants were producing approximately 2.5 bombers for every one produced in April 1942, while the increase of production workers during this period was only 10 percent.

Despite improved manufacturing methods, production was at this time experiencing many delays, the most important of which were as follows:

1) The local labor supply was becoming depleted; a considerable number of highly skilled personnel were entering the Armed Forces; and from 3,000 to 4,000 male employees were in job limbo, attempting to seek an occupational deferment. Many

male employees were uncertain of their draft status because of a lack of definite draft policy by local draft boards.
2) An unexpected workload was caused by the necessity of supplying the Fort Worth Plant with components which were to have been supplied by Ford Willow Run.
3) To avoid unnecessarily long moves of materials and parts through congested aisles, specific sub-assembly sections were relocated so that they could be fed into production flow and more directly into final assembly lines.
4) During December 1942 and February 1943, an interruption occurred in the flow of aircraft acceptances; caused by the failure correctly to evaluate the time required to incorporate the major engineering changes then underway.

B-24 production encountered 1,820 changes, which was a change for an average of every 3.6 bombers or about three changes per day average at peak production. For an item as structurally complex as a Liberator bomber consisting of over 45,000 parts and with such a high degree of inter-relationship of parts, components, and equipment, the engineering change program was by far the largest single factor of influence on production acceleration. The engineering department should have, but did not deal with the frequent and major ordered changes and the priorities of these changes and so it overloaded every department of the plant similarly. It should be mentioned that tooling changes caused 80 percent of the cost of the tooling department, while only 20 percent went into maintenance. Also, while for every employee engaged in procuring materials for the production program, one other was engaged in changing material procurement and delivering new materials to the line.

After the break in production caused by engineering changes, acceleration moved ahead more rapidly and smoothly until peak production was reached. Throughout this entire period, however, many material and GFE shortages frequently caused installations to be made out of order on the assembly lines. In early 1942, power plant installations caused delays; followed by the delayed installation of Sperry automatic pilots and Bendix tail turrets. As was common throughout the entire aircraft industry, aluminum extrusions and forgings were in serious short supply and some difficulties were encountered in obtaining steel items such as chromoly bar and tubing.

It was necessary to completely revise the pre-war concept of purchasing and the result produced a streamlined purchasing department, which reduced overall inventory from an early figure of $31 million to $18 million; reduced flow time by half; and prevented line stoppages. A new material system and the management incentive bonus system was initiated which awarded a direct financial gain to an individual for successful operation and penalties for failure.

Consolidated approached the complex and difficult problem of material procurement and storage by introducing innovative organizational methods that made a substantial contribution to production efficiency. The material system was straightforward, being divided into eight complete sections by classes of items procured and stocked the department. Basically, there were eight parallel and complete material departments with each section chief responsible for adequate purchasing, proper stocking, and timely delivery to the line of all items in the class.

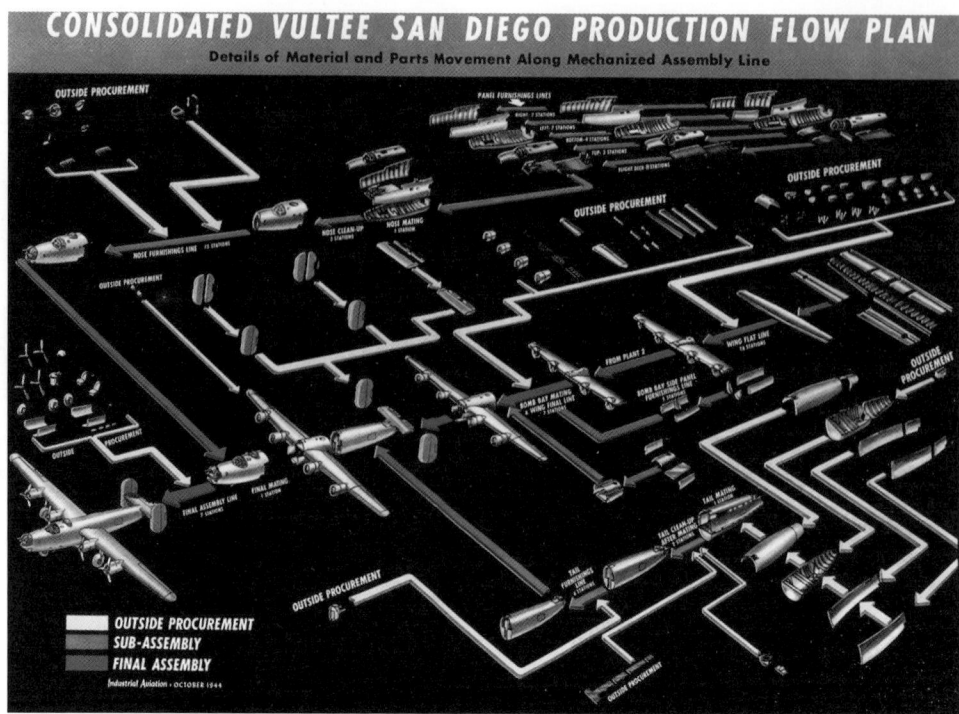

Again, the major difficulty in the material department was the engineering change program, and the resulting continuing short procurement of critical electrical and hydraulic valves, fittings, and accessories, and aluminum forgings and extrusions, all with long flow times even under normal uninterrupted procurement.

Production Control

From 30 November 1940 until September 1943, the delivery schedule of the B-24 was revised eleven times by the production planning and tooling departments. Production planning was divided between production control and tooling groups assisted by industrial engineering on methods, plant layout, etc. A new aircraft delivery schedule was separated into production requirements by weeks and days, and operations, routings, workloads, etc. The flow of work through the factory was by the lot system, each lot representing a month's production.

The first schedule that could be definitely associated with war production was the one issued on 1 July 1941, which planned a peak production of ninety bombers per month. To reach the schedule of ninety bombers per month, production plans resulted from decisions to incorporate moving production lines together with the breakdown of major components and the use of Plant #2. However, only approximately thirty of the scheduled ninety bombers was produced revealing the original planning, tooling, and production control to be inadequate to meet any future production schedules. Since this original plan was based on only a small quantity of sub-contracting, the later high production rate only became possible after the decision to sub-contract all major components other than the fuselage and center wing section was made.

The control of raw material and purchased parts into the plant and stockrooms was the role of the material department. The production control section prepared schedules for all materials to be purchased and distributed all materials when they were requisitioned and issued from stores.

The majority of the snowballing number of changes in detail, assembly, and installation planning were made by the AAF, which they found necessary through combat experience requirements or by aircraft improvements at the plants of other manufacturers. A relatively small number of change proposals were submitted either by supervisors or workers through industrial engineering recommendations and layouts or through the tooling section. Both detailed planning and detailed methods depended on continual revision during the entire war to meet peak production schedules.

Engineering changes were scheduled through the master change record (MCR) system, and while there were a large number of these engineering changes, an even larger number of miscellaneous changes resulted from engineering corrections, along with methods and planning changes, which made the institution of a system similar to the MCR system necessary for recording of these miscellaneous changes.

A lack of coordination with the shop by the master scheduling department caused a problem in making schedule changes in the production line and led to the formation of a master scheduling committee. This committee closely regulated and supervised MCR changes and authorized rescheduling when it became evident that schedule changes could not be met without disrupting the assembly lines. The number of miscellaneous changes grew so large that they could not be quickly processed and it became necessary to schedule these changes after the completion of planning and tooling since the heavy workloads in the tooling shops caused MCR changes to receive top priority there. To relieve this bottleneck, review boards for miscellaneous changes were organized to analyze and determine essential requirements with the authority to cancel unnecessary changes.

During 1943, as the production rate was accelerating, the lot system of manufacturing release caused a problem as the stores of material or sub-assemblies in one lot became too great to manage in the storage facilities available and on some items split lots had to be used. Some problems caused by the shortage of materials also necessitating split lots for the material on hand. To control the lot quantities, the second shift production control personnel (storekeepers) inventoried all parts and sub-assemblies actually on the line and stock at below minimum levels, posting these inventories on IBM equipment. These IBM shortage lists were analyzed by production control to determine the causes and were to correct them. If unaccountable inventory losses occurred, the necessary additional orders with advanced schedules were prepared and sent to the fabrication or material department as required.

Inspection

Consolidated described their Inspection policies as "at all times were commensurate with the quality to be expected in aircraft production." However, the lack of trained inspection personnel, both company and AAF, sometimes hampered the inspection process and the AAF also sometimes failed to coordinate their inspection directives with those of the company. Nonetheless, the company was able to provide almost 100 percent inspection on site and maintained the required standards without seriously inhibiting the flow of production materials to the line.

Consolidated's inspection department consisted of a division chief inspector in each plant, (Plants #1 and #2 and the Tucson Modification Center), who reported directly to the division manager. To assist the division chief inspector, inspection supervisors were placed in all major sections: receiving, fabrication, assembly, chipping, etc., and inspection personnel assigned to the job.

Because of the increased production in 1942 and 1943 and the loss of employees to the armed forces, Consolidated's personnel department initiated a training program to alleviate the impending shortage of inspectors. This training program was given in addition to the normal on-the-job training and significantly helped in supplying trained inspectors throughout the major portion of the production period.

After receiving preliminary training, all new employees in the inspection department were assigned to a particular station, given specified on-the-job training and tutored in the use of the *Inspector's Handbook*, which was to be the most important tool for their job. This *Handbook* delineated responsibilities and limits and at any time changes, deviations, or revisions were made. The inspector was notified and his *Handbook* was amended, to keep him current.

The AAF recruited their inspection personnel from other manufacturing facilities and from trade schools. All new AAF inspectors were also given the necessary in-plant training including use of the *AAF Inspection Manual* prior to being assigned to their stations. Many AAF inspectors were sufficiently trained to permit their successful operation in many different departments which increased their overall inspection efficiency. Whenever possible, all Consolidated and the AAF inspection personnel promotions were made from the ranks.

The proportion of production inspectors to the number of workers was less than the industry average which was due to Consolidated's inspection policy of not including the complete inspection of every production item as was normal in mass-production operations but did include a number of spot-check inspections. This inspection policy should have been supposed as questionable when considering the number of insufficiently skilled workers and the high turnover rate in the San Diego Plant.

AAF inspectors realized that it was necessary to conduct more thorough inspections of all assembly phases a throughout entire production period. This was necessary due to Consolidated's production department's control of inspection department and the constant stress placed upon company inspectors to accept components and assemblies before completion to assure that the scheduled flow of production would be maintained. The AAF continued to observe Consolidated's inspection procedure

Consolidated described their inspection policies as "at all times were commensurate with the quality to be expected in aircraft production." (*CAC/AAF*)

Consolidated engine testing stand and control house. (*ATSC*)

through systematic spot-checks. Each day AAF inspectors were assigned to a number of Consolidated's check lists on which 100 percent inspections were made. The items and procedures to be inspected were selected to give a complete average of all inspection points over a specific time period.

During early 1943, there were numerous rejections due to Consolidated's negligence in handling certain parts and materials including GFE (e.g. B-24's fuel cells were damaged from dirt and exposure). During July 1943, Consolidated's inspectors were not complying with specified inspection requirements, the most important of which affected engine cowling, inspection cover plates, and the coding of electrical cables. During October 1943, more inspection problems occurred during the careless installation of certain jigs and fixtures. The overall quality of production during October 1943 was found to be considerably below that of October 1942, but as production quantity and experience increased, so did production quality.

The Army-Navy "E" Award

Consolidated was presented The Army-Navy "E" award in September 1942, the first "Star" award in November 1943; the second "Star" award in January 1944; the third "Star" award in September 1944; and the fourth "Star" award in July 1945. The Army-Navy "E" Award (also known as the Army-Navy Production Award) was an accolade presented to a company during World War II for excellence in production of war equipment. The award consisted of a pennant for the company and an inch and a quarter long sterling silver lapel pins/broaches for all employees at the time the award was made. The large triangular swallowtail pennant was approximately 48 inches wide on the hoist edge, and approximately 97 inches long on the top and bottom edges. It had a white border, with a capital "E" within a yellow wreath of oak and laurel leaves on a vertical divided blue and red background. ARMY is on the red background and NAVY on the blue background.

Nominations for the Army-Navy "E" Award were the responsibility of the technical services of Army Service Forces, the Army Air Forces, and the Bureaus of the Navy Department, the Coast Guard, or the Marine Corps, whichever had the largest contractual interest in the plant. Thus, if the Army had the largest volume of business in the plant, it nominated the plant, and if the Navy had the prime interest, it nominated the plant. Considerations for the nomination were "quality and quantity of production in the light of available facilities are the factors which will be given the greatest weight in selecting recipients of the award." Other factors to be deliberated included:

1) Overcoming of production obstacles.
2) Avoidance of stoppages.
3) Maintenance of fair labor standards.
4) Training of additional labor forces.
5) Effective management.
6) Record on accidents, health sanitation, and plant protection.
7) Utilization of subcontracting facilities

Usually an Army and/or a Navy officer (usually of a rank suitable to the size and importance of the recipient company) would be present at a formal ceremony attended by company officials and employees. After the award of the pennant, it would be flown at the plant and the employees would wear their lapel/broach pins. Of the more than 85,000 companies involved in fabricating materials during the war, a total of 4,283 companies (about 5 percent) received the award during the course of the war. Plants that maintained an outstanding record of performance for six months after receiving the original Army-Navy "E" Award were granted a Star Award, indicated by a white star on their "E" Pennant. Additional stars could be won by continued outstanding performance for succeeding six-month periods until the flag carried four stars, after which the interval was increased to one year. Plants with continuing excellent work were awarded stars to add to their pennant. Of the 4,283 Awards, 763 had been granted one Star Award, 723 had been granted two Star Awards, 776 had been granted three Star Awards, 820 had been granted four Star Awards, and 206 had been granted five Star Awards (including Consolidated), and only eight had won six Star Awards when the program ended. Willow Run was awarded one Award in April 1945. The Army-Navy "E" Award program was terminated on 5 December 1945.

Army-Navy E Pennant consisted of white lettering and border trim, with the left Army half in red and the right Navy half black, and a gold wreath surrounding the E. (*Author's collection*)

Army-Navy E Pin consisted of a dark metal circle with a wreath surround and a central E. The four metal right and left horizontal outside stripes were red top and bottom and white two central. (*Author's collection*)

Raw Materials and Purchased Parts

Since Consolidated was a fabrication and assembly facility, all forgings, castings, extrusions, sheet aluminum, and steel had to be purchased from outside vendors. In addition, standard parts such as nuts, bolts, fittings, valves, etc. and special items such as landing gear, pumps, electric motors, etc., requiring skilled manufacture or special equipment were purchased from specialized sources. Before wartime production began, the Consolidated production plan functioned very satisfactorily as quantities on order were not large and suppliers could make deliveries from stock. However, as the program progressed, increasing shortages developed, and the expediting department became overloaded.

Once America entered the war, Consolidated planned to expand its existing purchasing department and also to change its purchasing policy as wartime purchasing necessitated finding a vendor with the desired materials readily available or one able to produce quickly rather than the one with the lowest cost. The initial orders for materials were placed on Bill of Material requirements for the entire contractual obligation, although there was some interchange of material between contracts. Generally, lead time for raw materials was six months and was two to five months for purchased parts, depending upon the item.

Early in the war, the material department was organized in three sections: purchasing, material control, and stores. Production control issued the production schedule to the material control section, which then placed orders with the purchasing section that purchased the material. When the material was received, the stores section took control and issued the material to the shop on production control's schedule. The buyer in the purchasing section was responsible for the material until it was received at the Consolidated Plant. However, when it was discovered that the Bill of Material was not reliable, the shop usage system of purchasing was initiated.

The Consolidated Bill of Material was never current, and it was determined that that the most practical method to purchase materials was on the basis of shop usage. This purchasing system functioned admirably and the incentive pay plan to the buyer, material control manager, and stockroom keeper encouraged inventory control. The follow-up agent located in major eastern cities was instrumental in expediting materials from vendors who were behind schedule and in obtaining materials on short notice for urgent engineering changes.

Difficulties increased, and it became apparent that assigned responsibilities were deficient within the functional organization. A thorough study was conducted and a totally new concept of a material procurement organization was created having vertical rather than horizontal divisions, consisting of eight material departments each directed by its own chief. Each of the eight department chiefs was wholly and only responsible for every item in his particular classification and for every phase from the initiation of the purchase request to the actual issue of the material to the line. This clear-cut responsibility made it possible to apply the new incentive earnings plan to material department personnel, which further improved operations, eliminating line stoppages, halving inventory, doubling production, while materials on hand became increasingly critical issue.

Consolidated was diligent about operating with minimum inventories. A detailed monthly list of every item in stock was tabulated, which indicated the past month's consumption, actual inventory, and standard inventory. A standard inventory was established based on scheduled production requirements for a fifteen-, thirty-, forty-five-, or sixty-day period, depending upon the character of the item. This tabulation was reviewed by the involved personnel in purchasing, stores, and material control and any necessary corrective actions were taken on "unbalanced" items. To avoid production delays by over-zealous inventory reductions, an incentive earnings program was established. In the calculation of incentive earnings, the maintenance of inventories at a "standard level" was a "plus" item while the cost of shortages was a "negative." After production was performed under this new control plan, lead time was reduced 50 percent without line stoppage.

The shortage of material, inventory restrictions, and information necessary to support allocation requests compelled a larger expansion of the material department than was anticipated. The expediting department was eliminated and its responsibilities were assumed by the buyers who were organized in local offices throughout the east to make personal contacts with vendors who were behind schedule. A material representative also contacted the aircraft scheduling unit in Dayton and War Production Board in Washington and maintained offices in those cities.

During the war, material shortages were the one of the greatest difficulties, however, under the CMP (Controlled Materials Plan) in 1943, the B-24's raised priority position eased the material situation.

Some of the early difficulties were caused by the late arrival or lack of aluminum and alloy tubing, which caused the delay of many shop orders in 1942. The aluminum forging situation was considered "unsatisfactory" and shortages also occurred in certain steel items such as tubing and chrome alloy bar stock. Many items were received in insufficient quantities and had to be ordered as emergency shipments for production to continue.

Some vendors were confused about material allocations and the filling of orders. Vendor-furnished parts also caused serious shortages, the most important of which were flexible engine mounts; electrical fittings; hydraulic pumps, valves, and fittings; flexible shafts and control cables. Vendors were unable to obtain sufficient quantities of nickel for night-landing light reflectors, brass for fittings, while roller and ball bearings were critical as steel allocations for their manufacture were inadequate

Difficulties in the receipt of parts from various sub-contractors were usually due to the following circumstances:

1) Consolidated furnished forgings, motors, valves, and hydraulic equipment to the sub-contractors which could not be delivered in time to permit the sub-contractors to complete fabrication as scheduled.
2) Certain sub-contractors, because of the lack of machine and die capacity, were compelled to, in turn, sub-contract a portion of their order.
3) Vendors were unable to quickly integrate the numerous engineering changes in their order and were unable to make timely delivery.

Most of these engineering changes necessitated the ordering of additional parts and materials and their vendors were unable to supply them on short notice. The result was that many of the changes were not incorporated as planned. When it was possible to alleviate these shortages by filing ASU-16s (critical shortage requests) that procedure was followed. Consolidated documents stated that the many engineering changes required a "superhuman effort" by Consolidated's material department or its eastern expediting offices as well as the ASU requests. Throughout the war, the obsolescence of material and parts caused by engineering changes became the prime obstruction in B-24 production.

Although many of those critical conditions were alleviated by the improved methods of material controls established in 1943, the material's problems continued. Many of the material or parts shortages, although mostly not delaying bomber delivery, had to be installed out of station on the assembly line at the cost of many man-hours. There were shortages of aluminum extrusions and steel forgings that continued to threaten production delays throughout the major portion of the production program. Substitutes for forgings were "hogged" (fabricated) out of bar stock; valves and fittings were made in Consolidated's machine shops, while the shortage of aluminum rivets became so critical that Consolidated had to acquire machine tools and make rivets in their shops. Some difficulties also arose due to the AAF, USN, and commercial contracts that Consolidated held, which caused the necessity of having three separate assignments of materials. There were difficulties caused by previous non-standardization when Consolidated attempted to standardize once mass-production had begun. Due to difficulties encountered in procurement, Consolidated made provisions so that standard item manufacturers could permit other producers or licensees to manufacture essential items, such as, electric motors, hydraulic pumps, valves, fittings, etc.

5
Feeder Shop Plan and Subcontracting

Feeder Shops

One year after Pearl Harbor, when manpower became critical at San Diego, Consolidated endeavored to help relieve the situation by developing Feeder Shops (also called Feeder Plants) and Plants in areas remote from the main plants, thus utilizing labor that could not be induced to come to San Diego to work.

The Feeder Shop Plan developed by Consolidated represented a considerable addition to the production at the San Diego Plant. All Feeder Shop personnel were on the Consolidated payroll and full control of these shops was consigned to the San Diego Division with these Feeder Plants considered as "removed Sections or Departments" of the main San Diego Plant. Although a large number of items that were sent to the Feeder Plants could have been easily sub-contracted as they were simple complete units, they were not attractive to most sub-contractors as the contract items in the volume available between changes were relatively small in size, weight, and man-hour cost. The principal Feeder Shop items were plastics, electric and hydraulic systems, and upholstery. Feeder Plants contributed approximately 10 percent of the total man-hours expended on the Liberator.

By pioneering the Feeder Shop concept, Consolidated was able to obtain the most desirable and least expensive locations available. The various Chambers of Commerce, municipal officials, and the Southern California Edison Electric Company were very helpful and cooperative in locating these Feeder sites.

Despite manpower shortages and difficulty in obtaining materials, many Feeder Plants were completely altered in only a few days to begin their contracted work. Almost all of the alteration work completed by local contractors was on a cost-plus-fixed-fee basis with alteration costs capitalized to be written off during the term of the leases. Some heating equipment and all the air compressors were owned by the Defense Plant Corporation. Materials for the alterations were obtained under a blanket priority list, approved by the WPB, and requested in advance for a "series of Feeder Plants." This was thought to be the first "blanket priority assistance" used for construction materials.

Consolidated's employment department established its own Feeder Shop hiring headquarters at Santa Ana, which was centrally located relating to the majority of the Feeder Plants. The Feeder Shops encountered few difficulties in finding employees except that there were a limited number of male workers but there sufficient women available who were described as "above average: and had a "marked enthusiasm to help in the war effort." Most of the new hires were referred to Consolidated's employment department by the U.S. Employment Service (USES) bureau office in the area and all new hires were cleared through this office for availability. Each Feeder Shop was given priority for labor procurement up to the shop's estimated maximum capacity. All of the general foremen and some of the foremen and assistant foremen were transferred to the Feeder Shops from main San Diego Plant. Fourteen assistant foreman, however, were developed from men hired locally, as were most of the assistant supervisors. A representative of the San Diego tooling department spent full time at the Feeder Shop where he was responsible for making repairs and minor alterations to sub-assembly production tooling (all major repairs were made in San Diego). Each Feeder Shop had production control personnel under a head dispatcher who reported to the superintendent of Feeder Shops. At five of the shops, the head dispatcher was hired locally as a stock clerk and promoted to assistant foreman in production control. The remainder of assistant foremen in this group were transferred from the production department in San Diego. The head inspector at most Feeder Shots was transferred from the San Diego inspection department and was responsible to that department. All assistant inspection personnel were developed from local hires.

All Feeder Shop requirements from San Diego and *vice versa* were managed through a chief coordinator's office located at Plant #2, San Diego. All matters pertaining to materials, completed parts, details, equipment, tools, etc. cleared through this office. To supply the Feeder Plants with materials, a 43,000-square-foot material warehouse was centrally established in Santa Ana to store all raw stock, Plexiglas, tubing, fabric, wire, commercial material and stores items, janitor supplies, etc.

The feeder facilities were usually rather small, innocuous buildings such as this Huntington Beach location. (*ATSC*)

The interior of the Huntington Beach facility which fabricated upholstery. (*ATSC*)

Above: Anaheim Plexiglas feeder plant. (*ATSC*)

Below: Santa Ana tube bending feeder plant. (*ATSC*)

Sub-Contracting

Sub-contracting at Consolidated during World War II conclusively proved that the prime contractor's facilities alone were not adequate to fulfill the company's production requirements.

Prior to 1942, Consolidated's policy was to sub-contract only those items for which other manufacturers had developed special tools and techniques. These items included exhaust manifold, engine mounts, assemblies, specialized punch press parts, and machine shop jobs. In addition, certain major components such as pontoons, wing panels, and attaching parts were sub-contracted, as a strategy to eliminate the need for plant expansion when the long-term use of these items was unknown.

Before Pearl Harbor, motivated by the war in Europe and the foreign aircraft orders, Consolidated began to realize the necessity for plant expansion to ensure meeting increasing aircraft demands. When it became evident in early 1942 that the production acceleration demanded of the company far exceeded its ability to obtain the necessary additional manpower, equipment, and space at the San Diego Plant, the decision to expand the sub-contracting program was made.

Consolidated sub-contracting prior to 1942 averaged approximately 10 percent of the total airframe man-hours, with some peaks reaching 15 percent to 20 percent. However, when the decision was made to expand the program, it was planned to quadruple the amount of sub-contracting to approximately 40 percent the total man-hours. This was to be done by sub-contracting large units, basically simple and complete in themselves such as wing leading edges, flaps, ailerons, elevators, rudders, stabilizers, tabs, bomb doors, gun turrets, bulkheads, and pilot's enclosures. In addition, sub-contractors for assembly of power plants and power plant equipment were to be developed.

While geographical location was a factor in the selection of sub-contractors, the decision to place the business usually involved its manufacturing ability, capacity, and the availability of labor. Mostly, the early selections were well-established as reliable sub-contractors and included such companies as Brewster Aeronautical, Long Island, New York; Bell Aircraft, Buffalo, New York; and Northrop Aircraft, Hawthorne, California. When the demands for aircraft increased in 1942, it became necessary to locate new sources which generally involved the conversion of commercial manufacturers into aircraft facilities with new processes, methods, and techniques. The managements, facilities, and operating conditions of these new sources were more closely analyzed than previously to determine to what degree they could be adapted to handle aircraft work.

Although the original plan was to sub-contract specialized items and those that were relatively simple and complete in themselves, the actual overall sub-contracting program reached its peak with regard to quality, volume, man-hour efficiency and cost during the early part of 1944. At this time, sub-contracting amounted to approximately 37 percent of total weight and 40 percent of total man-hours. During May 1944, at peak production, 2,175,650 pounds of airframe weight (120 equivalent bombers) were received from sub-contractors, representing 1,921,662 man-hours at a cost of $6.28 per man-hour, or $4.45 per pound. This was equivalent to 0.71 pounds per man-hour. This was later reduced by sub-contractor efficiency to 33 percent of total man-hours at

30 percent of the dollar value of the bomber after peak production had been passed. During sub-contracting, there were no reversals in the original plan at any time but any deviations were the result of "experience and aggressive initiative and were a growth toward improvement in coordination and methods to accomplish the utmost efficiency."

Previous to April 1942, all sub-contracting had been managed by the purchasing department, after which a separate sub-contract department was established separately from purchasing to specialize in the procurement of the larger units of the bomber. Basically those larger units such as wing panels, leading edges, control surfaces, bomb bay doors, and sections that were designed by the prime contractor, Consolidated, and which normally would have been built within its own plant, were included as sub-contract department units. Also, some items, such as the exhaust collector, engine mounts, and similar units which were generally procured from outside sources were also included in the sub-contract department. In effect, his organization consisted of three sections:

1) The procurement and negotiation sections employed approximately 80 percent of the sub-contract department's personnel and were engaged on procurement problems, negotiations, follow-up, and expediting.
2) The coordinating section employed about 10 percent of the personnel in engineering and tooling coordination engineering and tooling liaison.
3) The control section employed the remaining 10 percent of sub-contract personnel and were used on statistical and control work.

Although each sub-contracting section head was responsible for the execution of contracts, authorization was granted from a company officer. All final negotiations and contracts were very closely coordinated with Consolidated's legal and treasury departments. The sub-contract department initially consisted of approximately fifteen employees but was expanded during 1942 and 1943 to a maximum of 197 in January and March 1944. Because the department stressed the application of business, engineering, tooling, legal, and manufacturing aspects, sub-contract personnel were generally very capable and were relatively highly compensated.

When a sub-contractor was contracted, Consolidated instituted realistic scheduling by not only considering the sub-contractor's facilities but also by determining the necessary manpower required for the job, based on Consolidated's own experience in its plant. However, after the contract for an item was placed in the sub-contractor's plant, the efficiency or learning curve of that item in the new location was maintained, observed, and manpower and cost predictions were made based upon it. The manpower (man-hour) reports submitted by the sub-contractors supplied the data for interpretation of these learning curves. These reports were submitted periodically—weekly, semi-monthly, or monthly, depending upon the company's methods of timekeeping, although the majority of reports were received weekly, which was the most preferred reporting basis. There were a few cases where the sub-contractor refused or neglected to submit regular reports and personnel from Consolidated had to periodically visit the sub-contractor's plant and by careful observation were able to estimate the desired data. The normal manpower report disclosed three things:

1) The total number of man-hours expended on the quantity of assemblies produced during the defined time period
2) The average number of man-hours per aircraft allocated to the construction of each completed assembly during this period
3) The number of assemblies completed during this period

This basic data was used to chart the learning curve of each assembly in each sub-contractor's plant. These charts, in turn, made it possible to anticipate future performance of the sub-contractor in:

1) Determining future production costs in terms of man-hours.
2) Deriving projected labor loads indicating the number of workers required to meet the production schedule.
3) In predicting and, consequently, preventing bottlenecks, in delivery of assemblies to the prime contractor, due to over-optimistic commitments.

Generally, Consolidated's experience with the sub-contractors was decidedly satisfactory, particularly where sufficient liaison was and could be mutually maintained. The sub-contractors' managements aggressively instituted improvement programs and continually extended themselves to be more efficient and of more service to the prime contractor. The sub-contractor often improved the standard aircraft production methods, which was passed on to Consolidated. Thus, the exchange of ideas between the subs and the prime contractor proved to be mutually beneficial.

Often, the application of man-hour and learning curve data was entirely unknown to the sub-contractor. The original reluctance of a sub-contractor who was new to aircraft production in establishing fixed prices was shortly overcome when it was recognized that Consolidated's application of the aircraft industry's method of charting man-hour data and cost data was sound and that learning curve data not only gave a guide to the sub-contractor with respect to man-hour cost and rate of manufacture, but that it was also invaluable to him with respect to his financial requirements and in his financial negotiations with Consolidated.

Consolidated's experience indicated that, while it was preferable for the sub-contractor to be located close to the prime contractor, this was not essential provided that highways or rail facilities were available for the movement of raw materials and finished parts. In the early phases of sub-contracting, substantial pools or banks of parts were maintained as insurance against shortages or work stoppages due to transportation difficulties, However, as sub-contractors improved their control and handling procedures and as secondary sources were established in other areas, these problems were minimized, which enabled sizable reductions in the size of various banks of parts. Temporary manufacturing delays were seldom experienced—none of which were critical enough to actually hamper production.

The control of sub-contractors was achieved by "showing a competitive spirit, a free exchange of ideas and practices and proper consideration of all problems." Managerial control of the sub-contractors was by its own management unless the sub-contractor was to be wholly subsidized.

Often "clock-like precision" was achieved on the shipment of parts from the sub-contractor and receipt and usage by the prime. For the transportation of finished parts, rail services were used whenever possible when time permitted. Trucking services, however, allowed better control, fewer handling difficulties, and more flexibility in the operation. Sometimes, it was necessary to depend on alternative methods of transportation due to breakdowns, weather, and other localized situations. Rail express and air express were used more often when time was a factor. The cost of transportation was always secondary to the importance of delivery and production requirements as interruption of the final assembly line was not acceptable. Expediting the movement of parts was as important as expediting the manufacture of the part.

Inspection procedures of the sub-contractors were improved by Consolidated's liaison inspectors, although every effort was made to establish the sub-contractor's inspection as an independent and responsible unit. It was established that the education and improvement of the sub-contractor's inspection department was a much better approach to the quality control problem than to establish prime contractor/customer inspection at the sub-contractor/source. The necessity for the rework of subcontractor submissions by the prime contractor was established through his inspection department and coordinated through the negotiation section of the sub-contract department. Charges for necessary rework were billed back to the sub-contractor after coordination as to determination of responsibility and prevention of recurrence of the rejection through eliminating its cause.

Sub-contractor's objected to engineering changes that disrupted their production or caused a work stoppage. However, the sub-contractors became more amenable once they realized that these changes were made for the bomber's improvement or were made for military necessity.

San Diego Plant B-24 Sub-Contractors

Sub-Contractor	Location	Item
American Central Mfg.	Connersville, IN	Exhaust collector
		Tail stack
		Wing outer panel
		Top center section
Atlas Chromium Plating	Los Angeles, CA	Plating flap tracks
Baash-Ross Tool Co.	Los Angeles, CA	Flap tracks
Berger Mfg. Division	Canton, OH	Wing flap assembly
		Bomb bay door
		Stabilizers
Bobrick Mfg.	Los Angeles, CA	Check valve assembly
Carnice Steel and Supply	Los Angeles, CA	Bomb hoist support
Casper Aircraft	San Diego, CA	Electric harness
Castoloy of CA	Los Angeles, CA	Main entrance door
Continental Can	Los Angeles, CA	Leading win edges
		Trailing wing edges
Consolidated-Vultee	Nashville, TN	Center section front spar

Drayer and Hanson	Los Angeles, CA	Scavenging units
Engle Aircraft Specialties	Escondido, CA	Wing splice plates
		Elevator tab assembly
Essick Mfg.	Los Angeles, CA	Main beam and hoist
Firestone Aircraft	Los Angeles, CA	Oil cells
Gay Engineering	Los Angeles, CA	Engine mount supports
Gemmer Mfg.	Detroit. MI	Aileron gear unit
		Torque tube assembly
		Bellcrank assembly
		Bellcrank control system
General Fireproofing	Los Angeles, CA	Pilot seats
		Track assembly
Gilfillan Bros.	Los Angeles, CA	Arm drive mechanism
		Yoke nose drive mechanism
		Gear housing drive mechanism
Goodyear Tire and Rubber	Los Angeles, CA	Oil cells
Grand Rapids Store Eqpt.	Los Angeles, CA	Side gunner's door
		Control guards
		Life raft cradle
Hook Rubber	Watertown, MA	Rudder tabs
		Aileron tabs
Kawneer	Berkeley, CA	Bomb racks
Kaydon Engineering	Muskegon, MI	Wing splice fitting
La Porte	La Porte, IN	Fin assembly
Langley	San Diego, CA	Tab control
		Control column
		M.L.G. release
		Gear box assembly
Leonard Precision Prod.	Garden Grove, CA	Pump screen assembly
		Machining work
Mahl Mfg.	Huntington Pk, CA	Longerons
		Hangar assembly
Monarch Tool and Instr.	Los Angeles, CA	M.L.G Bumper
Motor Products	Detroit, MI	Tail turret
		Ammunition tracks
N-Mac Products	Hollywood, CA	Scavenging kits
Natl. Machine Products	Los Angeles, CA	Control column
		Sprocket assembly
		Machined parts
National Supply	Torrance, CA	Main landing gear
Pryne and Co.	Los Angeles, CA	Hydraulic tank
Rheem Mfg,	Los Angeles, CA	Nose bottom panels
Rocky Mt. Steel Products	Los Angeles, CA	Flap indicator

Company	Location	Parts
Rohr Aircraft	Chula Vista, CA	Power plant installation Quick change engine parts Nacelle rear
Ryan Aero	San Diego, CA	Aileron assembly Elevator assembly Outer wing panel Rudder
San Diego Machine	San Diego, CA	Handle Assembly Bellcrank control assembly Machining work
Schiefer and Sons	San Diego, CA	Amplifier cover Door panel Fuselage floors Map cases Cargo carriers
Shakespeare Products	Kalamazoo, MI	Throttle quadrant
Southern Aire	Garland, TX	Tail turret
Southern CA Airparts	Glendale, CA	Hydraulic tank assembly
Solar Aircraft	San Diego, CA	Exhaust collector Stack assembly
Spartan Aircraft	Tulsa, OK	Aileron assembly Elevator assembly Rudder
Super Cold	Los Angeles, CA	Bomb racks Pilot seat floors Tail bumper
Superior Machine	San Diego, CA	Machined forgings
Textile	Dallas, TX	Trailing edge over flap
Tidmarsh Machine	Tucson, AZ	Aileron tabs
Timm Aircraft	Van Nuys, CA	Hydraulic reservoir assembly
Vendo	Kansas City, MO	Ball turret guide
Vultee Field Division	Downey, CA	Wing tips Fins
Weaver Aircraft	San Diego, CA	Machining work
Welded Aircraft Parts	Huntington Pk, CA	Bomb supports Spare bomb chocks Flap track supports
Western Industrial	Los Angeles, CA	Pilot's enclosure

An example of an important Consolidated sub-contractor was neighboring Ryan Aeronautical Company, which had signed a fifty-year lease, starting in 1939, on land at the southeastern edge of Lindbergh Field along North Harbor Drive. Ryan sub-contracted aileron and elevator assemblies, the outer wing panel, and rudder. At peak wartime production, the Ryan plant had 8,500 employees and annual production exceeded $55 million.

Ryan Aeronautical. (*AFSHRC*)

Reuben Fleet (R) and Charles Van Dusen (L) pose with friend, neighbor, and subcontractor Claude Ryan. (*CAC/AAF*)

6

Government-Furnished Equipment and Spare Parts

Government-Furnished Equipment (GFE)

The B-24 included about 400 items of GFE, of which there were many severe shortages that often required special expedited delivery. GFE was a constant management problem both in the material department and in the production department. Compared to engineering changes, the lack of GFE did not affect aircraft deliveries to any appreciable degree during the five years of B-24 production.

In the early phases of the production program, Consolidated tried to operate a common supply system and common stockrooms for both company-owned and GFE items, which was at the time the only logical and suitable procedure for supplying a manufacturing plant. As the production rate was increased, the most serious problems of GFE procurement, storage, issue, and accountability occurred. To solve these GFE problems so that production would not be interrupted and to satisfy government property accountability regulations, the GFE unit was sent out of the material central general organization through its supervisor directly to the chief of material.

This plan was for managing GFE required personnel in addition to those employed in handling GFE items. Because of the different methods of issue and control, mistakes and uncertainty increased and the efficiency of shop personnel decreased. For instance, connector plugs of the same type and stock maker were issued as GFE and also as company-furnished equipment (CFE), which resulted in the employee never knowing exactly which part was to be used and if breakage occurred, whose part it was and who to charge. This was so common that in 1944, Consolidated was required to reimburse the government $500,000 for "material unaccounted for."

Consolidated desired a change in GFE accountability to be made to allow it to correspond with its own system of procurement, issuance, and controls and to deliver the GFE material to its plant and invoice the government for it at the time. This would allow Consolidated to acquire actual ownership of GFE and eliminate the separate elaborate and confusing accounting system but this never occurred.

Spare Parts

Spare parts were an important part of B-24 production when considering the total B-24 Program and basing it on its dollar value. Spare parts were shipped in an amount equal to 16.4 percent of production with 1 percent being shipped on emergency TWX orders and 2.4 percent on stock replenishment calls. The spare parts group grew from an insignificant unit and while passing through several evolutionary phases grew to a peak total of 327 employees. By the time of peak production, the spare parts program was able to supply the number of spare parts as required by any of the AAF contracts. Consolidated's failure to develop its spare parts program early enough caused it to become a definite burden on production acceleration.

As early problems of the control of spares developed it became necessary to split the duties of the spares group into several sections within the production and material control sections, which were assigned to handle all production requirements of similar items. The spares group as finally constituted focused on the final allocation of the spares items and their preparation for shipment. A separate 55,000-square-foot (with 80 percent used on the B-24 Program) depot was finally allotted with the spare parts department located directly over the shipping department where the packaging and shipping operations were performed. Later, another specialized depot operated under contract by the spare parts sub-contractors was located adjacent to the plant. This depot simplified the spares control problem as well as those of stocking, and packaging, and fixed the responsibility for supply.

Spares fulfillment slowly increased during the acceleration period to an 80 percent level at peak. The spares program began each contract with a serious handicap as the AAF did not freeze the list of spare parts items and quantities at the time of contracting nor for some time afterward, making planning difficult and fulfillment impossible. As time passed, the necessary changes in the list, further complicated spares control. Other major problems were fixing responsibility for spare parts provision; critical spare parts supply (i.e. the total available quantity of critical items); priority relative to the production program; and packaging; all of which added to the spares programs never being current. But in the face of these handicaps, the spare parts program was considered more than satisfactory as supported by the small 1 percent volume of emergency shipments. As the requirement for the Liberator decreased, the spares program became relatively less of a load on production and it rapidly reached the 100 percent fulfillment figure.

Rejected and Salvaged Items

All rejected items that were judged as unsuitable for further use were damaged to prevent any usage and identified by a rejection stamp. All rejected items were quickly examined to determine the cause for their rejection and later (about two weeks) engineering orders were issued and any faulty blueprints and tools were corrected. Items that were accepted as salvageable were identified by a Consolidated Inspection Salvage Stamp and their further disposition was usually made within twenty-four hours.

7

Consolidated Assembly Line

San Diego Liberator Construction Evolves

The first Liberators, like other aircraft of the late pre-war period, were mostly individually handbuilt. Three major expansions of 410,000 square feet (1939–40), 663,000 square feet (1940–41), and the enormous 1,700,000-square-foot expansion of 1941–42 about doubled the Consolidated San Diego Plant to 3,363,000 square feet. As production orders increased, Consolidated economically increased the amount of tooling to expand its production rate.

In 1943, Joseph Gwinn, Consolidated's supervisor of tooling and methods, described Consolidated B-24 assembly as more than a line but as a "philosophy of manufacture with its keynote being mobility with every element that has to do with the process moving with the aircraft themselves."

By 1944, ironically, after learning from the Ford-Willow Run mass production experience, the Consolidated San Diego Plant achieved true mass production, with nearly 600,000 separate component B-24 parts continuously gathered from many sources and systematically assembled. Production engineering allocated aircraft manufacture into small enough segments so that only enough personnel would work on construction of each segment at the same time. For example, a Liberator nose section began as ten separate panels, each on its own assembly line that merged into five lines with the panels merging into subsections, ultimately coming together as a single complete nose section.

The 3,000-foot-long San Diego final assembly line carried fifty-four Liberators, each canted at a 45-degree angle, to only thirty-one work stations including the work platforms that gave workers access to all sides of the aircraft. Production scheduling was so exact that a wing center section laid down in the jigs at 10 a.m. on 1 July would be ready for attachment to the fuselage on 9 July at 12:43 a.m. and would continue on as a finished Liberator at 2:53 p.m. on 14 July. This automation reduced the number of man-hours needed to manufacture a Liberator from 40,000 in 1943 to less than 8,000 in 1945.

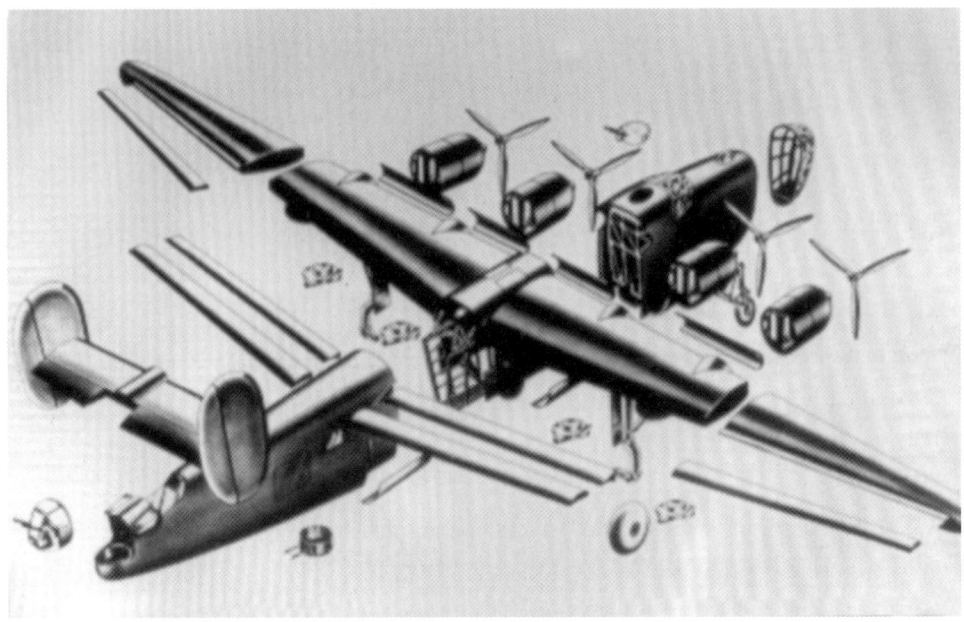

B-24 component breakdown. (*AAF*)

The first Liberators, like other aircraft of the late pre-war period, were mostly individually hand-built. (*CAC/AAF*)

The 3,000-foot-long San Diego final assembly line carried fifty-four Liberators. (*CAC/AAF*)

Nose Section Manufacture

The Liberator nose section was the most important and complex fuselage part and literally the Liberator's "nerve center" containing all the controls for the pilot, co-pilot, navigator, radio operator, and bombardier. Manufacture of the nose involved the use of almost 700,000 parts and rivets, plus installation of roughly 13,000 feet of wiring, 2,000 electrical and plumbing connections, and more than 2,000 feet of tubing of various types.

The new production system at the San Diego Plant for manufacturing the B-24 nose section required only one-third the number of workers to manufacture more than one-third more fuselage nose sections without a large increase in floor space. Instead of a sub-assembly line three-quarters of a mile long, only a few hundred feet of factory space were required for fuselage nose assembly. During the original production system, all these installations were undertaken by crews of six workers as no more could be contained into the nose section simultaneously and continue to work efficiently. Instead of the previous 6,000 man-hours and fifty working days, far less than 1,000 man-hours were now needed.

The basis of the new system was to build the nose section shells (from the rear line of the bombardier's transparent enclosure to the front wing spar) in stationary bucks as before but with the one exception involving leaving the rivets out along four cleavage lines, which separated the nose in four sections, one on each side from front to back just below the pilot's window, and one on each side near the bottom. All the necessary installations were then made on the moving assembly lines and then the sections then "buttoned" together again.

The job breakdown for each station was designed both to place installations next to the skin first and to permit the maximum number of workers to operate simultaneously without crowding, or without any one working directly above another. The lines had a varying number of stations to accommodate widely different numbers of installations. They were scheduled so the same segments that came out of stationary bucks were eventually remated.

The six sections were accommodated on four lines, one each for the side panels and flight deck with the top and bottom panels and top decks alternating on the remaining line. From breakdown to remating, the side panels proceeded along parallel lines through eleven stations, including cleanup and inspection, although installations were different in many cases. In every instance, however, the jobs to be done were broken down into the smallest possible operation. The flight deck section moved through sixteen stations, with Stations 8 and 12 for inspection and numbers fifteen and sixteen as auxiliary cleanup stations. Some of the largest installations, such as nose wheel landing gear fittings and two pilots' controls, were installed on the line. The pilots' controls, including throttle and mixture control column, elevator and aileron control wheels, rudder pedals, and all control cable leads, formed a complete subassembly. On this line, one station was exclusively for hydraulic operations, where all tubing previously installed was connected. At the same time, the top and bottom panels moved along their own line through five stations, the last for cleanup and inspection. The two-segmented top panel, with comparatively few installations, was placed on its side. The fixture for the bottom panel, however, had a swiveling arrangement whereby the segment was swung on its side through the first two stations to facilitate cleanup riveting that which could not be easily done in the buck and to simplify initial installations.

Mating of the sections required no special tooling as the units were simply rolled from their assembly lines into an open floor area adjacent to air and electric power lines and "buttoned up" with bolts and rivets. With the nose section being a single unit again, it was transferred to a rolling dolly to take its place on the third mechanized assembly line. Here, moving sidewise to conserve space, the nose traversed thirty stations. Since the majority of the installation work had been completed in Stations 5 to 16 preceding mating, these later operations consisted largely of connecting electric, hydraulic, and other lines that were routed through two or more of the segments, which could only be placed when the nose section was one unit. The last phase was installing the windshields, astrodome, and bombardier's enclosure; finishing all fabric, upholstery work, etc., and cleanup and inspections.

From the end of this line, the finished nose section was moved to the paint shop after which it was then moved by special truck trailer to the final assembly area where it is joined to center section and aft fuselage.

Above left: The Liberator nose section was the most important and complex fuselage part and literally the Liberator's "nerve center" containing all the controls for the pilot, co-pilot, navigator, radio operator, and bombardier. (*CAC/AAF*)

Above right: Manufacture of the nose involved the use of almost 700,000 parts and rivets, plus installation of roughly 13,000 feet of wiring, 2,000 electrical and plumbing connections, and more than 2,000 feet of tubing. (*CAC/AAF*)

Completed nose sections (and center sections) awaiting removal to the main assembly line. (*CAC/AAF*)

The Final Liberator Assembly Line

A day foreman and a night foreman supervised the work at each of the thirty-one stations on the Liberator line. Leadmen under the foreman in charge had direct control of each station. Consolidated always had the reputation of relying on the expertise of its floormen to resolve production problems and interpret engineering into production. A placard was hung on the side of each arriving assembly item denoting the station number, the name of the leadman in charge, and the name of the inspector. A portable shop clerk's desk was located at each station where the bill of materials and parts lists, as compiled by the tooling and methods department, were kept together with other essential shop records.

A bill of materials (BOM) was a list of the raw materials, sub-assemblies, intermediate assemblies, sub-components, parts and the quantities of each needed to manufacture an end product. A BOM could be used for communication between manufacturing partners or be confined to a single manufacturing plant. A BOM was often associated with a production order that could cause various factions to reserve components in the BOM that were in stock and requisition components that were not in stock. A BOM could define products as they are designed (engineering BOM), as they were ordered (sales BOM), as they were built (manufacturing BOM), or as they were maintained (service BOM).

When the assemblies were completed at their particular station they were transferred to their next station. A signalman, standing on the wing tip of every eighth bomber moving along the line, was supplied with two flags, red and white; the red flag gave the ready to move signal while the white one indicated that the line was in motion. Later, instead of stopping and starting, the line moved along at a constant speed of 7 inches per minute.

No essential tooling was fixed to the floor as the building housing the assembly line was considered only as a shelter for the operation. The line was oval-shaped, progressing up one side of the building and turning back to go down the other. Instead of being carried along abreast, to obtain economy of space, the aircraft traveled along the line at a 45-degree angle. While the finished B-24 had a wing span of over 100 feet, the 45-degree angle enabled it to be moved in a 74-foot bay and back again in a 116-foot bay while still providing an aisle and storage space.

The carriage that transported the future completed B-24 through its entire circuit of the assembly line was constructed of welded structural shapes and heavy tubing consisting of a framework having four vertical posts and eight wheels, one pair under each post. This square carriage moved along one of its diagonals on three tracks. The diagonally opposite two pairs of wheels that followed each other along the center track were pivoted and flanged to guide the carriage. The two outer pairs of wheels were fixed and had no flanges. All the carriages in each section of the line were linked together with tie bars that predetermined their spacing and moved them along when the carriage at the head of the line was pulled forward. For the first section of the line, the carriages were spaced on 46-foot centers, but for the return section, this dimension was increased to 65 feet. The tie bar was hinged to compensate for the change in the center distance and only a single solid length was used along the first part of the line.

The tie bar was disconnected as the carriage left this section to be swung around on a semi-circular length of track for its return trip. When the tie bar was reconnected it was swung on its hinged joint to its full length. A similar semicircular length of track at the end of the final half of the line made it possible to swing the carriage into the starting station without additional handling.

The 5-hp electric motors, backed up by a three-quarter-hp motor, for moving each section of the line, were connected so that the line could be moved either continuously or intermittently. The motors had suitable gear reductions to provide the proper speed. Two crane runways ran the entire length of the plant, one over each bay. Each runway supported two traveling cranes that were used for hoisting the large subassemblies into place. Electrical outlet boxes for were sunk in the floor along the entire length of the assembly line. Compressed air lines paralleled the two outer tracks with connections spaced at short intervals.

Sub-assemblies, being integral units with all wiring, piping, sheaves, and connections in place, arrived at the final assembly line with as much work as possible completed on them. All parts and sub-assemblies were given their last coat of paint before reaching the line with any retouching done with a spray gun if necessary.

An entire side of the assembly building had large doorways so these large units could be brought directly opposite the stations on which they were to be used. By placing of the aircraft at a 45-degree angle on the line, additional space was gained permitting the storage of engines, propellers, empennages, flaps, and turrets.

The underside of the carriage platform had racks on which certain detachable parts could be hung to remain with their particular bomber. For example, engines moved onto the line along with their removable cowl panels which were hung under the platform and moved along with the assembly while the engines were being installed.

A number of service shops were located on the opposite side of the building paralleling the first half of the line. Among these shops were a hydraulic and oxygen testing, inspection laboratory, an armament room used for preparing and sighting machine guns, an instrument department, a tooling and methods office, an electrical test room, and several stockrooms. There was a tool room where immediate adjustments could be made on templates and other tools without the paperwork and delay that would result if such work was sent to an outside department. Cribs, toilets, and a first aid room were located in the space between the two halves of the assembly line.

Stations 1–3, inclusive, united the three major aircraft sub-assemblies: the wing section, the fuselage nose section, and the fuselage tail section. These sub-assemblies were transported from the parts plant by truck on a specially constructed trailer that was adjustable to carry any one of these three sub-assemblies. The other sub-assemblies, such as outer wing panels, ailerons, and rudders, were transported by a truck using suitable wooden racks. Units furnished by outside vendors, including engines and propellers, were shipped in by rail or by truck, and could be unloaded directly opposite the station at which they were needed on the line.

The first step in assembly was to mount the wing section onto the carriage. It was picked up from its trailer by a sling from the traveling crane and was placed in the four supporting posts. The wing section was squared in position by Z-angle guides with adjustable buttons on all four posts. All posts were vertically adjusted by elevating screws used to level the wing section.

The mating jig was lifted by the traveling crane and placed over the wing section. As its name denoted, this jig located the wing and fuselage sections into their correct relative positions. Three welded tubular rigid jigs were used through the first three assembly stations. At the third station, the jig was released and carried back by crane to the start of the line to be used again.

Once the wing section was in place, the nose and tail fuselage sections arrived on their dollies. At each end of the mating jig, there were three chain hoists for elevating the fuselage sections into place. A positioning plate topped by a horizontal beam was bolted to locating holes in the bombardier's window mounting bulkhead of the nose section. The forward chain hoist hitched to this beam while a belly band was fastened between the other two hoists on the nose of the jig.

All hoists were movable along trolleys in the jig. The one at the forward end was actuated by a pulley through lead screws so that when the nose section was elevated it could be moved back into the wing section. The two other hoists were connected by cables and sheaves to maintain their relative positions on the trolleys, thus keeping the nose section square with the wings.

The same procedure was used to hoist the tail section of the fuselage but with the position of the pulleys reversed with the single pulley at the rear carrying a straight beam passed through plates attached to the empennage connecting holes. Hoisting and longitudinal movement was carried out like that for the nose section. For additional stability, nose and tail fuselage sections were held to the carriage with canvas straps.

The three major sub-assemblies, positioned on the center line of the fuselage in the mating jig, were then riveted together. The mating jig was wired and piped so that a single connection to each service provided adequate outlets for all working positions. There were three junction boxes, each with four outlets and three air valves on each of the four sides of the jig; allowing the pneumatic riveting tools to be easily connected.

The carriage was similarly wired but carried no air lines since most of the rivets had been driven at the first three stations. However, the floor air outlets could be used directly at any station. In moving the carriages from one station to the next, the air and electric lines were disconnected from the floor air outlets and wire and hose was cleared from the tracks.

At the right-hand side of each part was a data board with three columns: date below minimum, date listed, and date of next supply. As soon as the leadman used a part, he noted it in the first column. The stock chaser inspected these data boards daily and recorded his listing of the parts in the second column. When he determined the status of the next lot of parts in process, he placed its completion date in the third column.

Despite all precautions, shortages occurred, but an advantage of this moving assembly method was its flexibility and missing parts could be added at a later station. This practice was not desirable, however, as it interfered with the exact timing on which the performance of the line was dependent.

Every effort was made to pre-drill all parts by the use of jigs so that rivet hole drilling during assembly would be kept to a minimum. Pre-drilling was successfully completed on bomb well side panels and bomb racks but many components, made of sheet duralumin, were flexible and it was not possible to eliminate all the drilling required to mate holes during final assembly.

On the first part of the second section of the line, the engines, outer wing panel assemblies, stabilizers, and rudders were all added. Fowler flaps and propellers were then installed with all the fittings necessary for the wing and rudder control systems. The final stations were used to add the nose enclosure and radio instruments. When an assembly reached the end of the line, it was rolled out into the yard where any final adjustments were made. After air was pumped into the oleo-struts that lifted the bomber from its carriage; it was then ready for engine run ups and flight tests before delivery.

San Diego Liberator Construction Gallery

Outdoor monorail. (*CAC/AAF*)

Left: Indoor monorail carrying tail. (*CAC/AAF*)

Below: Crib storage. (*CAC/AAF*)

Component storage. (*CAC/AAF*)

Machine shop. (*CAC/AAF*)

Sheet metal department. (*CAC/AAF*)

Fuselage skinning. (*CAC/AAF*)

Part III: Consolidated San Diego and Fort Worth B-24 Plants 289

Right: Interior fuselage work. (*CAC/AAF*)

Below: Finished rear fuselage storage. (*CAC/AAF*)

Removal of lower center wing section from assembly dock. (*CAC/AAF*)

Upper center wing sections and outer wing panels awaiting removal to the assembly line. (*CAC/AAF*)

Fabric shop. (*CAC/AAF*)

Nose section assembly. (*CAC/AAF*)

Rear section being transported to the assembly line. (*CAC/AAF*)

Paint shop. (*CAC/AAF*)

Above and below: Attaching wing to fuselage. (CAC/AAF)

Attaching wing to fuselage. (*CAC/AAF*)

Attaching empennage. (*CAC/AAF*)

Above: Wing ready for engine attachment. (CAC/AAF)

Right: Engine attachment to wing. (CAC/AAF)

Above: Engines in place. (*CAC/AAF*)

Left: Engine connections. (*CAC/AAF*)

Part III: Consolidated San Diego and Fort Worth B-24 Plants 297

Right: Finishing touches. (*CAC/AAF*)

Below: Ready to leave factory for flight testing. (*CAC/AAF*)

The 5,000th Liberator, B-24J-195-CO 44-41064, produced by San Diego was aptly-named *V Grand* and received much media hoopla and many photo ops. (*CAC/AAF*)

Another view of *V Grand* showing the numerous signatures applied by Consolidated workers. The bomber would later serve with the 780BS/465BG/15AF bearing the signatures. (*CAC/AAF*)

Consolidated Wartime Aircraft Totals

In early 1944, the War Production Board officially cited Consolidated-Vultee and its subsidiaries as the largest aircraft manufacturer in the world; during that year, Consolidated-Vultee delivered over 12 percent by number and 16 percent by weight of all aircraft manufactured in the U.S. At the end of the war, Consolidated ranked fourth as the largest wartime contract recipient in dollars behind General Motors, Curtiss Wright, and Ford.

B-24 Production Costs

	B-24A	B-24J
Airframe	$225,125	$115,188
Engines	$53,840	$30,600
Government-Furnished Equipment (GFE)		
Propellers	$11,460	$4,220
Radio gear	$9,520	$7,092
Ordnance	$3,407	$3,152
GFE for airframe	$36,547	$48,235
GFE for engines	$2,061	$2,456
Totals	$341,960	$210,943

8

Consolidated San Diego: Summary and Conclusion

Facility Construction Period

In the late 1930s, when the Navy and Air Corps contracted Consolidated, the company was compelled to increase its production capacity and did so by increasing its existing facilities in two phases. The first phase, beginning in December 1939, provided additions costing $5 million and added 1,000,000 square feet by February 1941. The next phase, beginning in April 1940 and completed for use in February 1941, was the $23 million Plant #2 adding 1,876,000 square feet. Unlike later wartime construction projects, these pre-war projects proceeded rapidly aided by peacetime procuring and building along with Consolidated's early establishment of a complete and comprehensive engineering department, which delivered its designs and plans to the best of industrial architects and builders.

Pre-Production Period

If Consolidated had been contracted to build 270 B-24s in 1939 or even in 1940, keeping to a production schedule, it undoubtedly would have been completely incapable of doing so. But because the volume increases were contracted in relatively small increments, it was possible for the company to continue building aircraft with existing "handicraft" methods and then, as it became clearly impossible to meet requirements at various stages on the Acceleration Curve with the "old" methods then in use; it could slowly initiate improvements and introduce mass production technics.

The following factors prevented a more rapid production acceleration:

1) The pre-war B-24 design was not engineered for mass-production, the engineering information was incomplete, and the shop was relegated to resolve the details on many of the sub-assemblies.
2) Consolidated had no previous experience in volume production but it had capable engineers and mechanics who understood how to eventually build outstanding aircraft.

3) The pre-war B-24 design did not meet World War II combat requirements and was found to be unsatisfactory during the early years, either to the Air Corps or to the operation of the Consolidated production line. Company engineering was unable to ever catch up with production but fortunately other departments moved production along day-by-day but no long-range detailed planning was done.
4) The AAF never delineated its ultimate requirements for the Liberator, which could have caused serious production losses and schedule interruptions, except for Consolidated's policy of "playing it safe" which resulted in the "constant availability" of what the company called "just a little extra all along the line" which the company claimed to "help it meet production schedules which otherwise would have been impossible."
5) The "Catch-22" of forward planning on the B-24 program, which proved to be impossible due to the continuous engineering changes, the lack of engineering information, and the failure to make adequate planning assumptions, was that it caused a manpower situation that continually jeopardized the entire program. At no time in the early stages of production was there any "competent authoritative manpower planning" which resulted in too many unskilled applicants being hired as quickly as possible and placed on the production line. As the area's labor force became insufficient and outside hires proved to be inadequate to meet the steadily increasing demands of the B-24 and Navy programs; it became essential to gradually sub-contract 50 percent of the B-24 man-hours and establish Feeder Shops in order to maintain production schedules.

Production Period

In hindsight, Consolidated's production and daily acceleration curve was outstanding. The company's first two years of production contributed to hand-crafting the basic bomber and gained much valuable know-how, but there was no palpable progress toward mass production. If the demand for peak production had occurred at a later stage in the company's growth, a much more rapid production acceleration would have transpired because:

1) B-24 structural and tool designs would have been more complete.
2) Combat-inspired engineering changes would have been more limited and adequate controls and planning for their introduction would have been initiated.
3) Increased company experience and know how.
4) More and focused government control of all factors concerned with fulfilling its requirements.
5) The existence of adequate plant space and equipment, including one set of complete tooling.

Finally, a qualification on Consolidated production was that the manufacture of 270 B-24s per month did, in no way, signify mass-production as it was basically the large-volume manufacture of an aircraft designed by a company without mass-production experience. In practice, it can be said that Consolidated production engineering was a secondary and completely separate operation as actual mass-production would have been begun with a new bomber designed by engineers experienced in fabricating and assembling aircraft.

Conclusions and Evaluations

As a result of the experience Consolidated San Diego gained in the development and production of the B-24 heavy bomber, the following general conclusions can be made based on post-war evaluation:

1) Conceived late in 1938, the first B-24 was flown at the mid-1939, passed its 629 Inspection in February 1940 and was accepted in August 1940, which was considered exceptional for that time.
2) The B-24 was designed to meet pre-war standards and did not immediately meet the requirements revealed during combat, until many changes and improvements had been made. The problem of being current on technological developments, so that aircraft designed for the AAF would be tactically viable, required the leadership and intelligence of both the military services and the aircraft industry working together.
3) The large number of engineering changes that had to be introduced in the B-24 to make it combat-worthy, were an important reason but, by no means, the only one for delays in accelerating the production program. Coordination between the AAF and the company on the approval of the implementation of these changes was especially important in wartime to prevent aircraft production from being adversely affected. Some changes that were unrelated to safety could be postponed or omitted when considering that their introduction would create a "severe impediment" to production. The most significant causes for production delays was that the B-24 design was not frozen in order to speed up its manufacture and engineering changes continued to be complied with.
4) The pre-war B-24 design was not engineered for mass-production but because Consolidated's production engineers and production line workers had been long accustomed to building aircraft the "old way;" San Diego B-24 production did not lag very significantly. However, Consolidated's lack of production breakdown together with the very inadequate status of B-24 engineering would seriously handicap the start of the manufacturing program for these bombers in the Ford, Douglas, and North American Plants. The AAF should not have accepted an aircraft in service-test or production quantities where the designing contractor had not had its design and production engineers work together in developing a satisfactory production breakdown.
5) The experience that Consolidated acquired in building LB-30 for the French (and British), and the recommended engineering improvements found during its early combat experience, were invaluable in integrating their production organization and initiating the production program prior to Pearl Harbor.

6) The early expansion of the San Diego Plant, though largely based directly on Navy flying boat orders, was initiated because of the course of the war in Europe. The main part of the plant expansion had been completed and the required equipment purchased before materials and tools came in critical supply and no delays were caused in the production program.
7) The AAF did not, and undoubtedly could not, envisage the ultimate magnitude of the B-24 Program. From July 1941 to June 1942, there were three major upward changes in the forecasts for the monthly production goals for San Diego. These gradual increases in the size of the program did not delay the plant expansion program which was more easily achieved than if the entire project had been initiated at one time.
8) Consolidated's original production plan, which was based on the use of time-tested shop methods, was to expand existing tooling in sufficient quantities to meet the gradually increased production goals. "Modern industrial methods" were gradually introduced by Consolidated to some extent in the later phases of the production program. Even if the ultimate size of this program had been known at the beginning, no other production plan would have been feasible because of the lack of a satisfactory production breakdown, incomplete engineering, and inadequate dimensional control. The tooling dock was used at San Diego on the B-24 Program, but it was not applied in time to assist in developing true mass-production.
9) When an experimental aircraft design was accepted and approved for additional production quantities (service test, etc.), the master control gauges should have been be made and their accuracy verified. As changes were made in the B-24, the master control gauges were not kept current.
10) The several Consolidated Navy flying boat programs constituted a larger load proportionately on the company's engineering and tooling organizations and on its executive personnel than was supposed by their respective production output.
11) Consolidated's Feeder Shop Program successfully "took the work to the worker," thus supplementing the capacity of the San Diego Plant while simultaneously obtaining dispersion in case of then feared possibility of an enemy attack. The development of the Feeder Plant system included its own warehouse for materials and its own internal controls as a part of the on-site manufacturing department.
12) Consolidated's sub-contracting program proved to be remarkably successful and at peak production amounted to almost 40 percent of the total bomber construction. The development of a resourceful and very successful sub-contractor organization was based on the supply of all necessary and timely technical assistance and the application of the learner's curve to each sub-contractor. Sub-contracting extended maximum wartime production, expanded production workloads, and dispersed industry in case of an (then unlikely) enemy attack. Although sub-contracting never delayed production acceleration, some problems were encountered due to engineering changes and modifications and introduced correspondingly greater problems in transfer of engineering information, including design and scheduling changes, in expediting and control.

13) Both the sub-contractor and Feeder Shop methods of "taking the work to the worker" were beneficial, not only concerning the supply of materials to the main plant but also concerning main plant employee morale and efficiency with both being substantially higher and the cost being substantially lower than ever could be achieved in the over-congested conditions in and around the main plant.
14) The requirements for material supply in the B-24 Program were easily met due to the high priority assigned to this bomber.
15) The San Diego Plant, in building aircraft for both the Army and the Navy, was subject to the different inspection directives and procedures of both services on their respective contracts,
16) San Diego's manpower problem was severely exasperated by the lack of adequate housing which was the basic cause of the high rate of turnover among Consolidated personnel. To alleviate this housing problem, it was recommended that the company be given final control of all housing available for occupancy by its employees.
17) The AAF's spare parts requirements, amounting to over 15 percent, were of great importance in the over-all bomber program, and in January 1943, the company made changes on delivery and control of spare parts but nonetheless, the spare parts program never stayed current with production.
18) The company developed a very effective system of rewarding the management personnel of all echelons by the monthly payment to each man of a "carefully measured and clearly understood" incentive bonus.

The last of 6,724 San Diego Liberators forlornly waits to leave the assembly line on 31 May 1945. (CAC/AAF)

PART III

Consolidated San Diego and Fort Worth B-24 Plants

Section 2
Consolidated Fort Worth B-24 Plant

1
Fort Worth's Aviation Heritage

Fort Worth and World War I Aviation

By World War I, Fort Worth had grown from a "Cowtown" into a large city and a transportation hub of the Southwestern U.S., but its aviation experience only had consisted of a few aerial exhibitions. During the latter part of World War I, the British Royal Air Force faced a serious shortage of pilots and a demand to train the increasing numbers of cadets. The RAF looked to move its aviation training schools from Canada and considered Fort Worth, which offered more days of good flying weather. At the impetus of its Chamber of Commerce, led by upcoming city leader, Amon Carter, land leases were obtained and the infrastructure was built and Fort Worth would receive a boost in its economy from these bases for about a year until the bases were closed at the World War I Armistice.

Amon Carter: "Mr. Fort Worth"

Amon G. Carter had arrived in Fort Worth during May 1905 and would grow a newspaper, oil, and political empire; he befriended heads of state, political figures, corporate leaders, and entertainment personalities from around the world. Despite quitting school aged eleven, Carter would eventually control the business and political climate of vast and to-be-rich West Texas and was committed to selfless philanthropy and to a preoccupation with aviation. Most of all, Carter was deeply devoted to his adopted Fort Worth and acquired a contempt for neighboring Dallas, 30 miles to the east. Being raised in a small North Texas town, Carter had "no use for the Eastern dandies" he alleged were controlling Dallas. Soon after arriving in Fort Worth, Carter and four associates founded the *Star Newspaper* to compete with the already established *Telegram*. On 1 January 1909, Carter purchased the *Telegram* and merged it with the *Star* to create the *Fort Worth Star-Telegram*, which emblazoned "Where the West Begins" on its masthead to become one of the most influential U.S.

Amon Carter: "Mr. Fort Worth." (*CAC/AAF*)

newspapers of its day. Carter used his newspaper to flamboyantly promote both himself, Fort Worth, and West Texas and its small towns. Carter reveled in publicly upstaging and embarrassing neighboring Dallas ("Big-D," which he would disparage in his newspaper as "Big d"). Carter personally created the popular image of a larger-than-life Texan flaunting big cars, western attire, and stereotypical 10-gallon Stetson hats. He sported six-shooters during public events and opened all his speeches by proclaiming; "Texas forever! Fort Worth now and hereafter!"

Fort Worth and the 1920s

By the end of World War I, Fort Worth's infrastructure had developed to include a complex road, highway, and rail transportation system, a skilled labor force, and a developing political machine under Amon Carter, which would lead to the final components required to support a the forthcoming large petroleum and aviation industries. Large natural gas, oil, and helium deposits were discovered near Fort Worth, and the Lone Star Gas Company, working secretly with the War Department, laid hundreds of miles of pipe to Fort Worth from these new fields. New refineries were built in Fort Worth and nearby to process the oil and pipelines were laid to the Texas Gulf Coast to ship the refined petroleum. Because of this oil boom and the helium extraction plant, by 1920 Fort Worth had become a major petroleum pipeline hub and refining center. In August 1923, Fort Worth annexed the still-prosperous Armour and Swift meat-processing plants, bringing more revenue to the city. In July 1925, Fort Worth established itself as a major city when one of the abandoned World War I flight-training bases was renovated into Meacham Field Municipal Airport.

The Rise of Fort Worth's Aviation Industry

On 12 January 1939, with the looming possibility of Hitler's Germany going to war and the rise of his formidable *Luftwaffe*, President Roosevelt requested Congress to provide $300 million for the purchase of 3,000 aircraft for the Army. Soon the president ordered manufacturers to prepare for the production of 50,000 aircraft, nearly tripling their output, and to expedite the designs of new aircraft to replace the obsolete aircraft that were then being manufactured or in inventory.

In 1940, Roosevelt announced his defense plans for America's military aviation, which included decentralizing military construction and, for security reasons, building plants inland away from the Atlantic and Pacific Coasts. Because of this rapidly increasing demand for "defensive" military weapons and goods and the economic desperation caused by the Great Depression, Chambers of Commerce of inland American cities immediately began undertake campaigns to attract new factories. During the 1930s, simultaneously with the Depression, the southwestern Great Plains suffered the severe Dust Bowl drought that devastated Fort Worth bringing it to the verge of certain economic collapse by the end of the decade.

FDR's "Arsenal of Democracy" announcements quickly generated interest in the bidding for a government-constructed defense plant in North Texas. The area's labor pool was plentiful, although untrained in aircraft manufacturing, and housing problems could be solved more easily there than in the already crowded industrial areas on both coasts and the industrial Upper Midwest. Additionally, the area's flat terrain and temperate weather made for ideal flying.

The Federal Plant Site Board then directed aircraft manufacturers to implement site surveys in board-approved cities to determine locations suitable for the construction of plants that would be funded by the Defense Plant Corporation headed by powerful Texan Jesse Jones and leased back to the manufacturer. Maj. Gen. George Brett, chief of the Army Air Corps, ordered Consolidated's Reuben Fleet to immediately choose one primary and one alternate location from several "approved" cities where Consolidated would build its successful B-24 Liberator and PBY Catalina designs and were anticipating substantial orders for both.

Maj. Gen. George Brett, chief of the Army Air Corps. (AAF)

2

Enter Reuben Fleet

Reuben Fleet's Consolidated Aircraft Company was unquestionably one of America's preeminent aircraft enterprises as his plant facilities had doubled and then redoubled. Consolidated's sales had jumped from $3.6 million in 1939 and sales for the first eleven months of 1940 had reached $95.5 million, the greatest one-year growth in the history of American business.

After the government decreed that any new defense plants were to be built inland, Fleet realized that the government was not going to build a second Consolidated factory at coastal San Diego and decided to investigate inland sites adjacent to an inland lake (for the amphibian PBY) to build a new assembly plant. Charles Van Dusen, Consolidated's production manager, and Fleet's old friend, Thomas Bomar, director of San Diego's Chamber of Commerce, who had helped him move his plant from Buffalo to San Diego in 1935, was to accompany Fleet to Texas on a planned visit to consider potential sites in Dallas, Fort Worth, and Houston. Later, Fleet and Bomar were fly to New Orleans and also to send Consolidated Vice President Edgar Gott to examine sites at Tulsa Oklahoma and Atlanta Georgia as both were being considered by the government for aircraft factory construction.

Previous to Fleet's visit, the Fort Worth Chamber of Commerce wisely chose Amon Carter as its political affairs liaison to contact two California aircraft manufacturers that were deliberating building new factories: the Consolidated Aircraft Corporation of San Diego and the Vultee Aircraft Company of Downey. As described, by the late 1930s, the amiable Carter was internationally renowned for his bombastic cowboy persona, wealth, generosity, and love for Fort Worth. FDR's son, Elliott, a personal Carter friend, and Roosevelt's daughter, Anna, both resided in Fort Worth, and the president was their frequent visitor and also socialized at Carter's posh Fort Worth Club. Carter was granted almost *carte blanche* by the Fort Worth City Council to grant requests and allowances for significant legal and tax concessions and infrastructure improvements to sway their decision to build in Fort Worth.

On 22 November 1940, Carter had been informed by Bill Wheatley, Consolidated's chief test pilot, that the company needed to ferry 200 PBYs from San Diego to England and required a layover in the middle of the country. Consolidated Vice President Edgar Gott

FDR's son, Elliott Roosevelt, and wife, personal Amon Carter friends. (*CAC/AAF*)

sent Carter a letter detailing requirements for the temporary base on Lake Worth. Carter implored the Fort Worth Chamber of Commerce to meet Consolidated's requirements for flight crew's food and accommodations and to provide moorings and fuel the aircraft. On 27 November, only eight days after receiving Wheatley's request, Gott was notified that the requested facilities (which adjoined the proposed Lake Worth plant site) would be available on 30 November. Fort Worth's quick and efficient response impressed Gott and would later play a significant part in Consolidated's site selection decision.

Edgar Gott and the B-24

Consolidated Vice President Edgar Gott played an important part in winning Gen. Arnold's favor in the Liberator's development and later Consolidated's move to Fort Worth, but his influence in this and other Consolidated successes during his tenure have not been given full credit in company-generated literature despite his impressive resume. In 1909, Gott graduated with a bachelor of science in chemical engineering from the University of Michigan and worked for the Griffin Wheel Company in Washington until 1915 before becoming the agent in his cousin William Boeing's lumber business. In 1917, he was promoted to vice president of Pacific Aero Products Company, which became the Boeing Airplane Company during the next year. Gott served as Boeing president between 1922 and 1925, a time during which it and other aircraft companies were in a post-war scramble for business and survival. Gott was able to procure several military contracts making Boeing a major manufacturer of military biplanes, such as the Boeing NB trainer and the PW-9 fighter.

Edgar Gott, Consolidated vice president. (CAC/AAF)

Gott left Boeing in 1925 to become vice president of Fokker Aircraft Corporation of America, and during the following year, he became president of Keystone Aircraft where he negotiated its merger with Loening Aeronautical Engineering. Gott moved on and served as vice president of Consolidated Aircraft Corporation, playing an important role in initiating the B-24 project at San Diego and facilitating the establishment of Consolidated's Fort Worth Factory. He died in San Diego in 1947 at the age of sixty.

Ruben Fleet Romances Amon Carter and Consummates the Deal

In 1940, Reuben Fleet contacted Carter, one of his many business cronies, stating his interest in expanding his company's operations outside San Diego. In phone conversations and in writing, Fleet outlined what he was searching for in possible locations for a new plant citing "labor supply, wage scales, union activities, no labor disturbances ... state, county, and local taxations" among the considerations. The shrewd Fleet also explicitly mentioned that Consolidated was interested in other sites around the southern United States.

Once it became known that Fleet was interested in the North Texas area, the long-time Fort Worth-Dallas rivalry resurfaced as officials of both cities tried to attract a defense plant to their city. The Dallas Chamber of Commerce considered that Consolidated would be particularly interested in their area because of nearby Mountain Creek Lake, which might be appealing for the production of PBYs. In November 1939, Consolidated surveyors scouted a site west of Hensley Reserve Airfield, on Mountain Creek Lake, which was owned by the City of Dallas and leased to the War Department. Consolidated optioned the site through the Dallas Chamber of Commerce, contingent on a pending merger of Consolidated and the Hall Aluminum Aircraft Company.

Once aware of Consolidated's interest in Dallas, Carter continued his feud with that city by engaging an engineering firm to conduct a comparative study of the Dallas Mountain Creek Lake site and two Fort Worth lake sites, Lake Worth and Eagle Mountain Lake. Carter's study uncovered fluctuations in Dallas' Mountain Creek Lake water levels that would preclude its use for launching seaplanes during dry periods. The study also determined that the water levels of the two Fort Worth lakes could be maintained at any required level by the new dams that had been built on the Trinity River.

While the Consolidated/Hall merger was being negotiated, James "Dutch" Kindelberger, president of North American Aviation of Inglewood, California, also searched for a site in Dallas to build a new assembly plant. Kindelberger made a firm offer to Dallas for a site west of Hensley Reserve Airfield, which was also the same Mountain Creek Lake location optioned by Consolidated and already owned by the city. When the Consolidated/Hall merger collapsed, the Dallas Chamber of Commerce succeeded in having Consolidated relinquish its option and then leased the site to North American. Ironically, during World War II, North American would assemble and build 966 Liberators at its Dallas plant along with the intended AT-6 trainers and later P-51 fighters.

After Fleet's visit to Fort Worth, Carter remained in almost daily communication with Fleet, the Army and Navy, and U.S. government leaders. When Carter learned that Tulsa and Atlanta had been placed on the approved list for new aircraft factories, he increased communication with FDR and Fleet. Fleet informed Carter that the ideal situation would be to have the new B-24 factory built adjoining an airfield that could train pilots to fly the newly-built bombers. Harold Foster, manager of the Industrial Division of the Fort Worth Chamber of Commerce, offered to deed 1,450 acres of land near Lake Worth and the City of Fort Worth promised to clear the land and build all necessary roads. William Holden, executive vice president of the Fort Worth Chamber, then very much sweetened the deal by granting Consolidated 1,200 acres along Lake Worth, two runways with taxi strips, a water supply system with sewer mains and sewage disposal plant, necessary utility and railroads trunk lines, and help with highways and housing. Holden also stated that the Fort Worth City Council, Tarrant County officials, and Chamber of Commerce representatives were united in their efforts to bring Consolidated to Fort Worth.

Having convinced Fleet of the practicality of the Fort Worth location for his plant, Carter faced the major problem of Fort Worth not being on the government's approved location list. The undaunted Carter was determined to locate the B-24 plant in Fort Worth and began a siege on the Federal government beginning with persuading the Chamber of Commerce to engage *Fort Worth Star-Telegram* reporters to prepare a statement for government officials praising Fort Worth as an ideal location for a factory. Carter, joined by Cyrus Smith, president of Fort Worth-based American Airlines, utilized their political power and personal relationships within the U.S. government to cajole Washington for a favorable decision.

Nonetheless, the Federal government continued to advocate for a Consolidated plant in Tulsa, even though Fleet had strongly stated that Fort Worth would be a better location. Additionally, the government insisted that factories should be built in states that had not already benefited from defense dollars and Texas already had a sizable military presence and Dallas was about to procure a North American aircraft plant after Consolidated relinquished this option. Fleet remained adamant that Fort Worth should be selected and continued to urge Carter and Fort Worth officials to mount a last blitz against the War Department. As a last resort, Carter wired President Roosevelt reiterating that Fort Worth offered many advantages over Tulsa: better climate, better transportation (particularly railroads), better infrastructure, and a position along an established transcontinental air route (American Airlines). Also, Carter pointed out that Fort Worth would be the ideal site for Consolidated, the builder of the B-24 bomber and PBY amphibian, as Consolidated had continued using Lake Worth as a cross-continental stop for its flying boats. Carter offered Roosevelt an inspired solution, suggesting that Tulsa be granted another aircraft plant and Consolidated be allowed to come to Fort Worth.

After Fleet and his associates returned to San Diego, Gen. Brett pressed him for an immediate decision on a site to which Fleet responded that Fort Worth was his choice. Brett's telegrammed reply to Fleet repeated that Fort Worth was not an approved site and directed him to select Tulsa instead. Fleet apprised Brett that Consolidated had evaluated the Fort Worth location, was satisfied with it, and steadfastly insisted that the site be approved. Brett, piqued by the obstinate Fleet, told him that he could select any location he wanted, as long as it was Tulsa! The two debated via lengthy telegrams until Brett relented and agreed to discuss the situation with the Plant Site Board. Surprisingly, during that meeting, Dallas representatives actually recommended the selection of Fort Worth over Tulsa as Dallas owed Consolidated for giving up its Mountain Creek Lake lease to North American. As an ulterior motive for the recommendation was Dallas' anticipation that the new Dallas North American Plant would receive subcontracts for B-24 parts and wanted Consolidated to locate in nearby Fort Worth. Both the Fleet and Dallas appeals were for naught as on 21 December 1940, Brett announced that Tulsa was to be the location of a new $8–10 million aircraft manufacturing plant employing 5,000 operated by Consolidated.

When Amon Carter learned that Tulsa was to be granted his Consolidated factory contract, he became livid and telegrammed Roosevelt, telling him that to reject Fort Worth, "is almost a crime against national defense." He again maintained that Fort Worth had the best site, climate, size, labor supply, and infrastructure that included an operational airfield and an adjoining lake for Consolidated's seaplanes. After Roosevelt replied that he could not reverse the decision, Carter had the Fort Worth Chamber of Commerce file a formal objection with the War Department.

Having established a solid alliance and firm resolve with Fleet in attempting to finally locate a Consolidated plant in Fort Worth, Carter and his entourage turned their total attention to "priming" friends, politicians, and government officials. Upon arriving in Washington, Carter contacted Texas Senator Morris Sheppard (D), powerful chairman of the Senate Military Affairs Committee, urging him to pressure Assistant Secretary of War Robert Patterson to arrange a hearing with the War Department. In order to assist Sheppard in his duties, Carter sent him a brief detailing what Fort Worth had to offer.

Meanwhile, Carter again used his close connection with Elliott Roosevelt to influence various people in the government such as Gen. Edwin Watson, friend and senior aide to President Roosevelt, and of course, he contacted the president. At the

White House Carter pled his case to directly to Roosevelt, who promised Carter a one-week delay of a final decision while the War Department would reconsider Fort Worth. Carter ended the meeting by suggesting that FDR consider Tulsa as an alternate site for a proposed Douglas Aircraft Company bomber plant.

A 27 December 1940 release from the Associated Press explained the one-week moratorium:

Tulsa's Plane Plant Delayed by Fort Worth
Washington, Dec. 27 (AP) Groups from Texas personally interposed an objection and demanded that the Administration send the plant to Fort Worth. At the insistence of these powerful groups, the War Department granted a week's delay in completing the contract during which time briefs are to be filed by Texas against Tulsa in favor of Fort Worth.

In this interim, Carter began a siege on everyone he knew of importance in Washington with William Knudsen of the National Defense Advisory Committee (NDAC) topping Carter's list. The NDAC had recommended building four bomber plants, the third of which was to be built in Tulsa by Consolidated. However, Carter told Knudsen that Fleet and Consolidated believed Fort Worth to be the better site for the factory and that Tulsa should receive the fourth bomber plant to be run by some other aviation company.

The next Texas/Washington friend on Carter's list was Jesse Jones, owner of the *Houston Chronicle* newspaper and Texas' largest construction firm. During the 1920s, Jones' construction company built many of the buildings in the city centers of Fort Worth, Dallas, Houston, San Antonio, and New York City. During that time, Jones became a Carter crony, often as an overnight guest at the Fort Worth Club and in 1925, the Fort Worth Chamber of Commerce had named Jones as an honorary citizen. President Roosevelt had appointed Jones as chairman of the Reconstruction Finance Corporation (RFC), a position he held from 1933 until 1939. During his tenure, the RFC became the leading financial institution in America and the primary investor in the economy while Jones became one of the most powerful men in America, helping prevent the nationwide failure of farms, banks, railroads, and many other businesses during the Depression. Then, in 1940, he was appointed to head the Defense Plant Corporation (DPC), which placed him in charge of purchasing and building America's military plants during World War II. Jones had the inordinate discretionary authority to spend up to half billion dollars without presidential or Congressional approval or oversight and this powerful position gave Jones the reputation of being the "fourth branch of the government."

On 30 December 1940, the AP carried the following article:

Tulsa and Fort Worth May Get Plane Plants
Washington, Dec. 30 (AP) A possibility that Fort Worth, Texas, and Tulsa, Oklahoma, both might be selected as sites for aircraft assembly plants was seen Monday by Senator Morris Sheppard (Dem.) of Texas. He said plants would be constructed by the Consolidated Aircraft Corporation and the Douglas Aircraft Corporation and that there was a chance that each of the cities might get one.

Jesse Jones, chairman of the Reconstruction Finance Corporation. (*RFC*)

Senator Tom Connally said upon arriving from Texas, that he had recently sent telegrams to the War Department urging that Fort Worth be chosen as the site of the proposed Consolidated Aircraft Corporation plant. Connally said he had been informed that Fort Worth was preferred by the company but that someone in either the War Department or National Defense Commission preferred Tulsa and this had led to a recent report that the Oklahoma point had been chosen.

Carter continued "working his magic" and then on 3 January 1941 succeeded, as the War Department announced that bomber assembly plants would be built in Fort Worth, along with Kansas City, Omaha, and Tulsa.

On 3 January 1941, the AP released the following confirmation of Amon Carter's influence:

Plane Plants Given to Tulsa and Fort Worth
Controversy Ended By Double Award
Washington, Jan. 3 (AP) A plan to build thousands of bombers with the help of the automobile industry took definite form Friday night with the selection of Fort Worth as the site of a fourth assembly plant.

In a compromise of a contest between rival cities, a previous allotment of a similar plant to Tulsa was confirmed. Both the Tulsa and Fort Worth plants are to assemble long range, four-motor bombers. Each plant will be built by Army engineers, and is expected to cost up to $10,000,000.

The War Department said the Douglas Aircraft Corporation, Santa Monica, Calif., would operate the Tulsa plant and the Consolidated Corporation of San Diego. Calif., the Fort Worth establishment. There was no Indication when actual work would start on either.

The Fort Worth and Tulsa plants are designed to produce fifty four-motor planes a month.

3
The Consolidated Fort Worth Plant

The Fort Worth Plant would be known as Government Aircraft Plant 4 and would be operated by Consolidated. On 6 January 1941, War Department and Army Air Corps officials inspected and approved the Fort Worth location at Lake Worth.

Carter's role in securing the Fort Worth Consolidated Plant was crucial as without his participation the plant approval would have been highly unlikely. Reuben Fleet certainly was no supporter or friend of the FDR Administration and the New Deal, being forced to appear before Congressional Committees, denouncing high taxation and labor unions. While of some help, William Holden, executive vice president of the Fort Worth Chamber of Commerce, could not match Carter in persona or political clout at the Federal level. It was Carter who contacted Roosevelt and Knudsen about the situation and who urged Senator Sheppard to represent his views to Congress. Carter's concerted efforts at the end of December 1940 were pivotal in the War Department's decision to grant Fort Worth the Consolidated plant. Carter was so persistent that FDR's vice president, John Nance Garner, stated, "That man wants the entire government of the United States to run for the exclusive benefit of Fort Worth, and, if possible, to the detriment of Dallas."

The Chamber of Commerce and City administrators officially offered Fleet the Lake Worth site, and on 3 January 1941, the Federal government accepted. On 8 March 1941, the War Department awarded contracts for construction of aircraft plants at Fort Worth, Kansas City, Missouri, and Tulsa, Oklahoma. The Austin Company of Cleveland was awarded a $10,511,400 contract to build Government Aircraft Plant 4, while the L. J. Miles Company of Fort Worth was awarded a contract to build the adjacent Tarrant Field Airdrome. Fleet had purchased Hall-Aluminus Aircraft Corporation in August 1940 and Archibald Hall, former president of Hall-Aluminus, an experienced executive of the aircraft industry, was transferred to Fort Worth in early 1942 to supervise the completion of the plant and then the assembly of the first B-24s.

In a subsequent press release, Consolidated announced that while the Fort Worth Plant would first manufacture B-24s, it would also be large enough to construct a bomber that would far outsize the 50,000 pound Liberator. The press release described purported

B-32 bomber wrongly as having a wingspan of 195 feet and weighing 200,000 pounds (actual 135 feet and 100,000 pounds loaded). However, only a month later, on 11 April, the AAC requested preliminary design proposals from Boeing and Consolidated for an intercontinental bomber capable of delivering a 10,000-pound bombload over 5,000 miles, which dictated a bomber much larger than the B-32.

Once the site was selected, the Austin Company was contracted to design the building and to act as the construction contractor on the original assembly plant and also act as the construction manager on the construction of the parts plant. The Austin Company supervised lump sum construction contracts awarded by the government on the balance of the work. The Army Corps of Engineers established field offices and the L. J. Miles Construction Company of Fort Worth signed a contract to construct the landing area for the adjacent airfield. The government-owned/contractor-operated (GOCO) Aircraft Assembly Plant No. 4, its paint shop, hangar, pump house, cafeteria, and employment buildings were built in 1941 with the parts plant added in 1942. Minor additions were made during 1943, and during 1944, an experimental building was authorized and erected adjoining the original paint shop, which was remodeled to form a part of the experimental building.

In order to fulfill the agreement to build new streets and improve existing ones, Fort Worth voters approved a $3 million bond issue that also included storm sewers, drainage, streetlights, and traffic signals. Then, on 4 March 1941, by a 13:1 majority, Fort Worth voters then approved the bond issue needed to purchase the necessary additional land for the industrial airport. The owners of a 400-plus-acre farm did not want to sell but held out until their land was seized by Eminent Domain for a very lucrative $187 per acre as compared to the $38 per acre offer they had received in an earlier sale.

It was estimated that construction could take two years, but after Pearl Harbor, the Austin Company worked 24/7 in cooperation with Col. John Anderson of the Army Corps of Engineers, and in less than nine months, they completed construction of the huge factory. Local legend has that when Amon Carter learned that the Tulsa and his Fort Worth's plant would be identical, he persuaded Army architects to add 29 feet to the Fort Worth Plant's assembly line to make it the world's longest straight assembly line (Willow Run's "Tax Bend" would eliminate it from this accolade).

On 18 April 1941, during the rain-soaked ceremonies in a muddy cow pasture at the site of the future Government Aircraft Plant 4, Master of Ceremonies Amon Carter and Brig. Gen. Gerald Brant, commander of the Gulf Coast Air Training Center at Randolph Field, San Antonio, broke ground with a sterling silver shovel. Prefacing his remarks by saying that he was representing Maj. Gen. H. H. Arnold, chief of the Air Corps. In a *Fort Worth Star-Telegram* article about the ground breaking, Brig. Gen. Brant jibed:

> Only a few nights ago General Arnold arrived in London and made a radio address. The next evening the Nazis came over and gave London the worst raid of the war. I trust there will be no such reprisals after my speech.... We are learning. We have embarked on a truly American proposition of building our own planes and training our own pilots. This plant is a great thing. We're digging Hitler's grave here.

On 18 April 1941, during the rain-soaked ceremonies, Amon Carter and Brig. Gen. Gerald Brant broke ground for the Fort Worth factory. (CAC/AAF)

Brant also announced that a recommendation made by Carter for an AAC flight-training base adjacent to the plant would be forwarded to Washington. Within days after Pearl Harbor and the declaration of war, the War Department selected Fort Worth as a site for one of many flight-training bases to be established throughout the continental United States (CONUS). The base would be built on the east side of Tarrant Field Airdrome as previously recommended to Brig. Gen. Brant by Amon Carter.

At the ceremony, AAC Representative Col. F.M. Hopkins proclaimed that the project was "one of the most important in the country to the nation's defense program." Construction of the plant and airfield began three days later.

Once the factory had been approved, on 20 May 1941, Contract W535 ac-18723, between the government and Consolidated, became effective, approving 600 B-24D bombers. These bombers were to be manufactured and completed accordance with Consolidated's Specification ZD-32-009 in the Fort Worth Plant that was expected to be ready for occupancy on or before 1 January 1942. The components, knock-down kits, for the 600 bombers were to be manufactured by Ford Willow Run, the major sub-contractor and all bombers were to be delivered, completely set up, serviced, and ready for flight, to Fort Worth Airfield for acceptance by the government or Consolidated.

The government entered into supplemental Agreement No. 1 on 26 September 1941 providing for the delivery of an additional 800 B-24s. Ford had agreed to manufacture and/or supply and deliver to Consolidated the knock-downs and spare parts for the total of 1,400 model B-24Es now covered by contract ac-18723. The components called for under this contract were manufactured by Ford simultaneously with components called for by Douglas Contract ac-18722.

A special facilities contract between the government and Ford—covering the lease by Ford of specified government-owned trucks, trailers, and other special equipment used in delivering the knock-down assemblies to Fort Worth—was also in effect at Douglas Tulsa. The first B-24, a Model E, assembled by Fort Worth, using Ford components, was delivered in March 1943

Throughout the construction and organization of the Fort Worth Factory, Reuben Fleet was very (too) critical of bureaucratic red tape and his complaints were to be among the factors that would soon result in his leaving his own company. As has been described previously in the story of Fleet's sacking and the establishment of Consolidated-Vultee, that Fleet actually had not wanted to set up the plant in Fort Worth but wanted to expand in San Diego with government money and did not want to construct and run two factories in distant locations but had no other option.

While on a five-state inspection tour in July 1942, before the plant was completed, Gen. Arnold, made his first wartime trip to the Consolidated Fort Worth Plant. In his welcome speech, Arnold stated: "I look forward to the time when we can get the planes we need to win the war," and added that he was also "very favorably impressed with the plant, its type of construction, its layout, plans and production."

Construction of Government Aircraft Plant 4 had been completed in less than nine months and the facility was delivered to the new Consolidated-Vultee entity on 1 January 1942. Five weeks later, a $6.5 million expansion was approved that extended the length of the assembly building to nearly one mile and the plant's workforce would increase to an anticipated 25,000.

Once the plant was completed, Roosevelt and his Secret Service detail made a surprise visit to Fort Worth on 28 September 1942, arriving on a special train that pulled entirely into the building. Traveling in an open limousine with wife, Eleanor; son, Elliott, and his wife; and the grandchildren, FDR inspected the plant at a very slow speed. Also in the packed automobile was George Newman, the manager of Fort Worth/Consolidated, and Maj. Gen. Richard Donovan, commander of the Eighth Army Corps. The Fort Worth newspapers reported that FDR did not stop, only waved, and got to visit his grandkids!

The bomber plant was designed with no windows to satisfy the wartime blackout conditions and so the plant required extensive lighting ("its fluorescent light tubes could stretch from Fort Worth to Dallas") and air conditioning cost $1,250,000 of the plant's $10 million expenditure. About 14,000 gallons of water per minute ("enough to supply the average daily water consumption of Dallas and Fort Worth") were pumped from Lake Worth to supply the refrigeration system located on ten platforms, high in the ceiling trusses. The A/C "had a cooling capacity equal to 500,000 home refrigerators or that of Dallas and Fort Worth combined" while the "combined capacity of the giant fans in the air-conditioning units was great enough to remove all the air from every home in Dallas in a single day." The plant's monthly electric bill was equivalent to $275,000. Workers were also provided with four mezzanine lunchrooms with 50-foot-long tables and accessible toilet and first aid facilities.

Part III: Consolidated San Diego and Fort Worth B-24 Plants 321

Right: Aerial view of Fort Worth government-owned/contractor-operated (GOCO) Aircraft Assembly Plant No. 4 under construction. (*CAC/AAF*)

Below: Completed Fort Worth Plant, which was identical to the Douglas Tulsa Plant. (*CAC/AAF*)

The completed factory had no windows necessitating the installation of the world's largest industrial air conditioning system. (*CAC/AAF*)

Once the plant was completed, President Roosevelt made a surprise visit on 28 September 1942, arriving on a special train that pulled entirely into the building and then raveling in an open limousine with wife, Eleanor, and son, Elliott. (*CAC/AAF*)

Fort Worth Workforce

While the factory was being built, thousands of local workers were hired and trained. In employing a large workforce, the problem of transportation to and from the plant arose since automobile and bus manufacture had been paused for the duration of the war and gasoline and tire rationing was in effect. Public transportation became the only practical solution to transport employees to work. The Fort Worth Transit Company, a local bus company, converted unused automobile transport trailers into improvised buses by removing the top sections from the car haulers and replacing them with plywood enclosures and seats. These tractor-trailer contraptions transported thousands of workers to and from the plant from all parts of Fort Worth and surrounding counties.

Previously the North Texas economy provided more agricultural than industrial jobs, so accordingly there were few skilled assembly line workers available. As a solution, Consolidated hired a nucleus of 1,000 workers in Fort Worth in July 1941 and sent them to Consolidated's San Diego Plant for training. Consolidated also sent selected executives and half of the original San Diego engineering staff to organize the Fort Worth operation. Afterward, about half of the workers came to the factory upon graduation from a Texas vocational and industrial training schools. After Fleet purchased Hall-Aluminus Aircraft Corporation in August 1940, he transferred its key employees to Fort Worth. In 1941 alone, Consolidated added 6,000 jobs to the Fort Worth economy; to put that number in context, there were fewer than 10,000 manufacturing employees in Fort Worth in 1939. Consolidated not only added jobs but also payroll dollars, increasing its payroll from $10 million in 1942 to $60 million in 1944.

By May 1944, the military draft had steadily taken so many trained Consolidated employees that the Texas Headquarters for Selective Service granted a moratorium on the drafting of all male Consolidated employees between the ages of twenty-six and thirty-seven if they were "regularly engaged in an activity in war production for the national interest." The War Manpower Commission worked continually with Consolidated officials to train foremen and leadmen to cope with the continued employment requirements.

The overall proportion of women in the workforce in the United States in 1940 consisted of about 25 percent, but by 1945, at the peak of wartime production, women represented 36 percent of the total workforce. Before 1941, almost no women worked in the aircraft industry, but by 1942, women already comprised nearly 40 percent of Consolidated's total workforce. About half of the Fort Worth women employees were graduates of Texas vocational schools. While the Fort Worth Plant was known locally as the "Bomber Plant," the ever increasing number of women workers caused some reference to be made to it as the "Bloomer Plant." Chauvinist plant officials noted that women are "expert at doing the tedious, monotonous jobs. To them, working long and steadily at small and intricate work is down their alley."

The nearby government housing area for Consolidated/Fort Worth employees was Liberator Village consisting of 1,500 prefabricated dwelling units named after the

Above: Fort Worth triumvirate. *Left to right:* George Newman (Consolidated vice president), Amon Carter, and Harry Woodhead (Consolidated president). (*CAC/AAF*)

Left: While the Fort Worth Plant was known locally as the "Bomber Plant," the ever-increasing number of women workers caused some reference to be made to it as the "Bloomer Plant." (*CAC/AAF*)

B-24 bomber. The housing was built at a cost of $3.5 million and housed 6,000 near the new plant. The Village was built in three sections: the first were barracks built just across the road from the plant; the next two sections were built about a mile away and were brick apartment-type buildings and small housing units. The houses were described as "Ricky-ticky," but for some rural families, it was their first opportunity to use indoor toilets.

Liberator Village. (*CAC/AAF*)

4

Fort Worth B-24 Knock-Down Assembly and Production

Production of Fort Worth's B-24s required the Ford Michigan Willow Run Plant to ship knock-down kits to Fort Worth for assembly. A knock-down kit contained all the components and parts needed to assemble a completed Liberator. But once the Fort Worth Plant was ready for use in May 1942, the sets of components to be furnished by Ford were not even scheduled to be delivered and for Consolidated to preserve its valuable labor force, Supplemental Agreement No. 3 to Contract ac-18723 was granted, allowing it workforce to occupy the new plant to assemble knock-down kits supplied by Consolidated San Diego. Under this contract, Consolidated was to provide for the assembly of not more than 150 complete sets of component parts of B-24Ds as manufactured by San Diego under Contracts W535 ac-16005 and DA W535 ac-4, to be final-assembled at the government-owned plant at Fort Worth instead of the prime contractor's plant at San Diego. The government issued this supplemental agreement to utilize available facilities at Fort Worth, to expedite the assembly of Ford components when available and to permit the training of additional personnel. Consolidated was to final-assemble component parts into complete B-24Ds under substantially the same terms and conditions as provided in Contract ac-18723 when using Ford-furnished components. Change Order No. 5 to Contract ac-18723 provided that Consolidated should assemble only eight B-24Ds, using components furnished by Consolidated, San Diego. Knock-down kit manufacture and transport will be described and depicted as part of the Willow Run chapters.

The KD Kits Arrive from Willow Run

Production began in March 1942 with two parallel fully functional assembly lines. On 17 April 1942, one day less than one year after the 18 April 1941 ground breaking, the first B-24 built at Government Aircraft Plant 4 had been completed and the AAC accepted this first B-24 on 1 May 1942, an amazing 100 days ahead of schedule. The Associated Press (AP) announced the event:

KD truck/trailer arriving on its 1,250-mile journey from Willow Run, Michigan. (*CAC/AAF*)

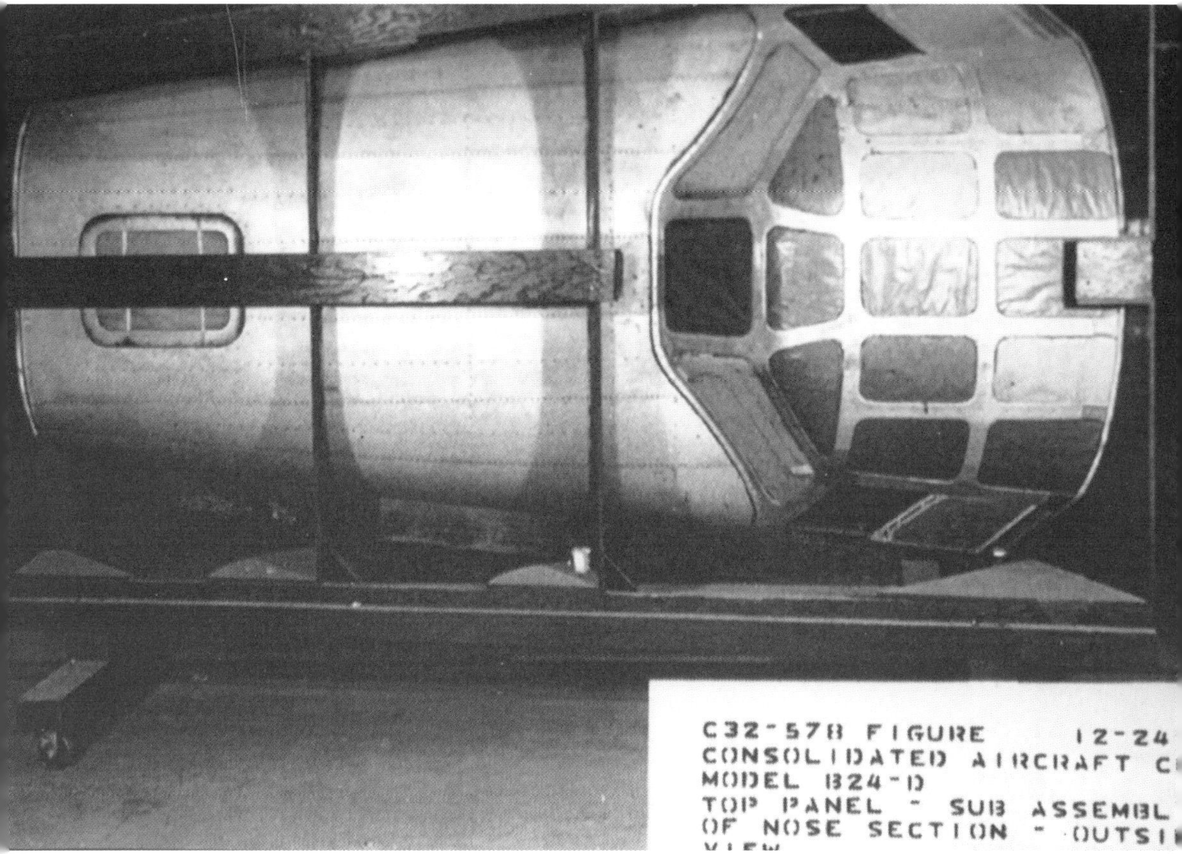

Nose sub-assembly in KD packing removed from trailer. (*CAC/AAF*)

Fuselage sub-assembly removed from trailer. (*CAC/AAF*)

Wing sub-assemblies being removed from trailer. (*CAC/AAF*)

Part III: Consolidated San Diego and Fort Worth B-24 Plants 329

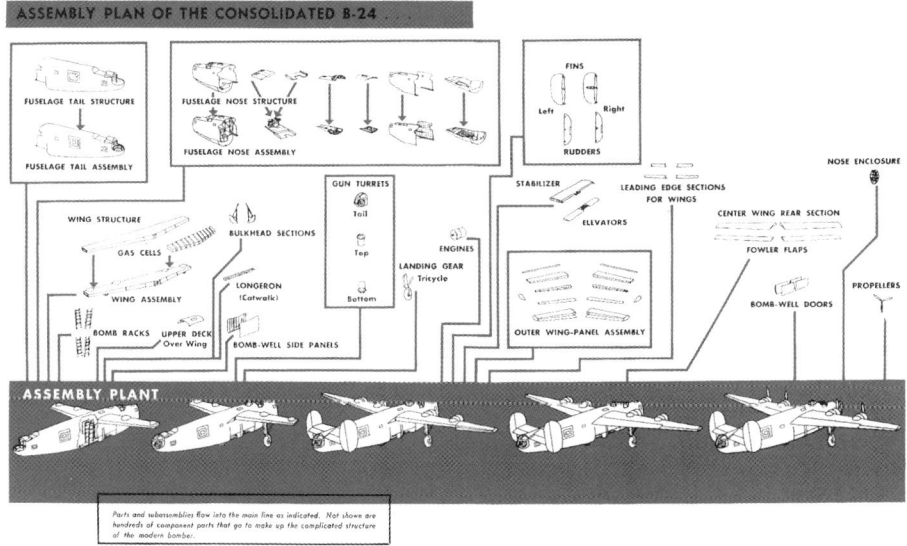

Big Bomber Launched Far Ahead of Time
Southwest Plant Turns It Out 100 Days Under Schedule
April 18 (AP) From a huge new plant somewhere in the Southwest. Tom M. Girdler, Chairman of the Board of Directors of Consolidated Aircraft Corporation. Friday announced that the first of a new series of four-motored B-24 land bombers had rolled from the assembly line 100 days ahead of the company's schedule.

The big plant formally was transferred at a brief ceremony from the Austin Company, builders, to the Army Corps of Engineers and then to the Army Air Forces. Girdler accepted the plant for Consolidated.

The first of the ships, capable of more than 300 miles an hour, a range of more than 3,000 miles and a bomb load of more than four tons, was taxied from the factory to the field immediately following its completion. It was given its initial test flight with George Newman, youthful Consolidated Vice-President in charge of the new plant, at the controls.

George Newman, who on 3 March 1942, became Vice President in Charge of Operations for Fort Worth Consolidated, flew a locally built B-24 airplane for the first time on 19 April as many workers and dignitaries watched. Newman, a former test pilot for Consolidated, had flown every type of airplane the company built, having worked for Consolidated since he was fifteen shortly after Fleet created it. In February 1941 Newman set a non-stop fight record of 9 hours, 57 minutes flying from San Diego to New York with the first B-24 to be delivered to Britain and named "Liberators" by the RAF when they arrived.

After Newman's first flight in the first Fort Worth-built B-24, production there began in earnest. Bomber assembly began at the plant's south end with the subassembly of smaller parts using Henry Ford's original assembly line technology as well as the auto

First Fort Worth B-24 flight on 17 April 1942 was piloted by George Newman. (*CAC/AAF*)

George Newman signing over the first B-24 to Consolidated President Tom Girdler. (*CAC/AAF*)

industry's use of interchangeable parts as described in detail elsewhere. An east–west aisle, 50 feet wide, separated the production line into two parts, and when assembly reached the aisle, bomber assembly into one piece started. The bomber structure was moved on a monorail attached to the ceiling and the station holding the bomber moved every other day, or sometimes every third day. Once the bomber's landing gear was installed, it moved on its undercarriage. A tram moved down the middle south–north aisle pulled by a tractor-type vehicle, which workers could step onto and ride to their work stations. A broadcast system was used to call workers to a telephone to receive instructions from a supervisor.

On 29 May 1942, the government and Consolidated entered into Contract W535 ac-26992, which called for 750 B-24Ds and spare parts that were not to exceed 15 percent of the total cost of the 750 aircraft. Supplemental Agreement No. 1 of 21 November 1942 increased number of bombers by 200, making a total of 950 B-24s to be manufactured by Fort Worth on Contract ac-26992.

Fort Worth was to final-assemble and deliver 107 Ford components on Contract ac-26992, leaving 843 B-24s to be actually manufactured and delivered by Fort Worth on Contract ac-26992. Due to constantly revised military requirements and developments, it became necessary from time to time, to change the model designations as production proceeded and Models D, E, H, and J would all be manufactured on this contract.

Fort Worth added a third shift in July 1942 for a 24/7 work week that rapidly began manufacturing B-24s and C-87 transports with the first C-87 ready on 24 August 1942, more than thirty days ahead of schedule. The 13 April 1943 Supplemental Agreement No. 7 between the government and Consolidated included the manufacture of 107 C-87s that was later increased until 169 C-87s were actually delivered against this supplement. Consolidated was to make "every effort" to deliver C-87s at the rate of twenty-five per month; however, production of the C-87s was not to interfere with regular production of the B-24. Fort Worth was authorized to use Ford-manufactured components of the B-24E model in the production of the 107 C-87s if possible to do so and in addition was "to manufacture such other parts as might be needed."

On 21 December 1943, the government and Consolidated, San Diego, entered into Contract W535 ac-40033 covering 4,500 B-24s and spare parts not to exceed $92,475,000. At about the same time, Fort Worth was engaged in the manufacture of the last of the B-24Hs and was preparing to start manufacture of the B-24J model; however, deliveries were made at a later date on this contract by Fort Worth.

Fort Worth Production

Above: Parts warehouse. (*CAC/AAF*)

Below: Nose and cockpit assembly. (*CAC/AAF*)

Wing KD being readied with wiring and tubing. (CAC/AAF)

Fuselage with partial wing attachment being lifted by overhead crane. (CAC/AAF)

Wing attachment. (*CAC/AAF*)

Engine being readied for attachment. (*CAC/AAF*)

Part III: Consolidated San Diego and Fort Worth B-24 Plants 335

Finished product leaving Fort Worth assembly line. (*CAC/AAF*)

During the war, Consolidated Fort Worth wanted to maintain high worker morale. On 20 May 1943, company newspaper, *The Eagle*, featured the following letter signed by "Eisenhower, General, Commander-in-Chief of the Allied Forces in Africa:"

> To the Men and Women of Consolidated Vultee Aircraft Fort Worth, Texas Division: Our fighting men, standing shoulder to shoulder with our gallant allies, the British and the French, have driven the enemy out of North Africa. In this victory the munitions made by American industry, labor and management, played a very important role. There is glory for us all in this achievement.

On Sunday 27 June 1943, between 9 a.m. and 6 p.m., a year and a half since its opening, Consolidated organized an open house. An *Eagle* newspaper ad invited each employee to bring one member of his or her immediate family, who was over eighteen years old to "walk down the world's longest airplane double assembly line and view the 'air might' for which their kin are responsible" and share the "pride in the planes that their loved ones helped build to further the war effort." An assembled B-24 and C-87 was also made available for viewing for the reported 32,400 visitors. Amon Carter, relishing being the center of attention and on this as on numerous other occasions, played the local press to great advantage.

The 18 February 1944 Contract W535 ac-40715 between the government and Consolidated covered 500 B-24Js and spare parts not to exceed $12,600,000. All J models delivered on this contract were manufactured and assembled by Fort Worth.

Above left: Amon Carter, always wearing his signature cowboy hat, seen christening a Liberator as "City of Fort Worth" after his beloved city.

Above right: George Newman (R) and Harry Woodhead (C) on, perhaps, a not-too-enjoyable inspection stroll with Harry Truman, the head of the influential and dreaded Truman Committee. (*CAC/AAF*)

On 21 March 1944, Contract W33-038 ac-811 covering 111 C-87s and spare parts became effective between the government and Consolidated San Diego. Due to early difficulties and confusion in production, it was necessary for Fort Worth to build the C-87s from B-24 parts furnished by Consolidated and modified as required for this transport version (Ford components were not used in the manufacture of C-87s). C-87s and B-24s ran on the same Fort Worth production line, however, it was necessary to partially hand-build the C-87, thereby, increasing their cost by approximately 11 percent over the B-24 cost.

Upon completion of the 500 B-24Js on Contract ac-40715, Fort Worth then manufactured 453 B-24 s on contract ac-40033 between August and December 1944. Many of the B-24s manufactured by Fort Worth were modified at Consolidated, Louisville, Kentucky, for the British and Canadian governments. Fort Worth manufactured 453 B-24Js on Contract ac-40033 for allocation to the British and Canadian governments prior to time they were produced. Fort Worth completed B-24 production on this contract when the last Fort Worth B-24 (44-44501) rolled through the doors of the assembly building on 26 December 1944. After a short ceremony commemorating the last of the 2,743 B-24s and 291 C-87s built at the plant, employees resumed work on the new B-32s already rolling on the production line. The Fort Worth Plant was then to be converted entirely to the manufacture of the B-32 and later to B-36 bombers.

Contracts called for 291 C-87s, the B-24 transport version, to be built at Fort Worth. (*AAF*)

The last of 2,743 B-24s and 291 C-87s built at Fort Worth was B-24 (44-44501) was completed on 26 December 1944 and was celebrated with a short ceremony commemorating the last of the Fort Worth (note the signatures of Fort Worth workers). (*CAC/AAF*)

5

B-24 Manufacture is Terminated and B-32 Production Begun

On 9 August 1944, the War Department officially announced that the Fort Worth Division had begun producing the B-32 bomber, issuing no specific information about this bomber other than its Dominator nickname. To meet Dominator production quotas, the Army Corps of Engineers approved a $2 million expansion program at the Fort Worth Division in 1944. Upon completion in the spring of 1945, the cost had reached $3 million. The largest additions were two new 100,000-square-foot buildings that became raw materials and process materials warehouses. Construction expanded the existing warehouse to become the salvage department and cafeteria. Also added were a road from the plant, a new employee parking lot, new road paving, relocation of floodlights, and excavation, grading, and installation of underground fire mains for the new buildings. Many manufacturing and training procedures developed for the B-24 were retained and expanded for the B-32, of which approximately 118–124 would be built

On 9 August 1944, the War Department officially announced that the Fort Worth Division had begun producing the B-32 Dominator bomber of which approximately 118 were built. (CAC/AAF)

6

Consolidated Fort Worth Plant Post-War to Present

Although post-war Consolidated underwent a few name changes and buyouts beginning with Convair, then General Dynamics, and finally Lockheed, the end of the war did not halt production at Consolidated Fort Worth as America remained militarily on alert throughout the Cold War.

After the war in Europe ended on 8 May 1945, B-32 production was greatly decreased, along with B-24 and B-32 training requirements. Despite the cutbacks, on 17 July 1945, the southwestern division of the Army Corps of Engineers issued a contract for a $2.23 million upgrade to the field's runway to accommodate the XB-36 Peacemaker. On 8 September 1945, this giant bomber was moved out of the experimental building at Government Aircraft Plant 4 and would keep the Fort Worth Plant viable for the next decade.

Chairman of the Board Tom M. Girdler, who took over from Fleet in December 1941, resigned on 27 April 1945, when he saw that the war was about to end aircraft production and his importance. He altruistically explained that he assumed the chairmanship three and a half years earlier, "only in service of the nation and in support of the government war effort." George Newman, who managed the Fort Worth Plant from its inception, resigned near the end of the war to accept a more lucrative and secure peacetime job. Newman was succeeded by Roland Mayer as manager of the Fort Worth Division, who had served as assistant division manager for fifteen months, after retiring from the Navy in 1940 and then continued on with Consolidated for twenty-two years of service.

In September 1945, Gen. Arnold sent a letter thanking Fort Worth: "Your plant in Fort Worth cooperated magnificently in meeting every changed or urgent production schedule. Without your outstanding services, our air plans against these two enemies could never have been accomplished." Mayer told employees that the work expected from Convair changed when the war ended: "During the war the United States Government wanted the best airplanes it could get the fastest and at any price. But our customers now, including the Government, want the best airplanes they can get the cheapest."

During the war, the Fort Worth Plant's impact on the city was significant. In the decade from 1940 to 1950, the population of Fort Worth increased 58.9 percent from 177,662 to 278,778, with wartime jobs attracting thousands of workers from surrounding small towns and rural areas. Consolidated-Vultee was the city's largest employer, reaching nearly 31,000 during the war. Also increasing Fort Worth employment were several aircraft parts suppliers and numerous community service providers that began business in the city.

After the cancellation of wartime contracts and the resulting lay-off, only five Convair divisions remained open, three of which would close during the next two years. By December 1945, only sixteen out of the sixty-six airframe plants that had been in business a year earlier still operated in America. Most of the branch factories that the major airline companies opened for war production shut down either before V-J Day or a few months after.

However, three major plants did not close: the Columbus Plant of Curtiss Aircraft, the Wichita Plant of Boeing, and the Fort Worth Plant of Convair. Employment at the Fort Worth Plant declined to 6,200 in 1946 as the plant would continue to work on three important experimental projects: the XB-36, the C-99 six-engined transport, and a third type of aircraft (B-58 Hustler) that was still classified by the War Department. The workweek was shortened to forty hours five days a week from forty-eight hours six days a week with only the experimental department to continue to work two shifts per day.

Between 1947 and 1954, Air Force Plant 4 produced 383 B-36s, the first intercontinental bomber; this maintained the Fort Worth Plant during the post-war era. The Peacemaker would operate as a USAF strategic bomber from 1949 to 1959, being the first bomber capable of delivering any of the nuclear weapons in the U.S. arsenal. It was the largest mass-produced piston-engined aircraft ever built, with the longest wingspan of any combat aircraft ever built (230 feet).

After B-36 manufacture ceased, Fort Worth built the F-58 Hustler, the first supersonic bomber. By 1966, the plant had expanded to 4.7 million square feet, and by 1968, it had expanded further to 6.5 million square feet to accommodate production of the F-111, the first swing-wing aircraft. At the end of the Cold War, in March 1992, Lockheed assumed operation of the facility and the plant was fabricating, assembling, and testing the F-16 fighter for the USAF and ten Allied nations. Later, the plant manufactured F-16 and F-22 aircraft components and, additionally, produced spare aircraft parts, radar units, and missile components. Today Air Force Plant 4 (AFP4) is a GOCO defense manufacturing facility that occupies 605 acres, bounded on the north by Lake Worth, on the south and west by the City of White Settlement, and on the east by Carswell Air Force Base with which the plant shares access to the runways and the support facilities. The plant includes 8 million square feet of industrial floor space (84 percent government-owned). It is a self-sufficient and self-contained fabrication and assembly operation with facilities that include a high bay structure and flyaway capability (from adjacent Carswell AFB). Support functions (logistics, engineering office space) are conducted from onsite trailers and leased offsite space.

The 383 Fort Worth B-36 Peacemakers would sustain that plant during the post-war era, as it operated as a USAF strategic bomber from 1949 to 1959. (*CAC/AAF*)

The first (B-36) and the last (C-87) at Fort Worth. (*CAC/AAF*)

Fort Worth Contract Deliveries

Contract	Model	Accepted Dates	#A/C
AC-18723	B-24D	April 1942 - July 1942	8*
AC-18723 (Supp.#7)	C-87	Sept. 1942 - Mar. 1944	169
AC-26992	B-24D	Sept. 1942 - Mar. 1944	295
AC-26992	B-24E	July 1943 - Aug. 1943	37
AC-18723 (Supp.#1)	B-24E	Mar. 1943 - July 1943	107
AC-26992	B-24H	Aug. 1943 - Nov. 1943	70
AC-18723 (Supp.#1)	B-24H	Aug. 1943 - Feb. 1944	493
AC-18723 (Supp.#1)	B-24H	Feb. 1944 - May 1944	175
AC-26992	B-24J	Sept. 1943 - Mar. 1944	348
AC-26992 (Supp.#1)	B-24J	Jan. 1944 - Mar. 1944	200
AC-40715	B-24J	Mar. 1944 - Aug. 1944	500
AC-40033	B-24J	Aug. 1944 - Dec. 1944	453
AC-18723 (Supp.#1)	B-24J	May 1944 - June 1944	57
AC-18723 (Supp.#7)	AT-22	June 1943 - Oct. 1943	5**
AC-18723 (Supp.#7)	C-87A	Apr. 1943 - Jan. 1944	6
AC-18723	C-87	Mar. 1944 - Aug. 1944	111
Total			3,034

Notes: 832 knock-down airframes built by Ford were final-assembled by Fort Worth and delivered on ac-18723. A total 107 airframes built by Ford were final-assembled by Fort Worth and contractually charged and delivered on ac-26992

*Assembled from components fabricated by Consolidated San Diego on Contract 16005

** Flight Engineering Trainer version of the B-24.

The average man-hour figure per plane for total of 3,034 airplanes was 14,075 production man-hours. The average direct man-hours per pound for same number of aircraft produced was 0.61

Summary of the Cost of Consolidated's Fort Worth Facility (5-23-44)

Schedule No.
I: Land and Land Improvements
- Land $20,010*
- Land Improvements $1,071,700
- Total I   1,091,700

II: Buildings and Etc.
- Buildings $18,748,400
- Building Installations (not mechanical) $11,242,000
- Leasehold Improvements $3,089,100
- Off Leasehold Improvements $278,800

Service Costs	$885,000
Total II	$34,243,300
III: Machinery, Equipment, Etc.	
Machine Tools	$6,269,547
Production Equipment	$1,199,824
Building Installations (Mechanical)	$1,280,900
Laboratory and Testing Equipment	$109,742
Furniture and Fixtures	$663,595
Total III	$9,523,609
IV: Portable Tools and Automotive Equipment	
Portable Tools	$12,000
Automotive Equipment	$367,564
Total IV	$379,565
V: Durable Tools	
Special Jigs and Fixtures	$35,500
Special Functional Gauges	$3,000
Special Dies and Patterns, Etc.	$23,000
Total V	$61,500
Total I-V	$45,299,684

*$20,010 was 50 acres or private land purchased for the pump house site and granting of a perpetual easement for the railway spur. All other land was donated to the government by the City of Fort Worth.

Tarrant/Carswell AAF

At the same time they courted Reuben Fleet's aircraft factory, the Fort Worth Chamber of Commerce acted to persuade the War Department to select their city as a site for a military airbase. A formal request for an airfield began when a member of the Civil Aeronautics Administration (CAA) in Fort Worth filed an application with the War Department in 1940, asking for a primary training base for the Army Air Corps even though San Antonio already had become an important center for aviation training at its Randolph and Kelly Fields. Once Fleet and Consolidated agreed to come to Fort Worth, organizers proceeded to coordinate and plan a facility that was to serve as a convenient training base to provide crews for Liberators coming off the adjacent assembly line. After the Japanese attack on Pearl Harbor, the construction of an AAC base on the east side of the factory area was authorized. Army Air Force Combat Crew School was opened on 1 July 1942 but was soon renamed Fort Worth Army Airfield on 29 July 1942; it was commonly referred to as Tarrant Field or also as Tarrant Field Airdrome during the war. The base began as a pilot transition school for the B-26 Marauder before becoming one of the first B-24 transition schools in operation. After more than 4,000 students were trained in B-24s at the base, its mission was changed to B-24 transition also because of the proximity to the Consolidated factory. In 1945, its mission was changed from B-24 to B-29 training.

In March 1946, Fort Worth Army Airfield was assigned to the newly formed Strategic Air Command and provided airmen and equipment during the post-war, Korean, Vietnam, and the Persian Gulf War. The base was renamed Carswell Air Base on 29 January 1948 after Medal of Honor recipient, B-24 pilot Maj. Horace Carswell, who received the medal for actions while returning from a mission on Japanese shipping in the South China Sea on 26 October 1944. He attempted to save a crewmember whose parachute had been destroyed by flak and remained at the controls of his crippled bomber and died while crash landing the Liberator near Tungchen, China. The base was officially closed as an active-duty installation on 1 October 1993 and was redesignated as Carswell Air Reserve Station and became the first joint reserve base and is now controlled by the Navy while a portion of the former air force base is station to the Texas National Guard.

Tarrant Field Airdrome (later Carswell AFB) was important addition to the Fort Worth facility as it would serve as a convenient training base for new crews, providing Liberators just off the adjacent assembly line. (*AAF*)

PART IV

The Magnificent Ford Willow Run Plant

The Ford Willow Run Bomber Plant is widely known and touted as an extraordinary modern manufacturing marvel, being the largest factory in the world under a single roof. It was constructed in 1941–42 to mass produce aircraft for the first time, ultimately constructing 8,685 Liberators, and during peak production in early 1944, an amazing one bomber per hour was produced. Willow Run's success can be attributed to Henry Ford's ground-breaking mass production technics in automobile production of inexpensive automobiles for the masses.

1
Henry Ford and Automobile Mass Production

The first automobile to be mass produced in America was in 1901 when American auto manufacturer Ransome Eli Olds produced 425 Curved Dash Oldsmobiles, making Olds America's leading auto manufacturer from 1901 to 1904. Henry Ford formed the Ford Motor Company in 1903 and, like other auto manufacturers, built his first automobiles by hand. Ford introduced the Model T in 1908, and after several years, he decided that an affordable automobile required automation production for mass consumption by the middle class. The Model T would become a great success when, about 1913, he introduced the first conveyor belt-based moving assembly lines with completely interchangeable parts. Ford and his engineers had developed machines to fabricate the large quantities of the parts required and devised methods of assembling these parts as quickly as they were made. At the Ford Highland Park, Detroit factory, workers were placed at appointed stations along a moving final assembly line, beginning with a bare chassis that stopped at each station, where parts were installed, until the Model T was finally completed and driven from the factory. This combination of accuracy, continuity, and speed introduced mass production to the world with Model T production reaching record levels; a completed auto leaving the line every ten seconds of every working day. Ford was able to cut prices, double the minimum daily wage to $5, produce a superior product, and still make a profit. By 1927, 15 million Model Ts had been manufactured at was Ford's showcase Highland Park assembly line.

By the early 1930s, it became apparent that the limits of the first generation of mass production, epitomized by the Model T's rigid production processes, had been reached and the era of flexible mass production began with the Model A. To produce the Model A, Ford mass production was moved to the River Rouge Plant, which was completed in 1928 as the world's largest integrated factory, measuring 1.5 miles wide by 1 mile long, including ninety-three buildings with nearly 16 million square feet of factory floor space. The Ford Model A, first produced at River Rouge on 20 October 1927, was Ford's second enormous success after its Model T predecessor, which had been produced for eighteen years. By 4 February 1929, 1 million Model As had been sold, and by 24 July, 2 million were sold in body styles ranging from the $500

Tudor to the $1,200 Town Car. In March 1930, Model A sales reached 3 million, and there were nine body styles available. Model A production ended in March, 1932, after 4,858,644 had been manufactured. Ford produced three completely new cars between 1932 and 1934: the Model B, Model 18, and Model 40, with substantial yearly model changes. Ford's main product introduced in 1935 was the Model 48, an update on Ford's V8-powered Model 40A. It was the 1935 Ford's combination of price, practicality, and appearance that vaulted the company ahead of rival Chevrolet for the sales. The Model 48 was given an annual cosmetic rejuvenation before being comprehensively redesigned for 1941 production. The production in 1942 was aborted for war production after only 160,000 were built, and the design was continued after the war for the 1946 year. By October 1941, it became apparent Willys-Overland could not meet production demand for its MA ("Military" model "A") and Ford was contracted to supplement production as the designated GPW, with the "G" for a "Government" type contract and "P" normally used by Ford to designate any passenger car with a wheelbase of 80 inches and the "W" referring to the "Willys" licensed design. The GP designation popularly became "Jeep" and during World War II, Willys produced 363,000 Jeeps and Ford 280,000.

HENRY FORD AND AUTOMOBILE MASS PRODUCTION

Ford Highland Park Plant. (*FMC*)

Highland Park Model T Production Line: Beginning with a bare chassis that stopped at each station, where parts were installed, 15 million Model Ts would be driven from Highland Park from 1910 to 1927. (*FMC*)

Ford River Rouge Plant. (*FMC*)

Henry (L) and Edsel Ford pose with their Model A successor to the Model T produced at the new Rouge Plant. (*FMC*)

Ford 1942 automobile production was aborted for war production after only 160,000 were built and Ford was contracted to supplement Willy's Jeep production. (*FMC*)

2

The Trimotor *Tin Goose*: Ford's First Aircraft Manufacturing Endeavor

During the 1920s, as 15 million Model Ts left his innovative mass production assembly lines at ever-lower prices, Henry Ford was identified with the automobile. At the time, Ford also assumed that he could that he could just as easily achieve the same results in the aircraft industry. During 1924, Henry Ford and his son, Edsel, along with eighteen other backers, invested $1,000 each in famous designer and entrepreneur William Stout's Stout Metal Airplane Company. In 1925, Ford engaged Stout and bought his aircraft designs, culminating in the cumbersome Model 3-AT prototype powered by three air-cooled Curtiss Wright radial engines. After being widely promoted by Henry Ford as the "airplane of the future," the Model 3-AT performed poorly in trials and was destroyed by a suspicious fire on 16 January 1926 that also destroyed the Stout factory. It was not long before the anticipated Ford-Stout parting took place and Ford replaced Stout with Harold Hicks and Tom Towle, who were credited with honing the 3-AT design into the Model 4-AT and then the definitive 5-AT, the renowned *Tin Goose* Trimotor (sometimes called the Tri-Motor).

The rugged, reliable, and remarkably maneuverable Trimotor, characterized by its corrugated aluminum fuselage skin, could carry ten to twelve passengers, seated on passably comfortable wicker seats in cabin that was penetrated by the deafening noise from the three 450-hp P&W R985 engines at a cruising speed of 110 to 115 mph. Although designed primarily for passenger use, the Trimotor could be easily adapted for hauling cargo, as its seats could be removed. Although similar in appearance to the popular Fokker transports, the Trimotor had two pronounced advantages: the Ford name and all-metal construction. Following its maiden flight in 1926, interest and demand for the Ford flourished, and by 1929, four aircraft were completed by the Ford factory each week. When production ceased on 7 June 1933, Ford had manufactured 199 Trimotors that served all three U.S. military branches, many airlines and corporations, and flew in twenty foreign countries. The Trimotor inaugurated U.S. transcontinental airline service while flying for Transcontinental Air Transport and is considered a ground-breaking airliner. The Trimotor was superseded as a passenger aircraft by more modern aircraft like the DC-3, but continued to be employed for decades carrying heavy freight to mining operations in jungles and mountains. It would not be until World War II broke out in Europe that Ford again considered aircraft manufacture.

Above: The Ford 5-AT, the renowned *Tin Goose*, was a rugged, reliable, and remarkably maneuverable ten to twelve passenger trimotor aircraft, of which 199 were built. (*FMC*)

Below: Left to right: William Stout, Edsel Ford, Henry Ford, and Trimotor pilot with the aircraft's characteristic corrugated aluminum fuselage skin as a backdrop. (*FMC*)

3

The Auto Industry Begins Aircraft Manufacture

The Reuther Report:
Touts the Automobile Industry's Manufacture of Aircraft

In the two-year period before America's entry into World War II, the American aircraft industry was unable to fulfill its commitments while the automobile industry had been underutilized. With a global war inevitable, Detroit realized the potential of airpower's role in modern warfare. Among those aware of and concerned by the disparity between aircraft promised and aircraft delivered by the American aircraft industry was a former highly-skilled machinist, Walter Reuther. As a CIO United Auto Workers (UAW) founder and president, Reuther, along with other labor leaders, was a powerful political force for the conversion of the auto industry into the "Arsenal of Democracy."

On 23 December 1940, Reuther, with the support of Philip Murray, president of the CIO, released his report, "500 Planes a Day, A Program for the Utilization of the Automobile Industry for the Mass Production of Defense Planes." In preparation for his program, Reuther gathered a group of skilled machinists who conducted a several month survey of the "shut-down capacity" (retooling) of various plants and their tool and die rooms.

The Reuther Report discussed how America could retool its auto industry, 50 percent of whose capacity was being underutilized:

> The workers in the automotive industry believe that the way to produce planes quickly is to manufacture them in automobile plants. The automotive industry today is operating at only half its potential capacity. This plan proposes that the unused potential of the industry, in machines and men, be utilized in the mass production of aircraft engines and planes. It is our considered opinion that it would be possible, after six months of preparation, to turn out five hundred of the most modern fighting planes a day, if the idle machines and the idle men of the automotive industry were fully mobilized, and private interests temporarily subordinated to the needs of this emergency.

At the time, American aircraft production was 30 percent behind the schedule required just to sustain Britain in its war effort, much less prepare America for a future war. Reuther maintained the U.S. would remain far behind schedule even if American aircraft plants were newly-built or expanded and then continued to use their slow and costly production systems geared to hand-tooled custom-made production: "New plants cannot be built and put into operation in less than 18 months. In 18 months Britain's battle ... may be lost, and our own country left to face a totalitarian Europe alone."

Reuther then expounded the key concept of his plan:

We propose, instead of building entirely new machines, to make the tools required to adapt existing automotive machinery to aircraft manufacture.... We propose to transform the entire unused capacity of the automotive industry into one huge plane production unit.... No industry in the world has the tremendous unused potential productive capacity of the American automotive industry, and no industry is as easily adaptable to the mass production of planes.

In conclusion, Reuther offered the total cooperation of labor:

The merit of our plan is that it saves time, and time is our problem. Normal methods can build all the planes we need if we wait until 1942 and 1943 to get them. This plan is put forward in the belief that the need for planes is immediate, and terrifying. Precious moments pass away as we delay. We dare not invite the disaster that may come with further delay.

During December 1940, Walter Reuther, United Auto Workers' founder and president, released his Reuther Report, which discussed how America could retool its underused auto industry for aircraft production. (*NA*)

Although Ford embraced the Reuther Plan as a means of implementing aircraft mass production, General Motors objected to Reuther's proposal, particularly the section in which he proposed that the U.S. Government would set up a tripartite aviation production committee, through which workers would participate in determining how retooling would be done, the levels of production, what goods would be produced, etc. In rebuttal, GM President Charles Wilson stated:

> Everyone admits that Reuther is smart but this is none of his business.... If Reuther wants to become part of management, GM will be happy to hire him. But so long as he remains Vice-President of the Union, he has no right to talk as if he were Vice President of a company.

However, even more serious opposition came from FBI Director J. Edgar Hoover, who circulated charges that Reuther and his brother, Victor, were Communists and placed them on the FBI's so-called "custodial list" of dangerous individuals slated for arrest should the president declare a national emergency. Several days after Reuther presented his "500 Planes a Day Plan," Hoover circulated a despicable dossier on Reuther to several individuals, including Roosevelt's secretary, Edwin Watson, GM's William Knudsen, "Dixiecrat" Representative Eugene Cox of Georgia, and others.

In response to Hoover and to promote his plan, Reuther gave forceful speeches defending the plan during a cross-country tour, while the UAW, aided by the CIO and others, actively circulated the plan to auto workers, others in the labor movement, and the American public. Reuther stressed the "machine-tool principle," and the "productive powers of labor," in the Plan as the "power that would uniquely protect and save freedom and the American Republic."

While Reuther oversimplified some points in his plan, for example, a fighter plane had ten times as many moving parts as an auto body and required frequent design changes, his fundamental emphasis on the need and the ability, to retool the auto industry on a crash basis, would be vindicated. The Reuther Plan was unquestionably instrumental in realizing Roosevelt's industrial conversion for Lend-Lease and then for war. Had Reuther not advanced proposals, retooling would have occurred far less quickly and efficiently.

The American Automobile Industry Becomes a Defense Industry

While the Reuther Plan was accepted by some in the government and many of the public, of course, neither the aircraft nor the automobile industries found even a little merit in the plan. Soon after Reuther released his proposal, the *Wall Street Journal* reported that holders of "aircraft shares are not particularly pleased at the prospect that the automobile industry may use some of its facilities for mass production of planes." Aircraft industry leaders were unconvinced or even ridiculed the notion of aircraft mass production by means similar to that of automobiles. Meanwhile, the automotive industry considered the Reuther Plan as technically flawed and certainly thought its proposal that labor participate in management as worrisome.

The Reuther Plan was based on the automobile industry's underutilization of its facilities as it had a potential production of eight million vehicles per year and was only producing four million per year, and thus, half its factories, labor, and equipment could be dedicated to aircraft manufacture without any reduction in civilian automobile production. Reuther maintained that this objective could be achieved if the auto manufacturers suspended their yearly model change to restrict tooling and also agree to pool their machine tools with other auto manufacturers to build aircraft. Reuther proposed that the administration of the program was to be assigned to a nine-man board consisting of three representatives each from government, management, and labor. This proposed administration would never be acceptable to the automobile establishment as the automotive industry could not be partially operated by its own management and partially by Reuther's proposed board. Reuther's Plan did not take into consideration that the automobile factories did not have the expansive floor areas required for aircraft assembly, even for smaller fighter aircraft. Moreover, neither America nor the United Kingdom would require the unrealistic 500 fighters a day. Alternatively, the wide publicity Reuther Plan received did call attention to the critical problem of machine tools. Both Reuther and automobile management mistakenly assumed that automotive production techniques would be readily adaptable to aircraft manufacture. Former GM President Gen. William Knudsen considered the Reuther Plan, but its advocates were unable to advance a comprehensive program without the cooperation of the automotive industry which was not accommodating. By the end of January 1941, the stagnating plan was shelved by the government and no longer held the attention of the public.

By the fall of 1940, the production of bombers, not fighters, had become a major problem, as a sufficient capacity for fighter manufacture already existed or could be readily provided. Manufacturing vast numbers of a standardized fighter, not required by either the American and British air forces, would have expended resources necessary for the production of other types of aircraft, particularly bombers. Aircraft manufacture by the automobile industry depended on the erroneous assumption that Air Corps aircraft designs could readily be frozen to facilitate mass production. However, as wartime experience continually proved, the rapid tempo of aeronautical and tactical advances prevented the freezing of a particular model for more than a very short time. If the existing 1940 models had been frozen for production on the scale proposed by Reuther, the consequences could have been calamitous.

However, the fundamentals of the Reuther Plan, the large-scale use of automotive facilities for airframe production and an effort to conserve machine tools, had previously been initiated by Knudsen whose incentive originated from the requirement for bombers, not fighters. On 15 October 1940, Knudsen spoke to automobile industry leaders at a meeting of the Automobile Manufacturers Association in New York and appealed to them first to suspend any auto model changes requiring new machine tools, and second, in secrecy, to undertake the manufacture of $500 million worth of aircraft parts and subassemblies. Then ten days later, at a meeting in Detroit, Knudsen succinctly portrayed the current automotive/aircraft conversion situation:

The present program calls for the delivery of some 33,000 airplanes by April 1, 1942. All plant expansion for this quantity is under way and the bottleneck is tools. Airplanes is a vague name for the product, as training planes weigh 4,000 pounds, and the biggest bomber, approximately 40,000 pounds. If we were to turn out 33,000 four thousand pound planes, there would be no problem, but only 30% are training planes, and the rest are combat planes and bombers.

Therefore you are asked to tackle the possible dies and stampings for four thousand four-motor bombers, weighing 40,000 pounds gross, and eight thousand two-motor bombers weighing 24,000 pounds gross, assembling to be done by airplane manufacturers. You are asked to consider not only pieces, but subassemblies for this quantity of planes. It should be remembered that planes to date have been more or less handmade and that, in order to transfer the operation to press and die work, production studies will have to be made.

It is therefore proposed to secure floor space in Detroit, in charge of Air Corps officials from Wright Field, and to secure a set of parts for each plane as designed now with the corresponding drawings, and study such production changes as are necessary to transfer manufacturing from bench to machine. To accomplish this we ask that a steering committee of four be appointed which, with two from the plane manufacturers, push this vigorously.

It is also proposed that while the parts and drawings are being secured, these six men visit the two airplane plants where the bombers are now being manufactured in order to get the proper picture of the method of jigging and manufacturing as now done in production.

It is proposed that a survey of equipment now in place be secured and as allocation of die work is made, the order for the required number of pieces follow the die order wherever possible so as to get immediate action after the try-out. Also a survey should be made of plant facilities available for jig assembly of minor assemblies such as wings, ailerons, tail surfaces, rudders, etc.

It is also desired that the steering committee investigate the forging situation, both aluminum and steel, plus the machining facilities available for such forgings, there being a serious shortage at the moment of facilities of this order. In other words, we are trying to get from the industry a coordinated branch of our Washington set-up to deal with sub-assemblies and pieces rather than the complete assembly as dealt with by us in Washington.

The result of Knudsen's requests was the formation of the Automotive Committee for Air Defense to coordinate the industry's aircraft manufacture undertakings and to begin surveys of available plants to determine what it could contribute to the program. Initially, its task was only educational, since the automotive production men were being requested to manufacture items that most of them had never encountered. At Knudsen's prompting, one of the committee's most valuable functions was to sponsor a Detroit exhibition of aircraft parts and components. An Air Corps officer and brilliant aeronautical mind, Maj. James Doolittle, was assigned by the Air Corps as its technical adviser for this exhibition and later as its liaison officer to assist the industry in its planning.

William Knudsen

Born in Copenhagen, Denmark, in 1879, twenty-year-old William Knudsen came to America where he worked in a New Jersey shipyard and for the Erie Railroad, before joining bicycle and auto parts maker John R. Keim in Buffalo, Kentucky, where he gained extensive shop experience. Keim was purchased by the Ford Motor Company in 1911, and by 1913, Knudsen was placed in charge of U.S. Ford assembly plants and later he was made the production manager at the Ford Detroit plant. During this time, he oversaw the initial development of the modern assembly line and mass production. After a disagreement with Henry Ford in 1921, Knudsen was recruited to join the Chevrolet division of General Motors in 1922 in an advisory capacity and soon afterward was made vice president in charge of operations of GM's Chevrolet Division. On 15 January 1924, Knudsen was elected president and general manager of Chevrolet and over the next decade, proceeded to turn Chevrolet from GM's worst performing division into the backbone of the corporation and then bettered the production levels set by his former employer Ford. On 16 October 1933, after his tenure at Chevrolet, he served four years as executive vice president in charge of all General Motors auto, truck, body, and accessory operations and became a member of the executive committee. On 3 May 1937, he was elected GM president, succeeding Alfred Sloan, Jr., who was named chairman of the board of directors. During his three-year tenure as president, Knudsen helped to guide General Motors through a period of intense labor unrest.

On 6 June 1940, Knudsen was granted a leave of absence by the General Motors board of directors and resigned on 3 September to accept an appointment by FDR. On the recommendation of Bernard Baruch, FDR named him as the chairman of the Office of Production Management (OPM) and as a member of the National Defense Advisory Commission (NDAC), for which he received a salary of $1 per year. In January 1942, Knudsen was commissioned a lieutenant general in the U.S. Army, the only civilian ever to join the Army at such a high initial rank, and was appointed as director of production, office of the undersecretary of war, as a consultant and a troubleshooter for the War Department. In both of these positions, Knudsen used his extensive experience in manufacturing and industry to expedite the largest production undertaking in history with America vastly out producing all the Axis combatants combined. As Knudsen said: "We won because we smothered the enemy in an avalanche of production, the like of which he had never seen, nor dreamed possible." He was appointed director of the Air Technical Service Command when it was founded in July 1944 and served in the Army until his resignation on 1 June 1945. Knudsen returned to the GM board of directors but had little to do as he had passed the mandatory retirement age of sixty-five years old. He died less than three years later on 27 April 1948. His son, Semon "Bunkie," served as GM executive vice president from 1966 to 1968, Ford president in 1968 and 1969, and White Motor Corporation chairman from 1971 to 1980.

Gen. William Knudsen, former General Motors president and chairman of the OPM. (NA)

The Bomber Program Develops

Over the next months as the bomber program developed, four bomber assembly plants were to be constructed to be operated by the aircraft companies, with Ford, Chrysler, Hudson, and General Motors' Fisher Body Division to be the subcontractors for the manufacture of parts and sub-assemblies for these plants. However, as the situation developed that the government discovered that it would have to finance much more for plants and machine tools than it had projected. Gen. Oliver Echols' original plan for auto/aircraft conversion was to have all existing facilities utilized to their the maximum use, and no new facilities were to be financed by the government or the automobile industry for the specific intent of manufacturing aircraft parts unless it was found to be absolutely necessary. Echols became concerned by the insistence of the so-called automobile industry "haves" General Motors, Ford, and Chrysler receive new facilities and machine tools; rather than to use, through subcontracting, the inactive facilities and machines of the "have nots" Willys-Overland, Graham-Paige, and others. During January 1941, after OPM had decided that there should be no reduction of automobile production during the first half of 1941, the larger auto companies obtained government authorization for new plants and machine tools on the assertion that they were required for the fulfillment of commitments to the aircraft program. Ford's new plant at Willow Run was financed by the government, and Chrysler, Hudson, and Fisher Body all obtained aid in the rehabilitation of existing plants while a new Chrysler plant was privately financed.

The real question was the extent to which automobile plants and tools could be converted to the production of aircraft. During October 1940, the Air Corps considered that automobile factories could not be used as aircraft assembly plants without extensive modifications because of their insufficient area and height clearances for large-scale aircraft assembly. As it would require as much as twenty months to build new dedicated aircraft assembly plants, there was no rush to convert the automobile plants to the manufacture of parts and sub-assemblies because, at the time, it would require much less than twenty months for that conversion.

Under the Reuther Plan, estimates of the degree to which automobile plants could be converted to munitions production ranged from 10 percent to as high as 50–60 percent. The automobile companies maintained that only 10–15 percent of their machine tools could be converted to the manufacture of munitions, while the machine tools industry and labor leaders placed the figure at 50 percent. However, in June 1942, there was an actual 66 percent conversion of machine tools in the automotive industry. Conversely, Reuther's assumption that such a large scale aircraft production/conversion program could have been undertaken without reducing the production of automobiles was questionable as it was his contention that unused facilities could be used with a resulting increase of employment and without cutback of normal production.

Meanwhile, more automobile companies were engaged in producing aircraft engines. In December 1940, the Studebaker Corporation received a contract for production of Wright R-2600 engines, and in January 1941, General Motors' Buick Division was contracted to build P&W R-1830 engines. Both these companies built new plants instead of using their existing ones as it became evident to both the Air Corps and the OPM that none of the automobile companies would forego its competitive position in the auto industry by converting its own existing facilities unless all of its competitors did also. Thus, the government found its only alternative was to provide them with new facilities and tools.

Even after the Reuther Plan was no longer a consideration, the auto industry continued to gain attention as a means to alleviate the increasing demand for aircraft production to come during 1941. In late December 1940, Assistant Secretary of War for Air Robert Lovett advocated:

> ... certain existing facilities (obviously the automotive industry-author), should be promptly diverted to war plane and engine production ... to compel, if necessary, the big aircraft companies to sub-contract their work where this can be done without jeopardizing quality.

Besides providing more facilities for aircraft manufacture, the rapid and continuous increase in automobile production was consuming huge amounts of metals and other materials required for aircraft and munitions production. During 1939, it was estimated that the auto industry used 18 percent of all the steel utilized in the U.S., 34 percent of the lead, 13.7 percent of the copper, 11.4 percent of the tin, 9.7 percent of the aluminum, 50 percent of the rubber, and 23 percent of the plate glass. The auto industry's economic power allowed it to successfully compete with defense production for these vital materials and also for the equipment and services essential to both. Soon the OPM realized the unavoidable necessity to readjust the existing balance between the two and, on 3 May 1941, dispensed an order curtailing automobile production by 20 percent for the model year beginning August 1941. The auto industry used this intervening period to stockpile materials, especially steel, and to increase auto and truck production to new records because the 20 percent reduction after 1 August would be based on the rate of production for the previous twelve months.

The reduction of production in the civilian durable goods industries, of which the automotive industry was the largest, assured no quick or certain solution to the munitions production problem. Knudsen was reluctant to reduce civilian production significantly because the defense orders already contracted were not adequate to utilize the industrial capacity and manpower, which would be released with the reduction, with the resulting unemployment and disbanding of skilled labor pools could have severe economic significance. Alternatively, shortages of tools and materials were delaying munitions production and the deficiency of productive capacity had discouraged the military from placing large orders on the industry, which the OPM believed should be placed on it. However, the gigantic character of the arms programs made it impossible to achieve a quick and smooth civilian to military transition but, nonetheless, action needed to be taken to meet military requirements. On 9 July 1941, FDR stated his belief that the durable goods industries had to be used for defense production, even though the conversion period might be costly to the government. By 21 August, the government and the auto industry had agreed on a gradual but rather large reduction of passenger car production totaling 43.4 percent during the year beginning 1 August 1941. It is evident that the main motivation for this curtailment was the conservation of critical materials rather than release of productive capacity. Consequently, it was not until after Pearl Harbor that there was a serious conversion of automobile plants to munitions production.

During the war, interaction between the aircraft and automotive industries were unavoidably close, if not always amiable. During 1940–41, the aircraft industry had manufactured almost all the aircraft and engines manufactured in America, while the auto companies continued to build the engine and airframe plants that would set production records during 1943–45. After the war, the aircraft manufacturer's fear of competition from the auto industry continued and had been echoed in their criticisms of the efforts of the automobile manufacturers. In May 1942, North American Aviation President James Kindelberger asserted that the automobile industry was a "bottleneck" in the production of parts and subassemblies for airframes. United Aircraft Chairman of the Board Frederick Rentschler was pleased with his company's role in bringing the automobile industry into the production of aircraft engines even if that industry "should turn out to be a Frankenstein's Monster and try to 'swallow up' the aviation industry after the war."

Aircraft Factory Conversion vs. New Construction?

Once war began in Europe, the American government and industrialists posed a hypothetical: if a war came quickly, would factory conversion or the construction of new airframe facilities be the best and ultimate choice? Also questioned was proving that the mass production approach of the automotive industry could be utilized for aircraft manufacture. Would the cost of a new factory and its time lag to production and the expenditure of tooling dollars be later offset by the savings in labor costs and the eventual realization of mass production? Studies found that considering the cost per square foot of floor space obtained, factory conversion to airframe manufacture cost approximately one-third of the initial expenditure by the government needed for new construction. However, since the long-term cost of new construction would have to consider rents paid, monies recovered by post-war plant sales, and the potentially better sales and profits because of the lower costs of end products sold by manufacturers using government-owned facilities as compared to those of manufacturers using their own facilities. Another consideration was the differences in taxes paid between contractors with government-owned facilities and private contractors. Although the AAF spent $3 billion in direct financing of airframe-manufacturing facilities during the war, only 35 percent was invested in new construction. An additional 4 percent purchased the land for the building sites and transportation such as railroad and roads. The remaining 61 percent was spent for the purchase of tools. For parts requiring special-purpose machine tools, which took months to fabricate, new facilities could be erected while these tools were on order, offsetting the most important time-saving offered by conversion that also required the same special tools. Where general-purpose tools were available and could adequately provide for the required manufacturing tasks, conversion was to be favored over new construction, with other things being equal. On the other hand, new factories could be built near the sources of available labor.

Before and during World War II, the AAF's major failure was its inability to foster an administrative organization that would gather information to determine if construction or conversion was best strategy for delivering a specific aircraft by a specific manufacturer. Thus, this complicated problem of aircraft procurement was consigned to the AAF procurement office and as a result, there were times when these procurement officers promoted government financing of new construction and the purchase of new tools when the conversion of existing plants and the utilization of existing general-purpose tools were entirely possible. Because their superiors compelled these officers to obtain quick results, they were especially susceptible to the aircraft manufacturers whose analyses indicated that new tools and new floor space financed by the government were required if production objectives were to be achieved. Some airframe contractors inflated their tooling and plant construction needs as they expected to purchase these facilities from the government at post-war bargain prices.

4

Ford and Charles Sorensen Enter the U.S. Air Defense Program

Before Pearl Harbor, the AAF had selected the B-24 for production utilizing automotive manufacturers and factories. Whereas Chrysler and General Motors considered converting their automotive assembly lines, Ford under the leadership the venerable eighty-year-old Henry Ford, his fifty-year-old son, Edsel, and their production head, Charles Sorensen, made the bold declaration that a new factory would be required to mass produce Liberators. The result would be the huge purpose-built Willow Run Michigan Liberator plant.

During December 1940, Dr. George Mead, director of procurement for the aeronautical section of the advisory council for National Defense and formerly with P&W, and Maj. Jimmy Doolittle of the Army Air Corps visited Henry Ford in Dearborn to determine his willingness to manufacture aircraft for the U.S. defense program. Previously, after accepting an order to build 9,000 English Rolls-Royce aircraft engines, Ford cancelled the order because of a report in England that inferred that Ford was supporting the British but also because of his disapproval of the war and of President Roosevelt. However, the businessman Ford posed no resistance to constructing aircraft, but the cantankerous Ford was adamant that he was not interested in collaborating with any aircraft company. Nonetheless, Sorensen and Dr. Mead decided to fly to San Diego on 8 January 1941 to visit Consolidated Aircraft whose goal was "to produce one B-24 bomber a day or 350 planes a year," which Sorensen considered as a very modest goal.

In San Diego, Sorensen was met by Edsel Ford and his two sons, Henry II and Benson, who had left Detroit four days earlier and was also joined by several of Ford's outstanding specialists: Harold Hanson, factory construction authority; Logan Miller, considered one of the industry's top sheet metal experts; Edward Scott, Ford's "Master of Tool and Die;" Roscoe Smith, manager of Ford's far-flung factories; and Ernest Walters, long-time head of Ford's production and engineering departments.

The entourage spent the day examining Consolidated's factory and facilities, their equipment, and their manufacturing methods and procedures. Sorensen soon realized that Consolidated did not have the facilities, equipment, or procedures to even realize

Ford chief executives. *Left to right*: Edsel Ford, Charles Sorensen, and Henry Ford greet Assistant Secretary of War Robert Patterson. (*FMC*)

Above left: Dr. George Mead, director of procurement for the aeronautical section of the Advisory Council for National Defense. (*NA*)

Above right: Reuben Fleet (C) greets Ford executives Charles Sorensen (L) and Edsel Ford (R) on their January 1941 visit to San Diego. (*CAC/AAF*)

the "bomber a day" goal as they were building the bomber using job shop procedures, virtually custom-building them in numbers which were far below the required quantity. Sorensen brazenly told Maj. Reuben Fleet, Consolidated president and general manager, no less, that his evaluation the production capacity of Fleet's plant was "very discouraging."

If Consolidated was to provide the thousands of bombers needed for the U.S. defense program, their factory would have to be enlarged and modernized for mass production, which the AAC opposed because of the plant's location and hypothetical vulnerability to attack from the sea. Also, upgrading this factory would require its closing, causing a loss of valuable production at time when production capacity could not even meet existing contractual requirements. Furthermore, Consolidated's final assembly process was completed outdoors on steel tubing fixtures where expansion and contraction from temperature changes would create distortions and production difficulties unsuitable for mass production.

It has been said that "Henry Ford took the praise for the Willow Run marvel but Charles Sorensen did the work." The obviously resentful Sorensen continued the thought in his 1956 autobiography, *My Forty Years with Ford*:

> Henry Ford is generally regarded as the father of mass production, he was not. He was the sponsor of it.... Henry Ford had no ideas on mass production. In later years, he was glorified as the originator of the mass production idea. Far from it; he just grew into it, like the rest of us. The essential tools and the final assembly line with its many integrated feeders resulted from an organisation, which was continually experimenting and improvising to get better production.... Mr. Ford had nothing to do with originating, planning, and carrying out the assembly line. He encouraged the work. His vision to try unorthodox methods was an example to us.

Charles Sorensen was undeniably the architect and father of the modern assembly line whose ground-breaking concept of moving an automobile in a straight line from one end of the factory and out the other, with parts supplied by stockrooms positioned strategically along the line being added by specialized workers performing repetitive tasks. This scheme would become the most efficient and therefore economical method to build an automobile as Sorensen's 1913 assembly line would transform the infant auto industry and abet Ford's domination of the automobile market for many years to come.

Sorensen acted as Ford's head of production for forty years, during which time he was responsible but largely uncredited for numerous innovations that markedly improved productivity and efficiency. Sorensen conceived the automated production methods and equipment that Ford used in its three most renowned factories: Highland Park, River Rouge, and Willow Run. Highland Park was Ford's showcase assembly line from 1910 to 1927 when it produced millions of redoubtable Model Ts. River Rouge then became the center of Ford automobile manufacturing in the early 1930s and continued the company's dominance of the automobile market. After visiting Consolidated San Diego, Sorensen realized that the assembly line method he had perfected in building more than 30 million Ford automobiles could be used to

Charles Sorensen was undeniably the architect and father of the modern assembly line and the moving force behind Willow Run. (*FMC*)

manufacture, not build, bombers and easily eclipse Reuben Fleet's modest goal of turning out one bomber per day, perhaps, to one bomber produced per hour.

During his career, Sorensen was noted not only for his organizational brilliance, self-confidence, and his hard-driving personality, but was also notorious for his insensitivity and explosive temper. After the factory tour and criticism of Consolidated's manufacturing methods, Sorensen was asked how he would manufacture the airplane. Sorensen confidently stated that he would have "something for them in the morning" and left for his luxurious room at the Coronado Hotel to concoct a plan for a new plant that could produce a bomber an hour. Sorensen observed in his autobiography (*My Forty Years with Ford*, Wayne State University, 2006):

> Inside the plant I watched men putting together wing sections and portions of the fuselage. The work of putting together a four-engine bomber was many times more complicated than assembling a 4-cylinder automobile, but what I saw reminded me of nearly 35 years previously when we were making Model A Fords at the Piquette Avenue Plant. This was before Walter Flanders rearranged our machines and eight years before we achieved the orderly sequence of the assembly line and mass production.
>
> The closer a B-24 came to its final assembly the fewer principles of mass production there were as we at Ford had developed and applied over the years. Here was a custom-made plane, put together as a tailor would cut and fit a suit of clothes.
>
> The B-24s final assembly was made out-of-doors under the bright California sun and on a structural steel fixture. The heat and temperature changes so distorted this fixture that it was impossible to turn out two planes alike without further adjustment.

The Consolidated and the Air Force people talked about an order from Ford Motor Company for center and outer wing sections, but it was obvious that if the wing sections had uniform measurements, the way we made parts for automobiles, they would not fit properly under out-of-doors assembly conditions.

All this was pretty discouraging, and I said so. Naturally, and quite properly, the reply was "How would you do it?" I had to put up or shut up. I'll have something for you tomorrow morning," I said.

I really did have something in mind. To compare a Ford V-8 with a four-engine Liberator bomber was like matching a garage with a skyscraper, but despite their great differences I knew the same fundamentals applied to high-volume production of both, the same as they would to an electric egg beater or to a wrist watch.

First, break the plane's design into essential units and make a separate production layout for each unit. Next, build as many units as are required, then deliver each unit in its proper sequence to the assembly line to make one whole unit; a finished plane.

To house all this and provide for efficient operation there should be a new plant specially designed to accommodate the progressive layout. I saw no impossibility in such an idea even though mass production of anything approaching the size and complexity of a B-24 never had been attempted before.

But who would accept such a wild notion? And instead of one bomber a day by the prevailing method I saw the possibility of one B-24 an hour by mass production assembly lines. How could the aviation people take that estimate seriously?

As soon as I returned to my room at the Coronado Hotel, I began figuring how to adapt Ford assembly methods to airplane construction and turn out one four-engine bomber an hour.

Throughout the day I had made copious notes. I listed all major units of the plane and the subunits and fractional units required for their assembly, and I had gathered figures on Consolidated's labor force and job performance. From these I computed each unit operation, its timing, and required floor space as I saw them, and paper began to fly. Figures for each unit I kept together in a separate pile, and soon there were little stacks of paper all over the floor of my room.

I was back, at my old game of sketching a series of manufacturing and subassembly operations and their orderly progression toward becoming major units-a game I had played many times since that morning in 1908 at the Piquette Avenue Plant when we first experimented with a moving assembly line.

Again I was practicing my production planning philosophy, which stemmed from my patternmaking days when I fashioned wooden models of Henry Ford's half-thought-out designs: "Unless you see a thing, you cannot simplify it. And unless you can simplify it, it's a good sign you can't make it?"

As I look back now upon that night, this was the biggest challenge of my production career-bigger than any Model T assembly line sequence for Highland Park, more momentous than the layout and construction of the great River Rouge plant in which I'd had a part. It took eight years to develop Ford's mass production system, and eight more years before we worked up to a production of 10,000 cars a day.

Now, in one night, I was applying thirty-five years of production experience to planning the layout for building not only something I had never put together before, but the largest and most complicated of all air transport and in numbers and at a rate never before thought possible.

Once again I was going on the principle I had enunciated many times at Ford; "The only thing we can't make is something we can't think about."

Through most of the night I set down figures and revised them. I arranged and rearranged the stacks of paper, as it became plainer to me which unit came after-the other in moving to final assembly and how much floor space was involved.

At length the whole picture became clear and simple. I knew I had the solution, and I was elated by the certainty that the Germans had neither the facilities nor the conception for greater bomber mass production.

Towards four o'clock, I was satisfied that my piles of paper were arranged in proper order and represented the most logical progress of units to the main assembly line; and I knew I could prove a construction rate of one big bomber an hour. Now I had something to talk about.

Standing over the papers, I roughed out on Coronado Hotel notepaper a pencil sketch of the floor plan of a bomber plant. It would be a mile long and a quarter mile wide, the biggest single industrial building ever. I still have that sketch, initialed by Edsel Ford, his two sons and others, and I still get a kick out of it.

The result of one night's hard work, it is the true outline of Willow Run, which took, two years to build and came through on schedule with one four-engine Liberator an hour, eighteen bombers a day, and by the end of the war a total of 8,800 big planes off the assembly lines and into the air. When I finished my sketch I went to bed, but was so carried away by enthusiasm for the project that I couldn't sleep. I was building planes the rest of the night.

At breakfast with Edsel the next morning I was somewhat woozy as I showed him the sketch and outlined the bomber-an-hour proposition. He was in complete accord and assured me that Ford Motor Company would build such a plant. My high respect for him went higher than ever. We spent an hour together, getting set for a meeting in Major Fleet's office to shoot the works on a $200,000,000 proposition backed only by a penciled sketch.

Government representative Dr. George Mead was pleased with the Ford (Sorensen) concept to be designated as Project A, but Consolidated President Reuben Fleet was not persuaded, and tendered a counteroffer contracting Ford to build only 1,000 wing sections. Sorensen replied flatly: "We'll make the complete airplane or nothing." Sorensen returned to Dearborn to personally present his plan to Henry Ford but first he had to listen to Ford's standard anti-war lecture and then sit through a tirade on how General Motors, the Du Ponts, and President Roosevelt were conspiring to drag America into war and to take over Ford. But ultimately, the tetchy elder Ford listened to Sorensen and agreed to the plan. Although Sorensen's management style was closer to that of the increasingly stubborn and volatile Henry Ford, he actually had more rapport with Edsel, whose heart and mind were not truly committed to his company presidency.

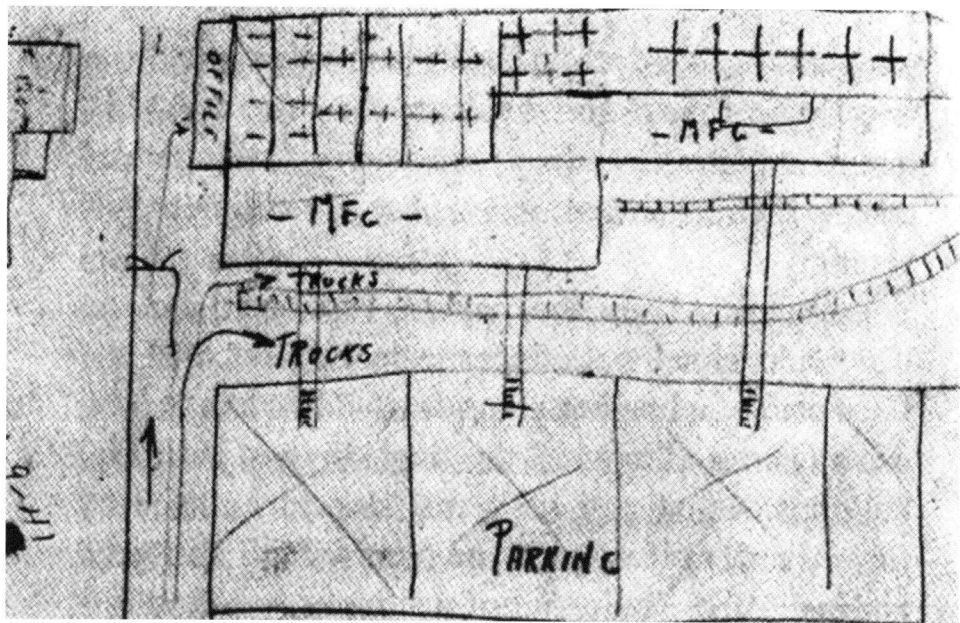

Sorensen's Willow Run layout sketch made in his San Diego hotel room over night after meeting with Reuben Fleet. (*FMC*)

Ford Top Management has Internal Problems

Thus as the Ford Motor Company was about to embark on its huge Willow Run enterprise, it was a house divided and not prepared to deal with the government, Reuben Fleet and the aircraft industry, and the United Auto Workers (UAW).

During the early 1940s, Sorensen had the responsibility for Ford's defense contracts, including Ford's Jeep and aircraft engine divisions and now assumed the production of the B-24 Liberator bomber. He led the design of the B-24 Willow Run Plant employing all of his prior experience in the development and refinement of mass production methods. Although each of Ford's B-24s was constructed from 488,193 parts, Sorensen's assembly line techniques would eventually increase Liberator production from one per day to an astonishing one per hour.

During the late 1930s, Pacifist and anti-Semite Henry Ford opposed America's entry into a European war and "insisted that war was the product of greedy financiers (the Jews) who sought profit in human destruction" and believed that "international business could generate the prosperity that would head off wars." Ford, like many other capitalists of the Great Depression, never supported or wholly trusted the Roosevelt administration, and thought FDR was inexorably moving America into war. Despite his pacifist claims, Henry Ford had accepted a contract from the Nazi government for the Ford-Werke Ford subsidiary. When Rolls-Royce looked for an American licensee manufacturer for its Merlin engine, Henry Ford rejected the Merlin contract because 60 percent of the Merlins were to be used to power British aircraft and Henry, an

Anglophobe, stated that Ford would only manufacture engines for American defense. William Knudsen, head of war procurement (OPM), contacted Henry to ask him to reconsider and was supposedly asked to leave Ford's office. Merlin production was then contracted to Packard, which built over 58,000, over half of which would engine AAF aircraft, including and transforming the P-51 Mustang into, arguably, the best fighter aircraft of the war. Once America entered the war in late 1941, Henry Ford's support of the American war effort remained problematic, but Willow Run had been approved and was slowly and uneasily moving ahead as the more rational Edsel Ford and Charles Sorensen prevailed at the Ford Motor Company—although not helped by internal soap opera-like company trials and tribulations.

Henry Bennett: Henry Ford Confidant and Enforcer

Over the years, Henry Ford increasingly relied on former boxer and ex-Navy sailor Henry Bennett as a confidant and, perhaps, friend to do his bidding. Bennett, who had been hired at age twenty-four in 1916, built Ford's notorious service department into what H. L. Mencken's *American Mercury* magazine called "the most powerful private police force in the world." Bennett's private *Gestapo* at one time employed 800 (Bennett described) "tough bastards" to monitor Ford employees, intimidate union organizers, deliver reprimands, cover Henry Ford's dalliances, and generally to protect Ford and his family over the next three decades. Despite his small stature, the red-headed, bowtie-wearing, gun-carrying Bennett projected a Hollywood tough-guy image and was said to have underworld connections. During the 1930s, Bennett took on the UAW and organized labor, overpowering union drives at plants in New Jersey and Pennsylvania during 1933; on 26 May 1937, he repressed UAW organizers gathered to distribute leaflets on an overpass at the Rouge Plant. During the Battle of the Overpass, Bennett's hooligans beat the union activists, including Walter Reuther, in front of photographers and reporters. However, four years later, a wildcat strike and Henry Ford's submission forced Bennett to sign a deal with the UAW.

Bennett had no qualms about playing irascible Henry against his meek and ailing son, Edsel. Even Henry Ford's most benevolent biographers concur that Henry treated Edsel, his only son and heir, unsympathetically and coldly. Thus, the Ford Motor Company divided into two camps: the Henry Ford–Harry Bennett faction and the Edsel Ford–Charles Sorensen faction.

At the time the government had concerns about the Willow Run concept, the feud between Ford Motor Company's top management echelons became common knowledge. Because of Henry Ford's age and Edsel Ford's failing health, Charles Sorensen had been appointed as Ford vice president in 1941, which was the first time in his long tenure that he held any titled position. The elder Ford trusted only the self-serving and ruthless Harry Bennett and began to feel (or was made to feel by Bennett) that Sorensen was an adversary. The powerful Bennett was feared by one and all at Ford and no one was safe from his wrath as Roscoe Smith, manager of Willow Run, would discover after a series of skirmishes with Bennett. In 1941, Smith

Above left: Henry Bennett, Henry Ford confidant and enforcer. *(FMC)*

Above right: Roscoe Smith, manager of Willow Run. *(FMC)*

ordered vending machines, from which Bennett personally profited, be removed from the plant. Then, in August 1942, the situation further deteriorated when Bennett had ordered specific machinery to be installed and Smith had it removed. The animosity peaked during a meeting concerning Bennett's plan to hire more black workers also attended by Smith and Sorensen who rejected Bennett's plan. Bennett who was a former boxer, lunged at Sorensen but punched Smith, who had tried to step in between the two antagonists and then as Smith tried to get up, Bennett hit him again. Afterwards, Bennett met with his patron, Henry Ford, and told "his" side of the story, and soon Smith was relieved as Willow Run manager. Only Sorensen's intercession saved Smith's position as a Ford employee, although as a much demoted one. However, Smith's sudden elimination from Willow Run management caused the powerful Truman Committee to call Smith to explain his removal. Meanwhile, Mead Bricker was appointed the unenviable job as Smith's successor as plant manager.

5

The Willow Run Factory is Conceived

The Willow Run Plant was first conceived only to manufacture knock-down sub-assemblies transported overland to assembly plants. As the war expanded and the role of military aircraft became more important, the Willow Run Bomber Plant concept changed from not only being a manufacturer of sub-assemblies but also to becoming an integrated venture which would build complete fly-away B-24s. In May 1941, the government agreed to allow Ford to also manufacture complete bombers and the company began plans for its huge Willow Run plant.

The Site

Ford was not only to find land to build its plant but was also able to supply enough land for an airfield as well. The location of the new plant was extremely important to Ford as it would have to meet what Sorensen called "industrial needs" and, once chosen, all planning and building would have to revolve around the site. Because of the complex engineering problems involved in the creation of all-new assembly lines for mass-producing Liberators, it was necessary for the new factory to be located near Ford's Dearborn, Michigan Headquarters.

The Ford Family Farm and Boy's Camp on the Willow Run Creek, purchased in the early 1930s, was an ideal location for both the plant and airfield as being under the personal ownership of Henry Ford made the problem of land acquisition much easier for the Defense Plant Corporation (DPC) and the AAC, for during this time, ten months before Pearl Harbor, there was no urgency to purchase of plant sites. The Ford Farm acreage was insufficient so Ford began to purchase additional surrounding land as covertly and cheaply as possible. Easements were acquired from landowners across the county line in Ypsilanti Township where the Liberator plant (and eventually the airport terminal) would be built Ford accumulated 1,384 acres at an undisclosed price and would sell it to the Government's Defense Plant Corporation for $293,570 ($212 per acre).

Part IV: The Magnificent Ford Willow Run Plant 375

Right: Willow Run aerial photo. (*ATSC*)

Below: Blueprint drawing of the proposed Willow Run Plant showing the L-shaped factory layout and adjacent 4-square-mile area including the area to become the world's largest airport. (*FMC*)

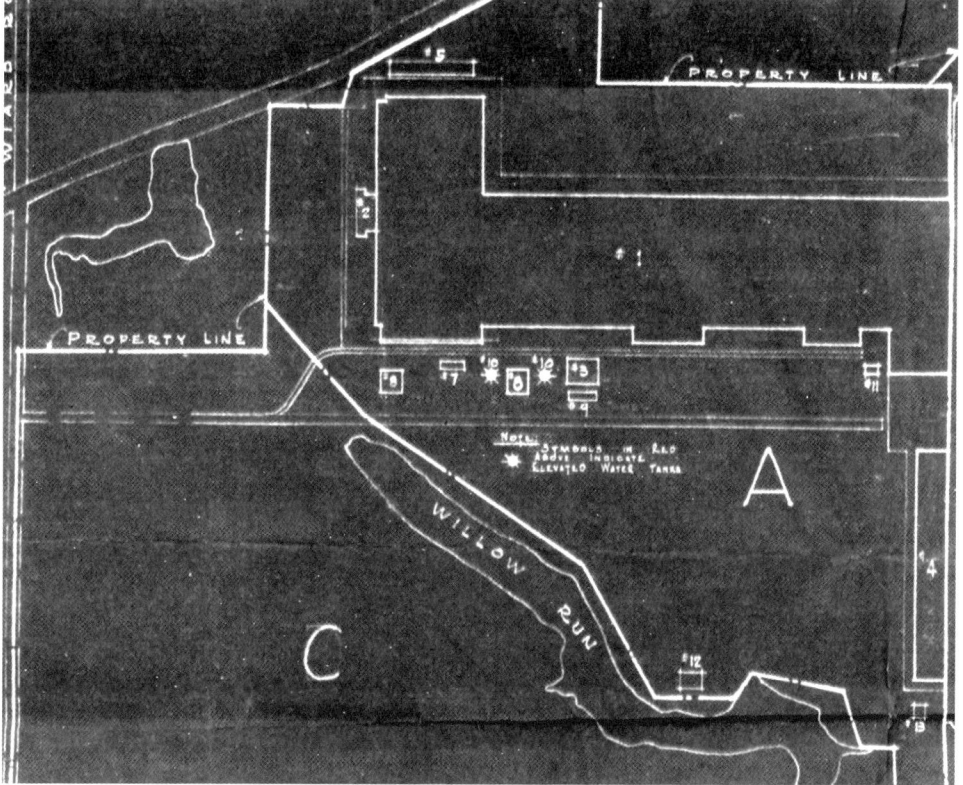

Location

The Willow Run Plant was built on a flat plain in southeastern Michigan near the Great Lakes, 35 miles from the nearest Canadian border; 650 air miles from the Atlantic Coast; and 1,300 air miles from the Gulf Coast. It was about 3 miles east of Ypsilanti, 21 miles west of Dearborn, and 35 miles west of downtown Detroit, 7–10 miles west of the outermost suburbs of Metropolitan Detroit between Ypsilanti and Belleville. It was in Washtenaw County on the Wayne County western border between the main roads and rail lines connecting Detroit with Ann Arbor and points to the west. The urban population of Washtenaw County was 42,000 in 1940 with only 4,852 persons engaged in manufacturing. The communities within about 10 miles of the plant had a population of 60,728 in 1940 with the two largest being Ann Arbor with a population of 30,000 and Ypsilanti with 12,000.

The location of the plant would later cause large manpower problems but at the time the site selection was made there was no rationing of tires and gasoline and there would supposedly be an adequate supply of workers because of the cutbacks in production of civilian goods when war came. While Ford management expected to obtain a considerable number of workers from communities surrounding Willow Run, it depended on obtaining most of its skilled labor force from the Detroit area, including many from its own plants.

Although officially retired since 1919 but still the company's actual controlling force, the shrewd Henry Ford refused government financing for Willow Run, preferring to have his company build the factory and sell it to the government, which would then lease it back to the company for the duration of the war and after the war Ford was to have first purchase option on the plant.

Sorensen presented Ford's proposal for the new plant's location and construction to the National Defense Advisory Commission (NDAC) whose duties were about to be assumed by the Office of Production Management (OPM). In the flux of this changeover and the powerful backing of government industrial czar, Gen. William Knudsen, and the enthusiasm of Air Corps, the Willow Run site proposal very quickly received a letter of intent on 21 February 1941.

On 28 March 1941, with the government letter of intent, 300 Ford laborers with saws, axes, and bulldozers cleared the first 100 forested acres where the plant would be built and would eventually cover 1,878 acres. The clear-cut trees were converted into 400,000 board feet of lumber by a steam-powered sawmill that was brought in from Henry Ford's Greenfield Village outdoor museum. Working against the natural slope of the site, the first construction for the plant and airfield began with a 74-mile drainage system on 13 August 1941. The east end of the plant was approximately 5 feet lower than the west end it as at the time it would have been exceedingly difficult to grade flat an area so large. Later this slope assisted with moving the Liberators inside the factory once their wheels were installed.

During the time that Ford officials were visiting San Diego in January 1941, they studied Consolidated's production operations, calculated the space required for the various types of jobs, estimated the size and type of plant that would be required, and formulated a preliminary plant layout.

After initial clearing, a 74-mile drainage system was begun for the factory and airport. (*ATSC*)

The Architect: Albert Kahn

Ford engaged renowned industrial architect Albert Kahn to design the largest factory in the world, which was almost a quarter of a mile wide and a half mile long and with 3,500,000 square feet under one roof (more square feet of usable floor space, than the Consolidated, Douglas, and Boeing facilities combined). Albert Kahn was born in Rhaunen Germany in 1869 and immigrated to America in 1880 where his family settled in Detroit. With little schooling, he began an architectural apprenticeship in 1883 and from there became associated with Henry Bacon, later the architect of the Lincoln Memorial, who Kahn credited with his architectural education. From 1900 until his death in 1942, Kahn maintained Kahn and Associates in Detroit, gaining his fame for his designs of significant commercial and industrial buildings but also for designing many other residences and non-commercial buildings. Today there are over sixty Kahn buildings on the National Register of Historic Buildings. Kahn and his designers and consultants are also noted for formulating the Russian Five-Year Plan of industrial construction in the 1930s. During his career, Kahn worked for the major American automotive and aircraft companies pioneering the use of reinforced concrete and metal sash windows. Kahn had earlier designed the Glenn Martin's 300,000-square-foot Middle River Plant (Baltimore) and would later design the 1937 and 1939 additions and Plant 2 (Middle River Depot) and later the Omaha plant, all of which manufactured the B-26 Marauder. He would design over 1,000 buildings for Ford, including its Highland Park automobile factory. Kahn culminated his brilliant career grandly with the gigantic Willow Run Bomber Factory. Kahn died on 8 December 1942 as America's foremost industrial designer.

Left: Albert Kahn was, perhaps, the premier industrial and commercial architect of the late 1930s and early 1940s working for the major American automotive and aircraft companies pioneering the use of reinforced concrete and metal sash windows.

Below: Architectural drawing of the Willow Run complex as it was to look in 1945. (*ATSC*)

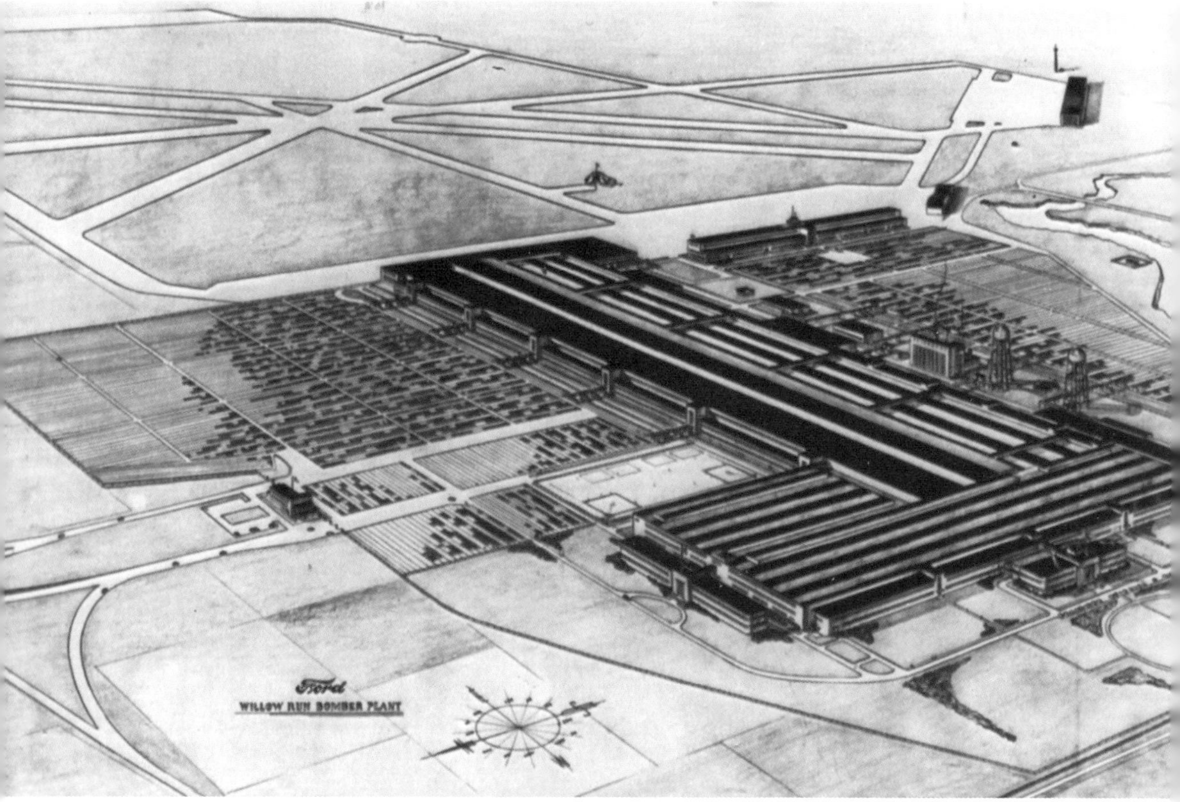

The Layout Board Model

A model of the proposed Willow Run Plant was built and divided the plant into bays representing 40 by 60-foot manufacturing areas and 40 by 150-foot assembly areas. Paper templates of machinery and other facilities were fabricated and moved on the layout board to determine their most advantageous location. The layout board also showed the installation of electric cables, cranes etc. The size and weight of a machine were important factors to be considered in the construction of the factory. Also taken into consideration were adequate toilet facilities for men and women, locker rooms, and large lunchrooms, which all needed to be close to employees' work stations.

Ground Breaking

On 18 April 1941, five weeks after receiving an initial $3.4 million contract to build B-24 sub-assemblies, Ford broke ground for the plant and named Roscoe Smith as plant manager. Previously, Smith, an electrical engineer, was best known as the manager of Ford Motor Company's outlying hydroelectric manufacturing plants and then as the manager of the Highland Park Automobile Starter Department. The plant was dedicated less than two months later, shortly before Henry Ford finally approved the first contract between the United Auto Workers and the Ford Motor Company. This period from Project A approval to ground breaking was several weeks shorter than the average for sixteen other airframe plants studied by the Air Technical Service Command (ATSC).

Willow Run Named

After six months into construction the new plant still did not have a name. Ford had a plant in nearby Ypsilanti, which caused confusion in the media and even in communications with the government. Finally, on 8 October, Ford issued a press release stating that the new bomber plant was to be known as the Willow Run Bomber Plant of the Ford Motor Company, taking its name from a small stream flowing nearby.

Layout board model. (*ATSC*)

Above left: On 18 April 1941, Edsel Ford (L) and Charles Sorensen (R) broke ground for the plant with Roscoe Smith who was named the plant manager.

Above right: Willow Run Creek, the plant's namesake. (*ATSC*)

6

Plant Construction

The Willow Run Bomber Plant was essentially completed eighteen months from the start of construction, which was a good result considering the enormous size of Project A and the changes in the production plan, which were made by the AAC while the building was in progress. Furthermore, construction time was not so important, in view of the time needed to prepare for the machinery and processes involved in mass production. The following discussion covers the planning for the project, the actual construction experience, and the changes and additions to the project.

Early Production Planning

The amount of effective planning for Willow Run prior to formal approval of the project 25 February 1941 was limited to some extent by uncertainty surrounding plans for production. Although the government proposed that Ford merely manufacture bombers in knock-down form for final assembly elsewhere, Ford also desired to undertake final assembly in the future as well. Consequently, when Ford officials made their exploratory visit to the Consolidated Plant in San Diego early in January 1941, preliminary planning was completed with the idea of building whole aircraft. These plans then had to be modified, when, early in February, the government reaffirmed its intention to limit Ford to production of knock-downs. While Willow Run's role as a final assembly plant did not emerge until some months after Project A approval, it is apparent both in Ford's selection of the plant site and the Army's approval of it, that such an eventuality was considered.

During this early period, Ford had contemplated use of its automotive plant facilities at River Rouge for fabrication of parts and planned the erection of a sub-assembly plant at the Willow Run site, which could be expanded into a final assembly plant if necessary. This plan was revised a short time later when it was decided that use of the existing facilities would not be feasible and erection of a fabrication plant of approximately 100,000 square feet at River Rouge was proposed to supply parts to

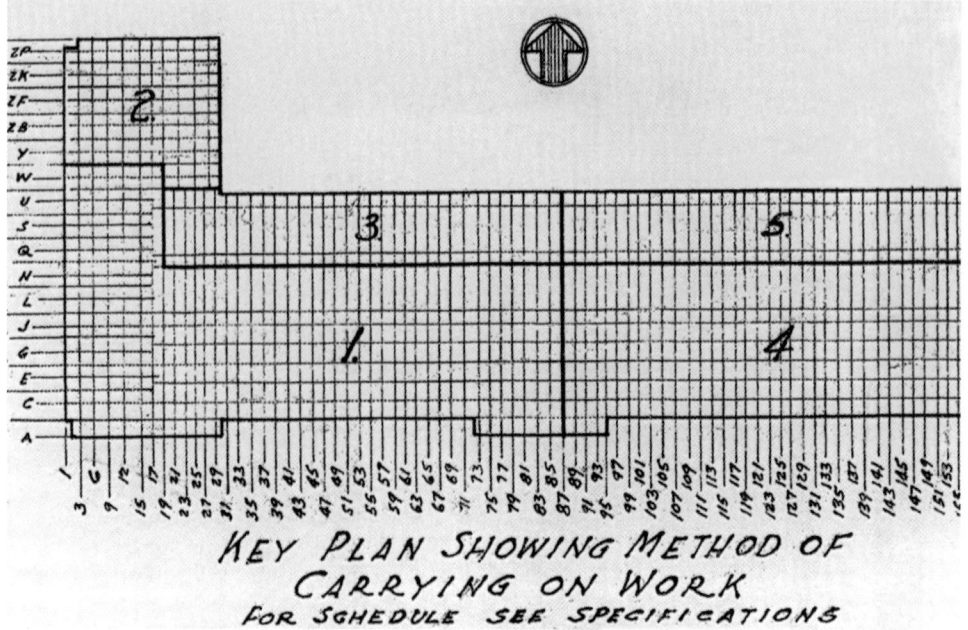

Construction Schedule: Because the Willow Run project was so large, five different contractors were awarded contracts to build five different sections of the plant under rigid timetables with staggered start dates. Sections 1, 2, and 3 were to be manufacturing and sub-assembly areas, while 4 and 5 were final assembly areas. (ATSC)

Willow Run. However, the idea of a fabrication plant in the midst of the Rouge works was discarded by Ford when it developed that the government proposed to take title to the Ford land. It was then that the decision was made to move the entire operation to Willow Run.

Ford, as one of the giants of the American industry, was in a singular position as a buyer of any commodity or service whether it was a raw material or a building contractor. Ford selected Willow Run contractors and negotiated terms with them. There were to be five main contractors as the job was too large to be let on an advertised competitive bid basis as there would have been no firm in Detroit big enough to undertake it. However, later, Bryant *and* Detweiler was made the responsible primary contractor for the entire Willow Run project. This was done at the suggestion of the Kahn architects in view of the difficulties involved in dealing with the many different contractors. The building sub-contractors were all Detroit firms with whom Ford had experience. Raw building materials were to some extent on hand and in stock. The steel fabricator had most of the structural steel on hand for most of the first portion of the building and the architect's plans were adjusted to new substitute sizes of available steel.

The "Tax Turn"

In a feature that was not in the original factory design layout, the main assembly line of the completed plant turned right at 90 degrees at one-third its length where a large turntable continued the line's progression until its end. Thus, the factory was "mirror L" shape, with the longer leg running 3,200 feet and the shorter leg being 1,279 feet, making the entire assembly line over a mile long at 5,460 feet. Willow Run lore has it that the original layout of the plant had been miscalculated and was located on Ford land in Wayne County where the taxes were five times that of adjacent Washtenaw County where Ford also owned land. The bend had to be introduced in order to keep the revenue-generating factory entirely in Washtenaw County with its lower taxes and the non-revenue-generating airport on the Wayne County side. Ford had the plant redesigned as an "L" at substantial cost and placed a giant turntable in the assembly line's floor that rotated the bombers 90 degrees at the junction of the "L" legs. Wayne County then placed a $2 tax on any aircraft that was delivered at the Wayne County airport, which would have meant that Ford would have to pay an extra $17,370 to Wayne County in taxes over the course of the war. True or not, since the plant was owned by the government, it paid no taxes. However, rumors purported that Ford wished to build lower-taxed commercial aircraft at Willow Run after the war, much to Consolidated President Reuben Fleet's chagrin. Ford had not manufactured aircraft since 1933 with the last of 199 reliable but unprofitable Trimotor airliners. However, Ford would not exercise its post-war option on the Willow Run Plant and Ford sold its land to the Reconstruction Finance Corporation's Defense Plant Corporation in July 1944, and shortly afterward, the Ford farms were transferred back to the company's ownership.

Tax Turn: The factory was "mirror L" shape with the longer leg running 3,200 feet and the shorter leg being 1,279 feet; the entire assembly line was 5,460 feet long. The bend of the "L" configuration was said to be due to tax considerations. (*ATSC*)

Construction Begins

On 3 May 1941, only two weeks after ground breaking, the first structural steel for the new plant was erected on its concrete foundation and footings. In the ATSC study of sixteen U.S. airframe plants, it required an average of over two months for this to occur and Willow Run's record in this respect was equaled only by the Republic-Evansville facility. Because of the frequent changes in plans by the AAF, construction of the new bomber plant became a matter of adaptation rather than construction of a building according to plan. To accommodate the changes, Ford developed the Willow Run facility in five separate building schemes.

Scheme No. 1: The first formal plan, provided for manufacture of 100 knock-down (KD) bombers per month, with approximately 22,000 workers. A manufacturing building to cost $17,369,239 was to be erected on the Willow Run site covering 1,176,300 square feet, to be financed by DPC as soon as the necessary paper work could be completed. The plans for this building were released for construction 6 March 1941, but the plan's appendix with the necessary details was not submitted to the government until 9 May 1941. Complete plans for the general trades had been issued as early as 14 April 1941 but were recalled because of pending changes.

Scheme No. 2: This scheme, incorporating the final assembly of B-24s as well as manufacturing of knock-downs, was drawn up on 19 May 1941 when Ford was formally asked to submit sketches for an expanded plant capable of producing 130 KDs and from seventy-five to 150 "fly-a-ways" per month. On 30 June 1941, this scheme was approved and plans were released with the increased area obtained by adding assembly areas to the already designed manufacturing building. The expanded building was to accommodate approximately 40,000 workers, with possible provision for 60,000. Under this scheme, plans were released for construction:

Assembly Plant	30 June 1941
Boiler House	14 July 1941
Office and Garage	15 August 1941
Hangar	19 September 1941

While these additions were based on a maximum of 280 aircraft per month, they were not changed when the actual schedule after several changes, decreased to 205 a month. The revised total estimated cost for the buildings grew to $47,620,171, providing in the factory building alone 3,475,567 square feet.

Scheme No. 3: The immediate result of the great increase in schedule following Pearl Harbor, was submitted as an Appendix on 22 December 1941 and again on 5 January 1942, and was released for construction on 30 January 1942, although it was not officially approved until 2 February 1942. This scheme accommodated the increased schedule of 255 KDs and 150 fly-a-way B-24s per month. Manpower requirements were increased to 80,000 and, whereas, Ford had previously planned on men workers only, at the Army's direction a provision now was made for 25 percent women. Added were a lengthened assembly line, a small manufacturing addition, and a $500,000 school building, plus additional toilet facilities, which raised the overall estimate to $63,328,000 and the total area of the factory building was increased to 3,595,567 square feet.

This scheme also covered additional buildings released for construction:

Dope and Paint	9 January 1942
Commissary	22 January 1942
Personnel	23 March 1942
Gas and Oil Pump	22 April 1942
Garage	18 May 1942

However, the appendix, increasing the over-all cost of buildings to $78,660,375, was not submitted until 21 August 1942.

Scheme No. 4: This scheme transferred to Willow Run such departments as tool design, engineering, pay office, material, cost department, employment and personnel, which Ford had intended to keep at Dearborn and Rouge. This move was prompted by Willow Run's wartime schedule increase and by the shortage of space at the automotive plants. In addition to the personnel building, considerable space was made available on the factory building balconies for the transferred departments.

Scheme No. 5: Issued 30 January 1943, it provided for a small special winter test hangar and increased the facilities for female employment, which it was now estimated would reach 40 percent or 32,000.

The first machine tools were installed at Willow Run in only five and a half months after Project A approval. Here, too, Ford's record was equaled only by Republic-Evansville. Ford, like Evansville, was able to secure steel from the fabricator's stock, with the architect's plans and drawings being adapted to the available sizes and shapes.

After nine months, only 30 percent of the building as originally planned had been erected, as the main delaying factor was the setting up of the complex mass production/manufacturing process making the speed of the plant erection less important. The first production at Willow Run occurred in seven and a half months after Project A approval and only two plants in the ATSC study bettered this record. In reaching production in this time period, the plant was then used to its fullest extent while construction was being completed. Portions of the plant were first put into use as early as September 1941 and thereafter, as portions of the plant were completed plywood, partitions were moved forward to close off the uncompleted portion from the space being used. The first acceptance of KDs came in July 1942, which was sixteen and a half months after Project A approval, at which time the plant was about 90 percent complete. First acceptance of completely assembled aircraft occurred in September 1942, eighteen months after Project A approval.

Chronology of Willow Run B-24 Manufacture, 1941–1945

1941

9 January: Sorensen submits Ford's proposal to San Diego.

12 January: Ford officials visit Wright Field and notify the Air Corps that Ford could start as soon as ordered by the government.

31 January: Gen. Oliver Echols, chief procurement officer, U.S. Army Air Corps, arrives in Dearborn suggesting that Ford draw up a Letter of Intent outlining their proposal for *Project A*:

  a) Manufacturing an "educational order" to acquaint Ford with the B-24

  b) Fabricating parts for Ford and Consolidated to assemble in Plants to be constructed in Tulsa and Fort Worth

  c) Manufacturing the complete airplane

4 February: Gen. Echols announces approval of steps one and two of Ford's proposal for Project A.

19 February: William Knudsen, director of the War Department, officially announces that the Ford Motor Company will erect a bomber plant at Ypsilanti to manufacture assemblies for Consolidated and Douglas.

21 February: Ford receives a letter of intent covering airframes for 1,200 bombers to be shipped to Tulsa and Fort Worth for assembly.

25 February: Project A approved in Washington.

11 March: 200 Ford engineers and draftsmen arrive in San Diego to begin work.

13 March: Ford receives a B-24 educational contract for $3,418,000.

24 March: Work Order request filed for first tooling.

28 March: Hundreds of workmen and numerous pieces of construction equipment begin to clear 5 square miles of land for the airfield and factory.

18 April: Ground-breaking for the factory begun.

20 April: First concrete poured in foundation footings.

3 May: Spur from New York Central Railroad reaches plant construction site.

5 May: Factory's first structural steel frame work raised.

5 June: AAC sends Ford a letter of intent for 800 complete B-24s.

13 August: First airfield drainage laid.

1 September: Willow Run receives its first machinery.

15 October: The River Rouge press shop produces its first bomber.

3 December: Airport drainage completed.

4 December: Last concrete runway poured.

8 December: First horizontal milling machine begins to operate and the first Willow Run part is manufactured.

24 December: The first center wing fixture is set up.

1942

16 April: The first center wing section is completed.

15 May: Ford's first assembled bomber, the educational aircraft, is completed and sent to the flight department.

10 December: First Ford-built B-24 completed.

1943

June: Ford manpower peak reaches a daily average of 42,331 employees.

1944

March: A monthly production peak of 462 bombers, sixty-two over Sorensen's original schedule, is reached.

April: 455 Liberators are produced in 450 hours (a bomber every 59.34 minutes).

1945

28 June: B-24 Production ceases (last bomber No. 8685).

Milestones

From the time Sorensen presented his $200 million proposal and hand-drawn sketch of Willow Run to Consolidated on 9 January 1941 until the government issued its final approval of the project on 25 February was only forty-seven days. Once final approval was received, additional land was procured under rights of eminent domain, and on 28 March 1941, ground-leveling operations began. Authorization to completion of the world's largest manufacturing structure and acceptance of the first B-24 completely assembled at Willow Run in September of 1942 required only nineteen months. From factory ground-breaking to the completion of the first center wing took two days less than a year, while the factory was still under construction.

7
The Plant

In his *Wartime Journals*, Charles Lindbergh called the new Willow Run Plant "the Grand Canyon of the mechanized world." A long-time friend of Henry Ford, Lindbergh was hired to work at the new Willow Run Plant as an aeronautical and engineering researcher. The Willow Run Plant and Air Field comprised of 1,878 acres; the plant was comprised of sixteen buildings on 444 acres. The 67-acre Willow Run main building was the country's largest aircraft plant and one of the largest ever built under one roof. The facility's total floor area was 4,750,000 square feet and factory area alone totaled 3,750,000 square feet of which 1,827,000 square feet were in direct production as of December 1944.

The main plant was a mirror L-shape with the longer leg running 3,200 feet (east to west) and the shorter leg being 1,279 feet (north to south); the entire assembly line was 5,460 feet long and 1,277 feet wide. It had a floor area of 3,503,016 square feet (80.25 acres) and a roof area of 67 acres. Expansion due to hot weather could be a problem as if the west wall were held firm, the east end would be moved 5.5 feet by the heat, but this was prevented by seven copper expansion joints—two across the width of plant.

The quantities of construction materials was enormous: steel: 38,000 tons; concrete: 317,000 cubic feet; brick: 10,000,000 pieces; gunite: 350,000 square feet; wood flooring blocks: 16,000,000 pieces; electric wire and cable: 2,000 miles; fiber conduit: 110 miles; steel conduit: 580 miles; conductor pipe: 6 miles; roof sumps: 6 miles; monorails (Mfg. Bldg.) 12 miles; monorails (for all buildings): 18 miles; sheet metal: 2,400 tons; steel-sash: 120,000 square feet; glass panes: 28,855 of thirty different types; fences: 11 miles. Landscaping included: 9,442 shrubs, 274 trees, and 53 tons of grass seed.

Ultimately there were sixteen structures, including an administration building and garage, three hangars, new materials building, a large school building, dope and paint storage building, commissary, transportation garage, and the utility structures: sewage disposal plant, gas house, incinerator, and power house. A personnel building was part of the main gate entrance to the plant. One special warehouse with a total inside

Part IV: The Magnificent Ford Willow Run Plant

In his *Wartime Journals*, Charles Lindbergh, standing with Henry Ford, called the new Willow Run Plant "the Grand Canyon of the mechanized world." (*FAM/AAF*)

storage space of over a million square feet, was added later to store spare parts, finished parts, and raw materials. Two large, long hangars were located along the edge of the airfield south from the assembly portion of the main building. The main production area, covering 80.25 acres (3.5 million square feet) under one roof, comprised of two major bays 150 feet wide, 36 feet high, with the North Bay extending 2,185 feet and the Center Bay at 1,825 feet. Their four primary lines had fourteen stations each.

Buildings and Floor Areas	Square Feet
Manufacturing and Assembly Bldgs.	3,503,016 (80.25 acres)
First Floor:	2,764, 836
Second Floor:	440,800
Mezzanine:	397,380
Administration Bldg. and Garage	36,739
Personnel Building	20,471
Hangar No. 1	268,570
Hangar No. 2	235,174
Winter Hangar	38,622
Spare Parts Building	481,770
Airplane School	49,494
Sewage Disposal Plant	20,900
Paint and Oil	12,000
Transportation Garage	9,900
Dope and Paint Storage	8,800
Commissary	6,050

Gas House	1,500
Incinerator	1,420
Power House	40,000
Total Square Footage	4,734,617 (109 acres)
Total Stock Areas	593, 502
Ground Floor	457,787
Mezzanine and Second Floor	135,715
New Materials Building	481,770
Total Square Footage	1,075, 272

Cost of Ford Willow Run (July 1945):

Schedule I:	Land and Land Improvements
Land	$441,930
Land Improvements	$4,177,827
Total Schedule I	$4,619,957
Schedule II:	Buildings, Structures, Etc.
Buildings, Structures	$23,539,409
Building Installations (not mechanical)	$20,627,974
Leasehold, Off Leasehold Improvements	$6,304,220
Service Costs	$3,236,490
Total Schedule II	$53,708,093
Schedule III:	Machinery, Equipment
Machinery, Equipment	$14,013,925
Building Installations (mechanical)	$5,378,139
Laboratory and Testing Equipment	$566,638
Furniture and Fixtures	$2,828,669
Freight	$109,606
Total Schedule III	$22,897,977
Schedule IV:	Portable Tools and Automobile Equipment
Portable Tools	$2.169,444
Automobile Equipment	$1,020,477
Freight	$5,028
Total Schedule IV	$3,154,949
Total Schedules I–IV	$84,420,776

Building the Enormous Willow Run Complex

A total 38,000 tons of steel framework and 2,400 tons of sheet metal stacked and ready to erect. (*ATSC*)

A total 317,000 cubic feet of concrete and 350,000 square feet of gunite were laid. (*ATSC*)

A total 10 million pieces of brick faced the buildings. (*ATSC*)

A total 28,855 glass panes of thirty different types and 120,000 square feet and steel-sash were used. (*ATSC*)

Part IV: The Magnificent Ford Willow Run Plant

A total 16 million wood flooring blocks ready to place. (*ATSC*)

A total 2,000 miles of electric wire and cable, 110 miles of fiber conduit, 580 miles of steel conduit: 6 miles of conductor pipe: 6 miles of roof sumps, 30 miles of monorails, and 11 miles of fencing completed Willow Run. (*ATSC*)

The unmatched completed product with 3,503,016 square feet (80.25 acres) of floor area of and 67 acres of roof area. (*ATSC*)

Willow Run Captures the Public's Imagination at Home and Abroad

In late 1941, the Willow Run Factory was virtually completed with nearly 10,000 workers employed and the first Liberator center wing section nearly finished. The extensive news coverage of the incredible Willow Run Plant helped to rekindle the American confidence and buoyed the spirits of many in the beleaguered United Kingdom. Roosevelt's many speeches, particularly his 1942 State of the Union Address, described how the war would be fought and won, not only in combat theaters but at home by industries such as famous American automobile companies, such as Ford and GM, which were being hailed as "self-contained Arsenals of Democracy." The news media looked to Detroit and its "Captains (not Generals?) of Industry" for America's war news.

Life magazine declared that "Henry Ford is still the greatest man in Detroit." Of all the Motor City's VIPs, the media designated Henry Ford as its main character in its "wartime industrial revolution" storyline, which was, of course, paradoxical. At the time, Henry Ford was little concerned with Ford Motor Company's war work and, in fact, was a vigorous pacifist who Edsel Ford and those around him had to continually convince of the importance of American military power. Nonetheless, Henry Ford and Willow Run were featured on the cover of the 23 March 1942 *TIME* magazine with the caption, "Mass Producer: Out of Enormous Rooms, Armies Will Roll and Fleets Will Fly." The inside article preamble stated:

> Something is happening that Adolf Hitler does not yet understand—a new reenactment of the old American miracle of wheels and machinery, but on a new scale. This time it is a miracle of war production, and its miracle-worker is the automobile industry.
>
> Even the American people do not appreciate the miracle, because it is too big for the eye to see in an hour, a day or a month. It is, in fact, too big to be described. It can only be understood by taking a sample.

Willow Run was considered Henry Ford's progeny and was lauded as for its great size and manufacturing potential. The *Christian Science Monitor* noted that the length of its assembly lines was "more than three times the height of the Empire State Building and four times that of the Eiffel Tower." The *Washington Post* reported that Willow Run was "the greatest single manufacturing plant the world had ever seen" while the *Wall Street Journal* termed the bomber plant as "the production miracle of the war."

Propaganda leaflets dropped on Nazi-occupied Europe by the RAF offered the giant Ford factory as a symbol of American industrial power. A leaflet stated:

> In one American factory alone, the new Ford plant at Willow Run, Detroit, they are already turning out one four-engined bomber able carry four tons of bombs to any part of the Reich every two hours.

However, at that time, Willow Run had yet to produce a single bomber.

Henry Ford (seen visiting the Willow Run construction site) was an ardent pacifist and was little involved with his company's war work; Edsel Ford and Charles Sorensen were responsible for the brunt of company management. (*FAM/AAF*)

The Bomber Plant: Manufacturing and Assembly

The bomber plant was divided into two sections: manufacturing and assembly. The manufacturing section initially produced the parts to supply knock-down kits and later the parts to assemble a complete Ford B-24E bomber. Of course, popular interest focused on the media hype and photos of the impressive Willow Run assembly line where a complete bomber was fabricated piece by piece and finally rolled off the line for AAF flight testing.

The assembly areas of the main building provided two clear 150-foot-wide areas, 30 feet high, with 33-foot clearances in final assembly. These two long clear areas extended for over 2,000 feet. The south half of the assembly area and the manufacturing portion had variously sized clear bay areas ranging from 20 feet by 20 feet to 80 feet by 80 feet, but the greater majority of columns were spaced so as to provide 40-foot by 60-foot bays. Doors either receded into the ceiling or were of the horizontal sliding type, providing 143-foot by 55-foot clearances.

There were nineteen cranes and hoists in the main building with a capacity of 5, 10, 15 tons and one crane in the main hangar that had a capacity of 20 tons, enough to hoist a loaded B-24.

Main Building

The 3,503,016-square-foot (80.25-acre) main building was built of steel frame construction (38,000 tons of structural steel were used) with large steel sash windows set in walls of combination brick and granite construction. The first floor area covered 2.76 million square feet. The Mezzanine floors covered 297,000 square feet (one-fifth of the floor area was over-lapped by mezzanines providing additional shop, office, and other space). The second floors covered 441,000 square feet while the total stock areas covered 593,000 square feet. The concrete flooring was covered with 16 million individual creosoted wood block flooring. There were 28,855 windows using thirty different types of glass. About twenty men were employed to wash windows in the main and other buildings. In addition to this natural light, lighting consisted of 76,000 fluorescent fixtures holding 152,000 4-foot tubes. The entire perimeter of the bomber plant was ringed by a small I-beam located above the plant's high windows for installation of to be unused black-out curtains. The center portion of the main building was four stories high and included offices, sleeping rooms and dormitories, restaurant, lounging, training, and special testing facilities. There was a link trainer and a pressure chamber to simulate high-altitude conditions.

Ford needed to maintain plant temperatures within a required range of 6 degrees, but in the summer, the plant's temperature became intolerable and the employees would only work with factory doors opened raising the temperatures even more. As a consequence, Ford B-24s built in the summer heat initially leaked fuel because of minute cracks in the aluminum skin that caused the need for fuel cells to be installed inside the wings of Ford-built B-24s, and this extra weight, which reduced operating range.

While the plant was built expressly for building B-24 bombers on a mass production basis, it could also be used for building and assembling almost any kind of aircraft or similar product in huge quantities (late in the war German V-1 Buzz Bomb copies were considered). The limiting factors were the 150 by 30-foot door clearances and the cranes in the manufacturing and assembly building, which had a maximum capacity of 15 tons.

Administrative Building

There was more than adequate office space provided including that in the administration building, the office space in the plant mezzanine, and in the special school building. The administration building was located in front of the main building and was connected to it by an executive garage. The administration building and garage totaled 36,739 square feet and the total factory and administrative parking space provided for over 15,300 automobiles.

IBM Service

IBM equipment was located on the second balcony of Building 18. There were fifty-six employees on two shifts operating three 405 alphabetic printers; three summary reproducers, five sorters, two collators, three multipliers, twenty key punches, and two interpreters. A daily production report was provided to the time office, production inspection office, and area offices. The report presented production totals by part number, by departments, and by division and also controlled all monthly

Administrative building. (*ATSC*)

scheduling for production and contract management plan on a six-month basis for the material department, showing production figures and balance to be built. There was a daily material review report for material control, salvage, and time.

Factory Supply Transportation

A main line NYC and Michigan Central Railroad was located alongside the main building and a spur track was routed into the receiving department. The receiving department could also accommodate trucks to load and unload without turning around.

Worker Transportation

Once war was declared and gasoline and tire rationing went into effect, the original plant layout of roads, designed solely for the accommodation of private automobiles, had to be revised to facilitate the movement of buses. A special "super-express" double-lane highway with no intersections was built by the Michigan State Highway Department to the Willow Run Plant, including the first U.S. double overpass. Arrangements were made for bus service between Detroit and other communities in the vicinity of Willow Run. The plant had 8.5 miles of concrete roads and three miles of perimeter gravel patrol roads.

With tire and gasoline rationing, Ford attempted to ease the transportation problem by establishing transportation and ride-sharing bureaus in the center of the plant to get the maximum from the available private transportation. During the war, 12,885 automobiles driving almost 275,000 miles per day were registered at the bureau, which at peak plant employment each carried 3.1 passengers per day. Detroit was divided into more than 200 zones to facilitate the ride-sharing arrangements and workers were canvassed to aid the formation of car pools. However, when the car owner was sick, it meant that one to three car-poolers were also absent.

Ford made no provision for public transportation to the factory until hiring was under way. After a conference of bus line representatives was held, arrangements were made for extra busses and extra runs with fifteen-minute bus service provided between the housing community and Willow Run. Public buses made thirty-five trips per day while private buses made 150 trips from 201 zones in Detroit and fifty from surrounding towns, all averaging about 2,850 passengers per day. However, there were never enough busses to fill the need, either between Willow Run and the housing community or between Willow Run and Detroit and other communities.

Factory-Based Transportation

Transport used by Willow Run included fifty-six passenger cars and twelve station wagons, 267 trucks of various types, seventy-two scooters, sixty-eight tractors and tugs, and seventy-four trailers of various types.

Public and private buses made 185 trips per day from Detroit and from surrounding towns, all averaging about 2,850 passengers per day. (*FAM/AAF*)

Aerial view of the Willow Run airfield and road network. (*ATSC*)

Airfields and Hangars

Since at that time of site selection there was no authorization for Ford to assemble complete aircraft, no airport would be necessary. However, Ford had always anticipated the building of complete aircraft and the selection of a site closer to Metropolitan Detroit and large enough for an airport would have necessitated many condemnation proceedings for which there was as yet no legal basis. As discussed, Ford's selection of the Willow Run site then included plans for an airport for Ford-built B-24s coming off the production line, which would need to be flight-tested. The last load of concrete for the adjoining mile-square airport was poured on 4 December, three days before Pearl Harbor.

The Willow Run Airfield covered 1,434 acres (828,000 square yards); it had six runways, all 160 feet wide, ranging in length from 6,510 to 7,366 feet, with 2.3 miles of 80-foot-wide taxiway. As a whole, the runways were the equivalent of a two-lane, 22-mile long, concrete highway. With 50 miles of electrical conduit, all or any part of the field could be floodlit and special lighting equipment enabled pilots to land during a blackout. The well-equipped control tower, opened on 24 June 1942 and operated 73,669 flights without an accident (through 1944). Two main hangars were located on the airfield.

The 270-acre AAF airbase could accommodate 3,700 men and at its peak graduated 240 men every four days in B-24 and P&W engine maintenance with a top enrollment of 1,500.

Hangar #1 was 1,256 feet long by 165 feet deep (268,570 square feet) and 79 feet high with eight bays enclosed by 45-ton, 144-foot-wide, and 42-foot doors moved by 10-hp motors. It had a forty bed dormitory (four private beds for officers). This hangar, that could house twenty B-24s, was used to prepare Liberators for delivery. Hangar #1 contained a 9 by 21-foot high-altitude chamber that had a 5-foot, 1-ton airlock door. The chamber could transfer its occupants from ground level to 40,000 feet in six minutes and from +70F to -70F in eight minutes.

Hangar #2 was 1,203 feet long by 161 feet deep (235,174 square feet) with eight bays, also with 45-ton, 144-foot-wide, and 42-foot doors moved by 10-hp motors. It was used for inspection and preparation for initial flight. So as not to shut down the main production line, Hangar #2 was later used to complete aircraft, which did not have orders for being implemented on the line.

Because of the severe Midwest winters, a special winter hangar was erected so that engine run-ups could be completed indoors. However, the flow of air through the hangar while the engines were being tested was so great that the temperature was as low inside the hangar as outside. Consequently, engine tests there were soon discontinued and the winter hangar was utilized for storage.

Utilities

Water, sewage, and other utilities were provided as specific facilities built as a part of the Willow Run complex. Henry Ford was a believer in hydroelectric as a source of electricity had previously built and managed as many as twenty-four hydro plants,

Part IV: The Magnificent Ford Willow Run Plant

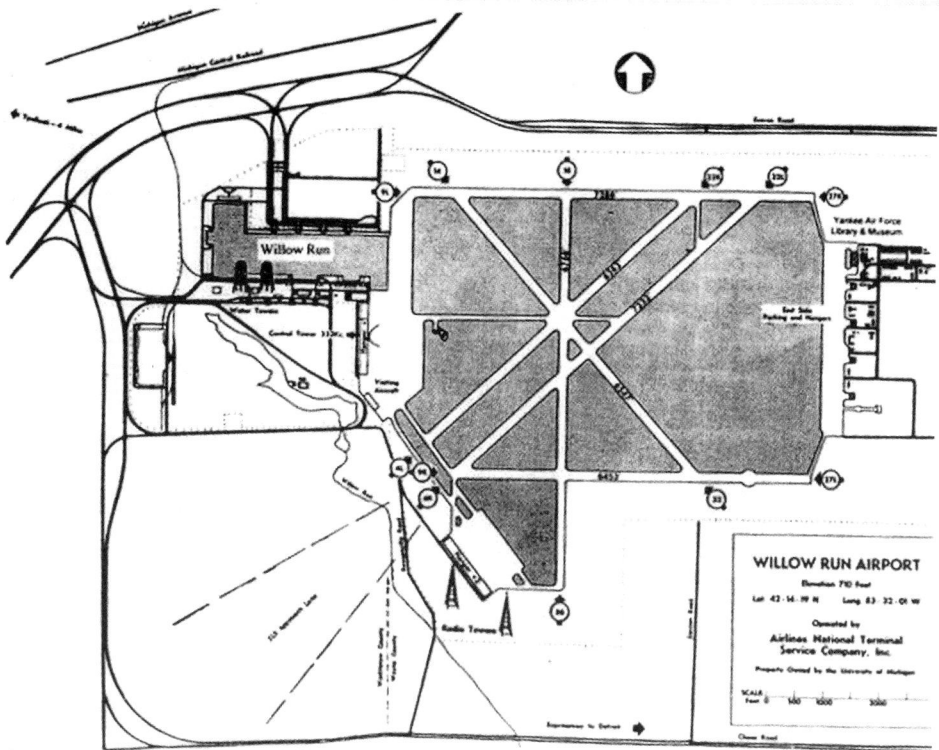

Willow Run airport.

Hangars 1 and 2 with B-24s on apron. (*FAM/AAF*)

Hangar 1. (*ATSC*)

Hangar 2. (*ATSC*)

Inside Hangar 2 with several Liberators undergoing modifications. (*FAM/AAF*)

each generating more than 16,000 horsepower. These plants known as "Henry Ford's Village Industries" provided not only electrical power, but also employment in rural areas. The Willow Run hydro plant opened in the spring of 1940 and provided power via 60 percent water wheel, 29 percent steam, and 11 percent generator. The Willow Run Power Plant provided 5,000 of the facilities required 13,200 KWH with Detroit Edison providing the remainder. The 160 by 130-foot power plant's four 80-hp boilers consumed 35,000 gallons on an average winter day. A small hydroelectric facility was also constructed on the grounds by damming Willow Creek.

The 3,300-square-foot sewage plant treated approximately 1–1.5 million gallons of waste daily through 18 miles of waste piping. There was 15 miles of drain tile from the parking lots and 85 miles from the airport which also had 72 miles of storm sewers.

Willow Run used approximately 5 million gallons of water daily supplied by three wells located at Rawsonville, which pumped 270,000 gallons per minute through two 24-inch mains. There were two 400,000-gallon water tanks and with 640,000-square-foot Tyler Lake, holding about 30 million gallons. The 70 by 71, 18,000-square-foot water treatment plant had a capacity of 6 million gallons per day but treated an average of 4.5 million gallons per day at 700 gallons per minute.

Power plant. (*ATSC*)

Hydro plant. (*ATSC*)

Specialized Buildings and Amenities

The cafeteria furnished 800 breakfasts, 1,500 lunches, and 500 dinners served by 110 waiters and prepared by twenty-three cooks and bakers. There also were twenty-four lunch rooms in the plant and hangar. Although sufficient cafeteria and dining room facilities were provided for the office employees, no cafeterias were available for shop workers who were generally fed from lunch wagons, which toured through the shop. The cafeteria building had a theater stage located in its rear

The hospital was staffed by eight doctors, one dentist, forty-four registered nurses, and twenty-five first aid men who were stationed at various factory and airfield locations.

Fire protection was furnished by 135 firemen and 1,200 trained auxiliaries; 2,182 fire extinguishers; 128 sprinkling systems with 51,212 sprinkler heads; and ninety-one fire hydrants with 21,825 feet of hose. Crash trucks, equipped with two-way radios, were equipped with ten 100-pound carbon-dioxide cylinders under 850-psi pressure and a 200-gallon per minute water pump. The plant was protected by a 335-man security force and eight automobiles, all Fords, of course.

There were about 750 employees on the daily maintenance staff. Three and a half carloads of paper towels were used every month along with 8,800 rolls of toilet paper.

Most of the 42,000 war time employees entered the plant via ten to twelve elevated cross-overs that led from the north parking lots and south bus roadway to interior of the plant. Each exterior tower serving these elevated cross-overs contained a roof mounted anti-aircraft gun. There was a superfluous air raid shelter located on the grounds.

The broadcasting studio, "B-24 Studio," opened on 3 November 1943, broadcasting to forty-four cafeterias, dining rooms, and lunchrooms in the plant, hangars, and six special first aid stations.

Cafeteria. (*FAM/AAF*)

Theater. (*FAM/AAF*)

Above left: Air raid shelter. (*ATSC*)

Above right: Security and fire protection. (*FAM/AAF*)

Broadcast studio. (*FAM/AAF*)

8

Mass Producing the B-24

Pre-production

Ford based its bold plan to mass produce B-24s on the expectation that the bomber's design could be frozen to allow long manufacturing runs of components and the bomber. Automobile manufacture was based on a year-long production run of identical vehicles, but aircraft manufacturers, especially during wartime when faced with rapidly changing technologies and combat tactics, had to continually modify their designs to keep them combat-contemporary.

As early as mid-1940, Ford engineers had proposed to build one Curtiss P-40 Warhawk fighter every hour, contingent on following an initial eight-month tooling period and on a frozen design. The proposal was correctly rejected by the assistant secretary of war who correctly believed that the mass production of a frozen design would only result in the air force flying large numbers of rapidly outdated aircraft. Nevertheless, Ford, the automobile manufacturer, already known for producing the acclaimed Ford Trimotor airliner in the late 1920s, remained adamant in its belief that warplanes could be mass manufactured. So, if Henry Kaiser could manufacture a Liberty Ship in forty-two days, Henry Ford would build a Liberator every hour.

Deciphering the Consolidated Data

As previously touched on, during March and April 1941, Ford sent representatives, ultimately as many as 200, to Consolidated's San Diego Plant where they made copies of all blueprints, bills of materials, and engineering releases; photographed every one of the 30,000 detailed drawings of every part, component, and assembly composing a completed B-24; and also made reproductions of the loft boards used by Consolidated. When they finished, they assumed that the two railway freight cars of accumulated data they sent back to Detroit would contain enough information to begin Liberator mass production.

However, once the data was organized and analyzed, it was determined that the Consolidated B-24 itself basically was not ready for mass production in the Ford system. The bomber was designed in 1938 and the XB-24 was built and flown in 1939. Although Consolidated had built 139 on a British contract, which was considered a "production order" by prewar criterion, the B-24 was, in fact, a "shop engineered" aircraft, not being initially designed for future mass production.

Upon examining the Consolidated's drawings and data arriving from San Diego, Ford found that they did not conform to Ford standards. Ford engineers noted many contradictions between the duplicate loft boards and the detailed drawings of parts. For Ford engineers trying to coordinate precision tooling for mass production, these inaccuracies were so significant that all 30,000 Consolidated drawings had to be redone. (Note: The engineering aspect of deciphering the Consolidated data is discussed in more detail later.)

Lofting and Pattern Shops

When Ford entered the bomber program in February 1941 and sent its engineers to the Consolidated plant, they not only found that there was no production breakdown for mass-production purposes but the bomber had never been lofted. Lofting was a drafting method using conic sections in which curved lines were systematically generated varying curves on a flat surface both graphically and mathematically to be used in plans for streamlined objects such as aircraft and boats. Lofting involved drawing full-sized patterns and was called so because it was often done in necessarily large, open mezzanines or lofts above the factory floor. Aircraft lofting was done on 16 by 64-foot, 16-gauge, white-painted steel-surfaced tables. Steel was used rather than using the older wood-surfaced tables as atmospheric conditions were reduced to .01 of an inch by using steel. Lofting was used to draw and cut pieces for fuselage and other curved structures, often in three dimensions. Aircraft loftsmen took dimensions and details from drawings and plans and translated this information into templates, battens, ordinates, cutting sketches, profiles, margins and other data. North American Aviation mathematician Roy Liming was responsible for putting aircraft lofting on a purely mathematical basis in the design of the superlative P-51 Mustang. Since the early 1970s computer-aided design (CAD) became standard for aircraft design and lofting processes.

At Willow Run, wood models were made from lofting specifications in the 200 by 37-foot pattern shop by thirty-four pattern makers. During a typical month at Willow Run, 25,000 board feet of lumber was used with mahogany used for master forms, pine and spruce for others.

From Building KDs to Building Complete B-24s

Being a secondary producer of parts for others had little appeal for Ford management, which had always been focused on mass producing completed aircraft on its own.

Ford engineers examining and attempting to decipher the 30,000 Consolidated drawings and data arriving from San Diego. (*FAM/AAF*)

Willow Run lofting department. (*FAM/AAF*)

Willow Run had ostensibly been erected as a knock-down/parts plant, but the immense building and its equipment made it obvious that Ford's intentions were to go far beyond manufacturing and shipping a few hundred KD units per month for Consolidated Fort Worth, North American Dallas, and Douglas Tulsa to assemble. Sorensen knew Willow Run was destined to manufacture complete Liberator airframes even before he sat down in the Coronado Hotel in San Diego, Henry Ford knew it, Gen. William Knudsen knew it, and the Air Corps knew this to be Ford's ultimate goal.

On 12 January 1941, looking toward the production of complete bombers, Ford officials visited Wright Field and notified the Air Corps that Ford could start production as soon as ordered by the government. On 5 February, Ford's offer to build complete bombers was declined by the office of production management (OPM) "at least for the present." War Department officials stated they would continue to adhere to the plan that had Ford manufacturing bomber parts only, to be assembled elsewhere. Thus, Ford's aspirations to build complete bombers were temporarily sidelined.

Ford is Contracted to Build One Complete "Educational" B-24

On 15 May 1941, even before it was contracted to be a KD supplier, Ford obtained a contract for one B-24 as an "education order," a method, without placing a contract, by which the government intended to test a manufacturer's ability to produce an unfamiliar and complicated military article and to aid development of manufacturer's work force capacity and skills. This education order not only tested the company's ability to produce the item, but also gave it the necessary experience to do so, while giving the sub-contracting company data relative to quality, quantity, and timely delivery. This educational B-24 was constructed from both Ford and Consolidated parts and was assigned to the flight test department at Willow Run. The company faced critical problems, especially of tooling, which could lead to costly delays in the realization of quantity production. By using this single educational aircraft, Ford was able to begin planning for the mass production of complete Liberators. In doing so, Ford virtually ignored the original schedules for its parts deliveries and all their production plans were premised upon their ultimate goal of producing one B-24 per hour at Willow Run. However, to reach this goal would be costly as the AAF did not authorize or include its expense and Ford had to use its own resources on their educational B-24.

Ford engineers had depended on the one B-24 received on the educational order for general engineering information and to develop know-how. But since the educational order was not received any earlier than the general project, it was not used in the general planning but was only beneficial to Ford's purchasing department to prepare a BOM, which gave them an indication of Liberator components and their cost.

The official designation for the first Ford Liberator was B-24E-FO (#.01) 42-6976 (1/1). FO referred to Ford Willow Run, where the bomber was assembled. (.01) was the bomber's unique production number with the decimal indicating that it was an

Ford obtained a contract for one B-24 as an "Education Order," a method, by which the government intended to test a manufacturer's ability to produce an unfamiliar and complicated military article and to aid development of manufacturer's workforce capacity and skills. (FAM/AAF)

educational aircraft. 42-6976 was the serial number identifier that remained with the bomber throughout its service. (1/1) indicated that there was only one aircraft in this production series as it was an Educational model. Beginning early 1942 .01 was assembled from components and parts supplied by Consolidated San Diego and the Ford Rouge Dearborn plant. Many parts were machined at the Willow Run plant beginning in October 1941, before the plant was completed. .01 was completed on 15 May 1942 and accepted by the AAF on 1 September 1942 for flight testing. After flight testing, it remained at Willow Run as an instructional reference point for the mass production of the next twenty-four Liberators and then became part of the AAF Ferry Command as a training aircraft based in the U.S.

Ford Gives in to the UAW Labor Union to Build Complete Liberators

During the late 1930s and into the early 1940s, Henry Ford was and continued to be labor's #1 enemy. The labor situation began to unravel even further when Ford lost a military truck contract and the UAW increased its pressure on Ford after the B-24 letter of intent was issued. Then, in February 1941, the Supreme Court ruled with the National Labor Relations Board (NLRB) that Ford should stop interfering with union organizing and with the court's ruling unionization accelerated and workers walked out of the Ford Rouge Plant. On 20 June 1941, as step toward building complete airframes Henry Ford reluctantly pacified the United Automobile Workers (UAW) and the National Labor Relations Board (NLRB) and astounded the industrial world by signing "the most generous contract it (UAW) had ever achieved." After this reluctant, but necessary, agreement with the UAW, Sorensen and Edsel Ford began to engage the AAC about building complete aircraft.

Ford's planning and scheming succeeded and in October 1941, it was authorized to produce complete bombers at Willow Run, and also was reimbursed for the previous outlay of its own funds. During February 1942, the AAC placed orders with Ford for 4,495 Liberators at a rate of 505 sub-assembles and 150 complete aircraft per month. By then, Ford certainly was in the position to succeed with its mass production plan as it possessed the resources required for large-scale production. It already had a large production staff, tool designers, engineers, expediters, and machinists. Its purchasing organization was experienced and was able to deal with vendors and suppliers. There were hundreds of machine tools in the Ford pool, which would be supplemented by the new equipment provided by the Defense Plant Corporation. However, the most important dynamic of the Ford mass production scheme would be the workforce and production tooling.

9

The Willow Run Workforce

Limiting Factors to Achieving Mass Production

While Ford Willow Run faced the problem of coordinating its mass production with both Consolidated and the AAF, its biggest challenge centered on an inadequate workforce, which also was the major problem faced by all American industry during 1942–43. Manpower was not only calculated in terms of the shortage and the poor quality of workers but also was reflected in low morale, high turnover, and absenteeism, which was to be a continuing problem at Willow Run and one which caused delays in production acceleration. The major difficulty was that, with the outbreak of war, the Detroit area's supposedly ample labor supply was quickly absorbed by an abundance of war orders. Another serious handicap was Willow Run's comparatively isolated location, which made it necessary for many workers to travel considerable distances at a time of stringent tire and gasoline rationing. Also contributing to the manpower problem were the long work weeks, the large number of workers without any previous production experience, the diversity of a labor force assembled from many parts of the country, management's unimaginative labor policy and its tendency to rely on high wages to maintain morale, and the loss of many trained men with special skills to Selective Service. In March 1943, Willow Run projected that a full complement of workers would be required in November 1943. By calculating the turnover rate, it was determined that 92,823 workers would have to be hired to fill the required 39,236 jobs. At times, during a single month, more workers left Ford than were available to be hired. Despite all of these factors, the rate of increase in Ford worker efficiency was generally better than the industry average, which was mainly the result of a high degree of factory mechanization, although considerable credit must go to the training program that was particularly aggressive and effective once it was fully organized and up and running.

Another limiting factor, in addition to the large number of workers, was adequate housing and facilities to support a workforce initially consisting of mostly white males. As Ford and the AAF battled over production schedules, the company attempted to increase hiring during a time when the government regulated worker's wages, hours, housing, and transportation. The government's perpetuation of its limited housing programs affected Ford, which would not only have to struggle to hire new workers but then have to find housing for them without government assistance. The Detroit area could not accommodate more arriving men, especially since men who were not draft-eligible probably would have families that would also need to be housed. To curtail the immigration of workers to Detroit and to maintain housing standards, the government urged Willow Run to hire white women and black men from the Detroit area's underutilized female and black male labor pools. These points will also be expanded upon.

The Ford Manpower Plan

Because of continual changes in the AAF's production plan for Willow Run, Ford's manpower planning was inevitably a process of evolution. It can, however, be correctly considered in two phases. First, the period before Pearl Harbor during which the plant's quota was finally set at 205 knock-downs and complete bombers per month. Second, the period immediately after Pearl Harbor when plans had to be modified considering wartime conditions and a new schedule of 405 bombers per month was set.

Prior to Pearl Harbor, Ford management believed that an almost unlimited supply of skilled labor would be available for Willow Run by transferring large numbers of surplus peacetime workers from the River Rouge Plant and other Ford plants and by drawing workers from other industries that had been sharply cut back in their production of civilian goods. With tire and gasoline rationing still in the future, it was considered quite feasible to depend entirely on private automobiles for the transportation of workers.

When Ford received its first contract for the manufacture of knock-down aircraft at the rate of 100 kits a month, management estimated employment requirements at 20,000 to 25,000 workers. By 1941, when the production plan had been revised to include assembly of complete aircraft and the quota had been raised to 205 a month the estimate of manpower needs was raised to 40,000–60,000.

In keeping with company policy, Ford planned to use men workers only. Some supervisors would be transferred from the Rouge Plant and others would be transferred from branch plants and agencies throughout the country. Consistent with a management plan to operate Willow Run almost entirely from the River Rouge Headquarters, departments concerned with manpower such as employment, payroll, and labor relations would be represented by only small branch units at Willow Run.

The attack on Pearl Harbor was followed by the doubling of Willow Run's schedules and also the conversion of much of private industry to war work, which resulted in an interference with most of Ford's employment plans. Management immediately raised its estimate of peak employment requirements to 80,000–100,000 dependent upon the length of the work week and number of shifts. However, at the same time that manpower requirements increased sharply, it became apparent that new war contracts at River Rouge and other Ford plants would mean that they could not supply Willow Run anywhere near the number of workers originally anticipated and that likewise the large pool of skilled workers from other industries would not materialize. During early 1942, management radically revised its manpower plans to keep pace with the rapidly changing situation. The AAF then directed Ford to prepare for the inclusion of 25 percent women in the workforce and this necessitated the revision of construction plans to incorporate women's rest rooms.

Build-up of the Labor Force at Willow Run

The original plan to retain Willow Run employment and associated departments at the River Rouge Plant complicated the recruiting and processing of new workers for Willow Run. Because of the expansion of the Willow Run Project A and the shortage of space at River Rouge as a result of other war work there, a decision was made early in 1942 to transfer the employment and payroll and labor relations departments to the rapidly developing Willow Run Plant. Also, Ford realized that the area within commuting distance of Willow Run would not yield sufficient workers and prepared to dispatch recruiting teams into other parts of the country.

Ford auto dealers throughout America helped in publicizing the need for workers, and newspaper advertising was used, although not in the critical Detroit area, which was controlled by the War Manpower Commission. Ford recruiters worked closely with the U.S. Employment Service, using a system of pooled interviews. The Ypsilanti Office of the War Manpower Commission retained a sub-office at Willow Run for clearance of recruited workers.

The original plans for the Willow Run Plant did not include a personnel building and the processing of employees was conducted in an improvised temporary employment office in the northeast corner of the Willow Run Plant where the earlier applicants were interviewed, classified, and processed. However, this temporary office soon became congested and a screening station was erected near the main gate where prospective employees were interviewed and if eligible, were taken to the main building for processing. The applicants had no protection from the weather while waiting to be interviewed. The boardwalk that bridged the muddy area between the screening station and the main building was so narrow that rejected applicants making the return trip often had to walk through the mud to pass incoming applicants. In May, the screening station operation was transferred away from the plant to a shed at Ford's generator plant in Ypsilanti, which was easier to reach. However, adequate employment facilities at Willow Run were unavailable until August 1942, when the new personnel building at the main gate was completed. But by that time, the most concerted hiring was nearly over and total employment remained at about 27,000.

Until peak employment was reached in June 1943, recruiting of workers was on a basis of a monthly labor requirement curve prepared by the plant superintendent's office, and checked against daily reports on department worker turnover. Normal procedure was to hire the prescribed number of workers, then train them for the jobs required. There were requisitions for some skilled jobs such as tool workers, pipefitters, hydraulics men, electricians, etc., although transfers from other Ford plants filled many of these jobs.

Workers were first hired for the manufacturing area of the plant, and when it was filled, hiring began for the assembly area. In July 1943, hiring was underway on requisitions originated by the foremen and cleared by the department head and plant superintendent. These requisitions were on the basis of job classifications corresponding to detailed job specifications maintained by the employment department.

The Willow Run workforce was expanded to a peak of approximately 42,500 in nineteen months. Hiring had begun in December 1941 when more than 1,500 men were employed, and then progressed very rapidly and consistently during the first ten months of 1942 when workers were added at an average monthly rate of nearly 3,000. From November 1942 until peak employment was reached in June 1943, the hiring rate was reduced significantly and averaged about 1,300 a month. Willow Run's peak employment was reached nine months before a peak production, largely due to a dispersal program during the summer of 1943, which was initiated to speed production acceleration and a substantial quantity of work was transferred to other plants.

The plant lost 10,000 workers in 1942 and needed to hire 44,000 workers to increase the work force to 34,000 in January 1943. Retention of new hires deteriorated to a mediocre 44 percent, and absenteeism, only 5 percent a day at the Ford Rouge Plant, rose to 10 percent at Willow Run. Of the 10,000 who left in 1942, 3,000 entered the military, which then took another 1,600 workers in January and February 1943; 1,300 left citing housing or transportation conditions; while and 1,500 just "disappeared," which Ford referred to as "ten-day quits." The company used the term "ten-day quit" for workers who failed to show up on ten consecutive days, but because of the government's attempts to stabilize the workforce, this meant that "ten-day quit" workers did not receive the release that regulations required for work in another war plant. At peak employment, instead of 100,000 workers, Willow Run employment numbered 60,000, with only 42,000 in the plant itself. At the desired peak production of a bomber an hour, fewer than 30,000 worked at Willow Run.

At the same time, the AAF was pressuring Ford to accept the new 405 Contract, ordering a monthly peak production of 405 complete bombers and 100 knock-downs by the end of 1943. Ford estimated that to complete this contract it would have to raise peak employment from 60,000 to 90,000 workers. Ford officials submitted the "Manpower Stabilization Plan" to the government. This was a plan "that concerned men taken by the military," in which Ford contended that because Willow Run was a new factory, young men comprised a greater than usual proportion of the work force. By assuring the government that it would continue to accelerate the recruitment of women, Ford requested that Willow Run's current male workers be exempted from the draft for as long as possible.

The Labor Supply

Willow Run was located seven to 10 miles from the outermost fringes of the metropolitan Detroit area and 35 miles from downtown Detroit. This vast industrial region had a pre-war population of about 2 million, which was then estimated to have increased to 2.5 million. It was from this supposedly unlimited labor supply that Willow Run was expected to draw the bulk of its workers.

Beyond the metropolitan Detroit area to the west of Willow Run there are only two sizeable communities: Ypsilanti, 3 miles away, with a 1940 population of 12,000, and Ann Arbor, 10 miles away, with a pre-war population of 30,000. Ypsilanti was the site of a generator plant operated by Ford and also a paper mill, two foundries, several wood-working shops, and a number of small, miscellaneous shops, which decreased the available labor supply.

The Detroit area, centered on the automobile production, was expected to be hit hard as a result of the cut back in civilian auto production, which actually was the case during the early months before the war and the supply of workers remained adequate. But the conversion of Detroit's resources to war production quickly altered the situation and produced a critical labor shortage. On a smaller scale, the same was true of Ypsilanti, Ann Arbor, and other communities closer to Willow Run.

The first 2,000 to 3,000 workers hired at Willow Run in December 1941 and January 1942, came from Ford's River Rouge Plant. Many of them were transferred, but others were former Rouge Ford employees rehired especially for the new bomber program. They included tool room workers, maintenance and machine set-up men, laborers, sweepers, etc. By 1 July 1942, when total employment was approximately 16,000, nearly 10,000 had been transferred from other Ford plants, including 6,000 from the Rouge Plant alone.

As the labor supply became increasingly critical, Willow Run had to extend its search boundaries to find new workers. Of 32,330 hires between mid-March 1943 and May 1944, there were 5,392 from local essential industries, 2,140 from other local industries, 4,016 local men and women not previously employed, and 1,561 commuters from outside the local area. The company referred to the workers from outside the area as "immigrants" and hired 4,528 immigrants from other sections of Michigan and 14,693 immigrants from other states. Most of the successful recruiting of immigrants was from Kentucky and Tennessee, which lacked war industries. During the period from 1 March 1943 through 13 May 1945, there were 6,491 immigrants from Kentucky and 1,971 from Tennessee. Ford privately referred to these particular immigrants as "Hillbillies." During this period, the list of immigrant employees also included 142 from Alabama, 397 from Arkansas, 116 from California, 115 from Florida, 125 from Georgia, 837 from Illinois, 342 from Indiana, 198 from Iowa, 179 from Louisiana, 128 from Minnesota, 179 from Mississippi, 314 from Missouri, 702 from New York, 262 from North Carolina, 600 from Ohio, 131 from Oklahoma, 325 from Pennsylvania, 714 from Texas, 246 from Virginia, 480 from West Virginia, 160 from Wisconsin, and smaller groups numbering from half a dozen to more than fifty from the other states.

Women

Detroit's automobile industry had previously been slow to recruit women because it had always had been able to hire from the surplus of male labor. Women comprised only 5 percent of the Detroit automobile workforce in 1941, with Ford excluding women almost entirely.

The percentage of women workers at both Ford's Willow Run and Rouge Plants never approached the higher percentages of other aircraft manufacturers. (*FAM/AAF*)

Between January 1940 and July 1942, women comprised only forty-five out of the 80,000 workers at the Ford River Rouge Plant. In addition, the conversion from civilian to military production delayed recognition for the need to recruit women as attention was fixed on reemploying men laid off during the conversion. Henry Ford who had always refused on principle to hire women finally had to give in, because of this employment crisis, and not due to any sudden development of a social conscience. So Ford began planning for women workers at the Willow Run in February 1942, and a year later, with the labor and housing shortage nearing crisis proportions, the company's planned proportion of women workers was increased to 60 percent. However, by August 1943, with just more than 41,000 employed and past peak employment levels, women workers still comprised only 35 percent of the workforce, even though women were considered productive workers and were dismissed for violations or inefficiency at half the rate of men. Anne Morrow Lindbergh, who lived in nearby Bloomfield Hills, while her husband, Charles, was assisting Ford in developing Liberator production, wrote in her diary after a tour of Willow Run: "One noticed chiefly the size and the number of women working, they all looked like housewives, quite ordinary Middle Western housewives, not a new breed of 'modern women,' as I had expected…"

Rosie the Riveter

Rosie the Riveter is a fictional cultural icon, featured in a U.S. government propaganda campaign created to encourage white middle-class women to work outside the home during World War II. Rosie the Riveter became most closely associated with Mrs. Rose Monroe, a Kentucky widow who moved to Michigan with her two daughters during World War II where she worked as a riveter at Willow Run. The Kay Kyser song, "Rosie the Riveter," inspired by a Long Island woman named Rosalind Walter, was popular at the time, and Hollywood actor Walter Pidgeon, discovered during a tour of the Willow Run factory as she happened to best fit the description of the worker depicted in the song, was asked to appeared in a promotional film for war bonds. Shortly thereafter, yet another real-life "Rosie" appeared, Rose Hicker, employed at the Eastern Aircraft Company. Both real and legendary "Rosies" were to become the basis for perhaps the most widely recognized icon of the time appearing in films and posters used to encourage women to go to work in support of the war effort. The song was soon followed by a rendering of Rosie by noted illustrator Norman Rockwell on the 29 May 1943 cover of *The Saturday Evening Post*. The iconic "We Can Do It!" poster by J. Howard Miller of the Rosie wearing a red bandana is the most well-known "Rosie" image.

Film actor Walter Pigeon discovered a women worker who best fit the description of Rosie the Riveter during a tour of the Willow Run factory. (*FAM/AAF*)

Above left: Mrs. Rose Monroe, the Willow Run Rosie the Riveter. (*FAM/AAF*)

Above right: Iconic "We Can Do It!" Rosie poster by J. Howard Miller. (*NA*)

Black Workers

Edsel Ford was often credited with the company's racially progressive hiring tradition but nonetheless only 2 percent of the Willow Run workers were black men who were not new hires but had transferred from other plants. The War Manpower Commission (WMC) periodically negotiated with Ford to boost black hiring but was generally ineffective. Early in 1943, the Ford Personnel Office backed by Harry Bennett agreed to hire at least 200 black men per week. However, Sorensen and Smith both rejected Bennett's plan to hire more black workers, which led to the infamous Bennett-Smith fight. Nonetheless, in June, Bennett ordered that no more black workers would be hired while Smith was demoted. It was because of the absence of any sizeable black community in the vicinity of Willow Run and the large number of white southern workers that the employment of black workers was kept at a rather low number throughout the war. The percentage of black workers was 1.7 percent in August 1942; 1.4 percent in December 1942; and rose to 2.8 percent by October 1944. It exceeded that figure slightly toward the end of B-24 production. Black women, however, would maintain only a very token presence at the Willow Run Plant. Moreover, Ford's ongoing discrimination against black women is credited with setting the standard for the entire automobile industry. In February 1943, there were only 1,000 black women among the 96,000 women working in major Detroit war industries.

The employment of blacks was kept at a rather low number throughout the war, reaching only 2.8 percent by October 1944. (*FAM/AAF*)

Little People

Ford and other aircraft manufacturers employed Little People to crawl into confined spaces, especially during the attachment of the center wing section.

Wages

Willow Run wages, while substantially higher than the prewar earnings for most of its workers and higher than the national average in the aircraft industry, were no higher than those at the other, less isolated, Michigan war plants as government regulations kept hourly wages stable from 1943 to 1945.

    The lowest Willow Run wage paid was 95 cents an hour for sweepers, moppers, and janitors; the highest, with the exception of supervision, was $1.80 an hour for toolmaker leaders. The rate for assemblers ranged from $1.10 to $1.15 an hour. The hourly rate among plant workers on 6 August 1943 was $1.15 per hour and, on 1 July 1944, $1.20 an hour. For women, especially, industrial wages were often several times higher the amounts they had previously earned before the war, with an unskilled woman worker earning $1.15 an hour.

    In 1943, the average annual wage for Willow Run's unskilled workers was $3,137, slightly less than the average for all Michigan workers employed in war manufacturing. For

Above left: Henry Ford greets several of the Little People workers at Willow Run. (*FAM/AAF*)

Above right: Willow Run wages, while substantially higher than the prewar earnings for most of its workers and higher than the national average in the aircraft industry, were no higher than those at the other war plants as government regulations kept hourly wages stable from 1943 to 1945. (*FAM/AAF*)

men with some industrial experience, a nine-hour day/six-day week, was the standard work week, and with overtime pay after forty hours; many worked more than the fifty-four-hour standard week. In 1943, unskilled men earned $3,376 annually on average at Willow Run, while women earned $2,792. In 1944, men who were by then more experienced earned slightly more but loss of overtime decreased men's average annual earnings. Often workers volunteered to have a portion of their wages dedicated to buying war bonds.

Work Week and Shift Distribution

Willow Run operated on a longer work week than most other airframe plants. From a forty-eight-hour week in January and February 1943, the plant went to a fifty-four-hour week in March and maintained it until the summer of 1944, after peak production had been reached, whereas the Industry average was about forty-five hours. However, the actual work week, allowing for absenteeism and overtime, fluctuated noticeably, ranging from nearly fifty-six hours in March and April 1943 to an average of forty-five hours and thirty-six minutes during the latter half of that year when absenteeism was extremely high. During 1943, the plant's ratio of Sunday work to week-day work was considerably below the industry average.

A ten-hour shift was adopted in September 1941 and continued until mid-May 1942. Shift length then remained at eight hours until mid-March 1943, when it

Willow Run operated on a longer work week than most other airframe plants. From a forty-eight-hour week in January and February 1943, the Plant went to a fifty-four-hour week in March and maintained it until the summer of 1944, after peak production had been reached, whereas the industry average was about forty-five hours. (*FAM/AAF*)

was increased to nine hours. Through 1943, which was a period of generally rapid production acceleration, the size of the second shift at Willow Run was steadily increased from 56 percent of the first shift to approximately 84 percent late that year. In 1944, about the time of peak production, the second shift went as high as 92 percent of the first. Throughout the period of greatest production acceleration, the size of the second shift was considerably above the industry average. Ford's third shift was generally a very small one and was used for maintenance and clean-up.

Employee Training

The Ford training plan was to provide one instructor for each eight to ten students so the teaching staff needed to be increased as quickly as possible. However, problems arose in obtaining qualified instructors, who, once hired, had to be trained in aircraft manufacture and mass production procedures. To fill shop instructor positions, new employees were screened and selected to be given special tutoring to become instructors themselves.

Classes in riveting were underway on a small-scale in the airframe building at Dearborn as early as May 1941, but generally, preparations for formulating a training program proceeded slowly and the decision that half a dozen general courses would suffice was influenced by the expectation that there would be a plentiful supply of skilled workers and that it would be a comparatively easy task to adapt these workers to the more specialized requirements of aircraft production.

Training became the dominant concern after Pearl Harbor with the expected sudden increase in labor requirements and the certainty that thousands of unskilled workers would have to be hired and trained. Thirteen temporary plywood classrooms were immediately built on one of the balconies of the plant, and within a few days, the training department, which then had a staff of only fifteen instructors, moved in. Work began at once on the writing of text books and an inspection manual.

One month after Pearl Harbor, there were only 174 students in training at Willow Run, including 102 in riveting, sixty-two in welding, and ten in apprenticeship classes. During the first quarter of 1942, approximately 2,000 new workers were trained or in training, including 1,279 who were graduated from riveting classes.

Preliminary plans for the school building near the plant had been made during the summer of 1941, and that fall, several representatives of the Ford schools were sent to the California to study training methods at Consolidated and other aircraft plants. General courses in hydraulics, inspection, electricity, blueprints, mechanical drawing, and engine mechanics were decided upon, and late that year, approximately a dozen instructors assigned to Willow Run from the Ford schools were trained in aircraft production methods in the airframe building at Dearborn

Finally, after the temporary classrooms had been used for nearly a year, ground was broken on 20 January 1942 for the $500,000 school building that was connected to the main plant by an overhead ramp. The first classroom was ready by 24 June and thereafter, classes were moved gradually into the new building as its construction continued. New employees, wearing trainee badges, were sent to the school from the employment office. On their arrival at the school, these new employees were given aptitude tests and were assigned jobs determined by these tests but also by the current demand for certain types of workers. Any student could voluntarily take any desired upgraded course on his own time to improve his job/wage status. The school kept a record of all students and their development and when workers were needed to fill certain jobs these records were accessed.

Generally, training was for ten days to three weeks of pre-job training, depending upon the job and the aptitude and progress of the student. Transition training of varying periods was provided to facilitate the move between the classroom and the workshop. During this period, the student engaged in an increasing number of hours of instruction each day under the supervision of an instructor on the type of job to which he would be later assigned. During the early part of 1942, before the manpower situation became critical, nearly 10 percent of the trainees were discharged because they were unable to become proficient in their job courses. Later, however, as manpower became scarce, trainees who failed the basic courses were returned to the employment department for assignment to more suitable jobs.

As manpower became limited, the quality of applicants also declined. The supply of skilled workmen was rapidly being absorbed elsewhere and the plant had to rely more and more on unskilled help: housewives, farmers, young men and women who had no mechanical experience of any kind. This decline in the caliber of workers in the latter part of 1942 revealed several underlying weaknesses in the original training program, as poor workmanship began to become a serious problem once the student moved to the job.

The deficiencies of the training program caused the training department to begin extensive course revisions. The original basic courses were found to be too general, too difficult for the unskilled trainees, and were too long. By teaching the new worker more than he needed to know to perform his job, he became disgruntled with his job. This was due to Willow Run mass production allocated only a few basic repetitive operations for the worker to perform. By inaugurating well-designed specialized courses, the trainees became better workers and were more satisfied with their jobs. So as not to be distracted during in-factory on-the-job training by the surrounding factory commotion, subsequently, a full-scale mock-up of the specific job area was built in the school and a concise on-site instruction was prepared.

In the revision and addition of courses, the training department worked closely with the production departments. The curriculum was kept flexible and the training staff was able to easily begin any type of training the various production departments required. Typically, an instructor was sent to the department concerned and discussed an appropriate new program or revision with the department head. When the instructor had outlined and developed the new or revised course, it was submitted to the department head for approval before being introduced for use in the school. Course material was printed in the school print shop and were bound so that they could be revised frequently with inserts to keep stride with the many engineering changes in the B-24.

Despite the vigorous renovation of the training program, significant retraining continued to be necessary into the early part of 1942 to compensate for the earlier failures. This retraining was achieved by a number of methods. For example, a bomber was taken off the assembly line, separated into sections, and placed on a balcony where groups of workers could review their specific job under the supervision of an instructor. If a foreman decided that a worker needed additional instruction in order to expedite production, he was returned to the school on company time for addition instruction. Also, instructors toured throughout the plant, looking for and correcting worker's faults and mistakes.

Supervisor training was not introduced at Willow Run until early in 1943 and this delay contributed to early production problems. Some supervisors, who had transferred from Ford branch plants and agencies, found that they had limited experience for performing their new job. Supervisors from the Rouge Plant, for example, had not previously dealt with women workers and found it difficult to adjust themselves to the new situation. Furthermore, up to that time, foremen and supervisors were not making use of their opportunity to instruct and correct workers on the job. In February 1943, the ratio of supervisors to workers was one to twelve while at the time of peak production there was one supervisor to each fifteen workers. Job improvement training (JIT) was given to nearly 1,400 foremen and group leaders in the production departments during the spring of 1943. That summer, job methods training (JMT) was given to all job foremen and a JMT appreciation course was given to all supervisors. During the fall of 1943, job relations training (JRT) was initiated and about 30 percent of the foremen took part. In the spring of 1944, another course in supervisory training was begun, starting with top supervisors and working down through the job foremen.

A large training school was finally organized to train new employees. The factory training program was a success with approximately 6,000 men and women enrolled in the various two week courses, training in four echelons of aircraft maintenance, taught by 200 instructors. At its peak, it graduated 240 men and women every four days. However, ultimately, it was found that much of the labor problem was solved by sub-contracting or moving the work back into Ford's Metropolitan Detroit plants.

Ford opened a large training school for new employees, graduating approximately 6,000 men and women enrolled in the various two-week courses. (*FAM/AAF*)

Apprentice training school. (*FAM/AAF*)

Worker Morale

Worker morale at Willow Run was never high as Ford management showed a lack of sympathetic and farsighted policy in dealing with its employees. Management had relied on better than average wages to maintain morale but failed to realize that it was managing all types of relocated workers from various parts of the country, who faced housing and transportation problems even before working long hours, all of which required unique methods by management beyond high wages. Prior to the spring of 1943, very little was done by management from a morale viewpoint, with the exception of the establishment of a ride-sharing bureau and a participation in a survey to learn the availability of rooms in nearby communities. Employee morale was further diminished in early 1943, when due to increase production acceleration, Ford transferred workers to other plants but then failed to explain the purpose of this dispersal program and give any assurances to the many affected insecure employees who were shifted from one department to another and afraid of losing their jobs.

With employee morale sinking rapidly, beginning in March 1943, management instituted various measures in an attempt to improve employee morale and job appreciation. Newly arrived workers, who had just traveled on the super highway through overpasses and underpasses up to the massive Ford Plant, were escorted to a special room in the new school building for a special orientation where the plant layout was explained and were then taken on an orientation tour of the overwhelming and gigantic plant. Before beginning their training, the workers were taken into the department in which they would later work and were introduced to their foreman.

Worker morale at Willow Run was never high, as Ford management showed a lack of sympathetic and farsighted policy in dealing with its employees. Women employees needed better childcare and housing opportunities more than a January 1943 visit from Eddie Rickenbacker. (FAM/AAF)

Also about this time, management generally adopted a more sympathetic attitude toward the workers and began to notify production departments in advance of changes, through bulletins and notices to foremen, so that workers would be kept informed. A public address system was also installed so that workers could be informed of plant activities in a more personal nature. A staff of counselors was established and employees were interviewed and counselled on any problems or grievances. About 150 "patients" were seen daily until late in 1943, after peak employment had been reached, when counselling was discontinued.

Worker Absenteeism

Absenteeism at Willow Run was considerably and consistently higher than the remainder of the aircraft industry. Throughout 1943, it rose from 6.4 percent in January to a very high 17.4 percent in December but then began dropping during 1944.

Factors contributing to the high absenteeism rate included:

1) Since more than 90 percent of the workers traveled to and from the plant in private automobiles and there was a high percentage of ride-sharing; consequently, the absence of a driver resulted in the enforced absence of one or more other worker/riders.
2) Difficulty in obtaining gasoline and tires when needed.
3) Thousands of workers came from Detroit, representing a round trip of approximately 70 miles a day while the industry average round trip traveled by workers was 40 miles.
4) Monthly rotation of workers between day and night shifts caused ride-sharing interruptions.
5) Management's sluggishness in adopting any real campaign to reduce absenteeism and promote morale.

Worker Turnover

Once Ford hired new workers, it found that workers with high wages did not always remain at the plant. During the build-up to peak employment, turnover at Willow Run compared favorably with that of the aircraft industry. During the early part of 1943, turnover was generally below the industry average, but then increasingly rose above it throughout the rest of the year as total employment was gradually reduced. Company statistics reveal that 32,718 workers left Willow Run during 1943, and over the plant's lifetime, the company hired over 80,000 workers, which was almost double its peak employment figure. The main reasons why men workers left in 1943 were entry to military service (26 percent), job-related (22 percent), "ten-day quits" (15 percent), and housing and transportation problems (6 percent). The main reasons why women workers left were "ten-day quits" (24 percent), medical (18 percent), needed at home/child care (16 percent), and housing and transportation problems (6 percent). During 1944, worker loss slowed somewhat as only 21,098 left. Nearly 40 percent of the plant's lifetime workforce worked at least a year. Over the plant's existence, the military drafted 11,000 men with the company allowed to retain only 150 potential draftees called "vital industrial workers" because of their "exceptional skills"

The Willow Run Manpower Problem and Worker Productivity

Before Willow Run's first bomber acceptance, 2,460,000 direct man-hours had been expended. This figure is indicative of the difficulties the plant experienced in beginning production. It was the opinion of many observers inside and outside the plant that Ford did not really have a manpower problem but a labor utilization problem. It took management time to attain the required number of workers, with the right skills, in the right place, at the right time, while simultaneously trying to correct the problems of a new production system that required frequent changes that left many workers with nothing to do for hours or even days. Direct workers in relation to total employment increased from 3 percent in January 1942 to 58 percent in September of that year, and up to peak employment, Willow Run maintained a higher proportion of direct workers than did the industry as a whole. Thereafter, the figure more nearly approached the industry average.

Productivity at Willow Run was considerably above the average for the industry, but it must be noted that the plant's elaborate tooling was designed with that end in mind. The increase in productivity was consistently good except for several months in the late spring and early summer of 1943 when there was a distinct decrease primarily the result of the 801 change, which called for a block of difficult engineering changes marked by a switch of the model designation from B-24E to H.

Worker Housing

Provision for public housing near Willow Run lagged far behind the construction of the plant. Even before public housing was available, Ford recruiting teams toured the U.S. with posters attractively describing the housing facilities. But eager workers arriving at Willow Run found that public housing had not been built and had to find temporary accommodations. Construction on the housing units was not started until 1942 and the first dormitory units were not opened until February 1943, a few months before peak employment was reached. Prior to that time, workers and their families lived wherever they could find accommodations. Of some help were the various agencies that had canvassed nearby communities for listings of spare rooms; some private homes had been converted into apartments; while garages and sheds became dwellings. By early 1942, every spare room between within a 15-mile radius of Willow Run was rented. Ingenious landlords often collected double or even triple rent for a single room as while one tenant worked a shift, the other slept. Many larger single-family homes were divided into rental rooms or apartments during this time. Conditions became so unhealthy that on 27 August 1942 Michigan State Police, because of the crowded, unsanitary conditions, evicted workers who had been forced to camp out near the plant.

Initially Ford did not want to build housing for its Willow Run employees, believing that Willow Run's manpower needs could be filled by workers living within a short distance of the plant, but under pressure from the Federal Public Housing Administration (PHA), Ford reluctantly conceded and the War Housing Community (WHC) was to be built. The PHA would build temporary housing; dormitories for single people and dwellings for family groups, which included ninety parcels of land totaling 2,641 acres. The PHA originally planned construction of 30,000 dwelling units based on early estimates of peak employment of 100,000 and purchased enough land for that many units, planning on permanent construction. As employment estimates declined, however, the number of units was reduced to 10,000 and because, by that time, building materials were becoming increasingly critical, temporary construction was decided upon.

Frederick Delano, FDR's uncle, was to organize housing for the projected 100,000 workers. Architect Oskar Stonorov extolled single family dwellings as "fortresses of individualism" and proposed a project-style "Bomber City," but Henry Ford refused to sell the land and the project was abandoned for dormitories.

In February 1943, the first dormitory, Willow Lodge, was opened, consisting of fifteen buildings containing 1,900 rooms, some single-occupancy and others double-occupancy, with occupancy for 3,000 people. Meanwhile, work continued until there were temporary flat-top buildings, known as Willow Village or as "The Village" by its tenants, which contained four, six, or eight apartments with one, two, or three bedrooms that would be home for 2,500 families. Some of these were ready for tenants in June 1943 and the project was finished later that year. It would not be until July 1944 that Willow Village accepted its first black tenants. The West Court buildings had peaked rooftops and its units were built for couples, or three adults. Of the 1,000 apartments in West Court, some had no bedrooms and were called "zero bedroom" apartments (i.e. "studio") and the remainder had one bedroom. The first of these apartments was ready for occupancy in August 1943. Another large 1,960 room dormitory project known as West Lodge was also ready for tenants at that time. There were also two trailer projects: one renting 960 "trailer-like" units for one or two people and another for privately-owned trailers. Each trailer community had communal laundry, shower, and toilet facilities.

Even with the new Willow Run housing that provided temporary shelter for 15,000 workers (about the same as the population of Ypsilanti at the time); by mid-1943, Willow Run employed over 42,000 causing many workers and their families to continue to live in converted abandoned commercial, buildings, ramshackle shelters, or tents, which when exposed became a national disgrace. At peak occupancy in late 1943 and months past peak plant production and employment, the War Housing Community had a population of 22,000–25,000 with approximately 6,500 of the 10,000 units occupied. Of these, approximately 75–80 percent were occupied by Willow Run employees, the remainder by workers from Ypsilanti and vicinity. At peak occupancy, there were 340 black families living in the community but only twenty-two of them included Willow Run workers while the remainder were employed in Detroit. The War Housing Community was finally completed early in 1944, but by that time,

Willow Run employment was well past its peak and was dropping steadily. The approximately 10,000 War Housing units included 4,960 dormitory rooms; 1,000 completely furnished family units; and 2,500 half-furnished, and the 960 trailer-like units for one or two persons. Dormitory rooms were rented for $5 a week for a single room and $5.50 each person for double rooms; family units ranged from $22.50 to $30, the trailer-like units rented for $28.50. Heating and cooking was done by coal in the family units while the trailer-like units were supplied with oil for heating and cooking. Ice boxes were provided and a functional ice plant was set up on community land and there was a shortage of ice only during one particularly warm week in 1944. It was not until late in 1943 and early 1944 that groceries and other goods were shipped into the housing community and a store was established so that workers would not have to travel outside the community to Ypsilanti to shop. Prior to that time there was only a temporary store set up in a shed on land provided by housing officials.

WILLOW RUN HOUSES ITS WORKERS

Willow Village would be home for 2,500 families. (*FAM/AAF*)

The "Village" consisted of temporary flat-top buildings containing four, six, or eight apartments with one, two, or three bedrooms. (*FAM/AAF*)

West Lodge was a large 1,960-room dormitory. (*FAM/AAF*)

West Court buildings had peaked rooftops and its 1,000 apartments were built for couples, or three adults. (*FAM/AAF*)

There were also two trailer projects: one renting 960 "trailer-like" units for one or two people and another for privately-owned trailers. (*FAM/AAF*)

By mid-1943, Willow Run employed over 42,000, causing many workers and their families to continue to live in converted abandoned commercial, ramshackle shelters, or tents that, when exposed, became a national disgrace. (*NA*)

Unions, Worker Grievances, and Race Riots

During the early morning of 2 April 1941, eight Ford workers called for a strike at the Ford Rouge Plant after being fired by Bennett's service men for "union activity." The workers claimed that their firings had violated Federal law and the strike gained momentum, and finally thousands and then tens of thousands of men walked off the job for the first ever strike at Rouge. Although the strike appeared to be spontaneous, the United Auto Workers (UAW) had planned ahead and encouraged thousands of outsiders who supported the auto unions, to converge on Dearborn. Armed with baseball bats and iron rods, they barricaded the three main entrances leading in and out of the plant. Inside the factory, Harry Bennett was prepared to "play out a daring, all-or-nothing strategy" using a previously organized "gang" (the Union description) of 2,500 blacks for his service department. These strikebreakers were also armed with knives and metal rods, and Bennett's promise to be paid around the clock to remain inside Rouge. An explosive racial standoff between white union men outside and black service men inside existed and the scheming Bennett sent a wire directly to Roosevelt, informing him that the Rouge was about to be seized by "Communist terrorists" and he needed the support of Federal troops maintaining that:

> Unlawful sit-down strikes, followed by seizure of highway approaches and entrances to the plant in a Communistic demonstration of violence and terrorism have prevented the vast majority of our 85,000 employees from going to work at the Rouge Plant.... Communist leaders are actively directing this lawlessness.

Soon the strike exploded into violence with Bennett's men throwing nuts and bolts from the roof at the union men below and several hundred blacks charged out of the Rouge main gate at the barricading pickets. A large number of these combatants were injured and Bennett held a press conference, proclaiming, "The unions seized our plant like burglars and if the Fords were to condone such actions it would be like saying 'come on, take us over.' Mr. Ford is convinced that his policies are just and right."

Union officials forcefully responded:

The Ford company is attempting to sabotage the defense program because of its Nazi connections.... It has sought to impede defense by turning down contracts for the British. The Ford Company incited violence during the strike and pitted race against race." Edsel Ford was in Florida on a brief trip, trying to regain his health and when he received news of the strike; he quickly returned to Detroit by company plane. Union-hater Henry Ford was adamant about facing the unions and urged Bennett to "fight the thing out ... to arm everyone we had in the plant and use tear gas if necessary.

Meanwhile, when Roosevelt received Bennett's cable, he was preoccupied with forcing the Congress to accept his Lend-Lease Bill, but he and his advisors became incensed that workers would walk off their critical defense work jobs. Then again, he was advised that the strike could become one of the worst race riots in American history and feared that if he sent in troops he would make the situation worse.

Instead, Roosevelt sent Walter White, head of the NAACP, and Thomas Dewey, a lawyer and future governor of New York, to Detroit. Republicans seized the circumstance to attack the Democratic president for not forcing an end to the Rouge strike with National Guard troops. When Edsel Ford arrived in Dearborn, he met with his father, Bennett, and Sorensen and insisted Ford do as the other automobile companies had done: sign a contract with the unions, as Federal law dictated and the Supreme Court had ruled. Of course, Henry Ford absolutely refused to sign any union contract and said he would close the plant down if necessary. Edsel pleaded with his father to sign saying if Ford did not sign, the government would take over the company.

But Henry remained adamant, and by day four, the strike had left all thirty-four U.S. Ford assembly plants and 130,000 workers on lockdown, for fear of further violence. Inside the Rouge Plant, Bennett's service men were becoming frightened and unruly, looting the plant for food. Around the Rouge gates, government sound trucks attempted to diffuse the standoff broadcasting: "The patriotic thing to do is to keep the wheels of our defense factories humming." At the Ford Fairlane mansion, at Roosevelt's behest, Bennett and Henry Ford meet with Michigan Governor Murray Van Wagoner. The two chided the governor by asking him what he was going to do with the Ford plants if he seized them.

Ten days into the strike, the governor brokered a settlement with the United Automobile Workers to which Henry reluctantly agreed, which certainly astonished everyone. Afterward, Henry recounted that when he told his wife, Clara, that he was going to close down the Rouge Plant she was "horrified that there would be riots and bloodshed" and that he then had no choice but to concede. Unknown to Henry, Edsel had met with his mother and his influence had led her to implore her cantankerous husband to sign the contract. Henry Ford later recounted that his concession to the union was "perhaps the greatest disappointment in all his business experience." In his continual struggle with Harry Bennett, the union contract was Edsel's greatest triumph to date and Ford had a contract at the time the Willow Run Project was undertaken and the new plant was automatically included in the Union contract.

Although Ford's so-called unionization "miracle" of 1941 happened quickly and expectantly, for the Union to change the Ford company management culture would take much longer. UAW Local 50, "the Bomber Local," had slight influence on the factory floor despite a series of wildcat strikes that briefly interrupted production. Local 50 was faced with the thousands of workers that Willow Run hired who were unaware of the pre-war unionization crusades. Many workers were also unaware that they even belonged to a union and few understood what union membership involved. While Ford led U.S. industry in production engineering, when it came to employee affairs, in the early 1940s, Ford followed other industry trendsetters, sometimes grudgingly.

Afterward, Willow Run was consistently free of serious labor troubles. Work stoppages occurred from time to time but were of brief duration, few lasting more than several hours. In July, there was a one-day foremen's strike over who would be allowed to use the plant's telephone. One of the most serious of these stoppages, affecting a large number of employees for several hours, was caused by a controversy over custody of a union committee room. Many of the stoppages affecting various

During early April 1941, the United Auto Workers called a strike that exploded into violence and left all thirty-four U.S. Ford assembly plants and 130,000 workers on lockdown, for fear of violence. (*NA*)

departments resulted from disciplinary action, such as the docking of employees who reported to work late. In all of 1942, there were six work stoppages, thirty-three in all 1943, but twenty-five in the first quarter of 1944. There were no stoppages on any matters that had been put through the approved grievance procedure, nor were there any that had Union authorization.

Grievance procedure was as follows:

1) The employee's grievance was written up by the Union's District Committeeman.
2) The grievance went to the foreman for disposition.
3) If the foreman could not settle it satisfactorily, it was re-written by the Union Committeeman and submitted to the Labor Relations Office, where disposition was made.
4) If disposition was still unsatisfactory, the grievance was put before the Plant Committee Meeting, attended by members of the union and labor relations office.
5) If it still was not settled it was referred to the appeal board at the Rouge Plant and it was discussed by officials of the Ford plant and the National Union Committeemen.
6) The final step, in the event of a disagreement, was the Umpire whose decision was final.

Most grievances were settled either by the Labor Relations Office or the Plant Committee.

Working conditions and in-plant services such as lighting, heating, restrooms, and toilets left little cause for complaint, but eating facilities were not entirely satisfactory. A large cafeteria in the administration building was available technically to plant workers; however, most of them were employed at such long distances from the cafeteria that to use it during the short lunch period was not feasible. The placing of lunch wagons throughout the plant was thought to be the solution, but there were some complaints that the service was unsanitary. Ford's long-standing "No Smoking" rule was relaxed in 1942 to permit smoking in cafeterias and in other designated smoking areas.

"Deconcentration:" Moving the Work to the Workers

Ultimately, the obvious solution to Willow Run's manpower problem, moving work away from Willow Run and Washtenaw County, could no longer be ignored by Ford and the AAF. In early 1943, the War Production Board, the War Manpower Commission, and the UAW all pressed Ford to reassess its original plan of concentrating all manufacturing and assembly at Willow Run, contending that work should be transferred to other Ford plants and to sub-contractors. There was an initial concern that transferring work from Willow Run could interfere with expected returns on the investment but as Willow Run's manpower problems continued to develop, on 5 April 1943, the Aircraft Production Board and Sorensen finally agreed to embark on a "Deconcentration" program and began to reduce the Willow Run workforce.

On 26 February 1942, the Willow Run production schedule was increased to 505 aircraft per month and to fulfil Sorensen's "a plane per hour" goal; Mead Bricker developed the "505 Plan" to sub-contract certain items to outside Ford plants beginning in early March 1943 and then transferred more work every month for the remainder of the year. By January 1944, Ford had moved 3,477 subassemblies and 6,182 dies from the plant, relocating most of the manufacturing mainly to their River Rouge, Highland Park, and Lincoln Plants. Ford also acquired parts from twenty-eight sub-contractors. Because of the worker hours saved through the new mass-production processes and exporting work, employment at Willow Run fell precipitously but, nonetheless, finally reached its targeted peak production in the spring of 1944. From a high of 42,000 workers in July 1943, the plant's employment numbers dropped to approximately 35,000 in December 1943 to under 30,000 in June 1944 and fewer than 25,000 in December. The Willow Run Plant never really solved its recruiting problems and even when the plant began to meet expectations, maintaining its workforce continued to frustrate the plant's management.

As the West Coast aircraft manufacturing centers also suffered from increasing production "congestion" and manpower problems, they also adopted "Moving work to workers." They built branch plants, sub-contracted work to manufacturers in areas with a better labor environment, and assigned small jobs to "feeder plants." Deconcentration eventually established that experimental engineering and final assembly were the only procedures that could not be successfully moved away from the parent aircraft factory.

10

Production at Willow Run

Production at Willow Run was planned around plant layout, and once the plant was completely and ideally laid out, the materials and parts flawlessly scheduled and the conveyors running, production was considered "synchronized to implement completely integrated airframe manufacture." The Ford concept of mechanized mass production depended on an efficient and uniform control of materials, and when based on an enormous tooling program, it functioned very efficiently for producing numerous airframes but involved a long period of preparation for production. The lack of complete engineering data necessary for the process and the number of engineering changes accompanying the B-24 caused pre-production delays, as the Ford mass production scheme was not flexible enough for use on a product that was not completely engineered and ready for mass production.

Ford's Plan for B-24 Production

Ford's plan for B-24 mass production was based on receiving an aircraft from Consolidated that was completely engineered and ready for manufacture, which could then be broken down with Consolidated's "advice and consent" into structurally complete components for mass production. Unofficially, Ford planned on producing bombers for complete assembly and fly-a-way in addition to the knock-downs and based its planning on eventually producing eight to twenty bombers per day depending on the number of shifts working, with an ultimate goal of one aircraft per hour. The plan envisaged that Consolidated would furnish all required engineering data, so that Ford personnel could visit San Diego, gather the necessary information and immediately proceed with tooling for production. Ford had planned on immediate tooling as it had one of the world's largest and best tool and die shops, which was equipped to provide all types of tools and was expected to design and fabricate its own tools. Ford tooling specialists carefully considered the standard light aircraft tooling used by Consolidated but decided in most instances to use the heavy hard dies and strong fixtures typical of automotive mass production.

Ford planned to manage material, controls, and production as it had previously operated its mass production of automobiles. The company expected to manufacture all the required parts at its new Willow Run Plant with no contributing outside manufacturing and then gather the component knock-downs for shipment to Fort Worth and Tulsa for final assembly. In order to save labor, there would be "automatic mass production based on completely rationalized tools with prefabrication carried to the greatest extent possible, and mechanical assembly including such new techniques as spot welding was to be used to the extent that the future safety of the aircraft would allow."

Workability of Ford's Plan

In order to apply automotive mass production to airframe production many requirements had to be met:

1) Engineering information had be current and set for production. Individual engineering drawings for each piece and part was to be quickly available. The bomber was to be completely and accurately lofted with a complete set of accurate templates were available.
2) Production engineering was to be completed sufficiently that relatively simple parts were available for manufacture and assembly by mass production workers.
3) Engineering changes were to be kept to a minimum and those changes made needed to be managed quickly and effectively with a double check record of the engineering drawings that were revised and made obsolete. The first lot of Liberators were to be frozen until production was in progress, so that engineering, tooling, production and assembly methods could be planned and initiated.
4) Tool designing could then to proceed quickly, provided a well-organized tool design "organization was set to go." A master copy of each engineering and tool design print which was filed by number was to be kept along with a record of the stage or place of the drawing tool, or part so that changes received could immediately incorporated.
5) Dies, jigs, and fixtures were to be accurate and durable so as to maintain accuracy and be tested before being put into use.
6) Master controls, control dummies, and checking gauges had to be fabricated accurately and available and used in all stages of production and assembly.
7) The plant was to have an adequately equipped tool shop available and was required to maintain thousands of tools and to make the necessary changes and modifications in the tooling program as they developed. Large tool making resources with many skilled workers were to be available.
8) Production and materials control to the smallest detail was required, with the control of the flow of materials and parts precisely timed.

Strengths of the Ford Plan

Ford understood that it would need to re-engineer the Liberator from a production perspective, at least to the point of being able to break it down into components that could be shipped long distances and then be easily assembled. The required dies, jigs, and fixtures were designed and built so as to be accurate, easy to maintain, and satisfactory for mass production.

Ford recognized the necessity for a complete set of master controls, control dummies, and checking gauges. An agreement was reached to have the Douglas Aircraft Company assist by assuming the design and engineering for these master controls and established the reference and locating points. Ford then built the master controls, control dummies, and checking gauges for Willow Run and for the assembly plants at Douglas Tulsa and Consolidated Fort Worth. Ford also built and then furnished the Tulsa and Fort Worth assembly plants with three complete sets of final assembly jigs and fixtures, in addition to the master controls and control dummies which avoided problems for these distant plants in in assembling Ford-made parts. Later studies showed that the use of Ford-made assembly parts caused fewer assembly problems than if Fort Worth and Tulsa would have fabricated their own.

Ford's plan for mass production and labor-saving through pre-fabrication and tool detailing for fabrication and assembly was based upon its vast tooling facilities. The Ford Rouge Plant had one of the largest tool shops in the world, operated by a large organization of very experienced tool engineering specialists and skilled tool and die makers. Ford intended to make the maximum use of these facilities to produce thousands of good, accurate, and long-lasting dies and thousands of heavy, well-built jigs and fixtures for sub-assembly and final assembly. Ford used its tooling facilities to complete large jobs in comparatively short times and consequently, it became possible to produce many pounds of aircraft with relatively little manpower once Willow Run had stabilized into efficient production.

Weaknesses in the Ford Plan

Ford's plan was based on its incorrect fundamental supposition that the engineering data received from Consolidated would be organized and complete. Any thorough pre-analysis by responsible Ford, AAF, and Consolidated officials should have indicated that Consolidated was not prepared to furnish engineering information to the extent and in the detail that Ford had expected.

One of Ford's initial errors had been to underestimate the complexity of the B-24 for mass production manufacture as it was confident that it could quickly apply its unequaled aptitude for production engineering tooling for mass production that it had used in automotive mass production. Although Ford would eventually be successful, the path to mass manufacture would require longer than planned because a heavy bomber is infinitely more complex than a Model T. Pre-engineering of the B-24 was incomplete, and the bomber had been neither production, nor combat-tested when

Ford began tooling up and as a result many unanticipated changes would become necessary. Ford soon realized that production engineering and simplification of parts needed to be carefully examined because of their eventual effect on design and stress-analysis.

For automobile manufacturing, Ford's large tooling organization had randomly included or excluded many records of engineering and production functions. Ford's tool designing group's administrative proficiencies were inadequate which increased problems after Ford received Consolidated's inadequate prints and data and then was besieged with change orders.

The Ford production plan also failed to recognize the necessity for complete and accurate shop scheduling for the fabrication of detail parts. Previously, Ford automotive detail parts were manufactured day after day with little attention paid to inventories or schedules since control was automatic with a steady flow of parts and production. When a change was contemplated or made in auto production any excess parts were used until depleted or set aside for renovation or a spare parts sale before the change was made. However, this procedure did not succeed in the production of airframe parts as a much closer control of production was required because of the constant engineering changes caused by both the demands of combat and production engineering.

11

Ford Implements the Plan

Ford's production specialists had observed Consolidated San Diego operations before deciding how they would perform the equivalent operations at Willow Run. All available Consolidated engineering drawings were submitted to Ford. Consolidated templates were duplicated by Ford in a special shop that was established at the San Diego Plant with about 800 templates duplicated there that were later found to be inaccurate and useless. Some preliminary work on space and machinery requirements was also performed in California.

Ford obtained a complete pilot line of the assembly tooling that Consolidated used and set it up in the airframe plant at Dearborn. This tooling line was not intended to be a model but rather was to be utilized for educational purposes and to check dimensions, locating points, and for the mating of parts. When Consolidated's drawings, lofts, templates, and charts were unusable, the final accurate dimensions for control masters were taken from this pilot line tooling.

Ford created a tool design engineering group of 800 to 1,000 men to design the required dies and fixtures and additionally would obtain assistance from outside tool designing firms. However, this tool designing group was inadequate as previously Ford was relatively indifferent about lines of authority, paper work, and organization, and this nonchalant attitude was continued by the new tool design engineering group. No records of prints, parts, work in progress, etc. were kept and a system was developed only very gradually. Meanwhile, progress was so slow that later a Federal grand jury indicted one of the leaders of this group who pleaded no contest for having purposely squandered the group's time and work while collaborating and profiting from the placement of design jobs with outside concerns.

Tool design commenced in March 1941 but very slow progress was made through January 1942, after which rapid but deliberate progress was made. A complete set of pilot line tools was ready by April 1942 and Ford's tooling was completed ahead of, or simultaneously with, engineering. Ford's deliberate policy was based on a decision made that about 15 percent of the tooling work done would be wasted, which would be worthwhile considering the time saved.

Assembly Tooling

The Willow Run mass assembly program of small sub-components, as well as the large final assemblies, was as completely well-structured as current mechanized mass-production techniques could conceive. There were fixtures for every assembly operation and for many parts fabrication operations that could not be done with dies. Drilling fixtures were made of heavy steel plates with removable guide bushings so that different-sized holes could be drilled where necessary. There were numerous holding fixtures for use on multiple drills. The traditional aircraft method had used a guide bushing attached to the drill, which resulted in inaccuracies of drilled parts. Small sub-assembly fixtures were built for almost every operation, wood, plastics, steel, and other materials all being used singly or in combination.

Dies

A die is a specialized tool (metal block) used to cut or shape material (like sheet metal and plastic) mostly by using a press, and like molds, are generally customized to the item they are used to create. Forming dies are typically fabricated by tool and die makers and put into production after mounting into a press. For the forming of sheet metal, such as aircraft parts, two parts may be used: one, called the "punch," performs the stretching, bending, and/or blanking operation, while another part, called the "die block," securely clamps the workpiece and provides similar stretching, bending, and/or blanking operation. The workpiece could go through several stages using different tools or operations to achieve the final form. In the case of an aircraft component, there will usually be a shearing operation after the main forming is done and then additional crimping or rolling operations were made to be sure that all sharp edges are hidden and to add rigidity to the panel.

Hard Dies

The success of Ford's "Bomber per Hour" plan was due to continuing their thirty-five-year use of hard steel dies in stamping presses to fabricate standardized aluminum parts as opposed to the aircraft industries use of soft Kirksite dies (see previous Consolidated San Diego dies). Simulating automobile production, Ford planned to use dies wherever possible in the manufacture of B-24 parts and much more extensively than had the aircraft industry as its tooling resources were far greater than those of any of the other aircraft manufacturers. The use of dies for blanking, piercing, forming, and drawing was intended to dramatically increase production. Once set up, tested, gauged, and placed into production, high-speed presses, operated by a relatively unskilled workforce, could fabricate extremely accurate parts in large quantities in a very short time. Dies were expensive and difficult to fabricate as they required highly-skilled die-sinkers and special machine tools that Ford had in profusion. Ford tool and die makers and its tool rooms were considered among the best in the world. The hard dies that Ford designed and used were a revolutionary innovation in aircraft production.

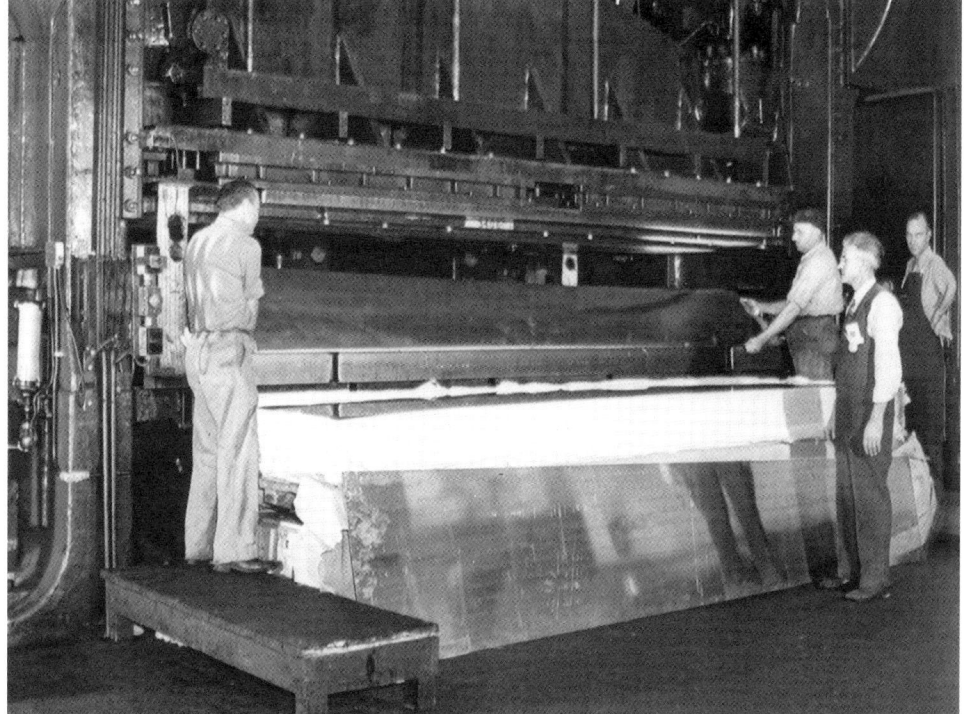

Hard dies. (FAM/AAF)

The Anticipated Advantages of Hard Dies

Just as it did for forming, Ford used hard dies in heavy presses for automotive manufacture. The advantages of Ford's hard dies used for forming and drawing were that once set up, tested, reworked if necessary, and in operation they produced parts more quickly, with greater accuracy, with less labor, and less maintenance than any other method. In forming thousands of parts, each part was just like the other and inter-changeability and mass assembly were thus made more practical.

The most important advantage was in the labor saved both through the speed of production and eliminating with the necessity for extensive hand-hammering of individual parts to knock out flaws, to bring them within tolerance, or to make the parts fit, which would have been necessary with the use of the rubber mat and soft cast metal dies and drop hammered drawn parts.

The so-called hard dies were not nearly as expensive for Ford to create as they would have been for any other tool maker. Conversely, Ford had no equipment nor experience with Kirksite dies and rubber mats. Ford considered an additional advantage of hard dies being that they had the equipment, know-how, and toolmakers for their manufacture. Ford River Rouge Plant had one of the largest tool making shops in the world and tooling was carried to its ultimate by Henry Ford who was interested in tooling for its own sake and did not have any stockholders or bankers to answer to, relative to his investment in tool-making facilities. For example, the Ford tool shop had a battery of twenty-three Kellett profilers, costing $80,000 each, and these machines were idle and available when the defense program started. The profiler was used to easily and quickly drill a large number of holes using a master drill sheet.

Overcoming the Disadvantages of Hard Dies

Ford found that the problems of manufacturing a new product, necessary learning errors, and numerous design and engineering changes, resulted in a waste of time, money, and effort expended on the tooling. The initial disadvantage in using hard dies was that they were very expensive to fabricate both in dollars and manpower expended, although this was partially offset when considering Ford's extensive die-making facilities. For production, Ford initially found that the maximum use of hard dies was unacceptable as the dies scratched and marred the surface of aluminum product, which was much softer than the steel used in manufacturing automobiles. Chrome-plated dies were tried and abandoned and after much costly experimentation, highly-polished steel dies were determined to be the solution. Changing the dies when a production run was at an end was also costly. However, this was sometimes offset by fabricating duplicate sets of dies in order to avoid switching double-purpose dies from top to bottom for right and left hand parts of the same design. The expense of changing these heavy dies was shown in that Ford considered it less costly to build an additional set of dies.

During early 1942, Ford recognized that the use of dies in presses was unsatisfactory as it had originally expected to economize and increase production by the extensive use of presses. As airframe manufacturers laboriously drilled holes one at a time, or sometimes faster with gang drills, Ford planned to punch out the holes for an entire skin section with one strike of a press. While this method seemed promising, the aluminum skin sheets would often stretch unevenly and the holes punched by hard dies would not line up when they reached their assembly point. A characteristic of aluminum, called "spring-back," caused it to try to return its original shape after being formed in a traditional die, not retaining the exact shape given it by a forming die. Spring-back had always been a problem in die making but proved especially problematic in working with aluminum, which is more difficult than steel to manipulate in this respect since it has twice the spring-back than steel. To correct spring-back Ford designed a sequence of two or more dies that made two deep draw passes to create a stable aluminum part.

Thus, Ford learned by doing and found that many more dies would be required than estimated since aluminum required two operations or draws, requiring two sets of dies where steel would have used only one. Consequently, these problems with the dies caused Ford engineers to have to fabricate 29,000 dies, although not more than 15,000 were actually used. Furthermore, about 2,400 of the "satisfactory" dies had to be reworked, some repeatedly, before they became satisfactory. These early delays prevented the supply of the mass production line with parts so that it was not until the end of 1942 that mass production really got under way.

One of the major economies Ford engineers depended on was a long production run producing the complete number of items on any given contract using semi-skilled labor using a single tool setting. Engineering and design changes were issued at a much higher rate than anticipated, and with Ford's lack of coordination, it was not always immediately possible to advise all persons and departments concerned. Dies were designed and built and then were found to be no longer needed, or were soon obsolete. With some 152,000 parts on the B-24, of which 30,000 were unlike, it was not unexpected that the designers and engineers sometimes duplicated tool design and manufacture for two parts in two different sections of the bomber that were actually identical. The margin of error in tooling completed without waiting for engineering was greater than anticipated. The press shops had to be definitely scheduled, so that the 10,000 or more stampings required would be fabricated and have a supply of each one available when they were needed on the assembly lines.

Also, this should-have-been predictable problem of continuing engineering design changes and uneven production combined with priority control of raw materials made it impossible to produce more than a sixty-day supply of parts, even though it would have been much more economical. Design changes became so frequent that Ford was reluctant to produce more than a sixty-day supply of any part as changes would make a larger inventory obsolete causing large scrap losses. However, there were times when shortages of vital materials made even a limited sixty-day run impossible.

In conclusion, the use of hard dies proved absolutely necessary in achieving mass production of a large number of standard interchangeable sheet metal parts.

Die Types

Blanking and Piercing Dies

Blanking and piercing are shearing processes in which a punch and die are used to modify long, thin, and flexible materials called webs (common webs include metal, foil, paper, textile, plastic film, and wire). The tooling and processes are identical between the two, only the terminology is different: in blanking, the punched-out piece is used and called a blank; in piercing, the punched-out piece is scrap. An alternative name for piercing is punching. The process for parts manufactured simultaneously with both techniques is often termed "blank and pierce."

Ford carried the use of these dies further than most airframe manufacturers, stamping out pieces that normally would be cut in a shears, saving Ford considerable labor that otherwise would have been used to make at least four separate cuts on each piece. Ford's original plan was to use old aircraft production methods of stamping, but Ford carried it further by using a plain steel punch, Kirksite die sections, rubber strippers, and a light three-sixteenth-inch steel backing plate. In order to get more accurate parts and better maintenance, guide pins were added to the die set up, the backing plates increased to half-inch thickness and spring-set heavy master die plates used. An additional later modification was the substitution of plain steel for Kirksite die sections. Later, a third plan, based on automotive technics for volume production, was instituted for those pieces were a large quantity was required. Alloy steel dies were made, steel punches were used, and the dies were set in heavy 1¼-inch die shoes with

Kirksite dies. (*FAM/AAF*)

half-inch steel visors and half-inch steel-spring pads with bolster pins. Metal strippers were substituted for rubber strippers where large quantity production was involved.

Forming Dies

Consolidated used several methods for forming parts, including brake presses, Kirksite and plastic dies in drop hammers, and Kirksite, other metals, and Masonite dies in a Hydropress using heavy rubber for the reverse of the dies.

However, Ford's most radical departure from accepted aircraft procedures was its method of forming parts. Ford decided, considering the large production demands, that it be totally dedicated to using mass production techniques in forming parts. It was decided to use no brake presses for forming work, which were commonly used by airframe manufacturers and not use any drop hammers, which it was felt were inaccurate and necessitated much more hand labor.

All forming was done in mechanical and hydraulic presses. The use of rubber as one part of each die set was completely abandoned, as was the use of Kirksite and other quickly produced, but not so accurate or long-lasting die materials. Instead heavy hard dies were made of rolled carbon or alloy steel, or cast steel or cast iron. There were both male and female dies, discarding the use of rubber and were backed up by heavy spring set master die blocks or plates.

Since the surface of the aluminum parts was supposed to be flawless, it was decided to chromium plate the steel surfaces of the dies; however, experience proved this to be impractical and unnecessary. The chrome plating was cleaned off and the polished steel surface was proven to be satisfactory.

Drawing Dies

For the drawing of parts that were more complicated than simple forming operations, Consolidated used a drop hammer with male and female Kirksite dies. If a deep draw was involved, plywood inserts were used in the female die to control the depth of the draw on the first few hammer blows.

Jigs: The Key to Mass Production

Although Ford engineers made extensive use of tooling to accelerate the fabrication of individual parts, it was in "jigging up" for final assembly that verified their philosophy of mass aircraft production as they built fixtures for every single assembly operation. Mostly these jigs were sturdy frames or benches of welded steel to ensure stability and rigidity while the work of assembly was in process. Since any military aircraft, built during a continuing war, experienced constant design changes, only about 11,000 jigs were used of the approximately 21,000 fabricated.

The magnitude and extent of the Willow Run tooling program can be judged from the number of tools designed, built and used:

	Dies	Fixtures
Designed	34,000	22,000
Ordered	31,000	19,000
Built	29,000	21,000*
In Production	15,000	11,000
Salvage and Storage	14,000	8,000–10,000

*Duplicates included

In final aircraft assembly alone, about 1,500 jigs and fixtures were used.

Machine Tools

Ford organized its machine tool program for the Willow Run Plant so effectively that the highest productivity per worker ever achieved by the aircraft industry was accomplished. While there were production delays, they were not caused by any shortage of machine tools.

The original Ford plan was developed during the Ford engineers and production men's visit to San Diego in early March 1941, where they examined Consolidated's operations and applied them to the Ford mass production scheme. This production plan envisaged a complete streamlining of production through tooling. Consequently, even though Ford had extensive tool making facilities, it foresaw an impending shortage and decided to buy, in addition to those needed for manufacturing, the machine tools necessary to equip a complete tool shop at Willow Run for intended maintenance and replacement. These machine tools were to be purchased from Ford's regular sources of supply.

Ford machine tool and production specialists observed each manufacturing operation at Consolidated San Diego, estimated the machines they would require, and then sent their requests for 4,000 to 5,000 machine tools to the purchasing engineering department at Dearborn.

The first machine tool orders for the tool room were placed as early as March 1941, at a time when Willow Run was contracted for the manufacturing of 100 knock-down kits of per month. The machine tools for this program only were completely ordered by the middle of 1941, five months before Pearl Harbor.

The purchasing engineering section was the machine tool engineering and buying division of the Ford purchasing department, which had many specialists for procurement of machine tools and their use and maintenance. Orders for machine tools were scheduled for specific delivery dates and were closely followed up. Ford's machine tool buyers, backed by the power of the vast Ford organization, assumed that they had the priorities and the cooperation of their suppliers in obtaining their machine tools. Also, after Pearl Harbor automotive production was ceased and Ford was able to move a large number of automotive presses and other tools that were then available to Willow Run or wherever else required. There were about 4,500 machine tools in the Willow Run Plant of which 1,554 were moved to Willow Run from other Ford plants. The bomber contract was charged with taxes and depreciation costs on these Ford-owned tools, with their title remaining with Ford. At the conclusion of the B-24 contract, many of these machines were immediately moved back to the River Rouge Plant for use in reconversion to peacetime production.

Ford was in a good position to the procure machine tools as, in addition to B-24 production, it had other contracts to build tanks, P&W aircraft engines, trucks, and other products. Ford was able to represent itself as one unit on all its war contracts, giving it the advantage of flexibility in its procurement program. If a tool was ordered for Willow Run but not needed because an old automotive tool was available, the specification was changed if necessary but its priority place was not lost. Delivery of the machine tool could then be switched for use in a Ford tank or aircraft engine plant. Contrariwise, if Willow Run was in urgent need of some general purpose tool it could be switched or borrowed from some other Ford war contract.

During the first few months of the Willow Run Project, Ford conveyed their concerns about the status of unavailable machine tools to the AAF, which then assigned high priorities for their purchases. Ford easily solved this problem due to the flexibility of its vast war production program that obtained these items from its many suppliers. There was some early difficulty in acquiring raw material machinery such as rivet-making machinery and Yoder Mills (that formed structural shapes from aluminum flat stock). However, the items produced by these machines were purchased from the outside manufacturers until Ford was able to procure these machines.

Joining of Parts and Components

Spot Welding

Joining of metal parts was done by spot welding as well as riveting. Ford was a pioneer in spot welding aluminum; however, being a new technique, it failed to obtain approval for spot welding aluminum items subject to structural stresses so that only about 10 percent of the total rivets were replaced by spot welding. Spot welding was employed on unstressed parts such as the bomb bay doors, escape doors, gun doors, life raft doors, and nose wheel doors.

Spot welding is a technique used to bond contacting metal surfaces shaped into sheets no thicker than three millimeters by the heat obtained from resistance to electric current. Unlike other welding techniques, spot welding can create accurate bonds without generating excessive heating that can affect the properties of the rest of the sheet. This is achieved by delivering a large amount of electric current in a short time, using two shaped copper alloy electrodes to concentrate current into a small "spot," melting the metal, creating controlled and dependable welds.

Riveting

In the beginning of the B-24 program, rivet holes were pre-punched to full size in order to save drilling on assembly. However, on larger parts expansion and contraction of the metal caused misalignment in final assembly. This problem was solved by pre-piercing of "pin" or undersize rivet holes. Prefabrication with pre-piercing of holes

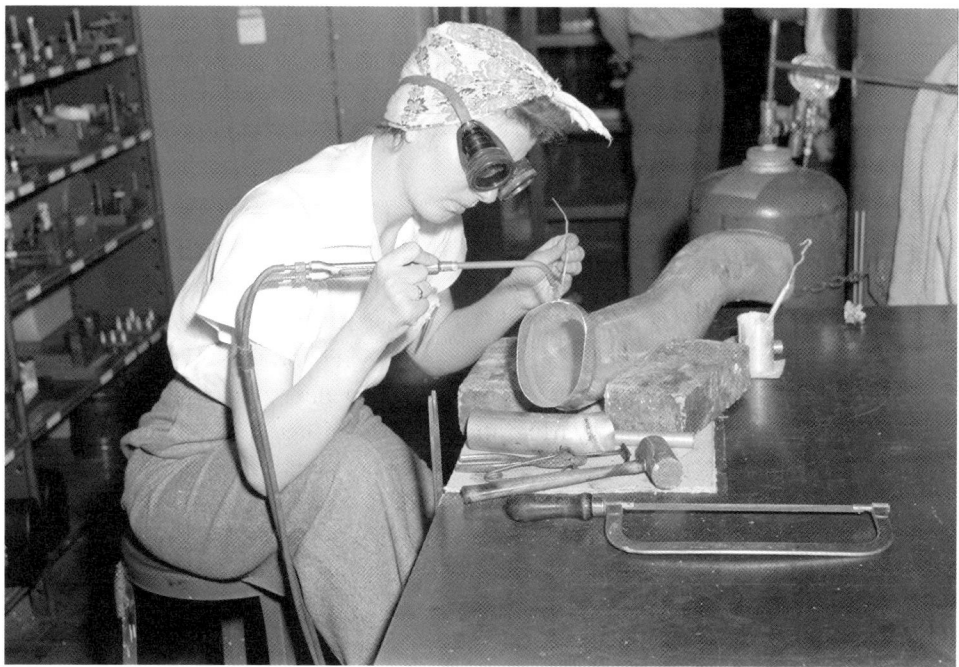

Spot welding. (*FAM/AAF*)

was performed in stamped and formed structural members. In many cases, locating holes and bolts were pre-pierced full size, provided that the gauge of the metal made it possible. Even with heavy accurate assembly jigs and fixtures, the 100 percent pre-piercing of full size rivet holes was found to be impossible. All detail parts were pre-pierced with pin holes or under size rivet holes with only the top piece of each series of assembly being pre-pierced and acting as a 100 percent location for rivet holes, which were drilled to full size for riveting in the assembly or riveting fixture. When circumstances warranted, pre-piercing of rivet holes to full size on items that were not structural parts was continued if there were no assembly problems. The blanking and piercing dies to perform these operations were carefully and accurately built. Many production short cuts were initiated, tested, and applied to production. It had been aircraft industry practice to carefully clean off all burrs resulting from drilling before riveting the aluminum. Ford laboratory tests showed that this was not only unnecessary but that riveting the sheets with the burrs left between the metal made a stronger bond than if the metal were cleaned smooth.

Heat Treatment

Willow Run's Ford-Holcraft recirculating hot air furnace, the only one of its kind in the aircraft industry, treated 12,800 pounds of rivets, 250,000 feet of drawn sections, and 55,000 miscellaneous parts daily.

Production Tooling: "Tooling Up"

Ford's basic premise for aircraft mass production at Willow Run was its application of "production tooling" that had made Ford the world's largest and most efficient industrial entity. The 1,000 plus men and a few women of the Ford tool design group worked continually for nearly a year to prepare the jigs, fixtures, and dies for production. However, there was a great difference in the amount of tooling required in building an aircraft then that of the automotive industries. More than 30,000 metal stamping dies, equivalent to eight or nine auto model changeovers, were ultimately required to manufacture the Liberator's multitude of parts. Ford spent $10 million for tooling up for a year's auto output while an aircraft manufacturer would invest only $150,000 as aircraft were mostly built by hand with the hundreds of thousands of rivets in a bomber mostly being individually driven. For this reason, aircraft production costs were estimated to range from $5 to $8 per pound versus the 15 or 20 cents per pound average of the automobile industry.

Ford management realized that there were risks in planning for tooling while the aircraft itself was still being engineered for production, as any subsequent design changes would require them to scrap the production tools already fabricated. Ford considered that these risks were warranted so as not to delay production and by April 1942 a complete set of production tools was ready. Ford's decision to tool up without

Above: Gang riveting. (*FAM/AAF*)

Right: Riveting team. (*FAM/AAF*)

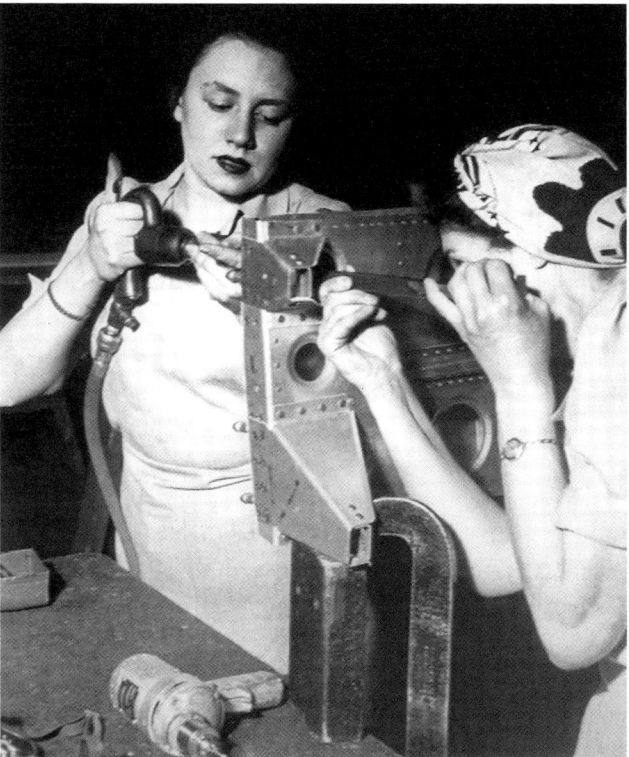

Metal stamping press. (*FAM/AAF*)

waiting for the B-24 to be thoroughly engineered for production was later justified even though 15 percent of the completed tools had to be scrapped or reworked because of design changes. Ford had fabricated a large number of tools long before the assembly line was scheduled to start allowing some significant problems to be resolved before production began and gave Ford the opportunity to determine that their basic assumption that the production techniques of the automobile industry could be directly applied to aircraft production.

There were two types of production tools: those designed to cut costs by simplifying and increasing the speed of production and those designed to ensure accuracy and interchangeability. Typical of the first type was the gang drill in which one worker controlled a single spindle that operated an entire bank of drills performing identical operations. Tooling for accuracy and interchangeability included a wide assortment of jigs and fixtures used for holding procedures to ensure perfect mating when separately fabricated parts were brought together for final assembly. As more tooling was added, the speed of production improved and the required skill level of a worker decreased and the use of trained labor became less important as a limiting factor. For example, a steel die in a press producing an intricately-shaped cowling or fuselage fillet obviously was more efficient than the most skillful workman making the same items by hand on a drop hammer. The Ford production program obligated the maximum use of both kinds of tooling and was based upon mechanization at every practicable production point. B-24 production was to be divided into seventy major component sections, each were to be completely prefabricated in their own special areas and then moved to the main assembly line. While production tooling was promising in concept, it was to be very difficult to implement.

Magnitude of Tooling

The tooling of the Willow Run Plant was probably the largest single tooling undertaking in one plant in America and the world during World War II. Basically, the single goal of this tooling program was to manufacture more aircraft with less labor. The tools were built to produce thousands of aircraft with the proviso for complete interchangeability of parts and easy mass assembly. An inclusive and accurate total of the capital invested in Willow Run tooling is not possible, but it is estimated that the templates, dies, jigs, fixtures, and mating bucks and special tools required totaled $75 to $100 million. Besides providing Willow Run with its tooling, Ford provided three complete sets of assembly jigs and fixtures for the B-24 assembly lines at Consolidated Fort Worth and the Douglas Tulsa.

Ultimately, the success of any tooling and manufacturing program is how much product is produced, compared to how much labor is expended. The Willow Run tooling program eventually produced a pound of airframe with less than .33 man-hours' work. In December 1944, Willow Run produced one pound of aircraft with .30 man-hours, whereas, the industry average was 50 percent higher at .47 man-hours. Expenditure *v.* the supply contracts in manufacturing B-24s at Willow Run totaled $1.25 billion. Nearly 9,000 complete B-24E and KDs were accepted at an average cost of about $148,000. Since these figures include all the tooling expenses, it appears that the overall program was successful.

Tooling Up Difficulties

The Ford plan for mass production at Willow Run did not progress as well as planned as the problem of tooling up was enormous and overwhelmed the vaunted Ford tooling department. Dies were required for some 10,000 sheet metal parts and with only a part of the necessary engineering information at hand, tool design and manufacture was begun.

The lack of efficient management in the tool engineering design division made it impossible to execute the enormous planned tooling program. Ford found it had inadequate capacity to design and build all the tools required and was obligated to subcontract 35–40 percent of the work. Between poor morale, lack of experience, and poor organization, plus lack of cooperation and specific well-organized information on the numerous changes from Consolidated, the entire tooling-up program was delayed and much time and energy was expended and wasted. The lack of organization and tooling capacity plus the unexpected problems of aircraft production and the engineering changes would make production acceleration a very gradual process throughout 1942. The character of the Ford system required a perfection of all details to make synchronized mechanized mass production work. The failure to make one die or the failure to make one stamping correctly in sufficient quantities meant a part missing on the assembly line, which for a long time meant not just a little less production, but practically no production.

Difficulties in Parts Manufacturing

Although Ford felt that the manufacturing parts was its most important problem, the assembling of finished aircraft and finishing the large sections of KD kits became a greater problem than had been anticipated. Although the conveyors and assembly lines were perfectly designed, aircraft assembly could not be reduced to the minimum of simple, but necessary, procedures that any workers without much supervision could carry out and so assembly slowed.

Among the difficulties were:

1) There were many unexpected engineering changes which made many items of tooling and manufactured parts obsolete by the time assembly was begun.
2) Dies were often inadequate or inaccurate and many formed parts were not found to fit on assembly,
3) Pre-pierced rivet holes did not fit on an assembly because of the accumulation of tolerance errors in the drawings, designs, dies, and assembly fixtures plus expansion and contraction of the metal caused by temperature changes.
4) There were inadequate production or inventory control and shortages were not discovered until parts were needed on the assembly line. The Ford concept in building automobiles had always been to have so many parts made in advance that there would be no shortages. During its thirty years' experience in building automobiles, Ford had developed methods of production and material control that were more automatic than Ford Executives had previously appreciated. In building the B-24, Ford had to learn by doing as it went along.
5) There was more poor workmanship than expected caused by inexperienced labor as much less good skilled labor was available than had been anticipated.

Ford learned from the problems and corrected them as they occurred. During 1943, new management took over at Willow Run and made major organizational changes. Engineering changes were organized into a Block System. The Ford engineering and tool design departments were reorganized and better systems and organizational controls were instituted. Material and stock control, especially of fabricated parts, and production scheduling were reorganized under new executive management, who realized the magnitude of the problems and the necessity for complete records.

To save labor during set up changes, dies were reworked and additional dies were made to correct aluminum spring-back. New tools for many operations were ordered and put into use. Pre-piercing of full-sized rivet holes was abandoned on most installations with an improved system of pre-pierced undersized rivet holes developed to be used on about half the pieces utilized. This system had the top sheet's pre-pierced undersized holes acting as a template for the under sheet. Installation drilling could then done accurately and with some saving in labor.

During automobile production at Ford, 90 percent of the parts had been run on a continuous daily basis, allowing the shop superintendent and machine operators to be able to schedule their own work. When aircraft failed to appear on schedule it was realized that other problems were involved. The Controlled Materials Plan (CMP) inventory was formulated with a sixty-day schedule so that when a machine was set up, it produced a sufficient supply of parts to last for two months after which the set up was changed and another job was started. A complete flow-time for all parts and operations in the plant was developed and thus a method of controlling production came into being.

12

Engineering at Willow Run

Engineering was one of the other major factors delaying production at Willow Run. The problem was multifaceted but basically was caused by Ford's inexperience in aircraft production and because of the exacting requirements of aircraft mass production. The initial volume of engineering information available on the B-24 was woefully inadequate and had to be meticulously developed over many months.

The Engineering Plan

The engineering plan, developed by Ford on their preliminary visit to the Consolidated Plant in January 1941, included these points:

1) Ford would send a group of engineers to Consolidated to familiarize themselves with the engineering problem, correlate data, and make the necessary reproductions.
2) Ford would organize an engineering department for Willow Run in two groups:
   a) Production engineering, built up around a nucleus of automotive engineers.
   b) Stress-analysis or design engineering, which several aeronautical engineers would be hired to head.
   Both groups would be expanded by canvassing universities in the Detroit Area for personnel with engineering ability.
3) A liaison office would be maintained at Consolidated San Diego.
4) Consolidated would furnish three sets of drawings, specifications, bills of materials, and parts lists; would permit Ford to reproduce loft boards, templates and tool masters; and on engineering changes would furnish new drawings and change analyses.
5) Since the B-24 was not engineered for mass production, Ford would break down the bomber into considerably more sub-assemblies than the **twenty** used by Consolidated.

6) Except as affected by this further breakdown of the aircraft Consolidated's drawings and engineering information would be used by Ford for production without significant change.

Assembling the Basic Engineering Material from Consolidated

Ford engineers began their move to Consolidated in early in March 1941. Among them were William Pioch, head of tool engineering; Edward Scott, chief body engineer, selected to head the new production engineering department for Willow Run; and W. F. DeGroat, one of the first aeronautical engineers hired by Ford, who was to organize the stress-analysis or design engineering group. Their task was to study Consolidated's engineering methods, develop a workable engineering procedure for Willow Run; collect all the data from Consolidated which Ford would need to go into production on the B-24; and begin working with Consolidated engineers to develop the further breakdown of the Liberator required by Ford's mass production methods.

However, it soon became apparent to the Ford team that in its existing form the status of Consolidated engineering data on the B-24 was not suitable for use by the new participating prime contractors: Ford, Douglas Tulsa, and North American Fort Worth. The data was far from meeting Ford's requirements and that adapting it for use at Willow Run would be very much more difficult than had been anticipated. For instance, when Ford engineers visited the Consolidated shops they found that there were discrepancies between loft boards and drawings and parts. Among the reasons for the discrepancies were that Consolidated, with only limited B-24 production up to that time, depended to a significant extent upon the know-how of its shop men and often omitted important details from its drawings. Furthermore, because of the unusually short time in which the B-24 had been designed and built by Consolidated, shortcuts had been taken and "shop engineering" was employed, with the result that the engineering department had been unable to keep pace.

William Pioch observed Consolidated's production of the center wing section for future fabrication by Ford and concluded:

> They had a very poor condition there at San Diego because the (nearby ocean) tides would change their floor levels and their fuselage fixtures were made of pipe. The tide would come in every day and go out and it would just raise that floor and let it down. They never knew where they were. That was a very poor condition which we noticed when we took a look at the job.
>
> Their major problem was to get their wings to line up with their fuselage and then drop them on. They would line the end of wings up on a transit and put them on. They used shims to make up the difference in their joints. When they joined the wings to the fuselage they used shims for that.
>
> They never made two wings alike. They never made two fuselages alike. They used to machine the ends of their wings to get them so they would be somewhere near right.

> I came to the conclusion that in order to make a good wing and make it accurate, make them identical and one right after another, we would have to make it like we do an automobile part; that is put it in a machine, machine it up, take it out, and put it on the assembly line.

The twenty-two-year-old William Pioch joined Ford as a die-maker in 1912 at Highland Park, then tool, die, fixture, and special machine designer, becoming head of the River Rouge plant production engineering department in 1926. From 1943 to 1945, he was the executive chief engineer at Willow Run. After the war he moved back to the Rouge Plant as its director of production engineering and developed several patents, machines for Henry Ford Hospital, and a five-year plan for tractor manufacture in China. He retired from the Ford Motor Company in 1953.

During March and April 1941, Ford engineers collected all the drawings and related data that Consolidated had available. After eliminating all duplicates, Ford reproduced them photographically. Simultaneously, the engineers of both companies collaborated to separate the B-24 into sub-assemblies. The huge center wing section, about which the B-24 was built, was selected first. Consolidated had been building the center wing piece by piece in a jig but Ford decided to build bulkhead and stringer sub-assemblies and then bring these units together in constructing the wing. This entailed cutting certain pieces to splice to other pieces and necessitated considerable redrawing and a continuing analysis of safety factors.

By the end of April 1941, Ford engineers had accumulated two railroad carloads of blueprints, releases, bills of materials, templates, reproductions of loft boards, and sample parts. It was decided to transfer the bulk of the engineering activities back to Dearborn so as to be nearer to the production departments. At that time, "little more than a good start" had been made on the aircraft's breakdown and what had been done consisted primarily of preliminary work on the center wing.

The Consolidated drawings showed the seven necessary mating stations but no fairing lines were available. Water and Butt lines and tail surface details were also not available, as were the detailed engineering on the offset charts. (Note: Water Lines (WL 0.0) define the height of important points (the floor or ceiling for instance) while Butt (Buttock) Lines (BL 0.0) measure left and right of the structure centerline.)

Other factors that also contributed to the inadequacy of Consolidated's data were the following:

1) Ford, with no recent aircraft production experience, frequently needed supplemental and clarifying information in addition to that normally used in the aircraft industry.
2) There was a wide divergence in engineering practice between the two companies. For example, Consolidated drawings were fractional and the entire Ford organization was used to decimal drawings.
3) Consolidated's production methods permitted rather extensive use of assembly drawings, while Ford's method of controlling tool manufacture required detailed drawings; one for each part to be tooled.

Putting the Consolidated Pieces Together

Because of the inadequacies of Consolidated's engineering information, Ford's inexperience in aircraft production methods, and the necessity for a complete analysis for mass production, absorbing the large accumulation of engineering data became a matter of tedious and time-consuming assembly, experimentation, and double-checking. When Ford Engineers were stumped, they discontinued work on that segment of the bomber and began work on another section. Discrepancies in Consolidated's data were resolved by using a set of assembly fixtures which Ford had purchased from Consolidated as a final authority for comparing and determining accurate dimensions.

Ford tooling and engineering, working together, continually experimented in an attempt to develop a satisfactory method of manufacturing some of the more complicated parts of the B-24. Many times, detailed engineering was delayed until the tool room had proved or disproved the feasibility of a proposed method of fabricating a part.

During August 1941, due to the complexity of the engineering problem and that some of the Consolidated lofts were only the size of a quarter coin, Ford engineers were forced to begin construction of a complete new set of lofts. Consolidated provided a staff of consultants and Consolidated's drawings, lofts, and templates were used as references.

Typical of engineering problems during this time were the problems caused by an innocuous toilet paper container. Ford engineers found that the drawing for the container had insufficient information regarding dimensions and shape and in requesting additional information they learned that Consolidated, which had produced only half a dozen B-24s at that time, had purchased the containers at a five-and-dime store.

With the realization that Consolidated's drawings were not sufficient for their purposes, Ford engineers immediately launched on an extensive, though somewhat haphazard redrawing program, that included 30,000 drawings that were made for the original Ford-built B-24; 10,000 more covering changes up to the 801 Change (B-24E to H) and 20,000 made subsequent to the 801 Change; for a total of 60,000 drawings made during the life of the contract.

Although considerable redrawing undoubtedly was necessary, later it became apparent that some redrawing could have been avoided if some of Willow Run's tooling had been completed from Consolidated drawings. In January 1943, Ford initiated reproducing some Consolidated drawings photographically and then used them for tooling without redrawing.

Throughout the summer of 1941, Ford engineers worked on the breakdown of the B-24, eventually arriving at seventy-two sub-assemblies for mass production and then confirmed the exact cleavage lines with Consolidated engineers. Ford's breakdown involved not only the separation of sections into sub-assemblies but in some cases eliminated sub-assemblies and introduced larger pieces. For example, Consolidated constructed the pilot's canopy from a series of small pieces welded together over a fixture while Ford fabricated it in two pieces, which could be lapped in and riveted. This breakdown was found to be thorough and correct with only three of the sub-assemblies eliminated as the project progressed.

Engineering was initially launched in Dearborn's airframe building but as soon as new construction at Willow Run was completed this department moved there. The new Ford aircraft engineering department was centered on automotive production where engineering played a relatively minor role and "served as a record of what had been done rather than planning what was to be done." Due to this downgrading of engineering, Ford was reluctant to allocate the responsibilities to its engineering department that the aircraft industry usually conferred its engineering departments, thus adding substantially to Willow Run's engineering coordination problems.

With production or process engineering headed by Edward Scott; design engineering by DeGroat; and tool engineering by Pioch; there were three separate engineering components operational in Willow Run production without any common or centralized control. Then adding more confusion, a fourth group, purchase specifications at the River Rouge Plant, was managed by engineering change control and for a while the blueprint and release groups were under the supervision of material control.

Like the previous Ford automotive practice, not only was production engineering considerably minimized by tool engineering, but it was often subordinated to design engineering because of the Ford's general lack of familiarity with building aircraft. Moreover, the production engineering department was under the strain of enormous expansion at a time when its engineering burden was already heavy.

The rapid expansion of the production engineering department and, to a lesser extent, design engineering caused each to locate and hire new personnel. Their search of Detroit area universities was successful in locating many engineers. An effort was made to locate former Ford employees who had worked on the manufacture of Trimotor Airliners in the 1930s but soon that notion was discontinued because most of these engineers were already working for other companies. From about seventy-five employees at the beginning of the project, production engineering was expanded to about 200 in the summer of 1941 and to about 450 when it was transferred from Dearborn to Willow Run in the spring of 1942. During this same period, design engineering grew to approximately fifty.

Initially, work was assigned to any available engineer, but eventually groups were formed that divided the aircraft into sub-assemblies and then engineered these sub-assemblies. However, the only two functional groups in the department were those concerned with hydraulics and electrical installations and consequently, a group leader in charge of one sub-assembly had changes to make involving several types of installations.

All these factors caused considerable disorder for Willow Run engineering management, but adding to the turmoil was the lack of coordination with Consolidated, which continued for almost a year following the return of the Ford group from Consolidated. Supposedly, the two companies cooperated but no actual attempt was made to sort out problems, no timely exchange of advice and assistance was made, and no effort to simplify some of the engineering difficulties was made. Although Ford maintained a liaison office at Consolidated, it was minimally effective and while Ford and Consolidated engineers communicated daily by telephone, the three-hour time zone difference was a definite hindrance.

Handling of Engineering Changes

The engineering deficiencies concerning coordination were especially noticeable in the management of the previously described flood of engineering changes which began almost as soon as the Ford engineers had returned to Dearborn.

At the same time Ford entered the B-24 program, Consolidated was undertaking the major change of the extension of the B-24's nose by 3 feet and a large number of other important changes that resulted as the bomber was put into service by the AAF. Approximately 130 master changes were incorporated in the first Ford-built B-24 and these changes, occurring at a time when Ford was attempting to perfect a complicated new product, created many difficulties.

Many early changes were attributable to the speed with which the B-24 had been built, since Consolidated engineers found it necessary to revise its drawings for various parts. Ford engineers and tool makers, on the other hand, also began contributing changes as they undertook the reproduction of Consolidated parts; so many, in fact, that in July 1941, the Ford engineering department banned such changes. This prohibition, considered necessary so that Ford production would not be delayed, remained in force more than six months.

Specific problems in connection with the handling of engineering changes included the following:

1) Consolidated had no orderly procedure for releasing information concerning changes and this information was sent to Ford in the form of meagre notifications that were not catalogued. Moreover, Ford sometimes did not receive this information until weeks after it had been received by the Consolidated shops. Ford, because of its unfamiliarity with aircraft engineering changes, found this method of transmitting information, particularly confusing.
2) Purchase specifications was given control over engineering changes at Ford, supplanting the engineering department which had been subordinated to a secondary role regarding changes. This change added to the problems of coordination with Consolidated and interfered with the efficiency of handling changes at Willow Run. Purchase specifications was later transferred to the engineering department that had been assigned additional personnel which alleviated the engineering changes problem. By that time Ford had gained more aircraft-building experience and more even control over these changes due to its insistence on subordinating changes to production.
3) Ford organized its engineering department according to components of the aircraft rather than along the functional lines of the aircraft industry, making it impossible for similar groups at the two plants to resolve a particular change together.

Some of Ford's engineering difficulties were alleviated by the spring of 1942 by the transfer of engineering from the Dearborn airframe building to Willow Run and the AAF's adoption of a block system for initiating changes and a method of numbering and giving priorities to them. However, the largest improvement resulted from the advent of the engineering sub-committee of the B-24 liaison committee.

Advent of the B-24 Liaison Committee and Sub-Committee

The formation of a B-24 liaison committee in March 1942, at the insistence of the AAF, was the first step toward satisfactory coordination Ford and Consolidated. In May 1942, the committee created an engineering sub-committee that immediately moved to San Diego and spent nearly six months at the Consolidated Plant organizing the flow of engineering change data and developing an aircraft analysis sheet, which listed all change drawings; identified by change letter; and itemized new and deleted drawings, new and deleted purchased parts, and new and deleted GFE items.

During this time the only change of any significance at Willow Run, concerning engineering, was the transfer of the blueprint and release groups from production engineering supervision to material control. While this transfer was made to reduce the amount of clerical work, the production engineering department was further weakened as a result

In the latter part of 1942, the engineering sub-committee moved to Willow Run and spent several months trying to improve the handling of engineering matters there. It concluded its study with a lengthy report at the close of 1942, criticizing Ford's engineering procedure.

Engineering Reorganization at Willow Run

The engineering sub-committee's negative report, plus a management reorganization that occurred about the same time, caused a complete overhauling of the engineering organization at Willow Run.

During early February 1943, Ford's first changes were the transfer of Edward Scott, the Ford liaison representative with Consolidated, to California and the consolidation of control over both design and production engineering under W. F. DeGroat. Simultaneously, William Pioch was assigned as the executive engineer and increasingly he began to bring all of the engineering components under centralized control. Several months later, in May 1943, DeGroat left Ford and Pioch assumed direct control of all engineering, tooling, production, and design.

During this period of extensive reorganization, the production engineering department was reorganized along functional lines, with leaders for wing, fuselage, radio, electrical, hydraulics, etc., and with sub-leaders for the various sub-assembly components.

Engineering change control was placed under the supervision of production engineering; the blueprint and release departments were removed from material control supervision and reinstated to production engineering; engineering field offices were established in the plant to put engineering in closer contact with production. An experimental group was formed within production engineering to devise a "pilot plane" installation on engineering changes before they were incorporated in production aircraft.

These changes resulted in a great improvement in the management of engineering matters at Willow Run. The experimental group, which had its first test in its handling of the 801 Change (B-24E to H), was so successful that it was made a permanent unit and was moved to Willow Run in August 1943, where it did much to facilitate the incorporation of subsequent engineering changes. The presence of Edward Scott at the San Diego Plant was very beneficial and for the first time an adequate liaison was realized between the two firms. Following the departure of DeGroat, there was a lessened emphasis on design engineering that helped to ease the progress of engineering.

For a time, Ford's decision to employ aeronautical engineers proved to be an astute choice, as the design group as an operating unit at times needlessly slowed production engineering. Primarily, its functions over-lapped those of Consolidated, the design prime contractor, and made Ford overly conscious of the importance of design and stress matters, but, as time passed, it contributed to the problem of coordination with Consolidated as Ford attempted to usurp certain phases of design responsibility.

Although it would be two years before engineering between Ford and Consolidated would become adequately coordinated; however, some of the difficulties Ford encountered in utilizing Consolidated data was a natural result in the exchange of large amounts of engineering information. This became apparent when North American entered B-24 production late in 1941 when North American found that many Ford drawings were unsatisfactory because of the inability of the Ford engineering department to keep pace with the rapidly changing situation.

The 801 Change: Model Designation Change from B-24E to B-24H

The most troublesome set of changes in production of the B-24 were those incorporated in Ford's Block No. 30, beginning with aircraft No. 801 (hence the "801 Change"). So comprehensive were the changes that they resulted in a change of the model designation from B-24E to B-24H. This change comprised fifty-six separate master changes including the addition of an Emerson nose turret (the first B-24 with a nose turret) and a Briggs retractable ball turret, the incorporation of a centralized fuel transfer system, cleared bombardier's passageway, and outward opening of the nose wheel doors. Furthermore, these changes had to be made as quickly as possible since the AAF in requesting the changes in mid-March called for fifty of these "H" bombers from Willow Run by 30 June. This goal proved to be unachievable as only six of the "Hs" were accepted in June and forty-two more in July, despite Ford declaring it was doing an "excellent and aggressive job" in incorporating these changes.

Among the reasons the goal of fifty H Models due in June could not be reached were:

1) Because of the short time allowed for the changes, engineering information from Consolidated was necessarily incomplete. For example, in the modification of the nose to accommodate the turret, Ford used sketches made at the modification center where Consolidated was developing the change and from these sketches

B-24E. (*AAF*)

B-24H. (*AAF*)

fabricated a plywood mock-up, and from the plywood mock-up made a plaster mock-up, from which the new tooling was designed.
2) Neither Ford nor outside vendors had sufficient time to tool up for the changes, consequently, even as late as the end of July many of the new parts were being made by hand.
3) The first Emerson turrets shipped to Ford for the 801 Change were originally designed as tail turrets and had to be changed before they could be installed in the nose.
4) The original Consolidated design of the new nose wheel doors were found to be unsatisfactory and had to be redesigned by Ford.

Master Changes B-24E and H

A total of 779 master changes were incorporated in Ford-built B-24s up to the time of peak production in March 1944.

B-24E and H Master Change Record (MCR) Changes: Block by Block

Model Block	Quantity	Date of 1st Aircraft	MCR Changes	KD Sequence	Aircraft Sequence
B-24E					
-1	29	9-1-42	129	1-40	1-29
-5	60	1-16-43	82	41-100	30-89
-10	57	3-15-43	95	101-200	90-146
-15	49	3-27-43	27	201-300	147-195
-20	58	4-21-43	23	301-400	196-253
-25	235	5-7-43	68	401-800	254-488
	488		424		
B-24H					
-1	253	6-30-43	51	801-1200	489-741
-5	89	9-18-43	4?	1201-1400	742-830
-10	189	10-6-43	37	1401-1800	831-1019
-15	540	11-11-43	75	1801-2800	1020-1559
-20	228	2-4-44	38	2801-3200	1560-1787
-25	266	2-24-44	18	3201-3600	1788-2053
-30	215	3-17-44	12	3601-3900	2054-2268
	1780		273		

13

Raw Materials and Purchased Parts

Ford's purchasing for the Willow Run Bomber Program was well-executed except for a brief period early in the program when Ford's inexperience and the constantly-changing bomber led to a large amount of over-buying, nonetheless the Ford purchasing department was generally efficient and well-organized.

Ford's Purchasing Plan

In purchasing, as in other phases of its operations, Ford's plan was to consider Willow Run as "just another small plant" in the Ford Empire and all procurement was controlled from River Rouge. Consequently, no provision was made for a purchasing department to be located at the new Willow Run Plant, which was an inconvenience as purchases for the B-24s were made from 965 suppliers located in 287 cities in thirty-three states. However, Ford did send representatives of the purchasing department to the Consolidated Plant in San Diego to observe Consolidated's purchasing practice and to determine the initial material requirements for B-24 mass production. Meanwhile, the educational order for the single B-24 was of benefit as Ford's purchasing department had to prepare a bill of materials that provided them with an idea of Liberator components and their cost.

In automobile production, Ford had managed much of its own raw material and fully planned to use these sources to supply Willow Run. Steel was to be provided from the Ford steel mills; castings from the Ford foundries; and forgings from the Rouge Plant. Two-thirds of the aluminum was to be purchased from Alcoa, America's largest aluminum company, and one-third from second largest Reynolds, completely utilizing the new Reynolds Alabama DPC aluminum facilities. Despite having Consolidated's consent granted to use their supply sources "to the extent of their excess capacity," Ford planned to depend almost entirely on its automotive suppliers. Ford anticipated that it would manage materials similarly as it had for automotive production; with large quantities ordered at one time and released for shipment by carloads according to a definite schedule.

The Ford Purchase Plan in Practice

During the visit to San Diego, Ford purchasing representatives studied Consolidated's purchasing methods, sources of supply, and prices. Consolidated had no complete bill of materials available for its B-24, but one was prepared in as much detail as possible from Consolidated's procurement records. Ford sent its expeditors to San Diego to determine which items Consolidated was having the most difficulties procuring, so that Ford purchasing could focus on them.

During this visit, Ford expeditors examined Consolidated's West Coast suppliers and determined them to be entirely inadequate to meet Ford's requirements. Contracts were then prepared and signed with local Willow Run suppliers formerly occupied in the automotive parts business, who had the ability to engineer, tool, and produce the required parts but lacked the training and the distinctive facilities particular to the aircraft industry. Purchasing for the first contracted 1,000 KD Kits was signed against engineering releases and Ford did not wait for the releases to clear through the stock department or for requisitions to be drawn up. Engineering blue prints were released to purchasing, which would furnish their buyer with information concerning the quantity required for one B-24, material specifications, dimensional tolerances, etc. to present to the potential supplier. For large quantities of one size aluminum sheet, some cross-checking with engineering and material control was done but normally orders were rushed to the suppliers and it was expected that amendments would be made later. Material control did develop a purchase notice that was used as a requisition by purchasing to fill emergency shortages, and to order items that had been omitted. Each buyer kept a master ledger record of all purchase orders, which provided a complete delineation of the procurement status of all material, including theoretical inventories, balances due, shipments promised, prices, etc.

The first large purchases were made in November 1941 for initial deliveries in February 1942. As the program was increased, additional purchase orders for large quantities of material were let, duplicating previous purchases but making it possible to adjust deliveries required in the latest production schedules.

Ford's use of automotive parts suppliers who were not familiar with aircraft requirements, led to new and higher prices than had originally been anticipated. However, Ford's buyers after completing purchases for the original 1,995 bombers successfully negotiated lower prices on subsequent purchases, which ultimately would return a total savings of $59 million by 1 April 1945. In addition, these buyers were influential in having some vendors absorb their tool costs and others to make return of surplus profits amounting to an additional $4.3 million.

Purchasing Difficulties

By mid-1942, largely due to Ford's large-scale buying and the unanticipated production delays, large surpluses of materials and parts accumulated at Willow Run and a critical shortage of storage space developed. One reason for the accumulation of these surpluses was once war was declared, it was impossible for Ford to control its suppliers as it had in peacetime. The priority system made it very difficult to schedule a supplier's output for Willow Run's convenience. When suppliers refused to hold shipments, Ford was forced to consider that it would be more advantageous to accept the material and place it in storage although it was not prepared to use it.

Because much of the material gathered and stored at Willow Run was urgently needed by other B-24 producers, Ford entered an agreement with the AAF basically making Willow Run a special warehouse for the B-24 pool. As the need for far more storage space evolved, Ford erected a large material's warehouse near the manufacturing building. Once this agreement was formalized as a supplement to Ford's contract, by June 1943 Willow Run had shipped $13 million of raw materials and parts to other Liberator manufacturers,

Order and supply problems were caused by the numerous engineering changes, which rendered many parts and materials useless. To reduce this loss, a special staff was selected to liaison directly with the engineering department in determining the effect of this problem on materials on order.

The purchasing department was based at the Rouge Plant rather than at Willow Run where the AAF representatives were based, which caused significant purchasing problems and instigated repeated requests from the AAF for the transfer of the department to Willow Run. Finally, during May 1943, during management reorganization that brought considerable autonomy to Willow Run, Ford agreed to transfer all purchasing to Willow Run, except those of aluminum and steel, which constituted the majority of the purchases, and remained at the Rouge Plant. As a result, there was significant improvement in the purchase and management of an assortment of smaller and more complicated articles at Willow Run. While this benefited the Ford aircraft program, overall it divided Ford purchasing, which was occupied with many additional contracts for the production of other war material.

Parts Storage

To quickly and efficiently build Liberators, Ford needed to manufacture (and later additionally import from sub-contractors) and then store the over 2.5 million parts produced per day, not including rivets. There were approximately 30,000 unique parts and a total of 150,000 manufactured parts in every Ford-built B-24. All parts were stored at the west end of the plant, although many of the same part numbers were used in various areas in each B-24 during its travel along the assembly line. The storage of components for the assembly line was in the north end of the building.

Storage space for raw materials and tools was provided by cribs in the main building. There were 487,186 square feet devoted to crib storage space on the main floor and mezzanines of the manufacturing and assembly building. There was a stock crib for every two workstations with each stock crib maintaining a ten-day parts float to insure the line was never shut down for lack of parts. Workers had to sign for parts, and if a part was damaged, it had to be returned before another one would be issued.

Parts storage west. (*FAM/AAF*)

Component storage north. (*FAM/AAF*)

Crib storage. (*FAM/AAF*)

IBM tabulating machines prepared parts inventory information for inventory control. When parts supply fell below a ten-day supply on hand, the parts replacement moved to a higher priority. There were various colors to indicate how short the supply had become and where efforts needed to be focused.

Material Control

Ford's pre-war system of material control, scheduling, etc. had been developed and used with its automotive production and was relatively straightforward. Basically, automobiles were built "out of a railroad box car," with the arrival of materials and the flow of production being controlled so thoroughly that storage and record-keeping presented no real problem. However, controlling materials for aircraft production was a problem and Ford's system was unable to manage it for several reasons: preparation for production required more time than had been projected; production acceleration was slower than anticipated; and chronic engineering changes affected the usefulness of materials and parts. Nevertheless, Ford developed a successful material control system that ultimately was judged to be as proficient as any in the aircraft industry.

In the original Ford plan, the purchasing department had the responsibility of scheduling raw materials and finished purchased parts, with the material control department providing delivery schedules and requirements and the engineering department providing specifications. Ford had examined Consolidated's materials control methods before launching its own procedures for its materials control and assumed that they would be able provide complete control. The material control department, while maintaining inventory and control of all material, was then to be responsible for requirements, planning, scheduling, production flow, plant stock control, general stores, etc. The requirements were to be determined from the BOM and from engineering releases.

Material Control's Operation

Materials delivery was scheduled in anticipation of Willow Run beginning significant production by May 1942. However, the plant did not accept its first bomber until July, and during the next six months bomber output accelerated very slowly. Furthermore, numerous engineering changes on which Ford had not assessed affected the usefulness of certain types of material and parts. Because only limited accommodations had been provided for the storage of raw stocks and finished parts, the material was stored anywhere there was available space.

The receiving department was in disorder as stock was unloaded upon receipt and because of the crowded conditions, inspections possibly would not be made for thirty to sixty days. Because the receiving report was prepared at the time of the inspection and forwarded to the material control department for entry into its records, this circumstance caused a thirty- to sixty-day delay in posting receipts. Consequently, any record of requirements compiled with inventory figures would be erroneous and almost unusable. An accurate inventory or visual stock check, was delayed due to material being haphazardly stored in every vacant space within the plant.

Also, at this time there were problems in production scheduling for material to be manufactured and processed in the plant. An airframe assembly conveyed down the line would be delayed by a shortage of parts, partially resulting from scheduling production from shortages rather than from production needs. Another result was frequent rescheduling, since parts were scheduled for a month at a time. At this time, the lot basis of scheduling was used with work divided into lots and a work order issued with the part accompanied to its destination.

By the end of 1942, Ford realized that to begin mass production, the existing materials control system was inadequate, and in early 1943, new controls and procedures to meet the requirements of aircraft production were initiated. Concurrently, the new materials building, designed for the storage of raw stock and also, in part, to store some excess inventories, began construction during June 1943 and would be completed in December. The large building had a floor space of 520 by 1,028 feet, totaling 577,120 square feet and contained: five stock departments; shearing; shipping; salvage; material conservation; receiving inspection; and maintenance departments; a carpenter shop; a blueprint crib, and an employee's garage. All component items, such as outer wings, stabilizers, rudders, fins, trailing edges, bomb bay doors, and bottom panels were shipped in 703 types of boxes ranging from a gross weight of 475 to 4,000 pounds that were export-packed to Army specifications with more than thirty-one carloads shipped each month. Emergency kits were packed for overseas shipment at an average rate of two to ten boxes daily. Rough stock such as sheet aluminum, coils, extrusions, wire, bar steel, and sheet steel were shipped to Ford plants, outside aircraft plants, and South America. The material conservation department shipped out surplus stock that was available to other aircraft plants.

The formation of a systems and tabulating department was the first stage in creating satisfactory parts controls. Since there are over 30,000 different parts in the B-24 with a total of approximately 465,000 separate parts, the tabulating equipment converted inaccurate manual controls to mechanized controls. Inventory procedures were changed so that complete control would be constantly maintained and a one-twelfth daily inventory was inaugurated so that every twelve days a complete inventory could be compiled on IBM machines. The tabulating department of material control used its equipment to compile monthly production schedules and later processed the required delivery schedule of finished purchased parts, the reordering of scrap and salvage statistics, and the compilation of daily production records by departments for use by the time and time study department, the production department, and the material department. IBM equipment was also utilized to deliver raw stock releases and gather station crib inventory records.

A parts and reference list was meticulously developed comprising 30,000 parts, specifying the number of each part as it was distributed for the manufacturing of the bomber, the name of the buyer, where purchased if outside, the department number if Ford-fabricated, area crib number where stocked, description, assembly in which used, and the effective point during production at which use started or stopped. Each concerned individual or department was provided a copy of this list, which helped to establish complete control of all material in the plant. This list was used in production and eliminated the causes of previous shortages as the Liberator moved from station to station.

A routing tag was attached to parts as they were manufactured, providing a description of the material and routing it to the appropriate assembly station or stock crib. The installation of Kardex card records in each crib provided improved material control and afforded a 100 percent check of material received as reported to the tabulating department. Disbursements of stock from area cribs to station cribs was recorded on a disbursement slip that balanced inventory records. Kardex was Remington-Rand's brand name and trademark for its cardstock system that was a desktop file (similar to a large rolodex) that had slots for multiple cardstock pages and were written on in pencil to be updated.

Raw Stock Material Control Department

The raw stock material control department was established to regulate the flow of material, prepare future requirements, check on incoming shipments, shortages, overages, scrap loss, etc. This department also consulted with the buyer of a particular material to regulate flow into the plant and maintain correct inventories. It consulted with the Rouge Plant contract material planning (CMP) department on all requirements and also with the engineering department on engineering changes affecting material.

Purchased Parts Control Department

This department operated closely with purchasing and with Ford vendors on inventories, scheduling, and control of finished parts.

Production Control Department

The production control department had the responsibility for material shortage or excessive inventories by use of the complete control of all material and parts.

Purchasing Specification Department

In the spring of 1943, the purchasing specification department of the material control department assumed the functions of determining the purchased part, size of sheets, requirements, and analyzing specifications to determine the type of material and grade to be used.

Material Control Liaison

The material control department joined management on overall planning as well as coordinating with all other departments concerned. Changes in plant layout, production sequences or installation were coordinated with the plant superintendent. Ultimately, Ford's material control program comprised the following numerous functions:
receiving and shipping; warehousing; rough stock control; general stores; tool and stock cribs; planning; production scheduling; distribution and control; spares division; property records division; purchased items; tabulating and systems; and salvage division.

A flow chart was developed by the material control department and presented an immediate graphic picture of production, showing the tempo of the flow of bombers along the assembly line as items were added to it. It also indicated the time needed to anticipate parts before they became items and the point at which they were to be added to the increasing bomber assembly.

Receiving and warehousing procedures were improved and standardized. All incoming shipments were immediately inspected and then transferred to an identified storage area. An item was marked for easy identification, grouped with similar items, and dated so that oldest stock was used first. By improved and correct stock handling, less material was scrapped and construction of the new materials building ultimately improved stock control.

14

Subcontracting: Other Ford Plants and Outside Sub-Contractors

Insufficient sub-contracting was one of the factors which hindered rapid production acceleration at Willow Run. The original Ford plan was to have its huge new bomber plant almost completely self-sufficient. The plan might have succeeded if a serious manpower shortage had not developed and forced Ford to initiate an extensive sub-contracting program. Fortunately, this occurred just as the plant was realizing perceptible production and subsequently was very effective.

Early Operation

The early Ford plan was for a minimum of sub-contracting, with 86 percent of all production to be retained at Willow Run and, of the remainder, 8 percent to be turned over to other Ford plants and only 6 percent going to outside vendors. This small proportion of outside production was essentially unchanged throughout the latter part of 1942 and the early part of 1943. Meanwhile, Willow Run began production in July 1942, which then began to accelerate at a very slow rate. While a number of factors contributed to the slow acceleration, one of the major causes was again the shortage of workers which developed rapidly as industry in the Detroit area was inundated with war contracts.

The AAF was convinced that an immediate increase in sub-contracting was the only solution of improving the Willow Run acceleration rate. In the spring of 1943, the AAF directed Ford to plan to increase the amount of outside production and Ford devised a detailed dispersal plan that went into effect beginning in September. Outside production in September rose from 17 percent to 26 percent, which increased to 33 percent by the end of the year and crested at 36 percent in March 1944 just as Willow Run was achieving peak production. Most of this sub-contracting went to other Ford plants while the amount sub-contracted to Ford vendors rose to only 9 percent during this same period.

Methods of Sub-contracting

There were five main phases in "farming out" a job to a sub-contractor:

1) A careful time-study was made of each job by the time study department, as a basis for determining costs.
2) A master breakdown sheet was prepared for each sub-contracted job, listing all dies, tools, jigs, fixtures, machinery, and, in some cases, the parts required. This outlined the issues to be considered in planning and establishing contracts for the jobs. Photographs of all parts or assemblies were used in negotiations with the vendors.
3) Interested companies and Ford plants were contacted and asked to quote prices on the job. After Ford was satisfied that the bidder could satisfactorily complete the job and at a cost comparable to that at Willow Run, contracts were let to the bidder.
4) A plan was to be developed for moving the job to the sub-contracting plant so that Willow Run production schedules would not be interrupted, as it was not possible to stop production while the fixtures and equipment were being moved and installed elsewhere. Most sub-contractors were not ready to immediately manufacture and ship the sub-contacted assembly in required quantities and planning was critical to assure a continuous supply of each assembly during the transfer to a Sub-Contractor's plant. Before a job was transferred, the length of time required to get the vendor into full production was considered. When possible, a pool or reserve of from seventy-five to 200 assemblies was accumulated to keep the assembly line running until the sub-contractor could entirely supply the final assembly lines.

   Specific items that were on "shortage lists" were in such short supply that it was impossible to build up a "float" on them. Since cancelling the sub-contractor or stopping Willow Run production was not an option, special provisions were made, such as moving during the night or on weekends after the sub-contractor had made necessary provisions to receive the fixtures, tools, and parts for the job such as electrical and air connections.

   Only a portion of the necessary equipment was moved to the sub-contractor's facility in order to construct a "pilot line" to acquaint and facilitate the manufacture of the first assemblies. A first assembly was submitted to Willow Run's inspection department for approval, after which the sub-contractor was authorized to proceed with production. After the sub-contractor was producing the anticipated output from the initial equipment, the remainder of the fixtures and machinery were delivered the sub-contractor then wholly adopted the job. Frequently, until the sub-contractor was able to complete the contracted item on its own, it would be produced at both at Willow Run and the sub-contractor plants for a time. Meanwhile, the reserve of finished assemblies was employed to keep Willow Run assembly lines operational if outside production falling below schedule.

   The sub-contracting companies were obliged to send their supervisors and sometimes workers to Willow Run for "on-the-job training." Also, some Willow

Run supervision and workers were sent to the sub-contractor to assist in helping to get the job on course. This was charged on an outside party work order and was paid for by the sub-contractor.

5) The final phase in this decentralization program involved completing the transfer, assisting the sub-contractor in production methods, operation, and maintenance of machinery and equipment, engineering changes, etc. A staff of from fifteen to twenty-five coordinators, each assigned to a particular plant, had the responsibility of assuring that the sub-contractor was supplied with sufficient fixtures, tools; machines, blueprints, and rough stock for the job.

Other Ford Plants as Sub-Contractors

Until August 1943, outside Ford plants had been producing between 8 percent and 9 percent of Willow Run's requirements, However, as the additional dies, fixtures, and tools were relocated, this increased to 18 percent in September; 23 percent in November; and by January 1944, 26 percent of production was placed outside Willow Run. From March 1944 onward until their closing, sub-contracting from Ford plants was approximately 27 percent.

The following Ford plants and branches contributed to the success of Willow Run's B-24 program.

Branch/Plant	Location	Parts Produced
Brooklyn Village Plant	Brooklyn, MI	Misc. machining
Clarkston Village Plant	Clarkston, MI	Misc. assembly
Dundee Village Plant	Dundee, MI	Brass foundry
Flatrock Village Plant	Flatrock, MI	Misc. electrical assemblies
Ford Airport and Airframe Bldg.	Dearborn, MI	Previously built the Tri-Motor 1924–31; also trained workers for Willow Run
Green Island Plant	Green Island, NY	P-1 aircraft generator
Hamilton Plant	Hamilton, MI	Outboard fuel accessory doors, Island and Oleo doors, nose wheel doors, side gunner doors, life raft and emergency escape doors
Hayden Mills Village Plant	Tecumash, MI	Misc. machining
Hydro Plant	Willow Run	Misc. machining
Highland Park	Highland Park, MI	Outer wing and nose enclosure, misc. small parts and machining, misc. electrical and hydraulic assemblies, nose side panel, tail cone

Iron Mountain Plant	Iron Mt. MI	Cargo floor
Lincoln Plant	Detroit, MI	Engine cowling assembly, air ducts, nose ring, center wing bulkheads, dressing of engines from Buick (Melrose Park, IL) and Chevrolet (Tonawanda, NY) for assembly into aircraft at Willow Run
Manchester Village Plant	Manchester, MI	Instruments, misc. assembly and machining
Milan Village Plant	Milan MI	Misc. assembly and machining
Milford Village Plant	Milford, MI	Misc. assembly and machining
Nankin Mills	Nankin Mills, MI	Engraving
Phoenix Plant	Plymouth, MI	Wired junction boxes
Rouge "B" Bldg.	Dearborn, MI	Truss bulkhead and radio operator's floor, side and bottom panels
Rouge Pressed Steel	Dearborn, MI	Stampings
Rouge Paper Mill	Dearborn, MI	Boxes, fillers, separators
Rouge Motor Bldg.	Dearborn, MI	Machining
Rouge Magnesium Foundry	Dearborn, MI	Castings
Rouge Rolling Mill	Dearborn, MI	Misc. small parts
Rouge Spring and Upset	Dearborn, MI	Forgings
Rouge Tire Plant	Dearborn, MI	Stabilizer, rudder, fins, elevator, aileron, oleo struts, canopy and upper deck

By January 1944, some 3,477 assemblies and 6,182 dies had been moved outside Willow Run. Wherever possible, dies were sent to enable the sub-contractor to stamp out and form its own parts for the jobs. These figures included 1,974 jobs and 4,448 dies sent to the Rouge Plant, 411 assemblies and 595 dies moved to Highland Park, 384 jobs and 575 dies sent to the Lincoln Plant, and eighty-five jobs and 125 dies moved to the Hamilton Plant in Ohio. Besides these four Ford plants, there were twenty-seven other main sub-contractors and numerous other Ford branches.

These 3,477 jobs ranged in size from miscellaneous small parts assemblies, which were let to Grand Rapids Metal Craft Company, Michigan to the entire outer wing section, which was built at Highland Park and also at Birmingham, Alabama. A total of 6,536 dies were used in the entire outside production program compared to 8,721 dies used at Willow Run. In January 1944, Ford was sub-contracting 35 percent of the work at Willow Run as was Consolidated, San Diego.

Ford's Highland Farm Tractor Plant builds spars and bulkheads for the outer wing to be shipped to Willow Run ready for installation. (*FAM/AAF*)

Under Mead Bricker's 505 Program, the building of nacelles was transferred from Willow Run Department 919 to the Lincoln Plant in Detroit with R-1830 engines were shipped directly to the Lincoln plant from Chevrolet's Tonawanda, New York, plant and Buick's Melrose, Illinois, plant. The Lincoln Plant then shipped over 100 complete, ready-to-install nacelles per day to Willow Run. (*FAM/AAF*)

Ford Rouge B-24 Sub-Assembly Plant

During January 1942, the Rouge Plant produced the first seventy-seven Ford Jeeps with Willys engines and then produced 1,460 Jeeps in February. Meanwhile, Ford's Chester, Dallas, Louisville, and Richmond branches each inaugurated their Jeep assembly lines. By the end of March, all these plants were producing at nearly their planned capacity with the company producing a total of 8,920 Jeeps; followed by a single month record of 11,159 in April. With Ford assembling Jeeps at six plants; the Rouge Plant terminated Jeep assembly in September 1942 and concentrated on producing 320,766 Jeep tires and 257,139 inner tubes before this enterprise was sold in June 1943 and shipped to the Soviet Union for reassembly. The building was then reconverted for manufacturing the B-24 sub-assemblies of which Willow Run was in continual short supply. The 440,000-square-foot building consisted of a basement, main ground floor area, and three balconies. At the peak of production there were 5,241 (about 3,000 women) employees, more than twice the number employed during the previous manufacture of tires.

After the reconversion, war production progressed rapidly in three critical areas: plastic parts production, strut and landing gear assembly, and the fabrication of seven major Liberator sub-assemblies. The former steering wheel and plastic department remained intact and was used for the manufacture of various plastic parts for war production. For the strut and landing gear manufacture, 477 new machine tools of all types were acquired for the machining and assembly process and a complete heat-treating and plating department was installed. The former tire builders, mill-men, and Banbury (an industrial mixer/blender) operators needed to undergo intensive retraining for the critical job of constructing the high-stressed strut and landing gear assemblies. In April 1943, in order to accelerate Willow Run bomber production, equipment was installed at the Rogue Plant to manufacture seven major assemblies, four of which comprised the entire tail assembly (stabilizers, fins, rudders, ailerons, elevators).

Vendor Sub-Contracting

Outside vendors, the other source of sub-contracting, were very minimal compared to the work completed by other Ford plants. From early 1942 until 1945, this outside source of production only increased from 6 percent to 9 percent, which finally compared to 27 percent for other Ford plants and consisted mostly of supplying smaller parts and assemblies.

Company	Location	Parts Produced
American Swiss Co	Toledo, OH	Turbo support, bomb hoist
Bechtel-McCone	Birmingham, AL	Outer wing
Brighton Auto and Aircraft	Brighton, Ml	Turbo support, bomb hoist
Brown Products	Detroit, MI	Rudder tab, pedestal assembly

Budd Co.	Detroit, MI	Wing tip, manifold and tail pipe, bomb doors
Dalrymple Mfg.	Detroit, MI	Elevator stabilizer tall skid assembly
Essex Wire Co.	Highland Park, MI	Electrical harness assembly and control boxes
Gibson Refrigerator	Greenville, MI	Center wing flap
Glenvale Products	Detroit, MI	Catwalk
Gorno Mfg.	Trenton, MI	Oxygen support brackets, tables
Lloyd Mfg.	Menominee, MI	Fuselage nose canopy
Prank McAllister	Birmingham, MI	Floor assembly
Metal Mouldings	Detroit, MI	Bomb racks <u>and</u> shackles
Park Mfg.	Highland Park, MI	Misc. cable assembly, elevator control cables
Pittsburgh Plate Glass	Crystal City, MO	Nose enclosure and pilot's enclosure
Quincy Mfg.	Quincy, MI	Bulkhead assembly, electric panels, fuse boxes, etc.
Reynolds Spring	Jackson, MI	Center wing trail edge and outer wing trail edge
United Stove	Ypsilanti, MI	Misc. stampings

The Ford Rouge Plant, Dearborn, MI, concluded assembling Jeeps in September 1942 and concentrated on producing Jeep tires and inner tubes before this enterprise was sold in June 1943 and shipped to the Soviet Union. The building was then reconverted for manufacturing the B-24 sub-assemblies. (FAM/AAF)

The Rouge Tire Plant became a major Willow Run supplier, providing the stabilizer, rudder, fins, elevator (seen on photo), and also the aileron, oleo struts, canopy, and upper deck. (FAM/AAF)

15

Spare Parts

Except for minor early problems, Ford managed the production of spare parts efficiently and in large quantities and was especially proficient in completing critical emergency spare parts shipments requested by overseas units. Willow Run supplied 50 percent of the total normal movement of B-24 spare parts and 85 percent of all emergency shipments and represented approximately 12 percent of the dollar value of all contracts.

Ford's Spare Parts Plan

Ford's plan for managing spare parts at Willow Run was developed about August 1941 when a "spare team" was set up by Ford, Consolidated, and the AAF to select the quantity and type of parts and assemblies, which would be classified as spare parts. However, at this time, only a few B-24s had been produced and with the lack of engineering information, this team could do little more than estimate spare parts requirements. The tentative list the team prepared showed 6,500 procured items for both the airframe and accessories and was put into effect in January 1942. Ford proposed separate shop scheduling of parts for spares and planned to ship them concurrent with aircraft production. A stove manufacturer's warehouse in Ypsilanti was procured to be used for crating, boxing, and shipping spares.

Ford Spare Parts Operation

At the outset Ford supplied spares to AAF bases throughout the country and also made emergency shipments overseas. However, this scheme involved considerable effort and a variety of packaging procedures. Early in 1943 authorization was obtained to send all shipments in standard domestic shipping packages in bulk to the AAF depots, where the parts would be packaged for export. This change in spare handling eliminated a bottleneck in packaging at Willow Run. However, certain large special items that were export-packed at Willow Run were excluded. In August 1943, the specialized depot at Shelby, Ohio, was completed as a stock warehouse and assigned as a Ford outlet and Willow Run was then able to send spares in larger quantities there.

In the summer of 1943, Ford set up a special spares division to manage all emergency requests from the AAF, to expedite all other orders, and to check the parts and drawings before the order was sent to the shop. Such checking avoided many wrong orders and revealed that it was sometimes more efficient to ship an entire assembly rather than a specific part of that assembly. The spares division called to Ford's attention certain essential items that had not been placed on the regular spare parts schedule and also enabled Ford to make suitable changes and additions to the list of authorized spare parts, which was checked weekly with Wright Field.

As Willow Run slowly began to accelerate production in the latter half of 1942 and emphasis was on producing KDs and completed bombers, the production of spare parts began to fall behind schedule. To remedy this situation, during the spring of 1943, management placed spare parts on an equal priority with production, allowing these spare parts to be either utilized for production or as spares as needed.

The spare parts situation was also improved in 1943 by the decentralization program, which increased the amount of outside production and provided more parts and assemblies for Willow Run. Also, when a new warehouse building was completed in January 1943, the handling and packaging of spares was improved and the excessive trucking and handling necessary on spares packed and shipped from the warehouse in Ypsilanti was eliminated. After January 1944, Ford was 94 percent to 99 percent procurement on all spare shipments and its spare parts problems were few. At peak, office personnel in the spares department totaled forty with shop personnel on packaging and shipping numbering 150.

16
Government-Furnished Equipment (GFE)

Willow Run Liberators were equipped with over 400 pieces of GFE. At no time were there GFE shortages or any serious GFE-caused production delays at Willow Run. Both the AAF and Ford ultimately had adequate follow-up systems and Ford was able to rework many types of equipment, once the AAF granted approval.

The Ford GFE Plan

Ford planned to match GFE handling the same as any other stock item, except that the AAF would place orders with the GFE sub-contractors, with scheduling and follow-up performed by Ford. Special Ford personnel were allotted to work with the AAF in scheduling deliveries, maintaining a current GFE list, and attempting to resolve any problems. The Ford radio screen room and instrument laboratory were to be equipped and staffed to make any repair or overhaul any piece of GFE equipment. All GFE that could be assembled to components were to be installed at Willow Run, and only engines, propellers, radios, and similar parts were to be sent to the assembly plants.

Ford GFE Operation

Early in 1942, because of the increase in production schedules following Pearl Harbor, Ford transferred a number of departments to Willow Run, which it had intended to keep at the River Rouge Plant. At the same time, Ford discontinued the plan to follow-up GFE sub-contractors, which was to be performed by the AAF.

Ford's requisitioning of GFE followed the example of its previous buying for automotive production, where large-scale purchases were made in preparation for carefully controlled production. In B-24 production, however, problems arose when preparation for production more time than anticipated and engineering changes often made quantity buying impracticable.

Consequently, during late 1942, as production acceleration fell substantially behind expectations, Willow Run accumulated a large surplus of many GFE articles while at the same time items in stock were either to many or too few and there were shortages of critical pieces of equipment. At this time, poor coordination between the AAF and Ford existed and moreover, Ford had no close stock control nor record-keeping and the amount of storage space available was inadequate.

Prior to mid-1943, physical inventory checks were almost non-existent. An overstock of tires, wheels, turrets, and bombsights was caused by Ford's not keeping an overall flow chart of the inventory, which would have enabled Ford to inform the GFE distribution organization that surpluses were developing but then GFE vendors did not keep the Wright Field schedules. However, during this first year of production, the Wright Field GFE organization was also undergoing growth and change and was unable to give Ford much support. After GFE items arrived at Willow Run, there was a shortage of storage space, which required stacking them on the production floor where these items were sometimes lost and unavailable when required.

Many problems occurred as a result of the lack of interchangeability on GFE items furnished by different sub-contractors. Additionally, the AAF had inflexible guidelines regarding the reworking GFE items and inspectors were reluctance, at times, to permit even minor repairs. These problems would have been insignificant when building "hand-made" aircraft or for very small production runs, but for Willow Run's mass production 1943 and 1944 efforts this became a serious problem.

GFE Reorganisation

By the end of July 1943, Willow Run's GFE problems crested and it sent the AAF resident representative's office a report delineating the need for a reorganization. During August, a Ford's Rouge Plant executive was transferred to Willow Run and given control of GFE and completely reorganized its management. GFE was organized as a separate department from the stock department, having its own receiving inspection handling procedures and its own storage space and cribs. Difficulties with inaccurate records and uneven stock supplies were also solved. During late 1943, the AAF established a GFE warehouse in Detroit, which helped solve the problem of critical items in short supply at Willow Run and made it possible to operate with a smaller inventory.

More than three-quarters of GFE parts were installed on Liberator final assembly lines while KD parts shipped to Fort Worth and Tulsa had only 25 percent of the GFE installed. So, most of the GFE parts on KD bombers was undertaken by the AAF with direct shipments to these assembly plants.

17

Inspection and Government Control

Willow Run encountered many inspection problems during the early stages of production. The underlying reason was poor workmanship, but the problem was exacerbated because Willow Run inspection was not independent of production. It was not until suitable local management was furnished during early 1943 that an effort was made toward an independently organized inspection department. With the resolution of the basic production problems and the establishment of independent inspection, these difficulties gradually were eliminated.

Ford's Inspection Plan

The original inspection plan for Willow Run did not provide for an effective inspection organization. There was no chief inspector; furthermore, the function of inspection was in effect, subordinate to production, which had been Ford's practice in its automotive production. Sixteen key inspection personnel were transferred from the Rouge Plant and sent to Consolidated and other aircraft plants for training. The remainder of the inspection organization was to be recruited and trained.

Willow Run Inspection in Operation

Ford selected quality personnel for their new inspection department, paying them high wages, equaling that of skilled production workers. Ford sent the new inspectors to San Diego in March 1941 where they remained for about four months, forming groups that concentrated on problems such as tooling, manufacturing, electrical, etc. Upon their return in July, the new inspection department was activated in the Dearborn airframe building and the San Diego-trained inspectors trained new inspectors there. Using good available equipment, the inspection procedure was complete and thorough using 15,000 gauges that were made by the inspection department's own gauge-maker.

All parts produced for the B-24 were 100 percent inspected and stamped and installed on the B-24, which had 120 inspection plates.

Throughout 1942, as Willow Run slowly progressed into production, there were numerous inspection difficulties, many of which were derived from the relatively secondary position of the inspection department in relation to production. The control of scrapped parts and items for salvage was inadequate and there were limited storage facilities, which led to finished parts shortages. Production could use previously inspected and rejected items if it considered them satisfactory.

In May 1942, Willow Run was given the barely adequate "C" inspection rating, but three months later in July when the plant went into production, the quality of Ford inspections had shown significant improvement. Also at that time, after AAF inspectors had received training, there was an increase in their inspection efficiency. At the beginning of January 1943, Willow Run established an independent local management organization that was the gateway toward developing an efficient enterprise. Then, in May 1943, the AAF conducted a complete survey of the plant that facilitated the correction of many inspection problems. The survey recommended various inspection procedure improvements and insisted that management immediately make the inspection department be completely independent from production department influence.

Even so, the quality of Willow Run's first bombers (and Fort Worth and Tulsa KD B-24Es) did not meet the increased combat requirements of the AAF and thus the entire production run of B-24Es was placed in an obsolescent "limited standard" service category on 18 September 1943 (the same day as the last E was delivered). Although only a very few Es saw overseas combat operations, their demotion gave the AAF a fleet of training aircraft. It also allowed Ford to reconsider its production philosophy while constructing a plentiful supply of needed B-24E trainers for the AAF. Ford was finally was on the path to achieving it mass assembly/production system but at great expense in fabricating and abandoning many dies and jigs.

In an effort to solve the inevitable clash between mass production and quality inspection, a salvage board was created consisting of company and AAF inspectors and manufacturing representatives who were to decide upon the disposition of rejected items. The establishment of a quality control division was another effort to resolve the poor quality problem. This division was to report directly to the plant manager, making it independent of both production and inspection but being able to coordinate their problems and solutions. After considering inspection's findings, the quality control division was to determine the causes of any problems and then to prompt corrective actions. This division also worked very closely with other Ford plants and sub-contractors to assist them in maintaining high quality standards.

While these changes were particularly valuable, the organization of the inspection department continued to remain unsatisfactory. In January 1943, one of the first changes to improve inspection was to divide it into two. One chief inspector was named to head manufacturing and sub-assembly, while the other was to direct final assembly and flight. Later, it was further divided into three departments: manufacturing, final assembly, and flight. The new inspection organization caused disagreements between the three inspection departments and frequently made it impossible to determine accountability for certain inspection problems. In August 1943, this situation was partially resolved when a chief inspector was to direct manufacturing, structural, and miscellaneous inspection. However, it was not until the end of 1944 that one chief inspector for the entire plant was assigned and all inspection activities coordinated and controlled by him.

X-ray inspections were an important part of the hundreds of checks in the Willow Run inspection process. Castings and forgings were x-rayed by two General Electric x-ray machines to divulge the slightest defect in castings. A large dark room could develop 3,000 feet of x-ray film daily. Defect-free forgings and castings were then routed through the machine department, where they were machined, gauged, inspected, and treated against corrosion. The plant also had a complete chemical laboratory and a metallurgical laboratory that had an apparatus for testing tensile strength up to 200,000 pounds' capacity.

Willow Run received a "B" inspection rating in February 1943, an "A" rating in February 1944 and the coveted Army and Navy E Award was conferred in May 1945. The ratio of AAF to company inspectors was one to twenty-three in the fall of 1942, but it fell to approximately one to thirty-five in the fall of 1943. When the plant reached peak production in the spring of 1944, it had 2,200 company inspectors, and at the end of 1944, there were 1,805 Ford factory inspectors and 109 AAF inspectors.

AAF Control at Willow Run

The control exercised by the AAF staff at Willow Run was under direction of the AAF resident representative (AAFRR). The efficiency of the AAFRR varied from AAF complaints that Ford and higher authorities often made decisions or made changes without clearing the AAFRR's office and that it had insufficient authority over Ford. Meanwhile Ford complained that AAFRR "frequently showed an inclination to take over the prerogatives of Management."

Since factory inspection was not a particularly coveted position, inadequately trained and inexperienced AAF personnel sent to Willow Run contributed to delays in production as did the frequent shifting of AAF plant representatives and other AAF personnel, together with the loss of time required for their orientation into the program. Unconfirmed verbal instructions from headquarters, Wright Field, caused considerable confusion for the AAFRR in carrying out his duties.

Willow Run Visitors

The Willow Run Plant was constantly besieged by official and celebrity visitors who occupied the valuable time of an overworked Ford and AAF staff, resulting in the loss of many man-hours. The visitors, transported by an electric-powered train, were followed and photographed by the Ford PR department.

FDR visits Willow Run during 1942, riding in his 1939 Lincoln, the "Sunshine Special." (*FAM/AAF*)

Above left: Henry Ford, signature straw hat in hand, greets Vice President Henry Wallace who has just signed the B-24. (*FAM/AAF*)

Above right: Charles Sorensen (L) and Edsel Ford (R) visit with William Knudsen. (*FAM/AAF*)

Henry Ford and Gen. Henri Giraud, Free French co-president and C-in-C French Forces. (*FAM/AAF*)

Left to right: Henry Bennett, Mead Bricker, Hap Arnold, Henry Ford Sr., and Henry Ford II (R) confer with two RAF officials (2-3R). (*FAM/AAF*)

18

Rate of Production Acceleration

Willow Run had the following production contract orders during the war:

With Douglas (W 535-ac-18722) for 954 aircraft
With Consolidated-Vultee (W535-ac-18723) for 969 aircraft
With the Government (W353-ac-21216) for 8,709 aircraft
Total Bombers: 10,602

Overall, the rate of production acceleration at Willow Run was only considered fair while acceleration during the long early factory period was poor. However, once production started, acceleration became rapid but only over a relatively short period. The project was approved 25 February 1941 and three years and one month later during March 1944 Willow Run reached what may be considered peak production. In that month, the plant produced 309 completely assembled B-24s and 140 KD kits. The total, with a KD evaluated at 80 percent of a completed aircraft, was 421 complete bombers. While it is true that this total was exceeded several times in succeeding months, Willow Run by that time was actually "coasting" as the plant could have produced over 600 bombers per month had the AAF needed them.

Elapsed time from Project A approval to first acceptance in July 1942 was slightly less than seventeen months and was better than the average of the sixteen aircraft plants selected for the ATSC study, but acceleration for the six months after the first acceptance was exceedingly slow. Among other producers of heavy bombers, Boeing Seattle, Consolidated Fort Worth, Lockheed Burbank, Douglas Long Beach, and even a plant with a very poor record, Consolidated San Diego, all accelerated in their early months much more rapidly than Willow Run. Actual production, as indicated by the expenditure of direct man-hours, began in November 1941, first acceptance followed the first production by eight months, and peak production was attained twenty-six months later.

The Willow Run Mass Production Plan

Ford made detailed plans to get mass production at Willow Run under way as quickly as possible. The essential aspects were:

1) Production would be geared to the manufacture of one B-24 per hour, so that, depending on the number of shifts worked, from six to eighty planes per day would be produced. Ford picked this goal "out of the hat" so that there would be something on which "to hang mass production plans," since it was obvious in early 1941 that all official schedules were only stop-gaps with no known requirements.
2) Consolidated would furnish a complete set of drawings, blueprints, and related engineering data and be responsible for engineering. Engineering changes were to have been made through Consolidated but were to be effective at the same time at both plants.
3) The bomber to be built was the B-24D.
4) Willow Run would be a completely integrated airframe plant, manufacturing not only parts normally made in an aircraft plant but also such standard items as rivets and formed shapes normally purchased from outside sources.
5) Consolidated would furnish one KD B-24D to be used for educational purposes.
6) Consolidated would furnish one set of pilot line assembly jigs and fixtures to be used for education purposes.
7) Mass production was to be carried out to its fullest extent. Detail parts were to be 100 percent pre-fabricated for "conveyorized" assembly. The large process of tooling up was to be thorough and systematic, with all tools to be designed and built by the Ford tooling facility.
8) The basic Ford Motor Company executive and staff organization was to remain unchanged as Willow Run was considered as merely the adding of one more war contract and one more plant to its already vast empire.
9) Essential manpower, including supervisory personnel, was to be procured as much as possible from the Ford organization, but mass labor was expected to be drawn from the area around Willow Run, from Ypsilanti, and other communities plus the contiguous rural area outside of metropolitan Detroit. Some Ford supervisors were to be trained at Consolidated's San Diego Plant.
10) The resources of the "Ford Domain" were to be used wherever essential: to provide engineering and laboratory assistance, to design and build the tools, to begin manufacture of detailed parts, etc.
11) The Ford automotive system of production control, scheduling, cost control, etc., was to be used at Willow Run.

The 8- and W-Series KD and Complete Aircraft Production Plan

The original official production schedule expected Willow Run to furnish 100 sets of B-24D KD kits for shipment, half to Consolidated Fort Worth and the other half to Douglas Tulsa. Both of these plants were built and owned by the War Department as part of an expansion and dispersal program for the express intent of assembling B-24 components to be supplied by Ford. From the beginning, Ford had intended that it should provide complete bombers as well as KDs and built Willow Run on this basis, even though Ford's offer to do so had been officially turned down early in February 1941. Then, on 1 May 1941, the government informally gave Ford approval to proceed with final assembly concurrent with the production of KDs. Delivery schedules were constantly revised with the first official schedule, 8C of 1 March 1941, being a very unrealistic "bogey" schedule, calling for the delivery of KDs starting in January 1942 with two per month, reaching 100 per month in June, five months later.

The first sufficiently realistic schedule to be used for planning purposes was the 8D schedule of 21 April 1941, which required the first two sets of KDs in September 1942 reaching a peak of ninety in April 1943. This 8D schedule, drafted before it was decided that Ford was to manufacture complete bombers, proved to be the most accurate one issued. Ford, however, held it could start deliveries in May 1942, and accordingly, the first delivery date in later schedules was advanced.

The 8E schedule issued 5 May 1941 was the first to include complete bombers. It provided for the delivery of the first two sets of KDs in May 1942 plus one complete unit that same month. Peak production of 120 KDs was to be reached in April 1943 and peak production of 150 complete units was to be reached two months later in June 1943.

The 8F Schedules, drawn up in July 1941, did not change the first delivery date, but it halved the peak production of completed aircraft.

For the remainder of 1941 until 8H was issued at the end of the year, Ford's scheduled goal remained at a peak production of 205 bombers a month, consisting of 130 KDs and seventy-five fly-a-ways.

Later schedules from W-4 onward reduced KD production and at the same time increased the number of complete bombers to be produced. Peak production of KDs was specified at 178 for January and March 1945 in the W-9 schedule released in January 1944 and peak production of complete units was specified as 425 from August and September 1944 in the W-11 schedule. Peak production, for any schedule was the 437 specified in W-9 for five thirty-one-day months in 1945 with later schedules significantly decreased production, including the W-14 schedule released on 23 April 1945.

Preparation for Production

It was a tribute to the resources and decisiveness of the Ford organization that, despite the size of the Willow Run Project A and the elapsed time from Project A approval to first acceptance, the Willow Run Plant was still better than average according to the ATSC report. Nonetheless, Willow Run was anything but being in actual production with its first Liberator acceptance, as many of the pre-production problems stretched over nearly six months of very slow acceleration before the huge plant actually could be considered to begin to produce bombers.

Generally, Ford's production plans were deemed dependable and achievable. To reiterate, the importance of the early placement of more than 200 Ford department representatives to San Diego to observe Consolidated's production methods proved to be very beneficial as did purchases of a complete set of pilot line tooling from Consolidated; the manufacture of a pre-production model of the B-24 under an educational order from the government; and the hiring of aeronautical engineers to alleviate Ford's lack of recent aircraft production know-how.

Ford's purchasing power and automotive mass production experience were important factors in their B-24 project. Ford's well-developed tooling facilities were of great value and the decision to continue tooling concurrent with the engineering of the B-24 for mass production was practicable despite the wastage involved. Machine tools were ordered early and Ford supported its own program in the expansion following Pearl Harbor by transferring many critical machine tools to Willow Run from its automotive plants. Ford's early, May 1941, training of riveters would prove to be beneficial once production was under way. Unlike its more complicated rival B-17, the B-24 had many inherent qualities making it easier to manufacture.

Long, Slow Period of Production Acceleration

In May 1942, the original manufacturing Willow Run Plant had been completed and the expanded plant with the additional assembly line space made necessary by the Japanese attack on Pearl Harbor was 75 percent completed. At a time when the first KD kits and complete aircraft should have come off the Willow Run line, only half of the machine tools were in place. A few KD parts had been laboriously completed and sent to Douglas Tulsa but were rejected because of poor workmanship.

Willow Run's first acceptance was in July 1942 when two KD kits were produced. The next month, there were no acceptances, but in September, Willow Run turned out two KD kits and two complete bombers. During that fall, production accelerated very slowly, and by the end the year, Willow Run had produced only twenty-four complete aircraft and ten sets of KD assemblies. These bombers, although accepted as airworthy, did not meet the changing combat standards and the AAF decided to operate them for training. There were various reasons for this slow acceleration, while some were a continuation of pre-production problems discussed previously, others occurred as the project developed over the next years.

1) Willow Run was particularly designed for mass production with its successful operation requiring that every tool be in place, a store of manufactured parts on hand, and each part so accurately fabricated that fitting it to other parts would be a comparatively straightforward procedure. Willow Run was undoubtedly far more dependent upon the completeness of production preparations than the average aircraft plant with its trained shop men.
2) During this point of preparation for production, Ford's emphasis on manufacturing was to be detrimental to assembly. Ford's plan was that by using accurately-made

parts and accurate assembly fixtures, the Liberator assembly would be relatively straightforward. However, soon it was found that even under ideal conditions, assembly definitely was not a trouble-free process. Assembly slowed down so badly in the fall of 1942 that Ford was lent several assembly lead men and supervisors from Consolidated and other West Coast aircraft manufacturers to help the Willow Run assembly lines get into satisfactory operation.

3) Many other fundamentals of the Ford production plan were found to be faulty and needed to be revised. The hard metal dies were not accurate because of greater spring-back of aluminum compared with steel and had to be reworked, this, however, did not cause any significant delays in production. The 100 percent pre-piercing of rivet holes were impractical because of accumulated minor engineering and production errors and the expansion and shrinkage of the metal due to temperature changes. The punching of undersize holes in certain pieces so that they would provide a drilling pattern in assembly to other pieces was substituted. Ford's production control system was wholly inadequate to meet the demands of the constantly fluctuating production requirements.

4) The Detroit area's supposedly unlimited supply of skilled workers was being rapidly absorbed by the conversion of that city's industrial plants to war production. Moreover, Willow Run's isolated location placed it in a particularly poor situation to compete for the declining source of workers and the later rationing of gasoline and tires made it difficult to lure workers. Ford management acted quickly and determinedly in initiating a recruiting program, not only throughout Michigan but throughout other parts of the country, that was a difficult task.

5) Because of the decline in the quality of workmanship and increasing shortage of workers, Ford's plan for only limited sub-contracting was reassessed, and throughout the fall of 1942, the necessity for outside supplementary production became obvious.

6) After the first few months of operation Ford's worker training programs were revealed to be insufficient leading to a decrease in new worker proficiency. Shortcomings in the training program were found and the program was reorganized, but it would require several months for the changes to become effective.

7) Many of Ford's supervisors were transferred to Willow Run from company branch plants and agencies. Some Rouge Plant foremen without aircraft experience and some Ford salesmen without any supervisory or aircraft experience transferred to Willow Run. It was not until the spring of 1943 that supervisor training began, and meanwhile, supervisory deficiencies would add to Willow Run's production problems.

8) The exigencies of production trumped inspection, consequently problems evolving from poor workmanship could not be satisfactorily resolved. There was no control over scrapped items and salvage and production would commonly commandeer this type of material and use it to build aircraft.

9) The design, or stress-analysis group, that Ford created to "double check" its production engineers overlapped the functions of prime design contractor,

Consolidated, and sometimes even attempted to appropriate Consolidated's design perquisites. The AAF also contributed to the ambiguities concerning design responsibility by authorizing Ford to make certain design changes.

10) Worker morale at Willow Run was poor for a variety of reasons, of which housing, transportation inadequacies, and the management's uninspired labor policy were primary.

Reorganization at Willow Run

At the end of 1942, about twenty-two months after Project A approval, Willow Run's best production was only eleven bombers a month. Finally, the AAF insisted something be done and an extensive reorganization was launched early in 1943.

The main points of this reorganization were:

1) On 1 January 1943, after repeated AAF requests to institute acceptable local management at Willow Run, Henry Ford named Mead Bricker, an experienced Ford production man, as general manager and Logan Miller as plant superintendent. This change removed Willow Run from the "small plant" class in the Ford dominion and for the first time gave it recognized local management. More than any other single action, this change improved conditions at the stagnant Willow Run Plant and directed it toward palpable production. Bricker forcefully confronted the plant's many problems and was instrumental in implementing many of the improvements to be listed below.
2) The B-24 liaison committee's engineering sub-committee had reported that Willow Run engineering was being poorly conducted, causing the complete revamping of Ford's engineering procedure. Within a few months, W. F. Pioch, former tool engineering head, assumed control over all engineering; W. F. DeGroat, who had headed design engineering, left the Ford organization, after which decreased emphasis was placed on the design function; Edward Scott, who had headed production engineering was transferred to San Diego as liaison representative with Consolidated; the production engineering department was organized along functional lines; and engineering change control was removed from purchase specifications and transferred to production engineering.
3) At the AAF's request selected purchasing functions were moved from the River Rouge Plant to Willow Run. Improvements were made in the method of production control and scheduling, material, and stock control.
4) The AAF also insisted that a sub-contracting program be investigation and its foundation be laid. An extensive sub-contracting program was put into effect in the fall of 1943.
5) Supervisor training was initiated, and an extensive supervisor retraining program was undertaken.
6) The subordination of inspection to production was terminated, and the inspection department was strengthened. A salvage board and quality control division were

created to promote an improved relationship between production and inspection.
7) An adequate employee morale-raising program was presented and accepted. Orientation periods were initiated, counselors provided, and a public address system was installed. While this program was somewhat beneficial, it was begun too late to be really effective and the shortcomings of inadequate housing and transportation, long hours, etc., were too much to be overcome completely.

On 1 January 1943, Henry Ford (L) named Mead Bricker, an experienced Ford production man, as general manager. (*FAM/AAF*)

19

Willow Run Crises

Production Crisis

For Ford to mass produce Liberators depended on their successful collaboration with Consolidated and the aircraft industry, which Ford complicated by insisting on being a licensee for complete aircraft instead of remaining as a sub-contractor. Because of Willow Run's slow start in late 1942, the War Production Board's new Aircraft Production Board (APB) considered bringing in Consolidated Manager Charles Perrelle who was experienced in aircraft assembly line techniques. But instead, the APB compelled Ford to initiate new management procedures that were to succeed before the end of January 1943 otherwise the government would bring in outside personnel.

During the summer of 1943, Willow Run was experiencing production problems that were not only caused by conflicting production expectations but also as a disagreement over production methods and manpower. As early as 1941, the AAC had promoted production schedules that Willow Run engineers considered as unworkable. In early September 1941, Roscoe Smith sent a draft contract to the AAC at Wright Field that included a schedule for manufacturing the first KDs in May 1942, with a monthly peak production of 130 KDs to be attained in March 1943. Smith estimated that the first "built unit" would be ready in September 1942 and reach ten per month by March 1943, but maximum production of seventy-five complete bombers per month would not occur until October 1943. Smith was "of the opinion that from a manufacturing point of view, it (this schedule) could be satisfactorily met." However, Wright Field's contract section maintained that Willow Run could reach full production earlier and requested that complete unit production begin in May 1942 and reach seventy-five complete bombers per month in February 1943, which was eight months earlier than Smith thought possible. After deliberation, Ford management responded that, while they "preferred" their own schedule, they would "endeavor" to meet AAC expectations. The Air Corps' contract section wrote the contract with Smith's lower production estimates, but Ford's top management, under a self-imposed need to impress the AAC and to prove Ford's mass production methods, insisted that Wright Field rewrite the contract with the more ambitious production goals. Ford promised the Office of Production Management (OPM) that they could meet the accelerated delivery schedule providing the company did not "run into difficulties on matters controlled by others, such as the labor situation or the availability of Government Furnished Equipment items." During 1942, the first year of the war, the AAF continually accelerated production expectations for Willow Run. In January 1942, the 405 Contract scheduled peak production consisting of 255 KD kits and 150 complete bombers for November 1943. In the April 1942 revision, peak production moved to August 1943, while the August 1942 revision moved peak production up to July 1943. As of December 1942, however, Ford still forecasted peak production for November 1943. It should be noted that Smith's original October 1943 production schedule would be a surprisingly accurate forecast.

In late 1942, the AAF and the Aircraft Production Board (APB) approved a new production schedule, Schedule 8-L, which established production schedules based on political objectives rather than manufacturing expectations. With Schedule 8-L, the APB set production goals that were to help meet President Roosevelt's January 1942 directive for 125,000 aircraft manufactured in America in 1943 that was also cited in his State of the Union address. Schedule 8-L put the APB in an armaments planning Catch-22: whether to use its stated goals to goad aircraft industry production and to satisfy the politicians or use the realistic production goals? The APB moved ahead with Schedule 8-L, even though it was fully aware that materials and particularly, manpower, were unavailable to meet the demands of Schedule 8-L.

The APB instructed William Knudsen, the War Department's APB representative, to examine the companies "where the maximum effort must be made to accelerate production" in order to meet Schedule 8-L goals. He concluded that Douglas and Ford should apply their maximum effort, which caused Ford and the APB to continually be at odds over production schedules during the first three quarters of 1943.

Knudsen was a knowledgeable representative as he had worked first for Ford where he became an expert on mass production and a skilled manager. After leaving Ford, Knudsen became president of General Motors' Chevrolet Division from 1924 to 1937 and then served as General Motors' president from 1937 to 1940. In 1940, President Roosevelt appointed Knudsen as chairman of the OPM and member of the National Defense Advisory Commission. In January 1942, Knudsen was commissioned as a lieutenant general in the U.S. Army and was appointed as the War Department's director of production and undersecretary of war, Robert Patterson's troubleshooter. In both positions, Knudsen used his vast manufacturing experience to help America to become a wartime industrial behemoth. Total U.S. military aircraft production for the year 1939 was less than 3,000 aircraft, and by the end of the war, it had expanded 100 fold to over 300,000 aircraft.

The War Department's December 1942 proposed 405 Contract, part of Schedule 8-L, delayed peak production until December 1943 but increased the plant's maximum monthly delivery of complete aircraft from 150 to 405. Sorensen, knowing that Ford could not meet the increase, requested a reduction, but Brig. Gen. Arthur Vanaman at Wright Field refused: "It is realized that tremendous effort must be expended on the part of the Ford Motor Company to achieve the 8-L delivery schedule. But it is likewise felt that the company is equal to the challenge given in the schedule."

In March 1943, Sorensen contacted Knudsen to complain that, in reference to Schedule 8-L, "there has been no definite understanding on any program like this." Sorensen made it clear that the disputed production numbers and accelerated peak production could not be met. In July, after being given an advance copy of the Truman Committee report critical of Willow Run, Sorensen defended the plant's record and asked that the report not imply "that all this expansion was expected to go into Willow Run."

During March 1943, the AAF chose Ford to incorporate changes gathered from combat reports into a model change from the B-24E to the B-24H, leaving Consolidated to continue to produce the B-24D (the Ford B-24E equivalent). The AAF wanted fifty Ford B-24Hs by 1 July, but neither the design nor the equipment to be provided by outside suppliers had yet been finalized. In order to deliver six B-24Hs in June and forty-two in July, Ford was forced to fabricate parts by hand, while simultaneously retooling for full mass production. Once completed, the AAF immediately sent these improved Liberators into combat over Europe.

At that time, labor contended that Ford mismanagement not labor was the cause for H Model production delays ridiculously asserting that "the newspaper announcements that the assembly line for bombers at Willow Run was in full operation and planes were being turned out so many per day, were all fakes" and that "old man Henry Ford's decision to keep adequate worker's housing away from Willow Run" was because "he plans to tear down the place when the emergency is over and return the land to his dearly beloved squirrels."

Truman Committee Investigation

In late 1942, there were reports that the Ford Willow Run Bomber Plant was not meeting its production schedule, and the media began to refer to the plant as "Willit Run?" Not helping the situation was that neither Ford, the government, nor the AAF would release any production figures because the plant, in fact, did not come even close to meeting AAF expectations to the embarrassment of everyone. The original October 1941 contract mandated September 1942 production to have reached thirty-six KDs and twenty complete bombers per month. Actually, during the entire last half of 1942, Willow Run built only twenty-four complete bombers and ten KDs. The May 1943 monthly peak production of 150 complete aircraft and 255 KDs scheduled in the 405 Contract was obviously unachievable.

With the (non) production rumors gaining credence, the War Production Board publicly acknowledged that Willow Run had "fallen short of its goals," concluding that "Willow Run exemplifies the manpower problems of Detroit, a shortage of highly skilled machinists who are key men and a tremendous turnover of workers because of housing and transportation congestion."

Reacting to the reports of missed production deadlines, the Senate Special Committee Investigating the National Defense Program, popularly known as the "Truman Committee," scheduled an inspection tour of the plant. The Truman Committee was a bipartisan Congressional investigative body formed in March 1941 and headed by Missouri Senator Harry S. Truman. The committee was charged with finding and correcting problems in U.S. war production: waste, inefficiency, and war profiteering. The Truman Committee was to launch one of the most successful investigative efforts ever by the U.S. government, with an initial budget of $15,000 that expanded over next three years to $360,000 yearly; the Truman Committee saved an estimated $10–15 billion in military spending and the lives of thousands of U.S. servicemen.

The Truman Committee had conducted earlier hearings on 22 July 1942 regarding the reduced Willow Run housing program. However, at that time the committee's senators were mainly interested in the strategic materials used in constructing housing, and their transportation and utility systems. Only days before the Truman Committee's 19 February 1943 visit, the Office of War Information (OWI) issued its appraisal of the plant's problems, both to anticipate what the Truman Committee would find and to give the public reassurance that all four assembly lines were now in production. The OWI Report found that workforce problems, housing and transportation conditions, the slow delivery of materials, the method that Ford tooled the plant, and the multitude of design changes ordered by the AAF had all contributed to the plant's production problems. Also, mentioned was that Ford had agreed not to "poach" the skilled workforce of other aircraft plants and that its workforce required intensive training, which made high employee turnover especially costly. The OWI also released photographs of the plant's assembly lines showing B-24s lined up from one end to the other, which gave the impression that Willow Run was in full production. In commenting on the OWI Report, *Business Week* concluded that "after a siege of growing pains which almost shattered the Ford myth ... Willow Run Runs."

Ford received advanced notice that the Truman Committee was going to investigate allegations that the plant was hoarding materials and that worker housing and transportation was substandard. Ford anticipated that the committee would be particularly interested in the Ford mass production assembly line, and that the company's firm resolve on installing full production line methods had actually slowed production and would make it difficult if not impossible to adapt to future design changes. Ford considered the Truman Committee visit as an opportunity to correct the committee's pre-conceptions about Willow Run and to demonstrate the viability of the mass production of aircraft.

During the tour of the factory, Ford officials seemed to have impressed the committee's senators and persuaded them to delay any conclusions about the company's production methods. After the tour, Washington Democrat Senator Mon Wallgren, a known sympathizer for his home state Boeing Aircraft Company, stated: "Willow Run compares very favorably with any plant in the country on actual work being done." Newly elected Republican Michigan Senator Homer Ferguson stated this about his home state industry: "We might say at this time that the Willow Run

Truman Committee. *Left to right*: Senators Homer Ferguson (R. senator, Michigan), Harold Burton (R. senator, Ohio), Senator Harry Truman (chairman D. senator, Missouri), Thomas Connally (D. senator, Texas), and Ralph Brewster (R. senator, Maine). (*NA*)

Charles Sorensen (L) meeting with Harry Truman considered the Truman Committee's visit as an opportunity to correct the committee's preconceptions about Willow Run and to demonstrate the viability of the mass production of aircraft. (*FAM/AAF*)

Plant is not as bad as painted by some, and not too bad when measured against the job undertaken." Ford officials expressed their concerns about the labor situation to the committee, and at breakfast with the senators, Edsel Ford appealed directly to Senator Truman, asking for Federal assistance to fill the thousands of open positions at Willow Run.

A May 1943 article in *Flying Magazine* stated:

> The Truman Committee, which came to Detroit with blood in its eye, felt better after touring the plant and talking to Ford officials, and left with the pronouncement that Willow Run compares favorably with any other airplane plant in the country as far as actual production work is concerned; and we have seen them all.

The Truman Committee took no further formal actions or ordered any official testimonies from Henry or Edsel Ford as they had against Glenn L. Martin personally but would "keep a watchful and skeptical eye on Willow Run."

Ford and the 1943 Detroit Race Riots

During June 1943, a heatwave enveloped Detroit and racial tensions flared. This was a period of dramatic population increase associated with the defense buildup as Detroit's auto industry was converted to the war effort; nearly 400,000 migrants, both black and white, came from the south from 1941 to 1943 and were competing for jobs and housing in an already crowded city, where ethnic immigrants also competed for jobs and housing. Although whites had long worked with blacks in the same plant, during June 1943, Packard Motor Car Company finally promoted three blacks to work next to whites in the assembly lines, in abiding with the anti-segregation policy required for the defense industry. In response, 25,000 whites staged a wildcat strike that slowed critical war production.

Meanwhile, Ford workers sweltered, rumors grew that violence was about to break out in Ford's factories after racial tensions had smoldered for months. On the hot and humid morning of 20 June 1943, foremen at Willow Run and the Rouge stopped work and walked off the job, complaining of poor conditions and intimidation by Harry Bennett's service men. State and local police were called to the factory and carefully maintained the labor–management standoff. But as dusk fell, word came that a fight between blacks and whites had broken out in downtown Detroit and autos full of men sped from the Rouge and Willow Run Plants and headed toward the downtown and inner city where the riot was escalating.

The riots and looting lasted for three days until Detroit Mayor Edward Jeffries and Governor Harry Kelly asked Roosevelt to restore order by ordering 6,000 Federal troops to Detroit on 22 June. During the riots thirty-four people were killed, twenty-five black and most at the hands of police or National Guardsmen; 433 were wounded, 75 percent of them black while property worth $30 million (2021 USD) was destroyed, most of it in black areas. Simultaneously, there were also racial riots

The Detroit riots continued for three days until Roosevelt restored order by ordering 6,000 Federal troops to Detroit. During the riots, thirty-four people were killed and 433 were wounded, mostly black. (*NA*)

in Los Angeles, which had a burgeoning defense industry; Mobile, Alabama; and Beaumont, Texas. Roosevelt's administration had prohibited racial segregation among federal defense contractors in an effort to improve opportunities for all citizens during the war effort. At Ford there was no such confrontation as Bennett's service men had kept tight control of the situation with minor disruption.

20

Period of Rapid Production Acceleration

Beginning early in 1943, Willow Run finally achieved rapid production acceleration and subsequently, until peak production was reached in March 1944, there were only two breaks in this rapid upward production trend. One break occurred in June and July 1943, when production fell off sharply primarily as a result of the "801 Change." The other came in November 1943, when production increased only by a few bombers over October, which was mainly due to the temporary disruption caused by the dispersal of a substantial amount of work to sub-contractors.

As described earlier, the 801 Change (B-24E to H) was a rush change ordered by the AAF which consisted of separate master changes that were significant enough to temporarily disrupt the entire Willow Run production process. A technical order change grounding aircraft pending changes in the fuel system also was responsible to suppress production at the time of the 801 Change. Except for these two periods, however, Willow Run production increased without interruption throughout 1943 and the early part of 1944; then, beginning in March 1944 production was intentionally leveled off because the AAF no longer required larger numbers of bombers.

While this rapid acceleration was facilitated by increased worker efficiency and the "passing of the shakedown stage" in the huge plant, it was also largely due to the management and department reorganization and the increase in outside Ford production and by sub-contractors.

Ford and Willow Run Management

The Management Plan

Ford decided to operate Willow Run as one of its so-called "Small Plants" under the direct control of the superintendent of small plants, with top management and virtually all staff functions, such as purchasing, engineering, material control, etc., centered in the River Rouge Plant, and with only nominal authority delegated to the plant officials at Willow Run.

This management plan was in no way affected by early indecisions as to whether Ford would be limited to manufacture of KD bombers for assembly elsewhere, or would produce complete bombers as well. However, Ford had hoped to build complete aircraft and planned accordingly and consequently, Ford would not have to revise its management plan when, within a relatively few months, Willow Run production would be expanded to include assembled bombers.

Originally Ford had decided to depend mainly on its own production workmen for B-24 manufacture but, also, to employ aeronautical engineers to check on them considering their lack of experience in aircraft design and production. Beginning in March 1941, to acquaint Ford personnel with aircraft production, a representative group of 200 key men in engineering, tooling, production, purchasing, plant layout, inspection, etc. were posted to Consolidated, San Diego on visits that continued through the fall and largely were considered "quite successful."

Initial Organization

Because of Ford's dislike of organization charts and titles, the original management organization of Willow Run and its relationship to upper management at the River Rouge Plant is difficult to determine in any detail. From the information available, Ford management appears to have been organized as follows:

1) Functions such as purchasing and contract coordination were controlled entirely at the River Rouge Plant.
2) Departments such as payroll, material control, employment, and personnel were retained at the Rouge Plant but small branch offices were opened at Willow Run.
3) Engineering, tool design, etc., were set up in the airframe building at Dearborn, since space was not available at the Rouge Plant.
4) Engineering was organized in two groups:
    a) Design engineering under W. F. DeGroat, an aeronautical engineer hired from the outside.
    b) Production or process engineering under Edward Scott, head of the body engineering department.
    Engineering changes were managed by a third group: purchase specifications.
5) Willow Run, as one of the "small plants" was placed under Roscoe Smith, superintendent of small plants. Under him were two plant superintendents:
    a) Walter Wagner, in charge of the manufacturing area and sub-assembly.
    b) Walter Johnson, in charge of final assembly.
    Also assigned to the plant and seemingly under Smith was Logan Miller, who supervised the development of production methods and tooling.
6) Various Ford officials from the Rouge Plant were assigned to Willow Run on a part-time basis to provide their expertise in the operation of that plant.

Edsel Ford, who died in May 1943, spent substantial time at Willow Run until his health began to fail at the end of 1942. Of course, Charles Sorensen, vice president in charge of production for the entire Ford domain, was closely associated with the

Willow Run Project. While occasionally visiting the plant, Henry Ford did not play an active role there because of his age, but as in other Ford operations, his mere specter remained an authoritative influence. The powerful, Henry Ford-backed Harry Bennett supervised security and labor relations and, as the trusted confidant, frequently represented Henry Ford on policy matters. The retention of control at River Rouge and the activity of leading Ford officials in the actual operation of Willow Run limited Roscoe Smith's role to that of a plant superintendent, even though as this program developed he spent almost full time at Willow Run.

This concept of management, while probably satisfactory for Ford's other normal operations, was shown to be unsatisfactory at Willow Run; first, because of the size and complex character of the Project A and second, because of the necessity for an inordinate amount of outside coordination and control. Among the disadvantages of this arrangement were:

1) The lack of centralized authority and the absence of a compact, clearly defined organization, which "worked against the development of team spirit and unity of purpose at Willow Run."
2) Production problems on the complex and rapidly changing B-24 were so numerous and so convoluted that the effort to control the entire Willow Run operation from the Rouge Plant created a "bottleneck" within the Ford organization.
3) The AAC, in its need to control a number of matters related to Liberator production was obstructed by the absence of an autonomous organization at Willow Run and the necessity to consult with officials at both Willow Run and River Rouge.
4) Coordination with Consolidated on the huge quantity of engineering and production data was thwarted by the lack of any independent management structure at Willow Run.

However, it was not until after America entered the war, when Willow Run's production schedule had been raised from 205 to 405 bombers per month, that there was any revision on the original management plan. Then, early in 1942, after plans were laid for expansion of the manufacturing department and extension of the assembly line, Ford upper management also decided to transfer some of the staff functions to Willow Run. Among the departments moved gradually during the balance of 1942 were process engineering, design engineering, tool design (both from Dearborn), payroll, material control, employment, and personnel (all from River Rouge).

Several factors were involved in this first move toward centralization at Willow Run with probably the single most important factor being the lack of space at the Rouge Plant and Dearborn because of increase in other war work at those plants. Other influencing factors were the AAF's continual pressure for more autonomy at Willow Run and the realization that with this expanded program, consolidation of the management functions at Willow Run promised increased efficiency. This change did not affect such important functions as purchasing and contract coordination, which remained at the Rouge Plant. Nor was there any attempt to provide Willow Run with independent management—a deficiency that became increasingly serious as the plant slowly began production.

During the latter part of 1942, Edsel Ford's health began to fail and he was unable to spend much time at Willow Run. Sorensen, whose production talent had played a large part in the prodigious task of tooling up for aircraft mass production, thus became the principal figure in its operation. Sorensen, a demanding production man with little sympathy for anything or anyone that threatened to interfere with production, continually battled the requirements for engineering changes and inspection. Finally, late in December 1942, in response to repeated requests, Henry Ford informed AAF representatives that he would depart from custom and specifically assign a new "No. 1 and No. 2 man" to Willow Run, and that the cantankerous Sorensen would be withdrawn from active participation in the Willow Run Project.

21

The Passing of Edsel Ford and Its Aftermath

Edsel Ford Passes

On 26 May 1943, the forty-nine-year-old Edsel Ford died of stomach cancer and the ailing eighty-one-year-old Henry Ford reassumed the presidency, a position he had not held since 1919. By this point in his life, the elder Ford was mentally unreliable, distrusting, and no longer adequate for the job, which caused most of the company's directors to not want him as president. However, for the previous two decades, although he had long been without any official executive title, he always had been in *de facto* control over the company as the board and the management had never seriously confronted him and now was no different as the directors elected him as company president and he would continue to serve, ineffectively, until the end of the war. During this period, the company began to seriously decline, losing over $10 million a month, and caused the Roosevelt Administration to consider a government takeover in order to ensure continued war production. Influential journalist and radio commentator Drew Pearson, who wrote the syndicated column *Washington Merry Go Round*, fueled the fire when he suggested that Henry Ford was too old to run his company and Roosevelt was prepared to take over Ford at any moment.

Upon his passing, Edsel had left behind a massive Ford wartime empire manufacturing bombers, aircraft engines, superchargers, gliders, tanks, tank engines, trucks, Jeeps, generators, gun mounts, and a huge inventory of spare aircraft and tank parts. Without Edsel and with elder Henry in control, there was no competent top echelon leadership and the Ford Motor Company was left without effective direction. There was discontent in upper echelon management and engineering; racial tensions in the factories and Detroit were high; while important income and all communication with Ford factories in Axis territories had long been severed.

On 26 May 1943, the forty-nine-year-old Edsel Ford died of stomach cancer and the ailing eighty-one-year-old Henry Ford (seen at the funeral with wife, Clara) reassumed the company presidency. (*FAM/AAF*)

Henry Ford II: (Only) Ford Motor Company Heir Apparent

When President Edsel Ford died in May 1943, Edsel's oldest son, the twenty-five-year-old Henry Ford II, was serving in the Navy and was thus unable to take over the presidency of the family-owned business controlled by his grandfather, Henry I. Henry Ford II was born in Detroit on 4 September 1917 and after graduation from the Hotchkiss School in Lakeville, Connecticut in 1936, he attended Yale University, where he specialized in sociology, a study that would palpably influence him. He lacked sufficient credits to graduate but left college anyway in 1940 to marry and begin work at the family automobile business. In 1941, Ford was drafted and became an ensign at the Great Lakes Naval Training School. Meanwhile, under the autocratic control of his grandfather financial conditions at Ford, which had been losing money, had deteriorated even further with the death of Ford II's father, Edsel, in 1943. President Roosevelt's Cabinet deactivated Ford II from the Navy, allowing him to assist in managing the company at the age of twenty-five, a situation for which he had little preparation.

After he was returned to Ford management, Ford II received little help from his grandfather and was given few duties. The young Ford studied his father's papers and files and was fortunate that Sorensen took an interest in him and advised him to "be seen around the factory." With no job responsibilities as such, Henry II dedicated himself to ousting Harry Bennett who, in his memoirs, Ford considered "a dirty, lousy SOB." However, after Edsel died, there was no protection from Bennett and his henchmen, and Henry II and the old-line Edsel "loyalists" were left vulnerable. During the first weeks after Edsel's death, several of Ford's top engineers, who had shown allegiance to Edsel, left the company. William Pioch who had headed Willow Run tool design, threatened to resign as he no longer felt he had any respect or influence, but Ford II convinced Pioch to remain on as favor to him and his father. Nonetheless, the departure of Edsel-loyalists, such as long-time, prominent Ford "auto men" Joseph Galamb and Laurence Sheldrick, continued and they were replaced by "Bennett men." The Ford power struggle became so apparent that the June 1944 *Fortune Magazine* published a long feature article that stated:

> In Detroit today, a casual passing mention of the Ford name will elicit tales and elaborations of tales about portentous goings-on inside the Ford empire.... A visitor to Detroit encounters them everywhere. They all say that Henry Ford, who will be eighty-one on July 30, is dominated by Harry Bennett, the man who has run Ford's private police for more than 20 years, and that all Ford executives who would not bend the knee to Bennett have 'resigned.'

Edsel, with mother, Clara, and father, Henry, virtually ran the company, and with his death, the company was left without effective direction; in the power struggle that followed, Clara would back Henry II relentlessly. (*FAM/AAF*)

Henry Ford II. (*FAM/AAF*)

Henry Ford II Postscript

On 21 September 1945, after Sorensen's tutelage and shelter and much perseverance, Henry II was finally able to win his grandfather's confidence and become the president of a chaotic, tenuous organization with its domestic sales in decline and facing the bleak prospect of a post-war revamping. To make matters worse, Ford's profitable pre-war European factories were destroyed. Once Henry Ford II became company president, to compensate for his lack of experience, he wisely began recruiting a skilled management team of ten young "up-and-comers," known as the "Whiz Kids." By 1949, the company had been revitalized and restructured and had introduced its renowned new 1949 model auto that was considered comparable to the Model T and Model A. During the 1950s, Ford moved into second place in automobile sales behind General Motors and became the industry's leader in product innovation. During 1956, under his leadership, the company became a publicly traded corporation. By 1960, Henry Ford assumed one-man control reminiscent of that of his grandfather as when he resigned the presidency, he became CEO and was also elected chairman. He resigned as CEO in October 1979 and as chairman in 1980. On 1 October 1982, upon reaching the company's mandatory retirement age of sixty-five, he formally retired from all positions at Ford but remained the "ultimate source of authority" at Ford until his death on 29 September 1987.

Ford Motor Company after the Demise of Edsel Ford

After Edsel Ford died in May 1943, Henry Ford wanted to name Bennett as Ford Motor president, but Clara Ford and Edsel's widow, Eleanor, aggressively opposed the idea and, instead, Bennett joined the board of directors in June 1943. The wily Bennett conspired with the elder Henry Ford to draft a codicil to his will that would effectively give Bennett control of Ford Motor after Henry's death, to the elimination of Ford's grandsons. However, when Henry II, the eldest grandson, became aware of the codicil, his confidant John Bugas confronted Bennett, who then destroyed the document. At this time, the Ford women again intervened and convinced Henry Ford I to give control to Henry II. On 21 September 1945, newly-named President Henry Ford II fired Bennett and thus Bennett departed, ending his bizarre thirty-year career with Ford.

Willow Run after the Demise of Edsel Ford

Edsel's death isolated Sorensen and severely weakened his influence to engage the capriciously willful senior Ford and the cunning Bennett who controlled the elder Ford. While his position with the company was currently secure, Sorensen realized that his days at Ford were eventually numbered and in his memoir stated that "there was only one thing for me to do; see that Henry II stayed on." However, upon Edsel's death, Mead Bricker was named Ford vice president and as the authority and responsibility for Willow Run's operation was increasingly centralized in Bricker, the influence of Sorensen at the plant gradually diminished until in March 1944, he resigned/retired/was forced out from the Ford Motor Company—ironically, just as Willow Run was attaining peak production. While illness from overwork was a factor for his "retirement", it appears that the resignation was largely the outgrowth of an accumulation of AAF complaints about his uncompromising attitude in production matters and an increase in the Bennett–Sorensen rivalry following the death of Edsel Ford. Sorensen then accepted a position as president of automaker Willys-Overland, presiding over the transition from wartime production back to civilian market production. Sorensen retired after clashes with the Willys' board but retained a title and salary as vice chairman from 1946 until full retirement in 1950. Sorensen retired to Florida and U.S. Virgin Islands. He died on 28 August 1968 and is buried in Miami Beach, Florida

Mead Bricker, who was elected as a vice president of the Ford Company upon the death of Edsel Ford in May 1943, was named as Willow Run general manager and for the first time gave the huge bomber factory qualified and recognized top management. Bricker soon corrected many of Willow Run's difficulties and brought the plant into efficient production and greatly diminished the role of Sorensen at Willow Run. Under Bricker, Logan Miller was named plant superintendent, and Roscoe Smith resumed his assignment as supervisor of small plants. Walter Wagner and Walter Johnson were retained in charge of the manufacturing and sub-assembly and final assembly, respectively. In the spring of 1943, engineering, including engineering changes, was consolidated under one head, W. F. DeGroat, and later combined with tooling under William Pioch.

Mead Bricker was elected as a vice president of the Ford Company upon the death of Edsel Ford in May 1943, and then was named as Willow Run general manager. Bricker (R) meets with (L-R) Henry Ford II, Louis Mayer (MGM CEO), and K. T. Keller (Chrysler CEO). (*FAM/AAF*)

The final steps toward the detachment of Willow Run from River Rouge came early in 1943 when, in response to continuing AAF requests, the contract and coordination office and most of the purchasing function were moved to Willow Run. The transfer of purchasing was opposed by A. M. Wibel, vice president in charge of purchasing and consequently he was dismissed early in May 1943.

22

The Fabled Willow Run Production Line

An Improbable Description

The total length of the production line was 5,450 feet with the length of each of the four primary lines being 720 feet with fourteen stations on each. The bays were 150 feet wide and 36 feet high with the transfer bay being 40 feet wide and 16 feet high. The mezzanine between the lines was 15 feet wide. There were 136 separate conveyors in plant powered by seventy-five drive units, which moved material 4,000 feet from the manufacturing section to supply the assembly line. The conveyors used approximately 5,000 feet of chain of which two to four links were removed in hot weather because of expansion of chain. There were sixty-eight traveling cranes of 5- and 15-ton capacity with a combined lifting capacity 520 tons. A total of 309 lifts were made in building a bomber. Some 124,200 feet of cable, ranging in size from three-sixteenths of an inch to $3\frac{1}{8}$ inches in diameter was required for cranes, conveyors, elevators, etc. with over 6,000 feet used for replacement every two weeks. There was 18 total miles of monorail lines in all buildings.

Movement of the Assembly Lines

The assembly line was originally planned as an eight-hour movement for Stations 1–12 inclusive and a four-hour movement for Stations 13–28 inclusive. The time was reduced to under four hours for Stations 1–14 inclusive and two hours for Stations 15–28. A master control panel was located at east end of balcony at K-54 and H-54. A schedule of movement was regulated by final assembly office and was based on production requirements.

There was a steady flow of unit assemblies consisting of preformed parts such as bulkheads, hat stringers, belt frames, floors, bomb and hatch doors, skin and stringer assemblies, fuselage panels, center wing flaps, and tail surfaces. Major units moved in from various departments along conveyors, or by crane, being formed into larger units until; finally, they met up with the center wing section. Similar sub-assemblies were

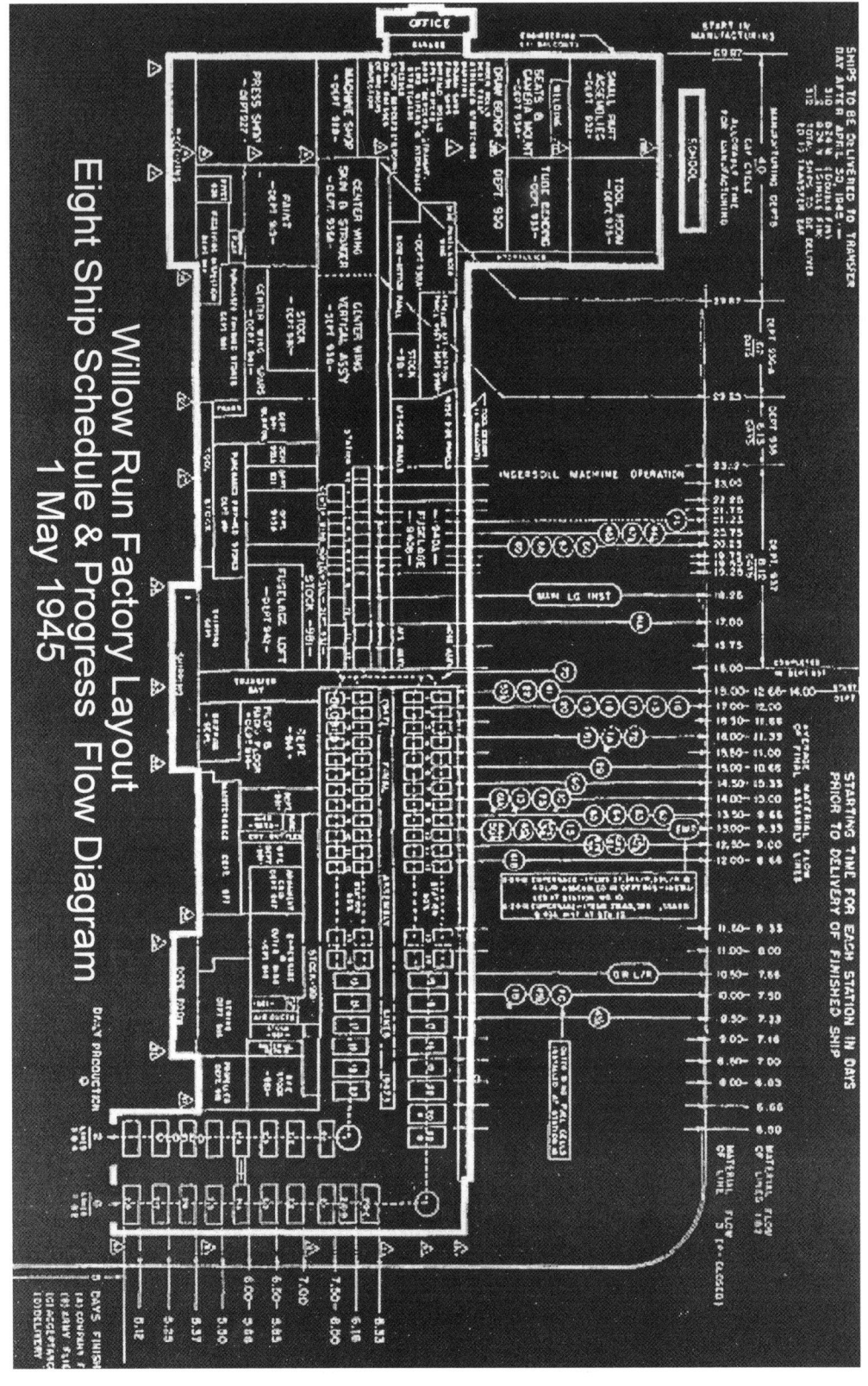

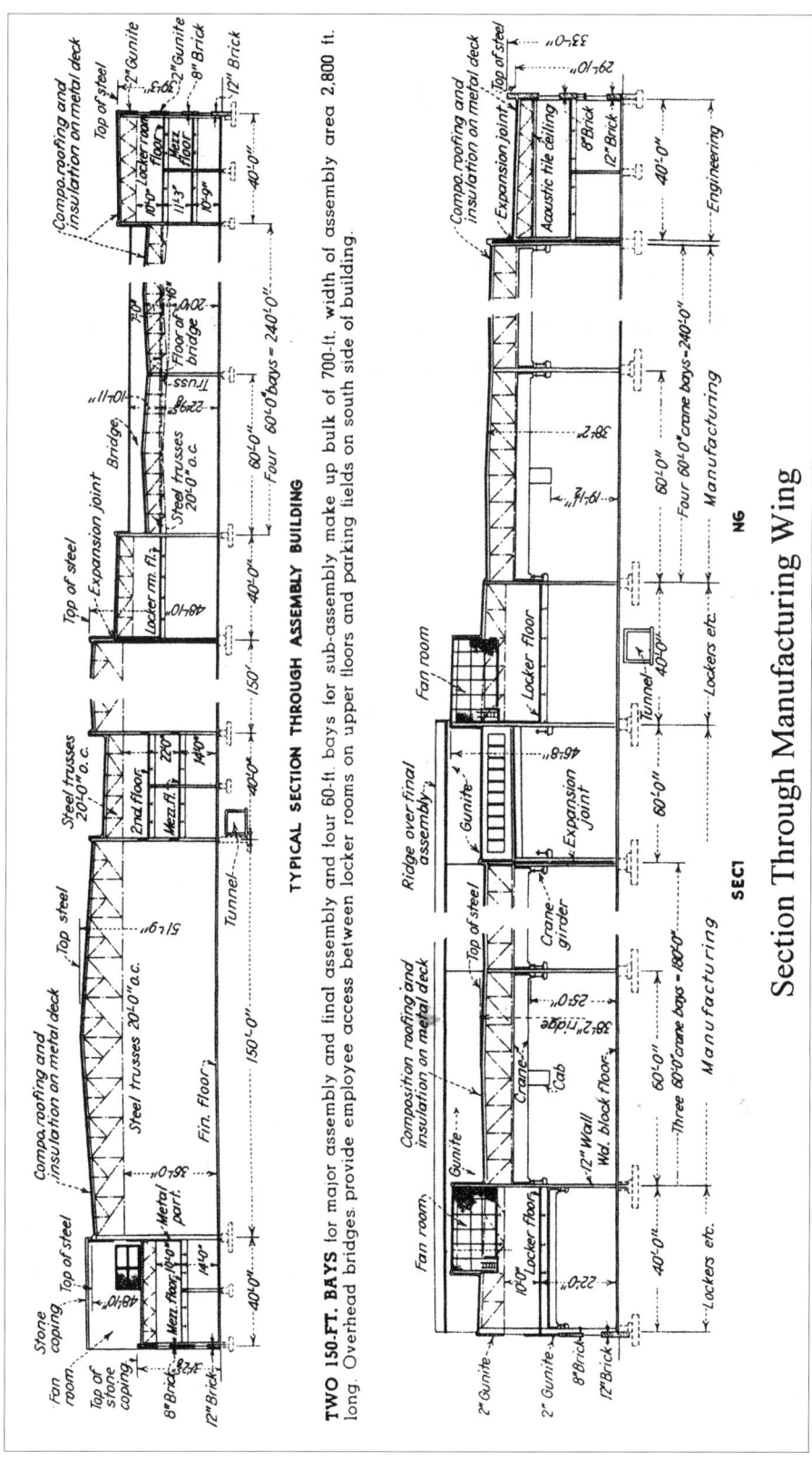

mated as they traveled down the final assembly lines. At other stations, forward and aft fuselage sections were mated to the center wing, the four engines descended from an overhead balcony to be installed. The tail surfaces followed to be installed. Various conveyors, from those moving the center wing section to the ones where the bomber was moved forward by its nose wheel, marked its progress down the line.

The Division of the Fuselage for Mass Production

The main difference between the Consolidated and Ford production lines was in the breakdown in the fuselage. The Ford engineers allocated the fuselage into thirty-three sections with the main nose and tail fuselage sections separated by the center wing. To facilitate mass production, the fuselage was divided into panels that allowed greater access.

The nose enclosure and the pilot's enclosure were natural divisions of the nose fuselage and were broken down into twelve pieces (called the "merry-go-round") that formed around the pilot's floor and included the two top decks, side panels, and a bottom panel.

The long tail fuselage was easily subdivided into four components: a tail cone, a bottom panel, and two side panels, which provided more accessibility for more personnel to work side by side and for easier installation of electrical and hydraulic equipment.

The wing was divided into three main sections, the 55-foot center wing, which extended from one outboard engine to the other and the two outer wing panels. The leading and trailing edges and the wing grips were assembled separately and attached later. Connecting the nose and tail fuselages across the wing were the canopy on top and the bomb bay side panels under the center wing.

Willow Run Manufacturing Section

The manufacturing section had been then key to Ford's automobile mass production and for bomber mass production materials such as Alclad sheet aluminum and castings and forgings were routed from the receiving department through laboratory and inspection departments to this department. Also, this section manufactured many of the necessary parts and sent them to the assembly line. In the layout of the factory, the manufacturing area was located near the first two assembly departments: the center wing skin and stringer and nose-bottom panel departments. The Willow Run manufacturing section was comprised of a number of departments that supplied parts transported by conveyor and delivered first to the plant shop and then to the assembly lines. The manufacturing section included:

The press shop, department 927, manufactured 120,000 pieces daily on 345 presses with fifty-six of the heavy presses ranging in capacity from 150 to 1,000 tons. Thirteen presses (Williams-White and Cincinnati) were hydraulic, ranging in size from 100 to 1,000-ton capacity and required 1,500 gallons of oil as the hydraulic agent. The weight of a 1,000-ton press was 350 tons, which was 320 tons more than the weight of the bomber itself. A press (press brake) is a machine tool used for bending sheet and plate material, most commonly sheet metal. It forms predetermined bends by clamping the workpiece between a matching punch and die. There were 109 Ferracute, Niagara, and Cleveland punch presses which ranged from 30 to 750-ton capacity. A punch press is a machine used to cut holes in material. It can be small and manually operated and hold one simple die set, or be very large with a multi-station turret and hold a much larger and complex die set.

The machine shop, department 928, located on half an acre of floor space in the southwest corner of the factory, produced 25,000 pieces of 500 different parts daily beginning with a part manufactured on a horizontal milling machine on 8 December 1941. There were 220 different types of equipment in the machine shop including lathes, milling machines, drill presses, and screw machines.

Milling is one of the most commonly used processes in industry and machine shops and is accomplished by a wide range of machine tools using rotary cutters to remove material from a workpiece by advancing (or feeding) in a direction at an angle with the axis of the tool.

A lathe is a tool that rotates the workpiece on its axis to perform various operations such as cutting, sanding, knurling (a pattern of straight, angled or crossed lines cut or rolled into the material), drilling, deformation, facing (cutting onto the flat workpiece surface), turning (describes a helix toolpath by moving more or less linearly while the workpiece rotates) with tools that are applied to the workpiece to create an object with symmetry about an axis of rotation.

A drill press is a fixed style of drill that may be mounted on a stand or bolted to the floor or workbench. A drill press consists of a base, column (or pillar), table, spindle (or quill), and drill head, usually driven by an induction motor. The head has a set of handles radiating from a central hub that, when turned, move the spindle and chuck vertically, parallel to the axis of the column into the workpiece.

Screw machines are specialized automated metalworking lathes used to produce large numbers of small identical precision-made parts such as shafts, bolts, screws, and pins. Essentially, they machine components by spinning on a very quickly rotating lathe, which shaves metal down to a desired size.

Draw bench, department 930, manufactured stringers for the wings that employed 300 workers operating 265 machines to manufacture 185,000 parts of 3,700 different types daily. They also rolled 260,000 feet of "Y" stock daily and approximately 5,000,000 parts were formed, stretched, or pierced each month. A draw bench is a machine used to perform cold work on metal, such as changing the shape of the metal by applying only pressure without applying heat.

A stringer, a longeron, or stiffener, is a thin strip of material to which the aircraft skin is fastened. In aircraft fuselage, stringers are attached to formers (also called frames) and run longitudinally to transfer the aerodynamic loads acting on the skin onto the frames and formers. In the wings or horizontal stabilizer, they run span wise and attach between the ribs and transfer the bending loads acting on the wings onto the ribs and spar. Sometimes the terms longeron and stringer are used interchangeably, but there is a subtle difference between the two. If there only a few longitudinal members in a fuselage that run all along the fuselage length (usually four to eight),

Large Williams-White hydraulic press used to form aluminum parts. (*FAM/AAF*)

Cincinnati press brake. (*FAM/AAF*)

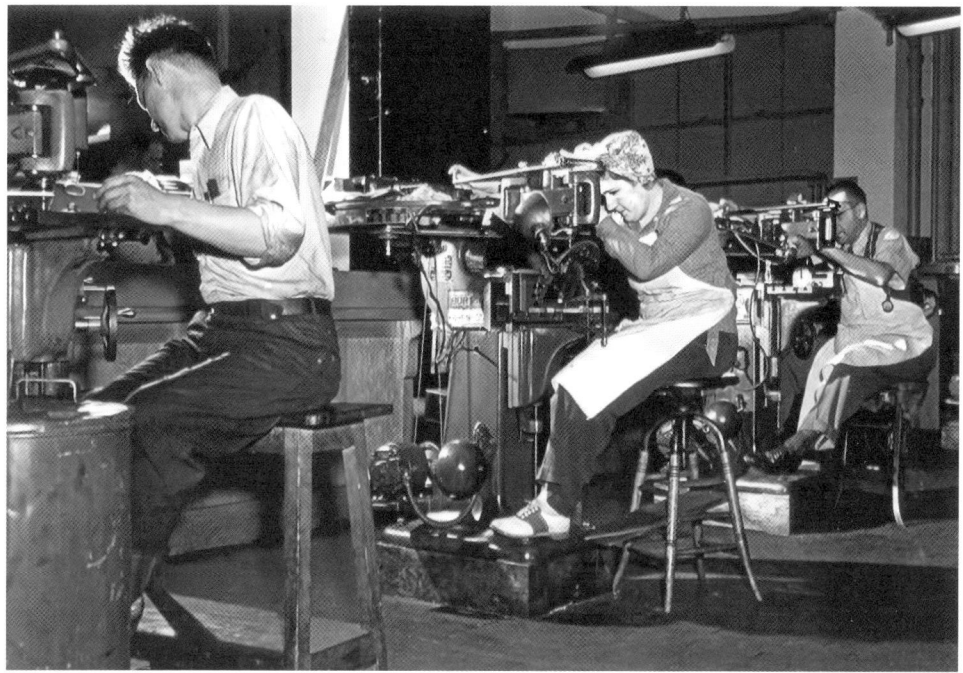

Machine shop. (*FAM/AAF*)

Lathe. (*FAM/AAF*)

Drill press. (*FAM/AAF*)

Screw machine. (*FAM/AAF*)

then they are called longerons. The longeron system also requires that the fuselage frames be closely spaced (about every 4–6 inches). If there are many longitudinal members (usually fifty to 100) and are only placed between two formers/frames, then they are called stringers. In the stringer system, the longitudinal members are smaller and the frames are spaced farther apart (about 15–20 inches). Generally, longerons are of larger cross-section when compared to stringers and often carry larger loads than stringers and also help to transfer skin loads to internal structure. Longerons almost always attach to frames or ribs while stringers often are not attached to anything but the skin, where they carry a portion of the fuselage bending moment through axial loading. It is not uncommon to have a mixture of longerons and stringers in the same major structural component.

Small parts assemblies, department 932, manufactured the Emerson nose turret and numerous small parts such as covered controls, doors, door air ducts, motor nacelles, cowling, and camera mounts. This department occupied more than an acre of floor space in the northwest corner of the manufacturing area.

Rivet department, 926, manufactured nearly two billion rivets (1,921,922,810) during the war or about 7 million per day that were the most numerous of all parts used in building the B-24. There were 313,237 rivets holding a Liberator together, of which 242,752 were required to build the major sections of the bomber: 78,606 were used in the center wing; 22,844 in the outer panel; 126,651 in the fuselage; and 14,651 in the tail assembly. There were 520 different kinds of rivets weighing 530 pounds used in each B-24. They ranged in sizes from one-sixteenth of an inch long (weighing .00005 pounds) to 3¼ inches long (weighing .05 pounds). There were about 100 rivet ice boxes located throughout the plant which kept a two day supply of rivets at temperatures of 10–20 degrees below 0 to keep them from age hardening.

The tool room, department 975, occupying an acre of floor space, was set up in the northeast comer of the manufacturing area as soon as construction permitted in January 1942. By that summer, 350 tool and die makers had moved from Dearborn into Willow Run and most of the 200 pieces of equipment ranging from the simplest of drill presses to a precise engraving machine had been installed.

Tool makers, die makers, mold makers, and tool fitters are machinists who make jigs, fixtures, dies, molds, machine tools, cutting tools, gauges, and other tools used in manufacturing processes. Usually, working from engineering drawings developed by engineers and technologists, tool makers lay out (mark out) the design on the raw material (usually metal), then cut it to size and shape using manually controlled machine tools (such as lathes, milling machines, grinding machines, and jig grinders), power tools (such as die grinders and rotary tools), and hand tools (such as files and honing stones). Tool making usually involves making tooling used to produce products. Common tooling includes metal forming rolls, cutting tools (such as tool bits and milling cutters), fixtures, or even whole machine tools used to manufacture, hold, or test products during their fabrication. Due to the unique nature of a tool maker's work, it is often necessary to fabricate custom tools or modify standard tools. Die making is a sub-category of tool making that mainly involves the making and maintaining of dies, often including the making of punches, dies, steel rule dies, and die sets.

Draw bench. (*FAM/AAF*)

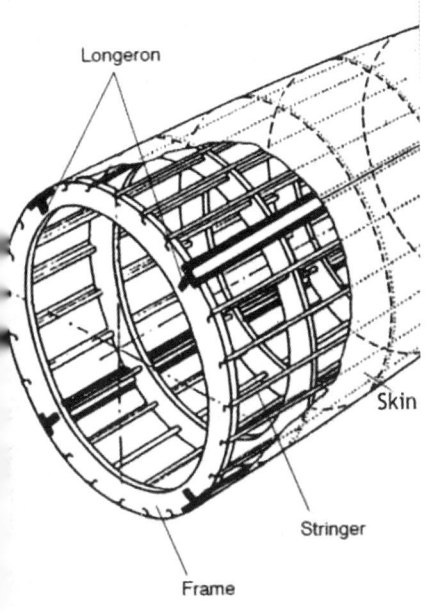

Above left: Stringer. (*Author's collection*)

Above right: Rivet Machine: The rivet department manufactured nearly 2 billion rivets during the war or about 7 million per day. (*FAM/AAF*)

Precision, with tolerances of less than one-thousandth of an inch, is crucial in die making; punches and dies must maintain proper clearance to produce parts accurately. One person often performed all the skills of both, which is why tool and die making is often regarded as one field. Although tool and die training programs varied, most tool and die makers began an apprenticeship with the employer, often including a combination of some classroom training but more hands-on experience. Some prior qualification and proficiency in basic mathematics, science, and an engineering aptitude were considered a valuable asset. Many tool and die makers attended a four- to five-year apprenticeship program to reach the position of a journeyman tool and die maker. (Note: My father was a master tool and die maker from 1940 onward and headed the tool room for the Outboard Marine Corp. prototype department. Since he was considered a vital industrial worker, he was rejected by the Air Corps despite his previous five-year experience training pre-war want-to-be civilian pilots and having multi-engine rating).

 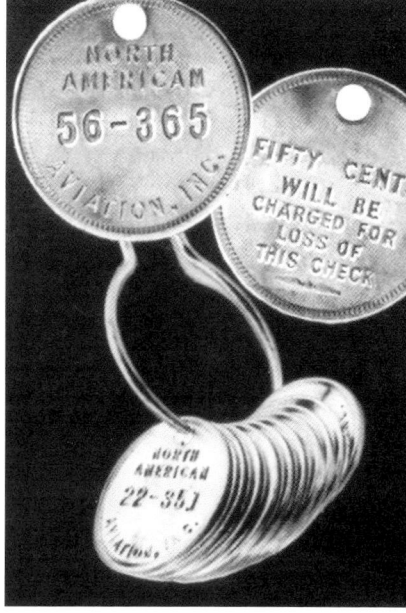

Above left: Tool room. (*FAM/AAF*)

Above right: Tool Check-Out Token: Workers checking out tools from the tool crib were given a metal token to be returned with the tool (there was a $.50 charge for a lost taken). (*FAM/AAF*)

23

The Center Wing Section: The Essence of Liberator Manufacture

The center wing section, about which the B-24 was built, demonstrated Ford's use of jigs, fixtures, mating bucks in its mass production methods on the two 468-foot parallel lines. One of the most important and impressive assembly jigs was the massive apparatus used in assembling the B-24 center wing section, the wing root on both sides, and the heavy structure where these roots joined the fuselage. The 6,652-pound center wing contained twenty-seven different bulkheads, 78,606 rivets, 1,000 bolts, and 6,439 different parts (exclusive of rivets and bolts). When the completed center wing left the vertical fixtures they were less than .01 inch from being perfect.

It took Consolidated thirteen days to set up their center wing fixture, assemble the wing with its large aluminum skins, and then remove it. The center wing fixture required dismantling each time a wing was completed, and before another wing could be built, it had to be reassembled by sighting it in with a transit for alignment. The problem facing Ford's production team was how to reduce this procedure from Consolidated's thirteen days to one hour and maintain accuracy. Riveting the skin and stringers together at a location other than where they were joined to the bulkhead and spar was believed to be impossible by aircraft manufacturers as they considered that large skin surfaces could not be made to fit accurately unless all of the matching and riveting were done on the same fixture. Ford's experience with auto mass production, however, had shown the company that if the preliminary operations were properly oriented and fitted in relation to those that followed, the resulting parts should fit wherever they were assembled. Ford proceeded to divide the wing and skin surfaces into sections, which allowed more employees throughout the factory to work on their particular assembly.

Center Wing Skin and Stringer Assembly (Department 936A)

The first fixtures at the center wing section assembly area were those used to hold the long skin segments for both the upper and lower surfaces of the wing while they were riveted together.

All the jigs, fixtures, and mating bucks were of substantial, robust, long-lasting construction. Much of Ford's production success was due to use of heavy positive mating bucks and rigid fixtures. Ford's use of fixtures is demonstrated in the preparation of a large aluminum sheet for the top skin section of the center wing with pre-drilled riveting holes. The sheet was placed in:

Fixture No. 1: Allowed the rivets to be placed in the holes
Fixture No. 2: Held the skin in place
Fixture No. 3: Held splicer bars in position while they were riveted to the skin
Fixture No. 4: Held stringers in position
Fixture No. 5: Allowed stringers to be riveted to the skin
Fixture No. 6: Allowed the riveting of stringers and splicer bars to each other

The long stringers, made in the draw bench, department 930, were laid out on steel benches constructed of thick metal tops mounted on heavy cast-iron legs with jigs to hold the individual stringers firmly positioned. Because the wings tapered from the center of the wing outward, the stringers also tapered, and the thickness of the B-24 skin varied from .125 inches at the center to .025 inches at the wing tips. Locating points and jigs on the tables allowed workers to readily follow the different angles and junctions for supporting the stringers.

Since the upper surface of the wing applied Bernoulli's principle of lifting forces (slow-moving fluid exert more pressure than a fast-moving fluids), it differed greatly from the lower surface, and so did the assembly operations. One of the important differences was the countersinking of rivet holes to provide a smooth surface for the air to pass over the upper surface.

The upper skin sections were formed of large pieces of rectangular aluminum trimmed to the correct measurement on the routing machines and curved on Farnham forming rollers to conform to the contour of the wing. Farnham rollers were designed for fast accurate forming of leading edge skins and many other sheet metal parts of cylindrical shape, airfoil contours, and other cylindrical and truncated conical shapes used in the aircraft construction. These skins were later blanked and pierced by dies at the Ford River Rouge Plant and returned to Willow Run ready for the assembly. Ten of these sections comprised the upper wing surface and were riveted together on special curved fixtures before being moved and assembled to the stringers.

The skin on the lower wing surface differed from the upper because of the wheel wells into which the wheels were retracted during flight. Directly below and above the wheel wells, the skin had be much thicker than elsewhere to support the stress of the load at these points. There were also a number of small access doors in the under-surface that were routed in the press shop until the skins were blanked and pierced at River Rouge. A total of forty-four pieces of skin were required for the bottom surface of the wing, compared to ten for the upper surface.

After the skin surfaces had been joined together and the stringers correctly prepared, they were placed in a fixture specifically designed to hold the skin and stringers while they were riveted together. From the stringer side, workers drilled through pre-pierced holes in the stringers, through the upper skin surface while another crew working on the opposite side countersank the holes for rivets. Riveters then completed the operation. While performing these operations, workers stood on the electrically controlled platforms that paralleled the sides of the fixtures.

Upon completion of this operation, the skin/stringer sub-assembly was lifted from its fixture by one of the large cranes and moved forward to the center wing vertical fixture.

Center Wing Vertical Assembly (Department 936)

The center wing was the most complex assembly manufactured at Willow Run. The vertical center wing fixtures that joined the stringer and skin sub-assembly to the spars and bulkheads, were considered one of Willow Run's outstanding accomplishments. These huge 70-foot-long, 18-foot-high, and 13-foot-wide fixtures were so complex that they were fabricated in the Ford River Rouge machine shop rather than by an outside contractor. Each fixture weighed 18.44 tons and was supported on individual foundations that kept them from being affected by heat or cold fluctuations of the plant's floor. A flat base ran across the bottom on which seating pins and brackets were used to align the front spar the same position each time. The top carriage located the rear spar. The fixtures were installed in groups of five, covering a distance of 468 feet.

The driving of 78,606 rivets into each center wing made the noise in this department deafening. There were seven sets of these batteries providing for the final assembly of thirty-five center wings at once. A center wing was assembled in these special fixtures using one-sixth of the labor that was used in previous methods where the pre-assembly of sub-components was minimal.

The prefabrication layout benches had layout jigs installed inside a center wing for every part as it was being built to insure that identical assemblies were produced. The complete part and component inventory was stored forward of the center wing vertical assemblies behind the layout benches.

The precision-manufactured spars, stringers, and bulkheads were designed to mate exactly with adjoining parts and were placed vertically in one of the 27-ton cast-iron and steel center wing assembly fixtures. There were forty-three assembly fixtures and forty-three center wings were continuously under some stage of manufacture in order to supply the production line. The metal skin of the center wing was riveted to the stringers in this fixture. The stringers rested on curved uprights in the fixture to ensure the proper contour of the wing. To save time, the fixtures opened at the top to allow removal of the completed center wing without disassembly of the fixture. The wing machining combine and the final wing dress-up station were located in the center behind the vertical fixtures.

While the center wings were in these vertical fixtures, four reference blocks were bolted onto the bottom of the front and rear spar. Later these blocks would be used to locate the wing in the mating fixture when it was joined with the fuselage. Upon completion of the center wing assembly, the end plates were moved back and a motor-driven carriage, on tracks above the fixture, would move its top bridge structure to one side. While the bridge was out of position, an overhead crane lifted the wing from its cradle, freeing it for the next one to be installed. Because this bridge structure was required to locate the spars in exactly the same position each time, it was designed not to sag more than .005 of an inch over a span of nearly 60 feet.

Ford's design of this fixture made it unnecessary to disassemble it and then reassemble it again, reducing Consolidated's down time from 250 man-hours to only one man-hour at Willow Run. Ford's fixture was so efficient that it reduced the number of man-hours to build a center wing section from an estimated 5,500 to 1,728 man-hours at first and reduced the number of fixtures used from ninety-eight to only thirty-five. By the time of the 600th wing center section left the line, the time was reduced to 800 man-hours; the 4,200th was produced in 500 man-hours; and by February 1945, the time was an amazing thirty-five man-hours. When the center wings were removed from the vertical fixtures, their ends were within .01 of an inch of being perfect. This eliminated the need for two milling machines to trim their ends, which was required at Consolidated before they could attach their outer wing.

ASSEMBLY OF THE CENTER WING SECTION

Departments 936, 936A, and 937 showing the entire center wing assembly area. Pre-fabrication benches are in foreground with layout jigs for every part to be assembled, with the completed inventory stored behind the benches and forward of the forty-three center wing vertical fixtures weighing 27 tons, which were in various states of assembly moving toward the rear of the photo. Behind the vertical assemblies are the wing machining combine and final wing dress-up stations. (*FAM/AAF*)

Farnham forming rollers were designed for fast accurate forming of wing leading edge skins and many other sheet metal parts of cylindrical shape. (*FAM/AAF*)

Wing skin sections being riveted together in the center wing fixtures. (*FAM/AAF*)

Precision-crafted stringers, spars, and bulkheads are being vertically-placed in the center wing fixture, which is opened at the top to expedite removal of the completed wing. (*FAM/AAF*)

Center wing vertical assembly. (*FAM/AAF*)

Aluminum skin being riveted to the curved stringers in the fixture. (*FAM/AAF*)

A photo celebrating breaking the record for completing the center wing section. Note that the censor has redacted the hours. (*FAM/AAF*)

Ingersoll Center Wing Milling Machine

The completely assembled center wing was moved by a crane to the Ingersoll center wing milling machine, which was used in assembling the center wing section, the wing root on both sides, and the heavy structure where these roots joined the fuselage. This milling machine was designed by Ford engineers, W. F. Pioch and John Mistele, and built by Ingersoll Milling Machine Co., Rockford, Illinois, at the then enormous cost of $168,500. Originally two machines were ordered but the second was cancelled when one was found to be sufficient. The valuable machine, in cost and time-savings, was completely fenced off and well-guarded. A large supply of spare parts was kept on hand at all times for any type of repairs necessary as a shutdown would have severely disrupted production.

The huge 27-ton Ingersoll machine needed to be supported on individual 10 by 13-foot, cast-steel bases each weighing 12,500 pounds, which rested on four leveling jacks supported on a concrete foundation 18 inches deep, 20 feet wide, 70 feet long. The cast bases were keyed and bolted to each other, and then fastened to hold them in place. The individual castings for the foundation were so precisely cast and finished at the Rouge Plant that the assembly there was only .005-inch variation on the surface of the entire block.

This machine, which was considered to be a special combination fixture and machine tool, performed a total of forty-two operations, which were ultimately completed in thirty-five minutes for 3.5 man-hours (210 minutes) by a crew of six men, supervised by one foreman. The forty-two operations after positioning the wing in the machining fixture included:

1) Mill eight upper engine mounting pads. Eight operations.
2) Mill eight lower engine mounting pads. Eight operations.
3) Drill four three-eighth-inch holes in each of the eight lower engine pads. Eight operations.
4) Drill one thirteen-sixteenth-inch hole in each of the upper engine mounting pads. Eight operations.
5) Bore and spotface four landing gear needle bearings, two on each side. Four operations.
6) Bore and spotface six main landing gear bearings, three on each side. Six operations.
After which the wing was removed from the machining fixture.

Note: A spotface is a machined feature in which a certain region of the workpiece (a spot) is faced (providing a smooth, flat, accurately located surface). This is especially significant on workpieces, cast or forged, where the spotface's smooth, flat, accurately located surface is distinct from the surrounding surface whose roughness, flatness, and location are subject to wider tolerances and thus do not have level of precision machining. The most common application of spotfacing is facing the area around a bolt hole where the bolt's head will sit.

Time wise, the forty-two operations completed in thirty-five minutes included:

Five minutes:	Removing wing from repair bay and locking it in the fixture.
Ten minutes:	Setting up machine, milling and drilling the upper and lower motor mount forging.

Fifteen minutes: Locating machine, boring and spotfacing needle bearing and main landing gear forging.
Five minutes: Unlocking and removing wing from fixture.

All forty-two machining operations were performed to very precise tolerances. The main advantage from a quality standpoint was that all of the holes drilled had to be in perfect alignment with each other, whereas if they were drilled separately rather than one at a time, the possibility of errors was greatly increased. These forty-two operations were completed in 3.5 man-hours whereas the previous method would have required some 500 man-hours. But more than the saving in labor was its gain in accuracy as all four-engined mounting pads could be milled and drilled simultaneously in perfect alignment as could the landing gear bearing holes.

The milling machine increased the efficiency of operations that led to reduce the hours required in time to manufacture the center wing section: Wing #100 (11/12/1942) required 3:45 hours to machine; Wing #500 (4/21/1943) 2:00 hours; Wing #1,000 (7/12/1943) 1:00 hour; Wings #1,500 to #2,000 0:40 minutes; Wings #2,000 onward the average time was thirty-five minutes with a record time of seventeen minutes.

As the wing was removed from the Ingersoll unit, it was turned and moved forward toward the center wing horizontal department. The turning of the wing was accomplished by the use of one crane equipped with two hooks. One hook held the wing by a lifting strap bolted to center of the wing, near the trailing edge, and another strap attached near the leading edge. While the first remained stationary, the second was raised and the turned. This method eliminated a second crane and was done more quickly and with greater efficiency.

Center Wing Horizontal (Department 937)

From their development of the vertical machining operation, Ford engineers became convinced they could develop a faster production line after it left the machining combine. A moving line chain trolley conveyor was developed in which the center wing was lifted onto a conveyor which with semi-overhead inserts that fitted into each end of the wing to hold it while it moved horizontally through the next twelve stations down the assembly line in department 937. The wing was maintained at standing height in order to facilitate the installation of components at each station. As it moved through the twelve workstations, each station made various installations. At Station 6, the turbo dress-up for both the inboard and board engines were installed. At Station 10, the main landing gear was installed, and just before leaving the horizontal conveyor, at Station 12, fuel cells were installed in the center wing and sprayed with spark-inhibiting varnish. When the center wing reached the final department 937 station, it was a mostly complete wing assembly with landing gear, including wheels, tires, brakes, turbochargers, hydraulic and fuel lines, and cowl fairing, with all electrical wiring bundles and connectors installed. As the center wing dress-up procedure was completed and the wing was elevated to flow into the start of final assembly to be mated to the other major sections, which were being assembled nearby.

The huge 27-ton Ingersoll machine (side view) needed to be supported on 10 by 13-foot cast-steel bases and was considered to be a special combination fixture and machine tool, operated by a crew of six men, supervised by one foreman. (*FAM/AAF*)

The Ingersoll machine was used in assembling the center wing section, the wing root on both sides, and the heavy structure where these roots joined the fuselage. (*FAM/AAF*)

In Department 937 (center wing horizontal), the wing came off the Ingersoll machine and was attached to a chain trolley conveyor (seen here) and moved horizontally through twelve stations down the assembly line and leaving the twelfth station was a mostly complete wing assembly. (FAM/AAF)

Fuselage and its Component Assemblies

While the center wing was being assembled, workers in the parallel bay along the north wall of the factory were assembling the forward and aft fuselage sections and their component sub-assemblies. At the start of the fore-and-aft fuselage assemblies parts were organized into a series of buildup stations where parts were added to produce larger components that would be used to complete fuselage sections. The parts would move from the bottom to the top, where they would join the final assembly.

The forward fuselage nose section and side walls moved into department 938 where all of the interior equipment was installed. Ford again used fixtures to hold stringers and spacers in exact positions while the aluminum skin was attached. The completed side walls would then be moved to dress-up stations where essential equipment and accessories would be installed. Having the fuselage section broken down into four separate pieces—left and right side and top and bottom sections—allowed workers access to rapidly install parts. This avoided the crowded conditions that would be found in a complete forward fuselage, where workers access to interior walls would be limited due to crowded conditions.

The side panel under the wing and the nose bottom were assembled in department 938A, while the aft panel of the fuselage was assembled in department 939A.

In department 939, rear fuselage sections were assembled on the parallel south subassembly line where the nose fuselage sections had the side, floor, and top sections joined to form a fuselage subassembly. The rear of the fuselage nose section had an assortment of capped hydraulic fittings, control cables, and electrical connections, which were prepared for rapid linkup to the center wing section, where they were mated on the final assembly line. The fixtures here used the same assembling process as the forward fuselage, with side walls open on both sides to allow access by more workers in order to rapidly install needed equipment. Fuselage assemblies were attached to one of the overhead cranes ran throughout the factory to lift subassemblies out of fixtures. Metal bands circled the fuselage sections and workers would attach crane cables to eyelets on the metal bands.

The nose side panels and the aft side panels were assembled the fuselage departments 940A and 940B, respectively. The internal wiring circuits and tubing clusters were assembled in another part of the Willow Run complex. The 1,700 different tubes carrying twelve separate fluid circuits and required wiring were bunched in a large number of clusters and were installed into various parts of the aircraft as assembled units during this time.

In department 940, rear fuselage sections neared completion with major components attached, which included the horizontal stabilizer twin tail attachment points and tail gunner compartment.

The forward fuselage cockpit floor and pilot/co-pilot controls were built by a group of skilled personnel but with no mass production techniques being employed. To build the cockpit side walls, ribbing was assembled and then skinned, the completed wall had the relevant wiring and piping clusters added, and then the assembled side wall was secured to the cockpit floor. The cabin roof was added, together with the canopy. The Perspex for the canopy was soaked in a fluid to a temperature of 260 degrees Fahrenheit, which made it very pliable and in this flexible state it was placed on a former of the appropriate shape, where it cooled to that shape.

The nose and rear fuselage sections were positioned in the north south transfer bay for north final assembly bay operations. At the center was a turntable with rollers to feed subassemblies onto the structure that separated the north and south final assembly lines in the north final assembly bay and feed the subassemblies to their attachment stations.

The twin stabilizer and elevator assembly were completed in department 912. The rudders, elevator, and horizontal and vertical stabilizers were assembled as a single unit to minimize work on the final assembly line. As part of Bricker's 505 program, the tail stabilizer manufacture had been transferred to Ford River Rouge.

At this point, the assembly line divided in two, with one moving onward overhead while the other carrying the completed KD component for shipment and assembly elsewhere. At the end of the fuselage assembly area and Station 12 center wing horizontal there was a transfer bay these two major sub-assemblies crossed over into the department 947 final assembly lines. Architect Albert Kahn designed a large bridge-type conveyor system that crossed the entire work area and delivered the fuselage sections into the assembly line similar to auto bodies being lowered into the assembly line at the Rouge automobile factory. The fuselage sections intended for Fort Worth and Tulsa were transferred to the shipping department.

Final Assembly Line (Department 947) Stations 1 through 14

After the KD components were sent off, the main assembly line continued forward, the completed center wing being moved by an overhead crane conveyed from mating jig to mating jig and fixtures. The mating jigs were very strong and sizeable structures. The bottom jig sometimes was a heavy wheeled cart which was moved fractions of an inch at a time in almost any direction by a hand-turned geared-up knobs permitting a perfect mating of the fuselage and wing sections.

The fuselage side panels, front section, and other integral parts of the bomber's structures were added. The fuselage side panels were assembled and then hung in an individual section on a moving conveyor. The 1,700 different tubes carrying twelve separate fluid circuits and countless electrical wiring circuits, assembled in another part of Willow Run, were bunched in a large number of clusters and were installed into various parts of the aircraft during this time. These fully assembled units then needed only to be connected to one another, eliminating the need to complete all this intricate work inside the fuselage after it had been joined.

After the center wing was transferred by heavy crane into final assembly, department 947, other major sections and assemblies were added to the bomber. At Station 1, the top fuselage deck above the wing was installed. At Station 2, the front and rear bomb racks, catwalk, and side panels were added; at Station 4, the forward fuselage; at Station 6, the hydraulic reservoir tank; and at Station 7, the nose landing gear. At Station 8, the aft section of the fuselage was mated with the center wing section, with assembly the result took on the configuration of an airplane and started to move forward on its own wheels. At Station 9, the power plant dress-up units added, and at Station 11, the Emerson nose turret was installed.

Mating of the fuselage sections with the center wing was dispersed over several work stations, which required a method of allocating the fuselage to the correct work stations. The major dilemma faced by Ford engineers was to develop a fixture which could quickly and accurately "mate" the large fuselage section with the 55-foot center wing section. Consolidated's laborious method of sighting through a transit to obtain accurate alignments, was not feasible for mass production and needed to be eliminated. A method needed to be developed to automatically align these huge sections by only placing them in the fixture. This fixture had to be reliable during high speed mass production without continually having to check it for accuracy. Consolidated engineers who had previously had floor movement problems due to nearby Pacific Ocean tides, thought that Michigan's seasonal climate changes would made the development this fixture to be irresolvable. But Ford engineers did develop a workable fixture which was subsequently ordered by Consolidated for its new Fort Worth factory.

The Ford engineers designed and built a durable fixture consisting of a set of four large, 7-foot-high, cast-iron pillars or "leveling towers" arranged in pairs mounted on a block of reinforced concrete 18 feet deep that rested on solid hard-pan (a hardened impervious layer, typically of clay, occurring in or below the soil which impaired drainage). This foundation provided the best possible support for the mating fixture with little likelihood that the towers could move out of alignment. The towers were placed sufficiently apart to allow the fuselage to pass between them and low enough so that the center wing section could move over their tops. The first operation in positioning the 55-foot-wing was to place it on top of two additional towers that were employed as hydraulic jacks. The wing was then lowered onto the leveling towers where it engaged the reference blocks bolted onto the front and rear spars. The wings were then adjusted up or down and when this operation was completed the wing was automatically leveled to the inflight 3-degree, 26-minute angle of incidence position. Simultaneously, it was positioned at right angles to the center line of the fixture that was used to carry the fuselage.

Once the fixture for positioning and attaching the wing and center wing section together was developed, Ford engineers designed a method of handling the large fore and aft fuselage sections. The engineers designed two cast-iron mating cars, onto which each section of the fuselage would be lowered, leveled, and aligned by using mating straps. The straps, each with four foot-like projections, lowered the fuselage onto four machined surfaces located in each corner of the mating car and once they were in place the fuselage was ready to be mated.

At this time, the four assembly lines narrowed to two and the center and rear sections of the fuselage were joined together into a single component to which the bomb bay racks, catwalk, bomb bay doors, and ball turret were added. The nose section and complete fuselage sections were then assembled to the center wing section and the front and rear turrets installed. All four engines were installed with each engine being held in place by four five-eighth-inch-diameter bolts.

The aircraft, supported on its own under carriage was then moved sideways to the center of the factory floor, with the two assembly lines becoming one. The outer wing sections were attached to the center wing section, as ten specially trained Little People climbed inside the center wing, via the undercarriage recess, to bolt the outer wings into place as they were held, by hoists, against the center wing section. They also installed stiffener rods in auxiliary fuel cells and attached the outer wing assembly to center wing at the splice joint and served as inspectors of the process. The nearly completely assembled B-24 now had its four propellers, instruments, radio equipment, wing flaps, and sound proofing added.

Four-Hour Stations: Final Assembly (Stations 15 to 28)

When the bombers left Station 14, they arrived at the four-hour station, where they were moved to the center of a 150-foot bay that provided the width required to install the right and left outer wings at Station 15. The outer wing fuel tanks were installed at Station 16, and the right and left flaps were installed at the next station. Between Stations 20 and 21, the aircraft were turned 90 degrees as they passed over the Albert Kahn-designed turntable into the assembly line and changed the plant into its distinctive L-shaped "Tax Turn." The bombers then continued through the final phases of assembly at Stations 22 and 27 where the propellers were installed and many last small additions and the comprehensive final inspection occurred.

The finishing Station 28 was the final station, where the bombers passed through two of the largest painting and dope booths in the U.S. aircraft industry, measuring 324 feet long by 90 feet wide with 36-foot ceilings. Each of the eight spray booths measured 150 by 80 feet, and each had fireproof doors closing their entrances and exits. The Liberators were camouflaged, olive drab on top and blue-gray underneath with paint that dried in three minutes under infra-red lamps. Later in the war, from model J onwards, camouflage paint was not used and natural metal finish was standard, reducing aircraft weight and accelerating production. The last camouflaged B-24 to leave Willow Run was #3844 (KD 3190), after which the 4,200 square feet of aluminum skin of each fuselage was cleaned.

The dope room was kept at 80 degrees Fahrenheit and humidity at 50 percent (+/- 10 percent) was required at all times regulated by three 100-ton dehumidifiers that created ten air changes per hour for the entire room. The ailerons, rudders, and elevators were cloth-covered with grade "A" cotton to dampened vibration and were given six coats of dope (four to five ounces/square yard). More than 3,000 signs and decals were applied on each aircraft.

Willow Run pumped approximately 30,000 gallons of 100 octane and 1,100 gallons of oil daily to deliver flight-ready the completed B-24s. The gasoline and oil were pumped from the 162 by 67-foot gas and oil house, which Ford touted as the "World's Largest Gas Station."

The gas and oil handling system controlled 60,000 gallons of oil and 150,000 gallons of gasoline stored in six 25,000-gallon underground storage tanks and was able to fuel and oil an aircraft in twenty minutes and also complete forty-one other operations in this area. In addition to the 142 gallons of oil used for each engine, 3,745 gallons of oil and 300 pounds of grease was used each week for tool maintenance. Two 1,000-gallon-per-minute oil separators were used to separate oil from plant water, held in a detention basin for an hour and a half, before it was emptied into Willow Run Creek

Once a bomber had received its markings, it was moved outdoors to the compass rose to have its compasses calibrated. Willow Run's device was unique in America, measuring 52 feet in diameter, weighing 85 tons, and was driven by a 30-hp motor. The compass rose displayed lines marked on its turn table oriented to magnetic north. These lines were painted in the cardinal directions (north, east, south, and west), and their intermediate points and was used to perform a "compass swing." The guns of every fifth bomber were checked for accuracy at the gun butt as they were readied for both company and AAF flight test, acceptance, and delivery. The 20-foot-wide by 30-foot-deep by 30-foot-high gun butt had walls 20 inches thick. About 65,000 rounds were fired every month and the shell casings were collected from the sand floor by an electro-magnet. Every fiftieth bomber had its guns fired in flight.

Each bomber that left the Willow Run Plant was towed onto one of the three, one-of-a-kind, 52,000-pound-capacity weighing platforms located in the gas house where they were leveled and weighed in five minutes. Inside the plant, there were 134 scales ranging in size from 100 pounds to 60-ton capacity.

Flyaway of the completed B-24s from Willow Run was performed by many women pilots as well as the women and men of the Ferry Command located at Romulus, Michigan, who flew the new bombers to any location in the U.S., often modification centers, or any overseas theaters of war.

Fuselage and its Component Assemblies Gallery

The following photo gallery is a comprehensive survey of the assembly of the Liberator from stored component parts to flyaway:

Overlooking the Liberator components stored in Departments 939 and 940. The rear fuselage sections (foreground) and nose section (background) had their top, sides, and floor united to form their fuselage subassemblies that were banded together to be hauled away by an overhead crane (is attaching to rear fuselage in the left foreground). (*FAM/AAF*)

Department 940 completed nose/cockpit and center fuselages. (*FAM/AAF*)

Department 940 rear fuselage await attachment of tail cones, which had the attachment points for the horizontal stabilizer and rear gunner station. (*FAM/AAF*)

Department 914: complex cockpit instruments and components installed on a turntable that rotated slowly from station-to-station. (FAM/AAF)

Department 914: women installing components on the pilot's pedestal. Once the cockpit was completed it was transported by crane to Department 939.

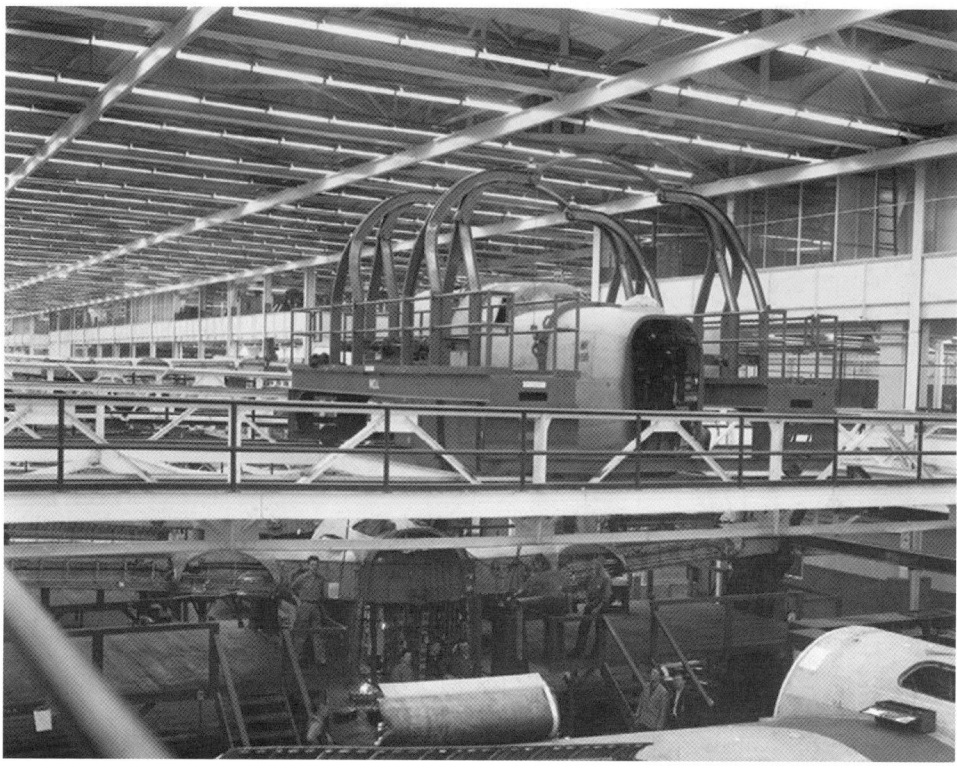

Nose fuselage section being transported by overhead crane. (*FAM/AAF*)

Nose and rea fuselage sections positioned for transport to the final assembly bay. In the center of the photo, a turntable can be seen; this delivered these sub-assemblies to their attachment stations. (*FAM/AAF*)

Center wing section being loaded on station 1 of the twenty-eight stations of the final assembly line. (*FAM/AAF*)

Nose section installed with tail sections waiting to be lowered (upper right). (*FAM/AAF*)

Center wing section being attached to the nose section, which is awaiting attachment of the nose turret mount (on floor). (*FAM/AAF*)

Rear fuselage being moved for attachment to rear of center wing.

Engine and nacelle being installed. (*FAM/AAF*)

Empennage assembly being dropped into place by a crane. (*FAM/AAF*)

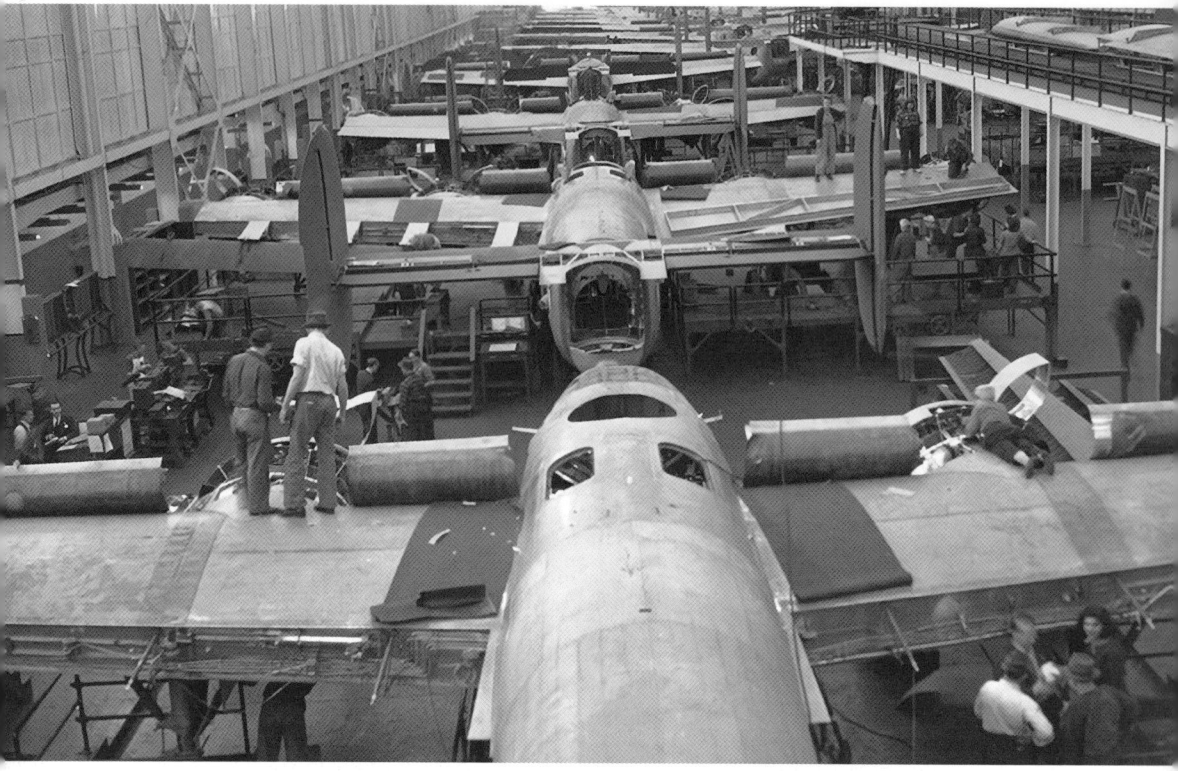

With the wings and fuselage sections are installed and the bomber moves to the last of the four-hour stations (stations 11–14). (*FAM/AAF*)

Empennage and engine dress-up and nose, dorsal, and tail turret installation. (*FAM/AAF*)

A day and a half from completion, the bombers, minus their outer wings move to a single assembly line. (*FAM/AAF*)

Outer wing attachment with a Little Person seen waiting inside the main wing. (*FAM/AAF*)

Each of the eight Willow Run spray booths measured 150 by 80 feet and each had fireproof doors closing their entrances and exits. (FAM/AAF)

Early Liberators were camouflaged, with dorsal olive drab and ventral blue-gray with paint that dried in three minutes under infrared lamps. (FAM/AAF)

Heading for the tax turn, the bomber has final components installed. (*FAM/AAF*)

Between stations 20 and 21, the aircraft were turned 90 degrees as they passed over the Albert Kahn-designed turntable into the assembly line and changed the plant into its characteristic L-shaped "tax turn." (*FAM/AAF*)

Early Liberators on the turntable and then continued through the final phases of assembly where the propellers were added and final inspection occurred. The structure in the center supports the factory roof. (*FAM/AAF*)

After being pulled by conveyers and tow tractors, the completed Liberators were filled with fuel and oil for their first flights. Fueling station balcony depicted on photo upper left with workers at wing filling openings. (*FAM/AAF*)

Another view of the fueling/oil station, which could fill the six wing tanks simultaneously in twenty minutes. (*FAM/AAF*)

Completed Liberators leave the assembly line through Willow Run's 150-foot-wide and 30-foot-high door clearances. (*FAM/AAF*)

After completion, the bombers were moved outdoors to Willow Run's unique compass rose to have their compasses calibrated. (*FAM/AAF*)

The guns of every fifth bomber were checked for accuracy at the gun butt. (*FAM/AAF*)

Flyaway of the completed B-24s from Willow Run, was performed by many company women pilots as well as the women and men of the Ferry Command. (*FAM/AAF*)

24

Knock-Down (KD) Kit Production and Transport

After Ford's initial proposal to mass produce aircraft was rejected, negotiations continued slowly for Ford to build aircraft engines. However, the auto industry was perceived as a large and potential source of parts and subassemblies for the aircraft industry establishment. From the end of 1940 and into early 1941, negotiations with Ford continued, and finally, in May 1941, Ford agreed to be a major sub-contractor supplying sets of KD parts or components for the B-24 heavy bomber to be assembled by Consolidated/Fort Worth and Douglas/Tulsa.

B-24Es Assembled from KD Kits

The early Willow Run Liberators were designated B-24Es to differentiate them from the Consolidated B-24Ds. The first KD from Willow Run arrived at Tulsa in late 1942, and by early 1943, Douglas Tulsa was in its own series production of the B-24E. Fort Worth received its first Ford KD in early 1943 and from mid-1943 was delivering assembled Willow Run B-24Es in addition to its own B-24D production. In March 1943, Consolidated merged with Vultee with the new company adopting the trade name Convair, but the B-24 continued to be referred to as a Consolidated product. By mid-summer of 1943, Consolidated at San Diego was manufacturing about 200 B-24Ds a month and assembling over 100 B-24Es at Fort Worth from KD assemblies supplied by Willow Run. Douglas was assembling B-24Es from KD components supplied by Ford and North American Aviation and was just beginning production on the B-24G. The first twenty-five G-models were slightly modified E-models, but from November 1943, the remaining 505 G-models had the electrically-powered Emerson nose turret installed.

Transporting KD Kits

A KD kit consisted of three large units: the aft fuselage section, the nose or forward section, and the center wing section, plus a variety of smaller assemblies. Shipment of all KDs by railroad (four cars) was considered at the outset but was rejected as too expensive and too slow in view of the large number to be shipped, although limited shipments could be made by railroad in case of disruption of the truck schedule because of weather conditions, accidents, etc.

To transport these units from Michigan to Consolidated Fort Worth (1,250 miles) and Douglas Tulsa (950 miles), two distinctive tractor-trailer sets would be required to test their viability as part of an initial fleet of sixty-four, which were to be followed by twenty more. Mechanical Handling Systems of Detroit was contracted to design the two trailers while E&L Transport Company in Dearborn, Michigan, was to design the two-truck tractors. The feasibility of the two experimental trailers and their tractors was to be proven in trial runs and then leased by the government to Ford, which would be responsible for their maintenance, but were contracted to be operated by an outside firm. The tractor-trailer combination, which could haul a maximum weight of about 27,000 pounds, had an overall length of about 75 feet, weighed 25 tons fully loaded, and ran on eighteen 8.25 by 20 tires.

E&L Transport Company was headed by Lloyd Lawson who designed the twin-engined, 12-foot, 4.5-ton truck tractors, which were basically two Ford ton-and-a-half trucks on one chassis using standard off-the-shelf cab-over-engine Ford truck parts, some of which were modified, but all were Ford. The truck was powered by two 100-hp Ford truck engines mounted side-by-side beneath the cab, driving four-speed Warner transmissions and Timken differentials. The engines ran in synchronization with single controls for the accelerator, clutch, and gear shift, however, each of the two engines had its own, ignition switch, gauges, radiator, transmission drive shaft and rear end. The tractor was equipped with a fuel and oiling system that permitted the trips to be made non-stop. There were oil consumption gauges in the cabs and oil could be fed into the engine from a reservoir controlled by the driver. Although Ford was often credited as the builder of the trucks, Thorco Dual Motors built them using Ford components.

The trailers, built by Mechanical Handling Systems, were 63 feet long with a wheel base measuring 40 feet. They were 12.5 feet high and 8 feet wide, and the overall length of the trailer/tractor combination was 75 feet. Dimensions of all the trailers were the same, but the interiors differed and all were loaded from the top by overhead cranes. One type was used to carry center wings, outer wings, and other related assemblies weighing 8 tons; another to carry fuselage sections, both forward and aft weighing about 4 tons; while the third was used to carry spare parts and purchase order items weighing 2 tons. The top of the trailer consisted of five sections of removable framework, covered with waterproof canvas, which were removed when loading or unloading.

Before the KD service was inaugurated, engineers inspected the entire route from Willow Run to the assembly factories. Intersections had to be surveyed to determine whether they allowed enough room for the trailers to negotiate the turn. Bridges in many states were found to be too narrow or weak, necessitating rerouting. At many points, arc-shaped overhead bridges made it necessary for the trailer to stay in the center where there was the most clearance causing oncoming traffic to be stopped or rerouted. Ideally, the trips to the assembly plants were made in four days at a maximum speed of about 40 mph but could take as many as seven days, depending on weather, route and traffic difficulties, and mechanical problems. The KD haulers did not travel at night and often were slowed while traveling through towns and cities and turning at intersections and bridge and narrow areas on the route. Two drivers were assigned to each KD hauler, each driving over five-hour intervals while the other driver took advantage of the built-in bed. The fleet of eighty-six KD haulers averaged 250 round trips per month, with 375 being the record number of round trips in one month. Poor weather conditions were the only serious operating problem as occasionally floods or a heavy snowfall, which once tied up as many as six to ten trailers at one point along the route.

KD Kit Gallery

KD kit components displayed in a Ford/Willow Run PR photo. (*FAM/AAF*)

KD components being diverted from Willow Run assembly line. (*FAM/AAF*)

KD wing sections being conveyed for truck loading. (*FAM/AAF*)

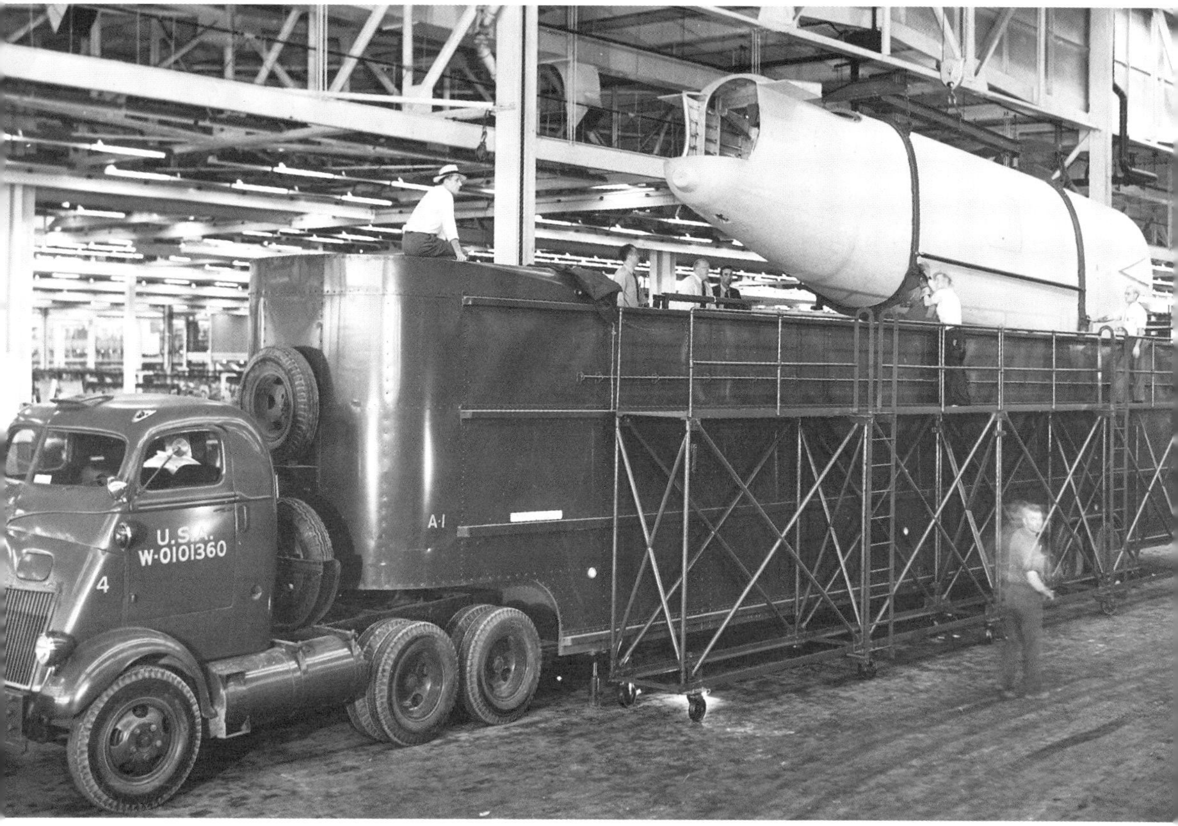

KD rear fuselage section being loaded into special truck trailer. (*FAM/AAF*)

Above left: 7 July 1944: Last of 1,893 KD kits shipped from Willow Run. (*FAM/AAF*)

Above right: E&L Transport Company twin-engined, 12-foot, 4.5-ton truck tractors that were basically two Ford ton and a half trucks on one chassis. (*FAM/AAF*)

Before the KD service was inaugurated, engineers inspected the entire route to the assembly factories measuring road widths, intersection turn radii, bridge height clearances, utility wires, etc. (*FAM/AAF*)

Trailer being unloaded at one of the KD assembly plants, either Douglas Tulsa or Consolidated Fort Worth. (*FAM/AAF*)

25

Was "Willit Run" a Success?

The B-24L, the last Liberator off the Willow Run production line, was certainly an entirely different aircraft from the initial educational B-24E. From the eighteen contracts that led to the last B-24L, there were 130 major changes and thousands of minor ones. The original Liberator design had ballooned from a gross weight of 41,000 pounds to 60,000 pounds as combat experience displayed the need for adding such improved equipment as turbo-superchargers, self-sealing fuel tanks, full-feathering constant-speed propellers, and three heavily armored power-operated gun turrets.

Ford management was willing and assertive in undertaking war work in an assortment of Army contracts, tanks, trucks, Jeeps, etc. This was particularly true in the case of Willow Run where Ford, with virtually no experience in aircraft production, confidently embarked on the mass production of the B-24 Liberator bomber. Ford ultimately achieved B-24 mass production despite many obstacles and delays, many of which were caused by itself.

The entire Ford mass production plan was based on two major assumptions. One was that the B-24 design would be reasonably stable; the other was that there would be a continuous flow of parts and semi-finished components to the assembly line. But Ford would find that both of these assumptions would be wrong. During the war, none of the U.S. military aircraft that were required in large numbers would have their design frozen and frequent, almost continual, design changes characterized the entire production life of the B-24. Most of these changes required revisions in the complex tooling that was created to increase the production rate at each station along the production line. Each time a major tooling change became mandatory, the entire production line stopped. Ford and the AAF finally compromised on design changes and Ford was permitted to produce the semi-frozen B-24E design, but this occurred long past the time when this variant was still a viable combat aircraft.

So was "Willit Run" a success? By assessing success by airframe pounds produced with the least dollar cost and man-hours expended, near the end of 1944, Willow Run produced one airframe pound with 0.30 man-hours of labor, which was far superior to the industry average of 0.47 man-hours. The cost per one Willow Run B-24 averaged approximately $167,000, which was calculated by dividing the 7,000 complete Liberators and the 2,000 KD kits into the total Ford outlay (including tooling) of about $1.5 billion. However, there were too many variables to make an accurate comparison especially since Willow Run never really operated at maximum capacity. Chronic labor shortages and the inexperience and high turnover of the existing labor force, tooling problems, and materials shortages colluded to hamper production. However, Willow Run was not operated at maximum capacity for another reason. By the time the plant finally was operating efficiently, the AAF no longer needed B-24 bombers in unlimited quantities as it had earlier. By March 1944, monthly Ford production had reached 309 bombers plus parts equivalent to 112 more for a total of 421 aircraft. Subsequently, increases in output up to 600 per month were theoretically possible, but combat units required nowhere near that number of aircraft at that point in the war. Consequently, large numbers of Liberators began to accumulate on airfields around the country. If Ford had been permitted to operate at maximum capacity until the end of the war, the ratio of airframe pounds to man-hours and the ratio of units to dollar costs would certainly have been markedly better.

Production of combat-suitable aircraft in the time required (i.e. rate of acceleration) is another measure of production success when compared with some of the established aircraft manufacturers. Considering the eighteen-month "maturation" period at Willow Run—which included the time between start up and delivery of the first production Liberator, the virtually obsolete B-24E, accepted in July 1942—the time to achieve a full-scale production schedule was thirty-eight months for Willow Run, compared with twenty-five to thirty-two months at other plants that built Liberators and Flying Fortresses "the old way." However, to be considered was the delay in receiving and deciphering design data from Consolidated had seriously hindered Ford's rate of acceleration.

Ford found that its production scheme was not flexible enough to build an aircraft that had not been completely engineered and ready for mass production and then incorrectly presumed that a design freeze was possible. The AAF should also be held responsible for permitting Ford to proceed with production under these conditions. The result of the Willow Run "experience" was that automobile makers realized that military aircraft could not be mass produced like passenger vehicles while at the same time traditional airframe manufacturers became aware of practical mass production methods. Automobile engineers were disposed to emphasize quantity while the conventional engineering departments of the traditional aircraft builders were principally involved with quality. Essentially aircraft engineers were designers rather than producers as they directed their attention to achieving aircraft of high performance, even to the neglect of such critical considerations as armament as was the case with the B-24. Combat experience continually demonstrated that both quantity and quality were necessary in aircraft manufacture. Both the production-oriented automobile makers and the performance-oriented aircraft designers finally recognized that real success lay in their ability to incorporate design changes on the production line without reducing productivity.

In less than three years, Ford had built 6,792 B-24s and furnished 1,893 others in KD form to Tulsa and Fort Worth, produced a multitude of spare parts and yet never operated Willow Run at full capacity. The complete B-24s built at Willow Run or supplied in Kit form represented 48 percent of the total Liberator production. The H-model was the pinnacle of Ford mass production success as nearly 1,800 Hs were built and by early 1944 Willow Run was completing a B-24H at an average rate of nearly one every hour (best: sixty-three minutes), twenty-four hours a day, and seven days a week and could have produced 600 per month but by this time B-24 supply was exceeding demand.

GALLERY WILLOW RUN B-24 MILESTONES

First Willow Run **B-24E-FO (#.01), S/N 42-7770 (1/1)** was an "Educational" model. (*FAM/AAF*)

The 1,000th Willow Run B-24 (an H-model). (*FAM/AAF*)

The 2,000th B-24. (*FAM/AAF*)

The 5,000th B-24. (*FAM/AAF*)

The 5,000th B-24 being signed by Henry and Edsel Ford. (*FAM/AAF*)

The 6,000th B-24. (*FAM/AAF*)

The 7,000th B-24. (*FAM/AAF*)

The 8,000th B-24. (*FAM/AAF*)

The 8,000th B-24 being signed by Henry Ford II. (*FAM/AAF*)

The 8,645th and last Willow Run B-24. (*FAM/AAF*)

Last Willow Run B-24 was B-24M-30-FO 44-51928 being towed from the factory by Henry Ford II. (*FAM/AAF*)

26

Willow Run Post-War

Ford Does Not Exercise Its Plant Option

Although Ford had an option to purchase the Willow Run Plant once it was no longer needed for war production, the company declined to exercise it and ended its association with Willow Run. There were about 2,300 government defense plant corporation owned machine tools in the plant with Ford providing over 1,500 machine tools from its automotive plants, all of which were removed from Willow Run after it ceased production.

Kaiser Takes Control

After war production ended, the plant was sold to the Kaiser-Frazer Corporation, a partnership of construction and shipbuilding magnate Henry J. Kaiser and Graham-Paige executive Joseph Frazer. The plant produced both Kaiser and Frazer automobile models, including the compact Henry J, which with minor differences was also innovatively sold through Sears-Roebuck as the Allstate. In 1951, Frazier's last year in business, only 131 Frazer Manhattan Convertibles, which were advertised as the "Pride of Willow Run," were produced. The luxury model of the Frazier Manhattan set new industry standards in coordination of color and fabric and was introduced as America's only four-door convertible, featuring a fully automatic top. During the 1952 model year, the Manhattan name was transferred to the Kaiser line. From 1947 through 1953, Willow Run produced 739,000 automobiles as part of Kaiser-Frazer and Kaiser Motors, but after years of losses, the company (called Kaiser Motors after Frazer's 1951 exit from the partnership) purchased Willys-Overland and began moving its production at Willow Run to the Willys plant in Toledo, Ohio. Kaiser Motors would give up on the passenger car business in 1955 and would became Kaiser Jeep in 1962, which would be purchased by American Motors in 1970, which in turn became part of Chrysler Corporation in 1987, as the Jeep-Eagle division.

After war production ended, the plant was sold to the Kaiser-Frazer Corporation, which produced both Kaiser and Frazer automobile models and the C-119 Flying Boxcar—seen on promotional display. (*Kaiser-Frazer Corporation*)

Renewed Aircraft Production at Willow Run

Although Willow Run is synonymous with the Liberator bomber, B-24s were not the only warplanes manufactured at Willow Run. As the U.S. Air Force struggled to expand its airlift capacity during the Korean War, Kaiser-Frazer built C-119 Flying Boxcar cargo planes at Willow Run under license from Fairchild Aircraft, producing an estimated eighty-eight C-119s between 1951 and 1953. Kaiser also built two C-123 Provider airframes at Willow Run, which were scrapped before delivery, as a procurement scandal involving the company put an end to any chance for future air force contracts.

MARC and Willow Run Laboratories

On the other side of the Willow Run Airport across from the assembly plant were a group of World War II hangars, which were sold to the University of Michigan in 1946. The university operated the Michigan Aeronautical Research Center (MARC), later known as Willow Run Laboratories (WRL), from 1946 to 1972. MARC and WRL produced many innovations, including the first ruby laser and operation of the ruby maser, as well as early research into antiballistic missile defense and advanced remote sensing. In 1972, the university spun off WRL into the Environmental Research Institute of Michigan, which eventually left Willow Run for offices in Ann Arbor.

General Motors Operations

Later in 1953, after a fire on 12 August destroyed General Motors' Detroit transmission factory in Livonia, Michigan, the Willow Run complex was leased to GM, which eventually purchased it. The salvaged Hydramatic transmission tooling and machinery was relocated to Willow Run and transmission production began in just nine weeks after the fire. Over the years, GM spent several hundred million dollars expanding the former bomber plant by roughly half, into the nearly 5 million-square-foot GM powertrain factory and engineering center. A parcel of land to the south of the powertrain factory was reserved for assembly operations that began in 1959, including a Fisher body plant that built bodies for the Chevrolet models assembled there, including the Corvair and Nova. In 1968, General Motors began reorganizing its body and assembly operations into the GM assembly division (GMAD). GMAD required sixteen years to completely absorb Fisher body's operations as Fisher would continue to manufacture auto bodies at Willow Run Assembly until the 1970s and vehicles would roll off the line there until 1992. In addition to making automatic transmissions, Willow Run also produced the M16A1 rifle and the M39A1 20-mm autocannon for the U.S. military during the Vietnam War. By the time General Motors entered bankruptcy in 2009, manufacturing and assembly operations at Willow Run had dwindled to almost naught and the GM powertrain plant closed in December 2010.

General Motors purchased the plant and expanded it to nearly 5 million square feet to accommodate its powertrain factory and engineering center. (*GM*)

RACER Trust

On 31 March 2011, the Revitalizing Auto Communities Environmental Response (RACER) Trust, created by a settlement agreement in the U.S. Bankruptcy Court with the U.S. government and took control of eighty-nine abandoned GM properties in fourteen states, principally in the Midwest and Northeast. RACER was created to restore and position these properties and other facilities owned by the former General Motors Corporation for redevelopment before its 2009 bankruptcy. RACER is one of the largest holders of industrial property in the U.S. and is the largest environmental response and remediation trust in U.S. history. Among the reasons the GM Willow Run site is attractive to redevelopers is that GM spent hundreds of millions of dollars developing the hydramatic/powertrain plant and the RACER Trust is spending $35.8 million to clean up the environmental problems there. In April 2013, a redevelopment manager for the RACER Trust announced that unused portions of the plant would likely be razed as a step toward redeveloping the property. The remainder of the property as of 2016 is under the control of Devon Industrial Group, which is demolishing the plant and Walbridge Development LLC, which has previously indicated that it intends to turn the property into a connected vehicle research facility.

Yankee Air Museum

On 23 June 2014, the Yankee Air Museum signed a purchase agreement with the RACER Trust to buy 150,000-square-foot section of the GM Willow Run powertrain plant, saving it from demolition. RACER Trust extended deadlines for the museum numerous times to help the deal come to realization. As part of the Willow Run revitalization, the 7,526-foot runway had all of the existing runway pavement and its lighting system was removed and replaced in a $45 million project. Yankee Air Museum leased Hangar 1 to display its B-17 and C-47. However, during 2019, it was announced that Hangar 1 was closing and Yankee Air Museum needed to build its own hangar. The Museum is currently focused on building and opening its own Aeronautics Center that will provide a permanent home for their Historic Flying Aircraft Collection, which is, only blocks away from the current Museum.

Future Autonomous Vehicle Testing Site

In January 2016, Michigan Gov. Rick Snyder announced the launch of lifelike proving ground for self-driving vehicle testing by the American Center for Mobility at the former Willow Run Factory. Construction began during January 2019, leveling the factory buildings and constructing a new infrastructure or updating what is on site. The center would include a 2½-mile high-speed highway test track; multilane intersections, alleys, and traffic circles; a 700-foot curving tunnel; two triple-decker overpasses; a cybersecurity lab; an electrical substation large enough to power a city; and driverless shuttles to connect at least some of the pieces.

During 2017, the Yankee Air Museum transferred its operations to Hangar 1, but in 2019, its lease was bought for the autonomous vehicle testing site. (*Yankee Air Museum*)

The future autonomous, self-driving, vehicle testing site began construction on the Willow Run site during 2019. (*National Highway Traffic and Safety Administration*)

PART V

North American Dallas Plant

1

Planning and Building the Dallas Plant

During 1940, President Roosevelt revealed his defense plans for military aviation, the decentralization of military construction, and the construction of plants inland away from the Atlantic and Pacific Coasts for security reasons. The aircraft industry, particularly North American and Consolidated, were interested in the North Texas area, including Dallas-Fort Worth, to build new plants. Texas was one of the states that was most ravaged by the Depression with oil production stalled and area's agriculture base still suffering. However, the Depression left an abundant labor pool of available, albeit, unskilled workers, untrained in aircraft manufacturing. Housing problems could be solved more easily in North Texas than in the already crowded industrial areas on both coasts and the industrial Upper Midwest. Additionally, the area's flat terrain, temperate climate, and ideal flying weather were important advantages. Popular cowboy philosopher Will Rogers lobbied for a major aircraft manufacturer to come to the Dallas area.

At the time, Consolidated had contractual and financial commitments to Dallas but was also bound to its Fort Worth facility. Meanwhile, financially flush North American Aviation, which had only been building aircraft for six years, was looking to build a new factory to manufacture aircraft to fill present and future orders. NAA President James "Dutch" Kindelberger decided to look to Dallas because of its moderate climate, the possibility of some outdoor construction, and the availability of land and low taxes. There was an abundance of electric power available as nearby artificial Mountain Creek Lake was a cooling lake for an under-utilized power plant. Kindelberger approached Rueben Fleet and Consolidated and offered to shoulder Consolidated's Dallas commitments, allowing Fleet to proceed with its Fort Worth factory.

Dallas heralded luring the NAA as "From Plains to Planes" in its pitch to Dallas voters. NAA and Dallas proclaimed that during 1940 only 4 percent of the Dallas population was factory-employed but that would potentially be raised to 8 percent during NAA's first year and would employ an anticipated 17,000 once the factory was in full production. NAA brought to light that it could not import labor from California and would have to train the local population.

Above: James "Dutch" Kindelberger, NAA president (L), and Leland "Lee" Atwood, NAA vice president. (*NAA/AAF*)

Left: NAA ad extolling "From Plain to Planes in 120 Days. The Dallas achievement is a tribute to individual teamwork supported by enthusiastic community cooperation." (*NAA/AAF*)

North American made a firm offer to a group representing the Dallas Chamber of Commerce, which was led by R. L. Thornton for a site under lease to the Army by the City of Dallas. The site was adjacent to Hensley Reserve Airfield located at Grand Prairie, Texas, approximately 11 miles west of downtown Dallas and not far from Consolidated's Fort Worth operation. The airfield was named for Major William Hensley, an air officer for the 8th Corps Army Area who aided the base site selection before his death. Kindelberger then negotiated with the City of Dallas to extend the Hensley Field runways and requested that the AAF grant access in perpetuity to the field. The City of Dallas, not wanting to have the NAA offer slip away, actually transferred machinery and labor from a dam project underway to lengthen the runways.

On 23 August 1940, contracts were signed with the City of Dallas committing NAA to build a factory, and from August into November, NAA concentrated on buying land parcels around Hensley Field that were not already owned by Dallas with the entire site finally encompassing 152.5 acres.

Meanwhile, on the opposite side of Hensley Field, the Navy was showing increased interest in expanding their operations there and the airfield became Naval Air Station (NAS) Dallas. NAA had already chosen its architectural and construction firms for its new factory, but the Defense Plant Corporation (DPC) insisted that NAA consent that it build the plant and lease it back to NAA for $1 per month and commit $7.9 million worth of installed equipment. NAA was allowed to use its selected architects and construction firms.

Ground breaking was on 28 September 1940, and soon the first structures built, which were the forge and hammer room that would be needed for both the construction of the plant and also would be used later for aircraft construction.

The concrete and steel Plant A would actually cover over 900,000 square feet, but Dallas and NAA PR hyped it a "million square foot" factory. The plant was built in 120 days, despite nearly 100 days of rainy weather at the time. It was the first plant in U.S. to feature artificial light exclusively with no outside windows or skylights, which were intended to maintain blackout conditions. With no windows, it was the first aircraft factory to be air conditioned.

Dallas T-6 construction began on the factory floor on 8 March 1941, before plant construction was completed and before plant dedication that would occur on 7 April. The 320 Texans slated to be constructed per month were chosen for manufacture as NAA decided not to build B-25 there as the Kansas City Plant met that demand. Soon 250 P-51Cs (and later a number of P-51Ds) would be built simultaneously with T-6s.

The Grand Prairie population increased from 2,000 in 1941 to over 16,000 a year later. Because there was not enough housing to accommodate the great influx of NAA employees, the DPC proposed building the 300-unit "Defense Housing Colony" in 100 days under the auspices of the Federal Works Agency. It was a pilot program that was part of a massive project to build 21,000 units of worker housing in proximity to critical defense industry sites across the country. The project was intended to lower the cost of "quality" housing by employing prefabrication and mass production building techniques. More agreeably renamed Avion Village, the project opened with high media attention in May 1941 when two construction teams competed to complete the

The concrete and steel Plant A would actually cover over 900,000 square feet, but Dallas and NAA PR hyped it a "million square foot" factory. It was the first plant in U.S. to feature artificial light exclusively with no outside windows or skylights, which were intended to maintain blackout conditions. With no windows, it was the first aircraft factory to be air conditioned. (NAA/AAF)

North American Aviation's main administrative building.

Above: A few of the 12,967 T-6 Texans being pulled along the Dallas assembly line by a cable system copied from the Ford Willow Run line. (*NAA/AAF*)

Right: A total 4,552 P-51 Mustangs and 299 F-6 Photo Mustangs were manufactured at Plant A. (*NAA/AAF*)

Avion Village was a Federal Works Agency pilot program to supply 300 quickly-built, low-cost worker housing. (*NAA/AAF*)

first house that was built in less than one hour. The entire development was finished in 100 days. The Avion design featured a large central open park area, which originally served as the on-site tented makeshift prefabrication area for the homes built on a ring of residential streets that terminated in cul-de-sacs at the edge of the park area. Avion housing included one-story houses, built mostly as duplexes, and two-story apartments with four units each. Each housing unit contained a living room, dining room, two bedrooms, a bath, and a kitchen. The Avion Village Mutual Housing Corporation purchased the development from the Federal government in 1948, and Avion Village continues to be mutually owned its residents.

2
NAA Builds Plant B for B-24 Production

Because NAA was so successful building T-6s and P-51s at Dallas and had underutilized its manufacturing space there, the DPC had NAA build B-24s in the new 1.4-million-square-foot Plant B across the way from Plant A, again using architects and construction companies selected by NAA.

A letter of intent dated 13 January 1942 advised North American that contract for B-24s would be issued. The contract AC-24663, issued 1 May 1942 was a cost-plus-a-fixed-fee type, specifying 750 B-24Bs complete and conforming to Consolidated's model specifications, and spare parts not to exceed 15 percent dollar value. On 1 February 1942, approval was granted for expanding the North American Dallas facility, which consisted of building a second plant adjacent to the first, the two installations being called Plants A and B. The purpose of Plant B was for production of B-24s at the rate of seventy-five per month. After much discussion as to the adequacy of Hensley Field for handling increased heavy air traffic, the project was approved under DPC Plancor No. 2

The planning of Plant B took place just after Pearl Harbor; the architect engineering firm Allen and Kelly, Indianapolis, Indiana, were named as architects for Plant B under a lump sum contract, and for Plant B, Cleveland, Ohio, architect engineering firm J. Gordon Turnbull under a fixed fee contract.

Since the quick completion of construction was of paramount importance, James Kindelberger and Lee Atwood, president and vice president of North American Aviation, requested authorization to award the construction to general contractor James Stewart Construction Company, Dallas, without competition on a lump sum contract for Plant B on a cost-plus-fixed-fee contract. The J. Gordon Turnbull Company was retained as consulting engineers. Ground was broken 15 March 1942, only six weeks after approval of Project A; four months later, the first steel of the 8,000 tons required for construction was erected. However, progress was hampered due to slow delivery of special building equipment and directives from Washington prohibiting use of steel in any but end products.

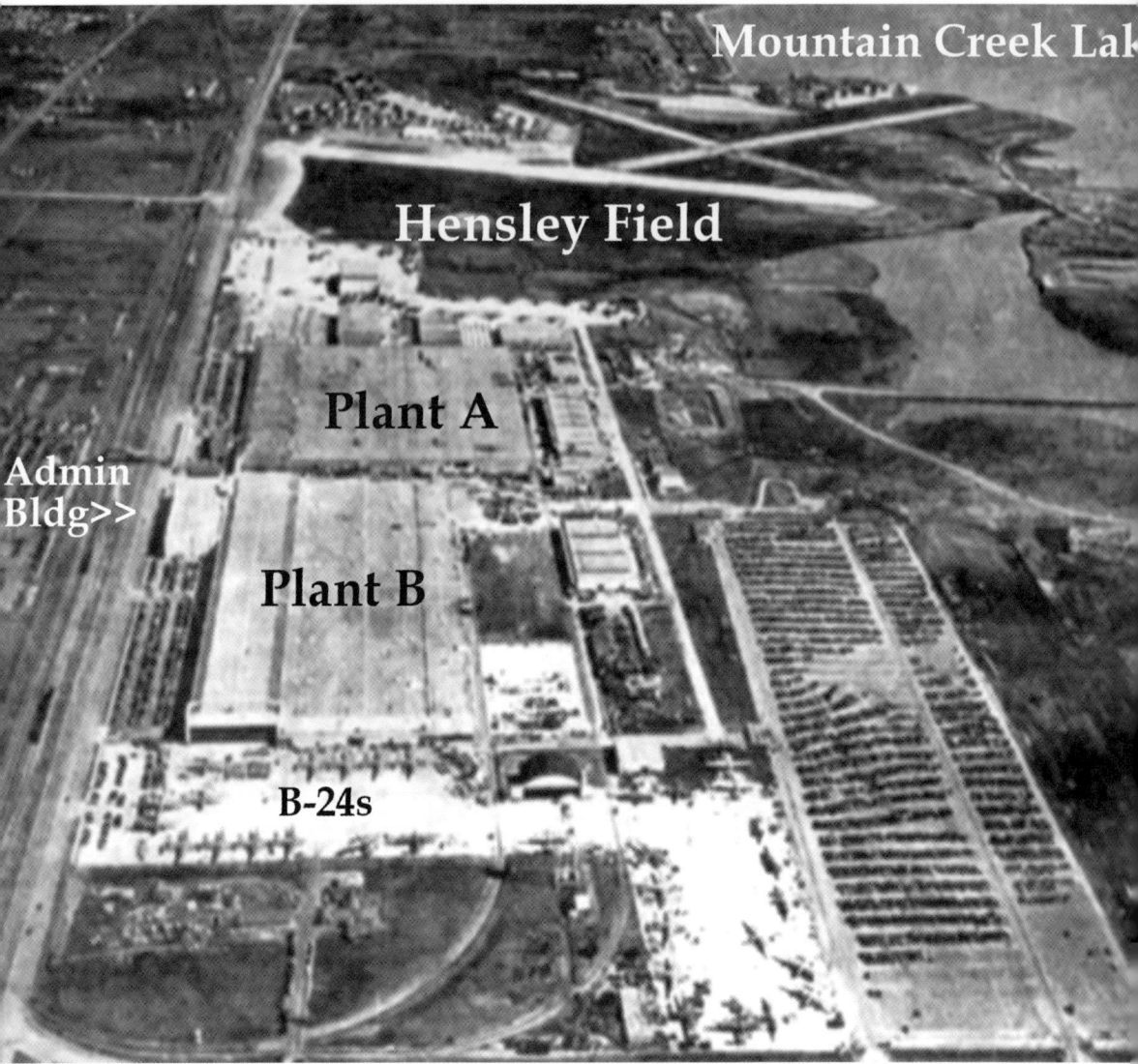

NAA Plant B was constructed adjacent to Plant A to build 966 Liberators. (*NAA/AAF*)

3

Assembling KD and Scratch B-24s

Finally, in January 1942, after the other members of the Liberator pool had been designated, NAA fabricated and assembled its own B-24G Liberators instead of assembling KD kits from Ford. When organizing its Dallas production, NAA engineers considered the problems caused when Ford had made use of Consolidated data when setting up their plant but, nonetheless, NAA/Dallas was delayed by faulty liaison between the two companies such as Ford drawings arriving in unsatisfactory condition. The experienced North American airframe engineers had fully expected design changes but became concerned by the 180,000 plus change notifications that had slowly cleared through Ford during the first few months of production. Just as Ford had restarted all the drawings they had received from Consolidated, the North American engineers finally decided to redraw all the prints sent to them from Willow Run.

During the early period of engineering design, North American agreed to depend on Ford but because of Ford's total use of production design for its mass-production methods, Ford's development of the necessary engineering data became very time intensive. NAA received the necessary Ford engineering data too slowly and, additionally, found that the Ford templates they received did not correlate with the control dimensions specified in about 500 drawings they obtained from Consolidated. Consequently, the arrangement for engineering responsibility was changed and North American was permitted to deal directly with Consolidated's engineering department.

North American's first B-24s were G-models, which were initially assembled in the Plant A hangar and moved during winter to the still incomplete final assembly floor of Plant B where the fuselage, wings, and control surface units were mated and the installations of fittings started. In August 1943, Plant B began production, approximately seven and one half months after Project A approval. In January 1943, the first NAA B-24 was flight-tested, and in March 1943, the first NAA B-24 was accepted by the AAF. In December 1943, Supplementary Agreement No. 10 was approved by the War Department calling for 650 additional B-24s, spare parts, and data. The contract was converted from cost-plus-a-fixed-fee to fixed price. Between

March 1943 and June 1944, only 430 B-24Gs of the original 650 would be delivered because the B-24J model came into production incorporating latest improvements.

The first twenty-five B-24Gs manufactured by North American Dallas were similar to the B-24D manufactured by Consolidated except for the installation with greenhouse noses, the A-5 automatic pilot, and S-1 bombsight in place of the C-1 and N-series equipment. These early G-models tended to be heavier than their counterparts from other factories, but NAA engineers devised a plan that resolved this problem. Later NAA B-24Gs were equipped with an Emerson A-15 nose turret installation beginning in October–November 1943 after the Ford B-24H had introduced them in June 1943. With addition of the nose turret on the twenty-sixth bomber, the remainder of the B-24Gs was similar to the B-24J except for the automatic pilot and bombsight. After delivery of camouflaged B-24Gs through Block 10, NAA Liberators were delivered in natural metal finish. North American exercised some innovation on its Liberators, including the introduction in January 1944 of bellcranks (a type of crank that changes motion through an angle) instead of gearboxes in aileron control linkages, which had the effect of reducing the amount of pilot muscle necessary to wrestle the control wheel for aileron inputs. Months later, Convair and Ford adopted this style as well. North American was occupied with heated anti-ice provisions to replace the black rubber de-icer boots when the switch from B-24G to B-24J production at Dallas caused postponement of this improvement, which subsequently only appeared on San Diego Liberators beginning with the B-24J-150-CO and Ford-built aircraft starting with the B-24M-20-FO. When North American changed to C-1 autopilot and M-series bombsight, the model designation became J, which was similar to the B-24J manufactured by Consolidated.

By the middle of 1944, Ford's B-24 production capacity was finally palpable and the need for five Liberator assembly plants had past. In May 1944, the executive committee had announced in the San Diego Report that North American and Ford would continue to produce B-24s after San Diego and Fort Worth production had been terminated as these two facilities were to concentrate on building of other aircraft such as B-32 and B-36 bombers. In June 1944, the first B-24J model had been delivered to AAF with 536 B-24Js eventually produced by North American. North American ended its Liberator (B-24J) production by November 1944, followed by Convair Fort Worth by the end of that year. North American's Dallas Plant would then concentrate on building P-51 Mustangs and, for a while, consideration was given to the production of the Lockheed-designed P-80 Shooting Star jet fighters there under contract.

North American's first B-24s were G-models that were initially assembled in the Plant A hangar and moved during the winter to the still incomplete final assembly floor of Plant B; during August 1943, Plant B began production. (*NAA/AAF*)

The first 25 B-24Gs manufactured by North American Dallas were similar to the B-24D manufactured by Consolidated except for the installation with greenhouse noses, however, later NAA B-24Gs were equipped with an Emerson A-15 nose turret. (*NAA/AAF*)

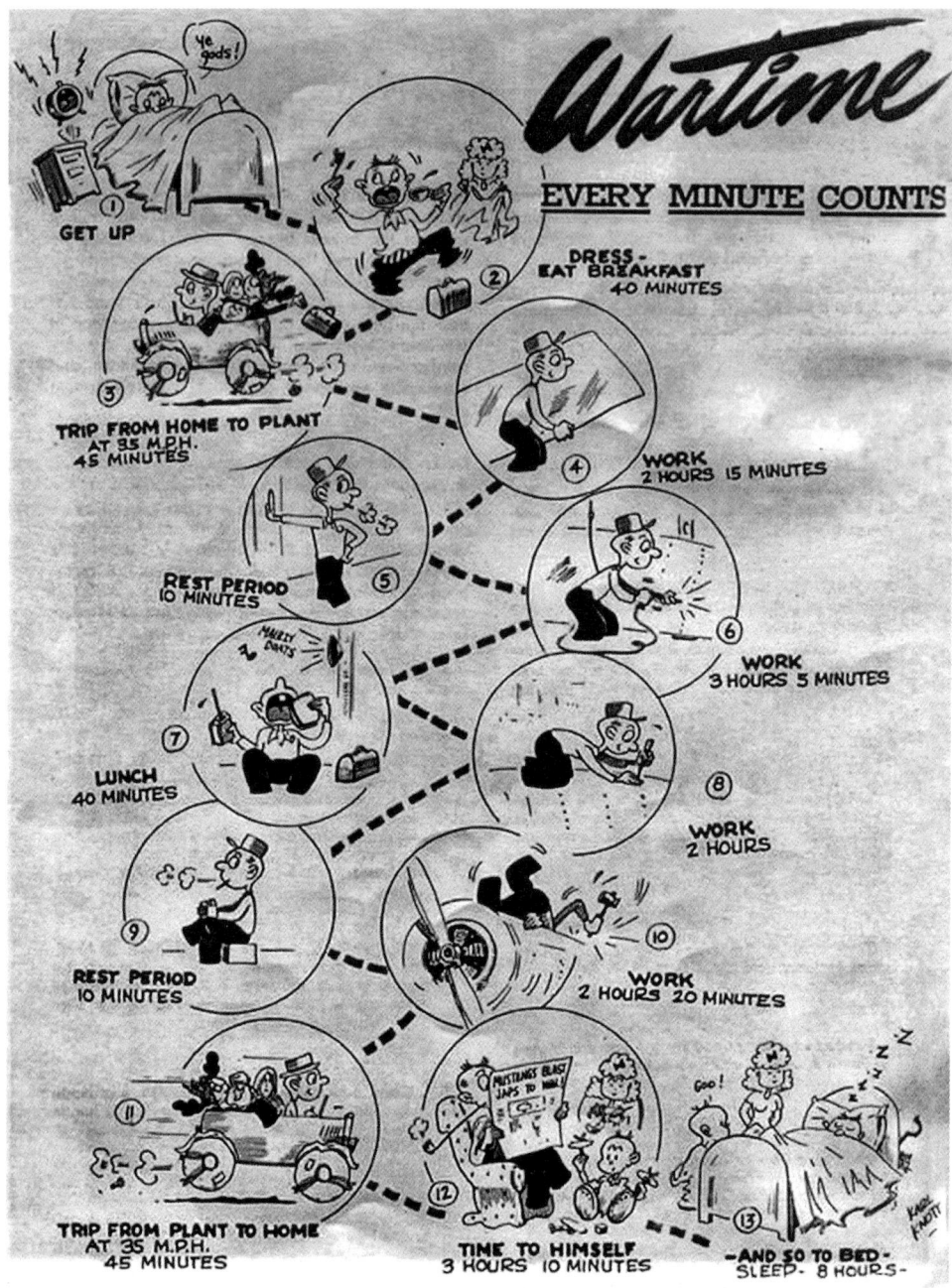

A NAA personnel poster chronicling an employee's typical workday. (*NAA/AAF*)

After delivery of camouflaged B-24Gs through Block 10, NAA Liberators were delivered in natural metal finish. (*NAA/AAF*)

The last of 966 NAA Dallas Liberators was *The Skies the Limit*, which was celebrated by being covered by worker signatures. (*NAA/AAF*)

4

NAA Dallas B-24 Production and Costs

North American B-24 Liberator Production

Contract	Model	Accepted	#A/C
AC-24663	B-24G	March 1943 to June 1944	430
AC-24665 (Supp. #10)	B-24J	May 1944 to November 1944	536
		Total	966

The average man-hour figure per bomber for the 966 aircraft was 14,818 production man-hours. The average direct man-hours per pound for the same number of aircraft produced was 0.64 $v.$ 0.49 for Douglas Tulsa. Maximum NAA Plant employment was approximately 29,000 and peak production was 109 B-24's per month, attained in June 1944.

Women workers known as plains women comprised 10 percent of the NAA workforce in 1941, but this figure rose dramatically to 60 percent during 1943 when the national average was about 35 percent.

The Wharf School conducted 24/7 training for 3,000 workers per month.

NAA coveted the Army-Navy E-Pennant for manufacturing excellence and was awarded it on 21 September 1941 for building 738 aircraft in thirty days (and was again awarded a second in April 1943). A 100 percent participation in War Bond purchase was a requirement to win an E-Pennant so smaller companies had a better chance at and were awarded more of them. With its thousands of employees, NAA had a few hold outs, who discovered that they had their pay docked for their reluctant war bond purchase.

Total Cost of Plancor No. 25 NAA Dallas (1 September 1944)

Schedule I: Land and Land Improvements

    Land $115,981
    Land Improvements $45,697
    Total Schedule I $161,679

Schedule II: Buildings, Structures, Etc.
    Buildings, Structures $6,309,361
    Building Installations (non-mechanical) $4,882,295
    Leasehold Improvements $1,685,115
    Off Leasehold Improvements   None
    Service Costs $1,419,982
    Undistributed Costs and Contingencies $2,502,912
    Total Schedule II $16,799,667

Schedule III: Machinery, Equipment, Etc.
    Machinery and Equipment $5,067,454
    Building Installations (mechanical) $932,614
    Laboratory and Testing Equipment $2,723
    Furniture and Fixtures $570,166
    Freight and Handling $183,165
    Installation Costs $60,150
    Undistributed Costs and Contingencies $4,228,823
Total Schedule III $11,045,096

Schedule IV: Portable Tools and Automotive Equipment
    Portable Tools $8,757
    Automotive Equipment $68,880
Total Schedule IV $77,837
Total Schedules I-IV $28,084,079

5

NAA Dallas Plant Epilog

North American's Plant A produced a total of 12,967 AT-6s, 4,552 P-51s, and 299 F-6s, while Plant B contributed 966 B-24s during World War II, which were the most "fly way aircraft" produced by any other U.S. aircraft plant. After Liberator production stopped, three initial Fairchild C-82 Packet a heavy-lift cargo aircraft were built to keep Plant B viable as part of 1,000 C-82 contract, which was cancelled as the atomic bombs abruptly ended the war, leaving 977 unfinished C-82 airframes. NAA then abruptly laid off half of its 34,000 employees while the remaining 17,000 were to continue for fifteen days, only long enough to complete remaining unfinished Texan and Mustang airframes and clean the factory for plant deactivation. The NAA shutdown severely affected the Dallas economy as the total Dallas manufacturing productivity was $350 million of which NAA contributed $236 million. Of $25 million of salaries paid in Dallas County, NAA accounted for $10.5 million.

In 1945, several North American employees left the company to form their own venture, the Texas Engineering and Manufacturing Company (TEMCO), which used the former North American Aviation plant. TEMCO specialized in airframe-oriented work such as subcontract manufacturing of aircraft assemblies, general aircraft overhaul, aircraft conversion, and other special modifications. TEMCO then built Globe Swifts under a license from nearby Globe Aircraft Company in Fort Worth, as well as other small civil and military aircraft. As Swift production and demand increased rapidly, TEMCO also saw a rapid expansion with its military contracts, involving production of 400 C-82 subassemblies and 200 F-24W46 four-seat, single-engined monoplane light transport subassemblies both for the Fairchild Aircraft Company. After TEMCO acquired additional facilities in Greenville, the Grand Prairie plant focused primarily on Navy programs.

In 1946, the government attempted to interest major aircraft contractors located in congested pre-war plants to relocate to the more modern facilities constructed during the war. During 1948, the Navy announced that the Chance Vought Aircraft plant at Stratford, Connecticut, would move its entire operation to NAA Plant B in Dallas. The move was initiated by the Navy, which did not want both of its main aircraft suppliers (the other being Grumman) located on the East Coast. The move, completed

After Liberator production stopped, three initial Fairchild C-82 Packets, a heavy-lift cargo aircraft, were built to keep Plant B viable as part of 1,000 C-82 contract. (*Fairchild/AAF*)

NAA Plants A and B after Vought occupancy with two Vought F4U Corsairs flying over Plant B. (*Vought/USN*)

by mid-1949, was the largest industrial move of its kind up to that time. Some 27 million pounds of equipment and 1,300 key personnel and their families were moved 1,700 miles. In the 1950s, the Vought plant was expanded and additional facilities were constructed, including several wind tunnels. Hensley's runway was lengthened to 8,000 feet at this time to support jet operations.

Vought built 320 of the under-powered, accident-prone, F7U Cutlass during the early 1950s. The Cutlass was succeeded by the F8U Crusader, which first flew in March 1955. Later designated as the F-8, it was the USN's first single-engined supersonic fighter and remained in production until 1965 and in the fleet service for thirty-one years after 1,263 had been built. From a post-World War II low of 3,600, Vought employment increased to 17,000 by 1957.

The company became part of a Conglomerate Rage in the 1960s and 1970s becoming Ling-Temco-Vought Corporation in August 1961 and was the majority of the LTV Aerosystems Corporation in 1965 where it produced the F-8 cousin, the A-7 Corsair II. The A-7 first flew in 1965, and 1,569 went on to see widespread service with the Navy, air force, and foreign militaries. The Vought Company remained part of the LTV conglomerate until mid-1992 when the aircraft division was equally purchased by Northrop and the Carlyle Group.

Most of the original NAA aircraft manufacturing complex survives today consisting of 25,272 acres; eighty-five buildings/2,985,000 square feet: seventeen major, sixteen minor, and fifty-two miscellaneous. The Dallas Global industrial center currently has control and is attempting to lease the space.

Vought moved its entire facility from Connecticut to occupy the Dallas plant to build 320 F7U Cutlasses, 1,263 F8U Crusaders, and 1,569 A-7 Corsair IIs (depicted). (*Vought/USN*)

PART VI

Douglas Tulsa Plant

1

Planning and Building the Tulsa Plant

In the 1930s, Oklahoma aviation was only distinguished as being the home to two U.S. aviation pioneers: cowboy humorist, social commentator, and motion picture actor Will Rogers and famed American aviator, innovator, and record-breaking round-the-world pilot Wiley Post, who died together in 1935 when their Lockheed Explorer floatplane crashed on take-off near Barrow, Alaska. Nonetheless, in the late 1930s as war approached in Europe and America mobilized its war industry, Tulsa's civic leaders vigorously promoted the construction of a new aircraft assembly facility in their city.

While the Federal government continued to advocate for a Consolidated plant in Tulsa, Reuben Fleet continued to strongly promote Fort Worth as a better location. At the time, the government insisted that factories should be built in states that had not already benefited from defense spending, and Texas already had a sizable military presence and Dallas was about to be granted the North American aircraft plant. Fleet remained adamant that Fort Worth should be selected and Amon Carter offered Roosevelt a solution, suggesting that Tulsa be granted another aircraft plant and Consolidated be allowed to come to Fort Worth.

The War Department agreed to construct a factory if Tulsa provided the land and required runways. Tulsa voters quickly passed a $750,000 bond issue in March 1941, authorizing the city to purchase 750 acres east of the Municipal Airport and to construct the runways. Title to the 343 acre plant site was deeded to the U.S. government by the City of Tulsa for the consideration of $1.

On 20 May 1941, Contract W535-ac-18722 (Contract 18722) was entered into by the government represented by its contracting officer and Douglas Aircraft Company, Inc. with the Ford Motor Company as the major sub-contractor. The contract was originally awarded to include 600 heavy bombardment B-24D Model bombers each to be completed and manufactured in accordance with Consolidated Aircraft Corporation Model Specification ZD-32-009 dated 18 March 1941. These bombers were to be assembled by Douglas from components manufactured by major sub-contractor Ford Willow Run in the government-owned plant at Tulsa that was to have been ready for occupancy on or before 1 January 1942. During July 1941, the model designation of the 600 B-24s of the initial Contract 18722 was changed from B-24D to B-24E by Change

Order No. 1 dated 29 July 1941. A letter of intent addressed by the War Department to Douglas dated 16 January 1942 authorized Douglas to proceed with the manufacture and delivery of 1,000 additional model B-24Es and spare parts.

Supplemental Agreement No. 1 to Contract W535 ac-18722 was granted on 11 April 1942, which superseded the letter of intent dated 16 January 1942. This Supplemental Agreement increased the number of B-24s on Contract AC-18722 to a total of 1,600 B-24s to be completed and delivered by Douglas in accordance with Consolidated's Specification ZD-32-009. The total estimated cost of the quantity of spare parts was to be equal to the estimated cost of approximately 15 percent of the 1,600 bombers. In *lieu* of the requirements of the *Handbook of Instructions for Airplane Designers* setting forth requirements for weight data, Douglas was to furnish weight data in the "Weight Empty" condition only on the fifth and 100th bomber and on every 100th thereafter up to the 1,600th. The government was to furnish without cost to the contractor, f.o.b. to Willow Run or Tulsa, all equipment listed as government-furnished (GFI) in Consolidated's Specification Report ZD- 32-009. All of such items and equipment were to be installed in accordance with Reports ZI-32-006 and ZI-32-007 (both dated 16 April 1941) as amended or revised and Consolidated Model Specification as amended.

Douglas Aircraft was to manage the plant assembling Ford Willow Run manufactured Liberator KD kits. The logistics of delivering these Ford components to their final assembly site made the Douglas Tulsa facility a better choice than any of the more distant three Douglas California options (Santa Monica, Long Beach, and El Segundo). Groundbreaking for Air Force Plant 3 took place on 2 May 1941 and company President Donald Douglas and Gen. Hap Arnold dedicated the Plant on 15 August 1942. Douglas Aircraft became the only manufacturer to build both the B-17 Flying Fortress (at its Long Beach plant as part of the Boeing-Vega-Douglas (BVD) consortium) and the B-24 Liberator under license.

The Tulsa facility, named Tulsa Aircraft Assembly Plant No. 3 on 3 May 1942, was located about 7.5 miles northwest of downtown Tulsa. The entire project consisted of a developed site, airfield, all buildings and facilities including the necessary utilities comprising a complete aircraft assembly plant designed to construct large, multi-engined aircraft. The Austin Company of Cleveland, the architects of the Consolidated Fort Worth Plant, was chosen as the architects of the Tulsa Plant, which was to be similar to the Fort Worth Plant. The new plant had a total production floor area of 803,310 square feet with the main manufacturing building measuring 320 feet wide and 4,004 feet long. Its 40-foot-high ceilings facilitated a material handling system consisting of five monorail craneways, each 4,000 feet long. The plant was built without windows and operated under blackout conditions even though it was located mid-continent, far from any possible enemy attack. In addition to the assembly building, the plant included an office building, hangar, paint shop, maintenance building, boiler house, guardhouse, police station, pump house, and cafeteria building. A Burlington Northern Railroad spur line transported aircraft sub-assemblies and raw materials into one end of the building and completed aircraft emerged from the other end. An airfield adjacent to the plant site was constructed at government expense on approximately 750 acres leased from the City of Tulsa. This airfield adjoining the Tulsa Municipal Airport #1 was designed to make the two flying fields correlated and connected.

Company President Donald Douglas initiated groundbreaking for Air Force Plant 3 on 2 May 1941 and Gen. Hap Arnold met Douglas in Tulsa to dedicate the completed Plant on 15 August 1942. (*DAC/AAF*)

After the citizens of Tulsa voted virtually free land and a $750,000 bond issue and construction on the Tulsa facility, named Tulsa Aircraft Assembly Plant No. 3, was begun. (*DAC/AAF*)

The Douglas B-24 plant was located about 7.5 miles northwest of downtown Tulsa, consisted of a developed site, airfield, all buildings and facilities including the necessary utilities. (*DAC/AAF*)

Truscon Steel Company ad of a drawing of the completed building, touting its use of "Revolutionary Ferroglas in the construction of the Plant that had a total production floor area of 803,310 square feet, including a Main Manufacturing Building that was 320 feet wide and 4,004 feet long and had 40 foot high ceilings." (DAC/AAF)

The Tulsa Plant airfield was designated for the final government inspection and acceptance of all B-24 bombers completed under contract AC-18722. Major sub-contractor Ford's Willow Run Plant was designated for the final inspection and acceptance of spare parts that were manufactured completely by Ford. Headquarters, materiel center, AAF, Wright Field, Dayton, Ohio, was designated for the final inspection and acceptance by the government of the data furnished under contract AC-18722. By June 1942, the Tulsa Plant was ready for operation but the sub-contracted Ford-furnished KD kits of component parts for B-24Es were not scheduled to be delivered to enable the Tulsa Plant to begin operations at that time. Supplemental Agreement No. 4 provided that the "assembly of not to exceed ten sets of component parts of B-24D airplanes at the Government-Owned Plant at Tulsa, Oklahoma, became effective on the fifth of June 1942." The government then arranged to obtain "sets of component parts not to exceed ten B-24D airplanes from Consolidated Aircraft Corporation at San Diego under fixed price contract, W535-ac-16005 dated 18 September 1940." The reason the government wanted component parts for these ten B-24Ds to be assembled at Tulsa instead of San Diego was to expedite assembly of the Ford B-24E components when they became available and to establish employment for the new plant in the interim. The Douglas Plant was to assemble component parts into complete B-24Ds under substantially the same terms and conditions as provided in contract AC-18722 covering the assembly and completion of B-24s from component parts to be furnished by Ford. The government and Ford entered into a special facilities contract in which specialized trucks, trailers, and equipment owned by the government and leased by Ford would be used to deliver parts and assemblies to Tulsa as they were to North American Dallas. This increased the work to be done by Ford, reducing costs to the government of the B-24 as called for under the prime contract and reducing the amount of fixed fee to be paid contractor.

2
Assembling B-24s

Meanwhile, Ford had supplied Tulsa with four complete sets of component parts for B-24Es during September 1942, after which monthly deliveries of component parts continually increased. The first "completed article" assembled from Ford B-24E components was delivered in February 1943. Douglas found itself in a unique situation concerning the delivery of its B-24s. As an assembly facility for Ford-built KD kits, the Douglas Tulsa assembly line was remote from the design of the bomber by Consolidated San Diego as well as from fabrication of the KD kits by Ford in Michigan. Yet Douglas was responsible for the quality of the finished product that rolled out of the Oklahoma Plant.

Supplemental Agreement No. 20 to contract AC-18722 reduced the quantity of B-24s from 1,600 to 954 and, in turn, reduced the quantity of spare parts. This reduction, plus the ten B-24Ds assembled from component parts supplied by San Diego, gave a final total delivery of 964 B-24s from Tulsa.

Besides the KD kits supplied by Ford, all other materials and labor required by Douglas to fully complete Contract AC-18722 were to be furnished and supplied by Douglas. All detachable blade propellers were to be assembled and balanced by Douglas. Serial numbers for the aircraft as mandated by the contract were furnished in writing to Douglas by the contracting officer. The delivery schedule established for the 1,600 airplanes was as follows:

Quantity	During Month of
2 Aircraft	July 1942
6 additional	August 1942
12	September 1942
20	September 1942
30	November 1942
40	December 1942
50	January 1943
65	January 1943
75	April 1943

85   May 1943
95   June 1943
100   July 1943
120   August 1943
130   September 1943
140   October 1943

Then 155 per month thereafter until 1,600 delivered

First Tulsa Liberator was the first of ten B-24Ds, after which the B-24E was built. (*DAC/AAF*)

The B-24E was the most produced Tulsa Liberator with 749 of the 964 (ten B-24Ds and 205 B-24Js) which ended Tulsa production. (*DAC/AAF*)

The last of 1,893 Willow Run KD kits was shipped to Tulsa on 7 July 1944, which assembled 954 from Ford and ten from Consolidated San Diego. (*DAC/AAF*)

B-24J Tulsa production ended alongside of the SBD-5/A-24B Dauntless. (*DAC/AAF*)

Contract Deliveries by Douglas Tulsa

Contract*	Model	Accepted Date	No.
18722	B-24D	Aug. 1942–Jan. 1943	10**
18722	B-24E	Feb. 1943–Sept. 1943	167
18722	B-24E	Aug. 1943–Mar. 1944	433
18722***	B-24E	Mar. 1944–May 1944	149
18722***	B-24J	May 1944–July 1944	205
Total			964

* W535 ac-18722

** Assembled by Douglas Tulsa from components of contract 16005 and DA-4 as fabricated by San Diego. The other 954 KD airframes built by Ford were assembled by Douglas Tulsa and delivered on 18722.

*** W535 ac-18722 Supplement #1

The average man-hour figure per plane for each of the 964 bombers was 11,350 production man-hours. The average direct man-hours per pound for same number of bombers produced was 0.49 $v.$ 0.64 for NAA Dallas

Summary of Cost of the Douglas Tulsa Facility (20 May 1944)

Schedule I: Land and Land Improvements	
Land	$1.00
Land Improvements	$878,830
Total Schedule I	$878,831
Schedule II: Buildings, Etc.	
Buildings	$10,003,734
Building Installations	$4,958,720
Leasehold Improvements	$3,352,849
Service Costs	$1,398,731
Total Schedule II	$19,714,034
Schedule III Machinery, Equipment, Etc.	
Machine Tools and Equipment	
Machine Tools	$2,231,376
Productive Equipment	$932,590
Building Installations (non-mechanical)	$1,721,456
Laboratory and Testing Equipment	$90,959
Furniture and Fixtures	$373,403
Office Equipment	$492,207
Dispensary Equipment	$7,646
Cafeteria Equipment	$88,406
Total Schedule III	$5,973,145

Schedule IV: Portable Tools, Automotive and Material Handling Equipment
Portable Tools $471,892
Automobile Equipment $175,692
Material Handling Equipment $188,691
Total Schedule IV $836,275
Schedule V: Durable Tools   None
Grand Total $27,366,285

When B-24 production ceased at Tulsa in July 1944, 964 Liberators had been delivered by Douglas. The last Tulsa B-24 was built in July 1944 and named *The Tulsamerican* by the employees, and the crews that flew it in Italy retained the name. *The Tulsamerican* was shot down by German fighters on 17 December 1944 after a bombing run over German-occupied Poland and crashed, killing three of the ten-man crew. When *The Tulsamerican* was lost in combat, the employees at the plant contributed enough in war bonds to purchase an entire squadron of the new Douglas A-26 then being built at Tulsa. During August 2010, the wreckage of the B-24 *Tulsamerican* was discovered by Croatian divers in the Adriatic Sea.

When B-24 production was discontinued, work at the Tulsa Plant then expanded to construction of 1,313 Douglas A-26s Invaders and 615 A-24s Banshees (AAF versions of the Navy SBD Dauntless Dive Bomber). The A-24 contract approved on 1 December 1942 was to provide for 1,200 A-24Bs (SBD-5) and deliveries began in March 1943 but cancellations on 30 October reduced the total to 615 A-24Bs completed by December 1943. The Tulsa Plant also carried out the modification of B-25s, C-47s, the conversation of B-17s into YB-40 gunships, and converting forty-seven A-20s into P-70 night fighters. Some of the modifications were completed at both the main building and four separate modification hangars that were built across the runway from the main building.

The Douglas plant produced 5,354 C-47s from March 1943 until August 1945. The plant built thirteen per day during peak performance and fabricated spare parts for 500 more Gooney Birds. The plant also assembled parts for 400 C-54 Skymaster military transports and 900 A-26 Invader attack bombers. As many as 38,000 Oklahomans labored at the Douglas Plant, and more than half were women.

The Douglas Plant officially closed on 17 August 1945 and 22,000 people became unemployed. Part of the plant was redesignated as Building 3001 and transferred to the Oklahoma City Air Technical Service Command (OCATSC) on 1 November 1945 where it served as the headquarters, modification, and maintenance building for the OCATSC, now the Oklahoma City Air Logistics Center. Tinker Air Force Base in Oklahoma City used the plant for storage for a time, and in June 1946, American Airlines occupied two of the four modification hangars to perform maintenance on its DC-6s. As the Cold War with the Soviet Union intensified in 1952, Douglas reopened the plant to manufacture licensed Boeing B-47 Stratojet long-range strategic bombers, along with modifications to B-47s and Lockheed T-33s. Concurrent with B-47 production was a second assembly line to build the Douglas RB-66 Destroyer light attack bomber. Douglas also built Delta rockets at the Tulsa Plant along with

The last of 964 Tulsa B-24s was built in July 1944 and named *The Tulsamerican* by the employees; the crews that flew it in Italy retained the name but the Liberator was lost in combat. (*DAC/AAF*)

After B-24 production ceased, the plant continued to build the last of 615 Army A-24B Banshees (the Navy SBD-5 Dauntless), which was the most produced version. (*DAC/AAF*)

During mid-1944, the plant began construction of 1,313 Douglas A-26s Invaders. (*AAF*)

Between March 1943 and August 1945, the Oklahoma City plant produced 5,354 C-47s. (*AAF*)

later modifying A-4s, B-52s, DC-8s, C-17s, and C-135s into EC-134s. Later, as part of McDonnell Douglas, F-15 conformable fuel tanks were fabricated at the factory. In 1962, North American Aviation leased a portion of Plant No. 3 from Douglas and eventually built Hound Dog and Minuteman Missiles, Saturn Lander Adaptors, and sections of the Space Shuttle. When all of the above-named companies or their derivatives were acquired by Boeing, they used the facility to build parts for the International Space Station. In 2005, investment firm Onex purchased the Boeing Wichita, Kansas, and Tulsa operations, which was then formed into the world's largest tier-one aerospace supplier, Spirit AeroSystems. Only the North American portion of the original plant was included in the purchase while the Douglas portion was razed and replaced by a brand-new state-of-the-art school bus factory owned by Navistar International Corporation.

In 1952, Douglas reopened the plant to manufacture Boeing B-47 Stratojet long-range strategic bombers. (*USAF*)

Bibliography

Magazine, Newspaper, and Internet Articles

Aeroplane, "The Box the B-17 Came In," *Aeroplane*, December 2002
Anderson, J., "Ludwig Prantl's Boundary Layer," *Physics Today*, December 2005
Aviation, "How Fewer Build More Bomber Nose Sections," *Aviation*, September 1943; "Flying Equipment," *Aviation*, May 1945
Bhargava, K., "India's Reclaimed B-24 Bombers," *www.bharat-rakshak.com*
Boone, A., "The Liberator," *Popular Science*, May 1943
Christensen, H., "Flying the Green Dragon, 389th Bomb Group Assembly Aircraft," *Friend's Journal*, Winter 1992
Dorr, R., "Data Base," *Aeroplane*, December 2002; "Flying the Banana Boat," *Aeroplane*, December 2002; "Liberator Goes to War," *Aeroplane*, December 2002
Fast, H., They Remember Tom Girdler, *New Masses*, July 1947
Fenelon, J., "Low, Slow, and Vulnerable," *FlyPast*, April, 2015
Flight, "A Novel Fighter Design," *Flight*, 29 January 1942
FlyPast, "Spotlight: Consolidated B-24 Liberator," *FlyPast*. November 2014; "Alpine Sanctuary," *FlyPast*. November 2014
Freeman, R., "Judas Goats," *FlyPast*, May 1996
Gunderson, B., "8th Air Force Newsboys: Cheddington Revisited," *Aerospace Historian*, Winter 1984
Gwinn, J., "B-24s in Quantity Production," *Aviation*, April 1942
Hamilton, D., "B-24 Production in San Diego, California," *San Diego Magazine*, n.d.
Hotchkiss, G., "Modification Centers, An American Military Innovation," *Aviation*, April 1943
Johnsen, F., "Single-Tail Liberators," *FlyPast*, April, 1996
Kelley, J., "Consolidated Vultee San Diego Production Plan," *Industrial Aviation*, Vol. 1, no. 5, 1944
Kinner, B., "Carpetbaggers World War Two's Covert Operations in the ETO," Author's Blog, 2009
Laddon, I., "Reduction of Man-Hours in Aircraft Production," *Aviation*, May, 1943
Latimer-Needham, C., "Refueling in Flight," *Flight*, 22 November 1945
Laufer, M., "BTO, PFF, OBOE, H2S, H2X, MICKEY: Enter the Mystical World of Radar Navigational Bombing," *Flak News*, April 1995
Lewis, D., "Willow Run Runs," *Business Week*, 20 February 1943
McGowan, S., "The Air Transport Command: From Lend-Lease to the Hump," *Warfare History*, July 2015

Nakamura, N., "San Diego and the Pacific Theater," *Journal of San Diego History*, n.d.
Newman, G., "Liberators by Consolidated Vultee," *Aviation*, July, 1943
Pelley, R., "Mid-Air Refueling in Gander," *Flight*, n.d.
Persons, L., "Sweeping Planes off the Floor," *Flying Aces*, February 1943
Peterson; A., "Aircraft Breakdown for Increased Production," *Industrial Aviation*, March 1945
Planes of the Past, "Aircraft Boneyards," *www.planes of the past.com.aircraft-boneyards.html*
Popular Mechanics, "Battle Log of the Liberators," *Popular Mechanics*, September 1943; "Tomorrow's Plane Takes Shape," *Popular Mechanics*, March 1942
Popular Science, "Liberator," *Popular Science*, June 1942; "Manta Fighter has Contra-Rotating Props, *Popular Science*, May 1942

Powell, H., "Lookout Hitler Here Comes the Flood," *Popular Science*, May 1943
Sebold, R., "Single Assembly Line Produces both Bombers and Transports," *Aviation*, April 1943
Sloat, C., "The Unknown Liberator: RY-3," *Warbirds International*, May/June 1988
Snell, K., "Tulsa Bomber Plant," *Oklahoma State, Digital Library*, n.d.
Swanger, A., "The Luftwaffe's Secret KG 200 Squadron," *World War II Magazine*, September 1997
Taylor, C., "American Air Operations in Sweden: 1943-1945," *AAHS Journal. Spring,* 1977
Thompson, S., "Post-War Aircraft Disposal," *AAHS Journal*, Winter 1992
Turpin, T., "C-87 Liberator Express," *World at War*, August-September, 2013
Veronico, V., "Rearming the Liberator," *Air Classics*, May 2012
Vincenti, W., "The Davis Wing and the Problem of Airfoil Design: Uncertainty and Growth in Engineering Knowledge," *Technology and Culture, Special Issue: Engineering in the Twentieth Century*, October 1986

Books

Aeronautical Chamber of Commerce of America, *The Aircraft Yearbook for 1942* (NY, Colonial Press, 1942)
Andrade, J., *US Military Aircraft Designations and Serials since 1909* (UK, Midland, 1979)
Baime, A, *The Arsenal of Democracy* (MA, Houghton Mifflin, 2014)
Bernad, D., *Rumanian Air Force: The Prime Decade 1938–1947* (TX, Squadron/Signal, 1999)
Birdsall, S, *B-24 Liberator* (NY, Arco, 1968); *B-24 Liberator in Action* (TX, Squadron/Signal, 1975); *Log of the Liberators* (NY, Doubleday, 1973)
Blue, A., *B-24 Liberator: A Pictorial History* (UK, Ian Allan, 1976)
Bond, S., and Forder, R., *Special Ops Liberators* (UK, Grub Street, 2011)
Bowers, P., *Boeing Aircraft since 1916* (UK, Putman, 1966)
Bowman, M., *100 Group (Bomber Support)* (UK, Pen and Sword, 2006); *B-24 Liberator: 1939–1945* (UK, Wensum, 1979); *Combat Legend: B-24 Liberator* (UK, Airlife, 2003); *Consolidated B-24 Liberator* (UK, Crowood, 1990)
Bradley, R., *Convair Advanced Designs* (MN, Specialty, 2010)
Campbell, J. and D., *Consolidated B-24 Liberator* (PA, Schiffer, 1993)
Carey, A., *Consolidated-Vultee PB4Y-2 Privateer* (PA, Schiffer, 2005); *US Navy PB4Y-1 (B-24) Liberator Squadrons in Great Britain during World War II* (PA, Schiffer, 2013)
Carty, *Secret Squadrons of the Eighth* (UK, Ian Allan, 1990)
Cate, J., and Craven W., *The Army Air Forces in World War II: Volume 6, Men and Planes* (IL, The University of Chicago Press, 1955)
Cervantez, B., *Amon Carter: The Founder of Modern Ft. Worth, 1930–1955* (TX, U. North Texas, MA Thesis, 2005)
Churchill, W., *The Second World War: The Hinge of Fate: Volume IV (History of the Second World War)* (NY, Houghton Mifflin, 1953)
Clarke, R., *The 802/492 Bomb Group: The Carpetbaggers* (UK, Carpetbagger Museum, 2001)
Cleveland, R., *Air Transport at War* (NY, Harper and Bros, 1946)
Compiled by Members of Plant Guide Staff, *Willow Run Plant Guide* (MI, 1 February 1945)
Davis. L., *B-24 Liberator in Action* (TX, Squadron/Signal, 1987)
Dmitri, I., *Flight to Everywhere* (NY, Whittlsey House, 1944)
Donald, D., (Editor), *Encyclopedia of World Aircraft* (Canada, Prospero Books, 1997)
Dorr, R., *Air Force One*, MBI (MN, 2001); *B-24 Liberator Units of the Eighth Air Force* (UK, Osprey, 1999); *B-24 Liberator Units of the Fifteenth Air Force* (UK, Osprey, 2000); *B-24 Liberator Units of the Pacific War* (UK, Osprey, 1999)
Douglas, G., *Consolidated B-24 Liberator: Owner's Workshop Manual* (UK, Haywood, 2013)
Doyle, D., *B-24 Liberator in Action* (TX, Squadron/Signal, 2012)
Ethell, J., *Aircraft of World War II* (UK, Harper Collins, 1995)
Feuer, A., *The B-24 in China* (PA, Stackpole, 1992)
Fleet, D., *Our Flight to Destiny* (NY, Vantage, 1964)
Freeman, R., *B-24 at War* (UK, Ian Allan, 1983); *Mighty Eighth* (NJ, Doubleday, 1970); *Mighty Eighth War Manual* (UK, Janes, 1984); *Mighty Eighth War Diary* (UK, Janes, 1981)
Girdler, T., *Boot Straps* (NY, Scribner, 1943)
Glines, C., *Chennault's Forgotten Warriors* (PA, Schiffer, 1995)
Green, W., *Famous Bombers of the Second World War* (NY, Doubleday, 1959)
Gunston, B., *World Encyclopedia of Aero Engines* (UK, Patrick Stephens, 1986)
Halley, J., *Squadrons of the Royal Air Force* (UK, Air Britain, 1980)
Harrington, J., *RAF 100 Group: Birth of Electronic Warfare* (UK, Fonthill, 2016)
Hendrie, A., *Cinderella Service: RAF Coastal Command: 1939–1945* (UK, Pen and Sword, 2006)
Herman, A., *Freedom's Forge* (NY, Random House, 2013)
Howell, F., *The Snoopers* (NY, Vantage, 1991)
Hutton, S., *Squadron of Deception: 36th Bomb Squadron in WWII* (PA, Schiffer, 1999)
Jackiewicz, J. and Bock, R., *Assembly Ships of the Mighty Eighth* (Poland, Kecam, n.d.)
Jackson, R., *The Secret Squadrons* (UK, Robson, 1983)
Johnsen, F., *Bombers in Blue: PB4Y-2 Privateers and PB4Y-1 Liberators* (WA, Bomber Books, 1979); *Consolidated B-24*

Liberator: Combat History and Development of the Liberator and Privateer (MN, Motorbooks, 1993); *Consolidated B-24 Liberator (Warbird Tech #1)* (MN, Specialty, 2001); *Consolidated B-24 Liberator, Rugged but Right* (NY, McGraw-Hill, 1999); *American Military Transport Aircraft since 1925* (NC, McFarland, 2013)

Jones, L., *U.S. Bombers, 1928–1980s* (CA, Aero, 1984)
Jones, W., *Bomber Intelligence* (UK, Midlands, 1988)
Kinzey, B., *B-24 Liberator in Detail* (TX, Squadron/Signal, 2000)
Kostenuk, S., and Griffin, J., *RCAF Squadrons and Aircraft* (Canada, Canadian War Museum, 1977)
Larkins, W., *Surplus WWII US Aircraft* (CA, BAC, 2005)
Lerche, H., *Luftwaffe Test Pilot* (UK, Janes, 1977)
Lloyd, A., Liberator, *America's Global Bomber* (MT, Pictorial Histories, 1993)
March, D.(ed.), *British Warplanes of World War II* (UK, Aerospace, 1998)
Mayo, L., and Thomson, H., *US Army in WWII: The Technical Services, The Ordnance Department: Procurement and Supply* (Washington, D.C., USGPO, 1959)
McDowell, E., *Consolidated B-24D-M Liberator in USAAF, RAF, RAAF, MLD, IAF, Czech AF and CNAF Service* (CA, ARCO, 1970)
Milward, A., *War, Economy and Society, 1939–1945* (CA, University of California Press, 1977)
Moyes, P., *Bomber Squadrons of the RAF and Their Aircraft* (UK, MacDonald, 1977); *Consolidated B-24 Liberator (Early Models)* (UK, Vintage Aviation, 1979); *Royal Air Force Bombers of WW2: Vol.1* (NY, Doubleday, 1968)
Nelmes, M., *Tocumwal to Tarakan, Australians and the Consolidated B-24 Liberator* (Australia, Banner Books, 1994)
Nelson, D., *Arsenal of Democracy: The Story of American Production* (NY, Harcourt Brace, 1946)
North, T. and Bailey, M., *Liberator Album: B-24s of the 2nd Air Division, 8th Air Force, Vol. 1* (UK, Norwich, 1979); *Liberator Album: B-24s of the 2nd Air Division, 8th Air Force, Vol. 2* (UK, Norwich, 1981)
Nowarra, H., *Fremde Vogel unterm Balkenkreuz* (Germany, Podzun Pallas-Verlag, 1981)
O'Leary, M., *Consolidated B-24 Liberator* (UK, Osprey, 2002)
Oliver, D., *Airborne Espionage* (UK, Sutton, 2005)
Parnell, B., *Air Commandos: Saga of the Carpetbaggers in WWII* (NY, ibooks, 1993); *Carpetbaggers America's Secret War in Europe* (TX, Eakin Press, 1987)
Pate, J., *Arsenal of Defense* (TX, Texas State Historical, 2011)
Pentland, G. and Malone, P., *Aircraft of the RAAF 1921–71* (Australia, Kookaburra, 1971)
Perrone, S., *B-24 Snoopers* (NJ, NJSG, 2001)
Peterson, S., *Planning the Home Front* (IL, U. of Chicago, 2013)
Rickenbacker, E., *Rickenbacker* (NY, Prentice Hall, 1967)
Roba, J., *Foreign Planes in the Service of the Luftwaffe* (UK, Pen and Sword, 2009)
Robertson, B., *British Military Aircraft Serials, 1912–1969* (UK, Ian Allan, 1969)
Serling, R., *When the Airlines Went to War* (NY, Kensington, 1997)
Shacklady, E., *Consolidated B-24 Liberator* (UK, Cerebus, 2002)
Skaarup, H., *Canadian Warbirds: Fighters, Bombers and Patrol Aircraft* (CA, Writers Club, 2012)
Sorensen, C. (with Williamson, S.), *My Forty Years with Ford* (IN, Wayne State, 2006)
Spight, E. and J., *Eagles in the Pacific: Consairways* (NY, Historical Aviation, 1980)
Stapler, H., *Strangers in a Strange Land* (TX, Squadron/Signal, 1988)
Streetly, M., *Aircraft of 100 Group* (UK, Robert Hale, 1984); *Confound and Destroy* (UK, McDonald and Janes, 1978)
Sullivan, M., *Dependable Engines: The Story of Pratt and Whitney* (Wash., D.C., Library of Flight, 2008)
Swanborough, G., and Bowers, P., *US Military Aircraft since 1909* (Wash., D.C., Smithsonian, 1982)
Swearngin, P., *Carpetbagger Project: Secret Heroes* (US, Create Space, 2009)
Swedish Aviation Historical Society, *Sweden: Haven of Refuge* (Sweden, SAHS, 1976)
Tanner, S., *Refuge from the Reich* (NY, Sharpedon, 2000)
Taylor, F., *Democracy's Air Arsenal* (Duell, NY, Sloan and Pearce, 1947)
Taylor, J., *Consolidated B-24/PG4Y Liberator: Combat Aircraft of the World from 1909 to Present* (NY, Putman, 1969)
Taylor, M., *Jane's American Fighting Aircraft of the 20th Century* (UK, Mallard, 1962)
Thomas, G. and Ketley, B., *KG 200: The Luftwaffe's Most Secret Unit* (UK, Hikoki, 2003)
Vander Meulen, J., *The Politics of Aircraft; Building an American Military Industry* (KS, University Press of Kansas, 1991)
Veronico, N. and Ginter, S., *Convair PB4T-2/P4Y-2 Privateer* (CA, Ginter, 2012)
Vincent, C., *Canada's Wings 2: Liberator and Fortress* (Canada, Canada's Wings, 1975)
Wagg, J., *General Dynamics Aircraft and Their Predecessors* (MD, NIP, 1990)
Wagner, Raymond, *American Combat Planes* (NY, Doubleday, 1982)
Walsh, K., *Air Force One* (NY, Hyperion, 2001)
Ward, R. and Munday, E., *USAAF Heavy Bomb Group Markings and Camouflage 1941–1945, Consolidated Liberator* (UK, Osprey, 1972)
Wegg, J., *General Dynamic Aircraft and their Predecessors* (UK, Putnam, 1990)
West, B., *The Man Who Flew Churchill* (NY, McGraw Hill, 1975)
White, G., *Allied Aircraft Piston Engines* (PA, SAE, 1995)
Wilson, S., *Boston, Mitchell, and Liberator in Australian Service* (Australia, Aerospace, 1992); *Military Aircraft of Australia* (Australia, Aerospace Publications, 1994)
Winchester, J., *Consolidated B-24 Liberator: Aircraft of WWII* (UK, Aviation Factfile, 2004)
Young, E., *B-24 Liberator Units of the CBI* (UK, Osprey, 2011)

Manuals

AAC, *Handbook of Operation and Flight Instructions for the B-24C and B-24D Bombardment Airplanes, AN 01-5EC-1*, 7 March 1942

AAC, *Handbook of Service Instructions for Models B-24C and B-24D Bombardment Airplanes*, 20 January 1942

AAF HQ, *How Not to Fly the B-24, Vol. 1 No. 1*, no date

AAF HQ, *Pilot Training Manual for the Liberator B-24, 50-12*, 1 May 1945

AAF HQ, *Pilot Training Manual for the Liberator B-24, 50-12*, 1 October 1944

AAF, *Erection and Maintenance Instructions for Army Models B-24D, G, H, and J; RB-24C and E/Navy Model PB4Y-1/British Models, AN 01-5EC-2*, 20 July 1943

AAF, *Erection and Maintenance Instructions for Army Models B-24D, G, H, and J; RB-24C and E/Navy Model PB4Y-1/British Models, AN 01-5E-2, 25*, October 1944

AAF, *Operation and Flight Instructions for the Model LB-30 Liberator II Airplane*, 30 December 1941

AAF, *Parts Catalog for the Army Model B-24M (Ford), AN 01-5EE-4B*, 1 August 1945

AAF, *Parts Catalog for the Army Models B-24D and J Airplanes, Navy Model PB4Y-1/British Models, AN 01-5E-4*, 25 July 1944.

AAF, *Parts Catalog for the Army Models B-24D and J Airplanes, Navy Model PB4Y-1/British Models, AN 01-5E-4*, 1 December 1944

AAF, *Parts Catalog for the Army Models B-24E and H Airplanes, AN 01-5E-4A*, 25 July 1944

AAF, *Pilot's Flight Operating Instructions for Army Models B-24G, H, J, L, and M Navy Model PB4Y-1 British Model Liberator GRVI and BVI Airplanes, AN 01-5EE-1*, 30 November 1944

AAF, *Pilot's Flight Operating Instructions for Army Models C-87, C87A, and C-87Band Navy Models RY-1 and RY-2 Airplanes, AN 01-5CA-1*, 15 December 1943

Air Ministry, *Liberator II, V, VI: Pilot and Engineer's Notes*, February 1944

Bureau of Aeronautics, *Pilot's Handbook of Flight Operating Instructions: Navy Model RY-3 Airplane, AN 01-5CB-1*, 1 December 1944

Consolidated Aircraft Company, *Flight Manual for the B-24D and J Heavy Bombardment Airplane*, 1943

Consolidated Aircraft Company, *Flight Manual for the B-24D*, 15 September 1942

Consolidated Aircraft Company, *Handbook of Erection and Maintenance for the Consolidated Liberator LB-30 "Liberator II" Bombardment Airplane*, 15 April 1941

Consolidated Aircraft Company, *Handbook of Operation and Flight Instruction for the Model B-24C and Bombardment Airplanes, 01-5EC-1*, 7 March 1942

Consolidated Aircraft Company, *Pilot's Notes for the Liberator II Airplane*, 21 May 1941

Consolidated Aircraft Company, *Service and Instruction Manual B-24D Airplane*, 1943

Consolidated Aircraft Company, *Service and Instruction Manual: Airplane General 24 Airplane*, 1 July 1941

Consolidated Aircraft Company, *Service and Instruction Manual: Airplane General 24D Airplane*, 1 October 1942

Ford Airplane School, *3509 AAF Base Unit, B-24 Job Sheet Manuals 1-6*, 1944

Second Air Force, *Standardization Handbook for B-24 Engineers*, 12 September 1944

Willow Run Plant Guide Staff, *Willow Run Reference Book*, 1945

Reports, Letters, Memorandum, Studies, and Analyses

Air Material Command, *North American Aviation, Inc., TX, AT-6, B-24, P-51 Construction and Production Analysis*, Logistics Planning Division: Industrial Plans Section, Wright Field, OH, undated

Air Materiel Command, *Consolidated Vultee Aircraft Corporation, CA, B-24, Construction and Production Analysis*, LA, AAF Procurement Field Office: Industrial Planning Branch, 1946

Air Materiel Command, *Consolidated Vultee Aircraft Corporation, TX, B-24, Construction and Production Analysis*. LA, AAF Procurement Field Office: Industrial Planning Branch, 1947

Air Materiel Command, *Douglas Aircraft Company, CA, B-17, Construction and Production Analysis*, LA, AAF Procurement Field Office: Industrial Planning Branch, 1946

Air Materiel Command, *Ford Motor Company Willow Run Bomber Plant, MI, B-24, Construction and Production Analysis*, Logistics Planning Division: Industrial Plans Section, Wright Field, OH, 1946

Air Materiel Command. *Boeing Aircraft Company, WA, Washington, B-17, Construction and Production Analysis*, LA, AAF Procurement Field Office: Industrial Planning Branch, 1946

Craig, H., Maj.Gen, AAF Assistant Chief of Staff, Operations, Commitments and Requirements. *Letter. Subject: Comparative Analysis of the B-17 and B-24 Airplanes, to Chief of the Air Staff*, 22 May 1944

Doolittle, J., Maj.Gen, Commander 8AF, *Letter: Subject: B-24 Modifications and Redesign. To Commanding General, U.S. Strategic Forces in Europe*, 14 February 1944

Holley, I., *United States Army in WWII: Special Studies, Buying Aircraft: Materiel Procurement for the Army Air Forces*, Washington, D.C.: U.S. Government Printing Office, 1962

Reuther, W., *500 Planes a Day, A Program for the Utilization of the Automobile Industry for the Mass Production of Defense Planes*, 23 December 1940

USAAF Board, *Tactical Application, and Test of Refueling in Flight of Heavy Bombardment Aircraft*, Project No. T-9, 10 March 1944.

USAAF Engineering Division Memorandum, *Appendix V: Sample Flight Plan Employing Flight Refueling (MX-204)*, Report No. ENG-50-914, 20 July 1943

USAAF Materiel Command Flight Section, *Memorandum Report on Pilot's Comments on Refueling Project (B-24D)*, ENG-19-1609-A, 18 June 1943

USAAF Materiel Command, *Appendix II: Operation of the Flight Refueling Equipment during Flight Tests at Eglin Field (MX-204)*, USAAF Materiel Command Engineering Division, 20 July 1943

USAF Historical Division, Air University, *Development of the Heavy Bomber, 1918-1944*, USAF Historical Study No. 6., AL, Maxwell AFB, 1951

USAF, Serial Search Number Search B-24, n.d.

Index

American Federation of Labor (AFL) 134-137, 139, 153
Anglo-French Purchasing Board 124
Arnold, Henry "Hap" 23-24, 101, 111, 116, 132, 138, 318, 320, 340, **492**(2), 600, **601**
"Arsenal of Democracy" 126, **127**, 309, 355, 394
Aviation Corporation (AVCO) 142, 145; Pursues Consolidated 146-148, 151, 154, 156-157, 164, 253

B-24 Committee 176-178; Established 176; Subcommittees 176-177; Liaison committee 178; Executive committee 178; Problems 178
Baker, Newton (War Department Secretary) 24
Bane, Col. Thurman 25, 27, 96
BDV (Boeing-Douglas-Vega) Committee 176, 600
Bell, Lawrence 60, **60**, 64, 71, 85-87, 94
Bennett, Henry 372-373, **373**, 420, 434-435, **492**, 506, 509, 513, 515
Bishop Fleet, Lillian (sister) 32, 162, 167-168
Bishop, Edward "Ned" (son-in-law) 32, 148, 162
Black, Senator Hugo L. 77, **80**
Black, Senator Hugo L. 77, **80**
Boeing Airplane Company 22, 27, 29, 56; of Canada 74; Boeing/United Airlines 77; Boeing Gets an Early Start in the Four-Engined Bomber Competition 92-93, **93**, 103, 112, 158, 179, 203
Boeing B-47 Stratojet 609, **612**
Boeing GA-1 46
Boeing Model 247 92
Boeing Model 299 92, **92**
Boeing Model 299 93, **93**, 215
Boeing PB-1 53
Boeing PT-13 Stearman 39
Boeing XB-17 92
Boeing Y1B-17 93
Boeing, William 22
Boeing/Laddon Model 50 47
Bomar, Thomas 85, **86**, 132, 310
British Air Commission (BAC) 124
British Purchasing Commission (BPC) 124, **124**
Brookins, Walter 94, **95**, 96, 102
Buenos Aires Line Inc. (NYRBA) 56, **57**, 66
Buffalo Plant 36, **37**(2), **38**, 44; XPY-1 Admiral 53, 55; Husky Junior 60; Fleet/Golem Flight to 64; P-30 (PB-2) Fighter 68; Model 24 72; XP3Y-1 prototype 73-74, **76**; Move to California 85, 85-87; Unions 134, 268, 310
Burlsen, A. S., (Post Master General) 24

Callery, Francis 146-147
Carter, Amon 132, 307-308, **308**, 310-319, **319**, **324**, 335, **336**
Clark, Virginius E. TW-3 designer 32-33; Biography 33-35, **35**; Consolidated resignation **38**, 39, **40**, 115

Commodore (Model 16) 55-56, **57**
Congress of Industrial Organisations (CIO) 134, 136
Consolidated Aircraft Company: Excess Profits 44; Enters large aircraft market 44-53; Enters the Latin American Market 55-59; Private Aircraft and Mail Market 60-64; Consolidated Acquires and Retires the Thomas-Morse Company 68; Consolidated Face the Depression Years 70; Navy investigates Admiral Flying Boat contract 74; House Naval Affairs Committee investigates Fleet 77-79; Consolidated moves to San Diego 84-89; The San Diego Plant Goes into Production 90-95; Pre-XB-24 Four-Engined Bomber Proposals 109-111; Acquires the Hall Aluminum Aircraft Company 123; New Contracts and Expands for B-24 Production 127-129; Confronts the West Coast Labor Unions 134-139; Merges with Vultee 140-160; Final Finances of the Merger 148; Merger: Aftermath and Clarification 149-152; New Consolidated Hierarchy 151-156; Girdler 152-154; Woodhead 154; Laddon 154-155; Wartime Contributions 156;

Knock-Down Kit Contracts 179-184; Consolidated Contracts 179-181; Joint Contracts 181; Ford Willow Run Contracts 182; Consolidated-Ford as a Subcontractor Contracts 182; Ford Prime Contract 183-184;

Consolidated Fort Worth B-24 Plant Prelude 307-316; Fort Worth and World War I Aviation 307; Amon Carter 307-308, **308**; Fort Worth and the 1920s 308; Rise of Fort Worth's Aviation Industry 309; Fleet Negotiates with Fort Worth 310-316; Edgar Gott 311-312, **312**, 318, 341, 493, 503; Fleet Closes Deal with Carter 312-316; Brett, Maj. Gen. George 309, **309**, 314; Jones, Jesse 132, 309, 315, **316**; Plant Description 316-345; Plant #4 Approval 317; Building Contracts 317; Groundbreaking 318, **319**; Roosevelt surprise visit 320, Description 320-322, **321**(2), **322**(2); Workforce 322-325, **324**(2); Liberator Village 323, **325**; B-24 Knock-Down Assembly and Production 326-338; KD Kits from Willow Run 326-329: **327**(2), **328**(2), **329**; First B-24 329-331, **329**(2); More contracts 331; Manufacture Photo Gallery **332-336**, **337**(2); B-24 Manufacture Terminated 338, **339**; Post-War 340-346, **342**; Contract Deliveries 343; Summary of the Cost of Fort Worth Facility 343-344; Tarrant/Carswell AAB 344-345, **345**

Consolidated San Diego B-24 Plant: Expansions 186-197: **186**, **187**(2); Plant Expansion 189; Early Planning 190; First Expansion 190-192; Taylor & Taylor 190-191; Chronology of the Highlights 191, **192**; Second Expansion 192-193; Taylor & Taylor 192, **193**; Chronology of the Highlights 193; Third Expansion 193-196, **194**(2), **195**; Taylor & Taylor 195, 196; Navy-sponsored Defense Plant Corporation (DPC) Lease Agreement 195; Chronology of the Highlights 196, **196**; Additional Expansions 197; Plant Description 198-214; Location and Access 198-200, **199**(2); Plant #1 Complex 200-201; Plant #1 Buildings 201, **201**; Plant #2 Complex 202-203; Plant #2 Buildings 202, **203**; Factory Camouflage 203-206, **204**, **205**(2), **206**; Lindbergh Airfield 206-209, **207**(2), **208**(2), **209**(2); Roads and Railways 210-211, **210**(2), **211**(2); Utilities and Services 212; Management 212-214; List 214; Labor Force 215-231; San Diego and the Labor Supply 215; Labor Build-up 216; Worker Training 217-218, **217**; Work Force Growth and Production 218; Utilization of the Available Work Force 218-221; Women 218-219, **218**; Black Workers 219-220, **220**; Military Personnel 220; Marginal Workers 220-221, **221**; Work Week and Shift Distribution 222; Employee Morale 222; "NOTHING SHORT OF RIGHT IS RIGHT" 222-223, **223**; Lodging and Housing 223-227; Rents 224; Dormitories 224; Women's Housing 224-225; Linda Vista 225-227, **226**(2), **227**; Housing Problems 227; Rationing 227, **227**; Company Services 229; *Consolidated News* 229, **229**; Community Factors 230; Labor Relations 230; Absenteeism and Turnover 230-231; Work Force Conclusions 231; Feeder Shop Plan and Subcontracting 265-274; Feeder Shops 265-267, **266**, **267**(3); Sub-Contracting 268-274; Sub-Contractors List 271- 273, **274**(2); Government-Furnished Equipment (GFE) and Spare Parts 275-276; GFE 275; Spare Parts 276; Rejected and Salvaged Items 276; Assembly Line 277-299; Construction Evolves 277, **278**(2), **279**; Nose Section Manufacture 279-281, **281**(3); Final Assembly Line 282-285; Manufacture Photo Galley 285-298; Wartime Aircraft Totals 299; Summary and Conclusion 300-304; Facility Construction Period 300; Pre-Production Period 300-301; Production Period 301-302; Conclusions and Evaluations 302-304, **304**

Cook, Adml. Arthur 101
Curtiss Aeroplane and Motor Company 29, 36, **37**, 341; Modification plants 640
Curtiss B-2 Condor 51, 82
Curtiss Challenger R-600 engine 39
Curtiss Chieftain engine 72
Curtiss Electric Propellers 687
Curtiss F9C Sparrowhawk 42, **43**
Curtiss JN-4-A Jenny 25, **26**, 31, 32, 35
Curtiss V-1570-27 engine 68

Davis Wing 96-103; Patent 98, **99**, 103-104; Davis Wing Considered 105; Consolidated Model 31 106-107, **107**
Davis, David 94, **95**, 96-103; After Consolidated 103-105, **105**; Manta aircraft 105, **105**
Dayton-Wright Airplane Company 25, 27; TW-3 31; PS-1 32; Patents to Consolidated 33; SJ-1 trainer 35
Deeds, Edward 25
Delaney, Representative John 77, **80**
Detroit-Lockheed XP-900 prototype 68
Diehl, Cdr. Walter 101
Douglas Cloudster 94
Douglas Tulsa B-24 Plant 597-612; Planning and Building 599-604; Background and Contracts 599-600, **601**; Plant Description 600, **602**(2), **603**; Airfield **602**, 603; Assembling B-24s 605-607; Monthly

Totals 605-606, **606(2)**, **607(2)**; Contract Deliveries 608; Summary of Cost of the Douglas Tulsa Facility 608-609; *Tulsamerican* (Last Tulsa B-24) 609, **610**; Post-B-24 Production 609, **610**, **611(2)**; Plant Closure 609-612; Oklahoma City Air Technical Service Command (OCATSC) 609; Douglas Reopens Plant (B-47) 609-610, **612**; North American Aviation Lease 612; Spirit AeroSystems 612; Navistar International Corporation 612

Emanuel, Victor 142, **142**, 146, 148, 152, 157, 253

Fleet Mitchell, Dorothy (Second wife) 65, 148, 162-166, **165**, 166
Fleet of Canada 62-63, **63(2)**, 64
Fleet, David (father) 18
Fleet, David (son) 18, **20**, 27, 64, 85, **86**, 155
Fleet, Eva Wiseman (Third wife) 163, 165, 167, **167**
Fleet, Lillian (mother) 18, **20**
Fleet, Phyllis (daughter) 18, **20**
Fleet, Reuben Early years 18-20, **18**, **19**, **20**; National Guard Service 21, 22; Army Pilot 21-24, **22**; Air Mail Service 24-25, **22(2)**; forms Consolidated Aircraft Co. 32-33; Fleet and Personal Secretary Lauretta Golem 64-65, **65(2)**, **130**, **133**; Fleet at the New Company 151; Post Merger and Retirement 161-168, **165**; Fleet and Family 162; Philanthropist 167, **167**
Fleet, Sandy (son with Dorothy) 162
Fleetster (Model 17) 66, **66**, **67(2)**
Fonck, Rene Sikorsky-Consolidated S-37B 49-52, **50**
Ford II, Henry 365, **513**; Bio 512-515, **514**, **491**, 513
Ford Willow Run Plant 348-575; Background: Henry Ford and Automobile Mass Production 349-352, **350**, **351(2)**, **352(2)**; Model T 349; Ford Trimotor 353-354, **354(2)**; Reuther Report 355-359, **356**; William Knudsen 360-361, **360**; Automotive Bomber Program 361-363; Aircraft Factory Conversion *v.* New Construction 363-364; Ford, Charles Sorensen, and the Willow Run Factory Development 365-373; Ford Top Management Internal Problems 371-372; Henry Bennett 372-373; Kahn, Albert Architect 377-378; Layout Board Model 379; Ground Breaking 379, **380**; Willow Run Named 379; Ford Willow Run Construction Introduction 381-388; Early Production Planning 381-382, **382**; "Tax Turn" 382-383, **383**; Construction Begins 384-385; Chronology of Willow Run B-24 Manufacture, 1941–1945 386-387; Milestones 388; Ford Willow Run Plant Construction 388-407; Buildings and Floor Areas Square Feet 389-390; Photo Gallery 391-394; Publicity 394-395; Main Building 396-397; Administrative Building 397, **397**; IBM Service 397; Factory Supply Transportation (RR) 398; Worker Transportation 398, **399**; Airfields and Hangars 399, 400, **401(2)**, **402(3)**; Utilities 400-404, **403**, **404**; Specialized Buildings and Amenities 404-406, **405(2)**, **406(3)**; Cafeteria 404, **405**; Hospital 404; Theater 404, **405**; Air Raid Shelter 404, **406**; Broadcast Studio 404, **406**; Ford Willow Run Pre-Mass Production 407-412; Pre-production 407; Consolidated Data 407-408, **409**; Lofting and Pattern Shops 408-409, **409**; Ford KD Kits 408-410; "Educational" B-24 410-411, **411**; UAW Labor Union 411-412; Ford Willow Run Workforce 413-438; Limiting Factors to Achieving Mass Production 413-415; Build-up of the Labor Force 415-416; Labor Supply 416-417; Women 417-420, **418**; Rosie the Riveter 419-420, **419**, **420(2)**; Black Workers 420-421, **421**; Little People 421, **422**; Wages 421-422, **422**; Work Week and Shift Distribution 422-423, **423**; Employee Training 423-426, **426(2)**; Worker Morale 427-428, **427**; Worker Absenteeism 428; Worker Turnover 428-429; Manpower Problem and Worker Productivity 429; Worker Housing 429-434; Federal Public Housing Administration (PHA) 430; Willow Lodge 430, **432**; Willow Village 430, **431**, **432**; West Court 430, **433**; War Housing Community 430-431: Unions, Worker Grievances, and Race Riots 435-437; United Auto Workers (UAW) 434, 435; "Communist terrorists" 434-435; Harry Bennett 420, 434-436; Violence 434-435, **436**; "Deconcentration:" Moving the Work to the Workers 437-438; Ford Willow Run Production Plan 439-442; Ford's Plan for B-24 Production 439; Ford's Plan Workability 440; Ford Plan's Strengths 441; Ford Plan's Weaknesses 441-442; Ford Willow Run Production 443-457; Implementation 443; Assembly Tooling 444; Dies 444; Hard Dies 444-447, **445**; Advantages 445-446; Disadvantages 446-447; Die Types 447-449; Blanking and Piercing Dies 447; Forming Dies 448; Kirksite Dies 448, **448**; Drawing Dies 449; Jigs 449; Machine Tools 449-450; Joining of Parts and Components 451-454; Spot Welding 451, **451**; Riveting 451-452, **453(2)**; Heat Treatment 452; Production Tooling 452-454; Tooling at Willow Run 455; Tooling Difficulties

455; Parts Manufacturing Difficulties 456-457; Raw Materials and Purchased Parts 469-475; Purchasing Plan 468; Purchase Plan in Practice 469; Purchasing Difficulties 469-470; Parts Storage 470-472, **471**(2), **472**; Material Control 472-474; Raw Stock Material Control Department 474; Purchased Parts Control Department 475; Production Control Department 475; Purchasing Specification Department 475; Material Control Liaison 475; Spare Parts 484-485; Government-Furnished Equipment (GFE) 485-487; GFE Plan 486; GFE Operation 486; GFE Reorganization 487; Ford Willow Run Engineering 458-467; Engineering Plan 458-459; Engineering Material from Consolidated 459-462; Engineering Changes 463; B-24 Liaison Committee and Sub-Committee 464; Engineering Reorganization 464-465; Change 465-467, **466**(2); Master Changes B-24E and H 467; Subcontracting 476-483; Early Operation 476; Sub-contracting Methods 477-478; Other Ford Plants as Sub-Contractors 478-480; List 478-479, **480**(2); Ford Rouge B-24 Sub-Assembly Plant 481, **483**(2); Vendor Sub-Contracting 481-482; List, Inspection and Government Control 488-492; Ford's Inspection Plan 488; Willow Run Inspection 488-490; AAF Control 490; Willow Run Visitors 490-492, **491**(3), **492**(2); Rate of Production Acceleration 493-499; Wartime Production Contract Orders 493; Mass Production Plan 494; KD and Complete Aircraft Production Plan 494-495; Preparation for Production 495-496; Long, Slow Period of Production Acceleration 496-498; Reorganization 498-499, **499**; Production Crisis 499-502; Rapid Production Acceleration 507-510; Management Plan 507; Management Plan 508-509; Disadvantages 509; Production Line 517-527; Description 517-519; Division of the Fuselage for Mass Production 520; Manufacturing Section 521-525; Press shop, Department 927 521-522, **522**(2); Machine shop, Department 928 521, **523**(2), **525**(2); Draw bench Department 930 521, 526: Small parts assemblies; Department 932 525; Rivet Department, 926 525, **526**; Tool room, Department 975 525, **527**(2); Center Wing Section 528-538; Description 528; Center Wing Skin and Stringer Assembly (Department 936A) 528-530; Center Wing Vertical Assembly (Department 936) 530-531; Center Wing Horizontal (Department 937) 536, **538**; Ingersoll Center Wing Milling Machine 535-536, **537**(2); Assembly of the Center Wing Section Photo Gallery **531-534**; Fuselage and its Component Assemblies 538-539; Final Assembly Line (Department 947) Stations 1 through 14 540-541; Final Assembly (Stations 15 to 28 541-543; Fuselage and its Component Assemblies Photo Gallery **543-556**; Knock-Down (KD) Kit Production and Transport 567-562; B-24Es Assembled from KD Kits 557; Transporting KD Kits 558-559; KD Kit Photo Gallery 559-562; Willow Run Appraisal 563-565; Willow Run B-24 Milestones Photo Gallery 565-570; Post-War 571-575; Ford 571; Kaiser 571-512, **572**; MARC and Willow Run Laboratories 572; General Motors 573, **573**; RACER Trust 574; Yankee Air Museum 574, **574**; Autonomous Vehicle Testing Site 575, **575**
Ford, Clara (wife) 513, 515
Ford, Edsel 352, 353, **354**, 365, **366**(2), 370, 372, **380**, 394-395, 412, 420, 435-436, **491**, 505, 508, 510; Death 511-512, **512**, **513**; Ford Co. after death 515; Willow run after death 515-516, **516**, **557**
Ford, Henry 349–350, **352**, 353, **354**, 360, **366**, 367, 369-374, 376-377, 379, 388, **389**, 394, 395, 400, 403, 407, 410-411, 418, **422**, 430, 435-436, 445, 460, **489**, **492**(2), 498, **499**, 502, 505, 509, **512**, **513**, 515, **567**
Frederick, Col. Alexander (uncle) 18, **19**
French Purchasing Commission 124

Gallaudet Aircraft Corporation/ Edson Gallaudet 29-33, **30**(2)
Gillmore, Brig. Gen. William 53
Girdler, Tom 140-141, **141**, 146, 151-154; On Reuben Fleet 166, 253, 329, **330**, 340
Girton, Elizabeth (first wife) 18, **20**, 27, 148, 167
Glenn Martin Company 54, 56, 60, 73, 77, 115, 129, 139, 222, 225, 377, 629, 640
Golem, Henry 55, 64, 165
Guggenheim Aeronautics Laboratory of the California Institute of Technology (GALCIT) 94, 97-98, 100-101, 104, 106, 116
Gwinn, Joseph 53, 60, 277

Hall Aluminum Aircraft Company 123,
Handbook for Aircraft Designers 81, 82, 115
Heinemann, Ed 47, 48
Hillman, Sidney 136-138, **138**
Hispano-Suiza V-8 (Hisso Vee) engine 32-33; Described 35-36, **36**
Husky Junior (Model 14)/Fleet 60, **61**

International Association of Machinists (IAM) 134-135

Jerry Vultee 143-144, **144**
Jones, Lt Col. Byron 23-24, **23**

Kahn, Albert Architect 377-378, **378**, 382, 539, 541, 553
Kelly, Lt. Oakley 94
Keys, Clement 29
Klicka, Emil 85

Laddon, Isaac 27, 33, Biography 45-49, 53, **57**, **86**, 87, 115, 789
LB-16 110, **110**
LB-29 110, **111**(2)
Leigh, Charles 55, **57**, 85, **86**, 87, 139, 155
Lewis, John L. 136, **138**
Liberator Production Pool 171-175; New plants 171-172; KD Kits 172, 174; Members 172; Maintenance and Parts Interchangeability 173
Lindbergh Field 64, 85, **119**, **186**, **187**, 197, 198, **199**(2), 206; Photo Gallery 207-209, 273
Lindbergh, Charles 34, 47, 49, 60, 143, 388, **389**, 418
Lockheed YP-24 68
Lovett, Robert 118, 138, **138**, 362

Macready, Lt. John 94
Manufacture 232-264; Engineering 232-233; Planning 233; Initial Difficulties 233-235, **234**(2), **235**; Engineering Changes 235-236; Master Change Record and the Treatment of Changes 236; Engineering Changes and the B-24 Committee 235-237; Production Methods and Tooling 237; Tooling Plan 237-240; Assembly Tooling 240, **240**(2); Changes Made 241-242, **242**, **243**(2); Tooling Difficulties 244; Cost of Tooling 244; Tooling Developments 244-245; Master Tooling Dock 245-247, **246**, **247**; Reproduction of Tooling Gauges by Tooling Docks 247-248; Manufacture of Tooling 248-249; Machine Tools 249; Machine Tool Procurement 249-250; Production Plan 250-252; Production Acceleration 252-253; Period of Production Acceleration 253-256, **256**; Production Control 256-257; Inspection 258-260, **259**(2); Army-Navy "E" Award 261-262, **261**, **262**; Raw Materials and Purchased Parts 262-264
Maroney, Terah 21, **22**
Marsh, Louis 53
McCook Field **24**, 25, 27, **28**, 33-34, 42, 45-47, 51, 53, 96, 115
Mead, George 129, **130**
Menoher Maj. Gen. Charles 25, **26**
Millar, Richard 144-145, 149, 151, 154
Miller, Roy 45, 49, 53, **86**, 115, 365
Millikan, Dr. Clark 98, 100, 101
Model 31 and Davis Wing 106-107, **107**
Model 32 112-118, **113**, **114**(2)
Moffett, R/Adml. William 42, 44, **45**, 53
Mounce, Gordon Biography/ Fleet of Canada 62, **64**

N2Y-1 42, **43**; As Sparrowhawk 42
Naming the LB 30 700
Naming the Liberator 700
National Labor Relations Board (NLRB) 134-135, 411-412
Naval Aircraft Factory (NAF) 47, 53, 74, 123
Newman, George Gallaudet Factory Manager 33 **38**, **57**, **86**, 87, 115; Fort Worth Plant Manager 320, **324**, 329, 330, **336**, 340
North American Dallas Plant 579-596; Planning and Building 579-584; Background 579, **580**(2); James "Dutch" Kindelberger 313, 363, 379, 380, 581, 585; Leland "Lee" Atwood **580**, 585; Offers to the City of Dallas 581; Defense Plant Corporation (DPC) 581; Groundbreaking 581; Construction 581; Plant A 581, **582**, **586**, 587, **589**, 594; Avion Village 581-582, **584**; Photo Gallery 582-584; Plant B for B-24 Production 585-586, **586**; KD Kits 587-581; Photo Gallery **589-591**; B-24 Production and Costs 592-593; Plant Epilog 594-596; Fairchild C-82 Packet 594, **595**; Texas Engineering and Manufacturing Company (TEMCO) 594; Chance Vought Aircraft 594-596, **595**, **596**
NY-1/-2/-3 Huskys 39-40, **41**, 42

O'Neill, Capt. Ralph 55-56, **57**
O-17 Courier 42, **43**
Odlum, Floyd 157-158, **158**

P2Y-1 and 2 Rangers (Model 22) 56-58, **59**, 73
P-30 (PB-2) Fighter 68-69, **69**, 87, 90
Palmer, Richard "Dick" 144-145
PB2Y-1 Coronado (Model 29) 90-91, **91**, 96
PBY Catalina 47, 70, 73-77, **75**(2), **76**(2), 90, 96, 102, 107, 115, 127-128, 190, 309, 314
Perelle, Charles 155, 245
"Project A" 92, 370
PT-1 (Model 1) Trusty 36-40, **37**, **38**(2); PT-3 (Model 2) Husky 39, **40**

Race Riots, Ford and the 1943 Detroit 505-506, **506**
Rand, James H. 56-58, **58**
Reconstruction Finance Corporation (RFC) 85, 315, **316**, 383
Richardson, Capt. Holden 47, 53-54
Rogers, Representative William 79, **81**
Ryan, T. Claude 94

Schairer, George 96, 98, 102
Sheahan, Bernard 45, 53, **86**, 115, 213
Sikorsky-Consolidated S-37B M 49, **50**(2), 51-52
Sorensen, Charles 129, 365, **366**(2), **368**, 371, 371-376, 380, 386, 387, 410, 412, 420, 435, 437, 438, **493**, 501-502, **504**, 508, 510, 513-515
Springer, Eric 94
Stinson Airplane Company 142-143

Thomas-Morse 27 (MB-3) 36, 68, 70, 72
Tonawanda Products Corporation 55

Tower, Les 92
Towers, Adml. John **35**, 127, **128**, 1**32**, **133**, 135, 138
Trippe, **Juan** 56, 139
Truman Committee Investigation 502-505, **504**(2)
Turbo-superchargers B-2 120
TW-3 Trainer 31, **31**, 32

Umstead, Maj. Stanley 118, **121**

Van Dusen, Charles 87, **88**, 112, 132, **275**, 310

Vickers (Montreal) 74
Vinson, Representative Carl 77
von Karman, Theodore 98
Vultee Aircraft Company 143-144; Trainers 45

Wade, Lt. Leigh Biography 51, **52**, 55, 57
War Department Aircraft Procurement Policy (1934) 80
Wheatley, William 74, **75**, 107, 118, **119**, 310-311

White, Capt. Earl 27
Whitman, Ray **38**, 87
Wilson, Woodrow **24**, 25
Woodring, Assistant Secretary of War Henry 79-80, **81**
Woods, Robert 68, 87

XB-24 118-122, **119**, **121** as XB-24B
XPY-1 Admiral (Model 9) 53-54, **54**